Controversies in CONSTITUTIONAL LAW

COLLECTIONS OF DOCUMENTS AND ARTICLES ON MAJOR QUESTIONS OF AMERICAN LAW

PAUL FINKELMAN

GENERAL EDITOR

Virginia Polytechnic Institute and State University

A Garland Series

HATE SPEECH AND THE CONSTITUTION

Volume 2

The Contemporary Debate: Reconciling Freedom of Expression and Equality of Citizenship

Edited with an introduction by

STEVEN J. HEYMAN

Chicago-Kent College of Law

Garland Publishing, Inc.
New York & London
1996

Library of Congress Cataloging-in-Publication Data

Hate Speech and the Constitution / edited with an introduction by
Steven J. Heyman.
      p.   cm. — (Controversies in constitutional law)
    Includes bibliographical references.
    Contents: v.1. The development of the hate speech debate —
v.2. The contemporary debate.
    ISBN 0–8153–2207–0 (alk. paper)
    1. Hate speech—United States.   2. Freedom of speech—United
States.   I. Heyman, Steven J. II. Series.
KF9345.H38   1996
342.73'0853—dc20
[347.302853]   95–25517
                                        CIP

Printed on acid-free, 250-year-life paper
Manufactured in the United States of America

For Kate

═CONTENTS═

Regulating Racist Speech on Campus: A Modest Proposal?
Nadine Strossen 2

Civil Rights vs. Civil Liberties: The Case of Discriminatory Verbal
    Harassment
Thomas C. Grey 93

Racist Speech, Democracy, and the First Amendment
Robert C. Post 119

There's No Such Thing as Free Speech and It's a Good Thing, Too
Stanley Fish 180

Excerpt from "The Coming Battles over Free Speech"
Ronald Dworkin 190

Brief *Amicus Curiae* of the National Black Women's Health Project in
    Support of Respondent, R.A.V. v. City of St. Paul 197

R.A.V. v. City of St. Paul 220

Excerpt from "The Case of the Missing Amendments: *R.A.V. v.
    City of St. Paul*"
Akhil Reed Amar 253

Liberalism and Campus Hate Speech: A Philosophical Examination
Andrew Altman 260

Harm Principle, Offence Principle, and the Skokie Affair
Raphael Cohen-Almagor 277

The Humanitarian Threat to Free Inquiry
Jonathan Rauch 295

Let Them Talk: Why Civil Liberties Pose No Threat to Civil Rights
Henry Louis Gates, Jr. 302

Wisconsin v. Mitchell 321

Excerpt from "Words, Conduct, Caste"
Cass R. Sunstein 330

Excerpt from "Freedom of Speech and International Norms:
    A Response to Hate Speech"
Elizabeth F. Defeis 338

Regina v. Keegstra
Edited by Lorraine E. Weinrib 361

Excerpt from "Hate Promotion in a Free and Democratic Society:
    R. v.Keegstra"
Lorraine Eisenstat Weinrib 382

Incitement to National and Racial Hatred: The Legal Situation in
    Germany
Rainer Hofmann 401

Confronting Racism by Law in Israel—Promises and Pitfalls
Amos Shapira 413

America's First "Hate Speech" Regulation
Michael W. McConnell 427

Toward a First Amendment Jurisprudence of Respect: A Comment on
    George Fletcher's Constitutional Identity
Robin West 435

Acknowledgments 443

Contents of the Series 447

Hate Speech and the Constitution

REGULATING RACIST SPEECH ON CAMPUS: A MODEST PROPOSAL?†

NADINE STROSSEN*

TABLE OF CONTENTS

Introduction 487

I. Some Limited Forms of Campus Hate Speech May Be
    Regulable Under Current Constitutional Doctrine 495
    A. *General Constitutional Principles Applicable to
        Regulating Campus Hate Speech* 495
    B. *Particular Speech-Limiting Doctrines Potentially
        Applicable to Campus Hate Speech* 507
        1. *Fighting Words* 508
        2. *Intentional Infliction of Emotional Distress* 514

---

† The title is drawn from Jonathan Swift's essay *A Modest Proposal for preventing the Children of poor People from being a Burthen to their Parents or the Country, and for Making them Beneficial to the Public* (Dublin 1729), in JONATHAN SWIFT 492 (A. Ross & D. Woolley eds. 1984). This Article not only responds to the specific points made in Lawrence, *If He Hollers Let Him Go: Regulating Racist Speech on Campus,* 1990 DUKE L.J. 431 [hereinafter Lawrence], but also addresses the general issues raised by the many recent proposals to regulate racist and other forms of hate speech on campus. Professor Strossen's Article, as well as Professor Lawrence's, are expanded versions of oral presentations that they made at the Biennial Conference of the American Civil Liberties Union (ACLU) in Madison, Wisconsin on June 16, 1989 (available from author). After discussion of these presentations, the Conference adopted the following resolution:

> The ACLU should undertake educational activities to counter incidents of racist, sexist, anti-semitic and homophobic behavior (including speech) on school campuses and should encourage school administrators to speak out vigorously against such incidents. At the same time, the ACLU should undertake educational activities to counter efforts to limit or punish speech on university campuses.

The ACLU has taken action to implement both prongs of this resolution. *See infra* note 17 and text accompanying notes 344-55.

* Professor of Law, New York Law School. A.B., 1972, Harvard-Radcliffe College; J.D., 1975, Harvard Law School. Professor Strossen is a General Counsel to the ACLU, and serves on its Executive Committee and National Board of Directors. She thanks Charles Baron, Jean Bond, Ava Chamberlain, Elsa Cole, Donald Downs, Eunice Edgar, Stephen France, Ira Glasser, David Goldberger, Thomas Grey, Gerald Gunther, Nat Hentoff, Mary Heston, Martin Margulies, Mari Matsuda, Michael Meyers, Gretchen Miller, Colleen O'Connor, Taggarty Patrick, john powell, John Roberts, Alan M. Schwartz, Judge Harvey Schwartz, Robert Sedler, Norman Siegel, Peter Siegel, William Van Alstyne, and Jane Whicher for information and insights they shared regarding the subject of this Article. For comments on earlier versions of the Article, she thanks Ralph Brown, Edward Chen, Norman Dorsen, Bernie Dushman, Stanley Engelstein, Eric Goldstein, Franklyn Haiman, Morton Halperin, Alon Harel, Leanne Katz, Martin Margulies, Maimon Schwarzschild, and Samuel Walker. For their research assistance, she expresses special thanks to Jennifer Colyer and Marie Newman, who provided help throughout this project. For additional research assistance, she thanks Marie Costello, Jayni Edelstein, Ramyar Moghadassi, and Julia Swanson.

484

2

3. *Group Defamation* 517

C. *Even a Narrow Regulation Could Have a Negative
   Symbolic Impact on Constitutional Values* 520

II. Professor Lawrence's Conception of Regulable Racist
    Speech Endangers Free Speech Principles 523

A. *The Proposed Regulations Would Not Pass
   Constitutional Muster* 524

1. *The Regulations Exceed the Bounds of the Fighting
   Words Doctrine* 524

2. *The Regulations Will Chill Protected Speech* 526

B. *The Proposed Regulations Would Endanger
   Fundamental Free Speech Principles* 531

1. *Protection of Speech Advocating Regulable
   Conduct.* 531

2. *Proscription on Content-Based Speech Regulations.*.. 533

a. *The indivisibility of free speech.* 533

b. *The slippery slope dangers of banning racist
   speech.* 537

c. *The content-neutrality principle reflects sensitivity
   to hate speech's hurtful power.* 539

III. Professor Lawrence's Rationales for Regulating Racist
     Speech Would Justify Sweeping Prohibitions, Contrary to
     Free Speech Principles 541

A. Brown *and Other Cases Invalidating Governmental
   Racist Conduct Do Not Justify Regulating Non-
   Governmental Racist Speech* 541

1. *The Speech/Conduct Distinction* 542

2. *The Private Action/State Action Distinction* 544

B. *The Non-Intellectual Content of Some Racist Speech
   Does Not Justify Its Prohibition* 547

IV. Prohibiting Racist Speech Would Not Effectively Counter,
    and Could Even Aggravate, the Underlying Problem of
    Racism 549

A. *Civil Libertarians Should Continue to Make Combating
   Racism a Priority* 549

B. *Punishing Racist Speech Would Not Effectively Counter
   Racism* 554

C. *Banning Racist Speech Could Aggravate Racism* 555

V. Means Consistent with the First Amendment Can Promote
   Racial Equality More Effectively Than Can Censorship...... 562

Conclusion 569

Freedom of speech is indivisible; unless we protect it for all, we will have it for none.[1]

—Harry Kalven, Jr.

If there be minority groups who hail this holding [rejecting a first amendment challenge to a group libel statute] as their victory, they might consider the possible relevancy of this ancient remark: "Another such victory and I am undone."[2]

—Hugo Black, Jr.

The civil rights movement would have been vastly different without the shield and spear of the First Amendment. The Bill of Rights . . . is of particular importance to those who have been the victims of oppression.[3]

—Benjamin L. Hooks

It is technically impossible to write an anti-speech code that cannot be twisted against speech nobody means to bar. It has been tried and tried and tried.[4]

—Eleanor Holmes Norton

The basic problem with all these regimes to protect various people is that the protection incapacitates. . . . To think that I [as a black man] will . . . be told that white folks have the moral character to shrug off insults, and I do not . . . . That is the most insidious, the most insulting, the most racist statement of all![5]

—Alan Keyes

Whom will we trust to censor communications and decide which ones are "too offensive" or "too inflammatory" or too devoid of intellectual content? . . . As a former president of the University of California once said: "The University is not engaged in making ideas safe for students. It is engaged in making students safe for ideas."[6]

—Derek Bok

[R]estrictive codes . . . may be expedient, even grounded in conviction, but the university cannot submit the two cherished ideals of freedom and equality to the legal system and expect both to be returned intact.[7]

—Carnegie Foundation for the Advancement of Teaching

---

1. Kalven, *Upon Rereading Mr. Justice Black on the First Amendment,* 14 UCLA L. REV. 428, 432 (1967).

2. Beauharnais v. Illinois, 343 U.S. 250, 275 (1952) (Black, J., dissenting).

3. Statement by Benjamin Hooks, *quoted in* Philip Morris Companies Inc., Press Release (May 7, 1990).

4. Gottlieb, *Banning bigoted speech: Stanford weighs rules,* San Jose (Cal.) Mercury-News, Jan. 7, 1990, at 3, col. 1.

5. Stanford News, Press Release (Mar. 19, 1990) (quoting Alan Keyes, a former assistant secretary of state and now president of Citizens Against Government Waste, criticizing Stanford hate speech regulation).

6. Bok, *Reflections on Free Speech: An Open Letter to the Harvard Community,* EDUC. REC., Winter 1985, at 4, 6.

7. CARNEGIE FOUNDATION FOR THE ADVANCEMENT OF TEACHING, A SPECIAL REPORT: CAMPUS LIFE, IN SEARCH OF COMMUNITY 20 (1990) [hereinafter CARNEGIE FOUND. SPECIAL REPORT].

In the political climate that surrounds [the race] issue[ ] on campus, principle often yields to expediency and clarity turns into ambiguity, and this is no less true for some of our finest scholars.[8]

—Joseph Grano

When language wounds, the natural and immediate impulse is to take steps to shut up those who utter the wounding words. When, as here, that impulse is likely to be felt by those who are normally the first amendment's staunchest defenders, free expression faces its greatest threat. At such times, it is important for those committed to principles of free expression to remind each other of what they have always known regarding the long term costs of short term victories bought through compromising first amendment principles.[9]

—Civil Liberties Union of Massachusetts

As a former student activist, and as a current black militant, [I] believe[ ] that free speech is the minority's strongest weapon. . . . [P]aternalism [and] censorship offer the college student a tranquilizer as the antidote to campus and societal racism. What we need is an alarm clock. . . . What we need is free speech . . . and more free speech![10]

—Michael Meyers

INTRODUCTION

Professor Lawrence has made a provocative contribution to the perennial debate concerning the extent to which courts and civil libertarians[11] should continue to construe the Constitution as protecting some

---

8. Grano, *Free Speech v. the University of Michigan,* ACADEMIC QUESTIONS, Spring 1990, at 1, 19-20.

9. Civil Liberties Union of Massachusetts, Policy Concerning Racist and Other Group-Based Harassing Speech Acts on Academic Campuses (adopted May 14, 1990) (principally drafted by Charles H. Baron, Professor of Law, Boston College Law School) (available from author).

10. M. Meyers, Banning Racist and Other Kinds of "Hate" Speech on the College Campus (outline for a debate with john a. powell at Hofstra University, Hempstead, Long Island, January 25, 1990) (available from author). Michael Meyers is a member of the ACLU's National Board of Directors and its Affirmative Action Officer; john a. powell is the ACLU's National Legal Director.

11. There is no single "civil libertarian" or ACLU position on many of the issues discussed in this Article. For example, Professors Lawrence and Strossen are both avowed civil libertarians and ACLU supporters, *see* Lawrence, at 434 n.20, 473, although they disagree on certain civil liberties issues.

On October 13, 1990, the ACLU's National Board of Directors adopted a policy opposing campus disciplinary codes against hate speech. For the text of this policy, which was adopted without dissent, see *infra* Appendix.

In addition to the national organization, the ACLU includes 51 state-wide or regional "affiliates," which may all adopt their own policies. Although an affiliate's policies must be "in accordance" with those of the national organization, this requirement is designed "to obtain general unity, rather than absolute uniformity." *See* Policy Guide of the American Civil Liberties Union, at Policy No. 501 (rev. ed. 1990) [hereinafter ACLU Policy Guide]. Accordingly, some ACLU affiliates may adopt policies concerning the regulation of campus hate speech that are to some extent divergent from each other, and from the national ACLU policy. The ACLU California affiliates have adopted a policy that does not oppose the regulation of a limited class of campus hate speech, *see* Policy of

forms of racist expression.[12] This recurring issue resurfaced most recently in connection with the increase of racial incidents at colleges and universities around the country.[13] In response, many of these institutions have adopted, or are considering,[14] regulations that curb "hate speech"—i.e., speech that expresses hatred or bias toward members of racial, religious, or other groups.

Civil libertarians are committed to the eradication of racial discrimination and the promotion of free speech throughout society.[15] Civil libertarians have worked especially hard to combat both discrimination and free speech restrictions in educational institutions.[16] Educational institutions should be bastions of equal opportunity and unrestricted exchange. Therefore, we find the upsurge of both campus racism and regulation of

---

ACLU California Affiliates Concerning Racist and Other Group-Based Harassment on College Campuses (adopted by ACLU of Northern California, Mar. 8, 1990; ACLU of Southern California, Mar. 21, 1990; and ACLU of San Diego and Imperial Counties, May 24, 1990) (available from author). In contrast, for example, the Civil Liberties Union of Massachusetts has adopted a policy that opposes any content-based restrictions on campus speech. *See supra* note 9.

To reflect the fact that civil libertarians may differ about the specific issues discussed in this Article, the term "traditional civil libertarian" is used only to describe the general view that much hate speech is entitled to first amendment protection. All other, more specific views expressed in this Article reflect the author's opinions. She does not purport to speak either for the national ACLU or for civil libertarians generally.

12. Consistent with Professor Lawrence's approach, *see* Lawrence, at 436 n.27, this Article focuses on racist speech, although the analysis generally applies to other forms of hate speech as well, such as sexist and homophobic speech, and speech vilifying religious or ethnic groups.

13. *See* Leslie, *Lessons from Bigotry 101,* NEWSWEEK, Sept. 25, 1989, at 48 (documents incidents at 250 colleges and universities since Fall 1986). *See also* CIVIL RIGHTS DIVISION OF ANTI-DEFAMATION LEAGUE OF B'NAI B'RITH, POLICY BACKGROUND REPORT—CAMPUS ANTI-BIAS CODES: A NEW FORM OF CENSORSHIP? 1 (1989) (in 1988 there were more reported incidents of anti-Semitic harassment on United States campuses than in any prior year). For a listing of some specific recent incidents of campus racism, see Matsuda, *Public Response to Racist Speech: Considering the Victim's Story,* 87 MICH. L. REV. 2320, 2333 n.71 (1989).

For some possible explanations for this wave of campus racism, see Steele, *The Recoloring of Campus Life,* HARPER'S, Feb. 1989, at 47.

14. *See* CARNEGIE FOUND. SPECIAL REPORT, *supra* note 7, at 19 (60% of the chief student affairs officers surveyed in 1989 reported that their campuses had written policies on bigotry, racial harassment or intimidation, and another 11% said they are working on such policies).

15. *See generally* ACLU Policy Guide, *supra* note 11, at Policy Nos. 301-31 (ACLU policies advocating equality for racial and other historically disempowered groups). For a summary of the ACLU's efforts to implement these policies, see *infra* notes 16 & 334-55 and accompanying text.

16. It has long been an ACLU priority to combat racial discrimination in education. For example, during the 1920s and 1930s, the ACLU assisted with the NAACP's formulation of a nationwide legal campaign against segregated education. *See* S. WALKER, IN DEFENSE OF AMERICAN LIBERTIES: A HISTORY OF THE ACLU 88-90 (1990). The Southern California ACLU successfully challenged school segregation as early as 1946. *See id.* at 239. The ACLU's recent efforts in this category include its representation of the plaintiffs in Brown v. Board of Educ., 892 F.2d 851 (10th Cir. 1989) (*Brown III*), which challenged the de facto segregation of Topeka, Kansas public schools. *See also* Memorandum from john a. powell to Ira Glasser and the Executive Committee, March 10, 1990, at 3-4 [hereinafter powell, Memorandum] (listing cases in which ACLU National Legal Department currently is challenging racial discrimination in education) (available from author).

campus speech particularly disturbing, and we have undertaken efforts to counter both.[17]

Because civil libertarians have learned that free speech is an indispensable instrument for the promotion of other rights and freedoms—including racial equality—we fear that the movement to regulate campus expression will undermine equality, as well as free speech. Combating racial discrimination and protecting free speech should be viewed as mutually reinforcing, rather than antagonistic, goals.[18] A diminution in society's commitment to racial equality is neither a necessary nor an appropriate price for protecting free speech. Those who frame the debate in terms of this false dichotomy simply drive artificial wedges between would-be allies in what should be a common effort to promote civil rights and civil liberties.[19]

Professor Lawrence urges civil libertarians to "abandon[ ] . . . overstated rhetorical and legal attacks on individuals who conscientiously seek to frame a public response to racism while preserving our first amendment liberties."[20] I join in this invitation, and I extend a corresponding one: Those individuals who espouse "new perspectives" on the first amendment in an effort to justify hate speech regulations should avoid overstated attacks on those who conscientiously seek to preserve our first amendment liberties while responding to racism.

In important respects, Professor Lawrence inaccurately describes, and unfairly criticizes, both traditional civil libertarians in general and

---

17. For example, the ACLU represented the plaintiff in Doe v. University of Mich., 721 F. Supp. 852 (E.D. Mich. 1989), which successfully challenged the University of Michigan's anti-hate-speech policy as violating the first amendment. The ACLU also has initiated a lawsuit challenging the University of Wisconsin's hate speech regulation. *See* Gribble, *Student Coalition Sues UW Over Racial Harassment Rule*, Milwaukee J., March 30, 1990, at 8B, col. 1. Prior to the adoption of both rules, the ACLU sought to persuade the universities to formulate narrower restrictions. *See infra* note 353. *Compare* Lawrence, at 477, 478 & n.162 ("Traditional civil liberties lawyers typically have elected to stand by while universities" adopt "poorly drafted and obviously overbroad regulations.").

See also infra note 177 (discussion of Wu v. University of Conn., Civ. H-89-649 PCD (D. Conn. Jan. 25, 1990). The plaintiff, represented by the Connecticut ACLU affiliate, settled her lawsuit challenging the University of Connecticut's hate speech rule pursuant to an agreement about the wording of an alternative rule.

18. At times, Lawrence recognizes that these goals are in fact mutually reinforcing, *see* Lawrence, at 435, 436 & n.27, 453 n.92, 455, 480 n.167, but at other times, he seems to view them as incompatible, *see id.* at 434, 446-47, 457-58, 466-67, 471, 473-74. This is a major unresolved tension in his article.

19. *See* Gale & Strossen, *The Real ACLU,* 2 YALE J.L. & FEMINISM 161, 171-84 (1990); *see also infra* text accompanying notes 422-35 (discussing interdependence of civil rights and civil liberties). Some themes in the present Article were previously explored in the Gale & Strossen essay. Professor Strossen thanks Professor Gale for her permission to draw upon this earlier piece in the present one.

20. *See* Lawrence, at 481.

the American Civil Liberties Union (ACLU) in particular. His argument depends on a "straw civil libertarian" who can be easily knocked down, but who does not correspond to the flesh and blood reality.[21] For example, contrary to Professor Lawrence's assumption, traditional civil libertarians do not categorically reject every effort to regulate racist speech. The ACLU never has argued that harassing, intimidating, or assaultive conduct should be immunized simply because it is in part based on words.[22] Accordingly, traditional civil libertarians should agree with Professor Lawrence that some examples of racially harassing speech should be subject to regulation consistent with first amendment principles—for example, the group of white male students pursuing a black female student across campus shouting, "I've never tried a nigger."[23]

Of course, traditional civil libertarians have urged that any restrictions on expressive activity must be drawn narrowly, and carefully applied, to avoid chilling protected speech. But, to a substantial extent,

---

21. In Professor Lawrence's composite view, "traditional" civil libertarians display the following "typical" propensities. First, they argue that all speech should be absolutely protected, *see* Lawrence, at 436, 438, 449, 457, 461, 473-74, 476-77, at least if it "stops short of physical violence," *id.* at 449. *But see infra* text accompanying notes 56-77. Second, they recognize that no face-to-face insults or fighting words are protected free speech, unless they are racial in nature, *see* Lawrence, at 436-37, 476. *But see infra* text accompanying notes 56-83. Third, they do not acknowledge that racist speech inflicts real harm, *see* Lawrence, at 448, 457, 458, 478. *But see infra* text accompanying notes 275-86. Fourth, they are more committed to the values reflected in the Constitution's free speech clause than to those reflected in its equal protection clause, *see* Lawrence, at 448, 461, 477-78. *But see infra* text accompanying notes 334-57. Fifth, they do not support, and indeed "often" oppose, "group expressions of condemnation" of racist speech, *see* Lawrence, at 477. *But see infra* text accompanying notes 397-402. Sixth, they "typically . . . elect[ ] to stand by" while universities draft constitutionally vulnerable hate speech regulations, *see* Lawrence, at 477. They "wait [to] attack [such] poorly drafted and obviously overbroad regulations." *Id.* at 478 n.162. *But see infra* text accompanying note 353.

The foregoing stereotypes are presented through unsupported assertions and are belied by the facts recited throughout this Article. Professor Lawrence also makes incorrect and misleading statements specifically about the ACLU and its members. *See* Lawrence, at 473, 478 & nn.163-64. *But see infra* text accompanying notes 333-57.

Professor Lawrence qualifies his depiction of the "traditional" civil libertarian or ACLU member in one important respect: He repeatedly suggests that civil libertarians and ACLU members who are members of minority groups (or perhaps women) differ from others in their positions on free speech and equal protection issues. *See* Lawrence, at 466 (distinguishing "[m]ost blacks" from "many white civil libertarians"); *see also id.* at 458-59, 461 & n.113, 473-74, 477-78 & nn.163-64.

Such racial stereotyping is both factually inaccurate and antithetical to equality principles. The inaccuracy is illustrated by the fact that two ACLU officials, both black, recently engaged in a public debate against each other in which one opposed all campus hate speech regulations. *See* M. Meyers, *supra* note 10. Both of these officials agree that the effort to shape appropriately narrow hate speech restrictions entails an undesirable diversion of resources from the essential task of shaping underlying attitudes. Interviews with Michael Meyers and john a. powell, in New York City (August 18, 1990). *See also supra* text accompanying notes 3-5 & 10 (quoting black leaders criticizing hate speech regulations).

22. *See infra* text accompanying notes 53-77 and Appendix.

23. Lawrence, at 448 (quoting *A Step Toward Civility*, TIME, May 1, 1989, at 43).

Professor Lawrence appears to endorse a similarly cautious approach. He stresses that he supports only limited regulations and invokes the recently adopted Stanford University code as a model.[24]

Insofar as Professor Lawrence advocates relatively narrow rules that apply traditionally accepted limitations on expressive conduct to the campus setting, his position should not be alarming (although it is debatable). In portions of his article, Professor Lawrence seems to agree with traditional civil libertarians that only a small subset of the racist rhetoric that abounds in our society should be regulated.[25] Although we may disagree about the contours of such concepts as "captive audience," "fighting words," or "intentional infliction of emotional distress" in the context of racist speech on campus,[26] these differences should not obscure strong common goals. Surely our twin aims of civil rights and civil liberties would be advanced more effectively by fighting together against the common enemy of racism than by fighting against each other over which narrow subset of one symptom of racism—namely, verbal and symbolic expressions—should be regulated.

What is disquieting about Professor Lawrence's article is not the relatively limited Stanford code he defends, but rather his simultaneous defense of additional, substantially more sweeping, speech prohibitions.[27]

---

24. *See* Lawrence, at 450 & n.82, 481. Stanford University recently adopted a rule defining some expression as prohibited "harassment by vilification." Stanford University, Fundamental Standard Interpretation: Free Expression and Discriminatory Harassment (June 1990) [hereinafter Stanford Code and Comments]. The rule, which was principally drafted by Professor Thomas Grey, is quoted *infra* text accompanying note 197.

At various points in his article, Professor Lawrence endorses regulations of broader scope, *see infra* note 27. However, he stresses his proposed variation of the Stanford code, which would apply to "all common areas" and would "not . . . protect[ ] persons . . . vilified on the basis of their membership in dominant majority groups." Lawrence, at 450 n.82. Therefore, throughout the remainder of this Article, references to the regulation endorsed by Professor Lawrence refer to this formulation, unless expressly indicated otherwise.

25. *See* Lawrence, at 434-36, 450 & n.82, 472-73, 474 n.155, 481.

26. Civil libertarians have a range of opinions as to when, if ever, these concepts may legitimately be employed to restrict speech. *See infra* text accompanying notes 69-87 & 116-58. For relevant ACLU policies, see *infra* note 77. The only doctrinal concept advanced by Professor Lawrence as a justification for regulating campus hate speech that the ACLU expressly and categorically rejects is group defamation. *See* ACLU Policy Guide, *supra* note 11, at Policy No. 6(c).

27. *See, e.g.,* Lawrence, at 450 & n.82 (supports variation on Stanford code which was broader than the one adopted in that it would apply to all common areas); *id.* at 437, 456-57 (urges regulation of racial epithets that do not involve face-to-face encounters, where victim is captive audience); *id.* at 451 n.85 (argues that fighting words include not only those addressed face-to-face, as under current doctrine, but should "be expanded in the case of racist verbal assaults to include those words that are intentionally spoken in the presence of members of the denigrated group"); *id.* at 463 n.119, 464 n.120 (endorses regulation of group defamation); *id.* at 481 n.169 ("Mari Matsuda has made a more radical venture, which I believe may well in the long run prove more satisfactory [than Lawrence's own proposals]. She calls for a doctrinal change that would involve an explicit content-based rejection of narrowly defined racist speech . . . .").

The rationales that Professor Lawrence advances for the regulations he endorses are so open-ended that, if accepted, they would appear to warrant the prohibition of *all* racist speech, and thereby would cut to the core of our system of free expression.

Although Professor Lawrence's specific proposed code appears relatively modest, his supporting rationales depend on nothing less immodest than the abrogation of the traditional distinctions between speech and conduct and between state action and private action. He equates private racist speech with governmental racist conduct.[28] This approach offers no principled way to confine racist speech regulations to the particular contours of the Stanford code, or indeed to any particular contours at all. Professor Lawrence apparently acknowledges that, if accepted, his theories could warrant the prohibition of *all* private racist speech.[29] Moreover, although he stresses the particular evils of racism,[30] he also says that "much of my analysis applies to violent pornography and homophobic hate speech."[31] Thus, Professor Lawrence himself demonstrates that traditional civil libertarians are hardly paranoiac when we fear that any specific, seemingly modest proposal to regulate speech may in fact represent the proverbial "thin edge of the wedge" for initiating broader regulations.

As just explained, the relatively narrow Stanford code that Professor Lawrence endorses is incongruous with his broad theoretical rationale. The Stanford code also is at odds with Professor Lawrence's pragmatic rationale. The harms of racist speech that he seeks to redress largely remain untouched by the rule. For example, Professor Lawrence movingly recounts the pain suffered by his sister's family as a result of racist expression,[32] as well as the anxiety he endured as a boy even from the

---

28. *See* Lawrence, at 438-49.

29. *See id.* at 449 ("This precedent [Brown v. Board of Educ., 347 U.S. 483 (1954), and its progeny] may not mean that we should advocate the government regulation of all racist speech . . . .").

30. For example, Lawrence argues that racist speech and conduct are unique because of the direct link between speech or act and harm:

> I do not contend that *all* conduct with an expressive component should be treated as unprotected speech. To the contrary, my suggestion that racist conduct amounts to speech is premised upon a unique characteristic of racism—namely its reliance upon the defamatory message of white supremacy to achieve its injurious purpose.

Id. at 440 n.42.

It is difficult to understand how racism is unique in terms of the asserted link between its message and its harm. Surely the same connection would exist between any form of group hatred and its resulting harm. For example, sexism relies on the message of male supremacy; homophobia relies on the message of heterosexual supremacy.

31. *Id.* at 436 n.27. *See also supra* note 27.

32. *See* Lawrence, at 459-61.

possibility of racist expression.[33] Yet the Stanford code clearly would not apply to any of the unspoken racist expressions that may lurk beneath the surface of much parlance in American life. Moreover, the regulation also would not apply unless the speech was directly targeted at a specific victim.[34] Therefore, it would not have relieved Professor Lawrence or his family of the traumas they experienced. Furthermore, the Stanford code would not address the racist incident at Stanford that led to its adoption.[35] Likewise, many additional campus racist incidents catalogued by Professor Lawrence and others would be beyond the scope of the Stanford code.

Two problems arise from the disharmony between the breadth of the racist speech regulations endorsed by Professor Lawrence and the harm that inspires them. First, this disparity underscores the rules' ineffectiveness. The regulations do not even address much of racist speech, let alone the innumerable other manifestations of racism which—as Professor Lawrence himself stresses[36]—pervade our society. Second, this disharmony encourages the proponents of hate speech regulations to seek to narrow the gap between the underlying problem and their favored solution by recommending broader regulations. For example, Professor Mari Matsuda recently proposed a substantially more restrictive hate speech regulation on the theory that such a regulation is needed to redress the harm suffered by hate speech victims.[37] Professor Lawrence has indicated his approval of Professor Matsuda's approach.[38] And the wedge widens.

This Article attempts to bridge some of the gaps that Professor Lawrence believes separate advocates of equality from advocates of free speech. It shows that—insofar as proponents of hate speech regulations endorse relatively narrow rules that encompass only a limited category of racist expression—these gaps are not that significant in practical effect. It also demonstrates that the first and fourteenth amendments are allies rather than antagonists. Most importantly, this Article maintains that equality will be served most effectively by continuing to apply traditional,

---

33. *Id.* at 482-83.

34. *See infra* text accompanying note 197 (quoting Stanford code).

35. *See* Gottlieb, *supra* note 4, at 3 (Professor Thomas Grey, who drafted the Stanford code, said "his rule probably wouldn't apply to one of the most publicized racial incidents at Stanford, when a white student left on a black student's door a poster of Beethoven drawn as a black caricature."). The broader variation of the Stanford code which Professor Lawrence endorsed, *see* Lawrence, at 450 n.82, apparently would have applied to this Stanford incident, *see id.* at 456 n.101, but not to the incident endured by his sister or to his boyhood ordeal.

36. *See* Lawrence, at 467-71. *See, e.g., id.* at 468 ("Racism is ubiquitous. We are all racists.").

37. *See* Matsuda, *supra* note 13.

38. `See` Lawrence, at 481 n.169.

speech-protective precepts to racist speech, because a robust freedom of speech ultimately is necessary to combat racial discrimination. Professor Lawrence points out that free speech values as well as equality values may be promoted by regulating certain verbal harassment, and retarded by not regulating it.[39] But it also must be recognized that equality values may be promoted most effectively by not regulating certain hate speech and retarded by regulating it.[40]

Part I of this Article demonstrates that some traditional civil libertarians agree with Professor Lawrence's point that some speech amounts to verbal assault or harassment and may be subject to government regulation. Part II shows that Professor Lawrence's conception of regulable racist speech is broader than that permitted by established constitutional doctrine and would endanger fundamental free speech values. Part III explores the even greater danger to free speech values posed by Professor Lawrence's expansive rationales.[41] Of primary importance, Part III exposes the flaws in Professor Lawrence's major argument—the argument that *Brown v. Board of Education*[42] and other decisions that invalidate *governmental* racist *conduct* somehow legitimize regulation of *non-governmental* racist *speech.*

Notwithstanding my differences with Professor Lawrence about the boundaries of regulable racist expression, it is important to place these differences in proper perspective. Even the racist speech that he would regulate constitutes only a small fraction of all racist speech. Thus, most racist expression would remain untouched under both Professor Lawrence's approach and the approach traditionally endorsed by civil libertarians and the Supreme Court. More importantly, as Part IV discusses, Professor Lawrence's proposal would not effectively address the underlying problem of racism itself, of which racist speech is a symptom. Part IV shows that suppressing racist speech could even aggravate racially discriminatory attitudes. Thus, the goals of free speech and of eradicating racism are not incompatible, as Professor Lawrence sometimes suggests.[43] Rather, as he also recognizes,[44] these goals are mutually reinforcing. Although these points focus on Professor Lawrence's specific proposal, they apply as well to all other proposals to censor hate speech.

---

39. *See* Lawrence, at 437, 453 n.92, 455, 458.
40. *See infra* text accompanying notes 365-96.
41. *See supra* notes 27-31.
42. 347 U.S. 483 (1954).
43. *See supra* notes 18-19.
44. *See id.*

Finally, Part V maintains that we should channel our efforts toward devising means to combat racism that are consistent with the first amendment. This method ultimately will be more effective than censorship in promoting both equality and free speech. The resurgence of racist expression on American campuses has sparked a revitalized national dedication to promoting racial equality on college campuses and throughout our society and the forging of creative strategies for doing so.[45] In order to counter racist speech, Professor Lawrence urges us to "think creatively as lawyers."[46] But if we are to understand and eradicate the complex root causes of racial discrimination, then we must think creatively as *more* than just lawyers.[47] We must draw upon the insights and skills of educators, sociologists, and psychologists. To draft legal rules that address only one manifestation of these deeper problems of racial inequality is at best ineffective, and at worst counterproductive.

I. Some Limited Forms of Campus Hate Speech May Be Regulable Under Current Constitutional Doctrine

A. *General Constitutional Principles Applicable to Regulating Campus Hate Speech*

To put in proper perspective the specific points of disagreement between Professor Lawrence's analysis and traditional civil libertarian views, the points of agreement first should be noted. Professor Lawrence usefully rehearses the many shared understandings between advocates of a traditional doctrine, which protects much racist speech, and advocates of various less protective regulations. Professor Lawrence acknowledges that there are strong reasons for sheltering even racist speech, in terms of reinforcing society's commitment to tolerance and mobilizing its opposition to intolerance.[48] Consequently, he recognizes that to frame the debate in terms of a conflict between freedom of speech and the elimination of racism poses a false dichotomy.[49] Accordingly, he urges civil libertarians to examine not just the substance of our position on racist speech, but

---

45. In response to the recent wave of racist expressions on campus, many universities have adopted programs designed to counter racism and to promote intergroup relations. *See infra* note 409. This development illustrates one of the advantages of refusing to censor hate speech: Society is motivated to counter the underlying biases that it manifests. *See infra* text accompanying notes 391-96.

46. Lawrence, at 480.

47. I owe this formulation to Ira Glasser, Executive Director of the ACLU (and a non-lawyer).

48. *See* Lawrence, at 436, 458 & n.105.

49. *See id.* at 435-36.

also the way in which we enter the debate, to ensure that we condemn racist ideas at the same time as we defend the right to utter them.[50]

There may be even more common ground between Professor Lawrence and the traditional civil libertarian position than he expressly acknowledges. In presenting the civil libertarian position as absolute and uni-focused, he oversimplifies and thereby distorts it. For example, as previously noted, Professor Lawrence sets up a "straw civil libertarian" who purportedly would afford *absolute* protection to *all* racist speech— or at least "all racist speech that stops short of physical violence."[51] In fact, as evidenced by ACLU policies, traditional civil libertarians do not take such an extreme position. Indeed, some civil libertarians recently have charged that the ACLU has maintained an *insufficiently* absolutist position toward free speech in the context of campus hate speech, at the same time that Professor Lawrence, also a civil libertarian, charges that its position has been *too* absolutist.[52] Moreover, as a matter of both policy[53] and practice,[54] the ACLU already condemns the ideas expressed by racist and other anti-civil libertarian speakers at the same time that it defends their right to utter them. Thus, contrary to Professor Lawrence's implication,[55] such condemnation does not constitute an innovation.

Professor Lawrence also mischaracterizes traditional civil libertarians when he asserts that they tolerate the regulation of "garden variety" fighting words, but not racist fighting words.[56] Some civil libertarians might agree with the Supreme Court's formerly stated view[57] that a narrowly defined category of "fighting words" might not be constitutionally

---

50. *See id.* at 476-77.

51. *Id.* at 449. *See also id.* at 438, 457, 461, 473-74, 476-77.

52. *See, e.g.,* Hentoff, *If a Civil Liberties Union Can't Agree on Free Speech . . . ,* Wash. Post, June 2, 1990, at A19, col. 1; Hentoff, *The Different Faces of the ACLU,* Wash. Post, March 31, 1990, at A27, col. 1; Rohde, *Any Limitations Are Bound to Violate the First Amendment,* Los Angeles Daily J., July 19, 1990, at 6, col. 4 ("I urge the California chapters of the ACLU to withdraw their new policy [permitting narrow regulations on campus hate speech] and replace it with something that's worked for nearly 200 years—the First Amendment.").

53. *See* ACLU Policy Guide, *supra* note 11, at Policy No. 46. The Policy states that: "[T]he democratic standards in which the ACLU believes and for which it fights run directly counter to the philosophy of the Klan and other ultra-right groups"; therefore, the ACLU should deal "with the difficult dilemma of having to defend the civil liberties of groups whose activities do fundamental injury to civil liberties" [by] vigorously present[ing] its opposing views "while defending the group's right to speak." *See also id.* at Policy No. 312.

54. *See infra* notes 338-55.

55. *See* Lawrence, at 476-81.

56. *Id.* at 436-37.

57. *But see infra* text accompanying notes 116-31 (Court has construed fighting words exception to free speech protection so narrowly that some scholars believe there no longer is such an exception).

protected.[58] Other civil libertarians maintain that "fighting words" should not be excluded from first amendment protection.[59] They all agree, however, that racist fighting words should receive the same degree of protection (or nonprotection) as other fighting words.

Consistent with Professor Lawrence's free speech concerns, the category of racist speech he seeks to regulate under the Stanford code[60] is relatively narrow compared to other campus hate speech rules.[61] In important respects, this proposal overlaps with the traditional civil libertarian position. On the end of the spectrum where speech is constitutionally protected, Professor Lawrence agrees[62] with courts and traditional civil libertarians that the first amendment should protect racist speech in a *Skokie*-type context.[63] The essentials of a *Skokie*-type setting are that the offensive speech occurs in a public place and the event is announced in advance. Hence, the offensive speech can be either avoided or countered by opposing speech. Traditional civil libertarians

---

58. *See* T. EMERSON, THE SYSTEM OF FREE EXPRESSION 337-38 (1970) (" '[F]ighting words' can be considered the equivalent of knocking a chip off the shoulder—the traditional symbolic act that puts the parties in the role of physical combatants."); L. TRIBE, AMERICAN CONSTITUTIONAL LAW § 12-10, at 852-53 (2d ed. 1988) ("[I]t is not difficult to recognize the genuine dilemma that law enforcement officers may confront when violence is incipient; although free speech would be suppressed, silencing the speaker is certainly preferable to a blood bath.").

59. *See, e.g.,* F. HAIMAN, SPEECH AND LAW IN A FREE SOCIETY (1981). Haiman states that:

> [I]t is my contention that in *all* of the circumstances in which antagonistic crowds or individuals respond or threaten to respond violently to communicators, the *audience* should be held responsible for its behavior, and not the speaker . . . . [V]iolent *re*action, by definition, is born in the psyche of the respondent. The idea to attack the communicator is not implanted or urged by the speaker, as might an idea to commit illegal acts be initiated and advocated by one who incites a supportive audience . . . .
>
> . . . [I]f hostile audiences are not held responsible for their own behavior . . . they will soon learn that they have the power to exercise a "heckler's veto" over the speech of their antagonists.

Id. at 258; *see also id.* at 20-23, 132-35, 253-54, 256-58.

60. *See infra* text accompanying note 197.

61. For example, the Stanford code applies only to intentionally insulting words "addressed directly" to an individual or a small number of individuals. *See infra* text accompanying note 197. In contrast, the Michigan rule which was recently held to violate the first amendment, *see infra* text accompanying notes 208-12, did not require either that the penalized words be intentionally insulting or that they be addressed to specific individuals. Moreover, the Michigan rule originally proscribed speech that "[c]reates an intimidating, hostile, or demeaning environment." *See infra* note 203. The same overbroad, vague language is contained in the rule recently adopted by the University of Wisconsin Board of Regents. *See* UWS 17.06(2)(a)(2) (effective Sept. 1, 1990).

62. *See* Lawrence, at 457 & n.103.

63. The reference is to an American neo-Nazi group's efforts, in 1977-78, to gain permission to demonstrate in Skokie, Illinois, a community with a large Jewish population, including many Holocaust survivors. For the judicial opinions rejecting arguments that Skokie residents should be protected from such personally odious expressions, see, e.g., Collin v. Smith, 578 F.2d 1197, 1205-07 (7th Cir.), *cert. denied,* 439 U.S. 916 (1978); Village of Skokie v. National Socialist Party, 69 Ill. 2d 605, 612-18, 373 N.E.2d 21, 23-25 (1978). For an excellent account of both the specific Skokie controversy and the general issues it raised, see A. NEIER, DEFENDING MY ENEMY: AMERICAN NAZIS, THE SKOKIE CASE, AND THE RISKS OF FREEDOM (1979).

recognize that this speech causes psychic pain. We nonetheless agree with the decision of the Seventh Circuit in *Skokie*[64] that this pain is a necessary price for a system of free expression, which ultimately redounds to the benefit of racial and other minorities.[65] Professor Lawrence apparently shares this view.

On the other end of the spectrum, where expression may be prohibited, traditional civil libertarians agree with Professor Lawrence that the first amendment should not necessarily protect targeted individual harassment just because it happens to use the vehicle of speech. The ACLU maintains this non-absolutist position, for example, with regard to sexually harassing speech on campus or in the workplace. The ACLU recently adopted a policy that specifically addresses racist harassment on campus,[66] and it previously had adopted analogous policies concerning sexual harassment on campus and in the workplace. These earlier policies recognize that unlawful sex discrimination can consist of words specifically directed to a particular individual—words that undermine the individual's continued ability to function as a student or employee. With regard to sexual harassment on campus, ACLU policy provides:

> College[s] and universities should take those steps necessary to prevent the abuse of power which occurs . . . where a pattern and practice of sexual conduct or sexually demeaning or derogatory comments is directed at a specific student or gender [and] has definable consequences for the student that demonstrably hinders her or his learning experience as a student. This policy does not extend to verbal harassment that has no other effect on its recipient than to create an unpleasant learning environment.[67]

As the last sentence of this policy emphasizes, the ACLU demands evidence that harassing speech causes verifiable harm that directly interferes with a student's education in a more tangible, specific manner than creating an "unpleasant environment." A parallel limiting concept is embodied in the ACLU's definition of verbal sexual harassment in the workplace as:

> [E]xpression . . . directed at a specific employee [that] has definable consequences for the individual victim that demonstrably hinders or completely prevents her or his continuing to function as an employee.

---

64. *Collin*, 578 F.2d at 1197.

65. For an elaboration of this point, see *infra* text accompanying notes 408-34.

I use the term "minorities" rather than "people of color" because the groups I intend to signify include those differentiated by characteristics other than race or ethnicity, such as religion, sexual orientation, or physical disability. I recognize, however, that the term "minorities" may "impl[y] a certain delegitimacy in a majoritarian system" and in fact describes groups that in the aggregate are a majority. Williams, *Alchemical Notes: Reconstructing Ideals From Deconstructed Rights*, 22 HARV. C.R.-C.L. L. REV. 401, 404 n.4 (1987).

66. *See supra* note 11.

67. ACLU Policy Guide, *supra* note 11, at Policy No. 72; *see also supra* note 11 and Appendix.

Ordinarily these would be the sort of consequences that could give rise to an action for civil damages or a claim for workers' compensation, unemployment compensation or sick leave. This policy does not extend to verbal harassment that has no other effect on its recipient than to create an unpleasant working environment.[68]

These ACLU policies recognize that conduct that infringes on the right to equal educational (or employment) opportunities, regardless of gender (or other invidious classifications) should not be condoned simply because it includes expressive elements.

To be sure, there is no clear boundary between speech that "demonstrably hinders" a learning (or working) experience and speech that "creates an unpleasant learning" (or working) environment. Accordingly, even civil libertarians who agree that this is the appropriate line to draw between unprotected and protected speech in the harassment context still would be expected to disagree about whether particular speech fell on one side of this boundary or the other. Moreover, some civil libertarians might endorse broader definitions of unprotected harassing speech,[69] whereas others might insist on narrower definitions.[70] However, the essential underlying point still stands: In the analogous context of regulating sexually harassing speech, traditional civil libertarians share what Professor Lawrence describes as a "moderate" perspective with regard to racially harassing speech—i.e., that such speech should be neither absolutely protected nor absolutely prohibited.[71]

---

68. ACLU Policy Guide, *supra* note 11, at Policy No. 316.

69. *See supra* note 11.

70. *See, e.g.,* F. HAIMAN, *supra* note 59, at 148-56 (would limit sanctions for verbal infliction of emotional distress to cases of injury through intentional factual misrepresentation).

71. *See* C. Lawrence, Presentation at ACLU Biennial Conference, *supra* note †, at 7. The Supreme Court applies a more searching degree of scrutiny to race-based discrimination than to gender-based discrimination. *Compare* Korematsu v. United States, 323 U.S. 214 (1944) ("strict scrutiny" standard applies to race discrimination claims) *with* Craig v. Boren, 429 U.S. 190 (1976) ("intermediate scrutiny" standard applies to gender discrimination claims). Moreover, at least since Brown v. Board of Educ., 347 U.S. 483 (1954), the Supreme Court consistently has enforced the equal protection clause with particular vigor in the context of promoting racial equality in education. *See* Bob Jones Univ. v. United States, 461 U.S. 574, 593 (1983) ("An unbroken line of cases following *Brown v. Board of Education* establishes beyond doubt this Court's view that racial discrimination in education violates a most fundamental national public policy, as well as rights of individuals."). Therefore, the ACLU rationale for treating some verbal harassment of students as prohibited gender-based discrimination, coupled with Supreme Court decisions, warrants treating some expressive conduct as prohibited race-based discrimination.

Professor Lawrence inexplicably asserts that "the suggestion" that the ACLU "adopt a policy concerning racist speech on campus . . . . [t]hus far . . . has not found widespread support within the ranks of the organization." Lawrence, at 478 n.163. He cites no support for this assertion, nor is there any. Since no poll has been undertaken of the approximately 300,000 members who constitute the ACLU's "ranks," it would be impossible to prove any generalization about their position on the indicated suggestion. Moreover, three ACLU affiliates have adopted a policy that does not oppose campus regulations of certain verbal harassment. *See supra* note 11 and Appendix.

17

Specifically in the context of racist speech, the ACLU has recognized that otherwise punishable conduct should not be shielded simply because it relies in part on words. Some examples were provided by ACLU President Norman Dorsen:

> During the Skokie episode, the ACLU refused to defend a Nazi who was prosecuted for offering a cash bounty for killing a Jew. The reward linked the speech to action in an impermissible way. Nor would we defend a Nazi (or anyone else) whose speech interfered with a Jewish religious service, or who said, "There's a Jew; let's get him."[72]

The foregoing ACLU positions are informed by established principles that govern the protectibility of speech. Under these principles, speech may be regulated if it is an essential element of violent or unlawful conduct,[73] if it is likely to cause an immediate injury by its very utterance,[74] and if it is addressed to a "captive audience" unable to avoid assaultive messages.[75] It should be stressed that each of these criteria is ambiguous and difficult to apply in particular situations. Accordingly, the ACLU would insist that these exceptions to free speech be strictly construed and would probably find them to be satisfied only in rare factual circumstances.[76] Nevertheless, ACLU policies expressly recognize that if certain speech fits within these narrow parameters, then it could be regulable.[77]

---

72. Dorsen, *Is There a Right to Stop Offensive Speech? The Case of the Nazis in Skokie,* in CIVIL LIBERTIES IN CONFLICT 133-34 (L. Gostin ed. 1988); *see also* A. NEIER, *supra* note 63, at 89-90.

73. The law may sanction crimes and torts accomplished by words without violating the first amendment, although it is sometimes hard to distinguish between protected expression advocating the commission of criminal or civil offenses and unprotected expression that actually constitutes an element of such offenses. *See generally* Greenawalt, *Speech and Crime,* 1980 AM. B. FOUND. RES. J. 645 (examining the tension between the protective approach to advocacy of crime taken by the Supreme Court and criminal code solicitation provisions). Crimes and torts that may consist primarily of words include bribery, fraud, and libel. *See infra* note 321 (sex-designated advertisements for jobs or housing are unprotected, as integral elements of proscribed discriminatory conduct).

74. This category is illustrated by Oliver Wendell Holmes' proverbial example of "falsely shouting fire in a theater and causing a panic." Schenck v. United States, 249 U.S. 47, 52 (1919). This theory also is invoked to justify regulating "fighting words" and group defamation. *See infra* text accompanying notes 116-51 & 165-75. Although the ACLU has no policy expressly addressing the fighting words doctrine, it explicitly rejects group defamation laws as inconsistent with the first amendment. *See* ACLU Policy Guide, *supra* note 11, at Policy No. 6(c).

75. *See* L. TRIBE, *supra* note 58, § 12-18, at 941.

76. There is no basis for Professor Lawrence's implication that traditional civil libertarians might support "less protection [for captive audiences] when they are held captive by racist speakers." Lawrence, at 438. *Compare supra* text accompanying notes 56-59 (Professor Lawrence incorrectly suggests that traditional civil libertarians would support less constitutional protection for racist fighting words than for other fighting words).

77. Regarding speech that is an essential element of unlawful conduct, the ACLU Policy Guide, *supra* note 11, at Policy No. 16, states that, "[T]here is . . . [a] need for the regulation of selling practices to minimize fraud, deception, and misrepresentations . . . . If the sale or transaction

The captive audience concept in particular is an elusive and challenging one to apply. As Professor Tribe cautioned, this concept "is dangerously encompassing, and the Court has properly been reluctant to accept its implications whenever a regulation is not content-neutral."[78] Noting that we are "often 'captives' outside the sanctuary of the home and subject to objectionable speech,"[79] the Court has ruled that, in public places, we bear the burden of averting our attention from expression we find offensive.[80] Otherwise, the Court explained, "a majority [could] silence dissidents simply as a matter of personal predilections."[81] The Court has been less reluctant to apply the captive audience concept to

---

is one that can be validly regulated or prohibited, then communications that are an integral part of such a sale or transaction can be regulated."

Regarding speech that can cause an immediate injury by its very utterance, see ACLU Policy Guide, *supra* note 11, at Policy No. 6 (accepts limitations on expression that creates "clear and present danger" of immediate unlawful action); *id.* at Policy No. 37 (recognizing that, under strictly limited circumstances, certain lawsuits may be brought for libel and invasion of privacy through speech without violating first amendment).

Regarding captive audiences, the ACLU Policy Guide, *supra* note 11, at Policy No. 43, states that:

> [T]he First Amendment is not inconsistent with reasonable regulations designed to restrict sensory intrusions so intense as to be assaultive. Reasonable regulations are those that apply only to time, place and manner without regard to content. . . . What constitutes a "reasonable" regulation will necessarily vary depending upon such factors as (1) the size of the . . . area involved, (2) the duration [or] frequency with which an individual is in the area . . . , or (3) the extent to which alternatives exist so that the individual can reasonably be called upon to avoid the area. . . . Assaultive sensory intrusions are those that are objectionable to the average person because of an excessive degree of intensity, e.g., volume or brightness, and which cannot be avoided.
>
> In larger public spaces . . . all communication is permitted unless it interferes with the primary purpose of the space. . . .
>
> In open public areas . . . people are able to move away from communication which they consider offensive. So long as there is ample public space[ ] where communication is unrestricted, the government may creat[sic] and maintain reasonably limited sanctuaries in public places where people can go for quiet and contemplation.

78. L. TRIBE, *supra* note 58, § 12-19, at 949-50 n.24. For an argument that the captive audience concept should be construed narrowly, see Haiman, *Speech v. Privacy: Is There a Right Not to be Spoken To?*, 67 Nw. U.L. REV. 153, 184 (1972). Haiman argues that:

> [H]uman beings have a significant ability mentally to reject many assaultive stimuli. The process known as "selective perception" enables us to generally choose what we wish to assimilate from the multitude of sensory bombardments surrounding us. . . . [W]e also have a strong tendency to screen out or distort messages that are inconsistent with . . . our current beliefs.
>
> Given these tendencies . . . . one might argue that the possibilities of unwelcome messages penetrating the psychological armor of unwilling audiences are so small that we ought to be worrying more about how to help unpopular communicators get through to reluctant listeners than how to give further protection from speech to those who already know too well how to isolate themselves from alien ideas.

79. Rowan v. United States Post Office Dep't, 397 U.S. 728, 738 (1970).

80. *See. e.g.*, Erznoznik v. Jacksonville, 422 U.S. 205, 210 (1975) (ordinance banning movies showing nudity on drive-in screens visible from street could not be upheld to protect sensibilities of involuntary passers-by); Cohen v. California, 403 U.S. 15, 21 (1971) (Individuals offended by expression on defendant's jacket worn in courthouse corridor "could effectively avoid further bombardment of their sensibilities simply by averting their eyes.").

81. *Cohen.* 403 U.S. at 21.

private homes.[82] However, the Court has held that even in the home, free speech values may outweigh privacy concerns, requiring individuals to receive certain unwanted communications.[83]

The Court's application of the captive audience doctrine illustrates the general notion that an important factor in determining the protection granted to speech is the place where it occurs.[84] At one extreme, certain public places—such as public parks—have been deemed "public forums," where freedom of expression should be especially protected.[85] At the other extreme, some private domains—such as residential buildings—have been deemed places where freedom of expression should be subject to restriction in order to guard the occupants' privacy and tranquillity.[86] In between these two poles, certain public areas might be held not to be public forums because the people who occupy them might be viewed as "captive."[87]

The foregoing principles that govern the permissibility of speech regulations in general should guide our analysis of the permissibility of particular speech regulations in the academic setting. The Supreme Court has declared that within the academic environment freedom of expression should receive heightened protection[88] and that "a university

---

82. *See, e.g., Rowan*, 397 U.S. at 737 (upholding addressee's statutory right to compel mailer of material which is deemed erotic, at addressee's sole discretion, to remove addressee's name from mailing list and stop all future mailings); Kovacs v. Cooper, 336 U.S. 77, 87 (1949) (upholding ordinance proscribing use of sound trucks in "loud and raucous" manner, in part because individual in his home is "practically helpless to escape" noise).

83. *See* Consolidated Edison Co. v. Public Serv. Comm'n, 447 U.S. 530, 542 (1980) (Court rejected captive audience objection to utility company's insertion of materials advocating nuclear power development in its billings, reasoning that customers could "escape exposure to the objectionable material simply by transferring the bill insert from envelope to wastebasket").

84. *See* G. STONE, L. SEIDMAN, C. SUNSTEIN & M. TUSHNET, CONSTITUTIONAL LAW 1177-1201, 1267-73 (1986).

85. *See* L. TRIBE, *supra* note 58, § 12-20, at 955-65.

86. *See supra* note 82; *see also* Carey v. Brown, 447 U.S. 455, 471 (1980) ("Preserving the sanctity of the home, the one retreat to which men and women can repair to escape from the tribulations of their daily pursuits, is surely an important value. . . . Protecting the well-being, tranquility, and privacy of the home is certainly of the highest order in a free and civilized society.").

87. *See* Lehman v. City of Shaker Heights, 418 U.S. 298, 302 (1974) (plurality opinion) (transit system advertising space not public forums, because users were captive audience); *id.* at 306-07 (Douglas, J., concurring). *But see* Frisby v. Schultz, 487 U.S. 474, 480 (1988) (residential neighborhood streets are public forum).

88. *See, e.g.,* Sweeney v. New Hampshire, 354 U.S. 234, 250 (1957) ("Teachers and students must always remain free to inquire, to study and to evaluate, to gain new maturity and understanding; otherwise our civilization will stagnate and die."). *See also* Keyishian v. Board of Regents, 385 U.S. 589, 603 (1967) (the classroom is "peculiarly the marketplace of ideas"); Shelton v. Tucker, 364 U.S. 479, 487 (1960) (nowhere are constitutional freedoms more vital than in American schools).

In University of Pa. v. EEOC, 110 S. Ct. 577 (1990), the Court said that these earlier cases did not protect a university from disclosing to the EEOC confidential peer review materials regarding the tenure candidacy of a former faculty member who allegedly had suffered race- and gender-based discrimination. However, the Court acknowledged "the crucial role universities play in the dissemi-

campus . . . possesses many of the characteristics of a traditional public forum."[89] These considerations would suggest that hate speech should receive special protection within the university community. Conversely, Professor Mari Matsuda argues that equality guarantees and other principles that might weigh in favor of prohibiting racist speech also are particularly important in the academic context.[90]

The appropriate analysis is more complex than either set of generalizations assumes. In weighing the constitutional concerns of free speech, equality, and privacy that hate speech regulations implicate, decisionmakers must take into account the particular context within the university in which the speech occurs. For example, the Court's generalizations about the heightened protection due free speech in the academic world certainly are applicable to some campus areas, such as parks, malls, or other traditional gathering places. The generalizations, however, may not be applicable to other areas, such as students' dormitory rooms. These rooms constitute the students' homes. Accordingly, under established free speech tenets, students should have the right to avoid being exposed to others' expression by seeking refuge in their rooms.[91]

Some areas on campus present difficult problems concerning the appropriate level of speech protection because they share characteristics of both private homes and public forums. For example, one could argue that hallways, common rooms, and other common areas in dormitory buildings constitute extensions of the individual students' rooms.[92] On the other hand, one could argue that these common areas constitute traditional gathering places and should be regarded as public forums, open to expressive activities at least by all dormitory residents if not by

---

nation of ideas in our society," *id.* at 585, and it reaffirmed an "academic-freedom right against governmental attempts to influence the content of academic speech," *id.* at 586.

89. Cornelius v. NAACP Legal Defense and Educ. Fund, 473 U.S. 788, 803 (1985); *see also* Widmar v. Vincent, 454 U.S. 263, 267 & n.5 (1981) (through policy of accommodating students' meetings, public university created open forum for student groups).

90. *See* Matsuda, *supra* note 13. Professor Matsuda states that:

Many of the new adults who come to live and study at the major universities are away from home for the first time, and at a vulnerable stage of psychological development. Students are particularly dependent on the university for community, for intellectual development, and for self-definition. Official tolerance of racist speech in this setting is more harmful than generalized tolerance in the community-at-large. It is harmful to student perpetrators in that it is a lesson in getting-away-with-it that will have lifelong repercussions. It is harmful to targets, who perceive the university as taking sides through inaction, and who are left to their own resources in coping with the damage wrought. Finally, it is a harm to the goals of inclusion, education, development of knowledge, and ethics that universities exist and stand for. Lessons of cynicism and hate replace lessons in critical thought and inquiry.

Id. at 2370-71 (footnotes omitted).

91. *See supra* text accompanying notes 82-86.

92. Professor Lawrence so argues, *see* Lawrence, at 456.

21

the broader community. Such an argument would derive general support from Supreme Court decisions that uphold the free speech rights of demonstrators in residential neighborhoods on the theory that an individual resident's right of stopping "the flow of information into [his or her] household" does not allow him to impede the flow of this same information to his neighbors.[93] The Supreme Court, however, recently declined to resolve the specific issue of whether university dormitories constitute public forums for free speech purposes.[94]

Even in the areas of the university reserved for academic activities, such as classrooms, the calculus to determine the level of speech protection is complex. On the one hand, the classroom is the quintessential "marketplace of ideas,"[95] which should be open to the vigorous and robust exchange of even insulting or offensive words, on the theory that such an exchange ultimately will benefit not only the academic community, but also the larger community, in its pursuit of knowledge and understanding.[96]

On the other hand, some minority students[97] contend that in the long run, the academic dialogue might be stultified rather than stimulated by the inclusion of racist speech. They maintain that such speech not only interferes with equal educational opportunities, but also deters the exercise of other freedoms, including those secured by the first

---

93. Organization for a Better Austin v. Keefe, 402 U.S. 415, 420 (1971) (invalidating injunction against leafletting in suburban residential areas as unjustified prior restraint); *see also* Frisby v. Schultz, 487 U.S. 474, 485 (1988) (in upholding ordinance regulating residential picketing, Court stressed that it prohibited only focused picketing in front of single residence; no broader-gauged picketing was prohibited).

94. *See* Board of Trustees v. Fox, 109 S. Ct. 3028, 3031 n.2 (1989). The district court in the same case had characterized these dormitories as "limited public forums." Fox v. Board of Trustees, 649 F. Supp. 1393, 1401 (N.D.N.Y. 1986).

95. Keyishian v. Board of Regents, 385 U.S. 589, 603 (1967).

96. *See* Schmidt, *Freedom of Thought: A Principle in Peril?*, YALE ALUMNI MAG., Oct. 1989, at 66 ("On some other campuses in this country, values of civility and community have been offered by some as paramount values of the university, even to the point of superseding freedom of expression. Such a view is wrong in principle, and, if extended, disastrous to freedom of thought.").

97. It should be stressed that not all minorities take this position, or support campus hate speech regulations. *See supra* note 21. In any event, even if a majority of a particular group supported a certain position, this would not necessarily mean that the position was correct in any sense, including in the sense that it advanced the group's self-interest. Justice Brennan, in a dissenting opinion in Michigan Dep't of State Police v. Sitz, 110 S. Ct. 2481, 2490 (1990), recently made this point in another constitutional context:

> I would hazard a guess that today's opinion will be received favorably by a majority of our society, who would willingly suffer the minimal intrusion of a sobriety checkpoint stop in order to prevent drunk driving. But consensus that a particular law enforcement technique serves a laudable purpose has never been the touchstone of constitutional analysis. . . .
> . . . "Moved by whatever momentary evil has aroused their fears, officials—perhaps even supported by a majority of citizens—may be tempted to conduct searches that sacrifice the liberty of each citizen to assuage the perceived evil."

Id. (quoting Olmstead v. United States, 277 U.S. 438, 478 (1928) (Brandeis, J., dissenting)).

amendment.[98] Professor Lawrence argues that, as a consequence of hate speech, minority students are deprived of the opportunity to participate in the academic interchange, and that the exchange is impoverished by their exclusion.[99] It must be emphasized, though, that expression subject to regulation on this rationale would have to be narrowly defined in order to protect the free flow of ideas that is vital to the academic community; thus, much expression would remain unregulated—expression which could be sufficiently upsetting to interfere with students' educational opportunities.[100]

Another factor that might weigh in favor of imposing some regulations on speech in class is that students arguably constitute a captive audience.[101] This characterization is especially apt when the course is required and class attendance is mandatory. Likewise, the case for regulation becomes more compelling the more power the racist speaker wields over the audience.[102] For example, the law should afford students

---

98.   *See* Letter from David Lee (a Stanford law student writing on behalf of Asian Law Students Association, Black Law Students Association, Jewish Law Students Association, Native American Law Students Association and Asian American Students Association) to Student Conduct Legislative Council (May 8, 1989), *reprinted in* Stanford Univ. Campus Rep., May 10, 1989, at 13. Lee stated that:

> [T]hose most concerned about having the [university rule] cover attacks against minority students that take the form of discriminatory speech are not advocating reduction in the freedom of speech. Rather, they are advocating more freedom of speech, more vigorous debate. . . . [R]acist speech [is] designed to silence the recipients of the speech, not to encourage them to debate. Racist speech silences its victims by warning them that they will suffer some kind of harm if they dare to speak up for their rights to work for economic success, to try to get a quality education, or to take part in the political process.

See also Matsuda, *supra* note 13, at 2337 ("In order to avoid receiving hate messages, victims have had to quit jobs, forgo education, leave their homes, avoid certain public places, curtail their own exercise of speech rights, and otherwise modify their behavior and demeanor.").

99.   *See* Lawrence, at 437, 456, 471. Professor Lawrence also makes a related point that the marketplace of ideas is distorted, to the detriment of the entire community, by the inclusion of racist speech. *See id.* at 467-71.

100.   *See* Grano, *supra* note 8. Grano stated that:

> One of the harms posited in the University of Michigan case was that some students found the speech at issue so upsetting that they had difficulty concentrating on their studies. The same harm could be posited, of course, in many other circumstances. During the Vietnam War, for example, the frequent and often caustic antiwar protests, which sometimes even expressed support for those whom the United States was fighting, may have extremely upset students who had served in battle, who had lost family members or friends in the war, or who simply believed that an unwavering loyalty was owed to their country. Similarly, many students, especially on segregated campuses in the South, may have been deeply disturbed by the civil rights protests gripping the nation and many universities during the 1960s.

Id. at 17.

101.   Professor Lawrence so argues. *See* Lawrence, at 456-57.

102.   *See, e.g.,* Contreras v. Crown Zellerbach Corp., 88 Wash. 2d 735, 741, 565 P.2d 1173, 1176 (1977) (reversing lower court's dismissal of Mexican-American employee's suit claiming he had been subject to racist slurs on the job, the court noted, "[W]hen one in a position of authority, actual or apparent, over another has allegedly made racial slurs and jokes and comments, this abusive conduct gives added impetus to the claim").

special protection from racist insults directed at them by their professors.[103]

Even if various areas of a university are not classified as public forums, and even if occupants of such areas are designated captive audiences, any speech regulations in these areas still would be invalid if they discriminated on the basis of a speaker's viewpoint. Viewpoint-based discrimination constitutes the most egregious form of censorship[104] and almost always violates the first amendment.[105] Accordingly, viewpoint discrimination is proscribed even in regulations that govern non-public forum government property[106] and regulations that protect captive audiences.[107]

Many proposed or adopted campus hate speech regulations constitute unconstitutional discrimination against particular views, either as they are written or as they are applied. This is a constitutional defect of the rule advocated by Professor Lawrence, for example.[108] He endorsed a variation on the Stanford regulation that expressly would have ex-

---

The ACLU's policy endorsing restrictions on a limited category of verbal sexual harassment on campus is confined to situations that involve "the abuse of power." *See supra* text accompanying note 67.

103. Speech by professors or administrators of public universities might be distinguishable from that of other members of university communities on the ground that it is arguably government speech, and hence subject to greater regulation. *See infra* text accompanying notes 299-302. However, faculty members and administrators have free speech rights of their own, which would weigh against government regulation. *See* Tinker v. Des Moines Indep. Community School Dist., 393 U.S. 503, 506 (1969); James v. Board of Educ., 461 F.2d. 566 (2d Cir 1972), *cert. denied,* 409 U.S. 1042 (1973); Russo v. Central School Dist. No. 1, 469 F.2d. 623 (2d Cir. 1972), *cert. denied,* 411 U.S. 392 (1973); Van Alstyne, *The Specific Theory of Academic Freedom and the General Issue of Civil Liberty,* in THE CONCEPT OF ACADEMIC FREEDOM 59 (E. Pincoffs ed. 1975); Van Alstyne, *The Constitutional Rights of Teachers and Professors,* 1970 DUKE L.J. 841. Moreover, university students should not necessarily view the speech of such individuals as representing the government's position, as opposed to that of the individuals. *See generally* Widmar v. Vincent, 454 U.S. 263 (1981) (public university students should recognize that state does not necessarily endorse speech by school-approved student organization meeting on campus). In any event, both public and private universities should encourage all their employees to be sensitive to the feelings and concerns of minority group members and to voluntarily couch their speech accordingly. *See infra* text accompanying notes 403-05.

104. *See* First Nat'l Bank v. Bellotti, 435 U.S. 765, 785 (1978); Madison Joint School Dist. No. 8 v. Wisconsin Employment Relations Comm'n, 429 U.S. 167, 175-76 (1976).

105. *See* Members of the City Council v. Taxpayers for Vincent, 466 U.S. 789, 804 (1984) ("a desire . . . to exclude the expression of certain points of view from the marketplace of ideas" is "plainly illegitimate" absent a demonstrated compelling state interest).

106. *See, e.g.,* United States v. Kokinda, 110 S. Ct. 3115, 3121 (1990); Cornelius v. NAACP Legal Defense and Educ. Fund, 473 U.S. 788, 806 (1985); Perry Educ. Ass'n v. Perry Local Educators' Ass'n, 460 U.S. 37, 43 (1983).

107. *See* Lehman v. City of Shaker Heights, 418 U.S. 298, 305 (1974); American Booksellers Ass'n v. Hudnut, 771 F.2d 323, 333 (7th Cir. 1985), *aff'd,* 475 U.S. 1001 (1986).

108. *See supra* note 24.

cluded speech directed at "dominant majority groups."[109] Despite the absence of explicit viewpoint discrimination in the rule that Stanford adopted, the chair of the committee that propounded this rule indicated that, as applied, it would effect viewpoint discrimination.[110] Professor Lawrence concedes that the Stanford code is facially content discriminatory,[111] and, as applied, probably viewpoint discriminatory as well.[112]

As the foregoing discussion illustrates, the question whether any particular racist speech should be subject to regulation is a fact-specific inquiry.[113] We cannot define particular words as inherently off limits, but rather we must examine every word in the overall context in which it is uttered.[114]

B. *Particular Speech-Limiting Doctrines Potentially Applicable to Campus Hate Speech*

In addition to the foregoing general principles, Professor Lawrence and other proponents of campus hate speech regulation invoke three specific doctrines in an attempt to justify such rules: the fighting words doctrine; the tort of intentional infliction of emotional distress; and the tort of group defamation.[115] As the following discussion shows, the Supreme

---

109. Lawrence, at 450 n.82. For the problems of equality and enforceability that this exception would cause, see *infra* note 387.

110. *See* Hentoff, *Stanford and the Speech Police,* Wash. Post, July 21, 1990, at A19, col. 1. Hentoff stated that:

> During a debate in the Faculty Senate, Professor Michael Bratman offered a hypothetical: in an angry exchange with a white student, a black student calls him a "honky SOB." I assume, said Bratman, that language would be prohibited.
>
> "No," said Professor [Robert] Rabin [a law professor who chairs the Student Conduct Legislative Council, which propounded the code]. The proposed speech standard takes the position, Rabin explained, that the white majority as a whole is not in as much need of protection from discriminatory harassing speech as are those who have suffered discrimination.
>
> "Calling a white a 'honky,'" Rabin said, "is not the same as calling a black a 'nigger.'"

111. The prohibition against content bias, the suppression of expression about an entire subject, was an outgrowth of the core prohibition against viewpoint bias. *See* Stone, *Restrictions on Speech Because of its Content: The Peculiar Case of Subject-Matter Restrictions,* 46 U. CHI. L. REV. 81 (1978). *See also infra* note 246 (discussing presumptive unconstitutionality of content-based speech regulations).

112. *See* Lawrence, at 451 n.83.

113. *See* L. TRIBE, *supra* note 58, § 12-10, at 853-54 (When government suppresses what would otherwise be constitutionally protected speech because of imminent violence, "the result is necessarily sensitive to even slight variations in the facts of the particular case.").

114. *See id.* § 12-10, at 850 (modern Court has rejected assumption of original "fighting words" doctrine, that certain words could be proscribed regardless of context in which they were used).

115. The University of Michigan based its rule on yet another approach, which focused on stigmatization and victimization of students, interference with academic efforts, and the creation of an intimidating or hostile educational environment. In Doe v. University of Mich., 721 F. Supp. 852 (E.D. Mich. 1989), this rule was held to violate the first amendment. Accordingly, some universities that had been considering a similar approach have apparently abandoned it in response to the *Doe*

Court has recognized that each of these doctrines may well be inconsistent with free speech principles. Therefore, these doctrines may not support any campus hate speech restrictions whatsoever. In any event, they at most would support only restrictions that are both narrowly drawn and narrowly applied.

1. *Fighting Words.* The fighting words doctrine is the principal model for the Stanford code, which Professor Lawrence supports.[116] However, this doctrine provides a constitutionally shaky foundation for several reasons: it has been substantially limited in scope and may no longer be good law; even if the Supreme Court were to apply a narrowed version of the doctrine, such an application would threaten free speech principles; and, as actually implemented, the fighting words doctrine suppresses protectible speech and entails the inherent danger of discriminatory application to speech by members of minority groups and dissidents.

Although the Court originally defined constitutionally regulable fighting words in fairly broad terms in *Chaplinsky v. New Hampshire,*[117] subsequent decisions have narrowed the definition to such a point that the doctrine probably would not apply to any of the instances of campus racist speech that Professor Lawrence and others seek to regulate. As originally formulated in *Chaplinsky,* the fighting words doctrine excluded from first amendment protection "insulting or 'fighting' words, those which by their very utterance inflict injury *or* tend to incite an immediate breach of the peace."[118]

In light of subsequent developments, it is significant to note that the first prong of *Chaplinsky*'s fighting words definition, words "which by their very utterance inflict injury," was dictum. The Court's actual holding was that the state statute at issue was justified by the state's interest in preserving the public peace by prohibiting "words likely to cause an average addressee to fight."[119] The Court stressed that "no words were forbidden except such as have a direct tendency to cause acts of violence

---

ruling. *See* Report of President's Ad Hoc Committee on Racial Harassment, University of Texas at Austin 17 (Nov. 27, 1989) [hereinafter University of Texas Report] (authored by committee chaired by Mark G. Yudof, Dean and James A. Elkins Centennial Chair in Law, University of Texas School of Law) ("For all of the reasons identified by the [*Doe*] court, [this] Committee early on abandoned the idea of recommending a racial harassment policy grounded in the Michigan approach. After the court's decision, a number of other universities withdrew similar policies, thus corroborating the Committee's decision."). *But see supra* note 61 (University of Wisconsin adopted a rule similar to the one adopted by the University of Michigan). For a discussion of the constitutional flaws in the Michigan-Wisconsin approach, see *infra* notes 208-15 and accompanying text.

116. *See* Lawrence, at 450-51. *See also infra* text accompanying note 197.

117. 315 U.S. 568 (1942).

118. *Id.* at 572 (emphasis added).

119. *Id.* at 573.

by the person to whom, individually, [they are] addressed."[120] The Court also held that the statute had been applied appropriately to Mr. Chaplinsky, who had called a city marshal "a God damned racketeer" and "a damned Fascist."[121] It explained that these "epithets [are] likely to provoke the average person to retaliation, and thereby cause a breach of the peace."[122]

In *Gooding v. Wilson*, the Court substantially narrowed *Chaplinsky*'s definition of fighting words by bringing that definition into line with *Chaplinsky*'s actual holding.[123] In *Gooding*, as well as in every subsequent fighting words case, the Court disregarded the dictum in which the first prong of *Chaplinsky*'s definition was set forth and treated only those words that "tend to incite an immediate breach of the peace" as fighting words. Consistent with this narrowed definition, the Court has invalidated regulations that hold certain words to be per se proscribable and insisted that each challenged utterance be evaluated contextually.[124] Thus, under the Court's current view, even facially valid laws that restrict fighting words may be applied constitutionally only in circumstances where their utterance almost certainly will lead to immediate violence.[125] Professor Tribe described this doctrinal development as, in effect, incorporating the clear and present danger test into the fighting words doctrine.[126]

---

120. *Id.*

121. *Id.* at 569.

122. *Id.* at 574.

123. 405 U.S. 518, 523 (1972) (where appellant had said to police officers, "White son of a bitch, I'll kill you," "You son of a bitch, I'll choke you to death," and "You son of a bitch, if you ever put your hands on me again, I'll cut you all to pieces," Court reversed conviction under law that it found overbroad in light of *Chaplinsky*).

124. *See, e.g.,* Karlan v. City of Cincinnati, 416 U.S. 924 (1974); Rosen v. California, 416 U.S. 924 (1974); Kelly v. Ohio, 416 U.S. 923 (1974); Lucas v. Arkansas, 416 U.S. 919 (1974); Brown v. Oklahoma, 408 U.S. 914 (1972); Lewis v. New Orleans, 408 U.S. 913 (1972); Rosenfeld v. New Jersey, 408 U.S. 901 (1972). Professor Lawrence twice states that Cohen v. California, 403 U.S. 15 (1971), quoted approvingly *Chaplinsky*'s language that certain words could be classified as unprotected fighting words per se, without regard to the circumstances in which they were uttered. *See* Lawrence, at 437 n.29, 453 n.92. But this citation does not support the continuing validity of that language, in light of the Court's subsequent rulings in *Gooding* and other fighting words cases.

125. *See, e.g.,* Eaton v. City of Tulsa, 415 U.S. 697, 699 (1974) (per curiam) (reversing contempt of court conviction for witness' use of word "chickenshit," since there was no showing that it posed imminent threat to administration of justice); Hess v. Indiana, 414 U.S. 105, 109 (1973) (per curiam) (reversing disorderly conduct conviction where statement during antiwar demonstration—"We'll take the fucking street later [or again]"—was not directed at any particular person or group and there was no showing that violence was imminent).

126. L. TRIBE, *supra* note 58, § 12-18, at 929 & n.9. A strictly limited fighting words concept is consistent with the views of Zechariah Chafee, whose writings provided the definition of "fighting words" that the Court adopted in Chaplinsky v. New Hampshire, 315 U.S. 568, 572. *See* Z. CHAFEE, FREE SPEECH IN THE UNITED STATES 151-52 (1941). In the same book, shortly after the passage proposing this definition, Chafee qualified his account of fighting words:

In accordance with its narrow construction of constitutionally permissible prohibitions upon "fighting words," the Court has overturned every single fighting words conviction that it has reviewed since *Chaplinsky*.[127] Moreover, in a subsequent decision, the Court overturned an injunction that had been based on the very word underlying the *Chaplinsky* conviction.[128]

For the foregoing reasons, Supreme Court Justices[129] and constitutional scholars persuasively maintain that *Chaplinsky*'s fighting words doctrine is no longer good law.[130] More importantly, constitutional scholars have argued that this doctrine should no longer be good law, for

---

This breach of peace theory is peculiarly liable to abuse when applied against unpopular expressions and practices. It makes a man a criminal simply because his neighbors have no self-control. . . . Thus . . . these crimes of injurious words must be kept within very narrow limits if they are not to give excessive opportunities for outlawing heterodox ideas.

Id.

127. *See supra* notes 124-25.

128. *Compare* Cafeteria Employees Local 302 v. Angelos, 320 U.S. 293, 295 (1943) (use of word "fascist" is "part of the conventional give-and-take in our economic and political controversies" and hence protected under federal labor law) *with Chaplinsky*, 315 U.S. at 573-74 (conviction affirmed on ground that words "God damned racketeer" and "damned Fascist," when addressed to police officer, were likely to provoke violent response). *See also* Note, *First Amendment Limits on Tort Liability for Words Intended to Inflict Severe Emotional Distress*, 85 COLUM. L. REV. 1749 (1985). The author stated that:

The principle that the advocacy of ideas is subject to regulation when such advocacy is intended to and likely to incite immediate violence remains good law. The continued validity of the application of this principle to the facts in *Chaplinsky*, however, is questionable because the addressee in *Chaplinsky* was a police officer. It is possible that the Court would now hold that because of his special training, the likelihood of a police officer responding violently is too remote for words addressed to a police officer to constitute "fighting" words.

Id. at 1768 n.98 (citations omitted). *Accord* Lewis v. City of New Orleans, 408 U.S. 913, 913 (1972) (Powell, J., concurring) (suggested that Court should apply separate standard when addressee of alleged fighting words is police officer).

129. Gooding v. Wilson, 405 U.S. 518, 537 (1972) (Blackmun, J., dissenting, joined by Burger, C.J.) ("[T]he Court, despite its protestations to the contrary, is merely paying lip service to *Chaplinsky*.").

130. *See, e.g.,* Gard, *Fighting Words as Free Speech*, 58 WASH. U.L.Q. 531, 536 (1980) (post-*Chaplinsky* Supreme Court decisions have rendered fighting words doctrine "nothing more than a quaint remnant of an earlier morality that has no place in a democratic society dedicated to the principle of free expression"); Shea, *"Don't Bother to Smile When You Call Me That"—Fighting Words and the First Amendment*, 63 KY. L.J. 1, 1-2 (1975) ("majority of the U.S. Supreme Court has gradually concluded that fighting words, no matter how narrowly defined, are a protected form of speech"). *See also* Letter from Professor Gerald Gunther to Professor George Parker, Chair of the Student Conduct Legislative Council at Stanford University (May 1, 1989), *reprinted in* Stanford Univ. Campus Rep., May 3, 1989, at 18 [hereinafter Gunther letter (May 1, 1989)]. In his letter, Professor Gunther stated that:

[T]here has been only *one* case in the history of the Supreme Court in which a majority of the Justices has ever found a statement to be a punishable resort to "fighting words." (That case was *Chaplinsky v. New Hampshire*, a nearly 50-year-old case involving words which would very likely not be found punishable today.) More important, in the nearly half-century since *Chaplinsky*, there have been repeated appeals to the Court to recognize the applicability of the "fighting words" exception. . . . [I]n every one of the subsequent attempted reliances on that exception, the Supreme Court has refused to affirm the chal-

reasons that are particularly weighty in the context of racist slurs.[131] First, as Professor Gard concluded in a comprehensive review of both Supreme Court and lower court decisions that apply the fighting words doctrine, the asserted governmental interest in preventing a breach of the peace is not logically furthered by this doctrine. He explained that:

> [I]t is fallacious to believe that personally abusive epithets, even if addressed face-to-face to the object of the speaker's criticism, are likely to arouse the ordinary law abiding person beyond mere anger to uncontrollable reflexive violence. Further, even if one unrealistically assumes that reflexive violence will result, it is unlikely that the fighting words doctrine can successfully deter such lawless conduct.[132]

Second, just as the alleged peace-preserving purpose does not rationally justify the fighting words doctrine in general, that rationale also fails to justify the fighting words doctrine when applied to racial slurs in particular. As Professor Kalven noted, "outbursts of violence are not the necessary consequence of such speech and, more important, such violence when it does occur is not the serious evil of the speech."[133] Rather, as Professor Lawrence stresses, the serious evil of racial slurs consists of the ugliness of the ideas they express and the psychic injury they cause to their addressees.[134] Therefore, the fighting words doctrine does not address and will not prevent the injuries caused by campus racist speech.

Even if there were a real danger that racist or other fighting words would cause reflexive violence, and even if that danger would be reduced by the threat of legal sanction, the fighting words doctrine still would be problematic in terms of free speech principles. As Professor Chafee observed, this doctrine "makes a man a criminal simply because his neighbors have no self-control and cannot refrain from violence."[135] In other contexts, the Court appropriately has refused to allow the addressees of speech to exercise such a "heckler's veto."[136]

---

lenged convictions. In short, one must wonder about the strength of an exception which, while theoretically recognized, has ever since 1942 not been found apt in practice.

131. *See, e.g.,* Note, *supra* note 128, at 1757 n.44 (*Chaplinsky* may well reflect concerns peculiar to the decade when it was decided, rather than enduring first amendment principles).

132. *See* Gard, *supra* note 130, at 580.

133. H. KALVEN, THE NEGRO AND THE FIRST AMENDMENT 14-15 (1965).

134. *See* Lawrence, at 457-76.

135. Z. CHAFEE, *supra* note 126, at 151.

136. *See, e.g.,* Gregory v. City of Chicago, 394 U.S. 111 (1969) (holding that there was constitutionally insufficient evidence to support disorderly conduct convictions for civil rights demonstrators who failed to disperse upon police order; Court refused to consider evidence noted by Justice Black in dissent that hostile crowd of 1,000 spectators was growing unmanageable in spite of efforts of 100 uniformed police officers); Cox v. Louisiana, 379 U.S. 536, 550 (1965) (reversed civil rights demonstrators' breach of peace convictions, finding insufficient evidence to support local officials' claims that spectator violence was imminent, where there were 100 to 300 "muttering" spectators); Terminiello v. Chicago, 337 U.S. 1 (1949) (where race-baiting speaker attracted "angry and turbulent" crowd, Court reversed breach of peace conviction).

The fighting words doctrine is constitutionally flawed for the additional reasons that it suppresses much protectible speech and that the protectible speech of minority group members is particularly vulnerable. Notwithstanding the Supreme Court's limitation of the doctrine's scope, Professor Gard's survey reveals that the lower courts apply it much more broadly. Since the Supreme Court only reviews a fraction of such cases, the doctrine's actual impact on free speech must be assessed in terms of these speech-restrictive lower court rulings. Professor Gard concluded that, in the lower courts, the fighting words doctrine "is almost uniformly invoked in a selective and discriminatory manner by law enforcement officials to punish trivial violations of a constitutionally impermissible interest in preventing criticism of official conduct."[137] Indeed, Professor Gard reported, "it is virtually impossible to find fighting words cases that do not involve either the expression of opinion on issues of public policy or words directed toward a government official, usually a police officer."[138] Even more disturbing is that the reported cases indicate that blacks are often prosecuted and convicted for the use of fighting words.[139] Thus, the record of the actual implementation of the fighting words doctrine demonstrates that—as is the case with all speech restrictions—it endangers principles of equality as well as free speech.[140] That record substantiates the risk that such a speech restriction will be applied discriminatorily and disproportionately against the very minority group members whom it is intended to protect.[141]

---

137. Gard, *supra* note 130, at 580.

138. *Id.* at 548. *Accord id.* at 568. *Compare* Lawrence, at 437 n.29 ("[T]here is no evidence that the continued usage of [the fighting words doctrine] has led down the slippery slope to rampant censorship.").

139. *See, e.g.,* Lewis v. City of New Orleans, 415 U.S. 130 (1974) (state court upheld conviction on basis of fighting words doctrine in situation in which police officer said to young suspect's mother, "[g]et your black ass in the goddamned car," and she responded, "you god damn mother fucking police—I am going to [the Superintendent of Police] about this."); Street v. New York, 394 U.S. 576 (1969) (black man who protested against shooting of civil rights leader James Meredith by burning American flag and saying, "If they let that happen to Meredith we don't need an American flag," was convicted under statute that criminalized words casting contempt on United States flag; Supreme Court rejected contention that conviction could be justified on fighting words rationale, *id.* at 592); Edwards v. South Carolina, 372 U.S. 229, 236 (1963) (state court upheld convictions of civil rights demonstrators for holding placards stating "I am proud to be a Negro" and "Down with Segregation"; Supreme Court rejected contention that convictions could be justified on fighting words doctrine); Waller v. City of St. Petersburg, 245 So. 2d 685 (Fla. Dist. Ct. App. 1971), *rev'd,* City of St. Petersburg v. Waller, 261 So. 2d 151 (Fla. 1972) (black man was convicted for shouting "pig" at passing police car, and state supreme court upheld conviction based on fighting words doctrine).

140. *See infra* text accompanying notes 365-96.

141. *See* Gard, *supra* note 130, at 566 ("Many commentators have recognized that [the] problem of discriminatory enforcement is particularly acute in the fighting words context. [One very real] danger is . . . that the penal law will be selectively invoked against members of racial or other minority groups and speakers who espouse ideological views unpopular with enforcement officials.")

Professor Lawrence himself notes that many Supreme Court decisions that overruled fighting words convictions involved a "potentially offended party [who] was in a position of relative power when compared with the speaker."[142] As Professor Gard demonstrated, for each such conviction that was reviewed and overturned by the Supreme Court, many others were not.[143] Thus, Professor Lawrence and other proponents of Stanford's fighting words code must believe that the officials who enforce that code will do so in a manner that differs from the general enforcement pattern of similar regulations. They must have faith that Stanford officials, as opposed to other officials, are unusually sensitive to free speech rights in general, and to the free speech rights of minority group members and dissidents in particular.

Based on his analysis of the actual application of the fighting words doctrine, Professor Gard adheres to no such faith in the discretion of officials. In response to another legal academic's suggestion that the fighting words doctrine could be invoked to protect the aged and infirm from "the vilest personal verbal abuse,"[144] Professor Gard said that this was "a romantic vision that exists only in the imagination of a law professor."[145] Even assuming that Stanford officials might be unusually attentive to free speech values when implementing the fighting words doctrine, Stanford's use of that doctrine could fuel an increased use by other officials, who might well fail to implement it in a speech-sensitive fashion.[146]

Because of the problems with the fighting words doctrine, the committee that proposed a hate speech policy for the University of Texas expressly declined to use it as a model.[147] Likewise, recognizing the weakness of the public peace rationale, the proponents of the Stanford code have attempted to reinvigorate the other rationale that the Supreme Court enunciated in its *Chaplinsky* dictum, but has since abandoned— the notion that such words inflict psychic or emotional injury by their

---

(footnote omitted). *See also id.* at 571 (doctrine creates danger that the common meaning ascribed to words by certain subcultures will be punished based on "myopic ethnocentricity" of officials who enforce rules); Karst, *Equality as a Central Principle in the First Amendment,* 43 U. CHI. L. REV. 20, 38 (1975) ("[S]tatutes proscribing abusive words are applied to members of racial and political minorities more frequently than can be wholly explained by any special proclivity of those people to speak abusively.").

142. Lawrence, at 453 n.92.

143. *See* Gard, *supra* note 130, at 564.

144. Shea, *supra* note 130, at 22.

145. Gard, *supra* note 130, at 564.

146. Professor Lawrence recognizes the potential danger that any speech-restricting precedent "would pose for the speech of all dissenters," and that such a dangerous precedent "might . . . include general societal tolerance for the suppression of speech." Lawrence, at 458 & n.106.

147. See University of Texas Report, *supra* note 115, at 16-20.

very utterance.[148] But this attempted "solution" to the problems flowing from the breach of the peace rationale causes another set of problems. First, the Supreme Court has never relied upon *Chaplinsky's* psychic harm dictum to sustain a fighting words conviction.[149] Second, after it pronounced that dictum, the Court issued a line of decisions protecting speech that was allegedly offensive and that assertedly could have caused emotional or psychic injury.[150] Consequently, as Professor Gard stated, to revive *Chaplinsky's* long-since discredited second rationale "would turn the constitutional clock back at least [fifty] years."[151]

2. *Intentional Infliction of Emotional Distress.* A committee report that the University of Texas is currently considering recommends the common law tort of intentional infliction of emotional distress as a basis for regulating campus hate speech.[152] This doctrinal approach has

---

148. *See* Stanford Code and Comments, *supra* note 24, at 3. The pertinent part of the Stanford Code and Comments states that:

The Supreme Court's phrase [in *Chaplinsky*] "insulting or 'fighting' words" is often shortened to simply "fighting words," an expression which . . . may . . . have certain misleading connotations. First, the expression may imply that violence is considered an acceptable response to discriminatory vilification . . . . Second, exclusive focus on the actual likelihood of violence might suggest that opponents of controversial speech can transform it into forbidden "fighting words" by plausibly threatening violent response to it. . . . Finally, the "fighting words" terminology might be thought to imply that extreme forms of personal abuse become protected speech simply because the victims are, for example, such disciplined practitioners of non-violence . . . that they do not . . . pose an actual and imminent threat of violent retaliation. Such a limitation might be appropriate under a breach of peace statute, whose sole purpose is to prevent violence, but does not make sense in an anti-discrimination provision such as this one.

149. *See* Gard, *supra* note 130, at 577.

150. *See, e.g.,* United States v. Eichman, 110 S. Ct. 2404, 2409 (1990) (prosecution for burning American flag in violation of Flag Protection Act of 1989, Pub. L. No. 101-131, 103 Stat. 777, held inconsistent with First Amendment protection of expressive conduct); Hustler Magazine v. Falwell, 485 U.S. 46 (1988) (first and fourteenth amendments prohibit public figures from recovering damages for intentional infliction of emotional distress due to caricature publication without showing false statements of fact made with "actual malice"); Spence v. Washington, 418 U.S. 405 (1974) (conviction for hanging flag upside down with peace symbol taped on held invalid; statute held to be impermissible infringement on protected expression); Cohen v. California, 403 U.S. 15 (1971) (first and fourteenth amendments require state to show compelling reason to make public display of four-letter expletive a criminal offense); Street v. New York, 394 U.S. 576 (1969); Terminiello v. City of Chicago, 337 U.S. 1 (1949) (Court reversed breach of peace conviction where race-baiting speaker attracted "angry and turbulent" crowd). *See also infra* text accompanying note 164 (quoting passage from *Hustler* referring to Court's "longstanding refusal to allow damages to be awarded because the speech in question may have an adverse emotional impact on the audience").

151. Gard, *supra* note 130, at 577.

152. *See* University of Texas Report, *supra* note 115, at 7 (defines prohibited "racial harassment" as "extreme or outrageous acts or communications that are intended to harass, intimidate, or humiliate a student or students on account of race, color, or national origin and that reasonably cause them to suffer severe emotional distress").

The Report's proposal includes the following limitations on the availability of the intentional infliction of emotional distress theory for barring speech: "racial harassment by communication usually will require repeated verbal conduct," *id.*; liability should be found "only where the conduct

a logical appeal because it focuses on the type of harm potentially caused by racist speech that universities are most concerned with alleviating— namely, emotional or psychological harm that interferes with studies. In contrast, the harm at which the fighting words doctrine aims—potential violence by the addressee against the speaker—is of less concern to most universities.[153]

Traditional civil libertarians caution that the intentional infliction of emotional distress theory should almost never apply to verbal harassment.[154] A major problem with this approach is that,

> the innate vagueness of the interest in preventing emotional injury to listeners suggests that any attempt at judicial enforcement will inevitably result in the imposition of judges' subjective linguistic preferences on society, *discrimination against ethnic and racial minorities,* and ultimately the misuse of the rationale to justify the censorship of the ideological content of the speaker's message.[155]

Again, as was true for the fighting words doctrine, there is a particular danger that this speech restrictive doctrine also will be enforced to the detriment of the very minority groups whom it is designed to protect.

The general problems with the intentional infliction of emotional distress theory counsel against application in the campus context specifi-

---

has been so outrageous in character, and so extreme in degree, as to go beyond all possible bounds of decency, and to be regarded as atrocious, and utterly intolerable in a civilized community," *id.* at 14 (quoting RESTATEMENT (SECOND) OF TORTS § 46 comment d (1965)); "[t]he factual context is critical to the judgment as to what acts and words are extreme and outrageous," *id.*; the rule applies "only where the distress inflicted is so severe that no reasonable [person] could be expected to endure it," *id.* at 15 (quoting RESTATEMENT (SECOND) OF TORTS § 46 comment j (1965)); and the rule would not apply to either "[a]bstract statements not addressed to particular listeners," *id.* at 20, or "the assertion of opinions," *id.* at 21.

153. *See, e.g., id.* at 19-20. The Report stated that:

[S]evere emotional distress may be present even where the victim is unlikely to respond with violence, and violence may occur even where the emotional harm is slight.

. . . [Under] the "fighting words" approach. . . . there is an incongruity between the real reason for the policy (avoidance of racially discriminatory humiliation and emotional distress) and the constitutional reason (avoidance of violence), the doctrinal box into which the draftsmen are attempting to make the real reason fit. It is much preferable for a racial harassment policy to focus on the real injury of severe emotional distress.

154. *See* F. HAIMAN, *supra* note 59, at 152-56. According to Franklyn Haiman, the tort of intentional infliction of emotional distress endangers free speech: it involves "boundless subjectivity," *id.* at 152; subjects people to punishment because they violate "changing sensitivities" of particular community at particular time, *id.*; perpetuates stereotyping, invites "radically unpredictable" judicial decisionmaking, *id.* at 153; and incorrectly assumes that all members of racial or other groups have monolithic responses to challenged stimuli. Haiman recommends limiting such actions to knowingly false communication. *See also* Note, *supra* note 128, at 1749-50 (extreme and outrageous language should be object of tort liability only when such language constitutes fighting words or invades private area such as home; even latter speech should not be basis for tort recovery by public official or public figure unless defendant made it impossible for such person to avert attention).

155. Gard, *supra* note 130, at 578 (emphasis added).

cally.[156] Citing these reasons, Stanford University declined to base its hate speech regulation on this tort model.[157] Moreover, even though the University of Texas committee report concluded that the emotional distress approach was less problematical than the fighting words approach, it cautioned: "[T]here can be no guarantee as to the constitutionality of any university rule bearing on racial harassment and sensitive matters of freedom of expression."[158]

The position that the intentional infliction of emotional distress tort should virtually never apply to words recently received support in *Hustler Magazine v. Falwell.*[159] Chief Justice Rehnquist, writing for a unanimous Court, reversed a jury verdict which had awarded damages to the nationally-known minister, Jerry Falwell, for the intentional infliction of emotional distress. The Court held that a public figure may not "recover damages for emotional harm caused by the publication of an ad parody offensive to him, and doubtless gross and repugnant in the eyes of most."[160] The Court further ruled that public figures and public officials may not recover for this tort unless they could show that the publication contains a false statement of fact which was made with "actual malice," i.e., with knowledge that the statement was false or with reckless disregard as to whether or not it was false.[161] In other words, the Court required public officials or public figures who claim intentional infliction of

---

156. *See* Report of Workshop on Racist and Sexist Speech on College and University Campuses, Annenberg Washington Program of Northwestern University, Washington, D.C., at 3 (Apr. 12, 1990) [hereinafter Report of Annenberg Workshop] (available from author). The Report of the Annenberg Workshop stated that:

> Most members of the group had difficulty with the subjectivity involved in making judgments on the basis of the emotional pain suffered by the targets of [hate speech]. No one denied that real pain is often suffered and no one was unconcerned about the possible personal consequences of such pain or its negative impact on equality of educational opportunity. But the prevailing view seemed to be that emotional pain, by itself, cannot be measured with the precision and objectivity required of any rule restricting speech.

157. *See* Stanford Code and Comments, *supra* note 24, at 4. The pertinent part of the Code and Comments stated that:

> [T]he "emotional distress" rubric. . . . has drawbacks as the legal basis for a discriminatory harassment regulation. It is less well established in free speech law than is the fighting words concept. Further, taken as it is from tort law, it focuses primarily on the victim's reaction to abuse . . . . We think it better in defining a disciplinary offense to focus on the prohibited conduct; we prefer not to require the victims of personal vilification to display their psychic scars in order to establish that an offense has been committed.

Notwithstanding its recognition of the constitutional weaknesses of the emotional distress approach, Stanford adopted a rule that is modeled on the *Chaplinsky* dictum that also sought to protect against emotional distress. *See supra* notes 146-51 and accompanying text.

158. University of Texas Report, *supra* note 115, at 13.

159. 485 U.S. 46 (1988).

160. *Id.* at 50.

161. *Id.* at 56.

emotional distress to satisfy the same heavy burden of proof it imposes upon such individuals who bring defamation claims.[162]

Although the specific *Falwell* holding focused on public figure plaintiffs, much of the Court's language indicated that, because of first amendment concerns, it would strictly construe the intentional infliction of emotional distress tort in general, even when pursued by non-public plaintiffs. For example, the Court said, to require a statement to be "outrageous" as a prerequisite for imposing liability did not sufficiently protect first amendment values. Because the "outrageousness" of the challenged statement is a typical element of the tort (it is included in the *Restatement* definition[163]) the Court's indication that it is constitutionally suspect has ramifications beyond the sphere of public figure actions. The Court warned:

> "Outrageousness" in the area of political and social discourse has an inherent subjectiveness about it which would allow a jury to impose liability on the basis of the jurors' tastes or views, or perhaps on the basis of their dislike of a particular expression. An "outrageousness" standard thus runs afoul of our longstanding refusal to allow damages to be awarded because the speech in question may have an adverse emotional impact on the audience.[164]

For the reasons signalled by the unanimous Supreme Court in *Falwell,* any cause of action for intentional infliction of emotional distress that arises from words must be narrowly framed and strictly applied in order to satisfy first amendment dictates.

3. *Group Defamation.* Professor Lawrence does not elaborate on either the constitutionality or efficacy of the group defamation concept, yet he approvingly notes others' alleged support for it.[165] The group defamation concept, however, has been thoroughly discredited by others.[166]

---

162. *See* New York Times v. Sullivan, 376 U.S. 254 (1964).

163. *See* RESTATEMENT (SECOND) OF TORTS § 46 (1965).

164. *Falwell,* 485 U.S. at 55.

165. *See* Lawrence, at 464 n.124. *But see* Downs, Skokie *Revisited: Hate Group Speech and the First Amendment,* 60 NOTRE DAME L. REV. 629, 661-66 (1985) (argues that group defamation statutes are unconstitutional except for face-to-face harassment of individual or small group, similar to fighting words situation).

166. *See, e.g.,* Beauharnais v. Illinois, 343 U.S. 250, 271 (1952) (Black, J., dissenting) (the sugar-coated label "group libel law" does not make censorship less deadly); *id.* at 284 (Douglas, J., dissenting) (regulation of speech must always meet clear and present danger test); *see also id.* at 277 (Reed, J., dissenting); *id.* at 287 (Jackson, J., dissenting); Tanenhaus, *Group Libel,* 35 CORNELL L.Q. 261 (1950); Comment, *Race Defamation and the First Amendment,* 34 FORDHAM L. REV. 653 (1966). It also is noteworthy that Professor Riesman, who wrote an influential series of articles advocating group defamation laws in 1942, subsequently changed his position. *See* Riesman, *Democracy and Defamation: Fair Game and Fair Comment II,* 42 COLUM. L. REV. 1282 (1942); Riesman, *Democracy and Defamation: Fair Game and Fair Comment I,* 42 COLUM. L. REV. 1085 (1942); Riesman,

First, group defamation regulations are unconstitutional in terms of both Supreme Court doctrine and free speech principles. To be sure, the Supreme Court's only decision that expressly reviewed the issue, *Beauharnais v. Illinois*, [167] upheld a group libel statute against a first amendment challenge. However, that 5-4 decision was issued almost forty years ago, at a relatively early point in the Court's developing free speech jurisprudence. *Beauharnais* is widely assumed no longer to be good law in light of the Court's subsequent speech-protective decisions on related issues, notably its holdings that strictly limit individual defamation actions so as not to chill free speech. [168]

Statements that defame groups convey opinions or ideas on matters of public concern, [169] and therefore should be protected even if those statements also injure reputations or feelings. [170] The Supreme Court recently reaffirmed this principle in the context of an individual defamation action, in *Milkovich v. Lorain Journal Co.* [171]

Democracy and Defamation: Control of Group Libel, 42 COLUM. L. REV. 727 (1942). *But see* S. WALKER, *supra* note 16, at 330 n.23, 437.

167. 343 U.S. 250 (1952).

168. See, e.g., Collin v. Smith, 578 F.2d 1197, 1205 (7th Cir.), *cert. denied*, 439 U.S. 916 (1978) (citing cases expressing "doubt, which we share, that *Beauharnais* remains good law at all after the constitutional libel cases"). *See also* L. TRIBE, *supra* note 58, § 12-17, at 926-27 (In particular, New York Times Co. v. Sullivan, 376 U.S. 254 (1964), "seemed to some to eclipse *Beauharnais'* sensitivity to . . . group defamation claims . . . because *New York Times* required public officials bringing libel suits to prove that a defamatory statement was directed at the official personally, and not simply at a unit of government.").

169. The fact that statements that defame groups convey ideas concerning issues of public importance is illustrated by *Beauharnais* itself. The statements that were the basis for the defendant's conviction were set out on a petition addressed to city officials and seeking readers' signatures. *See Beauharnais*, 343 U.S. at 267, 276 (Black, J., dissenting).

170. *See* Letter from Professor William Cohen to Professor George Parker, chair of the Student Conduct Legislative Council of Stanford University (March 10, 1989), *reprinted in* Stanford Univ. Campus Rep., March 15, 1989, at 18 [hereinafter Cohen letter (March 10, 1989)]. In his letter, Professor Cohen stated that:

> I have been asked why it is so important to draw a distinction between personal abuse— where I concede the possibility of regulation—and similar speech that is more generally distributed. If there is harm in being the target of an individual racial epithet, is not the harm the same, or greater, when the epithet is addressed to a broader audience? Indeed, it is. . . . [H]owever, it is not appropriate to look only to one side of the balance. The problem is that there are larger interests in freedom of expression that loom when speech enters the public arena. These are interests that can not be rejected in the case of speech considered by the community to be erroneous, dangerous and harmful without limiting permissible expression to the true and the relatively harmless.

171. 110 S. Ct. 2695 (1990). Although the Court declined "to create a wholesale defamation exemption for anything that might be labeled 'opinion,' " *id.* at 2705, it stressed that statements would only be actionable in defamation suits if a reasonable factfinder could conclude that they "imply an assertion" of fact. *Id.* The Court also summarized the various existing doctrines limiting defamation actions which are designed to ensure that expressions of ideas or opinions would not be chilled:

> *Hepps* ensures that a statement of opinion relating to matters of public concern which does not contain a provably false factual connotation will receive full constitutional protection.

In addition to flouting constitutional doctrine and free speech principles, rules sanctioning group defamation are ineffective in curbing the specific class of hate speech that Professor Lawrence advocates restraining. Even Justice Frankfurter's opinion for the narrow *Beauharnais* majority repeatedly expressed doubt about the wisdom or efficacy of group libel laws. Justice Frankfurter stressed that the Court upheld the Illinois law in question only because of judicial deference to the state legislature's judgment about the law's effectiveness.[172]

The concept of defamation encompasses only false statements of fact that are made without a good faith belief in their truth. Therefore, any disparaging or insulting statement would be immune from this doctrine, unless it were factual in nature, demonstrably false in content, and made in bad faith. Members of minority groups that are disparaged by an allegedly libelous statement would hardly have their reputations or psyches enhanced by a process in which the maker of the statement sought to prove his good faith belief in its truth, and they were required to demonstrate the absence thereof.[173]

Next, the *Bresler-Letter Carriers-Falwell* line of cases provide protection for statements that cannot "reasonably [be] interpreted as stating actual facts" about an individual (citation omitted). This provides assurance that public debate will not suffer for lack of . . . the "rhetorical hyperbole" which has traditionally added much to the discourse of our Nation.

The *New York Times-Butts* and *Gertz* culpability requirements further ensure that debate on public issues remains "uninhibited, robust, and wide-open." Thus, where a statement of "opinion" on a matter of public concern reasonably implies false and defamatory facts regarding. . . . a private figure on a matter of public concern, a plaintiff must show that the false connotations were made with some level of fault as required by *Gertz*. Finally, the enhanced appellate review required by *Bose Corp.*, provides assurance that the foregoing determinations will be made in a manner so as not to "constitute a forbidden intrusion of the field of free expression."

Id. at 2706-07 (footnotes omitted).

172. *See Beauharnais*, 343 U.S. at 261-62. In *Beauharnais*, the Supreme Court stated that: "It may be argued, and weightily, that this legislation will not help matters; that tension and on occasion violence between racial and religious groups must be traced to causes more deeply embedded in our society than the rantings of modern Know-Nothings." Later in the opinion, the Supreme Court stated that: "[I]t bears repeating . . . that our finding that the law is not constitutionally objectionable carries no implication of approval of the wisdom of the legislation or of its efficacy. These questions may raise doubts in our minds as well as in others." *Id.* at 267.

173. *See, e.g.*, Tanenhaus, *supra* note 166, at 299. In his article, Tanenhaus stated that:

The defendant in his effort to convince the jury that his grounds for belief were reasonable would be justified in introducing into evidence every piece of hate-literature he could find. The courtroom would in effect be turned into a public forum for his views. Considering the countless tons of defamatory literature available, it is hard to think of anything that a jury might not be convinced was reasonably and honestly believed.

Professor Lawrence's recommendation that a group defamation cause of action contain "the equivalent of an actual malice requirement," Lawrence, at 463 n.119, would exacerbate the foregoing problems. *See id.* ("Discussions that attempt to explore an issue of public concern would be protected, but group defamations that intentionally vilify a group or individual for purposes of harassment or intimidation would receive no protection.").

One additional problem with group defamation statutes as a model for rules sanctioning campus hate speech should be noted. As with the other speech-restrictive doctrines asserted to justify such rules, group defamation laws introduce the risk that the rules will be enforced at the expense of the very minority groups sought to be protected. The Illinois statute[174] upheld in *Beauharnais* is illustrative. According to a leading article on group libel laws, during the 1940s, the Illinois statute was "a weapon for harassment of the Jehovah's Witnesses," who were then "a minority . . . very much more in need of protection than most."[175] Thus, a rule based on the group defamation theory provides no guarantee that it will not be used against minorities.

C. *Even a Narrow Regulation Could Have a Negative Symbolic Impact on Constitutional Values*

Taking into account the constraints imposed by free speech principles and doctrines potentially applicable to the regulation of campus hate speech, it might be possible—although difficult—to frame a sufficiently narrow rule to withstand a facial first amendment challenge. The federal judge who invalidated the University of Michigan's anti-hate speech regulation as overbroad and vague expressly noted this possibility.[176] ACLU affiliates that have challenged particular campus hate speech restrictions have proposed alternative policies that might pass constitutional muster as a facial matter.[177] However, it bears reemphasizing that,

---

174. The Illinois statute provided, in pertinent part: "It shall be unlawful . . . to . . . publish . . . in any public place . . . any . . . publication [which] . . . exposes citizens of any race, color, creed or religion to contempt, derision or obloquy." ILL. REV. STAT., ch. 38, para. 471 (1949).

175. Tanenhaus, *supra* note 166, at 279-80. *See also Beauharnais*, 343 U.S. at 274 (1952) (Black, J., dissenting) ("[T]he same kind of state law that makes Beauharnais a criminal for advocating segregation . . . can be utilized to send people to jail . . . for advocating equality and nonsegregation.").

176. *See* Doe v. University of Mich., 721 F. Supp. 852, 862 (E.D. Mich. 1989) ("Under certain circumstances racial and ethnic epithets, slurs, and insults might . . . constitutionally be prohibited [under the fighting words doctrine]. In addition, such speech may also be sufficient to state a claim for common law intentional infliction of emotional distress.").

177. For example, the lawsuit challenging the University of Connecticut's hate speech rule was settled pursuant to the parties' agreement about the wording of an alternative rule, which the Connecticut Civil Liberties Union deemed to comport with first amendment strictures. *See* Appendix to Judgment, Proposed Consent Decree, Exhibit A, Wu v. University of Conn., No. Civ. H-89-649 PCD (D. Conn. Jan. 25, 1990) (prohibits face to face use of "fighting words," defined as "personally abusive epithets which, when directly addressed to any ordinary person are, in the context used and as a matter of common knowledge, inherently likely to provoke an immediate violent reaction, whether or not they actually do so"). *See also* Plaintiffs' Reply Brief in Support of Motion for Preliminary Injunction at 9 n.9, *Doe*, 721 F. Supp. at 852 (No. 89-CV-71683-DT) (filed by ACLU of Michigan; dated Aug. 24, 1989) (proposed alternative to successfully challenged rule; alternative would prohibit "any action directed toward another student . . . with the specific intention of inflicting emotional distress . . . or interfering with . . . academic efforts. . . . The . . . expression of any

as the University of Texas report stressed, "[T]here can be no guarantee as to the constitutionality of any university rule bearing on racial harassment and sensitive matters of freedom of expression."[178]

Even assuming that a regulation could be crafted with sufficient precision to survive a facial constitutional challenge, several further problems would remain, which should give any university pause in evaluating whether to adopt such a rule. Although these inherent problems with any hate speech regulation are discussed in greater detail below,[179] they are summarized here. First, because of the discretion entailed in enforcing any such rule, they involve an inevitable danger of arbitrary or discriminatory enforcement.[180] Therefore, the rule's implementation would have to be monitored to ensure that it did not exceed the bounds of the regulations' terms or threaten content- and viewpoint-neutrality principles.[181] The experience with the University of Michigan's rule— the only campus hate speech rule that has an enforcement record— graphically illustrates this danger.[182]

Second, there is an inescapable risk that any hate speech regulation, no matter how narrowly drawn, will chill speech beyond its literal scope. Members of the university community may well err on the side of caution to avoid being charged with a violation. For example, there is evidence that the rule which the University of Wisconsin implemented in 1989 has had this effect, even though it has not yet been directly enforced.[183] A third problem inherent in any campus hate speech policy, as Professor Lawrence concedes,[184] is that such rules constitute a precedent that can be used to restrict other types of speech. As the Supreme Court

---

idea in any form, unaccompanied by any action . . . directed toward another student . . . shall not be violative."). *See also supra* note 11 (policies adopted by ACLU California affiliates do not oppose regulation of narrowly defined campus hate speech). *See also infra* note 353 and accompanying text.

178. University of Texas Report, *supra* note 115, at 13.

179. *See infra* text accompanying notes 227-74.

180. *See* Amsterdam, *Perspectives on the Fourth Amendment,* 58 MINN. L. REV. 349, 435 (1974) ("The dangers of abuse of a particular power are, certainly, a pertinent consideration in determining whether the power should be allowed in the first instance.").

181. *See* L. TRIBE, *supra* note 58, § 12-10, at 856 (Although the Constitution probably permits legislation punishing words that cause hurt by their mere utterance, such legislation "would be constitutionally problematic—the potential for content-specific regulation is always great.").

182. *See infra* text accompanying notes 203-25.

183. *See* Gribble, *supra* note 17. In his article, Gribble stated that:

Ron Novy, editor of the UWM Post [the student newspaper at the University of Wisconsin-Milwaukee], said he had the feeling that since the rule was put into effect, students had become less willing to speak frankly.

"Our letters to the editor are not quite as vehement as they've been in the past," he said.

Novy said the rule had not "consciously" affected how the Post's writers approached stories, "but it's in the back of your mind."

Id. at 8B, col. 1.

184. *See* Lawrence, at 458 n.106.

has recognized, the long-range precedential impact of any challenged governmental action should be a factor in evaluating its lawfulness.[185]

Further, in light of constitutional constraints, any campus hate speech policy inevitably would apply to only a tiny fraction of all racist expression, and accordingly it would have only a symbolic impact.[186] Therefore, in deciding whether to adopt such a rule, universities must ask whether that symbolic impact is, on balance, positive or negative in terms of constitutional values.[187] On the one hand, some advocates of hate speech regulations maintain that the regulations might play a valuable symbolic role in reaffirming our societal commitment to racial equality[188] (although this is debatable).[189] On the other hand, we must beware of even a symbolic or perceived diminution of our impartial commitment to free speech. Even a limitation that has a direct impact upon only a discrete category of speech may have a much more pervasive indirect impact—by undermining the first amendment's moral legitimacy.[190]

---

185. *See, e.g.*, West Virginia State Bd. of Educ. v. Barnette, 319 U.S. 624, 641 (1943) ("It seems trite but necessary to say that the First Amendment . . . was designed to avoid these [totalitarian] ends by avoiding these beginnings."); Boyd v. United States, 116 U.S. 616, 635 (1886) ("[I]llegitimate and unconstitutional practices get their first footing by slight . . . deviations from legal modes of procedure. This can only be obviated by adhering to the rule that constitutional provisions . . . should be liberally construed.").

186. *See infra* Part II.

187. *See* Gunther letter (May 1, 1989), *supra* note 130. In his letter, Gunther stated that:

> [Y]our entire enterprise—the recurrent effort to identify forbidden speech, now more narrowly defined—does not strike me as a significant part of a campus wide effort to eliminate discrimination and perhaps stems more from an interest in symbolic gestures rather than in concretely effective ones. This proposed symbolic victory inevitably casts some pall over the vigor of campus speech and beyond that may well set an unfortunate precedent for future institutional action curbing speech even more severely.

188. *See* Letter from Professor William Cohen to Professor George Parker, chair of the Student Conduct Legislative Council of Stanford University (May 1, 1989), *reprinted in* Stanford Univ. Campus Rep., May 3, 1989, at 18 [hereinafter Cohen letter (May 1, 1989)]. Cohen wrote that: "While no one pretends that silencing racist remarks cures racism, there might be substantial symbolic cost in giving up on a legislative solution to this problem after so much effort. A number of the affected groups would reasonably see abandonment as demonstrating lack of institutional concern." *See also* University of Texas Report, *supra* note 115, at 1 (quoting charge of President William H. Cunningham of University of Texas at Austin to President's Ad Hoc Committee on Racial Harassment). President Cunningham stated that: "[O]ne of the primary reasons for adopting racial harassment policies is to affirm symbolically The University's commitment to tolerance and nondiscrimination— even if the rules themselves cannot completely eliminate the problem." *Accord* Matsuda, *supra* note 13, at 2322 ("A legal response to racist speech is a statement that victims of racism are valued members of our polity.").

189. *See* Report of Annenberg Workshop, *supra* note 156, at 2. The Annenberg Report stated that: "The adoption of restrictions on derogatory speech. . . . may . . . give some symbolic support and reassurance to the victims of such communication. It is, however, . . . of dubious effectiveness, even symbolically, in improving intergroup relationships. Indeed, such a response may lead to a backlash or a perception of official heavy-handedness."

190. Professor Walter Dellinger tellingly made this point about another proposed exception to the first amendment of an ostensibly limited nature—for physical desecration of the U.S. flag:

Recently, the Supreme Court ringingly reaffirmed the core principle that a neutral commitment to free speech should trump competing symbolic concerns. In *United States v. Eichman,* which invalidated the Flag Protection Act of 1989, the Court declared:

> Government may create national symbols, promote them, and encourage their respectful treatment. But the Flag Protection Act goes well beyond this by criminally proscribing expressive conduct because of its likely communicative impact.
>
> We are aware that desecration of the flag is deeply offensive to many. But the same might be said, for example, of virulent ethnic and religious epithets, vulgar repudiations of the draft, and scurrilous caricatures. "If there is a bedrock principle underlying the First Amendment, it is that the Government may not prohibit the expression of an idea simply because society finds the idea itself offensive or disagreeable." Punishing desecration of the flag dilutes the very freedom that makes this emblem so revered, and worth revering.[191]

II. Professor Lawrence's Conception of Regulable Racist Speech Endangers Free Speech Principles

The preceding discussion of relevant constitutional doctrine points to several problems with the Stanford regulations, as well as other regulations adopted or advocated by other universities. As previously explained,[192] the Stanford regulations violate the cardinal principles that speech restrictions must be content- and viewpoint-neutral. Moreover, although these regulations purportedly incorporate the fighting words doctrine,[193] they in fact go well beyond the narrow bounds that the Court has imposed on that doctrine, and, as the University of Michigan example demonstrates, they threaten to chill protected speech.

What would this proposed act of constitutional revision do to the moral legitimacy of the stance our Constitution has taken (and will continue to take) in defense of expression that offends many Americans as deeply as flag burning offends the great majority of us? . . . Once we have quickly passed the Twenty-seventh amendment to protect the sensibilities of those who revere the flag, what do we say to those who are particularly offended by, but must continue to tolerate, the burning of crosses by hooded members of the Ku Klux Klan, a brazen reminder of the era of lynching and terror? And what do we say to those who find themselves silenced and marginalized by sexualized (but not constitutionally "obscene") portrayals of women? What enduring Constitutional principle will remain unimpaired that will legitimately surmount these claims . . . ?

Hearings on Measures to Protect the Physical Integrity of the American Flag, Before the Senate Committee on the Judiciary, 101st Cong., 1st Sess. 553 (1989) (statement of Walter Dellinger).

191. United States v. Eichman, 110 S. Ct. 2404, 2409-10 (1990) (footnote omitted).

192. *See supra* text accompanying notes 104-12.

193. *See* Stanford Code and Comment, *supra* note 24, at 1.

A. *The Proposed Regulations Would Not Pass Constitutional Muster*[194]

1. *The Regulations Exceed the Bounds of the Fighting Words Doctrine.* As discussed above,[195] the fighting words doctrine is fraught with constitutional problems. As a result, it either has been abrogated *sub silentio* or probably should be. In any event, even assuming that the doctrine is still good law, it has been severely circumscribed by Supreme Court rulings. Because those limits are necessitated by free speech principles, they must be strictly enforced. Professor Gard's thorough study of the law in this area summarizes the Court's limitations on the fighting words doctrine:

> The offending language (1) must constitute a personally abusive epithet, (2) must be addressed in a face-to-face manner, (3) must be directed to a specific individual and be descriptive of that individual, and (4) must be uttered under such circumstances that the words have a direct tendency to cause an immediate violent response by the average recipient. If any of these four elements is absent, the doctrine may not justifiably be invoked as a rationale for the suppression of the expression.[196]

The operative language of the Stanford code provides:

> Speech or other expression constitutes harassment by personal vilification if it:
> a) is intended to insult or stigmatize an individual or a small number of individuals on the basis of their sex, race, color, handicap, religion, sexual orientation, or national and ethnic origin; and
> b) is addressed directly to the individual or individuals whom it insults or stigmatizes; and
> c) makes use of insulting or "fighting" words or non-verbal symbols.
> In the context of discriminatory harassment by personal vilification, insulting or "fighting" words or non-verbal symbols are those "which by their very utterance inflict injury or tend to incite to an immediate breach of the peace," and which are commonly understood to convey direct and visceral hatred or contempt for human beings on the basis of their sex, race, color, handicap, religion, sexual orientation, or national and ethnic origin.[197]

A comparison of the Stanford code to the Supreme Court's four criteria for constitutional fighting words restrictions reveals that the code clearly does *not* satisfy one of the Court's criteria, and it may not satisfy the other three. Most importantly, as outlined above, since *Gooding v.*

---

194. As a private institution, Stanford University is not directly bound by first amendment standards. However, many private academic institutions make policy choices to adhere to standards that are consistent with their notions of academic freedom.

195. *See supra* text accompanying notes 116-51.

196. Gard, *supra* note 130, at 563-64.

197. Stanford Code and Comments, *supra* note 24.

Wilson the Court consistently has invalidated fighting words definitions that refer only to the content of words. Instead, it has insisted that these words must be evaluated contextually, to assess whether they are likely to cause an imminent breach of the peace under the circumstances in which they are uttered. Yet, the Stanford code punishes words which are commonly understood to convey" group-based hatred.[198] By proscribing certain words, without considering their context, the Stanford code violates Gard's fourth criterion, and for that reason alone falls afoul of the first amendment.

The Stanford code also may fail to satisfy the Court's strict parameters for the fighting words doctrine in other respects. First, it does not expressly require that the prohibited speech "must constitute a personally abusive epithet," the first criterion in Professor Gard's list. Based on his analysis of cases that address the fighting words doctrine, Professor Gard concluded that "the utterance must constitute an extremely provocative personal insult"[199] in order to comport with free speech principles.[200]

Although the Stanford code may comply with the Court's second and third requirements, by prescribing that the prohibited speech be "addressed directly to the individual or individuals whom it insults or stigmatizes," both of these elements have been construed so strictly that they may not be satisfied by this provision. Some judicial rulings indicate that the second requirement, the face-to-face element, "is not satisfied by mere technical physical presence, but contemplates an extremely close physical proximity."[201] The third requirement has been interpreted to mean that "the offensive words must be descriptive of a *particular* person and addressed to that person."[202] The Stanford code does not require that the prohibited words describe the individual to whom they are addressed. Instead, under the Stanford code, the words may convey hatred for broad groups of people.

---

198. *Id.* (emphasis added). *Compare* the University of Connecticut's rule, *supra* note 177 (defining fighting words as those "which . . . are, *in the context used* . . . inherently likely to provoke an immediate violent reaction") (emphasis added).

199. Gard, *supra* note 130, at 536.

200. *See also id.* at 541 ("The importance of the content-focused personally abusive epithet element cannot be overestimated. . . . In essence it guarantees that the expression of ideas, no matter how offensive or distasteful, will be afforded constitutional protection.").

201. *Id.* at 559 (citing *In re* S.L.J., 263 N.W.2d 412, 420 (Minn. 1978)) (when alleged fighting words were spoken "from more than fifteen feet away rather than eye-to-eye, there was no reasonable likelihood that they would tend to incite an immediate breach of the peace"); Garvey v. State, 537 S.W.2d 709, 710 (Tenn. Crim. App. 1975) (face-to-face requirement was not met when defendant, while driving past police station, shouted "sooey" at police officer).

202. Gard, *supra* note 130, at 561 (emphasis added).

2. *The Regulations Will Chill Protected Speech.* Beyond its facial problems of violating neutrality principles and fighting words limitations, the Stanford code also will dampen academic discourse. This inevitable outcome is indicated by the experience under the University of Michigan hate speech regulation.[203]

---

203. That regulation provided that, in certain "[e]ducational and academic centers," individuals were subject to discipline for:

> Any behavior, verbal or physical, that stigmatizes or victimizes an individual on the basis of race, ethnicity, religion, sex, sexual orientation, creed, national origin, ancestry, age, marital status, handicap or Vietnam-era veteran status, and that . . . [i]nvolves an express or implied threat to . . . or has the purpose or reasonably foreseeable effect of interfering with an individual's academic efforts, employment, participation in University sponsored extra-curricular activities or personal safety . . . .

Doe v. University of Mich., 721 F. Supp. 852, 856 (E.D. Mich. 1989) (quoting The University of Michigan Policy on Discriminatory Harrassment (adopted April 14, 1988)). As originally adopted and implemented, the regulation also sanctioned speech that "[c]reates an intimidating, hostile, or demeaning environment for educational pursuits, employment or participation in University sponsored extra-curricular activities." *Id.* After the regulation was legally challenged, however, the University announced that it was withdrawing that section on the grounds that "a need exists for further explanation and clarification" of it. *Id.* (quoting University of Michigan Public Announcement, August 22, 1989).

The Michigan rule was in effect for more than a year, and documents concerning its enforcement were produced during the litigation that ultimately led to its invalidation on first amendment grounds.

Professor Lawrence contends that it is unfair to judge the Stanford code in light of the experience under the Michigan rule, arguing that the latter was "clearly overbroad," and asserting that "it is difficult to believe that anyone at the University of Michigan Law School was consulted in drafting" it. Lawrence, at 477 n.161 & 478 n.162.

It is ironic that, in this particular context, Professor Lawrence seeks to focus the debate solely on the Stanford code. As previously observed, *see supra* note 27, throughout his article, he repeatedly defends alternative hate speech regulations that are not only broader than Stanford's but also broader than Michigan's. Moreover, his proffered rationales would justify sweeping prohibitions. *See infra* Part III. Therefore, perhaps Professor Lawrence should not be so quick to protest that the Michigan code was "obviously overbroad." Lawrence, at 478 n.162.

In any event, the record documents that the University did consult with law school faculty members, as well as university counsel and other lawyers. The University also received comments from numerous other individuals and groups, including the ACLU, in its drafting process. *See* Letter from Henry W. Saad (counsel to University in *Doe* litigation) to Honorable Avern Cohn, at 2 (Aug. 17, 1989) [hereinafter Saad letter] (available from author). Saad wrote that:

> [University of Michigan] President Fleming also consulted with internationally recognized constitutional scholar and Dean of The University of Michigan Law School, Lee Bollinger, and internationally recognized labor/civil rights expert and former Dean of the University of Michigan Law School, Theodore St. Antoine, regarding drafting of the Policy and reviewed the final draft with them.

See also Grano, *supra* note 8, at 9 ("President Fleming [said] that the university's lawyers and three of his colleagues from the law school, including First Amendment expert Dean Lee Bollinger, believed the proposed approach to be sound." Although the University believed the approach to be constitutional, "various individuals and organizations, including the American Civil Liberties Union, voiced objections on constitutional grounds to the provisions regulating speech.") *Id.* The Michigan ACLU affiliate "supported the concept [of regulating verbal harassment] with suggestions for improvement." *See* Regents of the University of Michigan, Minutes of March 1988 Meeting, at 19 (March 17, 1988) [hereinafter Michigan Regents' Minutes] (available from author). Therefore, Professor Lawrence's unsubstantiated assertion that the ACLU and "[t]raditional civil liberties law-

Even though the Michigan regulation was in some respects broader than its Stanford counterpart,[204] the latter rule also suffers from facial overbreadth and ambiguity.[205] One of the key terms in the Stanford regulation, the term "stigmatize," also was contained in the Michigan regulation and specifically was ruled unconstitutionally vague.[206] Accordingly, the Stanford code appears to be as constitutionally suspect as the Michigan rule, contrary to Professor Lawrence's assumption. As discussed in the preceding section, all the alternative theories that have been offered—the fighting words doctrine, the intentional infliction of emotional distress tort, and group defamation—also pose significant threats to free speech principles.[207]

In *Doe v. University of Michigan*,[208] the United States District Court for the Eastern District of Michigan held that the University of Michigan's anti-hate speech policy violated the first amendment because, as applied, it was overbroad[209] and impermissibly vague.[210] The court con-

---

yers typically have elected to stand by" while universities draft clearly unconstitutional rules, Lawrence, at 477, is directly belied by the Michigan experience. For further refutation of this undocumented generalization, see *infra* notes 353-55 and accompanying text.

Following the *Doe* ruling, the University of Michigan did not, as Professor Lawrence suggests, "say to the black students, 'We tried to help you but the courts just won't let us do it.' " Lawrence, at 477 n.161. Rather, promptly after the *Doe* decision, the University adopted an interim policy that was more sensitive to free speech concerns; the new policy has not been challenged by the ACLU or any other party. *See* Policy Statement: The University of Michigan Interim Policy on Discrimination and Discriminatory Conduct by Students in the University Environment (available from author). *See also supra* note 177 (during *Doe* litigation, ACLU suggested alternative policy language that might withstand constitutional scrutiny). More importantly, the University is working on a comprehensive educational program to deal with racist attitudes and to instill in students a multicultural perspective. Telephone interview with Elsa Cole, General Counsel, University of Michigan (August 22, 1990).

204. *See supra* note 61.

205. *See supra* text accompanying notes 195-202. *See also* Cohen letter (May 1, 1989), *supra* note 188. Cohen wrote that: "Given the ambiguities—ambiguities I believe to be inevitable—the question arises whether the proposed rule, even with amendments, will chill dialogue as speakers try to avoid the danger zone."

206. *See Doe,* 721 F. Supp. at 867. Another term that is central to the Stanford code, "harassment," *see supra* text accompanying note 197, also has been held to be unconstitutionally vague. *See* Dorman v. Satti, 862 F.2d 432, 433, 436 (2d Cir. 1988) (in invalidating statute that prohibited "harass[ment] of persons "engaged in the lawful taking of wildlife," court noted that "harass" "can mean anything").

207. *See supra* text accompanying notes 116-75.

208. 721 F. Supp. 852 (E.D. Mich. 1989).

209. *See* City of Houston v. Hill, 482 U.S. 451, 458 (1987) (regulation of speech will be unconstitutionally overbroad if it "reaches a substantial amount of constitutionally protected conduct") (citing Hoffman Estates v. The Flipside, Hoffman Estates, Inc., 455 U.S. 489, 494 (1982)).

210. In particular, the term "stigmatize," also used in the Stanford code, specifically was held to be unconstitutionally vague. *Doe,* 721 F. Supp. at 867.

The void-for-vagueness doctrine is enforced especially strictly in the first amendment context. *See* Kolender v. Lawson, 461 U.S. 352, 358 (1983); *Hoffman Estates,* 455 U.S. at 499; Smith v. Goguen, 415 U.S. 566, 573 (1974); Grayned v. City of Rockford, 408 U.S. 104, 109 (1972).

cluded that during the year when the policy was in effect, the University "consistently applied" it "to reach protected speech."[211] Moreover, because of the policy's vagueness, the court concluded that it did not give adequate notice of which particular expressions would be prohibited and which protected.[212] Consequently, the policy deterred members of the university community from engaging in protected expression for fear it might be sanctioned. This "chilling effect" of any hate speech regulation is particularly problematic in the academic environment, given the special importance of a free and robust exchange of ideas.[213]

Moreover, the judge who ultimately found the Michigan rule unconstitutional did not share Professor Lawrence's opinion that it was "poorly drafted and obviously overbroad."[214] To the contrary, his opinion expressly noted that he would not have found the rule unconstitutionally overbroad merely based on its language. Rather, he found it unconstitutional in light of the enforcement record.[215] These findings prove the relevance of the Michigan case not only to the Stanford situation, but also to all other campus hate speech regulations. Regardless of how carefully these rules are drafted, they inevitably are vague and unavoidably invest officials with substantial discretion in the enforcement process; thus, such regulations exert a chilling effect on speech beyond their literal bounds.

In the recent wave of college crackdowns on racist and other forms of hate speech, examples abound of attempts to censor speech conveying ideas that clearly play a legitimate role in academic discourse, although some of us might find them wrongheaded or even odious. For example, the University of Michigan's anti-hate speech policy could justify attacks on author Salman Rushdie because his book, *The Satanic Verses,*[216] was offensive to Muslims.[217]

---

211. *See Doe,* 721 F. Supp. at 865. The court cited the following examples of protected speech which had been subjected to the policy: a statement by a graduate student in the School of Social Work, in a research class, expressing his belief that homosexuality was a disease and that he intended to develop a counseling plan for changing gay clients to straight, *id.*; the reading of an allegedly homophobic limerick, which ridiculed a well-known athlete for his presumed sexual orientation, by a student in the School of Business Administration during a class public-speaking exercise, *id.*; and a statement by a student during an orientation session of a preclinical dentistry class, widely regarded as especially difficult, that he had heard that minorities had a hard time in the course and that they were not treated fairly, *id.* at 865-66.

212. *See id.* at 867.

213. *See supra* note 88.

214. Lawrence, at 478 n.162.

215. *See Id.*

216. S. RUSHDIE, THE SATANIC VERSES (1988).

217. *See* Statement of the Washtenaw County Branch, American Civil Liberties Union, on the University of Michigan Policy "Discrimination and Discriminatory Harassment by Students in the University Environment" 6 (May 25, 1989).

Such incidents are not aberrational. Any anti-hate speech rule inescapably entails some vagueness, due to the inherent imprecision of key words and concepts common to all such proposed rules. For example, most regulations employ one or more of the following terms: "demeaning," "disparaging," "harassing," "hostile," "insulting," "intimidating," and "stigmatizing."[218] Therefore, there is real danger that even a narrowly crafted rule will deter some expression that should be protected[219]—especially in the university environment.[220] In particular, such a rule probably will "add to the silence" on "gut issues" about racism, sexism, and other forms of bias that already impede interracial and other intergroup dialogues.[221]

Other examples of academic discourse that have been labeled censurable as hate speech include the following: a group of students complained that a faculty member had created a hostile atmosphere by quoting racist comments originally made at the turn of the century, even though the professor said that was not his intention, *see id.* at 4; another group of students contended that the former students' complaint about the professor had itself created a hostile atmosphere, *see id.* at 5; a law student suggested that judicial decisions reflecting adverse stereotypes about blacks should not be studied in law school courses, *see* Shaw, *Caveat Emptor,* N.Y.L. Sch. Rep., Apr. 1989, at 3; a Jewish professor was penalized for suggesting to his black students that they should celebrate the anniversary of their ancestors' liberation from slavery under the thirteenth amendment, just as Jews celebrate their ancestors' liberation from slavery during Passover, *see* Hentoff, *Campus Court-Martial,* Wash. Post, Dec. 15, 1988, at A25, col. 2; students complained about a professor's statement that black students are not sufficiently critical of human rights violations by black African governments, *see* McKinley, *Minority Students Walk Out Over a Teacher's Remarks,* N.Y. Times, Oct. 4, 1989, at B3, col. 5.

218. *See* Doe v. University of Mich., 721 F. Supp. 852, 867 (E.D. Mich. 1989) (holding unduly vague the terms "stigmatize," "victimize," " 'threat' to an individual's academic efforts," and "interfering with an individual's academic efforts"). Although Professor Lawrence protests that the Michigan regulation was "clearly overbroad," Lawrence, at 478 n.162, and hence cannot fairly be compared to the Stanford code, a key term in the latter is "stigmatize," which the *Doe* court held to be unconstitutionally vague. *See supra* text accompanying note 210. *See also supra* note 206 (citing decision holding the term "harass" to be unconstitutionally vague).

219. Regarding the chilling effect of a University of Connecticut anti-hate-speech rule utilizing some of these terms, see Brief of Amicus Curiae in Support of Plaintiff's Motion for Preliminary Injunction at 9-10 & n.10, Wu v. University of Conn., No. Civ. H-89-649 PCD (D. Conn. Jan. 25, 1990) (submitted by ACLU). In its brief, the ACLU stated that:

> Given [the rule's] ambiguities, a . . . student could plausibly fear prosecution for voicing an opinion that members of the Unification Church . . . are "cultists"; that Zionists are "imperialists" or that Palestinians are "terrorists"; that evangelical ministers are "hustlers" and their followers are "dupes"; or that homosexuals are "sick." Most ironically of all, a homosexual rights activist could perhaps be prosecuted for declaring that Catholics are "bigots" if they follow their Church's teaching that homosexuality is a sin . . . . Similarly, a black activist student leader might reasonably hesitate to characterize other black students, who are deemed insufficiently supportive of black causes, as "Uncle Toms" . . . .

220. *See* Cohen Letter (May 1, 1989), *supra* note 188.

221. *Id. See also* Letter from Pierre Bierre, research computer scientist in the Neuropsychology Laboratory of the departments of Psychiatry and Psychology, to George Parker, Chair of the Student Conduct Legislative Council, Stanford University (Mar. 16, 1989), *reprinted in* Stanford Univ. Campus Rep., Mar. 22, 1989, at 20 ("As any conflict counselor knows, the first step to resolve conflicts is to get people to open up and share unedited gut feelings, however irrational they may

Additionally, it must be recognized that silencing certain expressions may be tantamount to silencing certain ideas.[222] As the plaintiff in *Doe v. Michigan* argued:

> [T]he policy . . . is an official statement that at the University of Michigan, some arguments will no longer be tolerated. Rather than encourage her maturing students to question each other's beliefs on such diverse and controversial issues as the proper role of women in society, the merits of particular religions, or the moral propriety of homosexuality, the University has decided that it must protect its students from what it considers to be "unenlightened" ideas. In so doing, the University has established a secular orthodoxy by implying, among other things, that homosexuality is morally acceptable, [and] that . . . feminism [is] superior to the traditional view of women . . . .[223]

The Michigan plaintiff was victimized directly by the "pall of orthodoxy"[224] that the University's anti-hate speech policy cast over the campus. As a graduate student specializing in behavioral psychology, he felt that the rule deterred him from classroom discussion of theories that some psychological differences among racial groups and between the sexes are related to biological differences, for fear of being charged with racial or sexual harassment.[225]

In addition to their chilling effect on the ideas and expressions of university community members, policies that bar hate speech could engender broader forms of censorship. As noted by Professor William Cohen of Stanford Law School, an anti-hate speech rule such as the one adopted by his university "purports to create a personal right to be free from involuntary exposure to any form of expression that gives certain kinds of offense." Therefore, he explains, such a rule "could become a sword to challenge assigned readings in courses, the showing of films on campus, or the message of certain speakers."[226]

---

seem, and the second step is to remove the listening 'blocks' that prevent the other side from hearing those feelings.").

222. As Justice Harlan observed in Cohen v. California, 403 U.S. 15, 26 (1971), "[w]e cannot indulge in the facile assumption that one can forbid a particular word without also running the substantial risk of suppressing ideas in the process."

223. Affidavit of John Doe in Support of Plaintiff's Motion for Preliminary Injunction at para. 14, Doe v. University of Mich., 721 F. Supp. 852 (E.D. Mich. 1989) (No. 89-71683) [hereinafter Doe Affidavit].

224. Keyishian v. Board of Regents, 385 U.S. 589, 603 (1967). *See also* West Virginia State Bd. of Educ. v. Barnette, 319 U.S. 624, 642 (1943), which declared that:

> If there is any fixed star in our constitutional constellation, it is that no official, high or petty, can prescribe what shall be orthodox in politics, nationalism, religion or other matters of opinion or force citizens to confess by word or act their faith therein. If there are any circumstances which permit an exception, they do not now occur to us.

225. *See* Doe Affidavit, *supra* note 223, at paras. 7-11.

226. Cohen letter (March 10, 1989), *supra* note 170. Professor Cohen cited the following examples of potential censorship under this construction: a challenge by evangelical Christians to the film *The Last Temptation of Christ* (Barbara De Fina, released by Universal and Cineplex Odeon Films

B. *The Proposed Regulations Would Endanger Fundamental Free Speech Principles*

The various proposed campus hate speech regulations, including the Stanford code that Professor Lawrence endorses, are inconsistent with current Supreme Court doctrine prescribing permissible limits on speech. More importantly, they jeopardize basic free speech principles. Whereas certain conduct may be regulable, speech that advocates such conduct is not, and speech may not be regulated on the basis of its content, even if many of us strongly disagree with—or are repelled by—that content.

1. *Protection of Speech Advocating Regulable Conduct.* Civil libertarians, scholars, and judges consistently have distinguished between speech advocating unlawful conduct and the unlawful conduct itself.[227] Although this distinction has been drawn in numerous different factual settings, the fundamental underlying issues always are the same. For example, within recent years, some pro-choice activists have urged civil libertarians and courts to make an exception to free speech principles in order to restrain the expressive conduct of anti-abortion activists. Instead, civil libertarians have persuaded courts to prohibit assaults, blockages of clinic entrances, trespasses, and other illegal conduct by anti-choice activists.[228] Similarly, civil libertarians and courts[229] have rejected pleas by some feminists to censor pornography that reflects sexist attitudes.[230] Instead, civil libertarians have renewed their efforts to per-

---

1988); a challenge by blacks to D.W. Griffith's film *The Birth of a Nation* (Epoch Producing Corporation 1915); or a speech by Professor Shockley on racial differences.

227. *See* Brandenburg v. Ohio, 395 U.S. 444, 456-57 (1969) (Douglas, J., concurring) ("The line between what is permissible and not subject to control and what may be . . . subject to regulation is the line between ideas and overt acts."); *see also* A. NEIER, *supra* note 63, at 74 (ACLU did not represent American Nazis and Nazi sympathizers prosecuted under Smith Act during World War II, because defendants appeared to be enemy agents who had committed overt acts helpful to Germany).

228. *Compare* S. WALKER, *supra* note 16, at 349 (discussing ACLU representation of anti-abortion demonstrators) *with* National Abortion Fed'n v. Operation Rescue, No. CV 89-1181 AWT (C.D. Cal. Aug. 29, 1989) (holding anti-abortion demonstrators in contempt for violating order previously obtained by Southern California ACLU to protect abortion clinics and patients from assaults and other illegal conduct).

229. In *American Booksellers Ass'n v. Hudnut,* 771 F.2d 323, 334 (7th Cir.), *aff'd,* 475 U.S. 1001 (1985), the Supreme Court summarily affirmed the Seventh Circuit ruling invalidating an ordinance based upon model legislation drafted by feminist pro-censorship leaders Andrea Dworkin and Catharine MacKinnon.

230. *See generally* A. DWORKIN, PORNOGRAPHY: MEN POSSESSING WOMEN (1981) (pornography is not mere expression but method of domination of women); MacKinnon, *Pornography, Civil Rights, and Speech,* 20 HARV. C.R.-C.L. L. REV. 1 (1985) (same). Some feminists reject the notion that censoring pornography advances women's equality; they believe, to the contrary, that censoring pornography perpetuates archaic stereotypes about women. *See* Strossen, *The Convergence of Feminist and Civil Liberties Principles in the Pornography Debate* (Book Review), 62 N.Y.U. L. REV. 201

suade courts and legislatures to invalidate sexist actions.[231] A decade ago, civil libertarians and several courts—including the Supreme Court—rejected the plea of Holocaust survivors in Skokie, Illinois to prohibit neo-Nazis from demonstrating.[232] Instead, civil libertarians successfully have lobbied for the enactment and enforcement of laws against anti-Semitic vandalism and other hate-inspired conduct.[233]

A pervasive weakness in Professor Lawrence's analysis is his elision of the distinction between racist speech, on the one hand, and racist conduct, on the other.[234] It is certainly true that racist speech, like other speech, may have some causal connection to conduct. As Justice Holmes observed, "[e]very idea is an incitement" to action.[235] However, as Justice Holmes also noted, to protect speech that advocates conduct you oppose does not "indicate that you think the speech impotent, . . . or that you do not care wholeheartedly for the result."[236] Rather, this protection is based on the critical distinction between speech that has a direct and immediate link to unlawful conduct and all other speech, which has less direct and immediate links. In Holmes' immortal words:

> [W]e should be eternally vigilant against attempts to check the expression of opinions that we loathe and believe to be fraught with death, unless they so imminently threaten immediate interference with the lawful and pressing purposes of the law that an immediate check is required to save the country. . . . Only the emergency that makes it immediately dangerous to leave the correction of evil counsels to time warrants making any exception to the sweeping command, "Congress shall make no law . . . abridging the freedom of speech."[237]

Justice Holmes' stirring phrases were penned in dissenting opinions. However, the Court enshrined his view as the law of the land in 1969, in

---

(1987) (reviewing WOMEN AGAINST CENSORSHIP (V. Burstyn ed. 1985)) (book demonstrates falseness of dichotomy between feminist and civil libertarian principles, since goal of both is society in which individuals are treated justly).

231. For a description of ACLU efforts to combat sex discrimination, see Gale & Strossen, *supra* note 19, at 168-84.

232. Collin v. Smith, 447 F. Supp. 676 (N.D. Ill.), *aff'd,* 578 F.2d 1197 (7th Cir.), *cert. denied,* 439 U.S. 916 (1978); Village of Skokie v. National Socialist Party, 69 Ill. 2d 605, 373 N.E.2d 21 (1978).

233. *See* Letter from Morton Halperin to author, at 2 (Feb. 5, 1990) (ACLU strongly supported federal legislation directing FBI to gather statistics on hate crimes) (available from author).

234. *See* Lawrence, at 438-44. *See, e.g., id.* at 440 n.42 ("racist conduct amounts to speech"); *id.* at 441 ("*Brown*'s declaration that segregation is unconstitutional amounts to a regulation of the message of white supremacy."); *id.* at 443 n.58 ("I want to stress the complete overlap of the idea and practice of racism."); *id.* at 444 ("[T]he Court recognized the inseparability of idea and practice in the institution of slavery."); *id.* at 446 ("*Brown* mandates the abolition of racist speech."); *id.* at 463 ("*Brown* is a case about group defamation.").

235. Gitlow v. New York, 268 U.S. 652, 673 (1925) (Holmes, J., dissenting).

236. Abrams v. United States, 250 U.S. 616, 630 (1919) (Holmes, J., dissenting).

237. *Id.* at 630-31.

Brandenburg v. Ohio.[238] In a unanimous opinion overturning the conviction of a Ku Klux Klansman for an anti-black and anti-Semitic speech, the Court said that the first amendment does "not permit a state to forbid . . . advocacy of the use of force or of law violation except where such advocacy is directed to inciting or producing imminent lawless action and is likely to incite or produce such action."[239]

It is impossible to draw a bright line between speech and conduct. It also may be difficult to determine whether certain speech has a sufficiently tight nexus to conduct to justify regulating that speech. Professor Lawrence, however, abandons the attempt to make any such distinctions at all. He treats even the most extreme, blatant discriminatory conduct as speech, including slavery itself.[240] Although undoubtedly harmful, the utterance of disparaging remarks cannot be equated fairly with the systematic denial of all rights to a group of human beings.[241] Professor Lawrence recognizes this and appropriately chides anyone who insists that *all* racist conduct that includes an expressive component should be treated alike—namely, as protected speech.[242] However, Professor Lawrence himself engages in precisely the same kind of oversimplification when he suggests that all conduct with an expressive component—which, in his view, includes *all* racist conduct and *all* racist speech[243]—should be treated alike, namely, as *unprotected* speech. Those of us who reject either extreme as unreasonably rigid should join forces in undertaking the essential, albeit difficult, task of line-drawing.[244]

2. *Proscription on Content-Based Speech Regulations.*

   a.   The indivisibility of free speech.   It is important to place the current debate about campus racist speech in the context of earlier efforts to censor other forms of hate speech, including sexist and anti-Semitic

---

238. 395 U.S. 444 (1969) (per curiam).

239. *Id.* at 447.

240. *See supra* note 234.

241. Slavery, as well as de jure segregation and other phenomena that Professor Lawrence assimilates to hate speech by students or faculty members, also are distinguishable on the additional ground that the former emanated from the government, and the latter from private individuals. Regarding the significance of this distinction, see *infra* text accompanying notes 299-321.

242. *See* Lawrence, at 438, 449, 457, 461, 473-74, 476.

243. *See id.* at 438-49.

244. Indeed, Professor Lawrence himself emphasizes that he advocates regulating only a narrow class of racist speech. *See id.* at 435-36, 450 n.82, 458, 472. Therefore, he apparently recognizes that his equation between racist speech and racist conduct—whatever theoretical appeal it might have— is not relevant to the task of deciding *which* subset of racist speech should be restricted. However, while rejecting the speech/conduct line between protected and unprotected expressive activity, he offers no other. For a further discussion of this issue in the particular context of Professor Lawrence's argument that *Brown v. Board of Education* sanctions regulating racist speech, see *infra* text accompanying notes 289-98.

speech.[245] Such a broadened perspective suggests that consistent principles should be applied each time the issue resurfaces in any guise. Every person may find one particular type of speech especially odious and one message that most sorely tests his or her dedication to free speech values. But for each person who would exclude racist speech from the general proscription against content-based speech regulations, recent experience shows that there is another who would make such an exception only for anti-choice speech, another who would make it only for sexist speech, another who would make it only for anti-Semitic speech, another who would make it only for flag desecration, and so on.

The recognition that there is no principled basis for curbing speech expressing some particular ideas is reflected in the time-honored prohibition on any content-based[246] or viewpoint-based[247] regulations. As stated by Professor Tribe, "If the Constitution forces government to allow people to march, speak and write in favor of peace, brotherhood, and justice, then it must also require government to allow them to advocate hatred, racism, and even genocide."[248]

The position stated by Professor Tribe is not just the traditional civil libertarian view, but it also is the law of the land. The courts consistently have agreed with civil libertarian claims that the first amendment protects the right to engage in racist and other forms of hate speech.[249] Why is this so, and should it be so? Professor Lawrence rightly urges us to take a fresh look at this issue, no matter how well-settled it is as a matter of law. I have taken that invitation seriously and reflected long and hard upon his thought-provoking article and the questions it presents. Having done so, however, I conclude that the courts and traditional civil libertarians are correct in steadfastly rejecting laws that create additional new exceptions to free speech protections for racist expression.

---

245. *See supra* notes 227-33 and accompanying text.

246. *See, e.g.,* Police Dep't of Chicago v. Mosley, 408 U.S. 92, 95 (1972) ("[A]bove all else, the First Amendment means that government has no power to restrict expression because of its message, its ideas, its subject matter, or its content."). Courts will sustain a content-based speech regulation only where the government can prove that it "is necessary to serve a compelling state interest and that it is narrowly drawn to achieve that end." Widmar v. Vincent, 454 U.S. 263, 270 (1981). This stringent showing can rarely be made. *See, e.g.,* Carey v. Brown, 447 U.S. 455, 465 (1980) (statute prohibiting peaceful picketing in residential neighborhoods not narrowly tailored enough to promote State's asserted interests in (1) promoting privacy of home, and (2) providing special treatment for labor).

247. *See supra* quote accompanying note 1.

248. L. Tribe, *supra* note 58, § 12-8, at 838 n.17.

249. Justice Holmes enunciated this position in United States v. Schwimmer, 279 U.S. 644, 654 (1929) (Holmes, J., dissenting) ("If there is any principle of the Constitution that more imperatively calls for attachment than any other it is the principle of free thought—not free thought for those who agree with us, but freedom for the thought that we hate.").

One longstanding rationale for the view that speech must be pro-
.ected, regardless of its content, is the belief that we need a free market-
ɔlace of ideas, open even to the most odious and offensive ideas and
ʒxpressions,[250] because truth ultimately will triumph in an unrestricted
.narketplace.[251] The marketplace metaphor is subject to some criticism,
ıs Professor Lawrence notes.[252] Nevertheless, the marketplace of ideas
does sometimes work to improve society: This has been particularly true
with regard to promotion of racial equality.[253] Moreover, there are
other, independently sufficient, rationales for the content-neutral protection even of hate speech. Another important, more recently articulated,
rationale is that freedom of expression promotes individual autonomy
and dignity.[254] Professor Lawrence himself endorses an additional theory for the protection of racist speech, a view which recently was advanced by Dean Lee Bollinger: Free speech reinforces our society's
commitment to tolerance and to combating racist ideas.[255]

Although the foregoing theories may be acceptable in general, one
might ask why they do not permit exceptions for racist speech. Racism
in America is unique in important respects. For most of our country's
history, racism was enshrined legally through slavery or de jure discrimination. The post-Civil War constitutional amendments guaranteed racial
equality. More recently, all branches and levels of the government have

---

250. *See, e.g.,* Watts v. United States, 394 U.S. 705, 708 (1969) (per curiam) (refers to a
" 'profound national commitment to the principle that debate on public issues should be uninhibited,
robust, and wide-open, and that it may well include vehement, caustic, and sometimes unpleasantly
sharp attacks.' The language of the political arena . . . is often vituperative, abusive, and inexact"
(quoting New York Times Co. v. Sullivan, 376 U.S. 254, 270 (1964))). The Supreme Court recently
reaffirmed that the first amendment does not allow authorities to "prohibit the expression of an idea
simply because society finds the idea offensive or disagreeable." Texas v. Johnson, 109 S. Ct. 2533,
2544 (1989) (invalidating conviction for burning United States flag to express idea).

251. In a widely quoted dissent, Justice Holmes championed this rationale for free speech as
"the theory of our Constitution":

> [W]hen men have realized that time has upset many fighting faiths, they may come to
> believe even more than they believe the very foundations of their own conduct that the
> ultimate good desired is better reached by free trade in ideas—that the best test of truth is
> the power of the thought to get itself accepted in the competition of the market, and that
> truth is the only ground upon which their wishes safely can be carried out.

Abrams v. United States, 250 U.S. 616, 630 (1919) (Holmes, J., dissenting). *See also* Cohen v.
California, 403 U.S. 15, 24 (1971) (free expression "will ultimately produce a more capable citizenry
and more perfect polity"); *New York Times,* 376 U.S. at 270.

252. *See infra* text accompanying notes 416-21.

253. *See infra* text accompanying notes 429-36.

254. *See Cohen,* 403 U.S. at 24 ("[N]o other approach [than protecting free speech] would comport with the premise of individual dignity and choice upon which our political system rests."),
Richards, *Free Speech and Obscenity Law: Toward a Moral Theory of the First Amendment,* 123 U.
PA. L. REV. 45, 62 (1974) (freedom of expression permits and encourages individual's exercise of
autonomy).

255. *See* Lawrence, at 436.

sought to implement these constitutional guarantees by outlawing any vestiges of state-sponsored, as well as many forms of private, racial discrimination. Given our nation's special obligation to eradicate the "badges and incidents" of the formerly government-sanctioned institutions of racism, is it not appropriate to make broader exceptions than usual to free speech doctrines for racist speech? As Professor Rodney Smolla has noted, "Racist speech is arguably different in kind from other offensive speech, because the elimination of racism is *itself* enshrined in our Constitution as a public value of the highest order."[256]

The American commitment to eradicate racial discrimination is reinforced by a parallel international commitment, as expressed in such documents as the United Nations Charter,[257] the Universal Declaration of Human Rights,[258] and the International Convention on the Elimination of All Forms of Racial Discrimination.[259] Moreover, the United States is apparently alone in the world community in sheltering racist speech. Both under international agreements[260] and under the domestic law of many other countries[261] racist speech is outlawed.

In light of the universal condemnation of racial discrimination and the world-wide regulation of racist speech, it certainly is tempting to consider excepting racist speech from first amendment protection. Episodes of racist speech, such as those cited by Professor Lawrence and others, make a full commitment to free speech at times seem painful and difficult. Civil libertarians find such speech abhorrent, given our dedication to eradicating racial discrimination and other forms of bigotry. But experience has confirmed the truth of the indivisibility principle articulated above: History demonstrates that if the freedom of speech is weakened for one person, group, or message, then it is no longer there for others.[262] The free speech victories that civil libertarians have won in the context of defending the right to express racist and other anti-civil libertarian

---

256. R. SMOLLA, FREE SPEECH IN OPEN CULTURE (tentative title, forthcoming).

257. U.N. CHARTER art. 1, para. 3.

258. Universal Declaration of Human Rights, arts. 2, 7, 16, G.A. Res. 217 (III), 9 U.N. GAOR (3d Sess. pt. 1) at 71, U.N. Doc. A/810 (1948).

259. *Opened for signature* Mar. 7, 1966, 660 U.N.T.S. 195.

260. For example, the International Convention on the Elimination of All Forms of Racial Discrimination, *id.* art. 4(a), requires states to "declare as an offence punishable by law all dissemination of ideas based on racial superiority or hatred, [and] incitement to racial discrimination."

261. *See* Kretzmer, *Free Speech and Racism,* 8 CARDOZO L. REV. 445, 499-506 (1987) (reviewing European anti-hate speech laws).

262. *See supra* text accompanying note 1. As Thomas Paine wrote during our country's formative period: "He that would make his own liberty secure, must guard even his enemy from oppression, for if he violates this duty, he establishes a precedent that will reach himself." (quoted in AMERICAN CIVIL LIBERTIES UNION, WHY THE AMERICAN CIVIL LIBERTIES UNION DEFENDS FREE SPEECH FOR RACISTS AND TOTALITARIANS 2 (n.d.) [hereinafter ACLU pamphlet]).

nessages have been used to protect speech proclaiming anti-racist and ɪro-civil libertarian messages. For example, in 1949, the ACLU defended the right of Father Terminiello, a suspended Catholic priest, to ʒive a racist speech in Chicago. The Supreme Court agreed with that ɔosition in a decision that became a landmark in free speech history.[263] ʃime and again during the 1960s and 1970s, the ACLU and other civil ɪights groups were able to defend free speech rights for civil rights demɔnstrators by relying on the *Terminiello* decision.[264]

    b.   The slippery slope dangers of banning racist speech.   To attempt ɪo craft free speech exceptions only for racist speech would create a significant risk of a slide down the proverbial "slippery slope." To be sure, lawyers and judges are capable of—indeed, especially trained in—drawing distinctions between similar situations. Therefore, I agree with Professor Lawrence and other critics of the absolutist position[265] that slippery slope dangers should not be exaggerated. It is probably hyperbole to contend that if we ever stepped off the mountaintop where all speech is protected regardless of its content, then inevitably we would end up in the abyss where the government controls all our words.[266] On the other hand, critics of absolutism should not minimize the real danger: We would have a difficult time limiting our descent to a single downward step by attempting to prohibit only racist expression on campus.[267] Applicable rules and supporting rationales would need to be crafted carefully to distinguish this type of speech from others.

    First, we must think hard about the groups that should be protected. Should we regulate speech aimed only at racial and ethnic groups, as the University of Texas is considering?[268] Or should we also bar insults of religious groups, women, gays and lesbians, individuals with disabilities, Vietnam War veterans, and so on, as do the rules adopted by Stanford and the University of Michigan? As the committee that formulated the

---

263. Terminiello v. Chicago, 337 U.S. 1 (1949) (ACLU appeared amicus curiae); *see also* Brandenburg v. Ohio, 395 U.S. 444 (1969) (per curiam) (upholding free speech rights of Ku Klux Klan leader represented by ACLU).

264. *See, e.g.,* Brown v. Louisiana, 383 U.S. 131, 135 (1966); Cox v. Louisiana, 379 U.S. 536, 552 (1965). *See also infra* text accompanying notes 423-28 (discussing important role which first amendment rights played in the civil rights movement).

265. *See* Minow, *On Neutrality, Equality & Tolerance: New Norms for a Decade of Distinction,* CHANGE, Jan./Feb. 1990, at 17.

266. As Professor Lawrence notes, *see* C. Lawrence, Presentation at ACLU Biennial Conference, *supra* note †, at 20 n.42, the Court has long upheld certain content-based speech regulations, such as those governing obscenity, without eviscerating all free speech rights.

267. Professor Lawrence recognizes this danger. *See* Lawrence, at 458 & n.106 (general societal tolerance for suppressing speech would pose dangerous precedent for speech of all dissenters, even without case law).

268. *See* University of Texas Report, *supra* note 115, at 10.

University of Texas's proposed rule pointed out, each category requires a separate evaluation, since each "raise[s] different policy and legal concerns."[269] Therefore, we should not play fast and loose with the first amendment by casually expanding the categories of proscribed hate speech.

Second, we must carefully define proscribable harassing speech to avoid encompassing the important expression that inevitably is endangered by any hate speech restriction. Censorial consequences could result from many proposed or adopted university policies, including the Stanford code, which sanctions speech intended to "insult or stigmatize" on the basis of race or other prohibited grounds. For example, certain feminists suggest that all heterosexual sex is rape because heterosexual men are aggressors who operate in a cultural climate of pervasive sexism and violence against women.[270] Aren't these feminists insulting or stigmatizing heterosexual men on the basis of their sex and sexual orientation? And how about a Holocaust survivor who blames all ("Aryan") Germans for their collaboration during World War II? Doesn't this insinuation insult or stigmatize on the basis of national and ethnic origin? And surely we can think of numerous other examples that would have to give us pause.

The difficulty of formulating limited, clear definitions of prohibited hate speech, that do not encompass valuable contributions to societal discourse, is underscored by the seemingly intractable ambiguities in various campus rules.[271] Even proponents of campus hate speech regulations recognize their inevitable ambiguities and contextualized applications,[272] with the result that the individuals who enforce them must have substantial discretion to draw distinctions based upon the particular facts and circumstances involved in any given case. Professor Richard Delgado, an early advocate of rules proscribing hate speech, acknowledged that the offensiveness of even such a traditionally insulting epithet as "nigger" would depend on the context in which it was uttered, since it could be a term of affection when exchanged between friends.[273] The imprecise na-

---

269. *Id.*

270. *See* Duggan, Hunter & Vance, *False Promises: Feminist Antipornography Legislation in the U.S.,* in WOMEN AGAINST CENSORSHIP 130, 134, 138-39, 146-47 (V. Burstyn ed. 1985); Snitow, *Retrenchment Versus Transformation: The Politics of the Antipornography Movement,* in *id.* at 118.

271. *See supra* text accompanying notes 206-21.

272. *See* Matsuda, *supra* note 13, at 2373.

273. Delgado, *Words that Wound: A Tort Action for Racial Insults, Epithets, and Name-Calling,* 17 HARV. C.R.-C.L. L. REV. 133, 179-80 (1982). According to Professor Delgado,

[A]n epithet such as "You damn nigger" would almost always be found actionable, as it is highly insulting and highly racial . . . . "Boy," directed at a young black male, might be actionable, depending on the speaker's intent, the hearer's understanding, and whether a reasonable person would consider it a racial insult in the particular context. "Hey, nig-

:ure of racist speech regulations is underscored further by the fact that ?ven their proponents are unsure or disagree as to their applicability in particular situations.[274]

Once we acknowledge the substantial discretion that anti-hate speech rules will vest in those who enforce them, then we are ceding to the government the power to pick and choose whose words to protect and whose to punish. Such discretionary governmental power is fundamentally antithetical to the free speech guarantee. Once the government is allowed to punish any speech based upon its content, free expression exists only for those with power.

c. The content-neutrality principle reflects sensitivity to hate speech's hurtful power. Contrary to Professor Lawrence's apparent assumption,[275] the conclusion that free speech protections must remain indivisible, even for racist speech, has nothing to do with insensitivity to the feelings of minority group members who are vilified by hate speech and suffer acutely from it. Traditional civil libertarians recognize the power of words to inflict psychic and even physical wounds.[276] For example, precisely because the ACLU both acknowledges the power of speech and defends the exercise of that power even by those who express anti-civil libertarian ideas, the ACLU expressly dissociates itself from such ideas and makes it a priority to combat them through counterspeech and action.[277] Nor are traditional civil libertarians unconcerned with the rights of hate speech victims, as Professor Lawrence implies.[278] To the con-

---

ger," spoken affectionately between black persons and used as a greeting, would not be actionable. An insult such as "You dumb honkey," directed at a white person, could be actionable . . . but only in the unusual situations where the plaintiff would suffer harm from such an insult.

Id.

274. For example, during a discussion about the University of Wisconsin rule regulating hate speech, even advocates of the rule disagreed as to whether it would (or should) apply to the following hypothetical situation: A white student sits down next to a black student and says, "I want you to know that I'm a racist and hate the idea of blacks being here at the university," but does not use any racist epithet. Telephone interview with Eunice Edgar, Executive Director of ACLU of Wisconsin (Nov. 14, 1989). *See also* Gottlieb, *supra* note 4 (Professor Thomas Grey, who drafted Stanford code, "said his rule *probably* wouldn't apply to one of the most publicized racial incidents at Stanford, when a white student left on a black student's door a poster of Beethoven drawn as a black caricature.") (emphasis added).

275. *See* Lawrence, at 458-59.

276. *See* Matsuda, *supra* note 13, at 2336 ("Victims of vicious hate propaganda have experienced physiological symptoms and emotional distress ranging from fear in the gut, rapid pulse rate and difficulty in breathing, nightmares, post-traumatic stress disorder, hypertension, psychosis, and suicide.").

277. *See supra* note 53 (quoting relevant ACLU policy).

278. *See* Lawrence, at 448, 456, 458, 478.

trary, civil libertarians champion the rights of all individuals to live in a society untainted by racism and other forms of bias.[279]

I was appalled by Professor Lawrence's account of the vicious racist vilification to which his sister's family recently was subjected.[280] This account powerfully demonstrates that the old nursery rhyme is wrong: Maybe words are different from sticks and stones insofar as they cannot literally break our bones, but words can and do hurt—brutally.

Two prominent defenders of content-neutral protection for hate speech have described painful personal experiences as victims of such speech. I refer to Stanford Law Professor Gerald Gunther, who was a leading opponent of the proposed Stanford code which Professor Lawrence advocates,[281] and Aryeh Neier, who as Executive Director of the ACLU during the Skokie episode vigorously championed the free speech rights of racists and anti-Semites.[282] Far from opposing censorship *despite* the suffering they personally experienced as a result of hate speech, Messrs. Gunther[283] and Neier[284] oppose censorship precisely *because* of

---

279. For ACLU policies opposing racism and other types of bias, see *supra* notes 11 & 15 and Appendix; for ACLU efforts to combat discrimination, see *supra* note 16 and *infra* text accompanying notes 336-55.

280. *See* Lawrence, at 460. It should be stressed, however, that this expression would not be encompassed by either the Stanford code or Professor Lawrence's variation on it. *See supra* notes 205-06.

281. *See* Letter from Professor Gerald Gunther to Professor George Parker, Chair of the Student Conduct Legislative Council, Stanford University (Mar. 10, 1989), *reprinted in* Stanford Univ. Campus Rep., Mar. 15, 1989, at 17 [hereinafter Gunther letter (March 10, 1989)]. Gunther wrote that:

[L]est it be said that I unduly slight the pain imposed by expressions of racial or religious hatred let me add that I have suffered that pain. I empathize with others who have, and I rest my deep belief in the principles of the First Amendment in part on my own experiences.

I received my elementary education in a public school in a very small town in Nazi Germany. I was subjected to vehement anti-Semitic remarks, from my teacher, my classmates and others. "Judensau" (Jew pig) was far from the harshest.

282. *See* A. NEIER, *supra* note 63, at 2-3 (recounting his childhood as a Jew in Hitler's Germany, his narrow escape from the Nazi death camps, and the extermination of almost all his relatives, beyond his immediate family, during World War II).

283. Professor Gunther stated that:

My own experiences have certainly not led me to be insensitive to the myriad pains offensive speech can and often does impose. But the lesson I have drawn from my childhood in Nazi Germany and my happier adult life in this country is the need to walk the sometimes difficult path of denouncing the bigots' hateful ideas with all my power yet at the same time challenging any community's attempt to suppress hateful ideas by force of law.

Gunther letter (March 10, 1989), *supra* note 281.

284. Aryeh Neier, reflecting on his role in the Skokie incident, recalled that:

The most frequently repeated line of all in the many letters about Skokie that I received was: "How can you, a Jew, defend freedom for Nazis?". . . . The response I made . . . most often began with a question: "How can I, a Jew, refuse to defend freedom, even for Nazis? . . ." Because we Jews are uniquely vulnerable, I believe we can win only brief respite from persecution in a society in which encounters are settled by power. As a Jew, therefore . . . I want restraints placed on power . . . . I want restraints which prohibit those in power from interfering with my right to speak, my right to publish, or my right to gather with others

these personal experiences. The justification for not outlawing "words that wound"[285] is not based on a failure to recognize the injurious potential of words. The refusal to ban words is due precisely to our understanding both of how very powerful they are and of the critical role they play in our democratic society.[286]

III. Professor Lawrence's Rationales for Regulating Racist Speech Would Justify Sweeping Prohibitions, Contrary to Free Speech Principles

Although Professor Lawrence actually advocates regulating only a relatively narrow category of racist speech, his rationales could be asserted to justify broader rules. Indeed, he himself appears to recognize that, if accepted, his approach could lead to outlawing all racist speech, as well as other forms of hate speech.[287] Since many universities and individuals now advocate broader-ranging regulations—and since Professor Lawrence also endorses restrictions that have a "considerably broader reach" than the Stanford code[288]—it is important to consider the problems with Professor Lawrence's more expansive rationales. His general theories about racist speech entail substantial departures from traditional civil libertarian and constitutional law positions.

A. Brown *and Other Cases Invalidating Governmental Racist Conduct Do Not Justify Regulating Non-Governmental Racist Speech*

Professor Lawrence intriguingly posits that *Brown v. Board of Education,*[289] *Bob Jones University v. United States,*[290] and other civil rights cases justify regulation of private racist speech.[291] The problem with drawing an analogy between all of these cases and the subject at hand is that the cases involved either *government* speech, as opposed to speech

---

who also feel threatened. . . . To defend myself, I must restrain power with freedom, even if the temporary beneficiaries are the enemies of freedom.

A. Neier, *supra* note 63, at 4-5.

285. *See* Delgado, *supra* note 273, at 133.

286. *See* Gale & Strossen, *supra* note 19, at 171. In their article, the authors stated that:

We know that free speech poses great personal and societal risks, and that the risks are borne, unfairly and disproportionately, by individuals and groups that any just and humane society would single out instead for respect, compassion, help, and even reparation for past wrongs. But we also know that racism, sexism, and silence have combined too often to form an unholy trinity in the history of oppression in the United States.

287. *See supra* text accompanying notes 28-31.

288. Lawrence, at 456. *See also supra* note 27.

289. 347 U.S. 483 (1954).

290. 461 U.S. 574 (1983).

291. *See* Lawrence, at 438-49.

by private individuals, or *conduct,* as opposed to speech.[292] Indeed, *Brown* itself is distinguishable on both grounds.

1. *The Speech/Conduct Distinction.* First, the governmental defendant in *Brown*—the Topeka, Kansas Board of Education—was not simply saying that blacks are inferior. Rather, it was treating them as inferior through pervasive patterns of conduct, by maintaining systems and structures of segregated public schools. To be sure, a by-product of the challenged conduct was a message, but that message was only incidental. Saying that black children are unfit to attend school with whites is materially distinguishable from legally prohibiting them from doing so, despite the fact that the legal prohibition may convey the former message.

Professor Lawrence's point proves too much. If incidental messages could transform conduct into speech, then the distinction between speech and conduct would disappear completely, because *all* conduct conveys a message. To take an extreme example, a racially motivated lynching expresses the murderer's hatred or contempt for his victim. But the clearly unlawful act is not protected from punishment by virtue of the incidental message it conveys. And the converse also is true. Just because the government may suppress particular hate messages that are the by-product of unlawful conduct, it does not follow that it may suppress all hate messages. Those messages not tightly linked to conduct must still be protected.[293]

Professor Lawrence's argument is not advanced by his unexceptionable observation that all human activity may be described both as "speech" and as "conduct." All speech entails some activity (e.g., the act of talking) and all conduct expresses some message.[294] First, this fact does not justify treating *any* speech-conduct as unprotected; second, it does not justify eliminating protection from the particular class of speech-conduct that Professor Lawrence deems regulable.

The fact that there is no clear distinction between speech and conduct does not necessarily warrant *limiting* the scope of protected speech-conduct;[295] instead, the lack of a clear distinction could as logically war-

---

292. Regarding the significance of this distinction, see *supra* text accompanying notes 234–41.

293. *See supra* notes 73-74 and accompanying text.

294. *See* Lawrence, at 440 n.43.

295. For example, as Professor Lawrence observes, *id.*, John Hart Ely has described all communicative behavior as "100% action and 100% expression." Ely, *Flag Desecration: A Case Study in the Roles of Categorization and Balancing in First Amendment Analysis,* 88 HARV. L. REV. 1482, 1495-96 (1975). This does not lead Professor Ely, however, to conclude that all speech should be regulated. Nor does it lead him to conclude that the speech/conduct distinction is irrelevant to first amendment analysis. Rather, he suggests that, in evaluating the constitutionality of a government

rant *expanding* the scope of protection. Although one could argue—as does Professor Lawrence—that some speech is tantamount to conduct and should therefore be regulated, one could also argue that some conduct is tantamount to speech and therefore should *not* be regulated. This latter approach has characterized a line of Supreme Court decisions that protect various forms of conduct, ranging from labor picketing[296] to burning the American flag,[297] as "symbolic speech."

The absence of a clear distinction between speech and conduct also does not support Professor Lawrence's particular concept of regulable racist speech. Even assuming that his wholesale abandonment of the traditional distinction is warranted with respect to racist words and deeds, Professor Lawrence himself apparently concedes that this still would not justify the regulation of all racist words. To the contrary, he advocates regulating only a limited class of such words. But if Professor Lawrence does not draw the line between regulable and non-regulable racist speech on the basis of the speech/conduct dichotomy, on what basis does he draw that line? He does not offer a clear limiting principle

---

regulation of certain conduct, the analytical focus should not be on whether that conduct should be classified as "speech" or "action." Instead, he urges, the relevant inquiry should be whether the regulation is aimed at the expressive aspect of such conduct. If so, it is presumptively unconstitutional; if not, it is presumptively constitutional. *Id.* at 1496-97. This is the analysis that the Court enunciated in United States v. O'Brien, 391 U.S. 367, 381-82 (1968) (upholding statute that criminalized the destruction of draft cards where governmental interest was limited to the noncommunicative aspect of defendant's conduct).

Under the Ely-*O'Brien* analysis, *Brown* does not involve the regulation of the expressive aspect of speech-conduct. Under the *O'Brien* test, as Professor Ely paraphrased it, "[t]he critical question . . . [is] whether the harm that the state is seeking to avert is one that grows out of the fact that the defendant is communicating . . . or rather would arise even if the defendant's conduct had no communicative significance whatsoever." Ely, *supra*, at 1497. Analysis reveals that school segregation would be invalidated apart from its communicative significance.

One can imagine situations in which the act of requiring schools to be racially segregated did not convey the message of white supremacy which Professor Lawrence views as the central meaning of school segregation. *See* Lawrence, at 441, 462-64. Yet *Brown* surely would hold that such segregated schools violate the equal protection clause. For example, a black student who had been raised in a different culture marked by black supremacy, and then moved to the U.S. and attended a racially segregated school, might well interpret school segregation as conveying the message of white inferiority. Would *Brown* not demand that this student should nonetheless attend a desegregated school? As another example, a community might come to view racial diversity much the way it regards religious diversity, so that the choice to attend a religiously segregated school would be viewed as conveying no more stigmatizing a message than the choice to attend a religiously segregated school. Would *Brown* not insist, nevertheless, that no public schools could be racially segregated, even if the option of attending them was completely voluntary? *See* Green v. County School Bd., 391 U.S. 430 (1968) (rejected "freedom-of-choice" plan for desegregation).

296. *See, e.g.,* Thornhill v. Alabama, 310 U.S. 88 (1940) (peaceful picketing to publicize labor dispute is constitutionally protected free speech).

297. *See* United States v. Eichman, 110 S. Ct. 2404, 2409-18 (1990); Texas v. Johnson, 109 S. Ct. 2533, 2539 (1989) (Flag burning is "conduct sufficiently imbued with elements of communication to implicate the first amendment.").

for distinguishing the racist speech that should be regulated from the entire corpus of racist speech, which he views as conduct, and hence presumptively regulable under the speech/conduct approach.[298]

   2. *The Private Action/State Action Distinction.*   Even if *Brown* involved only a governmental message of racism, without any attendant conduct, that case still would be distinguishable in a crucial way from a private individual's conveyance of the same message. Under the post-Civil War constitutional amendments, the government is committed to eradicating all badges and incidents of slavery, including racial discrimination. Consistent with the paramount importance of this obligation, the Supreme Court has held that the equal protection clause bars the government from loaning textbooks to racially discriminatory private schools,[299] even though the Court had held previously that the establishment clause does *not* bar the government from loaning textbooks to private religious schools.[300] In this respect, the government's constitutional duty to dissociate itself from racism is even greater than its constitutional duty to dissociate itself from religion.[301] The government's supreme obligation to counter racism clearly is incompatible with racist speech promulgated by the government itself. Private individuals have no comparable duty.

   Professor Mari Matsuda has argued that the government's failure to punish private hate speech could be viewed as state action insofar as this failure conveys a message that the state tolerates such speech.[302] Because the Court construes the establishment clause as prohibiting government

---

   298. The fact that Professor Lawrence also rejects the state action doctrine as a limiting principle on government's regulatory power further expands the range of speech that he would allow to be restricted. *See* Lawrence, at 444-49.

   Scholars constantly grapple with the complex problems of how to separate regulable from non-regulable speech. For recent efforts, see C. BAKER, HUMAN LIBERTY AND FREEDOM OF SPEECH (1989); K. GREENAWALT, SPEECH, CRIME, AND THE USES OF LANGUAGE (1989); H. KALVEN, JR., A WORTHY TRADITION: FREEDOM OF SPEECH IN AMERICA (1988); F. SCHAUER, FREE SPEECH: A PHILOSOPHICAL ENQUIRY (1982). Yet I am unaware of any that provide a more coherent basic approach than the Court's current general framework: A government regulation aimed at speech or expressive conduct is presumptively unconstitutional unless "it furthers an important . . . governmental interest . . . [that] is unrelated to the suppression of free expression . . . [and] the incidental restriction on . . . . First Amendment freedoms is no greater than is essential to the furtherance of that interest." United States v. O'Brien, 391 U.S. 367, 377 (1968). If speech is integrally interrelated with, or incites, violent or otherwise unlawful conduct, government regulation would be permitted under the *O'Brien* formulation. *See supra* notes 73-74 and accompanying text.

   299. Norwood v. Harrison, 413 U.S. 455, 471 (1973).

   300. Board of Educ. v. Allen, 392 U.S. 236, 248 (1968).

   301. *See Norwood*, 413 U.S. at 470 ("However narrow may be the channel of permissible state aid to sectarian schools, . . . it permits a greater degree of state assistance than may be given to private schools which engage in discriminatory practices.").

   302. *See* Matsuda, *supra* note 13, at 2378-79.

action that conveys a message of state support for religion,[303] establishment clause cases constitute instructive precedents for evaluating Professor Matsuda's argument.[304] In the analogous establishment clause context, the Court repeatedly has held that the government's neutral tolerance and protection of private religious expression, along with all other expression, does not convey a message that the government endorses religion.[305] In its 1990 decision in *Board of Education of Westside Community Schools v. Mergens,*[306] the Court expressly reaffirmed the crucial distinction between government and private speech, in the establishment clause context, in terms fully applicable to the racist speech controversy. The Court declared, "[T]here is a crucial difference between *government* speech endorsing religion, which the Establishment Clause forbids, and *private* speech endorsing religion, which the Free Speech and Free Exercise Clauses protect."[307] Paraphrasing this language and applying it to the campus hate speech context, one could say, "There is a crucial difference between *government* speech endorsing racism, which the Equal Protection Clause forbids, and *private* speech endorsing racism, which the Free Speech Clause protects."

In light of the government's special duty to dissociate itself from racism, one might try to distinguish private religious speech from private racist speech—much as the Court distinguished textbook loans to racially discriminatory private schools from the same kind of loans to private religious schools.[308] However, the direct, tangible, explicit government support of racially discriminatory schools through textbook lending programs is critically different from the indirect, intangible, implicit government support allegedly lent to racist conduct by the government's failure to outlaw private racist speech.[309]

---

303. *See, e.g.,* County of Allegheny v. ACLU, 109 S. Ct. 3086, 3101 (1989) (establishment clause inquiry is whether government is "conveying or attempting to convey a message that religion or a particular religious belief is *favored* or *preferred*").

304. Professor Lawrence also suggests the analogy between establishment clause doctrine and the law governing race discrimination. *See* Lawrence, at 447 ("for over three hundred years, racist speech has been the liturgy of America's leading established religion, the religion of racism").

305. Board of Educ. v. Mergens, 110 S. Ct. 2356 (1990) (interpreting Equal Access Act, 20 U.S.C. §§ 4071-4074 (1988), which prohibits public secondary schools from denying meeting space to religious and other clubs on the basis of speech content, expresses neutrality towards religion); Widmar v. Vincent, 454 U.S. 263, 271-72 (1981) (when university has created a forum generally open to student groups, its content-based exclusion of religious speech violates principle that regulation should be content-neutral).

306. 110 S. Ct. 2356 (1990).

307. *Id.* at 2372 (emphasis added).

308. *See supra* text accompanying notes 299-300.

309. *See* Norwood v. Harrison, 413 U.S. 455, 466 (1973) (state may not grant "tangible financial aid . . . if [it] has a significant tendency to facilitate, reinforce, and support private discrimination");

Professor Lawrence makes a telling point when he says that our government never has repudiated the group libels it perpetrated for years against blacks and that it is insufficient for the government simply to cease uttering those libels.[310] One approach for promoting racial equality, which is consistent with free speech, is to urge the government to proclaim anti-racist messages.[311]

Professor Lawrence also makes the persuasive point that there is no absolute distinction between state and private action in the racist sphere, insofar as private acts of discrimination (as well as government acts) also are unlawful.[312] This point, however, raises the other distinction discussed above—the distinction between words and conduct. Civil libertarians vigorously support the civil rights laws that make private discriminatory *acts* illegal,[313] but that is a far cry from making private *speech* illegal. The *Bob Jones* case, upon which Professor Lawrence seeks to rely,[314] illustrates these distinctions. What was objectionable there was the government conduct that supported and endorsed the private racist conduct—namely, the government's making of financial contributions, through the tax system, to racially discriminatory private educational institutions. Moreover, even if a private university could be prohibited from *taking* discriminatory actions—in the case of Bob Jones University, barring interracial marriage and dating—it still could not be prohibited from *advocating* such actions. The ACLU amicus brief in the *Bob Jones* case[315] made precisely these points in countering the University's claim that withdrawing its tax benefits would violate its first amendment rights. The ACLU argued,[316] and the Court agreed,[317] that the University was still free to urge its students not to engage in interra-

---

id. at 467 (state must not give "significant aid" to racially discriminatory private institutions); *id.* at 469 (discriminatory private schools may not receive "material aid" from state).

310. Lawrence, at 447.

311. *See infra* text accompanying notes 397-402.

312. *See* Lawrence, at 449.

313. *See infra* text accompanying notes 338-55 (outlining ACLU's efforts to combat racism). The ACLU joined an amicus brief filed by a coalition of civil rights organizations in Patterson v. McLean Credit Union, 109 S. Ct. 2363 (1989), endorsing the Court's earlier interpretation of 42 U.S.C. § 1981 (1988) as outlawing private race discrimination, *see* Runyon v. McCrary, 427 U.S. 160, 173 (1976) (section 1981 reaches private acts of discrimination).

314. *See* Lawrence, at 449.

315. Brief of the American Civil Liberties Union and the American Jewish Committee, Amici Curiae in support of Affirmance at 37-38, Bob Jones Univ. v. United States, 461 U.S. 574 (1983) (Nos. 81-3, 81-1).

316. Professor Strossen was counsel of record for the ACLU and the American Jewish Committee, amici curiae, advocating government denial of tax benefits to racially discriminatory educational institutions.

317. *See Bob Jones,* 461 U.S. at 603-04 ("Denial of tax benefits will inevitably have a substantial impact on the operation of private religious schools, but will not prevent those schools from observing their religious tenets."). *Accord Runyon,* 427 U.S. at 177 (42 U.S.C. § 1981 (1988) forbids pri-

cial marriage or dating, and this was as far as its first amendment rights extended. Prohibited racist acts are no different from other prohibited acts. The government may punish the acts, but it may not punish words that advocate or endorse them.

The other cases upon which Professor Lawrence premises his argument also do not authorize the regulation of private racist speech. For example, he attempts to analogize private racist speech to a local government's financing of allegedly "private" segregated (all-white) schools, after the government had closed down public schools in defiance of desegregation orders.[318] Lawrence misreads these cases as standing for the proposition "that the defamatory message of segregation would not be insulated from constitutional proscription simply because the speaker was a non-government entity."[319] Another example is provided by *Griffin v. Prince Edward County School Board,* in which the Supreme Court held that the governmental financing of segregated schools constituted prohibited state action.[320] In contrast, had individual school district residents urged their government to undertake such action, or expressed this opinion to black residents, that would have constituted protected private speech.[321]

B. *The Non-Intellectual Content of Some Racist Speech Does Not Justify its Prohibition*

In addition to his principal argument that private racist speech can be regulated because it is indistinguishable from governmental racist conduct, Professor Lawrence offers a second justification. He contends that "[a] defining attribute of speech is that it appeals first to the mind of the hearer who can evaluate its truth or persuasiveness,"[322] and that because certain racist speech lacks this quality, it should not be viewed as speech. This position is inconsistent with fundamental free speech values.

---

vate, commercially operated, nonsectarian schools from denying admission based on race, but such schools remain free "to inculcate whatever values and standards they deem desirable.").

318. *See* Lawrence, at 448 & n.75.

319. *Id.* at 448.

320. 377 U.S. 218, 233 (1964).

321. Equally unpersuasive is Professor Lawrence's attempted reliance on cases upholding prohibitions upon race-designated advertisements for employees, home sales, and rentals, *see* Lawrence, at 449 & n.81, 464 n.123. As the Supreme Court ruled, in Pittsburgh Press Co. v. Human Relations Comm'n, 413 U.S. 376, 391 (1973), these advertisements constituted integral elements of the prohibited discriminatory conduct—i.e., refusing to hire women. *Id.* at 388-89. Therefore, these advertisements fit within the general category of speech that may be regulated on the ground that it constitutes an essential element of an unlawful act. *See supra* notes 73-74 and accompanying text.

322. Lawrence, at 452 n.87.

Lawrence's argument overlooks the teachings of such landmark Supreme Court decisions as *Terminiello v. Chicago* [323] and *Cohen v. California*, [324] which hold that protectible speech often appeals to the emotions as well as the mind. As early as 1948, the Court recognized that first amendment protection is not restricted to the "exposition of ideas." [325] As Justice Douglas declared in a celebrated passage in *Terminiello*:

> [A] function of free speech under our system of government is to invite dispute. It may indeed best serve its high purpose when it induces a condition of unrest, creates dissatisfaction with conditions as they are, or even stirs people to anger. Speech is often provocative and challenging. It may strike at prejudices and preconceptions and have profound unsettling effects as it presses for acceptance of an idea. That is why freedom of speech, though not absolute, is nevertheless protected against censorship or punishment, unless shown likely to produce a clear and present danger of a serious substantive evil that rises far above public inconvenience, annoyance, or unrest. There is no room under our Constitution for a more restrictive view. For the alternative would lead to standardization of ideas either by legislatures, courts, or dominant political or community groups. [326]

Justice Harlan [327] echoed this theme in *Cohen* when he explained that protectible expression

> conveys not only ideas capable of relatively precise, detached explication, but otherwise inexpressible emotions as well. In fact, words are often chosen as much for their emotive as their cognitive force. *We cannot sanction the view that the Constitution, while solicitous of the cognitive content of individual speech, has little or no regard for that emotive function which practically speaking, may often be the more important element of the overall message sought to be communicated.* [328]

---

323. 337 U.S. 1 (1949).

324. 403 U.S. 15 (1971).

325. Winters v. New York, 333 U.S. 507, 510 (1948) (reversing conviction for selling crime magazines under statute prohibiting publication of "stories of . . . bloodshed, lust or crime" as obscene, *id.* at 508). The Court concluded that expression devoid of "ideas," but with entertainment value, was protected, because "[t]he line between the informing and the entertaining is too elusive for the protection of that basic [first amendment] right. . . . What is one man's amusement, teaches another's doctrine." *Id.* at 510.

326. *Terminiello*, 337 U.S. at 4-5 (citations omitted). For a very different view, compare Lawrence, at 438 ("Regulations that require civility of discourse in certain designated forums are not incursions on intellectual and political debate.").

327. It is noteworthy that these two ringing endorsements of constitutional protection for offensive, provocative speech were written by Justices at opposite ends of the Court's ideological spectrum. The agreement on this issue between Justice Douglas, a noted liberal, and Justice Harlan, a respected conservative, indicates that their views represent a solidly entrenched consensus about free speech tenets.

328. *Cohen*, 403 U.S. at 26 (emphasis added). Professor Tribe eloquently described how *Cohen* supports a more generous vision of protectible speech than just the intellectually oriented speech that Professor Lawrence would protect: "Justice Harlan's opinion for the majority [in Cohen] implicitly

Together, *Terminiello* and *Cohen* recognize that speech often expresses the speaker's emotions and appeals to the audience's emotions. This generalization applies not only to the ugly words of racist vituperation, but also to the beautiful words of poetry. Indeed, much indisputably valuable language, as well as expressive conduct, has the intention and effect of appealing not directly or not only to the mind. Such language also seeks to and does engage the audience's emotions. If emotion-provoking discourse were denied protected status, then much political speech—which is usually viewed as being at the core of first amendment protection—would fall outside the protected realm. The Court in *Terminiello* and *Cohen* rejected the restricted first amendment paradigm of "a sedate assembly of speakers who calmly discussed the issues of the day and became ultimately persuaded by the logic of one of the competing positions."[329] Professor Lawrence reveals his narrower view when he asks, "[A]re racial insults ideas? Do they encourage wide-open debate?"[330] In light of the *Terminiello-Cohen* line of cases, Professor Lawrence wrongly implies that a negative response to these questions should remove racial insults from the domain of protected speech. Professor Lawrence also incorrectly implies that the response to these questions should be negative. Racial insults convey ideas of racial supremacy and inferiority. Objectionable and discredited as these ideas may be, they are ideas nonetheless.[331]

IV. PROHIBITING RACIST SPEECH WOULD NOT EFFECTIVELY COUNTER, AND COULD EVEN AGGRAVATE, THE UNDERLYING PROBLEM OF RACISM

A. *Civil Libertarians Should Continue to Make Combating Racism a Priority*

Despite Professor Lawrence's proffered justifications for regulating a broader spectrum of racist speech, he in fact advocates regulating only a limited category of speech.[332] Thus, even Professor Lawrence's views of

---

rejected the hoary dichotomy between reason and desire that so often constricts the reach of the first amendment." L. TRIBE, *supra* note 58, § 12-1 at 787-88.

329. Rutzick, *Offensive Language and the Evolution of First Amendment Protection,* 9 HARV. C.R.-C.L. L. REV. 1, 18 (1974). *Compare* Lawrence, at 452 ("The racial invective is experienced as a blow, not a proffered idea, and . . . it is unlikely that dialogue will follow.").

330. Lawrence, at 463 n.119.

331. Professor Matsuda, *supra* note 13, at 2360, acknowledged that racist speech conveys an idea when she stated that, "Racial supremacy is one of the *ideas* we have collectively and internationally considered and rejected." (emphasis added). Professor Lawrence recognized the same point when he quoted this sentence from Matsuda. Lawrence, at 463 n.119.

332. *See* Lawrence, at 435-36, 450 & n.82, 458 & nn.105-06.

regulable speech, although broader than those of the Supreme Court or traditional civil libertarians, would allow most racist speech on campus.

I do not think it is worth spending a great deal of time debating the fine points of specific rules or their particular applications to achieve what necessarily will be only marginal differences in the amount of racist insults that can be sanctioned. The larger problems of racist attitudes and conduct—of which all these words are symptoms—would remain. Those who share the dual goals of promoting racial equality and protecting free speech must concentrate on countering racial discrimination, rather than on defining the particular narrow subset of racist slurs that constitutionally might be regulable.

I welcome Professor Lawrence's encouragement to civil libertarians to "engage actively in speech and action that resists and counters the racist ideas the first amendment protects."[333] But Professor Lawrence need not urge traditional civil libertarians to "put[ ] at least as much effort and as many resources into fighting for the victims of racism as we put into protecting the rights of racists."[334] The ACLU, for example, puts far more effort and resources into assisting the victims of racism than into defending the rights of racists.

Although ACLU cases involving the Ku Klux Klan and other racist speakers often generate a disproportionate amount of publicity, they constitute only a tiny fraction of the ACLU's caseload. In the recent past, the ACLU has handled about six cases a year advocating the free speech rights of white supremacists, out of a total of more than six thousand cases,[335] and these white supremacist cases rarely consume significant resources.[336] Moreover, the resources the ACLU does expend to protect hatemongers' first amendment rights are well-invested. They ultimately preserve not only civil liberties, but also our democratic system, for the benefit of all.[337]

---

333. *Id.* at 480.

334. C. Lawrence, Presentation at ACLU Biennial Conference, *see supra* note †, at 30.

335. Less than one-tenth of one percent of the ACLU's cases involve the defense of groups that might be labeled white supremacists. *See* ACLU pamphlet, *supra* note 262, at 10.

336. *See* A. NEIER, *supra* note 63, at 148 (free speech cases rarely involve factual disputes and therefore can be litigated relatively inexpensively).

337. Aryeh Neier persuasively drew this conclusion with respect to the ACLU's defense of the American Nazi Party's right to demonstrate in Skokie:

[W]hen it was all over no one had been persuaded to join [the Nazis]. They had disseminated their message and it had been rejected.

Why did the Nazi message fall on such deaf ears? Revolutionaries and advocates of destruction attract followers readily when the society they wish to overturn loses legitimacy. Understanding this process, revolutionaries try to provoke the government into using repressive measures. They rejoice, as the American Nazis did, when their rights are denied to them; they count on repression to win them sympathizers.

In confronting the Nazis, however, American democracy did not lose, but preserved its legitimacy . . . .

The ACLU has devoted substantial resources to the struggle against racism.[338] The ACLU backed the civil rights movement in its early years, working with lawyers from the National Association for the Advancement of Colored People (NAACP) to plan the attack on segregation. In 1931, the ACLU published *Black Justice,* a comprehensive report on legalized racism.[339] Although the ACLU initially was not involved in the infamous Scottsboro cases—in which seven young black men were convicted of raping two white women after sham trials before an all-white jury—an ACLU attorney argued and won the first of these cases to reach the Supreme Court.[340]

During World War II, the ACLU sponsored a challenge to the segregated draft and organized the Committee Against Racial Discrimination.[341] In the 1950s, the ACLU successfully challenged state laws that made it a crime for a white woman to bear a child she had conceived with a black father.[342] In the 1960s, the ACLU provided funds and lawyers to defend civil rights activists, and since then it has lobbied extensively for civil rights legislation.[343]

The ACLU's Voting Rights Project has helped to empower black voters throughout the southern United States, facilitating the election of

---

The judges who devoted so much attention to the Nazis, the police departments that paid so much overtime, and the American Civil Liberties Union, which lost a half-million dollars in membership income as a consequence of its defense, used their time and money well. They defeated the Nazis by preserving the legitimacy of American democracy.

Id. at 170-71.

338. This paragraph, and the accompanying footnotes, are drawn substantially from Gale & Strossen, *supra* note 19, at 164, 170-71, 175-76.

339. *See* S. WALKER, *supra* note 16, at 88-90.

340. *See id.* at 91. *See also* Powell v. Alabama, 287 U.S. 45, 73 (1932) (conviction reversed because of denial of adequate counsel at trial).

341. *See* S. WALKER, *supra* note 16, at 162-66.

342. *See* American Civil Liberties Union, ACLU Women's Rights Report (Spring 1980) (available from author).

343. *See* S. WALKER, *supra* note 16, at 162-63, 262-70. *See also* Memorandum from Morton H. Halperin and Wade Henderson to ACLU Executive Committee (Feb. 22, 1990) (available from author). The ACLU's legislative office played a key role in lobbying for such major civil rights legislation as the Fair Housing Amendments Act of 1988, Pub. L. No. 100-430, 102 Stat. 1619 (codified as amended in scattered sections of 28 U.S.C. and 42 U.S.C.), Civil Rights Restoration Act of 1987, Pub. L. No. 100-259, 102 Stat. 28 (codified as amended in scattered sections of 20 U.S.C., 29 U.S.C. and 42 U.S.C.), and renewal of Voting Rights Act Amendments of 1982, Pub. L. No. 97-205, 96 Stat. 131 (codified as amended at 42 U.S.C. §§ 1971 to 1973aa-6 (1988)); it also took the lead in opposing various constitutional amendments and bills which would have restricted civil rights, including court stripping proposals; during the most recent legislative session it helped to draft and lobbied for numerous pieces of civil rights legislation, including the Racial Justice Act, S. 1696, 101st Cong., 2d Sess. (1990), H.R. 4618, 101st Cong., 2d Sess. (1990), which would prohibit imposition of the death penalty in a racially discriminatory manner, and the Civil Rights Act of 1990, S. 2104, 101st Cong., 2d Sess. (1990), H.R.4000, 101st Cong., 2d Sess. (1990) (veto message read to Senate, 136 CONG. REC. S16562 (daily ed. Oct. 24, 1990)), which would overturn several recent Supreme Court decisions constricting civil rights remedies.

hundreds of black officials.[344] The ACLU also maintains several other special "Projects" whose constituents or clients are predominantly black—for example, the National Prison Project, the Capital Punishment Project, and the Children's Rights Project. For the past several years, the ACLU's national legal department has focused on civil liberties issues related to race and poverty.[345] In 1988, ACLU President Norman Dorsen appointed a special commission to oversee and coordinate the national ACLU's multiple efforts to combat racial discrimination.[346] In addition, state and local-level branches of the ACLU consistently allocate substantial resources to civil rights cases.[347]

As indicated by both policy[348] and action, the ACLU is committed to eradicating racial discrimination on campus as an essential step toward its larger goal of eliminating racial discrimination from society at large.[349] For example, ACLU leaders have corresponded and met with university officials to recommend measures that universities could implement to combat campus racism, consistent with both equality and free speech values.[350] In the same vein, ACLU officials have worked for the implementation of educational programs designed to counter racist attitudes among college students,[351] as well as younger students.[352] Addi-

---

344. *See* S. WALKER, *supra* note 16, at 356-57.

345. *See* powell, Memorandum, *supra* note 16.

346. *See* ACLU Policy Guide, *supra* note 11, at Policy No. 312b, 389b.

347. For example, the Southern California ACLU (ACLU-SC) successfully challenged school and housing segregation and miscegenation laws as early as 1946. *See* S. WALKER, *supra* note 16, at 239. The ACLU-SC initiated and provided lead counsel for the major school desegregation cases in Los Angeles and Pasadena, which spanned more than two decades. See the cases that culminated in Crawford v. Board of Educ., 458 U.S. 527 (1982); Pasadena City Bd. of Educ. v. Spangler, 427 U.S. 424 (1976); Jackson v. Pasadena City School Dist., 59 Cal. 2d 876, 382 P.2d 878, 31 Cal. Rptr. 606 (1963).

348. *See supra* note 11 and Appendix.

349. *See supra* note 15.

350. *See, e.g.*, Rowan, "Apartheid" on U.S. Campuses, North America Syndicate, Press Release (June 28, 1989) (describes such proposals made by Ira Glasser, ACLU Executive Director); Letter from Ira Glasser to university presidents (July 12, 1989) (available from author).

351. *See generally* responses to survey of ACLU affiliates regarding efforts to promote diversity (June 15, 1990) [hereinafter ACLU Survey] (available from author). The following responses are of particular interest: Response of Massachusetts affiliate, at 3 (offering programs for dealing with racism on university campuses); Response of New Hampshire affiliate, at 3 (planning forum on campus hate speech and racism); Response of North Carolina affiliate, at 3 (seeking funding for project to counter underlying causes of campus hate speech); Response of Northern California affiliate, at 4 (working in coalition to develop program to educate undergraduates about value of affirmative action).

352. *See, e.g.*, ACLU Survey, *supra* note 351, Response of Arkansas affiliate, at 3 (working with coalition on developing programs for reducing racial tensions in high schools); Response of Colorado affiliate, at 3 (worked closely with minority groups to deal with racial incidents in schools); Response of Kentucky affiliate, at 3 (organized community and expert testimony on racism in public schools); Response of Massachusetts affiliate, at 3 (developed programs on racism for schools, held student-teacher conference on racism, and conducted summer institute for teachers on racism); Response of

tionally, ACLU representatives have participated in universities' deliberations about whether to adopt anti-hate-speech rules, and if so, how to frame them.[353] Representatives of the ACLU also have organized investigations of racist incidents at specific campuses, for purposes of advising university officials how to counter those problems.[354] Furthermore, ACLU officials have organized and participated in protests of racist incidents, both on campus and more generally.[355]

In light of these efforts, Professor Lawrence's suggestion that "the call for fighting racist attitudes and practices rather than speech [is] 'just a lot of cheap talk' "[356] is a cheap shot. In particular, it is noteworthy that the ACLU affiliates that have brought lawsuits challenging campus hate speech regulations also have undertaken specific efforts to counter

---

New York affiliate, at 3 (NYCLU official designed and co-teaches course at public high school about roots of racism and has trained other bi-racial teams to teach this course at other high schools throughout New York City); Response of Oregon affiliate, at 3 (working with Portland School District officials to include study of racism in curriculum). *See also* Goodstein, *Warding Off Intolerance in a Brooklyn School,* Wash. Post, Apr. 10, 1990, at A3, col. 1 (describes ACLU program to teach about racism in public schools).

353. *See, e.g.,* Mayers, *ACLU May Ask Court to Halt UW's Anti-Racism Proposal,* Wisconsin State J., July 11, 1989, B1, col. 1 (Wisconsin ACLU affiliate recommended specific changes to proposed rules and said that if changes were adopted, ACLU would not make facial challenge to them, but rather "would wait and see how the rules are working"); Michigan Regents' Minutes, *supra* note 203, at 19 (March 17, 1988) (at public hearing on proposed regulations, Michigan ACLU affiliate supported concept of discriminatory harassment policy but made suggestions for improving specific proposal); *see also* Appendix to Judgment, Wu v. University of Conn., No. Civ. H-89-649 PCD (D. Conn. Jan. 25, 1990) (Connecticut ACLU affiliate recommended specific language that was substituted for University of Connecticut's anti-hate-speech rule, pursuant to agreement settling lawsuit).

354. *See, e.g.,* ACLU Survey, *supra* note 351, Response of Wisconsin affiliate, at 3 (ACLU Wisconsin affiliate worked in coalition with black student organizations and other minority organizations for purposes of conducting state-wide investigation of racism on campus, including through use of public hearings, and making recommendations of appropriate responses to campus officials). *Compare* Lawrence, at 478 ("In the view of minority delegates [to the 1989 ACLU Biennial Conference], hearings should be held on university campuses where the incidence and nature of the injury of racist speech could be carefully documented and responses that were least restrictive of protected speech could be recommended. . . . But this approach . . . was rejected.").

355. For recent examples, see, e.g., Smothers, *New Coalition Condemns Howard Beach Assaults,* N.Y. Times, Dec. 24, 1986, at B4, col. 2. Smothers wrote that:

> The executive director of the New York Civil Liberties Union, Norman Siegel, an organizer of the New Civil Rights coalition, said it was a multi-racial effort to "let everyone know unequivocally that we will not tolerate incidents of racial bigotry or a climate that fosters anything but racial equality and harmony in our city."

See also ACLU Survey, *supra* note 351, Response of New Jersey affiliate, at 3 (co-sponsored March Against Racism in Newark during spring of 1990); Response of New York affiliate, at 3 (as co-founder of New York City Civil Rights Coalition, affiliate has organized and participated in marches and rallies against racism). In contrast, Lawrence argues without citing sources that "[t]hose who raise their voices in protest against public sanctions of racist speech have not organized private protests against the voices of racism. . . . [T]raditional civil libertarians have been conspicuous largely in their absence from . . . group expressions of condemnation [of racism]." Lawrence, at 476-77.

356. Lawrence, at 480 n.166.

campus and societal racism.[357] Moreover, the charge of "cheap talk" more appropriately might be leveled at those who focus their attention on hate speech regulations. Such regulations may appear to provide a relatively inexpensive "quick fix," but racist speech is only one symptom of the pervasive problem of racism, and this underlying problem will not be solved by banning one of its symptoms.

B. *Punishing Racist Speech Would Not Effectively Counter Racism*

Parts II and III of this Article emphasized the principled reasons, arising from first amendment theory, for concluding that racist speech should receive the same protection as other offensive speech. This conclusion also is supported by pragmatic or strategic considerations concerning the efficacious pursuit of equality goals. Not only would rules censoring racist speech fail to reduce racial bias, but they might even undermine that goal.

First, there is no persuasive psychological evidence that punishment for name-calling changes deeply held attitudes. To the contrary, psychological studies show that censored speech becomes more appealing and persuasive to many listeners merely by virtue of the censorship.[358]

Nor is there any empirical evidence, from the countries that do outlaw racist speech, that censorship is an effective means to counter racism. For example, Great Britain began to prohibit racist defamation in

---

357. The three affiliates that have challenged university hate speech rules are located in Connecticut, Michigan, and Wisconsin. *See supra* note 17. All three are engaged in ongoing efforts to counter race discrimination. *See* ACLU Survey, *supra* note 351, Response of Connecticut affiliate, at 3 (it is currently producing videotape and teacher's guide, dealing with equality, for secondary school teachers, for statewide distribution free or at a nominal charge; it also is initiating the development and institution of curriculum on bigotry for elementary schools statewide); Response of Michigan affiliate, at Attachment C (summarizes recent and upcoming litigation, legislative program, and public education efforts regarding racial discrimination and prejudice); *id.* at Attachment C (it won favorable settlement in case brought on behalf of two black University of Michigan graduate students who were asked to leave an all-white suburb where they were conducting research); Response of Wisconsin affiliate, at 3 (it organized and is working with coalition of civil rights groups to investigate and recommend University's response to campus racial incidents); *id.* at Appendix ("In March, 1988, the [Wisconsin affiliate] decided to devote the majority of the organization's resources to protecting the civil rights of racial minorities and the poor."); *id.* at Appendix (summarizes current activities of affiliate's "Poverty, Race and Civil Liberties Project").

Compare Lawrence, at 480 ("When the ACLU enters the debate by challenging the University of Michigan's efforts to provide a safe harbor for its [minority] students . . . , we should not be surprised that non-white students feel abandoned.").

358. *See* Brock, *Erotic Materials: A Commodity Theory Analysis of Availability and Desirability,* in 1 Technical Report of the U.S. Comm'n on Obscenity & Pornography 131, 132 (1971); Tannenbaum, *Emotional Arousal As a Mediator of Communication Effects,* in 8 Technical Report of the U.S. Comm'n on Obscenity & Pornography 326-56 (1971); Worchel & Arnold, *The Effects of Censorship and Attractiveness of the Censor on Attitudinal Change,* 9 J. Experimental Soc. Psychology 365 (1973).

1965.[359] A quarter century later, this law has had no discernible adverse impact on the National Front and other neo-Nazi groups active in Britain.[360] As discussed above,[361] it is impossible to draw narrow regulations that precisely specify the particular words and contexts that should lead to sanctions. Fact-bound determinations are required. For this reason, authorities have great discretion in determining precisely which speakers and which words to punish. Consequently, even vicious racist epithets have gone unpunished under the British law.[362] Moreover, even if actual or threatened enforcement of the law has deterred some overt racist insults, that enforcement has had no effect on more subtle, but nevertheless clear, signals of racism.[363] Some observers believe that racism is even more pervasive in Britain than in the United States.[364]

C. *Banning Racist Speech Could Aggravate Racism*

For several reasons banning the symptom of racist speech may compound the underlying problem of racism. Professor Lawrence sets up a false dichotomy when he urges us to balance equality goals against free speech goals. Just as he observes that free speech concerns should be weighed on the pro-regulation, as well as the anti-regulation, side of the balance,[365] he should recognize that equality concerns weigh on the anti-regulation, as well as the pro-regulation, side.[366]

---

359. *See infra* text accompanying notes 367-70 for discussion of the Race Relations Act, 1965, ch. 73.

360. *See* A. NEIER, *supra* note 63, at 154-55.

361. *See supra* text accompanying notes 218-21.

362. *See* Lasson, *Racism in Great Britain: Drawing the Line on Free Speech,* 7 B.C. THIRD WORLD L.J. 161, 166, 171-73 (1987) (Democratic National Party Chairman Kingsley Read was tried under Race Relations Act in 1978 for referring in a public speech to "niggers, wogs, and coons," and for commenting on an Asian who had been killed in a race riot, "One down, a million to go." The judge instructed the jury that Read's words were not in themselves unlawful, and the jury acquitted Read.).

363. *See id.* (in response to anti-hate speech laws, contemporary racist publications tend to be more cautiously worded). *See also* A. NEIER, *supra* note 63, at 155 (National Front speakers substitute code words, such as attacks on immigration and calls for law and order, for explicit racist references).

364. For example, a 1988 article in the *New York Times* discussed the many incidents of violence against blacks and Asians in London and quoted Paul Boateng, one of the four minority members of the 650-member House of Commons, as follows:

[This] violence is linked to the deeper patterns of prejudice in a society in which racist behavior is more socially acceptable than in the United States. . . . We should not underestimate the degree to which greed and racism have become legitimate in Britain . . . . [T]he basic difference between the United States and Britain is that no one in America questions the concept of the black American. In Britain we still have not won the argument of whether it is possible to be black and British.

Raines, *London Police Faulted as Racial Attacks Soar,* N.Y. Times, Mar. 24, 1988, at A1, col. 1.

365. *See* Lawrence, at 458.

366. In a passage cited by Professor Lawrence, *see id.* at 446 n.66, Professor Michelman recognizes this point with respect to the analogous debate over whether pornography should be regulated.

The first reason that laws censoring racist speech may undermine the goal of combating racism flows from the discretion such laws inevitably vest in prosecutors, judges, and the other individuals who implement them. One ironic, even tragic, result of this discretion is that members of minority groups themselves—the very people whom the law is intended to protect—are likely targets of punishment. For example, among the first individuals prosecuted under the British Race Relations Act of 1965[367] were black power leaders.[368] Their overtly racist messages undoubtedly expressed legitimate anger at real discrimination, yet the statute drew no such fine lines, nor could any similar statute possibly do so. Rather than curbing speech offensive to minorities, this British law instead has been regularly used to curb the speech of blacks, trade unionists, and anti-nuclear activists.[369] In perhaps the ultimate irony, this statute, which was intended to restrain the neo-Nazi National Front, instead has barred expression by the Anti-Nazi League.[370]

The British experience is not unique. History teaches us that anti-hate speech laws regularly have been used to oppress racial and other minorities. For example, none of the anti-Semites who were responsible for arousing France against Captain Alfred Dreyfus were ever prosecuted for group libel. But Emile Zola was prosecuted for libeling the French clergy and military in his "J'Accuse," and he had to flee to England to escape punishment.[371] Additionally, closer to home, the very doctrines that Professor Lawrence invokes to justify regulating campus hate speech—for example, the fighting words doctrine, upon which he

---

See Michelman, *Conceptions of Democracy in American Constitutional Argument: The Case of Pornography Regulations,* 56 TENN. L. REV. 291, 307 (1989) (state should weigh "the infringements of liberty *and equal protection*" that would result from regulating pornography against "the infringements of liberty and equal protection" that would result from non-regulation) (emphasis added). *See also infra* note 396 (feminists have argued that regulating pornography would violate equal protection clause and discriminate against women).

367. In 1965, Parliament adopted the Race Relations Act, 1965, ch. 73, which criminalized the intentional incitement of racial hatred. The Act was amended in 1976 to eliminate the intent requirement of proving intent. The amended law made it an offense to distribute literature or to use words likely to stir up hatred against any racial group. In 1986, Parliament enacted the Public Order Act, 1986, ch. 64, which was designed to further ease the prosecution's evidentiary burden in proving incitement to racial hatred. It criminalizes conduct which is *either* likely *or* intended to "stir up" racial hatred. *See* Lasson, *supra* note 362, at 166, 171-73.

368. *See* Lasson, *supra* note 362, at 169.

369. *See* A. NEIER, *supra* note 63, at 153-55.

370. *See id.* at 157.

371. *See* ACLU pamphlet, *supra* note 262, at 8-9. *See also* Stein, *History Against Free Speech: The New German Law Against the "Auschwitz"—and Other—"Lies,"* 85 MICH. L. REV. 277 (1986). Stein argues that although there was an article in the German Criminal Code in 1871 that punished offenses against personal honor,

 [T]he German Supreme Court . . . consistently refused to apply this article to insults against Jews as a group—although it gave the benefit of its protection to such groups as

chiefly relies—are particularly threatening to the speech of racial and political minorities.[372]

The general lesson that rules banning hate speech will be used to punish minority group members has proven true in the specific context of campus hate speech regulations. In 1974, in a move aimed at the National Front, the British National Union of Students (NUS) adopted a resolution that representatives of "openly racist and fascist organizations" were to be prevented from speaking on college campuses "by whatever means necessary (including disruption of the meeting)."[373] A substantial motivation for the rule had been to stem an increase in campus anti-Semitism. Ironically, however, following the United Nations' cue,[374] some British students deemed Zionism a form of racism beyond the bounds of permitted discussion. Accordingly, in 1975 British students invoked the NUS resolution to disrupt speeches by Israelis and Zionists, including the Israeli ambassador to England. The intended target of the NUS resolution, the National Front, applauded this result. However, the NUS itself became disenchanted by this and other unintended consequences of its resolution and repealed it in 1977.[375]

The British experience under its campus anti-hate speech rule parallels the experience in the United States under the one such rule that has led to a judicial decision. During the approximately one year that the University of Michigan rule was in effect, there were more than twenty cases of whites charging blacks with racist speech.[376] More importantly, the only two instances in which the rule was invoked to sanction racist speech (as opposed to sexist and other forms of hate speech) involved the punishment of speech by or on behalf of black students.[377] Additionally, the only student who was subjected to a full-fledged disciplinary hearing

---

"Germans living in Prussian provinces, large landowners, all Christian clerics, German officers, and Prussian troops who fought in Belgium and Northern France."

Id. at 286 (quoting P. Paepcke, Antisemitismus und Strafrecht 164 (dissertation, Albert-Ludwigs-Universität Freiburg i. Br., 1962)) (footnotes omitted).

372. *See supra* text accompanying notes 137-46 (fighting words), 52-53 (intentional infliction of emotional distress) & 174-75 (group defamation).

373. A. NEIER, *supra* note 63, at 155-56.

374. *See* G.A. Res. 3379, U.N. GAOR Supp. (No. 34) at 83, U.N. Doc. A/10034 (1975).

375. *See* Neier, *supra* note 63, at 156. Some conservatives who were "very far from being Fascists" also were barred from speaking under the NUS resolution. *Id.*

376. *See* Gottlieb, *supra* note 4.

377. *See* Plaintiff's Exhibit Submitted in Support of Motion for Preliminary Injunction at 1, Doe v. University of Mich., 721 F. Supp. 852 (E.D. Mich. 1989) (No. 89-CV-71683-DT) (black student used term "white trash" in conversation with white student); *id.* at 5 (at beginning of preclinical dentistry course, recognized as difficult, faculty member led small group discussion, designed to "identify concerns of students"; dental student said that he had heard, from his minority roommate, that minorities have a difficult time in the course and were not treated fairly; the faculty member, who was black, complained that the student was accusing her of racism).

under the Michigan rule was a black student accused of homophobic and sexist expression.[378] In seeking clemency from the sanctions imposed following this hearing, the student asserted he had been singled out because of his race and his political views.[379] Others who were punished for hate speech under the Michigan rule included several Jewish students accused of engaging in anti-Semitic expression[380] and an Asian-American student accused of making an anti-black comment.[381] Likewise, the student who recently brought a lawsuit challenging the University of Connecticut's hate speech policy, under which she had been penalized for an allegedly homophobic remark, was Asian-American.[382] She claimed that, among the other students who had engaged in similar expression, she had been singled out for punishment because of her ethnic background.[383]

Professor Lawrence himself recognizes that rules regulating racist speech might backfire and be invoked disproportionately against blacks and other traditionally oppressed groups. Indeed, he charges that other university rules already are used to silence anti-racist, but not racist, speakers.[384] Professor Lawrence proposes to avoid this danger by excluding from the rule's protection "persons who were vilified on the basis of their membership in dominant majority groups."[385] Even putting aside the fatal first amendment flaws in such a radical departure from

---

378. *See id.* at 6 (social work student was charged with saying in class that homosexuality is an illness that needs to be cured and that he had developed a model to move gay men and lesbians toward a heterosexual orientation; he also was charged with sexual harassment against particular women).

379. *See* letter to James J. Duderstadt, President, University of Michigan, from a student (whose name and signature were deleted from the copy produced during litigation, to protect the student's privacy) (May 23, 1989), *reprinted in* Plaintiff's Exhibit Submitted in Support of Motion for Preliminary Injunction, *Doe*, 721 F. Supp. at 852. The student claimed that:

[T]he charges were pretexual [sic] and a coverup for vindictiveness based on my refusal to support any radical movements. . . . Moreover, these few students knew that a black student would have no chance of wining [sic] a favorable decision against such charges. These charges will haunt me for the rest of my life. . . . [T]hey will be used against me to prevent me from becoming a certified Social Worker . . . .

380. *See id.* at 1-2 (students wrote graffiti, including swastika, on classroom blackboard, and said they intended it as a practical joke).

381. *See id.* at 2-3 (his allegedly offensive remark was the question why black people feel discriminated against; after being charged, he explained that he was attempting to complain that black students in his dormitory tended to socialize together, with the result that he felt socially isolated).

382. *See* Wu v. University of Conn. (No. Civ. H89-649 PCD) (D. Conn. 1989); *see also Black Talks Prompt Protest and Complaint*, N.Y. Times, Dec. 10, 1989, § 1, at 67, col. 1 (first complaint filed under Trinity College's new racial harassment policy was against black speaker sponsored by black student organization, Black-Power Serves Itself).

383. Letter from Martin Margulies, of Connecticut Civil Liberties Union, to author, at 5 (Jan. 23, 1990) (available from author).

384. *See* Lawrence, at 466 (noting "cruel irony" in Stanford's refusal to punish white students for hanging racist poster in dormitory, while punishing black students who engaged in peaceful sit-in to protest that refusal).

385. *Id.* at 450 n.82.

content- and viewpoint-neutrality principles,[386] the proposed exception would create far more problems of equality and enforceability than it would solve.[387]

A second reason why censorship of racist speech actually may subvert, rather than promote, the goal of eradicating racism is that such censorship measures often have the effect of glorifying racist speakers. Efforts at suppression result in racist speakers receiving attention and publicity which they otherwise would not have garnered. As previously noted, psychological studies reveal that whenever the government attempts to censor speech, the censored speech—for that very reason—becomes more appealing to many people.[388] Still worse, when pitted against the government, racist speakers may appear as martyrs or even heroes.

Advocates of hate speech regulations do not seem to realize that their own attempts to suppress speech increase public interest in the ideas they are trying to stamp out. Thus, Professor Lawrence wrongly suggests that the ACLU's defense of hatemongers' free speech rights "makes heroes out of bigots";[389] in actuality, experience demonstrates that it is the attempt to *suppress* racist speech that has this effect, not the attempt to *protect* such speech.[390]

There is a third reason why laws that proscribe racist speech could well undermine goals of reducing bigotry. As Professor Lawrence recog-

---

386. *See supra* text accompanying notes 105-14.

387. Just one such problem is how "dominant majority groups" would be defined. Would they be defined in the context of the particular academic community—for example, at Howard Law School, blacks would probably fit this definition, and at Cardozo Law School, Jews would—or in the context of the larger society?

This definitional problem is compounded by the fact that Professor Lawrence would require a ranking of the relative dominance or subordination of various groups. During an oral defense of this proposal, at Duke University School of Law on January 27, 1990, Professor Lawrence "clarified" that it would prohibit a white woman from disparaging a black or gay man, but not a white, heterosexual man. Professor Lawrence did not explain whether these outcomes would differ if the female speaker were lesbian. *See also* Cohen, *On Harassment,* ACADEMIC QUESTIONS, Spring 1990, at 23, 29 (criticizing proposition that campus hate speech regulations should be applied differentially to various groups, depending on their societal status). Cohen stated that:

> Even if there were moral and intellectual substance to the distinction between subordinate and nonsubordinate groups, the theoretical and operational barriers to determining the membership and privileges of these groups seem insurmountable. The better rule is for the university to remain agnostic, and treat all its members as individuals and equals.

388. *See supra* note 358 and accompanying text.

389. Lawrence, at 438; *accord id.* at 436, 480.

390. For example, when the American Nazi Party finally was allowed to march in Illinois in 1978, following the government's and Anti-Defamation League's attempts to prevent this demonstration, 2000 onlookers watched the 20 Nazis demonstrate. *See* A. NEIER, *supra* note 63, at 169. And throughout the protracted litigation that the Nazis predictably won, the case received extensive media attention all over the country. *See id.* at 8. The event probably would have received little if any attention had the Village of Skokie simply allowed the Nazis to demonstrate in the first place.

nizes, given the overriding importance of free speech in our society, any speech regulation must be narrowly drafted.[391] Therefore, it can affect only the most blatant, crudest forms of racism. The more subtle, and hence potentially more invidious, racist expressions will survive. Virtually all would agree that no law could possibly eliminate all racist speech, let alone racism itself. If the marketplace of ideas cannot be trusted to winnow out the hateful, then there is no reason to believe that censorship will do so. The most it could possibly achieve would be to drive some racist thought and expression underground, where it would be more difficult to respond to such speech and the underlying attitudes it expresses.[392] The British experience confirms this prediction.[393]

The positive effect of racist speech—in terms of making society aware of and mobilizing its opposition to the evils of racism—are illustrated by the wave of campus racist incidents now under discussion. Ugly and abominable as these expressions are, they undoubtedly have had the beneficial result of raising public consciousness about the underlying societal problem of racism. If these expressions had been chilled by virtue of university sanctions, then it is doubtful that there would be such widespread discussion on campuses, let alone more generally, about the real problem of racism.[394] Consequently, society would be less mobilized to attack this problem. Past experience confirms that the public airing of racist and other forms of hate speech catalyzes communal efforts to redress the bigotry that underlies such expression and to stave off any discriminatory conduct that might follow from it.[395]

---

391. *See* Lawrence, at 435, 450 n.82, 458 & n.105, 481.

392. *See* A. NEIER, *supra* note 63, at 158 (noting that, in British context, it is far more dangerous when a major party such as the Conservative Party engages in racist politics, even though it uses polite language, than when a minor party attracts attention through ugly racist epithets).

393. *See supra* text accompanying notes 367-75. *See also* Lasson, *supra* note 362, at 170. The Lasson article stated that:

> [A] major effect of [the British anti-hate-speech] act has been to leave certain organizations with but two choices: to restrict their circulation to the members of a specific club, or to be more careful in their language. However, although this seems a positive development, it is possible that provocatively racist messages, by being concealed in genteel, and outwardly acceptable language, could be disseminated to an even larger number of people—thereby promoting more racial ill-will rather than decreasing such feelings.

394. *See infra* notes 404-07 and accompanying text.

395. *See* S. WALKER, *supra* note 16, at 59-62 (the ACLU's content-neutral defense of free speech permitted the Ku Klux Klan—which in the 1920s dominated many state legislatures, played a major role at the 1924 national Democratic convention, and staged a massive march on Washington, D.C.—to diminish its own influence by exposing its vicious plans to public view). *See also* A. NEIER, *supra* note 63, at 34. Neier stated that:

> The Nazis deter the expression of anti-Semitism in forms that might be more palatable to the American public and, therefore, more threatening to the Jews. Other anti-Semites must impose restraints on themselves for fear of being bracketed with the almost univer-

Banning racist speech could undermine the goal of combating racism for additional reasons. Some black scholars and activists maintain that an anti-racist speech policy may perpetuate a paternalistic view of minority groups, suggesting that they are incapable of defending themselves against biased expressions.[396] Additionally, an anti-hate speech policy stultifies the candid intergroup dialogue concerning racism and other forms of bias that constitutes an essential precondition for reducing discrimination. In a related vein, education, free discussion, and the airing of misunderstandings and failures of sensitivity are more likely to promote positive intergroup relations than are legal battles. The rules barring hate speech will continue to generate litigation and other forms of controversy that will exacerbate intergroup tensions. Finally, the censorship approach is diversionary. It makes it easier for communities to avoid coming to grips with less convenient and more expensive, but ultimately more meaningful, approaches for combating racial discrimination.

---

sally hated Nazis. A strong Nazi movement would be a great danger to Jews in the United States; a weak Nazi movement with no potential for growth has its uses.

Similarly, the speech of anti-pornography feminists has had a discernible impact on public perceptions, as well as public policy, concerning the connection between gender discrimination and pornography. If the censorship strategy had driven anti-female pornography from public view, this impact may well have been lessened. For example, a major public education and lobbying tool employed by Women Against Pornography is the display of anti-female pornographic images. Ironically, such displays would be prohibited under censorship legislation proposed by some feminist pornography opponents. *See supra* notes 228-30 and accompanying text.

396. *See, e.g., supra* text accompanying note 5 (quote from Alan Keyes criticizing the Stanford code); *see also supra* text accompanying note 10 (quote from Michael Meyers).

Similarly, while some feminists have advocated the regulation of pornography, arguing that regulation would promote women's equality, *see, e.g.,* A. DWORKIN, PORNOGRAPHY: MEN POSSESSING WOMEN (1981), other feminists have argued that regulation would hinder that goal. *See, e.g.,* Hunter & Law, *Brief Amici Curiae of Feminist Anti-Censorship Taskforce, et al., in* American Booksellers Association v. Hudnut, 21 U. MICH. J.L. REF. 69 (1988) (arguing that anti-pornography ordinance suppresses constitutionally protected speech in a manner particularly detrimental to women, and unconstitutionally discriminates on the basis of sex and reinforces sexist stereotypes). The arguments made by this latter group of feminists appear in large part applicable to regulations of racist speech, as well. *See, e.g., id.* at 122. Hunter and Law stated that:

The [Indianapolis] ordinance presumes women as a class (and only women) are subordinated by virtually any sexually explicit image. . . .
Such assumptions reinforce and perpetuate central sexist stereotypes; they weaken, rather than enhance, women's struggles to free themselves of archaic notions of gender roles. . . . In treating women as a special class, [this ordinance] repeats the error of earlier protectionist legislation which gave women no significant benefits and denied their equality.

V. Means Consistent with the First Amendment Can Promote Racial Equality More Effectively Than Can Censorship

The Supreme Court recently reaffirmed the time-honored principle that the appropriate response to speech conveying ideas that we reject or find offensive is not to censor such speech, but rather to exercise our own speech rights. In *Texas v. Johnson,* [397] the Court urged this counter-speech strategy upon the many Americans who are deeply offended by the burning of their country's flag: "The way to preserve the flag's special role is not to punish those who feel differently about these matters. It is to persuade them that they are wrong."[398] In addition to persuasion, the types of private expressive conduct that could be invoked in response to racist speech include censure and boycotts.[399]

In the context of countering racism on campus, the strategy of increasing speech—rather than decreasing it—not only would be consistent with first amendment principles, but also would be more effective in advancing equality goals. All government agencies and officers, including state university officials, should condemn slavery, de jure segregation, and other racist institutions that the government formerly supported. State university and other government officials also should affirmatively endorse equality principles. Furthermore, these government representatives should condemn racist ideas expressed by private speakers.[400] In the same vein, private individuals and groups should exercise their first amendment rights by speaking out against racism. Traditional civil libertarians have exercised their own speech rights in this fashion[401] and also

---

397. 109 S. Ct. 2533 (1989).

398. *Id.* at 2567.

399. *See* Matsuda, *supra* note 13, at 2358 n.201 (cites recent exchanges among American-Arab Anti-Discrimination Committee, B'nai B'rith International, and other organizations which effectively remedied ethnically derogatory expressions).

400. *See* Bok, *supra* note 6, at 6. In response to a letter demeaning women that a student club had circulated, Derek Bok, President of Harvard University, argued that this letter should not be suppressed. He then issued the following public criticism of the letter:

> The wording of the letter was so extreme and derogatory to women that I wanted to communicate my disapproval publicly, if only to make sure that no one could gain the false impression that the Harvard administration harbored any sympathy or complacency toward the tone and substance of the letter. Such action does not infringe on free speech. Indeed, statements of disagreement are part and parcel of the open debate that freedom of speech is meant to encourage; the right to condemn a point of view is as protected as the right to express it. Of course, I recognize that even verbal disapproval by persons in positions of authority may have inhibiting effects on students. Nevertheless, this possibility is not sufficient to outweigh the need for officials to speak out on matters of significance to the community—provided, of course, that they take no action to penalize the speech of others.

401. For recent examples, see *supra* note 355. In contrast, Lawrence claims, without support, that "[t]hose who raise their voices in protest against public sanctions of racist speech have not organized private protests against the voices of racism. . . . Traditional civil libertarians have been

have defended the first amendment freedoms of others who have done so.[402]

In addition to the preceding measures, which could be implemented on a society-wide basis, other measures would be especially suited to the academic setting. First, regardless of the legal limitations on rules barring hate speech, universities should encourage members of their communities voluntarily to restrain the form of their expression in light of the feelings and concerns of various minority groups.[403] Universities could facilitate voluntary self-restraint by providing training in communications, information about diverse cultural perspectives, and other education designed to promote intergroup understanding. Members of both minority and majority groups should be encouraged to be mutually respectful. Individuals who violate these norms of civility should not be subject to any disciplinary action, but instead should be counseled.[404] These educational efforts should be extended to members of the faculty and administration, as well as students. Of course, universities must vigilantly ensure that even voluntary limits on the *manner* of academic discourse do not chill its *content.*

---

conspicuous largely in their absence from . . . group expressions of condemnation [of racism]." Lawrence, at 476-77.

402. *See, e.g.,* A. NEIER, *supra* note 63, at 170 (Illinois ACLU, which had represented neo-Nazi group seeking to demonstrate, also assisted anti-Nazi groups in securing their first amendment rights to counter-demonstrate). Professor Lawrence asserts, without supporting authorities, that "[w]hen racial minorities or other victims of hate speech hold counter-demonstrations . . . civil libertarians often accuse them of private censorship, of seeking to silence opposing points of view." Lawrence, at 477. This unsubstantiated generalization is at odds with the relevant ACLU policy, which protects "[h]eckling or any other interruption of a speaker, as a form of speech or expression," unless it is so "extreme . . . that [it] effectively prevents the speaker from speaking or the audience from hearing." ACLU Policy Guide, *supra* note 11, at Policy No. 44.

It should be noted that the above-quoted policy is yet another example, *see supra* text accompanying notes 52-77, of the ACLU's recognition that expressive conduct should not be deemed absolutely protected by the first amendment just because it is verbal in form. *See id.* (counterspeech that effectively prevents speaker from speaking or audience from hearing "cannot be classified as protected speech even though it is verbal in form. It has the same effect, in preventing communication, as acts of physical force.").

403. *See* University of Texas Report, *supra* note 115, at 4. The Report admonishes students and faculty that:

> [W]hatever the legal boundaries of free speech, the members of an educational community should voluntarily adopt standards of civility and good taste that reflect mutual respect, understanding, and sensitivity among its diverse racial, ethnic, and cultural groups. In particular, members of the faculty represent The University and have a special role and position of authority with respect to students. They should treat students with respect and should be sensitive to the impact of their words and opinions on them.

404. *See, e.g.,* Report of Annenberg Workshop, *supra* note 156, at 2. The Annenberg Workshop concluded that:

> [M]any . . . [incidents of derogatory communicative behavior on campus] are so entwined with the expression of political, religious or social points of view that they should not trigger any disciplinary response at all, or are in a sufficiently gray area . . . that the response of an educational institution should be counselling rather than punishment . . . .

In addition to the foregoing measures, universities also should create forums in which controversial race-related issues and ideas could be discussed in a candid but constructive way. Another possibility would be for universities to encourage students to receive education in the history of racism and the civil rights movement in the United States and an exposure to the culture and traditions of racial and ethnic groups other than their own. Consistent with free speech tenets, these courses must allow all faculty and students to express their own views and must not degenerate into "reeducation camps."[405]

The proposed measures for eliminating racism on campus are consistent not only with American constitutional norms of free speech and equality, but also with internationally recognized human rights. For example, the Universal Declaration of Human Rights provides that individuals have a right to receive, and states have an obligation to provide, education which "promote[s] understanding, tolerance and friendship among all nations, racial or religious groups."[406]

If universities adopt narrowly framed rules that regulate racist expression, then these rules should constitute one element of a broader program that includes the more positive, direct strategies outlined above. Many universities appear to be responding constructively to the recent upsurge in campus hate speech incidents by adopting some of the measures suggested here.[407] This development demonstrates the positive impact of racist speech, in terms of galvanizing community efforts to counter the underlying attitudes it expresses.

---

405. *See generally* Strossen, *"Secular Humanism" and "Scientific Creationism": Proposed Standards for Reviewing Curricular Decisions Affecting Students' Religious Freedom,* 47 OHIO ST. L.J. 333, 383 (1986) (listing characteristics of a non-indoctrinating mode of instruction).

406. Universal Declaration, *supra* note 258, at art. 26(2). *Accord* art. 13(1), International Covenant on Economic, Social, and Cultural Rights.

407. *See, e.g.,* CARNEGIE FOUND. SPECIAL REPORT, *supra* note 7, at 32 ("The University of Minnesota requires that all students take at least two courses on different American cultures. Mt. Holyoke and Tufts University have a similar requirement. The University of California, Berkeley, Faculty Senate recently ruled that all undergraduates must take at least one course in American Cultures."). The University of Texas Report, *supra* note 115, at 23-25, in addition to recommending a rule that punishes certain racist expressions, *see supra* note 152, recommends that the University of Texas take the following additional steps to promote intergroup relations: orientation for all new students should include sensitivity sessions to reduce misunderstanding among different cultural groups; student extracurricular programs on multiculturalism should be expanded; all faculty, as well as other university employees, should participate in seminars about how to exercise their responsibilities in a multicultural academic setting; degree programs should require courses that foster an understanding of the responsibilities of living in a multicultural community, nation, and world; the entire curriculum should be reexamined from this perspective, and the form and content of particular courses should be restructured where necessary; consideration should be given to including required courses that deal with the social sciences and the arts with respect to people of different cultural backgrounds.

It is particularly important to devise anti-racism strategies consistent with the first amendment because racial and other minority groups ultimately have far more to lose than to gain through a weakened free speech guarantee. History has demonstrated that minorities have been among the chief beneficiaries of a vigorous free speech safeguard.[408]

Professor Lawrence offers two rebuttals to the proposition that blacks are (on balance) benefited rather than hurt by a strong free speech guarantee. First, he notes that "[t]he first amendment coexisted with slavery."[409] It is undeniable that, until the Union won the Civil War, not only the first amendment, but also *all* of the Constitution's provisions guaranteeing liberty, coexisted with the total negation of liberty through the institution of slavery. It also is true, however, that the free speech guarantees of the federal Constitution and some state constitutions allowed abolitionists to advocate the end of slavery.[410] Moreover, it must be recalled that until the 1930s, the first amendment provided no protection whatsoever against speech or press restrictions enacted by state or local governments.[411] Further, although the first amendment from its adoption provided theoretical protection against actions by the national government, in practice it was not enforced judicially until the latter half of the 20th century. Not until 1965 did the Supreme Court initially exercise its power—which it had recognized 162 years earlier[412]—to invalidate unconstitutional congressional statutes in the first amendment

---

408. *See* A. NEIER, *supra* note 63, at 5-7. Neier stated that:

It is a matter of self-interest. The oppressed are the victims of power. If they are to end their oppression, they must either win freedom or take power themselves. . . .

Jews and friends of Jews may hold power in Skokie, but they do not hold power in the rest of the country. Nor will they ever. The Jews in Skokie require restraints on power to guard themselves. Keeping a few Nazis off the streets of Skokie will serve Jews poorly if it means that the freedoms to speak, publish, or assemble any place in the United States are thereby weakened. . . .

It is dangerous to let the Nazis have their say. But it is more dangerous by far to destroy the laws that deny anyone the power to silence Jews if Jews should need to cry out to each other and to the world for succor.

409. Lawrence, at 466.

410. *See* M. CURTIS, NO STATE SHALL ABRIDGE: THE FOURTEENTH AMENDMENT AND THE BILL OF RIGHTS 30-32 (1986).

411. Along with other provisions in the Bill of Rights, the first amendment did not purport to constrain state or local governments, but rather limited only the federal government. *See* Barron v. Baltimore, 32 U.S. (7 Pet.) 243 (1833). Not until 1931 did the Supreme Court hold that the fourteenth amendment (ratified in 1868) made the first amendment's free speech and press clauses binding on the states. *See* Near v. Minnesota, 283 U.S. 697, 707 (1931). *See also* Gitlow v. New York, 268 U.S. 652 (1925) (suggested in dicta that first amendment might be binding on states). Therefore, for general reasons of federalism, throughout much of U.S. history, the first amendment protected *no* speech against violations by state and local governments; it necessarily coexisted not only with slavery, but also with whatever other limitations states or local governments chose to impose on the speech and other rights of their citizens.

412. *See* Marbury v. Madison, 5 U.S. (1 Cranch) 137 (1803).

context.[413] Thus, under the Espionage Act of 1918 and similar state statutes, numerous individuals were punished for expressing unpopular political opinions. The first amendment did not prevent these laws from contributing to "the gravest period of political repression in American history."[414]

In short, although slavery coexisted with the theoretical guarantees enunciated in the first amendment, slavery did not coexist with the judicially enforceable version of those guarantees that emerged only after World War I. We never can know how much more quickly and peacefully the anti-slavery forces might have prevailed if free speech and press, as well as other rights, had been judicially protected against violations by all levels of government earlier in our history. That robust freedoms of speech and press ultimately might have threatened slavery is suggested by southern states' passage of laws limiting these freedoms, in an effort to undermine the abolitionist cause.[415]

The second basis for Professor Lawrence's lack of "faith in free speech as the most important vehicle for liberation"[416] is the notion that "equality [is] a precondition to free speech."[417] Professor Lawrence maintains that racism devalues the ideas of non-whites and of anti-racism in the marketplace of ideas.[418] Like the economic market, the ideological market sometimes works to improve society,[419] but not always.[420] Odious ideas, such as the idea of black inferiority, will not necessarily be driven from the marketplace. Therefore, the marketplace rationale alone might not justify free speech for racist thoughts.[421] But that rationale does not stand alone.

---

413. *See* Lamont v. Postmaster General, 381 U.S. 301 (1965). *See also* L. TRIBE, *supra* note 58, § 1-2, at 4 n.8 ("[S]uccessful invocation of the Bill of Rights to protect from Congress what would today be called 'civil rights' or 'civil liberties' dates from the 1950's.").

414. A. NEIER, *supra* note 63, at 110 (noting, for example, that Rose Pastor Stokes received a ten-year prison sentence for saying, "I am for the people and the government is for the profiteers," and that socialist leader Eugene V. Debs and Congressman Victor Berger went to prison for similar remarks; similarly, a man in Minnesota received a prison sentence for saying to volunteer knitters, "No soldier ever sees these socks.").

415. *See* M. CURTIS, *supra* note 410, at 40.

416. Lawrence, at 466.

417. *Id.* at 467.

418. *See id.* at 470.

419. *See* A. NEIER, *supra* note 63, at 170 (Although Nazis had received national press attention during 16 months of Skokie controversy, they gained no new adherents; "[t]hey had disseminated their message and it [was] rejected."); S. WALKER, *supra* note 16, at 59-62 (Ku Klux Klan's exercise of free speech rights led to decline in Klan's influence, which had been significant during 1920s).

420. This paragraph, the following paragraph, and the accompanying footnotes, are drawn in large part from Gale & Strossen, *supra* note 19, at 174-76.

421. For criticisms of this metaphor, see Baker, *Scope of the First Amendment Freedom of Speech*, 25 UCLA L. REV. 964 (1978); Ingber, *The Marketplace of Ideas: A Legitimizing Myth*, 1984 DUKE L.J. 1.

The civil libertarian and judicial defense of racist speech also is based on the knowledge that censors have stifled the voices of oppressed persons and groups far more often than those of their oppressors.[422] Censorship traditionally has been the tool of people who seek to subordinate minorities, not those who seek to liberate them. As Professor Kalven has shown, the civil rights movement of the 1960s depended upon free speech principles.[423] These principles allowed protestors to carry their messages to audiences who found such messages highly offensive and threatening to their most deeply cherished views of themselves and their way of life. Equating civil rights activists with Communists, subversives, and criminals, government officials mounted inquisitions against the NAACP, seeking compulsory disclosure of its membership lists and endangering the members' jobs and lives.[424] Only strong principles of free speech and association could—and did—protect the drive for desegregation.[425] Martin Luther King, Jr. wrote his historic letter from a Birmingham jail,[426] but the Birmingham parade ordinance that King and other demonstrators had violated eventually was declared an unconstitutional invasion of their free speech rights.[427] Moreover, the Civil Rights Act of 1964, which these demonstrators championed, did become law.[428]

The more disruptive forms of protest, which Professor Lawrence credits with having been more effective[429]—such as marches, sit-ins, and

---

422. *See, e.g.,* L. LEVY, EMERGENCE OF A FREE PRESS 6 (1985) (describing historical English system whereby "[t]he manuscript of any work intended for publication had to be submitted to royal officials empowered to censor objectionable passages . . . . Anything published without an *imprimatur* was criminal."); Dorsen, *supra* note 72, at 133 (discusses public attempts to censor the messages of Vietnam protestors, civil rights activists and labor unions); Strossen, *supra* note 230, at 220-22 (discusses the danger of government censorship of pornography being used to suppress any messages that are inconsistent with the personal value judgments of the government officials).

423. *See* H. KALVEN *supra* note 133, at 4 (looks "at the impact of the [civil rights movement] on . . . free speech . . . . trace[s] connections between civil rights and civil liberties"); *see also id.* at 6 ("[A]s a thumbnail summary of the last two or three decades of speech issues in the Supreme Court, we may come to see the Negro as winning back for us the freedoms the Communists seemed to have lost for us.").

424. T. BRANCH, PARTING THE WATERS: AMERICA IN THE KING YEARS 1954-63, at 181-82, 468-69 (1988). *See also* K. O'REILLY, "RACIAL MATTERS": THE FBI'S SECRET FILE ON BLACK AMERICA, 1960-72, at 125-55 (1989) (describing the FBI's attempt to link Martin Luther King, Jr. and other leaders of the civil rights movement with communism).

425. For Supreme Court decisions protecting the NAACP against forced disclosure of its membership lists, see Louisiana *ex rel.* Gremillion v. NAACP, 366 U.S. 293 (1961); Bates v. Little Rock, 361 U.S. 516 (1960); NAACP v. Alabama, 357 U.S. 449 (1958).

426. M. L. KING, *Letter From Birmingham Jail,* in WHY WE CAN'T WAIT 76 (1964). For a description of the circumstances in which the letter was written, see T. BRANCH, *supra* note 424, at 737-44.

427. Shuttlesworth v. Birmingham, 394 U.S. 147 (1969).

428. Pub. L. No. 88-352, 78 Stat. 241 (1964) (codified as amended in Title 28, § 1447; Title 42, §§ 1971, 1975a-1975d, 2000a to 2000h-6 (1988)).

429. *See* Lawrence, at 466 & n.129.

kneel-ins—were especially dependent on generous judicial constructions of the free speech guarantee.[430] Notably, many of these protective interpretations initially had been formulated in cases brought on behalf of anti-civil rights demonstrators. Similarly, the insulting and often racist language that more militant black activists hurled at police officers and other government officials also was protected under the same principles and precedents.[431]

The foregoing history does not prove conclusively that free speech is an essential precondition for equality, as some respected political philosophers have argued.[432] But it does belie Professor Lawrence's theory that

---

430. *See* S. WALKER, *supra* note 16, at 241. The author states that, "after 1960, the sit-ins and other forms of increasingly militant protest depended on new definitions of First Amendment rights. . . . [T]he early civil rights movement depended on the First Amendment. As Georgetown University Law School professor Eleanor Holmes Norton later put it, 'There was always the First.' " (quoting from interview).

The record does not support Professor Lawrence's assertion that "the disruption that renders this speech effective usually causes it to be considered undeserving of first amendment protection." Lawrence, at 467. First, some of the authorities he cites in support of this generalization involved demonstrations that were accompanied by violence—including violence that "seemed to emanate from the protestors"—and not just disruption. *Id.* at 467 n.130. It would be ironic if Professor Lawrence, who accuses traditional civil libertarians of being too absolutist in defending free speech, would be even more absolutist by suggesting that violent expressive conduct should be protected.

If one focuses on expressive conduct that "disrupt[ed] business as usual," *id.* at 466, but was not accompanied by protestor violence, one finds a consistent line of Supreme Court cases sheltering such conduct under the first amendment. *See, e.g.,* NAACP v. Claiborne Hardware Co., 458 U.S. 886 (1982) (protected nonviolent elements of black citizens' boycott of white merchants to press for civil rights goals, although boycott caused substantial economic losses); Edwards v. South Carolina, 372 U.S. 229 (1963) (reversed breach of breach of peace convictions of 187 civil rights protesters who had demonstrated on state capitol grounds, although there was evidence that some sidewalks had been blocked during demonstration). *See also* Gregory v. Chicago, 394 U.S. 111 (1969) (in reversing disorderly conduct convictions for civil rights demonstrators who failed to disperse upon police order, Court refused to consider evidence that hostile crowd of 1,000 spectators was growing unmanageable); Cox v. Louisiana, 379 U.S. 536, 550 (1965) (reversed breach of peace convictions of civil rights demonstrators, despite local officials' claims that spectator violence was imminent, where there were 100 to 300 "muttering" spectators).

431. *See* Brown v. Oklahoma, 408 U.S. 914 (1972) (during political meeting in university chapel, appellant, a Black Panther, had referred to specific policemen as "mother-fucking fascist pig cops"; Supreme Court summarily vacated conviction under law which it found unconstitutionally overbroad); Gooding v. Wilson, 405 U.S. 518, 523 (1972) (where appellant, a black demonstrator, had made several threatening statements to police officers, including "White son of a bitch, I'll kill you," Court reversed conviction under law which it found unconstitutionally overbroad); *see also* Lewis v. New Orleans, 415 U.S. 130 (1974) (where police officer said to young suspect, "Get your black ass in the goddam car," and suspect's mother responded, "You god damn mother fucking police—I am going to [the Superintendent of Police] about this," lower courts upheld mother's conviction on fighting words doctrine, but the Supreme Court reversed).

432. *See, e.g.,* Beck, *Liberty and Equality,* 10 IDEALISTIC STUD. 24, 36 (1980) (liberty is "more basic" than equality); Machan, *Equality's Dependence on Liberty,* in 2 EQUALITY & FREEDOM 663, 664-65 (G. Dorsey ed. 1977); Raphael, *Tensions Between the Goals of Equality and Freedom,* in *id.* at 543, 555 ("Freedom appears to be a greater value than equality."). For the contrary view (i.e., that equality is the source of all rights and liberties), see R. DWORKIN, TAKING RIGHTS SERIOUSLY

equality is an essential precondition for free speech.[433] Moreover, this history demonstrates the symbiotic interrelationship between free speech and equality, which parallels the relationship between civil liberties and civil rights more generally.[434] Both sets of aims must be pursued simultaneously because the pursuit of each aids the realization of the other. The mutual interdependence of equality and liberty was forcefully described by Professor Karst:

> [T]he constitutional values of equality and liberty are fundamentally linked by the notion that equal access to certain institutions and services is a prime component of any meaningful liberty. This link is reflected in the language of egalitarian movements. The civil rights movement of the 1960s, for example, marched under the banner of "Freedom" even though its chief objective was equal access—to the vote, to education, to housing, even to lunch counters. "Liberation" is today a theme of more than rhetorical significance in egalitarian causes such as the women's movement.[435]

CONCLUSION

Some traditional civil libertarians may agree with Professor Lawrence that a university rule banning a narrowly defined class of assaultive, harassing racist expression might comport with first amendment principles and make a symbolic contribution to the racial equality mandated by the fourteenth amendment. However, Professor Lawrence and other members of the academic community who advocate such steps must recognize that educators have a special responsibility to avoid the danger posed by focusing on symbols that obscure the real underlying issues.

The recent exploitation of the American flag as a symbol of patriotism, to distort the true nature of that concept, serves as a sobering reminder of this risk. Joseph S. Murphy, Chancellor of The City University of New York, recently offered lessons for educators from the flag-related controversies. His cautionary words apply even more powerfully to the campus hate speech controversy, since the general responsibility of academics to call for an honest and direct discourse about compelling societal problems is especially great within our own communities:

> As educators, we should be somewhat concerned [about the manipulation of such symbols as the flag for partisan political purposes]. At our

---

273-74 (1977); Rawls, *Justice as Fairness,* 67 PHIL. REV. 164, 165-66 (1958). *But see* Hart, *Between Utility and Rights,* 79 COLUM. L. REV. 828, 845-46 (1979) (criticizing Dworkin's view that all liberties derive from principle of equality).

433. *See* Lawrence, at 467.

434. *See* Gale & Strossen, *supra* note 19, at 184-86.

435. Karst, *supra* note 141, at 43-44.

best, we convey ideas in their full complexity, with ample appreciation of the ambiguity that attaches to most important concepts. We use symbols, but we do so to illuminate, not to obscure. . . . The real question is how we use our position in the university and in society to steer national discourse away from an obsessive fixation on the trivial representation of ideas, and toward a proper focus on the underlying conflicts that define our era.[436]

An exaggerated concern with racist speech creates a risk of elevating symbols over substance in two problematic respects. First, it may divert our attention from the causes of racism to its symptoms. Second, a focus on the hateful message conveyed by particular speech may distort our view of fundamental neutral principles applicable to our system of free expression generally. We should not let the racist veneer in which expression is cloaked obscure our recognition of how important free expression is and of how effectively it has advanced racial equality.

---

436. Murphy, *Opinion, The Supreme Court Flag-Burning Decision: The Symbol Versus the Reality,* HIGHER EDUC. & NAT'L AFF., Sept. 25, 1989, at 5.

APPENDIX: ACLU POLICY STATEMENT

FREE SPEECH AND BIAS ON COLLEGE CAMPUSES[437]

Preamble

The significant increase in reported incidents of racism and other forms of bias at colleges and universities is a matter of profound concern to the ACLU. Some have proposed that racism, sexism, homophobia and other such biases on campus must be addressed in whole or in part by restrictions on speech. The alternative to such restrictions, it is said, is to permit such bias to go unremedied and to subject the targets of such bias to a loss of equal educational opportunity. The ACLU rejects both these alternatives and reaffirms its traditional and unequivocal commitment both to free speech and to equal opportunity.

Policy

1.   Freedom of thought and expression are indispensable to the pursuit of knowledge and the dialogue and dispute that characterize meaningful education. All members of the academic community have the right to hold and to express views that others may find repugnant, offensive, or emotionally distressing. The ACLU opposes all campus regulations which interfere with the freedom of professors, students and administrators to teach, learn, discuss and debate or to express ideas, opinions or feelings in classroom, public or private discourse.[438]

2.   The ACLU has opposed and will continue to oppose and challenge disciplinary codes that reach beyond permissible boundaries into the realm of protected speech, even when those codes are directed at the problem of bias on campus.[439]

3.   This policy does not prohibit colleges and universities from enacting disciplinary codes aimed at restricting acts of harassment, intimidation and invasion of privacy.[440] The fact that words may be used in connection with otherwise actionable conduct does not immunize such conduct

---

437. Adopted by ACLU National Board of Directors, without dissent, on October 13, 1990.

438. *See generally* ACLU Policy Nos. 60, 63, 65, 71.

439. The ACLU to date has opposed overbroad student speech codes adopted by the University of Connecticut, University of Michigan and University of Wisconsin and the University of California.

440. Although "harassment", "intimidation", and "invasion of privacy" are imprecise terms susceptible of impermissibly overbroad application, each term defines a type of conduct which is legally proscribed in many jurisdictions when directed at a specific individual or individuals and when intended to frighten, coerce, or unreasonably harry or intrude upon its target. Threatening telephone calls to a minority student's dormitory room, for example, would be proscribable conduct under the terms of this policy. Expressive behavior which has no other effect than to create an unpleasant learning environment, however, would not be the proper subject of regulation. *See also* Policy No. 316.

from appropriate regulation.[441] As always, however, great care must be taken to avoid applying such provisions overbroadly to protected expression. The ACLU will continue to review such college codes and their application in specific situations on a case-by-case basis under the principles set forth in this policy and in Policy 72.[442]

4.   All students have the right to participate fully in the educational process on a nondiscriminatory basis. Colleges and universities have an affirmative obligation to combat racism, sexism, homophobia, and other forms of bias, and a responsibility to provide equal opportunities through education. To address these responsibilities and obligations, the ACLU advocates the following actions by colleges and universities:

(a)   to utilize every opportunity to communicate through its administrators, faculty, and students its commitment to the elimination of all forms of bigotry on campus;

(b)   to develop comprehensive plans aimed at reducing prejudice, responding promptly to incidents of bigotry and discriminatory harassment, and protecting students from any such further incidents;

(c)   to pursue vigorously efforts to attract enough minorities, women and members of other historically disadvantaged groups as students, faculty members and administrators to alleviate isolation and to ensure real integration and diversity in academic life;

(d)   to offer and consider whether to require all students to take courses in the history and meaning of prejudiuce, including racism, sexism, and other forms of invidious discrimination;[443]

(e)   to establish new-student orientation programs and continuing counseling programs that enable students of different races, sexes, religions, and sexual orientations to learn to live with each other outside the classroom;

(f)   to review and, where appropriate, revise course offerings as well as extracurricular programs in order to recognize the contributions of those whose art, music, literature and learning have been insufficiently reflected in the curriculum of many American colleges and universities;

(g)   to address the question of *de facto* segregation in dormitories and other university facilities; and

(h)   to take such other steps as are consistent with the goal of ensuring that all students have an equal opportunity to do their best work and to participate fully in campus life.

---

441.   For example, intimidating phone calls, threats of attack, extortion and blackmail are unprotected forms of conduct which include an element of verbal or written expression.

442.   In determining whether a university disciplinary code impermissibly restricts protected speech, there must be a searching analysis both of the language of the code and the manner in which it is applied. Many factors, which are heavily fact-oriented, must be considered, including time, place, pattern of conduct and, where relevant, the existence of an authority relationship between speaker and target.

443.   All courses and programs must be taught consistent with the principles prescribed in ACLU Policy 60.

This policy is issued in connection with, and is intended as an interpretation and enhancement of, the binding resolution on racist speech adopted at the 1989 Biennial Conference. That resolution provides:

> The ACLU should undertake educational activities to counter incidents of racist, sexist, anti-semitic, and homophobic behavior (including speech) on school campuses and should encourage school administrators to speak out vigorously against such incidents. At the same time the ACLU should undertake educational activities to counter efforts to limit or punish speech on university campuses.

Social Philosophy & Policy Vol. 8 Issue 2, ISSN 0265-0525

CIVIL RIGHTS VS. CIVIL LIBERTIES: THE CASE OF DISCRIMINATORY VERBAL HARASSMENT*

By Thomas C. Grey

The expression of a change of aspect is the expression of a *new* perception and at the same time of the perception's being unchanged.

Wittgenstein, *Philosophical Investigations*[1]

American liberals believe that both civil liberties and civil rights are harmonious aspects of a basic commitment to human rights. But recently these two clusters of values have seemed increasingly to conflict – as, for example, with the feminist claim that the legal toleration of pornography, long a goal sought by civil libertarians, actually violates civil rights as a form of sex discrimination.

Here I propose an interpretation of the conflict of civil rights and civil liberties in its latest manifestation: the controversy over how to treat discriminatory verbal harassment on American campuses. I was involved with the controversy in a practical way at Stanford, where I helped draft a harassment regulation that was recently adopted by the university.

Like the pornography issue, the harassment problem illustrates the element of paradox in the conflict of civil-liberties and civil-rights perspectives or mentalities. This problem does not simply trigger familiar disagreements between liberals of a classical or libertarian orientation as against those of a welfare state or social democratic one – though it does sometimes do that. In my experience, the issue also has the power to appear to a single person in different shapes and suggest different solutions as it oscillates between being framed in civil-liberties and in civil-rights terms. At the same time, however, it remains recognizably the same problem. It is thus a very practical and political example of the kind of tension noted by Wittgenstein in the aphorism that heads this essay – a puzzle of interpretive framing, of "seeing-as."

One of my aims in this essay is to bring the reader to share the sense of paradox that, for me, pervades the experience of trying to categorize and resolve the harassment issue. At the outset, let me sketch what I take to be the two main structural features of the clash between the civil-liberties and the civil-rights perspectives that this problem exemplifies.

* My thanks for excellent research assistance go to William Boyle, Jay Fowler, and John Tweedy. And I am also grateful for the editorial suggestions of Barbara Babcock, Barbara Fried, Mark Kelman, Richard Posner, Robert Rabin, Carol Rose, James Weinstein, Steven Shiffrin, and Steven Winter; of those who attended my faculty workshop at Boalt Hall, University of California, Berkeley; and of Ellen Paul and the other editors of *Social Philosophy & Policy*. Finally, special thanks, for inspiration, to Charles Lawrence III.

[1] Ludwig Wittgenstein, *Philosophical Investigations* 196e (New York: Macmillan, 1958).

First, the two approaches take contrasting views of intangible or psychic injury. The civil-liberties mentality, centrally concerned with protecting freedom of expression against censorship, tends to limit the kinds of harms that can justify abridgment of that freedom to traditionally recognized infringements of tangible interests in property and bodily security. In particular, claims that government can interfere with speech to protect sensibilities, emotional tranquillity, or self-esteem – in general, *feelings* – are strongly disfavored. It is a "bedrock principle" of civil liberties that censorship is not justified to prevent even what is "deeply offensive to many."[2] The civil-libertarian counsel to fellow citizens is the traditional parental advice to the child wounded by insult or rejection: "Sticks and stones may break my bones, but words will never hurt me" – not hurt *enough*, that is, to justify the known costs of censorship.

By contrast, the civil-rights approach, with its roots in anti-discrimination law and social policy, is centrally concerned with injuries of stigma and humiliation to those who are the victims of discrimination – conduct generating "feelings of inferiority" that damage "hearts and minds," in the language of the most famous American civil rights case.[3] The point is not so much to protect a sphere of autonomy or personal security from *intrusion* as to protect potentially marginal members of the community from *exclusion* – from relegation, that is, to the status of second-class citizens.

The second contrast is a related one: it comes in the treatment of the public-private distinction. The active state is traditionally conceived as the sole or dominant threat to civil liberties. Civil libertarians do not spend much of their time or energy seeking ways to positively empower dissenters, deviants, and nonconformists against the pressures brought on them by unorganized public opinion, or by private employers or landlords. The catalogue of civil liberties is certainly what Judge Richard Posner has called the Constitution: "a charter of negative rather than positive liberties."[4]

"But [to continue with the same quotation from Judge Posner] where the liberty asserted is the right to equal treatment irrespective of race or sex, the analysis is more complex."[5] Under the civil-rights perspective, defense of basic human rights is by no means simply a matter of limiting state power. Government may deny equal protection by omission as well as by action – for example, by refusing law enforcement protection to minorities. The tendency of the civil-rights mentality is to favor the prohibition of all invidious treatment that has the effect of "implying inferiority in civil society" to individuals on the basis of their membership in identifiable social groups.[6] This "anti-discrimination principle" goes beyond cleansing government action of bias; it also attacks discrimination on the suspect bases of race, sex, and so on, in the other major institutions of civil society. Thus the identification of a new form of invidious

<hr>

[2] *United States v. Eichman*, 110 S. Ct. 2404, 2410 (1990).
[3] *Brown v. Board of Education*, 347 U.S. 483, 494 (1954).
[4] *Bohen v. City of East Chicago*, 799 F.2d 1180, 1189–90 (7th Cir., 1986) (concurring opinion).
[5] *Ibid.*
[6] *Strauder v. West Virginia*, 100 U.S. (10 Otto) 303, 308 (1880).

discrimination today typically brings with it pressure for legislation against private as well as official discrimination of that kind in housing, employment, and education.[7]

When the conflict of civil-liberties and civil-rights perspectives is described in terms of the structural features just sketched, it resonates with a number of the binary oppositions of social philosophy: liberty against equality; liberty against democracy; individualism against collectivism; the methods of economics and rational choice theory against those of sociology and cultural anthropology. Though I hope what I have to say here may intrigue those interested in the practical implications of the standard theoretical dichotomies, I do not analyze the harassment issue in these terms.

This is partly to avoid one of the temptations of classic social philosophy, the urge to make it as nearly as possible like geometry or physics. One seeks, using this paradigm, to formulate contending theoretical positions as models, stated as broadly and at the same time as rigorously as possible. Adopting this approach, one then sees an actual controversy that brings these oppositions into play as simply a manifestation of underlying theoretical contradictions. The practical issue serves the purpose of forcing choice between the theories, just as crucial experiments are supposed to force choice between rival scientific hypotheses. On the harassment issue, the structural conflict between civil-liberties and civil-rights approaches then naturally appears as the vivid illustration of a contradiction between, for example, opposed libertarian and egalitarian theories of liberalism. Intellectual rigor and respect for consistency would then require forthright resolution of the contradiction, most readily achieved by rejecting one of the conflicting alternatives.

This seems to me the wrong way to deal with the harassment problem; indeed, it generally seems the wrong way to deal with most theoretical disagreements as they bear on social, political, and legal questions. Rarely can important theories in these areas be plausibly formulated as models or axiom-systems precise enough to give rise to "contradictions." Much more often the actual working theories are perspectives, approaches, or mentalities constituted of more or less vague (but never completely open-ended) clusters of goals, ideals, guidelines, and presumptions. When theories this imprecise clash, no principle of logic requires rejection of either one.

Methods of social philosophy that seek to formulate theories with maximum precision do so with an eye to determinacy – they seek theories that can actually *compel* results where they apply. Theories that conflict over a practical issue then compel conflicting results; when a contradiction arises, one theory must be chosen to the exclusion of the other. Yet in problematic practical situations, each of the conflicting theories (perspectives, approaches, mentalities) may have something valuable and even essential to contribute to a resolution. In such situations, oversharpened theories tend to produce incomplete and one-sided

[7] See Paul Brest, "Foreword: In Defense of the Antidiscrimination Principle," *Harvard Law Review*, vol. 90 (1976), p. 1.

THOMAS C. GREY

outcomes, whereas a pragmatist tolerance of theoretical ambiguity and imprecision can conduce to better results.

Such a situation is, it seems to me, presented by the issue of discriminatory harassment. This problem exemplifies something liberal pragmatists should accept as normal – a conflict between plural, sometimes incommensurable, structured clusters of values and principles, here the familiar ones surrounding the terms "civil liberties" and "civil rights." Where these conflicting approaches overlap, as they inevitably will, liberal democrats can identify a range of mediating solutions that respect the claims of both conflicting approaches. I offer the Stanford provision on discriminatory verbal harassment as an example of such a solution. But first I should more fully describe the practical issue and the opposed civil-rights and civil-liberties approaches to it.

I

There has recently been an upsurge in the number and intensity of reported incidents of racist, homophobic, and sexist abuse in American universities.[8] An extreme example was the incident reported at the University of Wisconsin in which white students followed a black woman student across campus shouting "We've never tried a nigger."[9] Perhaps less unequivocal in its implications was this exchange at Stanford: after a dormitory argument in which a black student had claimed that Ludwig van Beethoven was a mulatto and other students had objected to placing such stress on racial origins, two white students defaced a picture of the composer into a blackface caricature and posted it near the black student's room.[10]

The question is: what disciplinary action (if any) is appropriate in such cases? A pure civil-rights approach treats the conduct in question as discriminatory harassment. Then principles of equal treatment not only entitle but *require* universities to punish the behavior, at least if it becomes sufficiently widespread to create a pervasively hostile environment. The analogy is to employers' obligations to deal with racial or sexual harassment by fellow employees in the workplace. When black or female employees must endure a barrage of race- or sex-based insults from co-workers, an employer who ignores the situation

---

[8] I will often make the oversimplifying assumption that all these forms of discrimination can and should be treated the same. Each form of insult has its own unique features and problems, however, and may ultimately generate its own distinct body of legal doctrine, as does each form of discrimination recognized as "invidious" under equal protection law and civil rights statutes. I will, moreover, put discrimination against gays and lesbians in with the rest, though it has *not* yet been recognized as invidious under federal constitutional law. A number of state and local civil rights laws, and the anti-discrimination policies of many public and private institutions (including Stanford) do prohibit sexual-preference discrimination, as in my view all should.

[9] *Time*, May 23, 1989, p. 89.

[10] I was faculty co-chair of the campus judicial council at Stanford when this incident occurred; no disciplinary charges were ultimately brought. Thereafter I worked on the drafting of a disciplinary standard to deal with racial harassment, which was adopted by the campus legislative body and became effective in June of 1990. The Beethoven incident is treated eloquently, strictly from a civil-rights perspective, in Patricia Williams, "The Obliging Shell: An Informal Essay on Formal Equal Opportunity," *Michigan Law Review*, vol. 87 (1989), pp. 2128, 2133–37.

may be guilty of unlawful (and if a public employer, unconstitutional) race or sex discrimination.[11] Again I quote Judge Posner, certainly no civil-rights extremist:

> By taking no steps to prevent sexual harassment, the city created a worse working environment for women than for men . . . That is discrimination . . . It is as if the city decided to provide restrooms for male but not female employees, and when pressed for a reason said it simply didn't care whether its female employees were comfortable or not.[12]

In the case in question, the sexual harassment included some physical contact and coercive sexual proposals by supervisors, as well as sexist obscenities and epithets from fellow workers. In discriminatory harassment cases, however, courts have not sharply differentiated between action and verbal abuse in evaluating claims by black or female employees. Typically, action and speech are blended together in a course of conduct that gives rise to liability for the employer when it creates an intolerably "hostile environment" for women or racial minority employees. In some cases, which the courts have not singled out for special treatment on this ground, harassment is found from speech alone – typically a stream of racist or sexist jokes, pictures, and epithets. To avoid liability, the employer must take reasonable steps to keep verbal as well as physical or otherwise coercive abuse below the level of a "sustained pattern of harassment."[13] The decisive question is not whether the harassment constitutes speech or action, but whether it is widespread and serious enough to go beyond what the courts judge must be tolerated as part of life's ordinary rough and tumble.

A civil rights approach to the verbal abuse problem on campus simply applies the doctrine of hostile environment discrimination to the university. Most

[11] The applicable legal provisions are (for most private employers) Title VII of the Civil Rights Act of 1964, which prohibits employers from discriminating against employees on the basis of race or sex in the "terms or conditions of employment," and (for public employers) the Fourteenth Amendment's requirement that no state may "deny to any person the equal protection of the laws," which has been construed to prohibit race and sex discrimination in public employment.

[12] *Bohen v. East Chicago*, p. 1191. Judge Posner alternatively analyzed the employer's inaction as analogous to a selective withdrawal of protection, as if a government denied police protection to blacks, or failed to punish rapes alone among violent crimes.

[13] In sex discrimination cases under Title VII, the courts distinguish between *"quid pro quo"* harassment (efforts to extract sexual favors in return for job retention or promotion) and "hostile environment" harassment of the kind described in the text. Racial harassment takes only the latter form. The Supreme Court recognized hostile environment sexual harassment as a Title VII violation in *Meritor Savings Bank v. Vinson*, 477 U.S. 57 (1986). On hostile environment discrimination, see *Rogers v. EEOC*, 454 F.2d 234, 238 (5th Cir. 1971) ("sustained pattern of harassment"); *Bundy v. Jackson*, 641 F.2d 934 (D. C. Cir. 1981), and *Henson v. City of Dundee*, 682 F.2d 897 (11th Cir. 1982) (sexual harassment cases involving mixed *quid pro quo* and pure verbal harassment incidents); *Erebia v. Chrysler Plastics*, 722 F.2d 1250 (6th Cir. 1985); *EEOC v. Murphy Motor Freight Lines*, 488 F. Supp 381 (D. Minn. 1980) (employer failure to take action against racist insults of black employee by fellow workers held unlawful discrimination).

educators, like most employers, are required by law (as they should feel required by fairness) to provide equal opportunity to women and students of color. Campus harassment can make the educational environment hostile, just as workplace harassment makes the employment environment so. Many campuses have already recognized this with respect to sexual harassment and have adopted disciplinary restrictions accordingly. There is no good reason why racial or anti-homosexual harassment should not be treated in the same way. As a legal matter, an unremedied "sustained pattern of harassment" might make the university itself guilty of unlawful discrimination.[14] Prudent and sensitive administrators will prohibit acts of harassment before the point at which the conduct cumulates into a sustained pattern and thus creates a legally actionable hostile environment.

An analysis like this can easily lead to a prohibition defined purely in terms of civil rights. Thus the University of Michigan, faced with an upsurge in racial harassment, enacted a prohibition against any "behavior, verbal or physical" that "stigmatizes or victimizes" an individual on the basis of race, sex, or other characteristics protected under the university's non-discrimination policy and that has the "reasonably foreseeable effect of interfering with an individual's academic efforts," or "[c]reates an intimidating, hostile or demeaning environment for educational pursuits." This is a prohibition drafted to track the form of injury dealt with by the civil-rights approach – conduct contributing to a hostile environment that denies equal educational opportunity.[15]

And yet, in the first major case involving the regulation of campus verbal harassment, a federal district court struck this provision down on First Amendment grounds.[16] Civil libertarians applauded the opinion; they qualified their applause at the result only because the case seemed so easy that it did not establish a particularly powerful precedent for other cases of regulation of campus harassment. And an easy case it was – as soon as it was considered from the angle of a civil-liberties, rather than a civil-rights, approach.

Viewed through a First Amendment lens, the Michigan regulation – now seen as a "hate speech" or "group defamation" rule rather than a harassment prohibition – was a dramatically overbroad incursion into core areas of protected speech. Consider just one example of the kind of speech prohibited by the regulation, taken from the guidelines the university distributed to student to explain the new policy:

---

[14] As with public employers, the Fourteenth Amendment prohibits public universities from discriminating on the basis of race or sex in providing educational services. Private universities receiving federal grants are subject to similar prohibitions under Title IX of the Civil Rights Act of 1964. In some states, statutes also prohibit discriminatory practices by private universities. Finally, most private universities in the United States have committed themselves to non-discrimination policies, which may give rise to contractual liability when a student can show discrimination that would be unlawful for a public university.

[15] Indeed it was evidently drafted on the model of the Equal Employment Opportunity Commission guidelines, which define sexual harassment to include "verbal or physical conduct of a sexual nature" that "has the purpose or effect of unreasonably interfering with an individual's work performance or creating an intimidating, hostile, or offensive working environment." 29 CFR §1604.11(a).

[16] *Doe v. University of Michigan*, 721 F. Supp. 852 (E. D. Mich. 1989). See 856 for the text of the regulations.

> A male student makes remarks in class like 'Women just aren't as good in this field as men,' thus creating a hostile learning atmosphere for female classmates.[17]

From this one can readily extrapolate to other statements (made in class or in a dorm hallway debate) that would violate the standard: arguing on the basis of IQ data that blacks are less intelligent than whites; that homosexuality is "unnatural," or is a disease; that women are naturally less creative than men.[18] The expression of these opinions is certainly experienced as "stigmatizing" and "demeaning" by many, probably most, students belonging to the groups thus insulted; when cumulated to create a climate of opinion, comments like these might well foreseeably "interfere with the academic efforts" of the students whose basic humanity or equal mental capacity they deny.

Because the Michigan regulation has been so universally condemned, it is important to understand how campus authorities might have drafted and enforced it the way they did. They evidently viewed the problem of verbal harassment from one perspective only: the perspective of civil rights. Viewed solely through the lens provided by anti-discrimination law and policy, the kind of statements to which the regulation was applied might well appear as more polite but no less demeaning versions of the kind of racist, sexist, or homophobic insults routinely prohibited under anti-harassment codes in the employment area.

Indeed, the very "politeness" of these statements might rationally be thought to make them *more* disabling to the educational performance of those exposed to them than are the relatively rare incidents involving gutter epithets. At most universities, the victims of the crudest insults can partly discount them because they clearly transgress the dominant mores. By contrast, the more academically respectable forms of denigration of blacks, women, and gays can be supported by evidence and argument, the forms of discourse with maximum credibility in the university. And the damage such statements do is probably enhanced when the stereotypes they reinforce deny the ability of groups of students to study and learn whose members already feel marginal on many campuses. The discourse of "statistics show . . ." and "environmental factors cannot fully explain . . ." may much more effectively create a hostile educational environment than "[Epithet] go home!"

But as soon as a civil-liberties perspective is brought to bear, the kind of speech reached by the Michigan regulation is readily seen as close to the core of the First Amendment. The record in the federal court challenge to the regulation, with a large number of complaints processed, and many resolved

---

[17] *Doe v. Michigan*, p. 858. The Guide went on to warn students that "YOU are a harasser when . . . You comment in a derogatory way about a . . . group's . . . cultural origins, or religious beliefs" – a very sweeping restriction on the discussion of history and current events. Might not screening *The Last Temptation of Christ* or selling *The Satanic Verses* count as "derogatory comment" on a "group's religious beliefs"?

[18] Under the University of Michigan regulation, a social work student was in fact prosecuted for expressing the view that homosexuality was a disease, for which he hoped to develop a counseling plan in a research class; *Doe v. Michigan*, p. 865. The other two statements propound views that I trust my readers will admit are widely held, or at least entertained, if relatively rarely expressed, on American campuses.

informally to require apology (and, in some cases, what looks suspiciously like University of Beijing-style "re-education")[19] in response to speech expressing views on issues of public and campus concern, did indeed present an easy case. If questions that go to the core of human rights and social policy issues cannot be freely debated on campuses, what issues can?

The regulation established a general, content-based regime of censorship of politically and socially controversial speech, with speech concerning issues of race, gender, and sexual orientation subject to special restriction. Worse, within that content-defined field of regulation, the censorship regime imposed a viewpoint-specific orthodoxy: students were allowed to state radical or liberal, but not conservative or reactionary, views on controverted issues. They could say that the mental abilities of blacks were equal to or greater than those of whites, but not lesser; that homosexuality was a culturally formed category of sexual preference or a natural inclination, but not a disease or a sin; that women's genetic endowments made them equal or superior to men in socially valued activities, but not inferior.[20]

Viewed from the civil-liberties perspective, regulations such as these are highly suspect because they are aimed squarely at the content of speech rather than at its incidental injurious consequences. Under current First Amendment doctrine, no restriction focused on the communicative impact of speech is permissible unless it is necessary to prevent serious and imminent harm; the harm in question cannot be simply offense, however strong and justified, at what is said. Finally, any restriction within these narrow confines must be "viewpoint neutral."

The underlying idea is that there must be no ideological censorship – no official regime of screening utterances for the political, moral, or social acceptability of the message they deliver.[21] "The First Amendment recognizes no such thing as a 'false' idea."[22] The idea behind this slogan need not be a paralyzed relativism. It can be a historically-founded liberal suspicion that officials are peculiarly unlikely to accurately distinguish falsity from truth under a regime of censorship, as expressed in Justice Jackson's classic *Barnette* opinion:

[19] For example, a student who had recited a homophobic limerick in class plea-bargained the dropping of a charge against him under the Michigan regulations in return for a classroom apology, a letter of apology to the campus paper, and attendance at a "gay rap session;" *Doe v. University of Michigan*, p. 865. It has become a commonplace among civil-libertarian opponents of verbal harassment regulation to stress the utility of "education" (rather than disciplinary rules) as a remedy for campus discrimination, generally without much serious attention to the question of what such "education" may entail. In my own view, the worst of both worlds is achieved when multicultural sensitivity training (valuable as it can be when done well) is imposed as a penal sanction for harassment. I would sharply separate punishment of harassment (which should be confined to cases of intentional wrongdoing) from orientation efforts aimed at acquainting students and others with the diverse cultural backgrounds, expectations, and sensitivities they are likely to meet in the contemporary university.

[20] The plaintiff in the Michigan case was a psychology graduate student working on the biological basis of differences in personality traits and mental abilities. He alleged, quite plausibly, that certain theories in his field could be perceived as sexist or racist, so that their discussion might be sanctionable under the policy. *Doe v. Michigan*, p. 858.

[21] An excellent and often-cited doctrinal analysis, distinguishing the key terms of art's "communicative impact," "content," and "viewpoint," is Geoffrey Stone, "Content Regulation and the First Amendment," *William and Mary Law Review*, vol. 25 (1983), p. 189.

[22] *Hustler Magazine v. Falwell*, 108 S. Ct. 876, 879 (1988); compare *Gertz v. Robert Welch*, 418 U.S. 323, 339 (1974).

> If there is any star fixed in our constitutional constellation, it is that no official, high or petty, can prescribe what shall be orthodox in politics, nationalism, religion, or other matters of opinion . . .[23]

Or it can be a republican faith in the citizenry's ability to respond to bad speech with better speech, as in Justice Brandeis's equally classic *Whitney* opinion:

> Fear or serious injury alone cannot justify suppression of free speech . . . Those who won our independence by revolution were not cowards . . . If there be time to expose through discussion the falsehood and fallacies, to avert the evil by the processes of education, the remedy to be applied is more speech, not enforced silence."[24]

The civil-liberties analytical framework tends to confine regulation of campus verbal harassment to prohibiting conduct verging on assault, including perhaps tortious "intentional infliction of emotional distress" and certain face-to-face insults that are especially likely to provoke immediate violence – so-called "fighting words." Further, the civil-liberties framework requires that any speech regulations must be evenhanded; universities may not single out ideologically defined classes of provocations or verbal assaults for prohibition. This, let it be said, is the moderate civil-libertarian position. Civil-liberties purists find even the "emotional distress" and "fighting words" theories insufficiently content-neutral and so oppose *any* disciplinary measures against verbal harassment whatever – even in the extreme Wisconsin example I mentioned above.[25]

For some, of course, the civil-rights and civil-liberties approaches are not "perspectives" on this problem; rather, one or the other of these approaches simply states the reality of the situation. Thus on the civil-rights side, many students at Stanford were sincerely shocked when free speech concerns led university authorities not to prosecute the Beethoven poster episode at Stanford that I described above. A number of them described this as an instance of taking something that was clearly one thing – a racist atrocity, which if left unpunished established an officially condoned practice of discrimination – and "turning it into" a civil liberties issue. Later in the year, when members of a left-activist student coalition seized (forcibly, but without causing personal injury or property damage) the office of the president of the university, they cited the

---

[23] *West Virginia State Board of Education v. Barnette*, 319 U.S. 624, 643 (1943). Compare *Texas v. Johnson*, 109 S. Ct. 2533, 2544: "If there is a bedrock principle underlying the First Amendment, it is that the government may not prohibit the expression of an idea because society finds the idea itself offensive or disagreeable."

[24] *Whitney v. California*, 274 U. S. 357, 377 (1927).

[25] The moderate view is especially well articulated, by a present General Counsel of the ACLU, in Nadine Strossen, "Regulating Campus Speech: A Modest Proposal," *Duke Law Journal*, p. 483. Strossen, like other moderates, is more skeptical of the "fighting words" than of the "emotional distress" rationale. The purist view is inferrable from Franklyn Haiman, *Speech and Law in a Free Society* (Chicago: University of Chicago, 1981). Haiman altogether rejects the "insulting or fighting words" doctrine, (pp. 132–35, 256–59); he would confine sanctions for verbal infliction of emotional distress to cases of injury through intentional factual misrepresentation (pp. 148–56).

Beethoven incident as one of their main grievances; when they were charged (and ultimately found guilty) under the university disciplinary code for the takeover, they said it was an irony that their "peaceful protest" had been punished while this clear incident of racist persecution had been treated as protected free speech.

On the other side, many civil libertarians simply do not see the problem as involving issues of civil rights or discrimination at all. It is *not* a clash of equal protection and free speech, they insist, but a pure civil liberties issue, in which fragile free speech values are threatened by powerful political pressure groups on liberal campuses. For these civil libertarians, protecting discriminatory verbal harassment is no different from protecting flag-burning; it represents the principled defense of reason against the perennial collective emotional impulse to censor, rather than answer, the speech of unpopular and often unpleasant dissenters.[26]

My own view is that there are plenty of good reasons, and plenty of worthy passions, on both sides of the issue. And they seem to me really to be *sides* – mutually incommensurable perspectives – rather than the poles of a well-defined continuum along which negotiators may approach each other in search of a solution that measurably splits the difference between them.[27] The epigraph to this essay occurs in the course of Wittgenstein's famous discussion of the ambiguous "duck-rabbit" drawing, which can appear as either a duck or a rabbit, depending on how you look at it.[28] You can learn facility at shifting between seeing the figure as a duck and seeing it as a rabbit, but at any moment it appears only in one aspect or the other. The campus harassment issue has something of the same quality.

II

Let me now describe the proposal I originally drafted, which was recently adopted as a disciplinary rule covering discriminatory verbal harassment at Stanford.[29] The provision is an attempt to accommodate competing values, to mediate the incommensurable conflict of civil-liberties and civil-rights approaches on this issue. I am not confident that it is better than other mediating solutions, though I can give a reason for the choice of each of its elements. But I do

---

[26] It has been my personal experience in debating this issue with colleagues and students that few causes attract more powerful *emotional* adherence than does First Amendment absolutism. I make the point not to disparage this aspect of their commitment, but because civil libertarians frequently pose the verbal harassment issue (typically with analogy to the flag-burning issue) as a clash between "reason" on their side and "emotion" on the other. On the other side, not a few civil-rights egalitarians take up the same binary opposition between "reason" and "passion" and turn it around to accuse free speech defenders of the moral defect of cerebral and unfeeling elitism.

[27] Incommensurable conflicts are, roughly, those we have to resolve in the absence of a satisfactory determining norm (substantive rule, agreed procedure, or common metric). They are not contradictions and need not be resolved "irrationally." A good discussion of value-incommensurability in the context of individual action can be found in Joseph Raz, *The Morality of Freedom*, 321–66 (Oxford: Clarendon Press, 1986).

[28] Wittgenstein, *Philosophical Investigations*, p. 194.

[29] The text of the Stanford regulation is given in the Appendix.

believe that some such accommodating solution, as against a "principled" choice implementing one approach to the exclusion of the other, is needed.[30]

The first section of the provision restates Stanford's policy on free expression, including an insistence that students must learn to "tolerate even expression of opinions which they find abhorrent." Counterposed is a second section restating the university's existing policy against discrimination "in the administration of its educational policies" on the basis of "sex, race, color, handicap, religion, sexual orientation, or national and ethnic origin," and adding that harassment on the basis of these characteristics can, when cumulated, constitute hostile environment discrimination under the policy. The third section notes that the free expression and anti-discrimination policies conflict on the issue of verbal harassment; it provides that "protected free expression ends and prohibited discriminatory harassment begins" at the point where expression of opinion becomes "personal vilification" of a student on the basis of one of the characteristics stated in the anti-discrimination policy.

The operative part of the provision comes in the fourth and last section, which defines "personal vilification" as speech or other symbolic expression that (a) is intended to insult or stigmatize individuals on the basis of one of the designated characteristics; (b) is "addressed directly" to those insulted or stigmatized; and (c) makes use of "insulting or 'fighting' words," defined (quoting from *Chaplinsky v. New Hampshire*[31]) as words (or non-verbal symbols) that "by their very utterance inflict injury or tend to incite to an immediate breach of the peace."

Finally, the proposal adds a narrowing proviso designed to adapt the *Chaplinsky* insulting-or-fighting words concept to civil-rights enforcement. In the context of discriminatory harassment, punishable words (or symbols) are defined as those "commonly understood to convey direct and visceral hatred or contempt for human beings on the basis of" the characteristics specified in the anti-discrimination policy – a phrase meant to capture the sense of the common expression "racial epithets" and to extend it to other prohibited forms of discrimination.

To summarize, the rule would punish speech directed to individuals: speech meant to insult them on the basis of a protected characteristic that also makes use of one of the gutter epithets of bigotry. It thus adopts one element of what I have called the "moderate civil libertarian" view of harassment regulation; it prohibits only expression that falls roughly within the categories of fighting words or intentional infliction of emotional distress doctrines. The provision therefore only prohibits a very narrow category of expression, immunizing even

---

[30] One example of an alternative mediating solution was the situation at Stanford before adoption of the harassment provision. The university's president and general counsel had said publicly that face-to-face use of racial epithets could be considered to violate the long-standing "Fundamental Standard" which required of students conduct manifesting such "respect for the rights of others as is expected of good citizens." Though that solution gave too little guidance to satisfy civil liberties concerns in my view, it was in the same ballpark as the one later adopted. Other examples of mediating solutions include the regulation adopted at the University of California and the one proposed at the University of Texas. See note 32 below.

[31] 315 U.S. 568, 572 (1942).

the vilest hate-speech addressed generally to a campus audience as well as many serious face-to-face discriminatory verbal assaults. Many students of color and other civil-rights advocates at Stanford have opposed it, for these reasons, as too weak an anti-discrimination measure.

At the same time, narrow as it is, the proposal retains enough of the civil-rights approach to trouble most civil libertarians. It seems to violate the second central civil-liberties tenet: not only can speech be regulated only to the minimum extent necessary to prevent immediate and otherwise unremediable harm; further, any speech regulation must be *neutral* – generally neutral as to content, certainly neutral as to viewpoint. The provision's apparent violation of the neutrality constraint results directly from its being framed as civil-rights protection or anti-discrimination measure.

To bring out the neutrality problem, I need to describe more fully the legal underpinnings of the proposal. It does not precisely track either of the most common bases for narrow discriminatory harassment regulations: the "fighting words" or "intentional infliction of emotional distress" rationales, which have been adopted at other universities in the wake of the Michigan case.[32] Rather, it draws on the relevant common elements in those two theories, adapting them to the context of a civil-rights-based campus harassment regulation.

In the *Chaplinsky* case, a unanimous Supreme Court excluded from First Amendment protection "insulting or 'fighting' words," those which "by their very utterance inflict injury" *or* that "tend to incite an immediate breach of the peace." Subsequent cases have focused on the "breach of the peace" half of the category, and the Court has made clear that its reach is narrow indeed; it has never affirmed a conviction under the doctrine since *Chaplinsky* itself in 1942.[33] During those years, the Court has also developed the "heckler's veto" doctrine as a counterweight to its "fighting words" proviso, putting the burden on law enforcement to protect speakers against threatened violence, rather than avoiding the violence by silencing the speaker.[34]

The heckler's veto analysis brings out the weakness in the "fighting words" doctrine as it was traditionally formulated. The concept seems to ask purely factual and predictive questions. Can imminent violence be expected from an audience? Are available law enforcement resources insufficient to protect the speaker? As many civil libertarians have argued, however, it seems inconsistent with free speech values to punish a speaker simply because the heckler's veto

---

[32] The University of California has adopted a prohibition on student harassment by "fighting words," defined as "those personally abusive epithets which, when directly addressed to any ordinary person are, in the context used and as a matter of common knowledge, inherently likely to provoke a violent reaction whether or not they actually do so." These "include, but are not limited to" terms abusive in terms of race, sex, or the other categories of discrimination law. Harassment occurs when fighting words are used to "create a hostile and intimidating environment" which the utterer should know will interfere with the victim's education.

A committee at the University of Texas has proposed a regulation of "racial harassment" tracking the Restatement of Torts definition of intentional infliction of emotional distress, with the addition of the element of intent to "harass, intimidate, or humiliate . . . on account of race, color or national origin." Establishing a violation requires an actual showing of "severe emotional distress" on the part of the victim.

[33] See *Cohen v. California*, 403 U.S. 15 (1971); *Gooding v. Wilson*, 405 U.S. 518 (1972).

[34] Compare *Gregory v. Chicago*, 394 U.S. 111 (1969) with *Feiner v. New York*, 340 U.S. 315 (1951).

is made effective – because, that is, a sufficient number of thugs have plausibly threatened violence and available police protection is inadequate. A serious civil-libertarian presumption in favor of free speech seems to require some evaluation of what the speaker has said – are they really *"fighting* words"? – before silencing the speaker in the face of a hostile audience can be said to be a proper response.

The same requirement of normative evaluation of the speech must also apply, it seems, in the case of intentional infliction of emotional distress. And here, indeed, the evaluative element is explicitly built into the standard common law elements of the tort. The victim must foreseeably suffer severe emotional distress from what the defendant does or says, but this is not sufficient. In addition, the defendant's conduct must be, as Section 46 or the Torts Restatement puts it, in unmistakably evaluative terms, "beyond all possible bounds of decency" and "regarded as atrocious and utterly intolerable in a civilized community" – in short, "outrageous."[35]

I suggest that we interpret the *Chaplinsky* category of "insulting or 'fighting' words" as designating utterances that at least meet the standard set by Restatement Section 46. For free speech purposes, though, the Section 46 standard is *too* purely evaluative – too vague.[36] But if the vagueness problem can be met (by delineating a category of utterances that *are* "outrageous" and are given further and more objective definition), then it would be reasonable – under *Chaplinsky* – to treat those utterances as subject to prohibition because they are likely *either* to provoke violence or to cause severe emotional distress.

The Stanford provision thus interprets *Chaplinsky*'s dual formulation to suggest a category of speech, objectively "insulting" in character, that attacks the very identity of its victim in such a way as to stimulate the familiar "fight or flight reaction." Among certain classes of hearers, particularly young males socialized to be physically aggressive, the typical reaction to a vile personal insult may be "fight." For others – many men; perhaps most children, most older people, most women; invalids – the typical reaction to this kind of verbal assault is some combination of extreme fear, numbness, and impotent rage: reactions calculated to produce the sort of "severe emotional distress" to which the Restatement of Torts makes reference. We should read *Chaplinsky*, in my view, to have identified two distinct kinds of reactions (fight or flight) to the same category of intolerable speech when it speaks, respectively, of utterances that "tend to incite an immediate breach of the peace" and those that "by their very utterance inflict injury."

The Stanford provision identifies discriminatory "personal vilification" as a class of utterances of which any instance is particularly likely to produce one

---

[35] *Restatement of Torts*, 2d, sec. 46, comment (d).

[36] " 'Outrageousness' in the area of political and social discourse has an inherent subjectiveness about it which would allow a jury to impose liability on the basis of the jurors' tastes or views, or perhaps on the basis of their dislike of a particular expression." *Hustler Magazine v. Falwell*, 108 S. Ct. 876, 882. The Court's decision, however, does not foreclose granting tort damages under the "outrageousness" test for infliction of emotional distress through speech alone in a private or face-to-face context, rather than in a published and nationally distributed lampoon of an important public figure, such as was involved in *Falwell.*

or the other of the kinds of injury covered by the "fighting words" and "emotional distress" analysis. These are, in Richard Delgado's phrase, "words that wound" – utterances directed to members of groups specially subject to discrimination, intended to insult or stigmatize them, and making use of the small class of commonly recognized words or symbols that have no other function but to convey hatred and contempt for these groups.[37]

Professor Delgado offers as the test for liability under his proposal the requirement that the words directed to the victim be such as "a reasonable person would recognize as a racial insult." In a campus context, where claims of insult and ideological debate are often intertwined, this phrasing raises special, and I think avoidable, civil-liberties problems. Some ideas might be taken as racial or ethnic insults by virtue of their content alone: for example, claims that the Holocaust never happened, or that blacks are genetically inferior to whites. To avoid banning ideas as such on the basis of propositional content, on campus or elsewhere, the Stanford regulation prohibits only verbal abuse including actual racial epithets, or their equivalents for other forms of discrimination.[38] These are the all-too-familiar words that carry with them so inseparable a message of hatred and contempt that apologies are in order for the affront involved in even quoting them: "nigger," "kike," "faggot," "cunt," and the like.[39]

Racial and other discriminatory hatred and contempt can be effectively expressed without using these words, of course, but (partly in the interests of avoiding vagueness and its chilling effect) such cases are not included under the regulation. A white student can tell a black student, face-to-face, "you people are inferior and should not be here," but not be guilty of harassment. In addition, even gutter eipthets are immunized when uttered to the campus or public at large, in order to give the widest possible leeway for speech in the public forum; the Klan or the neo-Nazis may demonstrate and display their

[37] Richard Delgado, "Words that Wound: A Tort Action for Racial Insults, Epithets, and Name-calling," *Harvard Civil Rights-Civil Liberties Law Review*, vol. 17 (1982), pp. 133–81. Professor Delgado has assembled on pp. 136–49 an impressive body of evidence and argument that supports the identification of racial verbal abuse as inflicting a distinctive and identifiable form of injury, and so qualifying as a distinctive wrong. His proposal is limited to *racial* insults.

[38] Because I believe to this extent in the "no false ideas" strand of American First Amendment law, I reject group defamation and hate speech prohibitions of the kind called for by the International Convention on the Elimination of All Forms of Racial Discrimination: "States Parties . . . shall declare as an offence publishable by law all dissemination of ideas based on racial superiority or hatred. . . ." Mari Matsuda ably argues the contrary view, urging modification of First Amendment law to permit the extension of a limited version of the international standard to this country in "Public Response to Racist Speech: Considering the Victim's Story," *Michigan Law Review*, vol. 87 (1989), p. 2320. As Professor Matsuda's article documents, many Western countries have such laws. The Canadian hate-speech statute is currently under review by the Supreme Court of Canada for its consistency with the free expression guarantee of the recently adopted Canadian Charter of Rights and Freedoms.

[39] It would be possible, in the interests of maximum clarity, to attempt a comprehensive list of the "discriminatory fighting words" and equivalent visual symbols (swastikas, burning crosses, etc.). I think this would be a mistake; new examples of such words and symbols are constantly being invented by the creativity of the collective bigoted mind. Even without a definitive list, however, the Stanford regulation gives clearer notice of what will count as an offense than any other similar proposal I know. I should add that as I understand the provision, derogatory epithets aimed at (white) national origin groups ("dago," "Polack," etc.) would come within its terms to the extent they were determined to be still "commonly understood" to "convey direct and visceral hatred or contempt" on the basis of national origin.

symbols and shout their words of hatred with impunity. This very much narrows the reach of the proposal and exposes it to the charge, mentioned before, that it is mere tokenism. But at the same time, it helps meet traditional and legitimate civil-liberties concerns about public political expression, and about vagueness and its accompanying chilling effect.[40]

The Stanford provision has also been drafted with an eye on another concern – one rooted in the civil-rights perspective, and often noted as well in civil-libertarian objections to "hate speech" or "group defamation" regulations.[41] The concern is illustrated by one of the cases that occurred under the Michigan regulation. A black woman law student, in the course of a heated argument, called a classmate "white trash." She was charged with a violation of the harassment rule; she ultimately agreed to write a formal letter of apology to the classmate in settlement of the charge.

Under the Stanford provision, calling a white student "white trash" would not constitute harassment. In its commonly understood meaning, the term is (like "redneck") derogatory to the poor whites of the rural South by virtue of their class, not their race.[42] If the student addressed came from that social background, and if class bias were a form of discrimination covered by the proposal (as it is not), there might be a disciplinary case. But as a white person, she is not a victim of discriminatory *racial* harassment; the term "white trash" is clearly not "commonly understood" to convey hatred or contempt for whites on the basis of their race as such – a requirement for liability under the provision. This is not to deny that the black woman student intended to express race-based hatred or contempt, or that she may have effectively conveyed a racial insult, just as a white student does who tells a black student that "you people are inferior and shouldn't be here." In neither case, though, is the regulation violated, because in neither case is there use of one of the required "commonly understood" assaultive epithets or symbols of discriminatory contempt.

The point of the "white trash" case can be generalized, and in a way that is most troubling to civil libertarian defenders of viewpoint neutrality. As best I can see, there are *no* epithets in this society at this time that are "commonly understood" to convey hatred and contempt for whites *as such*. The same can be said, I believe, of males as such, and heterosexuals as such.[43] If this is

<hr>

[40] The narrow confinement of the harassment regulation to the use of the gutter epithets also emphasizes that it is meant as an anti-discrimination provision, not a "civility rule." As a teacher, I would not let students address each other in class using personally derogatory terms of any kind, and would exclude students who persisted in doing so. That is a civility rule, similar to those applied in most American parliamentary bodies. Such rules are not, in my opinion, appropriate for campus-wide enforcement. The campus should be thought of as primarily a general public forum, and secondarily as a workplace (the work of education). I would add that values of residential privacy may justify more stringent regulation of offensive speech in student dormitories than in classrooms or in public campus areas, but this is a complex issue which I cannot treat adequately here.

[41] This is the concern raised by Justice Black in his dissent from the Supreme Court's decision sustaining conviction of a white racist pamphleteer under a group libel statute: "If there be any minority groups who hail this holding as their victory, they might consider the possible relevance of this ancient remark: 'Another such victory and I am undone.'" *Beauharnais v. Illinois*, 343 U.S. 250, 275 (1952).

[42] Indeed in its usual sense, the term is implicitly racist toward people of color – with its implication of surprise that a *white* person would be "trash."

[43] I realize that others might disagree with this, citing terms such as "honky," "gringo," "breeder," etc. But I

indeed a socio-linguistic fact, it is of course one not fixed in stone; on the other hand, it is no accident. The denigrating epithets covered by the Stanford provision are able to inflict the serious and distinctive injuries characteristic of legally prohibited invidious discrimination because they strike at groups subjected to longstanding and deep-rooted prejudices widely held and disseminated throughout our culture. American children grow up with the negative stereotypes of blacks, women, and homosexuals in their bones and in their souls. This is tragically true, too, of children who are black, female, or later identify themselves as homosexual.

The denigrating epithets draw their capacity to impose the characteristic civil-rights injury to "hearts and minds" from the fact that they turn the whole socially and historically inculcated weight of these prejudices upon their victim. Each hatemonger who invokes one of these terms summons a vicious chorus in his support. It is because, given our cultural history, no such *general* prejudices strike against the dominant groups that there exist no comparable terms of universally understood hatred and contempt applicable to whites, males, and heterosexuals as such.[44]

III

The Stanford provision, then, while neutral on its face, will foreseeably be asymmetric in its application. This aspect of the provision allows its interpretation to reflect a state of affairs central to civil-rights analysis – the continued existence of asymmetric social relations of group domination and subjugation in the United States. Contrary to the democratic ideal, American society (like other societies) is still characterized by a hierarchy of relatively stable ascriptive status groups. To rephrase the point from the jargon of sociology to the rhetoric of movement politics, there still exist "oppressor" and "oppressed" (or, to lower the political pitch, "privileged" and "subordinated") groups, identified as such by characteristics such as race, gender, class, and sexual preference. Indeed, the civil-rights project can best be understood as at once premised on the existence of these groups' asymmetric power relations and aimed at the ultimate elimination of the asymmetries. (To describe it thus is not to decide in advance the debatable

---

myself do not know which of these terms are current and seriously-used epithets of hatred or contempt – evidence that they are not "commonly understood" as such. On the other side, no sentient black, Latino, or gay American has any doubt about the current standard insulting epithets for their groups.

[44] A similar analysis applies to the unjustified use of the term "white racist," which many of my white students have invoked as the equivalent, applied to them, of the standard racial epithets as applied to the students of color. Leaving to one side whether unjustified use of a term like this inflicts the same level of injury, it does not in any event come within the class of injuries that concern civil rights law and policy. The term "white racist" does not denigrate whites *as such*, any more than "black separatist racist" denigrates blacks as such. In addition, strong civil-liberties considerations distinguish the cases. Terms of *political* abuse like "white racist" (or "Stalinist," "Nazi," "terrorist") are sometimes accurately and appropriately applied to individuals in robust debate; exactly when they properly apply, however, is politically controversial. In contrast, the Stanford provision rests on the premise that the racial (and other) discriminatory gutter epithets it deals with are *never* appropriately directed at individuals; enforcement of the provision, therefore, does not involve the politically charged task of discriminating between justified and unjustified uses.

question of affirmative action – the question of whether symmetric or asymmetric policies are best suited to attain the goal.)

Given its narrow coverage, the Stanford provision obviously does not embody a particularly radical or utopian civil-rights approach. Its categories and its thrust largely reflect a civil-liberties perspective on the racial harassment problem. The exclusive remedy it contemplates for all but a tiny fraction of discriminatory speech is the one civil libertarians favor: more speech. But the features it adopts from a civil-rights approach still jar most civil libertarians; indeed, they jar me when I look at the problem through a civil-liberties lens. First, the provision lacks content-neutrality; it regulates only speech bearing on matters of race, gender, sexual orientation, and the like while neglecting other speech that might similarly provoke violence or cause similarly severe emotional distress. Second, and even more troubling, the rule bears asymmetrically on its restricted subject matter in a way that, to some, will seem inconsistent with viewpoint-neutrality.

That is, it may seem biased against the disfavored ideologies of racism, sexism, and homophobia, openly favoring "politically correct" egalitarians against their adversaries in the campus marketplace of opinion. It arguably takes from the bigots emotively powerful rhetorical weapons – the traditional hate epithets – without imposing comparable restrictions on the other side. It is as if terms like "commie" and "pinko" were barred from political debate, while "imperialist lackey" and "capitalist running dog" were allowed. This seems to violate official neutrality: the principle of "no orthodoxy in matters of opinion," "no such thing as a false idea."

This civil-libertarian objection helps bring out the deep structure of the conflict between the two approaches. From the civil rights perspective, there *are* false ideas and ideologies, among which white supremacy and related forms of bigotry are the paradigm examples. The insult and stigma involved in the imposition of supremacist ideologies on those whom they oppress and exclude from full citizenship attacks what John Rawls has called the most fundamental of those "primary goods" that government is established to allow individuals to pursue – those that form the basis of self-respect.[45] The protection of the basis of the individual's capacity for self-respect against violation by socially authoritative humiliation is as much at the heart of equal protection as is official viewpoint-neutrality in regulating the marketplace of ideas that is at the heart of free expression.

The analysis of the civil-rights approach in terms of preventing exclusion by the social imposition of caste-based stigma supplies the standard rationale for the central doctrine of modern anti-discrimination law: the rejection of the "separate but equal" version of Jim Crow.[46] The doctrinal problem was this: A state supplies equal (but separate) facilities to whites and blacks – schools, public parks, beaches, buses, amenities in public buildings, etc. How does this

---

[45] John Rawls, *A Theory of Justice* (Cambridge: Harvard, 1971), pp. 178–79, 440–46, 543–47.

[46] *Brown v. Board of Education,* 347 U.S. 483 (1954); see also *Mayor of Baltimore v. Dawson,* 350 U.S. 877 (1955) (beaches); *Gayle v. Browder,* 352 U.S. 903 (1956) (buses); *Holmes v. City of Atlanta,* 350 U.S. 879 (1955) (golf courses); *Johnson v. Virginia,* 373 U.S. 61 (1963) (courthouses).

equality-preserving separation of the races violate the Constitution's prohibition of racially *unequal* treatment? The *Brown* line of cases answers that the inequality inheres in the subordinating character of the *message* delivered by the separation – the material state action, separate but equal segregation, viewed in isolation from its communicative impact, fully preserves equality. *Plessy* had said that if black people felt insulted by the separation, that was only their interpretation; *Brown* finally (and realistically) accepted that the insulting interpretation was the only plausible one.[47]

But the *Plessy* formula is a quite appropriate response to a complaint of discriminatory segregation in some social contents. Separation sometimes stigmatizes no one. The maintenance of separate men's and women's restrooms in public buildings, for example, does not by itself constitute invidious sex discrimination. But in the context of this society and its history, the Jim Crow variety of racial segregation imposed inequality because it rested on the assumption, and hence delivered the message, that whites were a superior caste to be protected from the polluting contact of their black inferiors. The insulting message, the wound inflicted by the authoritative endorsement of the "false idea" of white supremacy and black unworthiness, was what made Jim Crow unconstitutional.[48]

Essentially the same wound is the injury inflicted on minority, female, and gay students or employees when endemic verbal abuse renders educational or work environment discriminatorily "hostile" within the terms of discrimination law. In this sense, the focus on symbolic injury to the "hearts and minds" of black children in the desegregation cases supplies the basic authority for campus verbal harassment regulation; *Brown*, as Charles Lawrence strikingly argues, "may be read as regulating the content of racist speech."[49]

The civil-libertarian, dedicated to a principle of liberal official neutrality in the marketplace of ideas, sees this as a perverse misstatement of *Brown*. It ignores two crucial distinctions, the argument runs: speech vs. action, and public vs. private.[50] First, the civil-libertarian insists that the *practice* of white (or male,

---

[47] *Plessy v. Ferguson*, 163 U.S. 537, 551 (1896), rejecting the claim that "the enforced separation of the two races stamps the colored race with a badge of inferiority" on the ground that "[i]f this be so, it is not by reason of anything found in the act, but solely because the colored race chooses to put that construction upon it." Compare *Brown v. Board of Education*, 347 U.S. 483, 494 (1954).

[48] Edmond Cahn early on offered this rationale as the proper interpretation of *Brown*:

> As is observed in the ancient Babylonian Talmud, to shame and degrade a fellow-creature is to commit a kind of psychic mayhem upon him. Like an assailant's knife, humiliation slashes his self-respect and human dignity. He grows pale, the blood rushes from his face just as thought it had been shed. That is why we are accustomed to say he feels "wounded." . . .
>
> So one speaks in terms of the most familiar and universally accepted standards of right and wrong when one remarks (1) that racial segregation under government auspices inevitably inflicts humiliation, and (2) that official humiliation of innocent, law-abiding citizens is psychologically injurious and morally evil . . .

"Jurisprudence," *New York University Law Review*, vol. 30 (1955), pp. 148–59.

[49] Charles Lawrence III, "If He Hollers Let Him Go: Regulating Racist Speech on Campus," *Duke Law Journal*, vol. 1990, pp. 901, 909. My treatment of *Brown* has been much influenced by this excellent article.

[50] Nadine Strossen contests the *Brown* analogy in these terms in her article cited above.

or heterosexual) supremacy must be kept distinct from its *preaching;* while the former violates the anti-discrimination principle, the latter is protected by the principle of free expression. Questions of the boundary between speech and action may present difficulty, but the structure is clear.

The point is quite general: the Constitution certainly requires the *practice* of republican government, due process, and non-establishment of religion, as well as non-discrimination. But equally central is the principle of free expression, which includes the freedom to *preach* dictatorship, summary justice, theocracy – or even universal censorship. And so, the argument continues, the same principle guarantees freedom to advocate racist and other inegalitarian doctrines – as, indeed, many First Amendment decisions firmly establish.[51]

Second, the argument continues, the invocation of *Brown* to support the suppression of racist speech ignores the public-private distinction, which is essential to the maintenance not only of free speech but also of such other civil liberties as freedom of religion. If *Brown* does perhaps strike at certain "speech" (more precisely, at the communicative element in certain actions), it is only at *official* speech, which has never been thought protected by a principle of free expression. What the First Amendment protects is the right of *private* individuals to deliver those same messages.

While the equal protection clause might, for example, prohibit a legislature from placing a white supremacist slogan on a state's seal, flag, public buildings, and the like, the First Amendment just as firmly protects the freedom of private individuals to put that slogan into free competition against more egalitarian ones in the marketplace of ideas. Not only the flag, but also a copy of the *Brown* decision, or a picture of Martin Luther King, can be defaced in public with impunity under the First Amendment – though of course, as the civil-libertarian usually adds, government officials should denounce such racist outrages, just as university authorities should denounce racist speech on campus while resolutely protecting it against coercive interference.

When we turn to look at the world through the civil-rights lens, though, we find much less clarity in the public-private distinction.[52] The civil-rights approach seeks to cleanse not only the state but civil society generally of racist and other bigoted practices. The formal constitutional expression of the public-private distinction, the state action doctrine, tends to break down in the area of discrimination law. Nothing approaching a clear line separates (prohibited) official

---

[51] *Collin v. Smith,* 578 F.2d 1197 (7th Cir. 1978), *cert. denied* 436 U.S. 953 (1978); *Brandenburg v. Ohio,* 395 U.S. 444 (1969); *Terminiello v. Chicago,* 337 U.S. 1 (1949). The Court has reiterated the point in significant dicta in the flag-burning cases. "The First Amendment does not guarantee that other concepts virtually sacred to our Nation as a whole – such as the principle that discrimination on the basis of race is odious and destructive – will go unchallenged in the marketplace of ideas." *Texas v. Johnson,* 109 S. Ct. 2533, 2544 (1989). "We are aware that desecration of the flag is deeply offensive to many. But the same might be said, for example, of virulent ethnic and religious epithets [citing *Terminiello*]. . . ." *United States v. Eichman,* 110 S. Ct. 2404, 2410 (1990).

[52] The reliance of traditional civil-liberties law on a public-private distinction much stronger than we recognize elsewhere is the theme of Frank Michelman, "Conceptions of Democracy in American Constitutional Argument: The Case of Pornography Regulation," *Tennessee Law Review,* vol. 56 (1989), p. 291.

encouragement or support of private discrimination on the one hand from (permissible) neutral toleration on the other. Judge Posner's words quoted earlier from the hostile environment discrimination case help make the point: states often deny the equal protection of the laws not by acting, but by omitting to act against private discriminatory action within such areas of responsibility as a government workplace. The point becomes more forceful as, with the growth of the modern welfare and regulatory state, government's sphere of activity broadens, and increased supervision of areas of private conduct brings with it more responsibility for that conduct.[53]

Further, when we look beyond formal constitutional doctrine, we find that our actual civil-rights practices place little weight on the public-private distinction. The social condemnation of a form of discrimination as invidious brings it within the anti-discrimination principle. This principle typically leads both to judicial prohibition of the official forms of prejudice and legislative prohibition where it appears "privately" in employment, housing, education, and public accommodations. By contrast, our civil-liberties practices exhibit no parallel tendency toward legislative protection of Nazis, Klansmen, and flag-burners against private discrimination. "Tolerance," a civil-rights word, and "toleration," a civil-liberties word, name quite different values.

And as I have already stressed, the civil-rights approach likewise does not sharply distinguish between speech and action. "Sticks and stones may break my bones, but words will never hurt me" – which expresses in homely form the First Amendment's Brandeisian ideal of self-reliant civic courage[54] – does not apply within a framework of analysis in which the central injury to be avoided is stigma and humiliation – injury to a socially constructed (and hence socially destructible) personality. Words and symbols are among the chief weapons for inflicting this form of injury. The point becomes clear when one reads the facts of some of the hostile environment discrimination cases; anyone will agree with Judge Posner that the victims in these cases have suffered discrimination in "terms and conditions of employment" as surely as if they had been made to do extra work for the same pay on account of their race or sex.[55]

---

[53] Thus in *Shelley v. Kraemer*, 334 U.S. 1 (1948), extensive legal supervision of the kinds of enforceable covenants running with the land rendered enforcement of a racially restrictive private covenant discriminatory state action; in *Terry v. Adams*, 345 U.S. 461 (1953), extensive state regulation of elections rendered the exclusionary practices of the formally private Texas Jaybird Democratic Club (in effect the white Democratic Party) discriminatory state action; in *Burton v. Wilmington Parking Authority*, 365 U.S. 715 (1961), public ownership and operation of a parking garage constitutionally entangled the state in the racial exclusion practiced by a privately-owned restaurant leasing space in the building.

[54] See the language from Justice Brandeis's opinion in *Whitney v. California*, quoted in text accompanying note 24 above.

[55] Thus in *Bohen v. East Chicago*, the plaintiff, a female fire department dispatcher, had to deal with a supervisor who was constantly "speaking to her entirely of sexual matters and describing his preferred sexual positions. Bohen's participation, and his expectations for her behavior." Further, she was "a continual target for obscene comments by firefighters and other male employees and was forced to listen to their filthy talk and descriptions of their sexual fantasies of which she was the object." A fire captain told her that "a forcible rape in some nearby flora would improve her disposition." 799 F.2d, pp. 1182–83.

In *EEOC v. Murphy Motor Freight Lines*, 488 F. Supp. 381 (D. Minn. 1980), Ray Wells, a black dockman, was subjected regularly to racial slurs on chalkboards attached to loading carts: "Ray Wells is a nigger," "The

These same hostile environment discrimination cases likewise provide some of the best examples of civil rights analysis that blur the "speech-action" as well as the "public-private" distinction. When a private employer is held liable under Title VII for not taking reasonable steps to prevent racist or sexist verbal assaults by employees on their fellow workers, the government is in effect imposing (as sovereign, not employer) a content- and viewpoint-specific regime of censorship on the speech of private employees. The American Civil Liberties Union has seen the point; it opposes liability for employers or schools who fail to prevent verbal sexual harassment that "has no other effect on its recipient than to create an unpleasant working [learning] environment."[56] But I have found that many good civil-libertarians see these hostile environment cases (at least in the employment context) through the civil-rights lens; they thus agree with current law in accepting that an employer should be obligated to police the workplace to some extent against even purely verbal abuse when it becomes so pervasive and differentially "unpleasant" on grounds of race or sex to affect employees' terms and conditions of employment.

IV

I have tried to suggest how the civil-liberties and civil-rights approaches overlap and clash on the issue of discriminatory harassment; apparently, no higher principle of comparable force and vitality can resolve their conflict.[57] Do these two approaches simply represent, respectively, right- and left-wing political tendencies within American liberalism? It is possible to tell the story that way: civil-liberties (and its marketplace of ideas) then represents a dying classical liberalism, while civil-rights (and its society of equal groups) represents a post-liberal social democracy struggling to be born. Or (to flip the political poles of the historical plot-line) civil liberties now represents the true liberal future at this moment of the end of history, while the asymmetric civil-rights project will be rejected along with other misguided attempts to inject communitarian ideals into the legal governance of free societies.

Both of these sketches operate on the "contradiction" hypothesis; they postulate, on the basis of the structural conflict between the civil-rights and civil-liberties approaches, that one should give way in the name of principled consistency. Following this analysis, one could press (from the right) toward a more formal

---

only good nigger is a dead nigger," "Niggers are a living example that Indians screwed buffalo." When Wells started eating in another room, his white co-workers wrote "niggers only" above the door. Management did nothing in response to complaints. See pp. 384–85.

[56] *Policy Guide of the ACLU* (rev. ed. 1989), at 142, 400. The ACLU position requires distinguishing between (protected) verbal abuse that merely renders the environment "unpleasant" and that which crosses the line to inflicting actionable emotional distress – hardly a bright line. My thanks to Nadine Strossen for providing me the text of these ACLU provisions.

[57] Which is not to say that verbal formulae may not be offered to supply formal or aesthetic resolution to liberal theory and hence present it as a closed system. John Rawls attempts such a closure with his lexical ordering of liberty over equal opportunity in *A Theory of Justice;* the difficulty is to defend the substance of this firm hierarchy. Joseph Raz supplies an attractive overarching account of "autonomy" as *the* supreme liberal value, resolving liberty-equality conflicts, in *The Morality of Freedom.* I myself prefer the frank pluralism of Isaiah Berlin in "Two Concepts of Liberty," *Four Essays on Liberty,* pp. 167–72 (London: Oxford, 1969).

and neutral "civil-liberties" style of anti-discrimination law or (from the left) toward a more substantive and result-oriented "civil-rights" version of free speech law.

The former move would incline toward an ideal of formal neutrality in civil-rights law, one that stressed not the abolition of caste or status-subordination but the elimination from law of "suspect classifications" – distinctions based upon individuals' immutable characteristics. The latter move would give a larger role in First Amendment law to correction of market imperfections in the marketplace of ideas, pursuing policies such as realistically equal access to media, opening debate to the participation of those previously silenced by social subordination, and so on. As this essay perhaps suggests, I am more inclined to go in the latter direction than in the former, but I am not inclined to go very far[58] – nothing like far enough to bring civil-liberties law into full consistency with the public-private and speech-action treatments characteristic of current civil-rights law.

What, then, is the alternative to seeing this incommensurable conflict as contradiction? My answer is already implicit in the body of the essay; it can be roughly captured by the slogan that the civil-rights approach embodies a *project*, which is to be carried on within a *framework* constituted by the civil-liberties approach. Civil rights has statable social goals, however utopian: the abolition of racism, sexism, and other forms of bigotry. It postulates disease-like social conditions and collective enemies; it then sets us the task of struggling against these and, ideally, eliminating them. The civil-rights mentality represents our collective self-commitment to a definite, though limited and negative, judgment about the nature of the good society, or at least the good society for us – it is one without castes (whether of race, or sex, or sexual orientation, or . . .). Civil-rights law is then conceived mainly as an *instrument* toward that end.

Note that this instrumental account of civil-rights doctrine characterizes even those who are unhappy with affirmative action and who tend to support a symmetric version of anti-discrimination law. First, in my experience, few adherents of this view support a wholehearted symmetry in practice. Second, the reason for this shows up in their arguments; they oppose affirmative action as counter-productive, as a poor strategy in the effort to attain what all concede to be the long-run goal: a caste-free society. To use race as a principle for distributing burdens and benefits, they argue, is to legitimize it as a ground for social action; this reinforces the tendency to revert to less benign uses in moments of social panic or pressure. These neutralists on civil rights are thus, at bottom, instrumentalists too; they share the same conception of the overriding goal, only disagreeing on the best means by which to pursue it.[59]

---

[58] Thus I sympathize with Owen Fiss's suggestions for moving First Amendment doctrine in a more realistically democratic direction in his "Free Speech and Social Structure," *Iowa Law Review*, vol. 71 (1986), p. 1405. On the other hand, I stop short of endorsing civil-rights-based bans on potentially broad content-defined categories of speech: racist speech, as endorsed by Mari Matsuda, "Public Response"; or sexist pornography, as in the trafficking provisions of the Indianapolis anti-pornography ordinance invalidated in *American Booksellers Assn'n v. Hudnut*, 771 F.2d 323 (7th Cir. 1985).

[59] Thus in the most "neutralist" of recent Supreme Court civil-rights decisions, *City of Richmond vs. J. A.*

The civil-liberties approach, whether in its right- or left-wing versions, postulates no goal for society in the same sense. What would society look like if the "aims" of the First Amendment were achieved? It would be a society where people could in general say what they have to say, but this merely restates First Amendment doctrine in summary form without articulating a social goal at which it aims. Attempts to state positive goals for the First Amendment typically produce vague and eclectic wish-lists that are of little help in shaping free speech doctrine. A similar point could be made, I believe, of the free exercise clause and some aspects of the right of privacy. We cannot say anything very definite about how society would look if these civil-libertarian rights were fully realized.

We might fairly say that these provisions aim at an open society, but that is to say only that they aim at a society that might look like anything at all. Their very goallessness is in a sense the point of these provisions. They capture our skeptical sense that we do not, in general, know where we are going; we have no dominant *overall* collective project, and we want to keep it that way. The First Amendment, along with the other "civil liberties,"[60] is there to maintain possibilities, to keep the future open to the presently unpredictable workings of the human imagination. Its effective enforcement requires a strong dose of skepticism – not (a self-contradictory) "absolute relativism," but a skeptical *attitude* toward collectively-imposed substantive moral judgments. (This skepticism is not inconsistent with a fair degree of romanticism about the possible achievements of the unchecked human imagination.)[61] By contrast, the civil-rights approach, on its more limited subject (the intolerability of a system of group subordination or caste), is not skeptical at all – no more skeptical than were the abolitionists. (Of course, a degree of skepticism about the possibility of authoritatively ranking human beings, hence of identifying "natural aristocrats," also lends support to this limited egalitarian absolutism.)

In this contrast between the dominant skepticism of the civil libertarian and the dominant confidence of the civil-rights advocate lies the best answer to the objection that a narrow prohibition of discriminatory harassment violates "viewpoint-neutrality" by discriminating in favor of the Left against the Right on issues relevant to civil-rights concerns. The answer is that if the prohibition has been framed narrowly enough, it does preserve practical neutrality – that is, it does *not* differentially deprive any significant element in American political life of its rhetorical capital. I would argue that this is the case with the Stanford provision. The Right has no special stake in the free face-to-face use of epithets

<hr />

Croson, 109 S. Ct. 706, 721 (1989), invalidating a municipal minority business set-aside program, the Court majority stated the grounds for treating even benign racial classifications as suspect in terms instrumental to an anti-caste goal: "Classifications based on race carry a danger of stigmatic harm. . . . They may in fact promote notions of racial inferiority and lead to a politics of racial hostility."

[60] The First Amendment is also tied (as the free exercise and privacy rights are not) to the preservation of a functioning democratic system of government; however, there could conceivably be a working free speech guarantee, justified along the lines I suggest, even in a liberal but undemocratic state.

[61] This romantic side of the civil-liberties mentality is very attractively presented in Steven Shiffrin, *The First Amendment, Democracy, and Romance* (Cambridge: Harvard University Press, 1990).

that perform no other function except to portray whole classes of Americans as subhuman and unworthy of full citizenship.

V

In conclusion, I must return to answer an objection to the Stanford provision that I have heard from critics of both the civil-rights and civil-liberties persuasions. This has to do with the charge that the regulation is drafted so narrowly as to make it "merely symbolic," a point that evidently engages one of the key differences between the two approaches. I readily agree that the provision prohibits very little of the behavior that creates the significantly discriminatory hostile environment that faces students of color and others on many campuses. So why bother with it? The point is made with special force by civil libertarians, who think the proposal exacts a high cost in principle through its incursions into the indivisible fabric of the first amendment. But egalitarians, on their side, can also object on principle to the provision as a form of tokenism.

I also concede that the main good the provision can do is through its educative or symbolic effect – though I would add that the harms its opponents see in it are likewise largely symbolic as well. The question then arises: why can we not get the same educative effect through official statements, declarations of concern, and the like, issued with appropriate vehemence by university authorities whenever serious incidents of racist verbal abuse occur? Let me suggest a partial answer by modifying a hypothetical situation I posed earlier.

Suppose a state legislature declared a "white supremacy day," perhaps invoking the descriptive and predictive terms of Justice Harlan's dissent in *Plessy v. Ferguson* as an ideal. ("The white race deems itself to be the dominant race in this country. And so it is. . . . So, I doubt not, it will continue for all time, if it remains true to its great heritage. . . .")[62] That would be a terrible thing, but would it be unconstitutional? I think it would be – but I also admit there is at least some doubt as to the answer. On the other hand, there is no doubt at all that state imposition of racial segregation in public facilities, even if they maintain perfect material equality, are unconstitutional. Yet by hypothesis the injury, the stigma of official racial insult, is the same in both cases – or, if anything, more explicit and obvious in the case of "white supremacy day." Why is segregation more obviously unconstitutional?

One answer: because the government delivers the insult with more force (and hence compounds the injury) when the action expressing the insult *does* something, even if the thing done is (apart from the insult) not itself discriminatory. We think of government as primarily an instrument for the maintenance of law and order and the provision of material public goods.[63] Its ideological centrality in our lives derives mainly from its role as the primary repository of legitimated power in society. It provides such a "bully pulpit" largely *because* it already has

---

[62] 163 U.S. 537, 559 (1896). Actual current controversies that raise this issue (though less starkly) include the continued official use by southern states of the Confederate flag.

[63] This isn't true of government in all societies; see Clifford Geertz, *Negara: The Theater State in Nineteenth Century Bali* (Princeton: Princeton University Press, 1980).

so firm a grip on our attention through its coercive powers of taxation and law enforcement.

For this reason, government speaks most clearly when its message is delivered through the exercise of one of those powers, such as the provision of schools, parks, and the like. We think of joint resolutions designating state flowers and mayoral proclamations of schoolteacher week as quite apart from the serious business of government. The adoption of a racist resolution or motto, then, though unconstitutional, would not be as obviously so as would, say, resegregating the seats in the courthouse. When the government acts – when it does something – it puts its money where its mouth is.

Similarly, when a university administration backs its anti-racist pronouncements with action, it puts *its* money where its mouth is. The action, if it is to serve this purpose, must be independently justifiable – independently, that is, of the symbolic purpose. Authorities make the most effective statement when they are honestly concerned to do something *beyond* making a statement. And the action of punishing persons who violate the Stanford harassment regulation *is* justifiable independent of the statement it makes. It provides a remedy for an action that causes real pain and harm to real individuals while doing no good, and it may serve to deter such actions in the future.

Notice that the idea of the "main business of government" advanced here is derived from the classical liberal conception of the state, which in turn lies at the heart of the civil-liberties approach. In that conception, government exists to prevent private force and fraud and to supply tangible public goods by taxing and spending. And that is basically *all* it is there for; its other functions are either suspect or "merely symbolic." Yet throughout this essay I have contrasted that conception of government to one implicit in the civil-rights approach, which undermines traditional public-private distinctions as well as denying the automatic association of "merely" with "symbolic" or "intangible" when discussing of the kind of effects law and government should be centrally concerned with.

And yet, at the end, I revert to slogans involving a distinction between real state action and mere gesture! The point is that neither the civil-liberties nor the civil-rights approach will go away; sometimes, as here, one of them even feeds on the other. With that suggestion of the sometimes paradoxical interweaving of these perspectives, incommensurably co-existing at the heart of modern liberalism, let me call a halt to this very limited examination of their mutual relations.

Law, Stanford University

RACIST SPEECH, DEMOCRACY, AND THE FIRST AMENDMENT

ROBERT C. POST*

The curse of racism continues to haunt the Nation. Everywhere we face its devastation, the bitter legacy of, in William Lloyd Garrison's prophetic words, our "covenant with death and . . . agreement with Hell."[1] This is the living consequence of the history that has produced us. We cannot overcome that history without changing ourselves and therefore also our legal order. Since *Brown v. Board of Education*[2] vast stretches of our law have passed through the flame of this challenge.[3] The question is always what to preserve, what to alter.

Now it is the turn of the first amendment. Largely inspired by Richard Delgado's article, *Words That Wound*,[4] the past few years have witnessed an extraordinary spate of articles analyzing the constitutionality of restrictions on racist speech.[5] This anal-

---

* Professor of Law, School of Law (Boalt Hall), University of California at Berkeley. B.A., Harvard College, 1969; J.D., Yale University, 1977; Ph.D., Harvard University, 1980. I am deeply indebted to the many friends and colleagues who read the manuscript of this essay: Alexander Aleinikoff, Richard Delgado, Melvin Eisenberg, Cynthia Fuchs Epstein, Bryan Ford, Angela Harris, Sanford Kadish, Kenneth Karst, Mari Matsuda, Frank Michelman, Martha Minow, Paul Mishkin, Rachel Moran, John Powell, Terrance Sandalow, Joseph Sax, Philip Selznick, Reva Siegel, Jerome Skolnick, Jan Vetter, James Weinstein, and Franklin Zimring.

1. D. DUMOND, ANTISLAVERY: THE CRUSADE FOR FREEDOM IN AMERICA 273 (1961) (quoting William Lloyd Garrison).

2. 347 U.S. 483 (1954).

3. For a representative discussion, see Fiss, *Foreword: The Forms of Justice*, 93 HARV. L. REV. 1 (1979).

4. Delgado, *Words That Wound: A Tort Action for Racial Insults, Epithets, and Name-Calling*, 17 HARV. C.R.-C.L. L. REV. 133 (1982) [hereinafter Delgado, *Words That Wound*]; see Heins, *Banning Words: A Comment on "Words That Wound*," 18 HARV. C.R.-C.L. L. REV. 585 (1983); Delgado, *Professor Delgado Replies*, 18 HARV. C.R.-C.L. L. REV. 593 (1983).

5. Delgado, *Campus Antiracism Rules: Constitutional Narratives in Collision*, 85 NW. U.L. REV. 343 (1990); Gale, *On Curbing Racial Speech*, RESPONSIVE COMMUNITY, Winter 1990-91, at 47; Glass, *Anti-Racism and Unlimited Freedom of Speech: An Untenable Dualism*, 8 CAN. J. PHIL. 559 (1978); Grano, *Free Speech v. the University of Michigan*, ACADEMIC QUESTIONS, Spring 1990, at 7; Greenawalt, *Insults and Epithets: Are They Protected Speech?*, 42 RUTGERS L. REV. 287 (1991); Grey, *Civil Rights vs. Civil Liberties: The Case of Discriminatory Verbal Harassment*, SOC. PHIL. & POL'Y, Spring 1991, at 81; Hughes, *Prohibiting Incitement to Racial Discrimination*, 16 U. TORONTO L.J. 361 (1966); Jones, *Article 4 of the International Convention on the Elimination of All Forms of Racial Discrimination and the First Amendment*, 23 HOW. L.J. 429 (1980); Kretzmer, *Freedom of Speech and Racism*, 8 CARDOZO L. REV. 445 (1987); *Language as Violence v. Freedom of Expression: Canadian and American Perspectives on Group Defamation*, 37 BUFFALO L.

ysis is not merely academic. Motivated by an alarming increase in racist incidents,[6] universities throughout the Nation have turned toward the task of restraining racist expression.[7] The justification for these restraints, and their relationship to first amendment values, has become a matter of intense controversy.[8]

One approach has been to attempt to use legal regulation to eradicate all visible signs of that "racist sentiment" which, in the view of some, our history has caused to "pervade[ ] the life of virtually all white Americans."[9] The rules of the University of

---

REV. 337 (1989) [hereinafter *Language as Violence*]; Lasson, *Racial Defamation as Free Speech: Abusing the First Amendment*, 17 COLUM. HUM. RTS. L. REV. 11 (1985) [hereinafter Lasson, *Racial Defamation*]; Lasson, *Group Libel Versus Free Speech: When Big Brother Should Butt In*, 23 DUQ. L. REV. 77 (1984) [hereinafter Lasson, *Group Libel*]; Lawrence, *If He Hollers Let Him Go: Regulating Racist Speech on Campus*, 1990 DUKE L.J. 431; Love, *Discriminatory Speech and the Tort of Intentional Infliction of Emotional Distress*, 47 WASH. & LEE L. REV. 123 (1990); Matsuda, *Public Response to Racist Speech: Considering the Victim's Story*, 87 MICH. L. REV. 2320 (1989); Minow, *On Neutrality, Equality, & Tolerance: New Norms for a Decade of Distinction*, CHANGE, Jan.-Feb. 1990, at 17; Partlett, *From Red Lion Square to Skokie to the Fatal Shore: Racial Defamation and Freedom of Speech*, 22 VAND. J. TRANSNAT'L L. 431 (1989); Richardson, *Racism: A Tort of Outrage*, 61 OR. L. REV. 267 (1982); Smolla, *Rethinking First Amendment Assumptions About Racist and Sexist Speech*, 47 WASH. & LEE L. REV. 171 (1990); Strossen, *Regulating Racist Speech on Campus: A Modest Proposal*, 1990 DUKE L.J. 484; Wedgwood, *Freedom of Expression and Racial Speech*, 8 TEL AVIV U. STUD. L. 325 (1988); Wright, *Racist Speech and the First Amendment*, 9 MISS. C. L. REV. 1 (1988); Note, *A Communitarian Defense of Group Libel Laws*, 101 HARV. L. REV. 682 (1988); Note, *The University of California Hate Speech Policy: A Good Heart in Ill-Fitting Garb*, 12 J. COMM. & ENT. L. 593 (1990); Comment, *Freedom From Fear*, 15 LINCOLN L. REV. 45 (1984) (authored by Kammy Au); Edelman, *Punishing Perpetrators of Racist Speech*, Legal Times, May 15, 1989, at 20.

6. *See, e.g.*, H. EHRLICH, CAMPUS ETHNOVIOLENCE AND THE POLICY OPTIONS 41-72 (1990); Gibbs, *Bigots in the Ivory Tower: An Alarming Rise in Hatred Roils U.S. Campuses*, TIME, May 7, 1990, at 104.

7. David Rieff writes that 137 American universities "have in the past two years passed proscriptions on hate speech." Rieff, *The Case Against Sensitivity*, 114 ESQUIRE 120, 124 (1990). *See Lessons From Bigotry 101*, NEWSWEEK, Sept. 25, 1989, at 48; Wilson, *Colleges' Anti-Harassment Policies Bring Controversy Over Free-Speech Issues*, Chronicle of Higher Educ., Oct. 4, 1989, at A1; Fields, *Colleges Advised to Develop Strong Procedures to Deal With Incidents of Racial Harassment*, Chronicle of Higher Educ., July 20, 1988, at A11.

8. For a chronicle of the effect of this controversy on the American Civil Liberties Union (ACLU), see Hentoff, *The Colleges: Fear, Loathing, and Suppression*, Village Voice, May 8, 1990, at 20; Hentoff, *What's Happening to the ACLU?*, Village Voice, May 15, 1990, at 20; Hentoff, *Putting the First Amendment on Trial*, Village Voice, May 22, 1990, at 24; Hentoff, *A Dissonant First Amendment Fugue*, Village Voice, June 5, 1990, at 16; Hentoff, *An Endangered Species: A First Amendment Absolutist*, Village Voice, June 12, 1990, at 24; Hentoff, *The Civil Liberties Shootout*, Village Voice, June 19, 1990, at 26; *Policy Concerning Racist and Other Group-Based Harassment on College Campuses*, ACLU NEWSL., Aug.-Sept. 1990, at 2.

9. J. KOVEL, WHITE RACISM: A PSYCHOHISTORY 34 (1970); *see* Lawrence, *The Id, the Ego, and Equal Protection: Reckoning with Unconscious Racism*, 39 STAN. L. REV. 317, 321-26 (1987).

Connecticut, for example, plainly evince this remarkable ambition. These rules prohibit "[b]ehavior that denigrates others because of their race [or] ethnicity."[10] They provide that the "use of derogatory names, inappropriately directed laughter, inconsiderate jokes, anonymous notes or phone calls, and conspicuous exclusion from conversations and/or classroom discussions are examples of harassing behaviors that are prohibited."[11] The rules list the "signs" of proscribed "Harassment, Discrimination and Intolerance," some of which are

> Stereotyping the experiences, background, and skills of individuals
> Treating people differently solely because they are in some way different from the majority
> Responding to behaviors or situations negatively because of the background of the participants . . .
> Imitating stereotypes in speech or mannerisms . . .
> Attributing objections to any of the above actions to "hypersensitivity" of the targeted individual or group.[12]

These rules are plainly not designed to regulate specific forms of behavior or expression, but rather to encompass and to forbid all exterior "signs" of an interior frame of mind. One can readily understand the logic of this purpose. If our "common historical and cultural heritage" has made us "all racists,"[13] then racism must be seen as an unredeemed form of identity, whose every manifestation ought to be challenged and sanctioned. Punitive legal regulations are thus faced with the task of attempting to imagine and specify every possible indication of racism. But because the racist personality can express itself in an infinite

---

10. Department of Student Affairs, University of Connecticut, Protect Campus Pluralism (available from the Dean of Students Office, University of Connecticut). The regulations provide that "[e]very member of the University is obligated to refrain from actions that intimidate, humiliate, or demean persons or groups or that undermine their security or self esteem." They define "harassment" as "abusive behavior directed toward an individual or group because of race, ethnicity, ancestry, national origin, religion, gender, sexual preference, age, physical or mental disabilities," and they prohibit "harassment that has the effect of interfering with an individual's performance or creating an intimidating, hostile or offensive environment." *Id.*

11. *Id.* The regulations continue: "All members of the University community are responsible for the maintenance of a positive environment in which everyone feels comfortable working and learning." *Id.*

12. *Id.* The regulations instruct a student to inform the "Discrimination and Intolerance Response Network" if "[y]ou have experienced or witnessed any of the signs" and to "[k]now that the University will not tolerate such behavior." *Id.*

13. Lawrence, *supra* note 9, at 322.

variety of ways, the task is intrinsically elusive. The University of Connecticut rules are clearly caught up in the frustrating spiral of this logic, a logic that, when carried to its conclusion, can end only in the complete legal subjugation of the individual.[14]

The incompatibility of this logic with even the most elementary standards of freedom of speech is obvious. Any communication can potentially express the racist self, and thus no communication can ever be safe from legal sanction. It is therefore no surprise that the University of Connecticut was forced to withdraw its regulations, although apparently with reluctance and distress, because of a threatened lawsuit.[15] If the ambition of legal regulation is to suppress manifestations of racist personality, the necessary consequence will be the wholesale abandonment of all principles of freedom of expression.

To the extent that we care about first amendment values, therefore, we must make do with more modest aspirations.[16] The possibility of effecting a reconciliation between principles of freedom of expression and restraints on racist speech depends upon deflecting our focus away from its spontaneous target, which is the racism of our cultural inheritance, and toward the redress of particular and distinct harms caused by racist expression. The specification of these harms will lead to the definition of discrete forms of speech, the legal regulation of which can then be assessed in light of relevant first amendment values.

---

14. One is reminded of the escalating efforts of the Inquisition in sixteenth-century Spain to discover and punish all external signs of inward backsliding on the part of Moors and Jews who had outwardly converted to Catholicism in order to avoid expulsion. These efforts eventually led the Inquisition to conclude that eating couscous or disliking pork were themselves punishable as heresy. *See* Root, *Speaking Christian: Orthodoxy and Difference in Sixteenth-Century Spain,* REPRESENTATIONS, Summer 1988, at 118, 126, 129.

15. Ravo, *Campus Slur Alters a Code Against Bias,* N.Y. Times, Dec. 11, 1989, at B1, B3.

16. Modest aspirations, however, will not be easy in the highly charged atmosphere of many universities. *See* Detlefsen, *White Like Me,* NEW REPUB., Apr. 10, 1989, at 18. The University of Connecticut is hardly unique in its use of punitive legal regulation to block all manifestations of racism. The Board of Regents of Higher Education of the Commonwealth of Massachusetts, for example, adopted on June 13, 1989 a "Policy Against Racism" that "prohibits all forms of racism." Board of Regents of Higher Education, Commonwealth of Massachusetts, Policy Against Racism and Guidelines for Campus Policies Against Racism 1 (June 13, 1989). This prohibition includes:

all conditions and all actions or omissions including all acts of verbal harassment or abuse which deny or have the effect of denying to anyone his or her rights to equality, dignity, and security on the basis of his or her race, color, ethnicity, culture, or religion. . . .

Racism in any form, expressed or implied, intentional or inadvertent, individual or institutional, constitutes an egregious offense to the tenets of human dignity and to the accords of civility guaranteed by law.

Id. at 2.

Such, in any event, will be the strategy of this essay. Its ambition is to be illustrative rather than comprehensive: the general issue of racist speech simply has too many facets to be encompassed by the small scope of this study. Although Part I attempts to isolate and describe five specific kinds of harm said to be caused by racist speech, Part II offers an account of only one of several possible relevant and important first amendment values, that of democratic self-governance. In my view this value is primarily responsible for the constitutional safeguards that currently protect public discourse. The major part of this essay, Part III, therefore addresses the narrow issue of the constitutionality of regulating public discourse to ameliorate specific harms caused by racist speech. Part IV then briefly compares the quite different constitutional issues posed by the regulation of racist speech within public institutions of higher learning.

One significant drawback of this analytic structure is that it renders the term "racist speech" into something of a cipher. As the University of Connecticut regulations illustrate, the term is inherently labile and ambiguous. It probably has as many different definitions as there are commentators, and it would be pointless to pursue its endlessly variegated shades of meaning. I have decided, therefore, to focus instead on the constitutional implications of specific justifications for restraining racist expression, and to let the term "racist speech" absorb the content implied by these various justifications.

I should add that writing this essay has been difficult and painful. I am committed both to principles of freedom of expression and to the fight against racism. The topic under consideration has forced me to set one aspiration against the other, which I can do only with reluctance and a heavy heart.

I. The Harms of Racist Speech

Even a brief survey of the contemporary debate reveals it to be rich with textured and complex characterizations of the harms of racist expression. It would be impossible within the limited scope of this essay to disentangle and evaluate each of the many harms suggested in this literature. It will therefore be necessary to group these harms into five rough categories that represent the most prominent lines of analysis and that are at the same time convenient for first amendment analysis.[17]

---

17. These categories by no means exhaust the field. The European literature, for

A. *The Intrinsic Harm of Racist Speech*

A recurring theme in the contemporary literature is that racist expression ought to be regulated because it creates what has been termed "deontic" harm.[18] The basic point is that there is an "elemental wrongness"[19] to racist expression, regardless of the presence or absence of particular empirical consequences such as "grievous, severe psychological injury."[20] It is argued that toleration for racist expression is inconsistent with respect for "the principle of equality"[21] that is at the heart of the fourteenth amendment.[22]

> The thrust of this argument is that a society committed to ideals of social and political equality cannot remain passive: it must issue unequivocal expressions of solidarity with vulnerable minority groups and make positive statements affirming its commitment to those ideals. Laws prohibiting racist speech must be regarded as important components of such expressions and statements.[23]

If the basic harm of racist expression lies in its intrinsic and symbolic incompatibility with egalitarian ideals, then the distinct class of communications subject to legal regulation will be defined by reference to those ideals. If the fourteenth amendment is thought to enshrine an antidiscrimination principle, then "any speech (in its widest sense) which supports racial prejudice or discrimination"[24] ought to be subject to regulation. If the relevant ideals are thought to embody substantive racial equality, then the relevant class of communications should be defined as speech containing a "message . . . of racial inferiority."[25]

---

example, contains a well-developed jurisprudence of regulating racist speech based upon the harm of potential violence. *See* Cotterrell, *Prosecuting Incitement to Racial Hatred*, 1982 PUB. L. 378; Kretzmer, *supra* note 5, at 456; Leopold, *Incitement to Hatred—The History of a Controversial Criminal Offense*, 1977 PUB. L. 389, 391-93. I do not discuss this category of harm because it is relatively unimportant in the American setting. I suspect that this is largely because of the accepted dominion of the *Brandenburg* version of the clear and present danger test. *See* Brandenburg v. Ohio, 395 U.S. 444, 447-49 (1969).

18. Wright, *supra* note 5, at 14-22.
19. *Id.* at 10.
20. *Id.* at 9.
21. Hughes, *supra* note 5, at 364.
22. Lawrence, *supra* note 5, at 438-49.
23. Kretzmer, *supra* note 5, at 456.
24. *Id.* at 454.
25. Matsuda, *supra* note 5, at 2357.

B. Harm to Identifiable Groups

A second theme in the current debate is that racist expression ought to be regulated because it harms those groups that are the target. There are two basic variations on this theme. One draws its inspiration from the tradition of group libel[26] and the decision of the Supreme Court in *Beauharnais v. Illinois.*[27] On this view speech likely to cast contempt or ridicule on identifiable groups ought to be regulated to prevent injury to the status and prospects of the members of those groups. A second variation derives from the more contemporary understanding of racism as "the structural subordination of a group based on an idea of racial inferiority."[28] Racist expression is viewed as especially unacceptable because it locks in the oppression of already marginalized groups: "Racist speech is particularly harmful because it is a mechanism of subordination, reinforcing a historical vertical relationship."[29]

If the prevention of group harm is the basis for the regulation of communication, the definition of legally proscribed speech will depend upon one's understanding of the nature of the group harm at issue and the way in which communication is seen as causing that harm. Regulation that derives from a theory of group defamation, for example, would tend to safeguard all groups,[30] whereas regulation that derives from a theory of subordinate groups would sanction only speech "directed against a historically oppressed group."[31]

C. Harm to Individuals

A third prominent theme in the contemporary literature is that racist expression harms individuals. This theme essentially analogizes racist expression to forms of communication that are regulated by the dignitary torts of defamation, invasion of privacy, and intentional infliction of emotional distress. The law

---

26. Riesman, *Democracy and Defamation: Control of Group Libel*, 42 Colum. L. Rev. 727 (1942).

27. 343 U.S. 250 (1952). For work in this vein, see Lasson, *Group Libel, supra* note 5; Lasson, *Racial Defamation, supra* note 5; Note, *Group Vilification Reconsidered*, 89 Yale L.J. 308 (1979).

28. Matsuda, *supra* note 5, at 2358.

29. *Id.*

30. *See, e.g.,* Lasson, *Racial Defamation, supra* note 5, at 48.

31. Matsuda, *supra* note 5, at 2357.

compensates persons for dignitary and emotional injuries caused by such communication, and it is argued that racist expression ought to be subject to regulation because it causes similar injuries. These injuries include "feelings of humiliation, isolation, and self-hatred,"[32] as well as "dignitary affront."[33] The injuries are particularly powerful because "racial insults . . . conjure up the entire history of racial discrimination in this country."[34] In Patricia Williams' striking phrase, racist expression is a form of "spirit-murder."[35]

Regulating racist expression because of its negative impact on particular persons would suggest that the class of communications subject to legal sanction be narrowed to those that are addressed to specific individuals or that in some other way can be demonstrated to have adversely affected specific individuals. The nature of that class would vary, however, depending upon the particular kind of harm sought to be redressed. If the focus is on preventing "dignitary harm,"[36] the injury might be understood to inhere in the very utterance of certain kinds of racist communications;[37] if the focus is instead on emotional damage, independent proof of distress might be required to sustain recovery.[38] Regulation will also vary depending upon whether harm to individuals is understood to flow from the ideational content of racist expression, or instead from its abusive nature.[39]

---

32. Delgado, *Words That Wound, supra* note 4, at 137.

33. *Id.* at 143.

34. *Id.* at 157.

35. Williams, *Spirit-Murdering the Messenger: The Discourse of Fingerpointing as the Law's Response to Racism,* 42 U. MIAMI L. REV. 127, 151 (1987).

36. Love, *supra* note 5, at 158.

37. Richard Delgado, for example, proposes that courts create a tort for racial insult whenever a plaintiff can prove that "[l]anguage was addressed to him or her by the defendant that was intended to demean through reference to race; that the plaintiff understood as intended to demean through reference to race; and that a reasonable person would recognize as a racial insult." Delgado, *Words That Wound, supra* note 4, at 179.

38. See, for example, the proposed regulation of The University of Texas at Austin, which prohibits racial harassment and which defines racial harassment "as extreme or outrageous acts or communications that are intended to harass, intimidate or humiliate a student or students on account of race, color, or national origin and that reasonably cause them to suffer severe emotional distress." President's Ad Hoc Committee on Racial Harassment, The University of Texas at Austin, Report of President's Ad Hoc Committee on Racial Harassment 4-5 (Nov. 27, 1989). The drafters of the proposed regulation state that it is "much preferable for a racial harassment policy to focus on the real injury of severe emotional distress." *Id.* at 20.

39. Compare, for example, the regulations of the University of Wisconsin, which reach "racist or discriminatory comments, epithets or other expressive behavior directed at an

D. Harm to the Marketplace of Ideas

A fourth theme in the current debate is that racist expression harms the very marketplace of ideas that the first amendment is designed to foster. A variety of different arguments have been brought forward to support this position. It is argued that racist expression ought to be "proscribed . . . as a form of assault, as conduct" inconsistent with the conditions of respect and noncoercion prerequisite to rational deliberation.[40] It is argued that racist expression is inconsistent with rational deliberation because it "infects, skews, and disables the operation of the market . . . . Racism is irrational and often unconscious."[41] Finally, it is argued that racism "systematically" silences "whole segments of the population,"[42] either through the "visceral" shock and "preemptive effect on further speech" of racist words,[43] or through the distortion of "the marketplace of ideas by muting or devaluing the speech of blacks and other non-whites."[44]

The class of communications subject to legal sanction would depend upon which of these various arguments is accepted. Depending upon exactly how racist expression is understood to damage the marketplace of ideas, the class might be confined to communication experienced as coercive and shocking, or it might be expanded to include communication perceived as unconsciously and irrationally racist, or it might be expanded still further to encompass speech explicitly devaluing and stigmatizing victim groups.

E. Harm to Educational Environment

Each of the four categories of harm so far discussed can be caused by racist expression within public discourse. There is,

---

individual." Board of Regents of the University of Wisconsin System, Wis. Admin. Code UWS § 17.06(2)(a) (Aug. 1989) (currently being challenged as a violation of the first amendment in UWM Post, Inc. v. Board of the Univ. of Wis. Sys., No. 90-C-0328 (E.D. Wis. filed Mar. 29, 1990)), with that of Stanford University, which reaches only racist speech that is "addressed directly to the individual or individuals whom it insults or stigmatizes" and that consists of "insulting or 'fighting' words." Stanford University, Fundamental Standard Interpretation: Free Expression and Discriminatory Harassment 2 (draft, Mar. 15, 1990).

40. Lasson, *Group Libel, supra* note 5, at 123. "The speech clause protects the marketplace of ideas, not the battleground." *Id.*

41. Lawrence, *supra* note 5, at 468.

42. *Id.* at 447 n.66 (quoting MacKinnon, *Not a Moral Issue,* 2 YALE L. & POL'Y REV. 321, 340 (1984)).

43. *Id.* at 452.

44. *Id.* at 470.

however, yet a fifth kind of harm which is quite important to the contemporary controversy, but which is relevant only to the specific educational environment of institutions of higher learning. This is the harm that racist expression is understood to cause to the educational mission of universities or colleges. The prevention of this harm is central to the definition of a great number of campus regulations.

Universities and colleges characteristically seek to regulate racist communications that "directly create a substantial and immediate interference with the educational processes of the University," without articulating exactly how racist expression can cause that interference.[45] Some campus regulations are more specific, focusing on the damage that racist expression is understood to cause to particular individuals or groups. For example, some regulations only proscribe racist expression that "will interfere with the victim's ability to pursue effectively his or her education or otherwise to participate fully in University programs and activities."[46] Presumably this interference will occur for reasons similar to those that we have already canvassed.

In a number of instances, however, college or university regulations enunciate special educational goals that are understood to be inherently incompatible with racist expression. For example, Mount Holyoke seeks to inculcate the value of diversity, which it views as plainly inconsistent with racist expression. Accordingly Mount Holyoke's regulations provide:

---

45. Office of Student Life Policy and Service, Rutgers University at New Brunswick, University Student Life Policy Against Insult, Defamation, and Harassment 1 (May 31, 1989) (revised); see also Doe v. University of Mich., 721 F. Supp. 852, 856 (E.D. Mich. 1989); Oberlin College, Policy on Race Relations and Informal Procedures for Racial Grievances; Office of the Dean for Student Affairs and the Special Assistants to the President, Massachusetts Institute of Technology, Information on Harassment (Sept. 1989); State University of New York College at Brockport, Discriminatory Harassment § 285.02; University of Pennsylvania, Harassment Policy (Almanac Supp., Sept. 29, 1987) (as published originally in the Almanac of June 2, 1987).

46. University of California, Universitywide Student Conduct: Harassment Policy (Sept. 21, 1989) (available from Office of the President). For an example of a regulation based upon group harm, see Clark University's Code of General Conduct: "Harassment includes any verbal or physical conduct which has the intent or effect of unreasonably interfering with any individual's or group's work or study, or creating an intimidating, hostile, or offensive environment." Clark University, Code of General Conduct and University Judicial Procedures 1 (Fall Semester 1988). For other examples of similar kinds of regulations, see Emory University, Policy Statement on Discriminatory Harassment; Marquette University, Racial Abuse and Harassment Policy (May 5, 1989); Office of University News and Information of Kent State University, Policy to Combat Harassment, For the Record, Vol. 5, No. 5 (Feb. 6, 1989).

> To enter Mount Holyoke College is to become a member of a
> community. . . .
>
>   . . . .
>
> Our community is committed to maintaining an environment
> in which diversity is not only tolerated, but is celebrated.
> Towards this end, each member of the Mount Holyoke com-
> munity is expected to treat all individuals with a common
> standard of decency.[47]

Marquette University defines itself "as a Christian and Catholic
institution . . . dedicated to the proposition that all human beings
possess an inherent dignity in the eyes of their Creator and
equality as children of God."[48] Accordingly Marquette's regulations seek to maintain "an environment in which the dignity and
worth of each member of its community is respected" and in
which "racial abuse or harassment . . . will not be tolerated."[49]
Mary Washington College sets forth what appears to be a secular
version of this same educational mission; its regulations provide
that the "goal of the College is to help all students achieve
academic success in an environment that nurtures, encourages
growth, and develops sensitivity and appreciation for all people."[50]
Accordingly "any activity or conduct that detracts from this
goal — such as racial or sexual harassment — is inconsistent with
the purposes of the college community."[51]

In such instances, racist expression interferes with education
not merely because of general harms that it may inflict on groups
or individuals or the marketplace of ideas,[52] but also, and more
intrinsically, because racist expression exemplifies conduct that
is contrary to the particular educational values that specific
colleges or universities seek to instill.[53]

---

47. Mount Holyoke College, The Honor Code: Academic and Community Responsibility
§ III, Community Responsibility, Introduction (reprinted from the Student Handbook).
48. Marquette University, Racial Abuse and Harassment Policy 1 (May 5, 1989).
49. Id.
50. Mary Washington College, Mary Washington College Student Handbook 20 (1990-
91) (available from Office of the Dean of Students).
51. Id.
52. "If the university stands for anything, it stands for freedom in the search for
truth. . . . [But] [c]an truth have its day in court when the courtroom is made into a
mud-wrestling pit where vicious epithets are flung?" Laney, Why Tolerate Campus Bigots?,
N.Y. Times, Apr. 6, 1990, at A35.
53. Thus James T. Laney, the President of Emory University, stated:
>   Educators are by definition professors of value. Through education we pass
>   on to the next generation not merely information but the habits and manners
>   of our civil society. The university differs from society at large in its
>   insistence on not only free expression but also an environment conducive to
>   mutual engagement.
Id.

II. The Values of the First Amendment

As any constitutional lawyer knows, first amendment doctrine is neither clear nor logical. It is a vast Sargasso Sea of drifting and entangled values, theories, rules, exceptions, predilections. It requires determined interpretive effort to derive a useful set of constitutional principles by which to evaluate regulations of expression. In recent years there has been an unfortunate tendency, by no means limited to the controversy surrounding racist speech, to avoid this difficult work by relying instead on formulaic invocations of first amendment "interests" which can be captured in such conclusory labels as "individual self-fulfillment," "truth," "democracy," and so forth.[54] These formulas cast an illusion of stability and order over first amendment jurisprudence, an illusion that can turn dangerous when it substitutes for serious engagement with the question of why we really care about protecting freedom of expression.

What is most disappointing about the expanding literature proposing restrictions on racist speech is the palpable absence of that engagement. The most original and significant articles in the genre concentrate on uncovering and displaying the manifold harms of racist communications; the harms of regulating expression are on the whole perfunctorily dismissed. Of course this emphasis is readily understandable. It is a formidable task to attempt to carve out a new exception to the general protection of speech afforded by the armor of first amendment doctrine. Even so staunch a defender of minority rights as Justice William Brennan might seem unsympathetic, given his recent observation in *United States v. Eichman*[55] that "virulent ethnic and religious epithets"[56] ought to receive constitutional protection because of the "'bedrock principle underlying the First Amendment . . . that the Government may not prohibit the expression of an idea simply because society finds the idea itself offensive or disagreeable.'"[57] In the face of such daunting obstacles, it is natural for

---

54. *See, e.g.,* Delgado, *Words That Wound, supra* note 4, at 175-79; Note, *A First Amendment Justification for Regulating Racist Speech on Campus,* 40 Case W. Res. 733 (1989-90).

55. 110 S. Ct. 2404 (1990).

56. *Id.* at 2410.

57. *Id.* (quoting Texas v. Johnson, 109 S. Ct. 2533, 2544 (1989)). See Brennan's remark in *Texas v. Johnson* to the same effect: "The First Amendment does not guarantee that . . . concepts virtually sacred to our Nation as a whole—such as the principle that discrimination on the basis of race is odious and destructive—will go unquestioned in the

proponents of restraints on racist speech to emphasize their affirmative case and to minimize countervailing considerations.

I agree, of course, that the question of regulating racist speech ought not to be settled simply by reference to present doctrine. But it is equally important that the question ought not to be settled without serious engagement with the values embodied in that doctrine. Regulations like those promulgated by the University of Connecticut and many other universities suggest that this lack of engagement is a real and practical problem.[58] Although earnest inquiry into the first amendment values involved in the restraint of racist speech cannot by itself definitively solve the difficult constitutional issues we face, it can at least illuminate what is most deeply at stake for us in this controversy, and to that extent clarify the choices we must make.

A. Democracy, Public Discourse, and the First Amendment

This essay concentrates on the relevance for the regulation of racist speech of only one strand of first amendment values. It is, however, an extraordinarily important strand, one which in my view accounts for a good deal of the shape of contemporary first amendment doctrine. It concerns the relationship between freedom of expression and democratic self-governance. Its basic thrust is to provide certain kinds of protection to communication deemed necessary for the processes of democracy, communication that the Court has labelled "public discourse."[59]

In protecting public discourse the first amendment serves the purposes of democracy, and the question at hand is what we believe those purposes to be. This is not a simple question. Even so powerful a first amendment theorist as Frederick Schauer can argue that "[a]ny distinct restraint on majority power, such as a

---

marketplace of ideas." *Johnson*, 109 S. Ct. at 2546. Brennan supported this remark by citing Brandenburg v. Ohio, 395 U.S. 444 (1969), in which the Court extended first amendment protection to a Ku Klux Klan rally featuring such revolting comments as: "Bury the n——s"; "A dirty n——r"; and "Send the Jews back to Israel." *Id.* at 446 n.1.

58. Charles Lawrence, for example, writes that the University of Michigan regulations recently invalidated by a federal court, see *supra* note 45, were so patently unconstitutional that "it is difficult to believe that anyone at the University of Michigan Law School was consulted" in their drafting. Lawrence, *supra* note 5, at 477 n.161. "It is almost as if the university purposefully wrote an unconstitutional regulation so that they could say to the black students, 'We tried to help but the courts just won't let us do it.'" *Id.* A great many contemporary university regulations are similar to those of the University of Michigan.

59. Hustler Magazine v. Falwell, 485 U.S. 46, 54 (1988).

principle of freedom of speech, is by its nature anti-democratic, anti-majoritarian."[60] If democracy means no more to us than that in each instance the majority ought to have its way, then of course Schauer is quite correct that speech comprising public discourse ought not for that reason to have any special exemption from majoritarian regulation.[61] But the underlying equation of democracy with the simple exercise of majority will is radically inadequate not only as an explanation of contours of contemporary doctrine, but also as an account of the normative attraction of democracy.[62]

A far more persuasive account is one that begins with

> the distinction between autonomy and heteronomy: democratic forms of government are those in which the laws are made by the same people to whom they apply (and for that reason they are autonomous norms), while in autocratic forms of government the law-makers are different from those to whom the laws are addressed (and are therefore heteronomous norms).[63]

This distinction between autonomy and heteronomy formed the basis of Hans Kelsen's definition of "democracy," which he viewed as a form of government resting on "the principle of self-determination."[64] The distinction is manifestly at the root of the Court's repudiation of seditious libel in *New York Times Co. v. Sullivan*,[65] which turned on Madison's differentiation of American and English forms of government: in England "the Crown was sovereign and the people were subjects," whereas in America "'[t]he people,

---

60. F. SCHAUER, FREE SPEECH: A PHILOSOPHICAL ENQUIRY 40 (1982). On the equation of democracy with majoritarianism, see A. DE TOCQUEVILLE, DEMOCRACY IN AMERICA 254 (F. Bowen trans. 1945): "The very essence of democratic government consists in the absolute sovereignty of the majority. . . ."

61. Schauer writes:

> The more we accept the premise of the argument from democracy, the less can we impinge on the right of self-government by restricting the power of the majority. If the argument from democracy would allow to be said things that the "people" do not want to hear, it is not so much an argument based on popular will as it is an argument against it.

F. SCHAUER, *supra* note 60, at 41.

62. The equation is nevertheless quite commonplace. *See, e.g.*, Partlett, *supra* note 5, at 458 (footnote omitted) ("I take it that a central tenet of democracy is majority rule. If the majority decides to suppress free speech, how can it be defended upon democratic lines?").

63. N. BOBBIO, DEMOCRACY AND DICTATORSHIP 137 (P. Kennealy trans. 1989).

64. H. KELSEN, GENERAL THEORY OF LAW AND STATE 284-86 (A. Wedberg trans. 1961).

65. 376 U.S. 254 (1964).

not the government, possess absolute sovereignty.'"[66] For this reason in America "'the censorial power is in the people over the Government, and not in the Government over the people.'"[67]

If democracy as a form of government is important to us because it embodies the value of self-determination, we must ask what it means for a collection of persons to decide governmental policy in a way that facilitates that value.[68] Kelsen answers the question in a way that begins with Rousseau's formulation in *The Social Contract*,[69] but that moves rapidly to a distinctively modern perspective:

> A subject is politically free insofar as his individual will is in harmony with the "collective" (or "general") will expressed in the social order. Such harmony of the "collective" and the individual will is guaranteed only if the social order is created by the individuals whose behavior it regulates. Social order means determination of the will of the individual. Political freedom, that is, freedom under social order, is self-determination of the individual by participating in the creation of the social order.[70]

Because it is unconvincing to imagine that the will of individuals can be "in harmony" with the general will in all matters of political moment, Kelsen ultimately locates the value of self-determination in the ability of persons to participate in the process by which the social order is created. He conceives that process as preeminently one of communication:

> The will of the community, in a democracy, is always created through a running discussion between majority and minority, through free consideration of arguments for and against a certain regulation of a subject matter. This discussion takes place not only in parliament, but also, and foremost, at political meetings, in newspapers, books, and other vehicles of public opinion. A democracy without public opinion is a contradiction in terms.[71]

---

66. *Id.* at 274 (quoting 4 ELLIOT'S DEBATES 569 (1876)) (citation omitted in original).

67. *Id.* at 275 (quoting 4 ANNALS OF CONGRESS 934 (1794)).

68. This is the central problematic of Alexander Meiklejohn's work. A. MEIKLEJOHN, POLITICAL FREEDOM: THE CONSTITUTIONAL POWERS OF THE PEOPLE 11 (1948). Meiklejohn was concerned to analyze "the difference between a political system in which men do govern themselves and a political system in which men, without their consent, are governed by others." *Id.*

69. J. ROUSSEAU, THE SOCIAL CONTRACT (C. Frankel trans. 1947).

70. H. KELSEN, *supra* note 64, at 285.

71. *Id.* at 287-88.

For Kelsen, then, democracy serves the principle of self-determination because it subjects the political and social order to public opinion, which is the product of a dialogic communicative exchange open to all. The normative essence of democracy is thus located in the communicative processes necessary to instill a sense of self-determination,[72] and in the subordination of political decisionmaking to those processes.

This logic is widely shared. It leads Benjamin Barber, for example, to conclude that "there can be no strong democratic legitimacy without ongoing talk."[73] It leads John Dewey to remark that "[d]emocracy begins in conversation."[74] It leads Durkheim to observe that "[t]he more that deliberation and reflection and a critical spirit play a considerable part in the course of public affairs, the more democratic the nation."[75] It leads Claude Lefort to claim that

> modern democracy invites us to replace the notion of a regime governed by laws, of a legitimate power, by the notion of a regime founded upon *the legitimacy of a debate as to what is legitimate and what is illegitimate* — a debate which is necessarily without any guarantor and without any end.[76]

In fact the notion that self-determination requires the maintenance of a structure of communication open to all commands a wide consensus. Jürgen Habermas characterizes that structure as determined by the effort to attain "a common will, communicatively shaped and discursively clarified in the political public sphere."[77] John Rawls views it as a process of "reconciliation through public reason."[78] Frank Michelman regards it as the practice of "jurisgenerative politics" through the "dialogic 'modulation' of participants' pre-political understandings."[79] For all three thinkers the goal of the structure is to facilitate the

---

72. For a good discussion of this point, see Freeman, *Reason and Agreement in Social Contract Views*, 19 PHIL. & PUB. AFF. 122, 154-57 (1990).

73. B. BARBER, STRONG DEMOCRACY: PARTICIPATORY POLITICS FOR A NEW AGE 136 (1984); *see* Pitkin & Shumer, *On Participation*, DEMOCRACY, Fall 1982, at 43, 43-54.

74. DIALOGUE ON JOHN DEWEY 58 (C. Lamont ed. 1959).

75. E. DURKHEIM, PROFESSIONAL ETHICS AND CIVIC MORALS 89 (C. Brookfield trans. 1958).

76. C. LEFORT, DEMOCRACY AND POLITICAL THEORY 39 (D. Macey trans. 1988).

77. 2 J. HABERMAS, THE THEORY OF COMMUNICATIVE ACTION 81 (T. McCarthy trans. 1987).

78. Rawls, *Justice as Fairness: Political not Metaphysical*, 14 PHIL. & PUB. AFF. 223, 230 (1985).

79. Michelman, *Law's Republic*, 97 YALE L.J. 1493, 1526-27 (1988).

attainment of "agreement" that is "uncoerced, and reached by citizens in ways consistent with their being viewed as free and equal persons."[80]

Coercion is precluded from public debate because the very purpose of that debate is the practice of self-determination. The goal is "agreement" (or the attainment of "a common will") because in such circumstances the individual will is by hypothesis completely reconciled with the general will. It is important to understand, however, that this goal is purely aspirational. In fact, it is precisely because absolute agreement can never actually be reached that the debate which constitutes democracy is necessarily "without any end," and hence must be independently maintained as an ongoing structure of communication.

Without this structure, the simple kind of majoritarian rule Schauer equates with democracy loses its grounding in the principle of self-determination and merely represents the heteronomous submission of a minority to the forceful command of a majority. With such a structure in place, on the other hand, both majority and minority can each be understood to have had the opportunity freely to participate within a "system"[81] of communication upon which the legitimacy of all political arrangements depends. Whether that opportunity will actually establish the value of autonomous self-determination for both majority and minority is a complex and contingent question, dependent upon specific historical circumstances. But, in the absence of that opportunity, realization of the value of autonomous self-determination will be precluded under conditions characteristic of the modern state.[82]

The first amendment principles that this essay considers are those that function to safeguard from majoritarian interference this structure of public discourse, so that our democracy will be able to serve the end of collective self-determination. Four aspects of that structure require emphasis, for they will be of importance when we subsequently examine in detail the regulation of racist speech.

---

80. Rawls, *supra* note 78, at 229-30; *see* 1 J. HABERMAS, THE THEORY OF COMMUNICATIVE ACTION 25-26 (T. McCarthy trans. 1984); Michelman, *supra* note 79, at 1526-27.

81. Fiss, *supra* note 3, at 38.

82. I do not mean to foreclose the possibility that, under special conditions of charismatic leadership or identification with traditional authority, the value of self-determination can be achieved in the absence of a communicative structure of public discourse. I mean only to imply that such conditions will not ordinarily obtain in the modern rational and bureaucratic state.

First, the function of public discourse is to reconcile, to the extent possible, the will of individuals with the general will. Public discourse is thus ultimately grounded upon a respect for individuals seen as "free and equal persons."[83] In the words of Jean Piaget,

> The essence of democracy resides in its attitude towards law as a product of the collective will, and not as something emanating from a transcendent will or from the authority established by divine right. It is therefore the essence of democracy to replace the unilateral respect of authority by the mutual respect of autonomous wills.[84]

The individualism so characteristic of first amendment doctrine[85] thus flows directly from the central project of democracy.[86]

Second, some form of public/private distinction is necessarily implied by democracy understood as a project of self-determination. This is because the state undermines the *raison d'être* of its own enterprise to the extent that it itself coercively forms the "autonomous wills" that democracy seeks to reconcile into public opinion.[87] If the adjective "private" is understood to designate that which is beyond the coercive formation of the state, public discourse must be conceptualized as a process through which "private" perspectives are transformed into public power.

Third, democracy is on this account inherently incomplete. This is because the "autonomous wills" postulated by democratic the-

---

83. Rawls, *supra* note 78, at 230.

84. J. PIAGET, THE MORAL JUDGMENT OF THE CHILD 366 (M. Gabain trans. 1948).

85. *See* Post, *Cultural Heterogeneity and Law: Pornography, Blasphemy, and the First Amendment*, 76 CALIF. L. REV. 297, 314-24 (1988).

86. See, for example, Kateb, *Democratic Individuality and the Claims of Politics*, 12 POL. THEORY 331, 332 (1984):

> To speak, therefore, of individualism is to speak of the most characteristically democratic political and moral commitment. It would be a sign of defection from modern democracy to posit some other entity as the necessary or desirable center of life. There is therefore nothing special (much less, arbitrary) in assuming that the doctrine of the individual has the preeminent place in the theory of democracy.

87. *See, e.g.*, Bowers v. Hardwick, 478 U.S. 186, 205-06 (1986) (Blackmun, J., dissenting). Such a public/private distinction must, of course, be understood as inherently unstable and problematic, for all government regulation influences, to one degree or another, the formation of individual identity. *See, e.g.*, Sunstein, *Legal Interference with Private Preferences*, 53 U. CHI. L. REV. 1129, 1138-39 (1986). For this reason, the distinction should be regarded as a pragmatic instrument for distinguishing those aspects of the self considered indispensable for the exercise of political and moral autonomy, and hence as beyond the coercive formation of the state.

ory do not and cannot appear *ex nihilo*. The only reason that a person possesses a personality capable of autonomous choice is because the person has internalized "the institutions of [the] community into his own conduct."[88] This process of socialization, which is prerequisite for personal identity, is not itself a matter of independent election, but rather is attributable to accidents of birth and acculturation. Democracy thus necessarily presupposes important (not to say foundational) aspects of the social world organized along nondemocratic lines. For this reason public discourse must always exist in tension with other forms of communication ("nonpublic speech").

Fourth, democracy, like all forms of government, must ultimately be capable of accomplishing the tasks of governance. As Alexander Meiklejohn notes, "Self-government is nonsense unless the 'self' which governs is able and determined to make its will effective."[89] Democratic governments must therefore have the power to regulate behavior. But because public discourse is understood as the communicative medium through which the democratic "self" is itself constituted, public discourse must in important respects remain exempt from democratic regulation. We use the speech/action distinction to mark the boundaries of this exemption. Because all "[w]ords are deeds,"[90] this distinction is purely pragmatic. We designate the communicative processes necessary to sustain the principle of collective self-determination "speech" and thus insulate it from majoritarian interference.

B. *Community, Civility Rules, and Public Discourse*

Restraints on racist speech characteristically involve certain general first amendment issues that I briefly review in this Section in light of the functional concerns of public discourse. In so doing I confine myself to summarizing conclusions, the detailed arguments for which I have developed elsewhere.[91]

If democratic self-governance presupposes a social world in which "autonomous wills" are to be coordinated and reconciled,

---

88. G. MEAD, MIND, SELF & SOCIETY 162 (C. Morris ed. 1934).

89. A. MEIKLEJOHN, *supra* note 68, at 14.

90. L. WITTGENSTEIN, CULTURE AND VALUE 46e (P. Winch trans. 1980).

91. *See generally* Post, *The Constitutional Concept of Public Discourse: Outrageous Opinion, Democratic Deliberation, and* Hustler Magazine v. Falwell, 103 HARV. L. REV. 601 (1990) [hereinafter Post, *The Constitutional Concept*]; Post, *The Social Foundations of Defamation Law: Reputation and the Constitution*, 74 CALIF. L. REV. 691 (1986) [hereinafter Post, *Defamation Law*]; Post, *The Social Foundations of Privacy: Community and Self in the Common Law Tort*, 77 CALIF. L. REV. 957 (1989) [hereinafter Post, *Privacy*].

there is an important form of social organization, which I call "community," that rests on exactly the opposite presupposition. Building on the work of Michael Sandel,[92] I define a "community" as a social formation that inculcates norms into the very identities of its members. So far from being considered autonomous, persons within a community are understood to depend, for the very integrity and dignity of their personalities, upon the observance of these norms.

For hundreds of years an important function of the common law has been to safeguard the most important of these norms, which I call "civility rules." These rules apply to communication as well as to action, and their enforcement lies at the foundation of such communicative torts as defamation,[93] invasion of privacy,[94] and intentional infliction of emotional distress.[95] Through these torts the common law not only protects the integrity of the personality of individual community members, but it also serves authoritatively to articulate a community's norms and hence to define a community's identity.

There is an obvious tension between community and democracy. Public discourse within a democracy is legally conceived as the communicative medium through which individuals choose the forms of their communal life; public discourse within a community is legally conceived as a medium through which the values of a particular life are displayed and enacted.[96] Democracy seeks to open the space of public discourse for collective self-constitution; community seeks to bound that space through the enforcement of civility rules. In the inevitable negotiation between democracy and community, the first amendment has, since the 1940's, generally served the purposes of democracy by suspending the enforcement of civility rules in such landmark cases as *Cantwell v. Connecticut*,[97] *New York Times Co. v. Sullivan*,[98] *Cohen v. California*,[99] and *Hustler Magazine v. Falwell*.[100]

---

92. *See* M. SANDEL, LIBERALISM AND THE LIMITS OF JUSTICE (1982).

93. *See* Post, *Defamation Law, supra* note 91, at 699-719.

94. *See* Post, *Privacy, supra* note 91, at 959-87.

95. *See* Post, *The Constitutional Concept, supra* note 91, at 616-46.

96. *See, e.g., id.* at 627-33.

97. 310 U.S. 296 (1940).

98. 376 U.S. 254 (1964).

99. 403 U.S. 15 (1971).

100. 485 U.S. 46 (1988). The American first amendment is unique in thus separating democracy from community. I suspect that the origins of this separation lie both in our tradition of individualism and in the fact of our cultural diversity. For instructive

There is, however, a complex and reciprocal relationship between democracy and community. Democracy necessarily presupposes some form of social institution, like community, through which the concrete identities of "autonomous" democratic citizens can be defined and instantiated. The paradigmatic examples of such institutions are the family and the elementary school. In these settings a child's identity is created in the first instance through decidedly undemocratic means; it "comes to be by way of the internalization of sanctions that are de facto threatened and carried out."[101]

This fact has important consequences for the practice of public discourse. The specific purpose of that discourse is the achievement of some form of "reconciliation through public reason,"[102] yet because the identity of democratic citizens will have been formed by reference to community norms, speech in violation of civility rules will characteristically be perceived as both irrational and coercive.[103] This creates what I have elsewhere termed the "paradox of public discourse": the first amendment, in the name of democracy, suspends legal enforcement of the very civility rules that make rational deliberation possible.[104] The upshot of the paradox is that the separation of public discourse from community depends in some measure upon the spontaneous persistence of civility. In the absence of such persistence, the use of legal regulation to enforce community standards of civility may be required as an unfortunate but necessary option of last resort. A paradigmatic example of this use may be found in the "fighting words" doctrine of *Chaplinsky v. New Hampshire*.[105]

If community norms thus infiltrate and make possible the practice of democracy, so the ethical imperatives of democracy can be expected to reshape the terms of community life. A stable and successful democratic state will regulate the lives of its citizens in ways consistent with the underlying principle of "their being viewed as free and equal persons."[106] Such regulation will influence community institutions, moving them closer toward the

---

contrasts, see Jacobsohn, *Alternative Pluralisms: Israeli and American Constitutionalism in Comparative Perspective*, REV. POL., Spring 1989, at 159; Kommers, *The Jurisprudence of Free Speech in the United States and the Federal Republic of Germany*, 53 S. CAL. L. REV. 657 (1980).

101. 2 J. HABERMAS, *supra* note 77, at 38.
102. Rawls, *supra* note 78, at 230.
103. Post, *The Constitutional Concept, supra* note 91, at 641-44.
104. *Id.*
105. 315 U.S. 568 (1942).
106. Rawls, *supra* note 78, at 230.

realization of specifically democratic principles. The only intrinsic limitation on the ability of the democratic state to regulate community institutions in this manner is the public/private distinction, which requires that at some point the coercive formation of the identity of individuals remain beyond the purview of the state.

C. The Domain of Public Discourse

This essay primarily concerns the regulation of racist expression within public discourse. "Public discourse" may be defined as encompassing the communicative processes necessary for the formation of public opinion, whether or not that opinion is directed toward specific government personnel, decisions, or policies. Democratic self-governance requires that public opinion be broadly conceived as a process of "collective self-definition"[107] that will necessarily precede and inform any specific government action or inaction. Public discourse cannot encompass all communication within a democracy, however, because both the public/private distinction and the paradox of public discourse imply that the processes of democratic self-governance depend upon the persistence of other nondemocratic forms of social organization, such as community.

Because the first amendment extends extraordinary protection to public discourse, it is important to demarcate the boundary between such discourse and other speech. I have discussed this issue in detail elsewhere[108] and will not repeat that analysis here. Suffice it to say that the boundary is inherently uncertain and subject to perennial reevaluation. Factors that the Supreme Court has used to delineate the boundary include the content of speech and the manner of its dissemination.[109] Speech that can be said to be about matters of "public concern" is ordinarily classified as public discourse,[110] as is speech that is widely distributed to the public at large through the mass media. There are exceptions, however, like commercial speech, which flow from the influence of traditional conventions that define for us a recognizable "genre" of public speech.[111]

---

107. Pitkin, *Justice: On Relating Private and Public*, 9 Pol. Theory 327, 346 (1981).
108. *See* Post, *The Constitutional Concept*, *supra* note 91, at 667-84.
109. *Id.* at 667.
110. *Id.*
111. *Id.* at 680.

It is difficult to discuss profitably the abstract question of setting the boundaries of public discourse. At the most general level, these boundaries mark the point at which our commitment to the dialogue of autonomous self-governing citizens shifts to other values, as for example to that of the socially implicated self characteristic of community. The particular points at which our commitments alter is a highly specific and contextual inquiry requiring case-by-case assessment.

I confine myself, therefore, to two preliminary observations. First, the constitutional protections extended to public discourse differ importantly from those extended to nonpublic speech. Thus even if the first amendment were to immunize from legal regulation the circulation of certain racist ideas in newspapers, it would not follow that the expression of those same ideas could not be restrained by the government within the workplace, where an image of dialogue among autonomous self-governing citizens would be patently out of place.[112] The first amendment values at stake in the regulation of nonpublic speech are complex and diverse,[113] and I will not be able to review them within the limited span of this essay.

Second, the category of racist expression cannot be excluded as such from the domain of public discourse. The racist content of a particular communication is only one of many factors relevant to the determination of whether the communication lies within or without of that domain. Thus the leaflet at issue in *Beauharnais v. Illinois*,[114] which was an effort "to petition the mayor and council of Chicago to pass laws for segregation,"[115] was plainly

---

112. *See, e.g.,* Rogers v. EEOC, 454 F.2d 234, 237-38 (5th Cir. 1971), *cert. denied,* 406 U.S. 957 (1972); EEOC v. Murphy Motor Freight Lines, 488 F. Supp. 381, 385 (D. Minn. 1980); *cf.* Meritor Sav. Bank v. Vinson, 477 U.S. 57, 65-66 (1986) (holding that speech that constitutes sexual harassment may be regulated). I do not mean to imply, however, that *all* speech within the workplace is excluded from public discourse. *See, e.g.,* Connick v. Myers, 461 U.S. 138, 149 (1983); Givhan v. Western Line Consol. School Dist., 439 U.S. 410, 415-16 (1979).

113. It should be emphasized that in text I am using the adjective "public" in a discrete and stipulative sense to refer to that speech necessary for democratic self-governance. Thus I do not mean to imply that speech within the workplace is "nonpublic" in the sense that it is unimportant, or that it is "private" in the sense of being intrinsically insulated from governmental control or regulation. *See* Karst, *Private Discrimination and Public Responsibility: Patterson in Context,* 1989 SUP. CT. REV. 1, 10-11; *supra* text accompanying notes 106-11. My point is instead that if the regulation of nonpublic speech is in fact protected by the first amendment, it will be on the basis of constitutional values other than democratic self-governance.

114. 343 U.S. 250 (1952). The leaflet is reproduced in Justice Black's dissenting opinion. *Id.* at 276 (Black, J., dissenting).

115. *Id.* at 267 (Black, J., dissenting).

an effort to engage in public discourse, despite its overt and virulent racism. Similarly, the infamous Nazi march in Skokie was also an attempt to participate in public discourse, notwithstanding its repulsive political symbolism.[116] In both cases racists used well-recognized media for the communication of ideas in order to address and affect public opinion.[117]

III. Racist Speech and Public Discourse

We are now in a position to assess the justifications for the regulation of racist expression in light of the first amendment values associated with public discourse. In some cases this assessment allows us to reach definite conclusions; in others it simply helps to clarify the issues raised by particular forms of regulation. In each case I use the term "racist speech" to encompass the class of communications that would have to be regulated in order to ameliorate the specific harm under consideration.

A. Public Discourse and the Intrinsic Harm of Racist Ideas

It is of course a commonplace of first amendment jurisprudence "that the government must remain neutral in the marketplace of ideas."[118] The justification for this principle as applied to public discourse is straightforward. Democracy serves the value of self-determination by establishing a communicative structure within which the varying perspectives of individuals can be reconciled through reason. If the state were to forbid the expression of a particular idea, the government would become, with respect to individuals holding that idea, heteronomous and nondemocratic. This is incompatible with a form of government predicated upon treating its citizens "in ways consistent with their being viewed as free and equal persons."[119]

For this reason the value of self-determination requires that public discourse be open to the opinions of all. "[S]ilence coerced by law—the argument of force in its worst form"[120] is constitu-

---

116. *See* Collin v. Smith, 447 F. Supp. 676 (N.D. Ill.), *aff'd*, 578 F.2d 1197 (7th Cir.), *cert. denied*, 439 U.S. 916 (1978).

117. To exclude from public discourse the category of racist speech as such would be equivalent to establishing a per se exclusion of racist ideas from public discourse, a form of regulation whose constitutionality is assessed in Section III(A), *infra*.

118. Hustler Magazine v. Falwell, 485 U.S. 46, 56 (1988) (quoting FCC v. Pacifica Found., 438 U.S. 726, 745-46 (1978)).

119. Rawls, *supra* note 78, at 230.

120. Whitney v. California, 274 U.S. 357, 375-76 (1927) (Brandeis, J., concurring).

tionally forbidden. In a democracy, as Piaget notes, "there are no more crimes of opinion, but only breaches of procedure. All opinions are tolerated so long as their protagonists urge their acceptance by legal methods."[121] The notion that racist ideas ought to be forbidden within public discourse because of their "elemental wrongness"[122] is thus fundamentally irreconcilable with the rationale for first amendment freedoms.

The contemporary debate nevertheless contains three distinct arguments that racist ideas ought to be proscribed because of their "deontic" harm. The first is that the idea of racism is "*sui generis*" because it is "universally condemned."[123] The same authors who make this claim, however, also stress "the structural reality of racism in America," a reality manifested not merely in an "epidemic of racist incidents," but also in the widespread racist beliefs characteristic of "upper-class whites" and important social "institutions."[124] In fact it is probably fair to characterize these authors as proponents of regulating racist speech precisely because of their urgent sense of the *prevalence* of racist practices. Although the nightmare of these practices ought to occasion strong public response, their prevalence substantially undermines the conclusion that racism is "universally condemned"[125] in any sense relevant for first amendment analysis. Such practices can be understood only as manifestations of strongly held but otherwise unarticulated racist ideas.[126]

A second argument is that the failure to regulate racist ideas amounts to a symbolic endorsement of racist speech, which is intolerable in "a society committed to ideals of social and political equality."[127] In essence this argument rejects the public/private

---

121. J. PIAGET, *supra* note 84, at 57; *see id.* at 63.

122. Wright, *supra* note 5, at 10.

123. Matsuda, *supra* note 5, at 2359; *see* Kretzmer, *supra* note 5, at 458.

124. Matsuda, *supra* note 5, at 2332-34. "Racist hate messages are rapidly increasing and are widely distributed in this country using a variety of low and high technologies." *Id.* at 2336. Kretzmer is also concerned with the potential spread of racist ideas. *See* Kretzmer, *supra* note 5, at 464-65.

125. *See supra* note 123 and accompanying text.

126. I thus do not reach the theoretically more fundamental question of why it should make a constitutional difference that racist ideas are "universally condemned." See, for example, the Court's rejection in United States v. Eichman, 110 S. Ct. 2404, 2409 (1990), of the Solicitor General's invitation to overrule Texas v. Johnson, 109 S. Ct. 2533 (1989), on the grounds of "Congress' recent recognition of a purported 'national consensus' favoring a prohibition on flag-burning. . . . Even assuming such a consensus exists, any suggestion that the Government's interest in suppressing speech becomes more weighty as popular opposition to that speech grows is foreign to the First Amendment." *Eichman*, 110 S. Ct. at 2409.

127. Kretzmer, *supra* note 5, at 456; *see* Matsuda, *supra* note 5, at 2338:

distinction required by democratic self-governance.[128] But if responsibility for ideas advanced by individuals in public discourse were to be attributed to government, the government could not then also be deemed *responsive* to those ideas in the way required by the principle of self-determination. Just as a library could not function if it were understood as endorsing the views of the authors whose books it collects and displays, so also in a democracy the government could not serve the value of autonomy if it were understood as endorsing the ideas expressed by private persons in public discourse.[129]

A third argument is that the free expression of racist ideas is inconsistent with our commitment to the egalitarian ideals of the fourteenth amendment. At root this argument rejects autonomy as the principal value of democracy and substitutes instead what Kenneth Karst has eloquently argued is "the substantive center of the fourteenth amendment: the principle of equal citizenship."[130] Although some political theorists have endorsed this position,[131] it runs against the overwhelming American commitment to the importance of "self-rule," to the fundamental belief "that the American people are politically free insomuch as they are governed by themselves collectively."[132]

Of course the principle of self-rule contains its own commitment to the value of equal citizenship, to the notion that, as a formal matter, citizens must be "viewed as free and equal persons."[133] But the meaning of this commitment is measured by the purpose of enabling the processes of self-determination. The appeal to the fourteenth amendment, on the other hand, is meant to signify

---

However irrational racist speech may be, it hits right at the emotional place where we feel the most pain. The aloneness comes not only from the hate message itself, but also from the government response of tolerance. When hundreds of police officers are called out to protect racist marchers, when the courts refuse redress for racial insult, ... the victim becomes a stateless person. Target-group members can either identify with a community that promotes racist speech, or they can admit that the community does not include them.

128. Matsuda, *supra* note 5, at 2378.

129. *See* Greenawalt, *supra* note 5, at 304-05.

130. Karst, *Citizenship, Race, and Marginality,* 30 WM. & MARY L. REV. 1, 1 (1988).

131. *See, e.g.,* N. BOBBIO, *supra* note 63, at 157-58; C. GOULD, RETHINKING DEMOCRACY: FREEDOM AND COOPERATION IN POLITICS, ECONOMY, AND SOCIETY 90 (1988); J. PENNOCK, DEMOCRATIC POLITICAL THEORY 3-161 (1979).

132. Michelman, *supra* note 79, at 1500-01. Michelman notes that "no earnest, non-disruptive participant in American constitutional debate is quite free to reject" this "belief." *Id.* at 1500.

133. Rawls, *supra* note 78, at 230.

commitment to a substantive value of equality that is not defined by reference to this purpose, so that the implementation of the value may adversely affect processes of self-determination.[134] The argument thus envisions the possibility of "balancing" fourteenth amendment values against first amendment principles.

In balancing the value of equal citizenship against the principle of self-determination, however, we must ask who is empowered to interpret the meaning of the highly contestable value of equal citizenship. To the extent that the value of equal citizenship is used to justify limiting public discourse, the interpreter of the value cannot be the people, because the very function of the appeal to the fourteenth amendment is to truncate the communicative processes by which the people clarify their collective will.[135] In such circumstances the Ultimate Interpreter, whoever or whatever it may finally turn out to be, must impose its will without popular accountability. Our government currently contains no such Interpreter, not even the Supreme Court, whose constitutional decisions are always shadowed by the potential of constitutional amendment or political reconstruction through subsequent appointments. The impossibility of locating such an Interpreter suggests the difficulties that attend the argument from the fourteenth amendment.[136]

B. Public Discourse and Harm to Identifiable Groups

The purpose of public discourse is to reconcile through reason the differences occasioned by a collection of "autonomous wills." Groups neither reason nor have an autonomous will; only persons do. This is the source of the profound individualism that characterizes first amendment doctrine. The question is whether that

---

134. See, for example, *Language as Violence, supra* note 5, at 360 (remarks of Mari Matsuda):

> I use the principle of equality as a starting point. . . . [I]f I were to give primacy to any one right, and if I were to create a hierarchy, I would put equality first, because the right of speech is meaningless to people who do not have equality. I mean substantive as well as procedural equality.

135. That members of minority groups are now embraced within the circle of the people and afforded the formal equality required by first amendment processes of self-determination is not, of course, due to any principle of the first amendment, but rather to the principle of equal citizenship embodied in the fourteenth amendment. In this fundamental sense, therefore, no hierarchical relationship between the first and fourteenth amendments can exist.

136. For fuller consideration of a sophisticated argument for "balancing" the values of the fourteenth amendment against those of the first, see *infra* text accompanying notes 210-19.

individualism is compatible with the regulation of public discourse in order to prevent harm to groups.

It is rather common for the laws of other countries to restrain speech deemed harmful to groups, speech that, in the words of the Illinois statute at issue in *Beauharnais*, casts "contempt, derision, or obloquy" on a particular group.[137] Such laws subordinate individual expression to the protection of group status and dignity, typically on the theory that group membership is an essential ingredient of personal identity. Hence, as Gary Jacobsohn notes in his description of Israeli law, groups are seen "as units whose corporate identity carries with it . . . claim[s] upon the state for specific entitlement."[138] Thus the law will in certain situations give "greater priority to fraternal and communal attachments over the subjective choices of individuals."[139]

In American law, by contrast, there is a tendency to view groups as mere "collections of individuals,"[140] whose claims are no greater than those of their constituent members.[141] This tendency is virtually fixed by the individualist presuppositions of public discourse. Thus in *Cantwell v. Connecticut*[142] the Court extended first amendment protection to an anti-Catholic diatribe so violent that it "would offend not only persons of that persuasion, but all others who respect the honestly held religious faith of their fellows."[143] The Court reasoned that this constitutional immunity was necessary so that "many types of life, character, opinion and belief can develop unmolested and unobstructed."[144] This reasoning presupposes that groups evolve through the informed choices of individuals.[145] The Court subordinated the sen-

---

137. Beauharnais v. Illinois, 343 U.S. 250, 251 (1952) (citing ILL. REV. STAT. ch. 38, ¶ 471 (1949)). Antiblasphemy regulations are a common example of such laws. *See* Post, *supra* note 85, at 305-17; THE LAW COMMISSION, OFFENCES AGAINST RELIGION AND PUBLIC WORSHIP 39-53 (Working Paper No. 79, 1981). Many countries also have laws prohibiting group defamation. *See, e.g.*, E. BARENDT, FREEDOM OF SPEECH 161-67 (1985); Lasson, *Group Libel, supra* note 5, at 88-89; Matsuda, *supra* note 5, at 2341-48.

138. Jacobsohn, *supra* note 100, at 175.

139. *Id.* at 170.

140. *Id.* at 175.

141. *See, e.g.*, City of Richmond v. J.A. Croson Co., 488 U.S. 469 (1989).

142. 310 U.S. 296 (1940).

143. *Id.* at 309.

144. *Id.* at 310.

145. For an excellent study of the efforts of contemporary Americans to forge new communities, like the Castro district in San Francisco, and hence to "reinvent themselves" by constructing "new lives, new families, even new societies," see F. FITZGERALD, CITIES ON A HILL: A JOURNAL THROUGH CONTEMPORARY AMERICAN CULTURES 23 (1986). FitzGerald views such efforts as "quintessentially American": try to imagine, she suggests, "Parisians

sibilities of members of established groups, such as Catholics, to the communicative structure necessary for these choices.[146] It thus refused to allow unattractive and highly offensive representations of the Church to be excluded from public discourse.

Cantwell makes special sense because American religious groups have since the nineteenth century been organized on the principle of "voluntarism,"[147] on the notion that "religion is . . . a matter of individual choice."[148] It might be argued, however, that race is quite another matter, one in which a certain kind of group identity is inescapably imposed upon a person by accident of birth. For this reason group identity might be seen as primary with respect to race, and the individualist foundations of public discourse—the assumption that racial groups are determined by processes of individual decisionmaking—repudiated as unrealistic.

This argument is powerful and requires close attention. In analyzing it, we can draw on the distinction that has emerged in feminist writings between "sex," which refers to biological facts, and "gender," which refers to socially constructed roles.[149] To confuse the two, to predicate the social content of gender upon the biological fact of sex, is to fall into "the determinist or essentialist trap."[150] The political point of the distinction is to keep perpetually open for discussion and analysis the social meaning of being born female and included within the group "women."[151] Even if one is not free to opt out of the group, the possibility ought nevertheless to be preserved that the identity of the group be ultimately determined, in the language of Nancy Fraser, "through dialogue and collective struggle."[152] Fraser writes that "[i]n a society as complex as ours, it does not seem to me wise or even possible to extrapolate" the outcome of that dialogue

---

creating a gay colony or a town for grandparents." *Id.* If in Europe or Canada group identity precedes the attempt to ask "the essential questions of who we . . . are, and how we ought to live," *id.* at 20, 389-90, FitzGerald's work illustrates the extent to which group identity in America tends to follow on that attempt, and hence ultimately to rest on individualist premises.

146. For a more detailed discussion, see Post, *supra* note 85, at 319-35.

147. *See* P. MILLER, THE LIFE OF THE MIND IN AMERICA 40-43 (1965).

148. R. BELLAH, R. MADSEN, W. SULLIVAN, A. SWIDLER, & S. TIPTON, HABITS OF THE HEART: INDIVIDUALISM AND COMMITMENT IN AMERICAN LIFE 225 (1985).

149. *See, e.g.,* D. RHODE, JUSTICE AND GENDER 5 (1989); Marcus, *Reflections on the Significance of the Sex/Gender System: Divorce Law Reform in New York,* 42 U. MIAMI L. REV. 55, 55-63 (1987).

150. Marcus, *supra* note 149, at 61; *see* Harris, *Race and Essentialism in Feminist Legal Theory,* 42 STAN. L. REV. 581 (1990).

151. *See* Harris, *supra* note 150, at 615-16.

152. Fraser, *Toward a Discourse Ethic of Solidarity,* 5 PRAXIS INT'L 425, 429 (1986).

"from the current, prepoliticized experiences and idiolects of women, especially since it is likely, in my view, that these will turn out to be the current prepoliticized experiences and idiolects only of *some* women."[153]

Fraser's point is that regardless of the biological basis of sex, the social meaning of gender is a political issue whose outcome, like that of all political issues, must be regarded as indeterminate. She thus applies the structure of democratic self-determination to the constitution of group identity. The individualist assumptions of that structure create a form of communication in which political indeterminacy is preserved; they guarantee that the dialogue envisioned by Fraser will remain open to the perspectives of *all* women. If the identity of the group "women" were understood to have a content determinate enough to employ the force of law to silence dissenting views, the law would hegemonically impose the perspective of only *some* women.

The same logic, I believe, holds true for racial groups. We must distinguish race as a biological category from race as a social category. Even if unfortunately "the attempt to establish a *biological* basis of race has not been swept into the dustbin of history,"[154] it would nevertheless be deplorable to construct first amendment principles on the basis of a biological view of race. What is most saliently at issue is rather "race as a social concept": "The effort must be made to understand race as *an unstable and 'decentered' complex of social meanings constantly being transformed by political struggle.*"[155] To the extent that the social meaning of race is thus profoundly controversial[156] — and it is controversial not merely for members of minority groups but also for the entire Nation[157] — the individualist premises of public

---

153. *Id.*

154. M. OMI & H. WINANT, RACIAL FORMATION IN THE UNITED STATES: FROM THE 1960s TO THE 1980s 59 (1986). For an example of the persistence of a biological model of race, see Herrnstein, *Still an American Dilemma*, PUB. INTEREST, Winter 1990, at 3.

155. M. OMI & H. WINANT, *supra* note 154, at 60, 68. Omi and Winant write of the "continuous temptation to think of race as an *essence*, as something fixed, concrete and objective." *Id.* at 68; *see* Appiah, *The Uncompleted Argument: Du Bois and the Illusion of Race*, in H. GATES, "RACE," WRITING AND DIFFERENCE 36 (1986): "Talk of 'race' is particularly distressing for those of us who take culture seriously. . . . What exists 'out there' in the world — communities of meaning, shading variously into each other in the rich structure of the social world — is the province not of biology but of hermeneutic understanding."

156. For a good example, see Scales-Trent, *Black Women and the Constitution: Finding Our Place, Asserting Our Rights*, 24 HARV. C.R.-C.L. L. REV. 9 (1989).

157. For a brief history of the interdependence of understandings of national identity

discourse will ensure that it remains open to democratic constitution.

This lack of closure may of course be threatening, for it casts the creation of group identity upon the uncertain currents of public discourse. The safe harbor of legal regulation may, by contrast, appear to promise members of minority groups more secure control over the meaning of their social experience. But that promise is illusory, for it is profoundly inconsistent with the analysis of racism prevalent in the contemporary literature. To the extent that racism is viewed as pervasive among whites, and to the extent that whites, as a dominant group, can be expected to hold the levers of legal power, there would seem little reason to trust the law to establish socially acceptable meanings for race. Such meanings cannot be determined by reference to easy or bright-line distinctions, as for example those between positive or negative ascriptions of group identity. The work of figures as diverse as William Julius Wilson,[158] Shelby Steele,[159] and Louis Farrakhan[160] illustrates how highly critical characterizations of racial groups can nevertheless serve constructive social purposes. To vest in an essentially white legal establishment the power to discriminate authoritatively among such characterizations and purposes would seem certain to be disempowering.[161]

---

and understandings of race, see Gleason, *American Identity and Americanization*, in W. PETERSEN, M. NOVAK, & P. GLEASON, CONCEPTS OF ETHNICITY 57 (1982). A small but I suspect paradigmatic example of this interdependence may be found in the following passage from a student letter to *The Daily Californian*:

> Advertising, television, schools and government are areas of society where racism is largely promoted. Its existence is not easily eradicated. Phrases like "blackmail," "black ball" and "black mood" are common ways "blackness" is communicated in negative terms. . . . One of my professors frequently employs terms like "black lie" to mean the worst of all lies. It takes a conscious effort to disregard these statements and prevent such negative influence on one's psyche. But we must understand that daily use of this terminology reinforces the attack on African-American identity and value.

Broughton, *Promote Afro-American Culture*, The Daily Californian, Sept. 12, 1989, at 4. The writer's point is relevant to the perspectives of members of *both* minority and majority groups; in fact the point effectively demonstrates the essential reciprocity of these perspectives.

158. Wilson, *Social Research and the Underclass Debate*, BULL. AM. ACAD. ARTS & SCI., Nov. 1989, at 30.

159. S. STEELE, THE CONTENT OF OUR CHARACTER: A NEW VISION OF RACE IN AMERICA (1990).

160. See *Black Power, Foul and Fragrant*, ECONOMIST, Oct. 12, 1985, at 25, for a summary of Farrakhan's critical assessment of the condition of many African-Americans.

161. Note, in this regard, Nadine Strossen's evidence that regulations of racist speech have historically proved to be "particularly threatening to the speech of racial and political minorities." Strossen, *supra* note 5, at 556-59.

The conclusion that group harm ought not to justify legal regulation is reflected in technical first amendment doctrine in the fact that virtually all communications likely to provoke a claim of group harm will be privileged as assertions of evaluative opinion.[162] The following language, for example, gave rise to legal liability in *Beauharnais*: "If persuasion and the need to prevent the white race from becoming mongrelized by the negro will not unite us, then the aggressions . . . rapes, robberies, knives, guns and marijuana of the negro, SURELY WILL."[163] Justice Frankfurter interpreted this language as a false factual assertion: "No one will gainsay that it is libelous falsely to charge another with being a rapist, robber, carrier of knives and guns, and user of marijuana."[164] This interpretation, however, seems plainly incorrect. To accuse an individual of using marijuana is to assert that she has committed certain specific acts, but to accuse the group "blacks" of using marijuana is not to make an analogous assertion. Some blacks will have used marijuana, and most will not have. The question is thus not the existence of certain specific acts, but rather whether those acts can appropriately be used to characterize the group. The fundamental issue is the nature of the group's identity, an issue that almost certainly ought to be characterized as one of evaluative opinion.

Because the social meaning of race is inherently controversial, most statements likely to give rise to actions for group harm will be negative assessments of the identity of racial groups, and hence statements of evaluative opinion. No serious commentator would advocate a trial to determine the truth or falsity of such statements; the point is rather that such statements should not be made at all because of the deep injury they cause. But in a context in which group identity is a matter for determination through political struggle and disagreement, the hypostatized injury of a group cannot, consistent with the processes that instantiate the principle of self-determination, be grounds to legally silence characterizations of group identity within public discourse.

---

162. Or, in the language that the Court recently proposed in Milkovich v. Lorain Journal Co., 110 S. Ct. 2695 (1990), claims of group harm will most likely be privileged as nonfactual assertions of "ideas." For a discussion of the first amendment distinction between fact and ideas, see Post, *The Constitutional Concept, supra* note 91, at 649-61. For a discussion of the close relationship between group defamation and nonfactual ideas. see D. RICHARDS, TOLERATION AND THE CONSTITUTION 190-93 (1986); Greenawalt, *supra* note 5, at 305-06.

163. Beauharnais v. Illinois, 343 U.S. 250, 276 (1952) (ellipsis in original).

164. *Id.* at 257-58.

Commentators who stress the theme of group harm vigorously emphasize the fact that racist speech does not injure random groups; it damages precisely those groups who have historically suffered egregious oppression and subordination.[165] But although the tragedy of this fact is obvious, its constitutional implications are not. Our history certainly warrants the assumption that racist speech will inflict terrible injuries on victim groups. But the question is whether these injuries are so unspeakable as to justify suspending the democratic constitution of group identities. One approach might be to avoid this tension by characterizing the injuries of racist speech in such a way that their legal redress would actually be required by the principles of public discourse. Thus it can be argued that the stigmatizing and disabling effects of racist speech effectively exclude its victims from participation in public discourse. This approach suggests an important line of analysis, but I wish to defer consideration of it until Section III(D), *infra*, when it can be placed in the context of other justifications for restraints on racist speech that turn on harms to the marketplace of ideas.

Another method of avoiding the tension between group harm and democratic principles would be to claim that racist speech ought to be characterized as a "mechanism of subordination" within a larger system of suppression, rather than as a form of communication.[166] This claim requires us to determine the criteria by which speech can be designated as action and hence excluded from public discourse. The standard implicitly advanced by the claim is that if communication is intimately connected to larger social relationships that are deeply undesirable, the communication can for that reason be characterized as action.

The difficulty with this standard is that all communication grows out of and embodies social relationships; for this reason all communication is both speech and action. The function of public discourse is to create a protected space within which communication, even if embodying social relationships, can be protected as speech if formulated and disseminated in ways relevant for democratic self-governance. Such a space opens up the possibility of subjecting social relationships to rational reflection, dialogue, and (hence) *self*-control. It thus enables "self-rule" to be reconciled with rule "by laws."[167] If communication

---

165. *See, e.g.,* Matsuda, *supra* note 5, at 2358.
166. *Id.*
167. Michelman, *supra* note 79, at 1501.

could be excluded from this space because it embodies social relations of which we disapprove, public discourse could no longer perform this function. There is no difference between excluding speech from public discourse because we condemn the social relationships it embodies and excluding speech from public discourse because we condemn the ideas by which those social relationships are embodied. In the end, therefore, the argument that racist speech is a form of action reduces to the claim, which we have already considered, that racist speech ought to be restrained because of its inconsistency with the egalitarian ideals of the fourteenth amendment.

C. Public Discourse and Harm to Individuals

There appear at first blush to be important differences between claims of group harm and claims of individual harm. To the extent group identity is understood to be a matter of political struggle (and hence dialogic interaction), speech containing negative ascriptions of that identity cannot be censored without undermining the democratic nature of that struggle. But individual identity does not seem to rest on political struggle and dialogue in this way. Indeed, one's spontaneous image is of fully formed individuals entering the realm of public discourse to reach agreement on issues that concern their collective, rather than personal, lives. Speech damaging personal life can thus be restricted without undercutting the very purposes of public discourse.

This perspective, however, rests on a rather sharp distinction between individual and collective identity, a distinction that simply cannot be maintained. The very reason that racist speech harms individual persons is because it so violently ruptures the forms of social respect that are necessary for the maintenance of individual personality. These forms of respect, when taken together, constitute a collective, community identity. Hence the state can prevent the individual harm caused by racist speech only by enforcing pertinent standards of community identity. The interdependence of individual and collective identity is thus presupposed in the very concept of individual harm.

This interdependence lies behind well-established constitutional prohibitions on restricting public discourse because it is "offensive"[168] or "outrageous,"[169] or because it affronts "dignity"

---

168. Cohen v. California, 403 U.S. 15, 16 (1971).
169. Hustler Magazine v. Falwell, 485 U.S. 46, 52 (1988).

or is "insulting" or causes "public odium" or "public disrepute."[170] Such speech causes intense individual suffering because it violates community norms, yet the Court has required its toleration in order to prevent the state from using the authority of law to enforce particular conceptions of collective life.[171]

Questions of personal identity are in fact always at stake in discussions of collective self-definition. For this reason effective political dialogue requires that participants be constantly willing to be transformed. As Frank Michelman points out, public discourse is impossible so long as "the participants' pre-political self-understandings and social perspectives must axiomatically be regarded as completely impervious to the persuasion of the process itself."[172] As our collective aspirations change, so will our respective personal identities. Thus restrictions on public discourse designed to protect those identities from harm will necessarily also restrict self-determination as to our collective life. If group harm is an inevitable price of the political constitution of group identity, individual injury is an unavoidable cost of the political constitution of community identity.

It is important to emphasize the narrowness of this conclusion. In recent years an important theme of our national life has been the opposition to racism. We have enacted that opposition by legally regulating racist behavior like discrimination. Because action both creates and manifests identity, this regulation inhibits the formation and expression of racist identities. So also does regulation prohibiting certain kinds of racist speech in nonpublic speech, as for example in the workplace.[173] In effect we have determined to use government force to reshape community institutions in order to combat racism. This is an appropriate and laudable use of democratic power.[174] But it is legitimate precisely

---

170. Boos v. Barry, 485 U.S. 312, 316, 322 (1988). "[I]n public debate our own citizens must tolerate insulting, and even outrageous, speech in order to provide 'adequate breathing space to the freedoms protected by the First Amendment.' " *Id.* at 322 (quoting *Hustler Magazine*, 485 U.S. at 56); *see* Texas v. Johnson, 109 S. Ct. 2533, 2543-47 (1989).

171. I elaborate on this argument in Post, *The Constitutional Concept, supra* note 91, at 626-46. The cases cited in notes 168-70 *supra* thus stand foursquare against the application to public discourse of the tort of racial insult as proposed by Delgado, *supra* note 4, Love, *supra* note 5, and Wright, *supra* note 5.

172. Michelman, *supra* note 79, at 1526; *see* F. CUNNINGHAM, DEMOCRATIC THEORY AND SOCIALISM 188-91 (1987).

173. *See supra* notes 112-13 and accompanying text.

174. It should be noted, however, that the public/private distinction necessary for democratic governance will require that at some point limitations be placed on the ability of the state coercively to form citizens with nonracist identities. *See supra* note 87.

because we have adopted it in a manner consistent with the principle of self-determination; it reflects a national identity that we have freely chosen.

This legitimacy is possible because of public discourse, which serves the value of self-determination because it is so structured that every call for national identity has the opportunity to make its case. There is a significant difference, therefore, between proscribing racial insults directed toward individuals in the workplace[175] and proscribing them in a political discussion or debate.[176] The harm to the individual victim may be the same, but for public discourse to enable *self*-government, racist speech within that discourse must be repudiated on the merits, rather than be silenced by force of law.

D. Public Discourse and Harm to the Marketplace of Ideas

The most effective arguments for regulating racist speech are those that double back on the concept of public discourse itself and contend that such regulation is necessary for public discourse truly to instantiate the principle of self-determination. On the surface there appear to be two distinct lines of analysis. The first stresses the irrational and coercive qualities of racist speech; the second the untoward effects of racist speech in silencing victim groups. In the end these lines of argumentation cross and depend upon each other.

1. Racist Speech as Irrational and Coercive

Public discourse must be more than simply a register of private preferences in order to serve as a medium for the enactment of collective autonomy. If persons communicated in public discourse merely through polling organizations to make known their "votes" on public issues, democracy would degenerate into the heteronomous system of majoritarian rule described by Schauer. The purposes of collective self-determination require instead that public action be founded upon a public opinion formed through open and interactive processes of rational deliberation. The argument that racist speech is irrational and coercive, that it is

---

175. *See, e.g.*, Contreras v. Crown Zellerbach Corp., 88 Wash. 2d 735, 565 P.2d 1173 (1977); Alcorn v. Anbro Eng'g, 2 Cal. 3d 493, 468 P.2d 216, 86 Cal. Rptr. 88 (1970); Love, *supra* note 5, at 128-33.

176. *Cf.* Dominguez v. Stone, 97 N.M. 211, 638 P.2d 423 (1981) (penalizing racist speech in political speech).

nothing more than a kind of "linguistic abuse (verbal abuse on an unwilling target),"[177] thus cuts to the very root of public discourse.

The argument, however, points to a more general problem, for all communication that violates civility rules is perceived as both irrational and coercive.[178] Because civility rules embody the norms of respect and reason we are accustomed to receive from members of our community, communication inconsistent with those rules is experienced as an instrument "of aggression and personal assault."[179] The argument from coercion and irrationality thus poses a generic dilemma for first amendment doctrine. If the state were permitted to enforce civility rules, it would in effect exclude from public discourse those whose speech advocated and exemplified unfamiliar and marginalized forms of life. But if the state were to suspend the enforcement of civility rules, it would endanger the possibility of rational deliberation by permitting the dissemination of abusive and coercive speech. This tension between the requirement that self-government respect all of its citizens "as free and equal persons," and the requirement that self-government proceed through processes of rational deliberation, creates the paradox of public discourse.[180]

It might be thought that the specific case of racist speech dissolves this paradox, for such speech by hypothesis violates norms of both equality and civility and hence appears to be suppressible without harm to public discourse. But this conclusion is not accurate. The principle of equality at issue in the paradox of public discourse is purely formal; its extension to all persons

---

177. Lasson, *Group Libel, supra* note 5, at 122.

178. Thus "fighting words" are understood to be those that "by their very utterance inflict injury." Chaplinsky v. New Hampshire, 315 U.S. 568, 572 (1942). Outrageous words intentionally inflicting emotional distress are "nothing more than a surrogate" for a "punch or kick." Wright, Hustler Magazine v. Falwell *and the Role of the First Amendment,* 19 Cumb. L. Rev. 19, 23 (1988). "Ridicule" is experienced as a form of "intimidation." Dewey, *Creative Democracy—The Task Before Us,* in Classic American Philosophers 389, 393 (M. Fisch ed. 1951). Pornography is received not as "expression depicting the subordination of women, but [as] the *practice of subordination* itself." Brest & Vandenberg, *Politics, Feminism, and the Constitution: The Anti-Pornography Movement in Minneapolis,* 39 Stan. L. Rev. 607, 659 (1987). And blasphemous communications are nothing more than a form of "brawls." F. Holt, The Law of Libel 70-71 (1816).

179. Time, Inc. v. Hill, 385 U.S. 374, 412 (1967) (Fortas, J., dissenting). Alexander Bickel once remarked that such communication "amounts to almost physical aggression." A. Bickel, The Morality of Consent 72 (1975); *see also* Cohen v. California, 403 U.S. 15, 27 (1971) (Blackmun, J., dissenting) (characterizing Cohen's actions as being more like conduct than speech).

180. *See supra* text accompanying notes 91-105.

is the fundamental precondition of the possibility of self-government. To the extent that the principle is circumscribed, so also
is the reach of self-determination. The norm of equality violated
by racist speech, on the other hand, is substantive; it reflects a
particular understanding of how we ought to live. It is the kind
of norm that ought to emerge from processes of public deliberation. Although the censorship of racist speech is consistent with
this substantive norm of equality, it is inconsistent with the
formal principle of equality, because such censorship would exclude from the medium of public discourse those who disagree
with a particular substantive norm of equality. Such persons
would thus be cut off from participation in the processes of
collective self-determination.

First amendment doctrine has tended to resolve the paradox
of public discourse in favor of the principle of formal equality,
largely because violations of that principle limit pro tanto the
domain of self-government, whereas protecting uncivil speech
does not automatically destroy the possibility of rational deliberation. The visceral shock of uncivil speech can sometimes
actually serve constructive purposes, as when it causes individuals to question the community standards into which they have
been socialized and hence enables them, perhaps for the first
time, to acknowledge the claims of others from radically different
cultural backgrounds.[181] There is in fact a long tradition of oppressed and marginalized groups using uncivil speech to force
recognition of the intensity and urgency of their needs.[182]

Tolerating uncivil speech, moreover, does not necessarily undermine the process of rational deliberation, so long as the extent
of such speech is confined and does not infect the process as a

---

181. Thus in *Terminiello v. Chicago*:

> [A] function of free speech under our system of government is to invite
> dispute. It may indeed best serve its high purpose when it induces a condition
> of unrest, creates dissatisfaction with conditions as they are, or even stirs
> people to anger. Speech is often provocative and challenging. It may strike
> at prejudices and preconceptions and have profound unsettling effects as it
> presses for acceptance of an idea. That is why freedom of speech, though
> not absolute . . . is nevertheless protected against censorship or punishment,
> unless shown likely to produce a clear and present danger of a serious
> substantive evil that rises far above public inconvenience, annoyance, or
> unrest. . . . There is no room under our Constitution for a more restrictive
> view. For the alternative would lead to standardization of ideas either by
> legislatures, courts, or dominant political or community groups.

337 U.S. 1, 4-5 (1949) (citations omitted).

182. For an excellent discussion, see Karst, *Boundaries and Reasons: Freedom of
Expression and the Subordination of Groups*, 1990 U. ILL. L. REV. 95.

whole. The judgment that rational deliberation can continue in spite of the presence of uncivil speech is exactly the point of Harlan's opinion in *Cohen v. California*,[183] in which the Court refused to permit the state to use the force of law "to maintain . . . a suitable level of discourse within the body politic":[184]

> The constitutional right of free expression is powerful medicine in a society as diverse and populous as ours. It is designed and intended to remove governmental restraints from the arena of public discussion, putting the decision as to what views shall be voiced largely into the hands of each of us, in the hope that use of such freedom will ultimately produce a more capable citizenry and more perfect polity and in the belief that no other approach would comport with the premise of individual dignity and choice upon which our political system rests. . . .
>
> To many, the immediate consequence of this freedom may often appear to be only verbal tumult, discord, and even offensive utterance. These are, however, within established limits, in truth necessary side effects of the broader enduring values which the process of open debate permits us to achieve. That the air may at times seem filled with verbal cacophony is, in this sense not a sign of weakness but of strength.[185]

It is of course a matter of judgment whether "open debate" within "the arena of public discussion" is indeed achieving "broader enduring values." How one makes that judgment will depend very much on one's circumstances. The call in recent literature to attend more carefully to "the victim's perspective"[186] is well taken in this regard. Members of dominant groups may be satisfied with the overall quality of public deliberation, but members of victim groups, at whom racist speech is systematically targeted, may feel quite otherwise.

It is at this point that the line of analysis stressing the irrational, coercive quality of racist speech crosses and depends upon the line of analysis stressing the silencing of victim groups. For when pressed the point is not that public discourse is pervasively disabled by racist speech, but rather that the concentrated effect of such speech on members of victim groups is to foreclose public discourse as an effective avenue of collective

---

183. 403 U.S. 15.
184. *Id.* at 23.
185. *Id.* at 24-25.
186. Matsuda, *supra* note 5, at 2340; *see* Lawrence, *supra* note 5, at 436.

self-determination. In the contemporary debate this effect has been addressed under the rubric of "silencing."

2. Racist Speech as Silencing Minority Groups

The literature on silencing has burgeoned. So far as I can make out the literature presents three distinct arguments to support the concept of silencing:[187] victim groups are silenced because their perspectives are systematically excluded from the dominant discourse;[188] victim groups are silenced because the pervasive stigma of racism systematically undermines and de-values their speech; and victim groups are silenced because the visceral "fear, rage, [and] shock" of racist speech systematically preempts response.[189] This Section analyzes each of these arguments separately; the following Section weaves them together into a more complex indictment of racist speech.

The first argument, more developed in the context of recent feminist literature than in that of racist speech, is that the language of public discourse, although seemingly neutral and objective, has a built-in bias that prevents the articulation of minority positions.[190] Thus racism in the dominant discourse is compressed into "the neutralized word 'discrimination,' " in which "the role of power, domination, and oppression as the source of the evil" is effaced, and "[m]uch of the political, historical, and moral content of 'equality' has been dropped."[191] Similarly, the understanding of whites that racism is an "intentional belief in white supremacy"—the perpetrators' perspective—has been folded into the very language of public debate, whereas the understanding of minorities that racism " 'refers *solely* to minority subordination' "—the victims' perspective—is banished from the language.[192]

Although the premise of this argument seems to me true, it does not by itself support the conclusion that racist speech ought

---

187. I omit discussion of speech that silences through outright intimidation and threats. The regulation of such speech is not problematic under any theory.

188. For a good introduction to the concept of "discourse," see Bové, *Discourse*, in CRITICAL TERMS FOR LITERARY STUDY 50 (F. Lentricchia & T. McLaughlin eds. 1990).

189. Lawrence, *supra* note 5, at 452.

190. *Id.* at 474-75; *see* Crenshaw, *Race, Reform, and Retrenchment: Transformation and Legitimation in Antidiscrimination Law,* 101 HARV. L. REV. 1331, 1370-81 (1988).

191. Finley, *Breaking Women's Silence in Law: The Dilemma of the Gendered Nature of Legal Reasoning,* 64 NOTRE DAME L. REV. 886, 889 (1989).

192. Note, *Racism and Race Relations in the University,* 76 VA. L. REV. 295, 304 n.32 (1990) (quoting Brooks, *Anti-Minority Mindset in the Law School Personnel Process: Toward an Understanding of Racial Mindsets,* 5 J.L. & INEQUALITY 1, 8-11 (1987)).

to be regulated. All communication rests on foundations of unarticulated assumptions. The very function of dialogue is often to move toward enlightenment by uncovering and exposing these assumptions. Enlightenment can be gradual and progressive, or it can result from the shock of intense political struggle. That our language always encompasses both more and less than our intentions is thus not an argument for the suppression of racist speech, but rather for the encouragement of further public debate.

The point might be made, however, that public debate fails to achieve such enlightenment because the pervasive racism of American society devalues and stigmatizes minority contributions to this debate. The voice of the victims goes unheard. There is thus a call for an "outsider jurisprudence"[193] which will legitimate that voice and enable "[l]egal insiders . . . [to] imagine a life disabled in a significant way by hate propaganda."[194]

Once again, the premise of this argument appears sound, but its conclusion does not. Audiences always evaluate communication on the basis of their understanding of its social context.[195] This is not a deformity of public discourse, but one of its generic characteristics.[196] It poses the question of how an audience's prepolitical understanding of social context may be altered, a question that confronts all participants in public dialogue. The urgency of the question does not justify restricting public discourse; it is rather a call for more articulate and persuasive speech, for more intense and effective political engagement.

Taken together, the argument from the inherent bias of accepted discourse and the argument from the stigmatic devaluation of minority speech fuse into a single indictment of public discourse as irrational. The systematic derogation of the specific perspectives of victim groups is said to be caused by the Nation's particular history of racial oppression, rather than by concerns that would properly affect a legitimately rational public dialogue. Both arguments thus ultimately appeal to the concept of false consciousness,[197] to the notion that there is an ideal vantage from

---

193. Matsuda, *supra* note 5, at 2323-26.

194. *Id.* at 2375; *see* Lawrence, *supra* note 5, at 458-61.

195. Riesman, *Democracy and Defamation: Fair Game and Fair Comment II*, 42 COLUM. L. REV. 1282, 1306-07 (1942).

196. *See* P. CHEVIGNY, MORE SPEECH: DIALOGUE RIGHTS AND MODERN LIBERTY 53-72 (1988); Michelman, *Conceptions of Democracy in American Constitutional Argument: The Case of Pornography Regulation*, 56 TENN. L. REV. 291, 313 (1989).

197. For a general discussion of the concept of "false consciousness," see R. GEUSS, THE IDEA OF A CRITICAL THEORY: HABERMAS AND THE FRANKFURT SCHOOL (1981).

which the rationality of discourse can be "objectively" assessed.

But it is one thing to use the idea of false consciousness as a weapon *within* public discourse to convince others of the need to break with the prejudices of the past, and it is quite another to use the idea as a justification to limit public discourse itself. The first is a familiar rhetorical strategy. It is consistent with the processes of public discourse because its effectiveness ultimately depends upon its persuasive power. The second, however, presupposes an intimacy with truth so vital as to foreclose opposing positions. The very point of using the idea of false consciousness to limit public discourse is to justify legally disregarding certain perspectives, on the grounds that these perspectives could not possibly be respected as true expressions of autonomous individuality. Circumscribing public discourse to ameliorate false consciousness thus does not protect public discourse from harm, but rather contradicts its very purpose of providing a medium for the reconciliation of autonomous wills.

The third argument for restraining racist speech does not turn on the characterization of public discourse as irrational, but rather as coercive. Recent literature contains searing documentation of the profound personal injury of racist speech, and this injury may in particular circumstances be so shocking as to literally preempt responsive speech. Although the analogous harm of uncivil speech is randomly scattered throughout the population, the disabilities attendant upon racist speech are concentrated upon members of victim groups. Hence, where members of dominant groups perceive "isolated incidents,"[198] members of victim groups perceive instead a suffocating and inescapable "racism that is a persistent and constituent part of the social order, woven into the fabric of society and everyday life."[199]

Under such conditions it is to be expected that members of dominant and victim groups may well come to conflicting judgments about whether racist speech shocks significant segments of victim group population into silence. The recent literature proposing restraints on racist speech is eloquent on the need to "listen[ ] to the real victims" of such speech and to display "empathy or understanding for their injury."[200] And of course any fair and just determination about the regulation of public discourse would require exactly this kind of sensitivity. But there

---

198. Matsuda, *supra* note 5, at 2331.
199. Note, *supra* note 192, at 295.
200. Lawrence, *supra* note 5, at 436.

is also a tendency in recent literature to move from the proposition that a fair determination cannot be made unless "the victims of racist speech are heard,"[201] to the very different proposition that such a determination ought to use "the experience of victim-group members [as] a guide."[202] The latter proposition seems to me plainly false.

The issue on the table is whether irrationality and coercion have so tainted the medium of public discourse as to require shrinking the scope of self-government. That issue significantly affects every citizen, and its resolution therefore cannot be ceded to the control of any particular group. In fact I do not see how the issue can be adequately resolved at all unless some notion of civic membership is invoked that transcends mere group identification. Unless we can strive to deliberate together as citizens, distancing ourselves from (but not abandoning) our specific cultural backgrounds, the issue can be resolved only through the exercise of naked group power, a solution not at all advantageous to the marginalized and oppressed.[203]

Paradoxically, therefore, the question of whether public discourse is irretrievably damaged by racist speech must itself ultimately be addressed through the medium of public discourse. Because those participating in public discourse will not themselves have been silenced (almost by definition), a heavy, frus-

---

201. *Id.* at 481.

202. Matsuda, *supra* note 5, at 2369. This tendency is explicitly thematized in Iris Marion Young's artless proposal that "a democratic public" should cede to "constituent groups that are oppressed or disadvantaged" a "veto power regarding specific policies that affect a group directly." Young, *Polity and Group Difference,* 99 ETHICS 250, 261-62 (1989).

203. The "grand tradition" of republican participation, the notion that "we can lift our public life above the fallen and compromised realm of factional politics," thus does not seem to me so easily abandoned as would appear from recent literature stressing fidelity to the particular cultural "tradition" of minority groups. *See* Lopez, *The Idea of a Constitution in the Chicano Tradition,* 37 J. LEGAL EDUC. 162, 163-64 (1987). Even Young notes that a "heterogeneous public . . . is a *public,* where participants discuss together the issues before them and are supposed to come to a decision that they determine as best or most just." Young, *supra* note 202, at 267.

> It is possible for persons to maintain their group identity and to be influenced by their perceptions of social events derived from their group-specific experience, and at the same time to be public spirited, in the sense of being open to listening to the claims of others and not being concerned for their own gain alone. It is possible and necessary for people to take a critical distance from their own immediate desires and gut reactions in order to discuss public proposals. Doing so, however, cannot require that citizens abandon their particular affiliations, experiences, and social location.

Id. at 257-58.

trating burden is de facto placed on those who would truncate public discourse in order to save it. They must represent themselves as "speaking for" those who have been deprived of their voice. But the negative space of that silence reigns inscrutable, neither confirming nor denying this claim. And the more eloquent the appeal, the less compelling the claim, for the more accessible public discourse will then appear to exactly the perspectives racist speech is said to repress.

Even if this burden is lifted, however, and it is simply accepted that members of victim groups are intimidated into silence, it would still not follow that restraints on racist speech within public discourse are justified. One might believe, for example, that such silencing occurs chiefly through the structural conditions of racism, rather than specifically through the shock of racist speech. "The problem," as the Chairman of the Black Studies Department of New York's City College recently remarked apropos of the racist comments of an academic colleague, does not lie with specific communicative acts, but rather with "racism" itself, "insidious in our society and built into our culture."[204] If that were true, restraints on racist speech would impair public discourse without at the same time repairing the silence of victim groups.

Alternatively, one might believe that racist speech silences victim groups primarily because of its "ideas," because of its messages of racial inferiority, rather than because of its incivility. The distinction is important for the following reason: although it is consistent with the internal logic of public discourse to excise in extreme circumstances certain kinds of uncivil speech that are experienced as coercive,[205] it is fundamentally incompatible with public discourse to excise specific ideas because they are "analogously" deemed to be coercive. Public discourse is the medium within which our society assesses the democratic acceptability of ideas; to exclude certain ideas as prima facie "coercive" and hence destructive of public discourse is to contradict precisely this function. Therefore "harm" to public discourse cannot justify restraints on racist ideas on the grounds that such ideas are perceived to be threatening or coercive.[206]

---

204. Berger, *Professors' Theories on Race Stir Turmoil at City College*, N.Y. Times, Apr. 20, 1990, at B1, col. 2.

205. *See supra* text accompanying notes 178-80.

206. Note that the argument in text does not hold against the contention that certain ideas should be excluded from public discourse because they cause extensive harm to

There are also other possibilities. One might believe, for example, that because it is difficult to distinguish ideas from incivility, and because it is vitally important to collective self-determination to protect all ideas, the law will as a practical matter be able to restrain only a small category of blatant racist epithets, which, although deeply offensive and lacking in ideational content, have relatively little to do with the more widespread phenomenon of silencing. Or one might believe that racist speech silences primarily when shocking racist epithets are used in the face-to-face confrontations characteristic of the "fighting words" doctrine of *Chaplinsky*,[207] so that the essential insight of the argument from silencing is already reflected within first amendment doctrine.

My own conclusion, in light of these alternative considerations, is that the case has not yet been made for circumscribing public discourse to prevent the kind of preemptive silencing that occurs when members of victim groups experience "fear, rage, [and] shock." I say this with some hesitation, and with considerable ambivalence. But even if the empirical claim of systematic preemptive silencing were accepted (and I am not sure that I do accept it), it is in my view most directly the result of the social and structural conditions of racism, rather than specifically of racist speech. Because the logic of the argument from preemptive silencing does not impeach the necessity of preserving the free expression of ideas,[208] public discourse could at most be regulated in a largely symbolic manner so as to purge it of outrageous racist epithets and names. It seems to me highly implausible to claim that such symbolic regulation will eliminate the preemptive silencing that is said to justify restraints on public discourse.

---

individuals or victim groups. Such harm is extrinsic to the function of public discourse. To evaluate the contention that public discourse ought to be limited because of harm to individuals or groups, therefore, we must assess the importance of democratic self-governance in light of our commitment to protecting stable personal and group identities. *See supra* Sections III(B) & (C).

The argument considered in text that certain ideas ought to be excluded from public discourse because they are intrinsically coercive, on the other hand, turns upon harm to the function of public discourse itself. The argument is unsatisfactory because the concept of "coercion" must itself be defined by reference to a "moral baseline" determined by the practice in question. *See* A. WERTHEIMER, COERCION 217 (1987). Within the practice of public discourse, no idea can be deemed intrinsically coercive because the very function of public discourse presupposes a formal equality of persons and hence of ideas.

207. Chaplinsky v. New Hampshire, 315 U.S. 568 (1942).

208. *See supra* note 206.

3. Racist Speech as Symbolic Cultural Oppression

When distinguished and parsed in this analytic manner, therefore, the various arguments for restraining racist speech in order to preserve the integrity of public discourse do not in my judgment support their desired conclusion. But the arguments can be braided together to fund an accusation more powerful than its separate strands.

In ordinary life, members of victim groups do not experience a string of distinct disadvantages. Rather, if representations in the current literature are accepted as true, these groups confront in public discourse an undifferentiated complex of circumstances in which they are systematically demeaned, stigmatized, ignored; in which the very language of debate resists the articulation of their claims; in which they are harassed, abused, intimidated, and systematically and egregiously injured both individually and collectively. The question is not whether these liabilities, when taken individually and singly, justify restraining racist speech within public discourse, but rather whether, when taken together as a complex whole, they render public discourse unfit as an instrument of collective self-determination for members of victim groups, and whether this unacceptable situation would be cured by restraints on racist speech.

What makes this question so very formidable is that it turns on the nexus between public discourse and the value of collective self-determination. Although the formal preconditions of that nexus can be described, its actual substantive realization must remain contingent upon conditions of history, culture, and social structure. Thus when members of victim groups claim that public discourse no longer serves for them the value of self-government, it is no answer to reply that they have been embraced within its formal preconditions. If members of victim groups in fact perceive themselves to be systematically excluded from public dialogue, that dialogue can scarcely achieve for them those "broader enduring values" that are its democratic justification. The very legitimacy of democratic self-governance is thus called into question.

The dependence of the value of public discourse upon matters of social perception poses complex and delicate questions, but the difficulty of these questions is profoundly magnified in the context of the controversy over racist speech. First, the truth of the claim that members of victim groups are cut off from meaningful participation within public discourse cannot be directly experienced and hence evaluated by members of dominant groups. Its resolution must therefore depend, to one degree or another, upon acceptance of the representations of members of victim groups. As a practical political matter, therefore, what is called into question is not merely the truth of these representations, but also the trust and respect with which they are received by members of dominant groups.[209] Second, the focus on trust and respect is reinforced by the remedial claim that racist speech ought to be censored so as to open up public discourse to victim groups. Essentially this claim requires that self-determination be denied to some so that it may be made available to others. Thus society's willingness to circumscribe public discourse is transformed into a touchstone of the esteem with which it regards victim groups.

In fact it is this transformation that most precisely supports the argument. The argument turns on the interpretive meaning that members of victim groups ascribe to their place in American life; the contention is that this meaning is one of exclusion. Such an interpretation cannot be reduced to any specific empirical claims or conditions. Instead the need of those who feel alienated is most exactly met by a gesture of social esteem. By conveying in the strongest possible terms messages of respect and welcome, the censorship of racist speech might go a long way toward allowing members of victim groups to reinterpret their experience as one of inclusion within the dialogue of public discourse. The objection we noted earlier, that the regulation of racist speech within public discourse could at most restrict the publication of highly offensive racist epithets and names, and that such regulation could only serve symbolic purposes, is thus no longer pertinent. For the argument now turns squarely on the politics of cultural symbolism.

The most salient characteristic of such politics is that the particular content of government regulation is less important than its perceived meaning. We have already noted how claims like those of individual injury or preemptive silencing define concrete classes of communications that are said empirically to cause a particular harm. But the claim of cultural exclusion is fundamentally different, for it implies no such specific referent.

---

209. *See* Lawrence, *supra* note 5, at 474-75. That this is a general characteristic of group claims can be seen by the development of an analogous dynamic among those who support the regulation of pornography. *See, e.g.,* C. MACKINNON, *On Collaboration,* in FEMINISM UNMODIFIED: DISCOURSES ON LIFE AND LAW 198 (1987).

The claim, when pressed, is not that any specific class of communications actually causes members of victim groups to feel excluded, but rather that a particular regulatory gesture will be the occasion for members of victim groups to feel included.[210]

This suggests, however, that restraints on public discourse are only one of a wide variety of strategies that government can pursue to ameliorate the sense of cultural exclusion experienced by victim groups. Other alternatives might include antidiscrimination laws, affirmative action programs, redistribution of economic resources, restraints on racist forms of nonpublic speech, and so forth. All these modifications of community life could be interpreted as significant gestures of respect and inclusion. It is a matter of political choice and characterization to reject these alternatives as insufficient and to deem the limitation of public discourse as necessary to overcome the alienation of victim groups.

At root, therefore, the argument from cultural exclusion seeks to subordinate public discourse, whose very purpose is to serve as the framework for all possible forms of politics, to a particular political perspective. The argument begins with the sound premise that a cultural sense of participation is necessary for public discourse to serve the value of collective self-determination. But instead of conceiving public discourse as a means of rousing the Nation's political will to actions designed to facilitate that sense of participation, the argument instead turns on public discourse itself, and, as a matter of political perception and assertion, deems the limitation of that discourse to be prerequisite for the elimination of disabling alienation. The argument therefore does not ultimately rest on the importance of protecting public discourse from harm, but rather on the need to sacrifice public discourse in order to recuperate profound social dislocations.

Bluntly expressed, the argument requires us to balance the integrity of public discourse as a general structure of communication against the importance of enhancing the experience of political participation by members of victim groups. The argument thus reiterates the position that public discourse ought to be subordinated to the egalitarian ideals of the fourteenth amend-

---

210. The success or failure of the gesture will depend entirely on the perception of members of victim groups. There is thus no guarantee that any particular regulatory scheme will in fact actually cause members of victim groups to reinterpret their position within public discourse. This inherent gap between regulatory design and the achievement of regulatory purpose, coupled with the fact that only members of victim groups can experience and evaluate the claim of cultural exclusion, creates disturbing possibilities for strategic manipulation.

ment. It adopts a sophisticated version of that position, however, for it is able to contend that public discourse need be impaired in only slight and symbolic ways. Even so minimal a gesture as purging outrageous and shocking racist epithets could be sufficient to make members of victim groups feel welcome within the arena of public discourse, and thus to enable public discourse to serve for them the value of self-determination.[211] In this form the argument is analogous to that advanced in the controversy over prohibiting flag burning, in which it is also urged that public discourse ought to be minimally impaired for highly important symbolic reasons.[212] Just as it has been contended that any idea can be expressed without burning a flag,[213] so it can be asserted that any idea can be expressed without recourse to vile racist epithets.[214] In both cases, therefore, it can be argued that the de minimis effects on public discourse are outweighed by the significance of the interests at stake.[215]

I believe, however, that this invitation to balance ought to be declined. This is not because balancing can be ruled out in advance by some "absolutist" algorithm; the attraction of a purely formal democracy may itself in extreme circumstances no longer command limitless conviction. It is rather because, in the American context, the temptation to balance rests on what might be termed the fallacy of immaculate isolation.[216] The effect on public

---

211. Of course so minimal a gesture might not be sufficient to achieve this purpose. The intrinsically speculative quality of the argument must be taken into account in its evaluation.

212. According to the Solicitor General, the state's interest in prohibiting flag burning turns on the importance of "safeguard[ing] the flag's identity 'as the unique and unalloyed symbol of the Nation.'" United States v. Eichman, 110 S. Ct. 2404, 2408 (1990) (quoting Brief for United States at 28, 29).

213. Texas v. Johnson, 109 S. Ct. 2533, 2553-54 (1989) (Rehnquist, C.J., dissenting).

214. I should be plain that I myself reject the premise of this argument and do not believe that the rhetorical meaning of speech can be disentangled from the manner of its presentation. Style and substance are always interdependent, for, in the words of Georg Lukács, "[c]ontent determines form." G. LUKÁCS, REALISM IN OUR TIME: LITERATURE AND THE CLASS STRUGGLE 19 (J. & N. Mander trans. 1962). For a discussion, see Post, *The Constitutional Concept, supra* note 91, at 663 n.314. I therefore do not think that the impact on public discourse of prohibiting certain kinds of words can ever properly be said to be de minimis. I nevertheless want to evaluate the case for balancing on the strong assumption of this kind of de minimis impact.

215. For a discussion of this argument in the context of flag burning, see *Eichman,* 110 S. Ct. at 2410-12 (Stevens, J., dissenting).

216. In evaluating this balance, I do not mean to call into question the holding of *Chaplinsky,* which in my view attempts to distinguish private fracases from political debate. *See* Post, *The Constitutional Concept, supra* note 91, at 679-81. It is clear enough that racial epithets, when uttered in certain face-to-face situations, would constitute

discourse is acceptable only if it is de minimis, and it is arguably de minimis only when a specific claim is evaluated in isolation from other, similar claims. But no claim is in practice immaculately isolated in this manner. As the flag burning example suggests, there is no shortage of powerful groups contending that uncivil speech within public discourse ought to be "minimally" regulated for highly pressing symbolic reasons.[217]

This is evident even if the focus of analysis is narrowly limited to the structure of the claim at issue in the debate over racist speech. In a large heterogeneous country populated by assertive and conflicting groups, the logic of circumscribing public discourse to reduce political estrangement is virtually unstoppable. The Nation is filled with those who feel displaced and who would feel less so if given the chance symbolically to truncate public discourse. This is already plain in the regulations that have proliferated on college campuses, which commonly proscribe not merely speech that degrades persons on the basis of their race, but also, to pick a typical list, speech that demeans persons on the basis of their "color, national origin, religion, sex, sexual orientation, age, handicap, or veteran's status."[218] The claim of de minimis impact loses credibility as the list of claimants to special protection grows longer.

"fighting words" and hence not form part of public discourse. *See* Greenawalt, *supra* note 5, at 306. The point of the argument in text, however, is to evaluate restraints on racist epithets in what would otherwise clearly be deemed public discourse, as for example in political debates, newspapers, pamphlets, magazines, novels, movies, records, and so forth.

217. Anyone inclined to doubt this proposition should review again the current controversy over funding for the National Endowment for the Arts, or the recent prosecutions occasioned by the Mapplethorpe exhibition or the recordings of 2 Live Crew. *See Rap Band Members Found Not Guilty in Obscenity Trial,* N.Y. Times, Oct. 21, 1990, § 1, at 1, col. 1 (discussing 2 Live Crew's acquittal after being charged with giving obscene performance and record store owner's conviction after being charged with selling obscene 2 Live Crew album); *Cincinnati Jury Acquits Museum in* Mapplethorpe *Obscenity Case,* N.Y. Times, Oct. 6, 1990, § 1, at 1, col. 1; *Reverend Wildman's War on the Arts,* N.Y. Times, Sept. 2, 1990, § 6 (Magazine), at 22, col. 1.

218. Emory University, Policy Statement on Discriminatory Harassment (1988); *see* Doe v. University of Mich., 721 F. Supp. 852, 856 (E.D. Mich. 1989) (concerning sanctions for speech victimizing an individual "on the basis of race, ethnicity, religion, sex, sexual orientation, creed, national origin, ancestry, age, marital status, handicap or Vietnam-era veteran status"). The regulations of Michigan State University include the prohibited category of "political persuasion." Michigan State University, Your Ticket to an Adventure in Understanding (1988) (available from University Housing Programs). The regulations of West Chester University include the category of "lifestyle." West Chester University, Ram's Eye View: Every Student's Guide to West Chester University 61 (1990) (available from Student Development Office). The regulations of Hampshire College include that of "socio-economic class." Hampshire College, College Policies: Updates and Revisions (1988-89).

The point I want to press does not depend upon the intellectual difficulty of drawing lines to separate similar claims. It is rather that the remedial and political logic of equal participation applies with analogous force to a broad and growing spectrum of group claims. One might, of course, devise arguments, perhaps based on the specific history of the fourteenth amendment, to distinguish racial epithets from blasphemous imprecations, or from degrading and pornographic characterizations of women, or from vicious antigay slurs, or from gross ethnic insults. But the question is whether such arguments can withstand the compelling egalitarian logic that unites these various situations. My strong intuition is that they cannot, and hence that the claim of de minimis impact on public discourse is implausible.[219]

In the specific context of the argument from cultural exclusion, moreover, a refusal to balance is far less harsh than it might superficially appear. The fundamental challenge is to enable members of victim groups to reinterpret their experience within the American political and cultural order as one of genuine participation. There are a host of ways to address this challenge short of truncating public discourse. The most obvious and potentially effective strategy would be to dismantle systematically and forcefully the structural conditions of racism. If we were so blessed as to be able to accomplish that feat—if we were truly able to eliminate such conditions as chronic unemployment, inadequate health care, segregated housing, or disproportionately low incomes—then we would no doubt also have succeeded in ameliorating the experience of cultural exclusion.

IV. THE FIRST AMENDMENT AND HARM TO THE EDUCATIONAL ENVIRONMENT

If public discourse is bounded on one side by the necessary structures of community life, it is bounded on the other by the need of the state to create organizations to achieve explicit public objectives. These organizations, which are nonpublic forums, regulate speech in ways that are fundamentally incompatible with the requirements of public discourse.[220] Public discourse is the

---

219. This claim is also implausible, as I noted earlier, because of its vulnerable assumption that style can be sharply distinguished from substance. *See supra* note 214.

220. The argument in this and the following two paragraphs is developed in detail in Post, *Between Governance and Management: The History and Theory of the Public Forum*, 34 UCLA L. REV. 1713 (1987) [hereinafter Post, *Between Governance*]. *See also* Post, *The Constitutional Concept, supra* note 91, at 684-85.

medium through which our democracy determines its purposes, and for this reason the legal structure of public discourse requires that all such purposes be kept open to question and reevaluation. Within nonpublic forums, on the other hand, government objectives are taken as established, and communication is regulated as necessary to achieve those objectives.

Although the Supreme Court has often held that "the First Amendment rights of speech and association extend to the campuses of state universities," and even that "the campus of a public university, at least for its students, possesses many of the characteristics of a public forum,"[221] in fact state institutions of higher learning are public organizations established for the express purpose of education. The Court has always held that "a university's mission is education" and has never construed the first amendment to deny a university's "authority to impose reasonable regulations compatible with that mission upon the use of its campus and facilities."[222] The Court has explicitly recognized "a university's right to exclude . . . First Amendment activities that . . . substantially interfere with the opportunity of other students to obtain an education."[223] Thus student speech incompatible with classroom processes may be censored; faculty publications inconsistent with academic standards may be evaluated and judged; and so forth.

The regulation of racist speech within public institutions of higher learning, therefore, does not turn on the value of democratic self-governance and its realization in public discourse. Instead the constitutionality of such regulation depends upon the logic of instrumental rationality, and specifically upon three factors: (1) the nature of the educational mission of the university; (2) the instrumental connection of the regulation to the attainment of that mission; and (3) the deference that courts ought to display toward the instrumental judgment of institutional authorities.[224] The current controversy regarding the constitutionality of regulating racist speech on university and college campuses may most helpfully be interpreted as a debate about the first of these factors, the constitutionally permissible educational objectives of public institutions of higher learning.[225]

---

221. Widmar v. Vincent, 454 U.S. 263, 267 n.5, 268-69 (1981).

222. *Id.* at 268 n.5.

223. *Id.* at 277 (citing Healy v. James, 408 U.S. 169, 189 (1972)).

224. Judicial application of these factors in nonpublic fora like universities is discussed in greater detail in Post, *Between Governance, supra* note 220, at 1765-1824.

225. This short discussion considers only issues pertaining to the *constitutionality* of

Courts have advanced at least three different concepts of those objectives. The most traditional concept, which I refer to as "civic education," views public education as an instrument of community life, and holds "that respect for constituted authority and obedience thereto is an essential lesson to qualify one for the duties of citizenship, and that the schoolroom is an appropriate place to teach that lesson."[226] Civic education conceptualizes instruction as a process of cultural reproduction, whereby community values are authoritatively handed down to the young. The validity of those values is largely taken for granted, and there is a strong tendency to use them as a basis for the regulation of speech in the manner of the traditional common law.

The concept of civic education held sway in the years before the Warren Court and has recently been forcefully resurrected with regard to the regulation of speech within high schools. Thus in *Bethel School District No. 403 v. Fraser*[227] the Court upheld the punishment of a high school student for having delivered an "offensive" and "indecent" student-government speech.[228] The Court reasoned that "the objectives of public education" included "the 'inculcat[ion of] fundamental values necessary to the maintenance of a democratic political system.' "[229] Among these values were "the habits and manners of civility as . . . indispensable to the practice of self-government."[230]

> The undoubted freedom to advocate unpopular and controversial views in schools and classrooms must be balanced against the society's countervailing interest in teaching students the boundaries of socially appropriate behavior. . . .
>
>   . . . .
>   . . . [S]chools must teach by example the shared values of a civilized social order. . . . The schools, as instruments of the state, may determine that the essential lessons of civil, mature conduct cannot be conveyed in a school that tolerates lewd, indecent, or offensive speech and conduct such as that indulged in by this confused boy.[231]

---

the regulation of racist speech. It does not consider the *educational* issues raised by such regulation. These issues are, however, profound and revolve around the question of whether legal restraint is the heuristically most effective response to racist speech.

226. Pugsley v. Sellmeyer, 158 Ark. 247, 253, 250 S.W. 538, 539 (1923).

227. 478 U.S. 675 (1986).

228. *Id.* at 678.

229. *Id.* at 681 (quoting Ambach v. Norwick, 441 U.S. 68, 77 (1979)).

230. *Id.* (quoting C. BEARD & M. BEARD, NEW BASIC HISTORY OF THE UNITED STATES 228 (1968)).

231. *Id.* at 681, 683. For a more recent example of the same kind of reasoning, see Hazelwood School Dist. v. Kuhlmeier, 484 U.S. 260, 271-72 (1988).

That the concept of civic education would lead to similar conclusions if applied to institutions of higher learning is evidenced by Chief Justice Burger's 1973 dissent in *Papish v. University of Missouri Curators*:[232]

> In theory, at least, a university is not merely an arena for the discussion of ideas by students and faculty; it is also an institution where individuals learn to express themselves in acceptable, civil terms. We provide that environment to the end that students may learn the self-restraint necessary to the functioning of a civilized society and understand the need for those external restraints to which we must all submit if group existence is to be tolerable.[233]

Because racist speech is both deeply uncivil and contrary to "the shared values of [our] civilized social order,"[234] its restraint would be relatively unproblematic if civic education were understood to constitute a constitutionally acceptable purpose of public institutions of higher learning.[235] A number of public universities have fashioned their regulations on exactly this understanding. For example, the Policy Against Racism of the Board of Regents of Higher Education of the Commonwealth of Massachusetts argues that "institutions must vigorously strive to achieve diversity in race, ethnicity, and culture sufficiently reflective of our society. However, diversity alone will not suffice":

> There must be a unity and cohesion in the diversity which we seek to achieve, thereby creating an environment of pluralism. Racism in any form, expressed or implied, intentional or inadvertent, individual or institutional, constitutes an egregious offense to the tenets of human dignity and to the accords of civility guaranteed by law. Consequently, racism undermines the establishment of a social and academic environment of genuine racial pluralism.[236]

The policy clearly postulates the fundamental task of the university to be the inculcation of the value of "genuine racial plural-

---

232. 410 U.S. 667 (1973).

233. *Id.* at 672 (Burger, C.J., dissenting).

234. Bethel v. School Dist. No. 403 v. Frazer, 478 U.S. 675, 681 (1986).

235. For the development of this logic at the pre-university level, see, for example, Clarke v. Board of Educ., 215 Neb. 250, 338 N.W.2d 272 (1983).

236. Commonwealth of Massachusetts Board of Regents of Higher Education, Policy Against Racism and Guidelines for Campus Policies Against Racism 2 (June 13, 1989).

ism," and it proscribes racist speech because of its incompatibility with that value.

A second concept of the mission of public education, which I refer to as "democratic education," begins with the very different premise that the "public school" is "in most respects the cradle of our democracy,"[237] and it therefore understands the purpose of public education to be the creation of autonomous citizens, capable of fully participating in the rough and tumble world of public discourse.[238] Democratic education strives to introduce that world into the generically more sheltered environment of the school.

The concept of democratic education was most fully expressed during the era of the Warren Court in *Tinker v. Des Moines School District*,[239] in which the Court held that the purpose of public education is to prepare students for the "sort of hazardous freedom . . . that is the basis of our national strength and of the independence and vigor of Americans who grow up and live in this relatively permissive, often disputatious, society."[240] The majority in *Tinker* explicitly rejected the premise of civic education that the purpose of public schooling is the transmission of canonical values. It concluded instead that "[i]n our system, state-operated schools may not be enclaves of totalitarianism. . . . [S]tudents may not be regarded as closed-circuit recipients of only that which the [s]tate chooses to communicate. They may not be confined to the expression of those sentiments that are officially approved."[241] According to *Tinker* the object of public education is to lead students to think for themselves.

The chief characteristic of democratic education is its tendency to assimilate speech within public educational institutions to a model of public discourse. Recognizing that this ambition is "not without its costs in terms of the risk to the maintenance of civility and an ordered society," the Court nevertheless strongly advanced the concept of democratic education during the late

---

237. Adler v. Board of Educ., 342 U.S. 485, 508 (1952) (Douglas, J., dissenting). For a fully developed statement of this position, see Abington School Dist. v. Schempp, 374 U.S. 203, 241-42 (1963) (Brennan, J., concurring).

238. The tension between the concepts of democratic and civic education closely recapitulates the informative debate between Piaget and Durkheim over the question of how to teach moral values. Durkheim stressed the importance of discipline, authority, and constraint, whereas Piaget emphasized cooperation, agreement, and autonomy. *See* J. PIAGET, *supra* note 84, at 341-71.

239. 393 U.S. 503 (1969).

240. *Id.* at 508-09.

241. *Id.* at 511.

1960's and early 1970's, in part because it believed the concept essential to the maintenance of "our vigorous and free society."[242] If, as I have argued, racist speech is and ought to be immune from regulation within public discourse, we can expect courts guided by the concept of democratic education to be quite hostile to the regulation of racist speech within universities, preferring instead to see students realistically prepared for participation in the harsh but inevitable world of public discourse.

There is yet a third concept of public education, one most often specifically associated with institutions of higher learning. This concept, which I refer to as "critical education," views the university as an institution whose distinctive "primary function" is "to discover and disseminate knowledge by means of research and teaching."[243] Critical education locates the principal prerequisite for university life in "the need for unfettered freedom, the right to think the unthinkable, discuss the unmentionable, and challenge the unchallengeable."[244]

> [I]f a university is a place for knowledge, it is also a special kind of small society. Yet it is not primarily a fellowship, a club, a circle of friends, a replica of the civil society outside it. Without sacrificing its central purpose, it cannot make its primary and dominant value the fostering of friendship, solidarity, harmony, civility, or mutual respect. To be sure, these are important values; other institutions may properly assign them the highest, and not merely a subordinate priority; and a good university will seek and in some significant measure attain these ends. But it will never let these values, important as they are, override its central purpose. We value freedom of expression precisely because it provides a forum for the new, the provocative, the disturbing, and the unorthodox. Free speech is a barrier to the tyranny of authoritarian or even majority opinion as to the rightness or wrongness of particular doctrines or thoughts.[245]

The university as the purveyor of critical education serves important social purposes. These include not only the disciplined

---

242. Healy v. James, 408 U.S. 169, 194 (1972).

243. *Report of the Committee on Freedom of Expression at Yale*, 4 HUM. RTS. 357, 357 (1975) [hereinafter *Report of the Committee*]. This function is not one that we ordinarily attribute to high schools, much less elementary schools.

244. *Id.*

245. *Id.* at 357-58; *see* Schmidt, *Freedom of Thought: A Principle in Peril?*, YALE ALUMNI MAG., Oct. 1989, at 65, 65-66.

pursuit of truth, but also the exemplary enactment of a "model of expression that is meaningful as well as free, coherent yet diverse, critical and inspirational."[246] The concept of critical education has strong affinities to the traditional "marketplace of ideas" theory of the first amendment, and it is not uncommon for courts who use the concept to speak of the "classroom" as "peculiarly the 'marketplace of ideas,'" deserving of protection because the "Nation's future depends upon leaders trained through wide exposure to that robust exchange of ideas which discovers truth 'out of a multitude of tongues, [rather] than through any kind of authoritative selection.'"[247]

The concept of critical education differs significantly from both civic and democratic education. In contrast to civic education, it rejects the notion of canonical values that are to be reproduced in the young. Hence public universities committed to critical education are not free to posit certain values (apart from the value of critical education itself) and to punish those who disagree. The logic of critical education would constitutionally require that a public university "not restrict speech . . . simply because it finds the views expressed by any group to be abhorrent."[248] This stands in stark contrast to the educational project of institutions like the University of Massachusetts, Mount Holyoke, Marquette, or Mary Washington,[249] which are committed to the mission of civic education.

The concept of critical education would also sharply limit the ability of universities to censor uncivil speech. Speech can be uncivil for many reasons, including the assertion of ideas that are perceived to be offensive, revolting, demeaning, and stigmatizing. Critical education, however, would require the toleration

---

246. Byrne, *Academic Freedom: A "Special Concern of the First Amendment,"* 99 YALE L.J. 251, 261 (1989). The presence of such a model

> contributes profoundly to society at large. We employ the expositors of academic speech to train nearly everyone who exercises leadership within our society. Beyond whatever specialized learning our graduates assimilate, they ought to be persuaded that careful, honest expression demands an answer in kind. The experience of academic freedom helps secure broader, positive liberties of expression.

Id.

247. Keyishian v. Board of Regents, 385 U.S. 589, 603 (1967) (quoting United States v. Associated Press, 52 F. Supp. 362, 372 (S.D.N.Y. 1943)); *see* Healy v. James, 408 U.S. 169, 180-81 (1972).

248. *Healy,* 408 U.S. at 187-88.

249. *See supra* notes 47-51 and accompanying text.

of all ideas, however uncivil.[250] This toleration would be consistent with the Court's 1973 holding that "the mere dissemination of ideas—no matter how offensive to good taste—on a state university campus may not be shut off in the name alone of 'conventions of decency.' "[251]

Critical education also differs in important respects from democratic education. The telos of critical education lies in the pursuit of truth, rather than in the instantiation of the responsible autonomy of the citizen. The pursuit of truth requires not only an unfettered freedom of ideas, but also honesty, fidelity to reason, and respect for method and procedures. Reason, as we have seen, carries its own special requirements of civility, which preclude coercion and abuse.[252] Although enforcement of these requirements and values would be inconsistent with democratic education, it may well be required by critical education. Moreover critical education requires freedom of ideas only with respect to that speech which forms part of the truth-seeking dialogue of the university. Thus, for example, nothing in the concept of critical education would prevent a university from penalizing malicious racist speech communicated *solely for the purpose* of harassing, humiliating, or degrading a victim.[253] The trick, of course, would be to distinguish such speech in a manner that does not chill communication intended to form part of a truth-seeking exchange.[254] This represents a formidable technical challenge, for it is all too easy to permit revulsion with the content of speech to infect regulation ostensibly justified by other reasons.[255]

Although there is not space in this short essay to engage in a full-scale exploration of the purposes of higher education, some conclusions are clear enough. The Constitution would not permit a public university, in the name of civic education, to prohibit

---

250. "If the university's overriding commitment to free expression is to be sustained, secondary social and ethical responsibilities must be left to the informal processes of suasion, example, and argument." *Report of the Committee, supra* note 243, at 360.

251. Papish v. University of Mo. Curators, 410 U.S. 667, 670 (1973).

252. *See supra* Section III(D)(1).

253. As a matter of policy, however, it is always dangerous to make the legality of speech depend primarily upon an assessment of a speaker's intent, for there is a powerful tendency to attribute bad motives to those with whom we fundamentally disagree.

254. The inability to make this distinction contributed to a court's recent decision to strike down as unconstitutional the regulations of the University of Michigan. *See* Doe v. University of Mich., 721 F. Supp. 852 (E.D. Mich. 1989); Grano, *supra* note 5, at 7.

255. For an admirable attempt to meet this challenge, see Grey, *supra* note 5, and the regulations that Professor Grey drafted for Stanford University.

the teaching of communism because of its conflict with community values. Nor would the Constitution, in the name of democratic education, preclude a public university from enforcing regulations against highly offensive racial epithets within a classroom.

Examples like these incline me toward the concept of critical education, yet the extent to which state universities ought constitutionally to be *required* to pursue one or the other of these educational missions does not seem to me without difficulties.[256] The analysis is complicated by the possibility that public universities may have various educational functions with constitutionally distinct characteristics. Thus it is conceivable that public universities may be permitted to pursue the mission of civic education within their dormitories, but be required to follow the requirements of democratic education with regard to their open spaces.[257] These are matters that require further and careful consideration.

I conclude, therefore, by stressing two brief points. First, the constitutionality of restraints on racist speech within public universities does not depend upon the constitutionality of such regulation within public discourse. Second, the constitutionality of restraints on racist speech within public universities will depend to a very great extent upon the educational purposes that we constitutionally attribute to public institutions of higher learning, and upon the various modalities through which such institutions are understood to pursue those purposes. We ought to see debate turn toward the achievement of a fuller and more reflective comprehension of these questions.

V. CONCLUSION: THE QUESTION OF FORMAL DEMOCRACY

This account of the constitutionality of university restrictions on racist speech suggests that a principal flaw of the contemporary debate has been its pervasive assumption that the relationship of racist speech to the first amendment can be assessed

---

256. Cases like *Tinker* and *Healy* make clear, however, that the Supreme Court's first amendment jurisprudence has rested on the assumption that there are constitutional limits to the freedom of public educational institutions to define their own educational mission.

257. Some universities have regulated racist speech in ways that turn on similar functional and geographic considerations. *See Doe*, 721 F. Supp. at 856; *Tufts Restores Free Speech After T-Shirt Confrontation*, San Francisco Chron., Dec. 9, 1989, at B6, col. 1; Wilson, *Colleges Take 2 Basic Approaches in Adopting Anti-Harassment Plans*, Chron. Higher Educ., Oct. 4, 1989, at A38, col. 1; Russo, *Free Speech at Tufts: Zoned Out*, N.Y. Times, Sept. 27, 1989, at A29.

independently of social context. Communication, however, does not form a constitutionally undifferentiated terrain. The standards of first amendment protection afforded to public discourse will not be the same as those applied to nonpublic speech, and these in turn will differ from those that govern the regulation of speech within instrumental governmental institutions like universities. The concrete circumstances of racist speech thus figure prominently in the constitutional equation.

Public discourse is the realm of communication we deem necessary to facilitate the process of self-determination. As that process is open-ended, reflecting the boundless possibility of social self-constitution, so we fashion public discourse to be as free from legal constraint as is feasible to sustain. But as self-determination requires the antecedent formation of a "self" through socialization into the particularity of a given community life, so public discourse must at some point be bounded by nonpublic speech, in which community values are embodied and enforced. And as the decisions of a self-determining democracy require actual implementation, so public discourse must at some other point be bounded by the instrumentally regulated speech of the nonpublic forum.

I have attempted to explain the unique protections that American first amendment jurisprudence affords to public discourse through a self-consciously formal analysis; that is, I have attempted to uncover the formal prerequisites for the instantiation of the value of democracy as self-determination. Although this kind of formal analysis has the advantage of forcing us to clearly articulate the values in whose name we purport to act, it has the disadvantage of obscuring the messy complications of the world. Formal analysis is always subject to the critique that actual, substantive conditions have undermined its very point and meaning.

From a formal perspective, democracy fulfills the purposes of autonomous self-government because we accept an image of independent citizens deliberating together to form public opinion. We therefore structure constitutional policy according to the requirements of that image. But it is an image blatantly vulnerable to the most forceful empirical attack.[258] Citizens are not autonomous; they are manipulated by the media, coerced by private corporations, immured in the toils of racism. Citizens do

---

258. *See, e.g.,* E. PURCELL, THE CRISIS OF DEMOCRATIC THEORY: SCIENTIFIC NATURALISM AND THE PROBLEM OF VALUE (1973).

not communicate together; they are passive, irrational, and voiceless. Deliberation is impossible because of the technical and economic structure of the mass media; public opinion is therefore imposed upon citizens rather than spontaneously arising from them. The very aspiration to self-determination reinforces pre-existing inequalities by empowering those with the resources and competence to take advantage of democratic processes; it systematically handicaps socially marginalized groups who lack this easy and familiar access to the media of democratic deliberation. And so forth: the litany is by now depressingly familiar.

Of course these criticisms, and others like them, contain important elements of truth. They therefore force us to choose: either we decide to retain the ideal of democracy as deliberative self-determination and work to minimize the debilitating consequences of these criticisms, or we decide that these criticisms have so undermined the ideal of deliberative self-determination that it must be abandoned and a different value for democracy embraced. If we choose the second alternative, we have the responsibility of articulating and defending a new vision of democracy. But if we choose the first, we have the responsibility of working to foster the constitutional values upon which we rely. We have the obligation of doing so, however, in ways that do not themselves contravene the necessary preconditions of the ideal of deliberative self-determination.[259] The function of formal analysis is to make clear the content of that obligation.

The strict implication of this essay, then, is not that racist speech ought not to be regulated in public discourse, but rather that those who advocate its regulation in ways incompatible with the value of deliberative self-governance carry the burden of moving us to a different and more attractive vision of democracy. Or, in the alternative, they carry the burden of justifying suspensions of our fundamental democratic commitments. Neither burden is light.

---

259. For a striking illustration of the untoward (and in retrospect horrifying) consequences of repudiating that obligation, see Marcuse, *Repressive Tolerance*, in R. WOLFF, B. MOORE, & H. MARCUSE, A CRITIQUE OF PURE TOLERANCE 81 (1965).

BOSTON REVIEW

FEBRUARY 1992

THERE'S NO SUCH THING AS FREE SPEECH AND IT'S A GOOD THING TOO

STANLEY FISH

"Nowadays the First Amendment is the First refuge of Scoundrels."
—S. Johnson and S. Fish

Lately many on the liberal and progressive left have been disconcerted to find that words, phrases and concepts thought to be their property and generative of their politics have been appropriated by the forces of neoconservatism. This is particularly true of the concept of free speech, for in recent years First Amendment rhetoric has been used to justify policies and actions the left finds problematical if not abhorrent: pornography, sexist language, campus hate-speech. How has this happened? The answer I shall give in this essay is that abstract concepts like free speech do not have any "natural" content but are filled with whatever content and direction one can manage to give them. Free speech, in short, is not an independent value but a political prize, and if that prize has been captured by a politics opposed to yours, it can no longer be invoked in ways that further your purposes for it is now an obstacle to those purposes. This is something that the liberal left has yet to understand and what follows is an attempt to pry its members loose from a vocabulary that may now be a disservice to them.

Not far from the end of his *Aereopagitica,* and after having celebrated the virtues of toleration and unregulated publication in passages that find their way into every discussion of free speech and the First Amendment, John Milton catches himself up short and says, of course I didn't mean Catholics, *them* we exterminate:

> I mean not tolerated popery, and open superstition, which as it extirpates all religious and civil supremacies, so itself should be extirpate . . . that also which is impious or evil absolutely against faith or manners no law can possibly permit that intends not to unlaw itself.

Notice that Milton is not simply stipulating a single exception to a rule generally in place; the kinds of utterance that might be regulated and even prohibited on pain of trial and punishment comprise an open set; popery is named only as a particularly perspicuous instance of the advocacy that cannot be tolerated. No doubt there are other forms of speech and action that might be categorized as "open superstitions" or as subversive of piety, faith, and manners, and presumably these too would be candidates for "extirpation." Nor would Milton think himself culpable for having failed to provide a list of unprotected utterances. The list will fill itself out as utterances are put to the test implied by his formulation: would this form of speech or advocacy, if permitted to flourish, tend to undermine the very purposes for which our society is constituted? One cannot answer this question with respect to a particular utterance in advance of its emergence on the world's stage; rather one must wait and ask the question in the full context of its production and (possible) dissemination. It might appear that the result would be ad hoc and unprincipled, but for Milton the principle inheres in the core values in whose name men of like mind came together in the first place. Those values, which include the search for truth and the promotion of virtue, are capacious enough to accommodate a diversity of views. But at some point—again impossible of advance specification—capaciousness will threaten to become shapelessness, and at that point fidelity to the original values will demand acts of extirpation.

I want to say that all affirmations of freedom of expression are like Milton's, dependent for their force on an exception that literally carves out the space in which expression can then emerge. I do not mean that expression (saying something) is a realm whose integrity is sometimes compromised by certain restrictions, but that restriction, in the form of an underlying articulation of the world that necessarily (if silently) negates alternatively possible articulations, is constitutive of expression. Without restriction, without an in-built sense of what it would be meaningless to say or wrong to say, there could be no assertion and no reason for asserting it.

The exception to unregulated expression is not a negative restriction, but a positive hollowing out of value—we are for this, which means we are against *that*—in relation to which meaningful assertion can then occur. It is in reference to that value—constituted as all values are by an act of exclusion—that some forms of speech will be heard as (quite literally) intolerable. Speech, in short, is never a value in and of itself, but is always produced within the precincts of some assumed conception of the good to which it must yield in the event of conflict. When the pinch comes (and sooner or later it will always come) and the institution (be it church, state, or university) is confronted by behavior subversive of its core rationale, it will respond by declaring "of course we mean not tolerated _____, that we extirpate"; not because an exception to a general freedom has suddenly and contradictorily been announced, but because the freedom has never been general and has always been understood against the background of an originary exclusion that gives it meaning.

This is a large thesis, but before tackling it directly I want to buttress my case with another example, taken not from the seventeenth century but from the Charter and case law of Canada. Canadian thinking about freedom of expression departs from the line usually taken in the United States in ways that bring that country very close to the *Aereopagitica* as I have expounded it. The differences are fully on display in a recent landmark case, *R. v. Keegstra*.[1] James Keegstra was a high school teacher in Alberta who, it was established by evidence, "systematically denigrated Jews and Judaism in his classes." He described Jews as treacherous, subversive, sadistic, money-loving, power hungry, and child-killers. He declared them "responsible for depressions, anarchy, chaos, wars, and revolution," and required his students "to regurgitate these notions in essays and examinations." Keegstra was indicted under section 319(2) of the Criminal Code and convicted. The Court of Appeal reversed and the Crown appealed to the Supreme Court, which reinstated the lower court's verdict.

Section 319(2) reads in part, "Everyone who, by communicating statements other than in private conversation, willfully promotes hatred against any identifiable group is guilty of . . . an indictable offense and is liable to imprisonment for a term not exceeding two years." In the United States, this provision of the code would almost certainly be struck down because, under the First Amendment, restrictions on speech are apparently prohibited without qualification. To be sure, the Canadian Charter has its own version of the First Amendment, in section 2(b): "Everyone has the following fundamental freedoms . . . (b) freedom of thought, belief, opinion, and expression, including freedom of the press and other media of communication." But section 2(b), like every other section of the Charter, is qualified by section 1: "The Canadian Charter of Rights and Freedoms guarantees the rights and freedoms set out in it subject only to such reasonable limits prescribed by law as can be demonstrably justified in a free and democratic society." Or in other words, every right and freedom herein granted can be trumped if its exercise is found to be in conflict with the principles that underwrite the society.

This is what happens in *Keegstra* as the majority finds that section 319(2) of the Criminal Code does in fact violate the right of freedom of expression guaranteed by the Charter, but is nevertheless a *per-*

missible restriction because it accords with the principles proclaimed in section 1. There is, of course, a dissent that reaches the conclusion that would have been reached by most, if not all, U.S. courts; but even in dissent the minority is faithful to Canadian ways of reasoning. "The question," it declares, "is always one of balance," and thus even when a particular infringement of Charter section 2(b) has been declared unconstitutional, as it would have been by the minority, the question remains open with respect to the next case. In the United States the question is presumed closed and can only be pried open by special tools. In our legal culture as it is presently constituted, if one yells "free speech" in a crowded courtroom and makes it stick, the case is over.

Of course, it is not that simple. Despite the apparent absoluteness of the First Amendment, there are any number of ways of getting around it, ways that are known to every student of the law. In general, the preferred strategy is to manipulate the distinction, essential to First Amendment jurisprudence, between speech and action. The distinction is essential because no one would think to frame a First Amendment that began "Congress shall make no law abridging freedom of action;" for that would amount to saying "Congress shall make no law," which would amount to saying "There shall be no law," only actions uninhibited and unregulated. If the First Amendment is to make any sense, have any bite, speech must be declared not to be a species of action, or to be a special form of action lacking the aspects of action that cause it to be the object of regulation. The latter strategy is the favored one and usually involves the separation of speech from consequences. This is what Archibald Cox does when he assigns to the First Amendment the job of protecting "expressions separable from conduct harmful to other individuals and the community." The difficulty of managing this segregation is well known: speech always seems to be crossing the line into action where it becomes, at least potentially, consequential. In the face of this categorical instability, First Amendment theorists and jurists fashion a distinction within the distinction: some forms of speech are not really speech because they have a tendency to incite violence; they are, as the court declares in *Chaplinsky v. New Hampshire* (1942), "fighting words," words "likely to provoke the average person to retaliation, and thereby cause a breach of the peace."

The trouble with this definition is that it distinguishes not between fighting words and words that remain safely and merely expressive, but between words that are provocative to one group (the group that falls under the rubric "average person") and words that might be provocative to other groups, groups of persons not now considered average. And if you ask what words are likely to be provocative to those non-average groups, what are likely to be *their* fighting words, the answer is anything and everything, for as Justice Holmes said long ago (in *Gitlow v. New York*), every idea is an incitement to somebody, and since ideas come packaged in sentences, in words, every sentence is potentially, in some situation that might occur tomorrow, a fighting word and therefore a candidate for regulation. That may be why the doctrine of "fighting words" has been more invoked than honored since 1942. If the category is not a formal one, but one that varies with the varying sensitivities of different groups, there is no utterance that it does not include, and we are led to the conclusion that there is nothing for the First Amendment to protect, no such thing as "speech alone" or speech separable from harmful conduct, no such thing as "mere speech" or the simple non-consequential expression of ideas. It would follow from this conclusion that when a court rules in the name of these non-existent things, it is really doing something else; it is deciding to permit certain harms done by words because it believes that by permitting them it upholds a value greater than the value of preventing them. That value will not, however, be the value of speech, per se, but of whatever set of concerns is judged by the court to override the concerns of those who find a particular form of speech harmful.

At this point a First Amendment purist might ask, "Why couldn't that overriding concern be the protection of speech? Why couldn't freedom of speech be the greater value to which other values must yield in the event of a clash?" The answer is that freedom of expression would only be a primary value if it didn't matter what was said; didn't matter in the sense that no one gave a damn, but just liked to hear talk. There are contexts like that, a Hyde Park corner or a call-in talk show where people get to sound off for the sheer fun of it. These, however, are special contexts, artificially bounded spaces designed to assure that talking is not taken seriously. In ordinary contexts, talk is produced with the goal of trying to move the world in one direction rather than another. In these contexts—the contexts of everyday life—you go to the trouble of asserting that x is y only because you suspect that some people are wrongly asserting that x is z or that x doesn't exist. You assert, in short, because you give a damn, not about assertion—as if it were a value in and of itself—but about what your assertion is about. It may seem paradoxical, but free expression could only be a primary value if what you are valuing is the right to make noise, but if you are engaged in some purposive activity in the course of which speech happens to be produced, sooner or later you will come to a point when you decide that some forms of speech do not further but endanger that purpose.

Take the case of universities and colleges. Could it be the purpose of such places to encourage free expression? If the answer were "yes" it would be hard to say why there would be any need for classes, or examinations, or departments, or disciplines, or libraries, since freedom of expression requires nothing but a soapbox or an open telephone line. The very fact of the university's machinery—of the events, rituals, and procedures that fill its calendar—argues for some other, more substantive, purpose. In relation to that purpose (which will be realized differently in different kinds of institutions), the flourishing of free expression will in almost all circumstances be an obvious good; but in some circumstances, freedom of expression may pose a threat to that purpose, and at that point, it may be necessary to discipline or regulate speech, lest, to paraphrase Milton, the institution sacrifice itself to one of its *accidental* features.

Interestingly enough, the same conclusion is reached (inadvertently) by Congressman Henry Hyde, who is addressing these very issues in a recently offered amendment to Title VI of the Civil Rights Act. The first section of the amendment states its purpose, to protect "the free speech rights of college students" by prohibiting private as well as public educational institutions from "subjecting any student to disciplinary sanctions solely on the basis of conduct that is speech." The second section enumerates the remedies available to students whose speech rights may have been abridged; and the third, which is to my mind the nub of the matter, declares as an exception to the amendment's jurisdiction any "educational institution that is controlled by a religious organization," on the reasoning that the application of the amendment to such institutions "would not be consistent with the religious tenets of such organization." In effect, what Congressman Hyde is saying is that at the heart of these colleges and universities is a set of beliefs, and it would be wrong to require them to tolerate behavior, including speech behavior, inimical to those beliefs. But insofar as this logic is persuasive, it applies across the board; for all educational institutions rest on some set of beliefs—no institution is "just there" independent of any purpose—and it is hard to see why the rights of an institution to protect and preserve its basic "tenets" should be restricted only to those that are religiously controlled. Read strongly, the third section of the amendment undoes sections one and two—the exception becomes, as it always was, the rule—and points us to a balancing test very much like that employed in Canadian law: given that any college or university is informed by a core rationale, an administrator faced with complaints about offensive speech should ask whether damage to the core would be greater if the speech were tolerated or regulated.

The objection to this line of reasoning is well known and has recently been reformulated by Benno Schmidt, president of Yale University. According to Schmidt, speech-codes on campuses constitute "well-intentioned but misguided efforts to give values of community and harmony a higher place than freedom" (*Wall Street Journal,* May 6, 1991). "When the goals of harmony collide with freedom of expression,"

184

he continues, "freedom must be the paramount obligation of an academic community." The flaw in this logic is on display in the phrase "academic community"; for the phrase recognizes what Schmidt would deny, that expression only occurs in communities; if not in an academic community, then in a shopping mall community or a dinner-party community or an airplane-ride community or an office community. Arguments like Schmidt's only get their purchase by imagining expression occurring in *no* community, in an environment without the pervasive pressures and pressurings that come along with any socially organizing activity. The same (impossibly) quarantined and pristine space is the location of his preferred value, freedom, which in his conception is not freedom *for* anything, but just "freedom," an urge without direction, as expression is for him an emission without assertive content. Of course the speech to which campus codes are a response is full of content and productive of injury; but Schmidt is able to skirt this difficulty by reducing the content to a matter of style and the injury to an offense against sensibility. This is the work done by the word "obnoxious" when Schmidt urges us to protect speech "no matter how obnoxious in content." In this formulation, obnoxiousness becomes the content of the speech and the deeper affront that might provoke efforts to curtail it is pushed into the background. "Obnoxious" suggests that the injury or offense is a surface one that a large-minded ("liberated and humane") person should be able to tolerate if not embrace. The idea that the effects of speech can penetrate to the core—either for good or for ill—is never entertained; everything is kept on the level of weightless verbal exchange; there is no sense of the lacerating harms

that speech of certain kinds can inflict.

To this Schmidt would no doubt reply, as he does in his essay, that harmful speech should be answered not by regulation, but by more speech; but that would make sense only if the effects of speech could be canceled out by additional speech, only if the pain and humiliation caused by racial or religious epithets could be ameliorated by saying something like "So's your old man." What Schmidt fails to realize at every level of his argument is that expression is more than a matter of proffering and receiving propositions, that words do work in the world of a kind that cannot be confined to a purely cognitive realm of "mere" ideas.

It could be said, however, that I myself mistake the nature of the work done by freely tolerated speech because I am too focused on short-run outcomes and fail to understand that the good effects of speech will be realized not in the present, but in a future whose emergence regulation could only inhibit. This line of reasoning would also weaken one of my key points, that speech in and of itself cannot be a value and is only worth worrying about if it is in the service of something with which it cannot be identical. My mistake, one could argue, is to equate the "something" in whose service speech is with some locally espoused value (e.g., the end of racism, the empowerment of disadvantaged minorities), whereas in fact we should think of that "something" as a now inchoate shape that will be given firm lines only by time's pencil. That is why the shape now receives such indeterminate characterizations (e.g. true self-fulfillment, a more perfect polity, a more capable citizenry, a less partial truth); we cannot now know it, and therefore we must not prematurely fix it in ways that will bind successive generations to error.

This forward-looking view of what the First Amendment protects has a great appeal, in part because it continues in a secular form the Puritan celebration of millenarian hopes, but it imposes a requirement so severe that one would expect more justification than is usually provided. The requirement is that we endure whatever pain racist and hate speech inflicts for the sake of a future whose emergence we can only take on faith. In a specifically religious vision like Milton's this makes perfect sense (it is indeed the whole of Christianity), but in the context of a politics that puts its trust in the world and not in the Holy Spirit, it raises more questions than it answers and could be seen as the other prong of a strategy designed to delegitimize the complaints of victimized groups. The first strategy, as I have noted, is to define speech in such a way as to render it inconsequential (on the model of "sticks and stones will break my bones, but . . ."); the second strategy is to acknowledge the (often grievous) consequences of speech, but declare that we must suffer them in the name of something that cannot be named. The two strategies are denials from slightly different directions of the present effects of racist speech; one confines those effects to a closed and safe realm of pure mental activity; the other imagines the effects of speech spilling over into the world, but only in an ever-receding future for whose sake we must forever defer taking action.

I find both strategies unpersuasive, but my own skepticism concerning them is less important than the fact that in general they seem to have worked; in the parlance of the marketplace (a parlance First Amendment commentators love), many in the society seemed to have bought them. Why? The answer, I think, is that people cling to

First Amendment pieties because they do not wish to face what they correctly take to be the alternative. That alternative is *politics,* the realization (at which I have already hinted) that decisions about what is and is not protected in the realm of expression will rest not on principle or firm doctrine, but on the ability of some persons to interpret—recharacterize or rewrite— principle and doctrine in ways that lead to the protection of speech they want heard and the regulation of speech they want silenced. (That is how George Bush can argue *for* flag-burning statutes and *against* campus hate-speech codes.) When the First Amendment is successfully invoked the result is not a victory for free speech in the face of a challenge from politics, but a *political victory* won by the party that has managed to wrap its agenda in the mantle of free speech. It is from just such a conclusion—a conclusion that would put politics *inside* the First Amendment—that commentators recoil, saying things like "this could render the First Amendment a dead letter," or "this would leave us with no normative guidance in determining when and what speech to protect," or "this effaces the distinction between speech and action," or "this is incompatible with any viable notion of freedom of expression." To these statements (culled more or less at random from recent law review pieces) I would reply that the First Amendment has always been a dead letter if one understood its "liveness" to depend on the identification and protection of a realm of "mere" expression or discussion distinct from the realm of regulatable conduct; the distinction between speech and action has always been effaced in principle, although in practice it can take whatever form the prevailing political conditions mandate; we have never had any normative guidance for marking off protected from unprotected speech; rather the guidance we have has been fashioned (and refashioned) in the very political struggles over which it then (for a time) presides. In short, the name of the game has always been politics, even when (indeed, especially when) it is played by stigmatizing politics as the area to be avoided.

It is important to be clear as to what this means. It does *not* mean that in the absence of normative guidelines we should throw up our hands and either regulate everything or allow everything. Rather it means that the question of whether or not to regulate will always be a local one and that we can not rely on abstractions that are either empty of content or filled with the content of some partisan agenda to generate a "principled" answer. Instead we must consider in every case what is at stake and what are the risks and gains of alternative courses of action. In the course of this consideration many things many be of help, but among them will not be phrases like "freedom of speech" or "the right of individual expression," because as they are used now, these phrases tend to obscure rather than clarify our dilemmas. Once they are deprived of their talismanic force, once it is no longer strategically effective simply to invoke them in the act of walking away from a problem, the conversation could continue in directions that are now blocked by a First Amendment absolutism that has only been honored in the breach anyway. To the student reporter who complains that in the wake of the promulgation of a speech code at the University of Wisconsin there is now something in the back of his mind as he writes, one could reply, "There was always something in the back of your mind and perhaps it might be better to have this code in the back of your mind than whatever was in there before." And when someone warns about the slippery slope and predicts mournfully that if you restrict one form of speech, you never know what will be restricted next, one could reply, "some form of speech is always being restricted; else there could be no meaningful assertion; we have always and already slid down the slippery slope; someone is always going to be restricted next, and it is your job to make sure that the someone is not you." And when someone observes, as someone surely will, that anti-harassment codes chill speech, one could reply that since speech only becomes intelligible against the background of what isn't being said, the background of what has already been silenced, the only question is the political one of which speech is going to be chilled, and, all things considered, it seems a good thing to chill speech like "nigger," "cunt," "kike," and "faggot." And if someone then says, "But what happened to free speech principles?" one could say what I have now said a dozen times, free speech principles don't exist except as a component in a bad argument in which such principles are invoked to mask motives that would not withstand close scrutiny.

An example of a wolf wrapped in First Amendment clothing is an advertisement that ran recently in the Duke University student newspaper, *The Chronicle*. Signed by Bradley R. Smith, well-known as a purveyor of anti-Semitic neo-Nazi propaganda, the ad is packaged as a scholarly treatise: four densely packed columns complete with "learned" references, undocumented statistics, and an array of so-called authorities. The message of the ad is that the Holocaust never occurred and that the German state never "had a policy to exterminate the Jewish people (or anyone else) by putting them to death in gas chambers."

In a spectacular instance of the increasingly popular "blame the victim" strategy, the Holocaust "story" or "myth" is said to have been fabricated in order "to drum up world sympathy for Jewish causes." The "evidence" supporting these assertions is a slick blend of supposedly probative facts— "not a single autopsied body has been shown to be gassed"—and sly insinuations of a kind familiar to readers of *Mein Kampf* and *The Protocols of the Elders of Zion.*

The slickest thing of all, however, is the presentation of the argument as an exercise in free speech—the ad is subtitled *The Case for Open Debate*—that could be objected to only by "thought police" and censors. This strategy bore immediate fruit in the decision of the newspaper staff to accept the ad despite a longstanding (and historically honored) policy of refusing materials that contain ethnic and racial slurs or are otherwise offensive. The reasoning of the staff (explained by the editor in a special column) was that under the First Amendment advertisers have the "right" to be published. "American newspapers are built on the principles of free speech and free press, so how can a newspaper deny these rights to anyone?" The answer to this question is that an advertiser is not denied his rights simply because a single media organ declines his copy, so long as other avenues of publication are available and there has been no state suppression of his views. This is not to say that there could not be a case for printing the ad; only that the case cannot rest on a supposed First Amendment obligation. One might argue for example that printing the ad would foster healthy debate or that lies are more likely to be shown up for what they are if they are brought to the light of day, but these are precisely the arguments the editor *disclaims* in her eagerness to

take a "principled" free speech stand. By running the First Amendment up the nearest flagpole and rushing to salute it, the editor and her staff short-circuited their thought processes and threw away the opportunity to take the serious measure of a complicated issue. They allowed First Amendment slogans to blur the distinction between the positive effects of the exchange of ideas and the harm done—a harm to which they contribute—when flat-out lies are able to merchandise themselves as ideas. They rented the dignity of their publication to a hatemonger masquerading as a scholar because they were bamboozled by the invocation of a doctrine that did not really apply and was certainly not dispositive. In this case, at least, the First Amendment did bad work, first in the mouth (or pen) of Mr. Smith and then in the collective brain of the student editors.

Let me be clear. I am not saying that First Amendment principles are inherently bad (they are *inherently* nothing), only that independent of some particular partisan vision, they have no necessary content; and if the vision by which they have been appropriated is hostile to your interests, you would be well advised not to rely on them. This does not mean that you would be better off if they were not available; like any other formulas embedded in the process by which decisions are made, free speech principles function to protect society against over-hasty outcomes; they serve as channels through which an argument must pass on its way to ratification. But the channels are not, as they are sometimes said to be, merely and reassuringly procedural. They have as much content as the contents they "filter," and therefore one must be alert to the content they presently bear and not look to them for a deliverance from politics, for it is politics, either your own or someone else's, that is responsible for the form free speech principles now have. My counsel is therefore pragmatic rather than draconian: so long as so-called "free speech principles" have been fashioned by your enemies, contest their relevance to the issue at hand; but if you manage to refashion them in line with your purposes, urge them with a vengeance.

It is a counsel that follows from the thesis that there is no such thing as free speech, which is not, after all, a thesis as startling or corrosive as may first have seemed. It merely says that there is no class of utterances separable from the world of conduct, and that therefore the identifications of some utterances as members of that non-existent class will always be evidence that a political line has been drawn rather than a line that denies politics entry into the forum of public discourse. It is the job of the First Amendment to mark out an area in which competing views can be considered without state interference; but if the very marking out of that area is itself an interference (as it always will be), First Amendment jurisprudence is inevitably self-defeating and subversive of its own aspirations. That's the bad news. The good news is that precisely *because* speech is never "free" in the two senses required—free of consequences and free from state pressure—speech always matters, is always doing work; because everything we say impinges on the world in ways indistinguishable from the effects of physical action, we must take responsibility for our verbal performances—*all* of them—and not assume that they are being taken care of by a clause in the Constitution. Of course, with responsibility comes risks, but the

have always been our risks and no doctrine of free speech has ever insulated us from them. They are the risks of either allowing or policing the flow of discourse. They are the risks, respectively, of permitting speech that does obvious harm and of shutting off speech in ways that might deny us the benefit of Joyce's *Ulysses* or Lawrence's *Lady Chatterly's Lover* or Titian's paintings. Nothing, I repeat, can insulate us from those risks. (If there is no normative guidance in determining when and what speech to protect, there is no normative guidance in determining what is art—like free speech a category that includes everything and nothing—and what is obscenity.) And, moreover, nothing can provide us with a principle for deciding which risk in the long run is the best to take. I am persuaded that at the present moment, right now, the risk of not attending to hate speech is greater than the risk that by regulating it we will deprive ourselves of valuable voices and insights or slide down the slippery slope toward tyranny. This is a judgment for which I can offer reasons but no guarantees. All I am saying is that the judgments of those who would come down on the other side carry no guarantees either since the abstractions that usually accompany such guarantees are malleable political constructs. It is not that there are no choices to make or means of making them; it is just that the choices as well as the means are inextricable from the din and confusion of partisan struggle. There is no safe place.

NOTES

1. Reprinted in Volume 2 of this series.

THE NEW YORK REVIEW OF BOOKS

JUNE 11, 1992

THE COMING BATTLES OVER FREE SPEECH*

RONALD DWORKIN

The First Amendment, like the other great clauses of the Bill of Rights, is very abstract. It cannot be applied to concrete cases except by assigning some overall *point* or *purpose* to the Amendment's abstract guarantee of "freedom of speech or of the press." That is not just a matter of asking what the statesmen who drafted, debated, and adopted the First Amendment thought their clauses would accomplish. Contemporary lawyers and judges must try to find a political justification of the First Amendment that fits most past constitutional practice, including past decisions of the Supreme Court, but also provides a compelling reason *why* we should grant freedom of speech such a special and privileged place among our liberties. . . .

. . . Constitutional lawyers and scholars have proposed many different justifications for the free speech and press clauses. Most of them fall into one or the other of two main groups, however. The first treats free speech as important *instrumentally*, that is, not because people have any intrinsic moral right to say what they wish, but because allowing them to do so will produce good effects for the rest of us. Free speech is said to be important, for ex-ample, because, as Holmes declared in his *Abrams* dissent, politics is more likely to discover truth and eliminate error, or to produce good rather than bad policies, if political discussion is free and uninhibited. Or for the reason Madison emphasized: that free speech helps to protect the power of the people to govern themselves. Or for the more common-sense reason that government is less likely to become corrupt if it lacks the power to punish criticism. According to these various instrumental views, America's special commitment to free speech is based on a national endorsement of a strategy, a collective bet that free speech will do us more good than harm over the long run.

The second kind of justification of free speech supposes that freedom of speech is valuable, not just in virtue of the consequences that it has, but because it is an essential and "constitutive" feature of a just political society that government treat all its adult members, except those who are incompetent, as responsible moral agents. That requirement has two dimensions. First, morally responsible people insist on making up their own minds about what is good or bad in life or in politics, or what is true

---

* Reviewing Anthony Lewis, *Make No Law: The Sullivan Case and the First Amendment* (1992). Endnotes have been renumbered.

190

and false in matters of justice or faith. Government insults its citizens, and denies their moral responsibility, when it decrees that they cannot be trusted to hear opinions that might persuade them to dangerous or offensive convictions. We retain our dignity, as individuals, only by insisting that no one—no official and no majority—has the right to withhold opinion from us on the ground that we are not fit to hear and consider it.

For many people moral responsibility has another, more active, aspect as well: a responsibility not only to form convictions of one's own, but to express these to others, out of respect and concern for them, and out of a compelling desire that truth be known, justice served, and the good secured. Government frustrates and denies that aspect of moral personality when it disqualifies some people from exercising these responsibilities on the ground that their convictions make them unworthy participants. So long as government exercises political dominion over a person, and demands political obedience from him, it may not deny him either of these two attributes of moral responsibility, no matter how hateful the opinions he wishes to consider or propagate, any more than it may deny him an equal vote. If it does, it forfeits a substantial ground of its claim to legitimate power over him. The wrong is just as great when government forbids the expression of some social attitude or taste as when it censors explicitly political speech; citizens have as much right to contribute to the formation of the moral or aesthetic climate as they do to participate in politics.

Of course, the instrumental and constitutive justifications of free speech are not mutually exclusive.[1] John Stuart Mill endorsed both of them in *On Liberty*. So did Brandeis in his remarkably insightful and comprehensive dissent in *Whitney*: he said that "those who won our independence believed that the final end of the state was to make men free to develop their faculties" and that "free speech is valuable both as an end and as a means," which is a classic endorsement of the constitutive view. Brandeis was right that both kinds of justification are needed in order fully to explain First Amendment law; it is hardly surprising that so complex and fundamental a constitutional right as the right of free speech should reflect a variety of overlapping justifications.

The two kinds of justification are moreover similar in many ways. Neither claims that freedom of speech is absolute; both allow that the values they cite may be overridden in special cases: in deciding, for example, how far military information may be censored. But the two justifications are nevertheless crucially different, because the instrumental justification is both more fragile and more limited. It is more fragile because, as we shall see, there are circumstances in which the strategic goals it appeals to might well be thought to argue for restricting rather than protecting speech. It is more limited because, while the constitutive justification extends, in principle, to all aspects of speech or reflection in which moral responsibility demands independence, the instrumental one, at least in its most popular versions, concentrates mainly on the protection of political speech.

If the point of freedom of speech is only to ensure that democracy works well—that people have the information they need in order to vote properly, or to protect democracy from usurping officials, or to ensure that government is not corrupt or incompetent—then free speech is much less important in matters of art or social or personal decisions. The First Amendment then protects sexually explicit literature, for example, only on the strained and easily resisted assumption that people need to read such literature in order to vote intelligently in national or local elections. Indeed, some scholars who accept the instrumental view as the exclusive justification of free speech have argued, as Robert Bork did, that the First Amendment protects nothing *but* plainly political speech, and does not extend to art or literature or science at all.[2] Even those who reject that view, on the ground that literature and science can sometimes bear on politics, nevertheless insist that the main burden of the First Amendment is the protection of political speech, and that any protection the Amendment offers for other kinds of discourse is derivative from that principal function.

[Justice] Brennan seemed to rely almost exclusively on the instrumental justification in his opinion for the Court in [*New York Times v. Sullivan* (1964)]. He limited First Amendment protection to cases involving libel of "public officials" rather than extending protection to all libel defendants. He quoted Madison's instrumental argument that free speech is necessary in order to make the people rulers of the government rather than the other way around. He quoted passages from earlier Supreme Court decisions emphasizing the different instrumental argument Holmes had made in his *Abrams* dissent, in which he said that truth emerges in a free market of ideas. . . . Only at one point did Brennan suggest a constitutive justification for free speech. He spoke of "the citizen-critic" of government; he said, "It is as much his duty to criticize as it is the official's duty to administer," and cited Brandeis's opinion in *Whitney*, which, as I said, recognized that free speech is an end as well as a means. But Brennan limited even this isolated suggestion of a constitutive justification to the political context.[3] . . .

In retrospect, however, Brennan's near exclusive reliance on the instrumental justification, and his emphasis on the special role of political speech, seems regrettable even if it was necessary to collect a majority, because it may, unwittingly, have reinforced the popular but dangerous assumption that that is all there is to the First Amendment, and that the constitutive justification is either misplaced or unnecessary. In fact, relying exclusively on the instrumental justification is dangerous for free speech in ways that have already begun to be realized. . . .

We should start, in considering that danger, by noticing that the Madisonian version of the instrumental justification, on which Brennan particularly relied, cannot provide an intellectually acceptable justification even for the First Amendment's political core. Madison's argument that free speech is necessary if the people are to be in charge of their own government does explain why government must not be allowed to practice clandestine censorship which the people would reject if they were aware of it. But that argument does not explain why the majority of people should not be allowed to impose censorship that it approves and wants. A referendum might well reveal, for example, that a majority of Americans would prefer government to have the power to censor what it deems to be politically and diplomatically sensitive material, such as the *Pentagon Papers*. If so, then the Court's obviously correct decision that government does not have that power[4] can hardly be justified by Madison's instrumental argument, except on the most implausibly paternalistic grounds. The great expansion of First Amendment protection in the decades after World War I plainly contracted, rather than expanded, the majority's power to have the form of government it itself wants.

Some of that expanded protection can of course be justified on the different instrumental argument made by Hand and Holmes: that the truth about political issues is more likely to emerge if no idea is excluded from the discussion. It is certainly plausible that the public will make more intelligent decisions about race and civil rights if newspapers are free to write about these matters without fear of libel suits, and better decisions about war and peace if newspapers cannot be stopped from publishing documents like the *Pentagon Papers*.

But even this form of the instrumental argument cannot justify some of the most important of the federal court decisions expanding First Amendment protection in recent decades, including the Supreme Court's decision, in *Brandenburg v. Ohio*, that states may not punish someone who says, wearing a hood at a Ku Klux Klan rally, that "the nigger should be returned to Africa, the Jew returned to Israel,"[5] and the Seventh Circuit's decision that a small band of neo-Nazis could not be prevented from marching with swastikas in Skokie, Illinois, where many Holocaust survivors lived.[6] Is our electorate really in a better position to choose its leaders or its policies because it permits speech of that kind? Would we be in a worse position to sift truth from falsity—would the marketplace of ideas be less efficient—if klansmen or Nazis or sexist bigots were silent?

It might be said that we cannot trust legislators or judges to draw distinctions between valuable and worthless political comment, so that in order to protect seri-

ous newspapers discussing serious issues we must also protect klansmen and Nazis spreading hate and causing pain. But that slippery-slope argument ignores the ability of lawyers to draw difficult distinctions here as they do in every other part of the law. If the Supreme Court can distinguish political speech from commercial speech, which it has decided enjoys much weaker constitutional protection, then it could also distinguish racist or sexist speech from other forms of political comment. It could uphold a statute carefully drafted to outlaw only speech that insults people on grounds of race, religion, or gender, in the manner of the British Race Relations Act, for example.

I emphasize this point not, of course, to recommend such a course, but to show that the instrumental justification does not offer much genuine protection against a statute of that character. In fact, the Supreme Court will soon rule on just such a statute. Last December, it heard oral argument in *R.A.V. v. St. Paul* and will presumably announce its decision sometime this spring. The City of St. Paul adopted an ordinance prohibiting display of a symbol that can be expected to cause "anger, alarm or resentment in others" on the basis of their race, religion, or sex, and providing a ninety-day jail sentence for that offense. Robert Viktoria was prosecuted, under that ordinance, for burning a cross on a black family's lawn. Of course, burning a cross on someone else's lawn is forbidden by ordinary criminal law, and Viktoria will be tried for that ordinary crime even if the Supreme Court decides that he cannot be punished under the special ordinance. The *Viktoria* case raises the question whether a state may constitutionally make an assault a special crime, carrying a larger sentence, because it is intended to express a conviction the community disapproves of. The Court's decision will undoubtedly have repercussions for the constitutionality of the regulations that many state universities, which are subject to the First Amendment, have recently adopted forbidding speech that expresses racial or sexual hatred or bias.

It is very important that the Supreme Court confirm that the First Amendment protects even such speech; that it protects, as Holmes said, even speech that we loathe. That is crucial for the reason that the constitutive justification of free speech emphasizes: because we are a liberal society committed to individual moral responsibility, and *any* censorship on grounds of content is inconsistent with that commitment. The instrumental arguments Brennan relied on in *Sullivan* are now being widely used, however, not to support but to undermine that view of liberal society. In a recent defense of campus constraints on "politically incorrect" speech, for example, Stanley Fish insisted, "Speech, in short, is never and could not be an independent value, but is always asserted against a background of some assumed conception of the good to which it must yield in the event of conflict." Fish rejects the very possibility of what I called a constitutive defense of free speech; he insists that any defense must be instrumental, and that censoring politically incorrect speech will serve the instrumental purpose better than freedom will.[7]

Catherine MacKinnon, Frank Michelman, and others have offered a similar argument for censoring pornography and other material offensive to women. They say that since women are more effective participants in the political process when they are not insulted by offensive material, the instrumental goal of effective de-

mocracy is actually better served by invading than protecting freedom of speech. They suggest, for example, that the ordinance Indianapolis adopted in response to a feminist campaign, which prohibited, among other kinds of literature, materials that "present women as enjoying pain or humiliation or rape," would have improved rather than compromised democracy, because such literature "silences" women and so decreases their voice and role in democratic politics. The Seventh Circuit Court of Appeals, in an opinion by Judge Frank Easterbrook which I have discussed in these pages,[8] rejected that argument, and held the statute unconstitutional because it outlawed not obscene publications generally, but just those promoting a particular idea or attitude. Easterbrook tacitly relied on the constitutive rather than the instrumental justification for free speech, and the Supreme Court can honestly declare the St. Paul ordinance invalid, as it should, only if it too recognizes that justification as well as repeating the old instrumental rhetoric. . . .

In a recent decision, the Supreme Court of Canada accepted a different instrumental argument for upholding a statute censoring certain forms of pornography.[9] The Canadian Charter of Rights and Freedoms protects freedom of expression, though with qualifications the First Amendment does not recognize. The Canadian Court conceded that the effect of its ruling was to narrow that constitutional protection, but said that "the proliferation of materials which seriously offend the values fundamental to our society is a substantial concern which justifies restricting the otherwise full exercise of the freedom of expression." That is an amazing statement. It is the central, defining, premise of freedom of speech that the offensiveness of ideas, or the challenge they offer to traditional ideas, cannot be a valid reason for censorship; once that premise is abandoned it is difficult to see what free speech means. The Court added that some sexually explicit material harms women because "materials portraying women as a class as objects for sexual exploitation and abuse have a negative impact on the individual's sense of self-worth and acceptance." But that kind of harm is so close to mere offensiveness that it cannot count, by itself, as a valid reason for censorship either. Every powerful and controversial idea has a potential negative impact on someone's self-esteem. The Canadian Court, presumably, would not uphold a ban on non-pornographic literature whose purpose was explicitly to deny the equal worth of women, no matter how persuasive or effective that objectionable literature might be.[10]

These trends are ominous for liberty and for democracy. If Brennan had given a more prominent place to the constitutive justification in his restatement of the First Amendment premises in *Sullivan*, it would now be easier for American courts to reject the arguments that appealed to the Canadian Supreme Court, and to hold statutes like the St. Paul ordinance and laws [restricting sexually explicit literature] unconstitutional.

NOTES

1. See an important pair of articles by the Harvard philosopher Thomas Scanlon. In the first, "A Theory of Freedom of Expression," *Philosophy and Public Affairs*, Vol. 1, p. 204 (1972), he developed a Kantian argument for the constitutive justification. In the second, "Freedom of Expression and Categories of Expression," *University of Pittsburgh Law Review*, Vol. 40 (1979), p. 519, partly in criticism of the first article, he emphasized the complex character of any adequate account of the right to free speech, in which constitutive and instrumental factors must both figure.

2. Robert Bork, "Neutral Principles and Some First Amendment Problems," *Indiana Law Journal*, Vol. 47 (1971). In the Senate hearings considering his nomination to the Supreme Court, Bork said he had abandoned this view.

3. Lewis points out that this remark reflected the opinions of Alexander Meiklejohn, a political scientist who had long been a passionate defender of the view—which merges aspects of the instrumental and constitutive justification—that censorship of political opinion is unjustified because citizens are entitled to as much information as possible in order to fulfill their responsibilities to govern themselves. . . .

4. *New York Times v. United States*, 403 US 713 (1971).

5. 395 US 444 (1969).

6. *Collin v. Smith*, 578 F. 2d 1197 [(1978)]. The Supreme Court refused to stay the Seventh Circuit's decision. 436 US 953 (1978).

7. See Stanley Fish, "There's no Such Thing as Free Speech and It's a Good Thing, Too" [reproduced in Volume 2 of this series]. Fish claims to consider and reject the argument that "freedom of speech is the greater value to which other values must yield." But he construes that argument as the preposterous claim that the point of speaking is just speaking for its own sake. He confuses people's reasons for speaking, which are of course to promote some other purpose, with the reasons government might have for protecting their right to speak, which may include constitutive as well as instrumental reasons.

8. "Liberty and Pornography," *The New York Review*, August 15, 1991.

9. *Butler v. Her Majesty the Queen,* decided February 27, 1992.

10. I discuss the argument that pornography can be banned because it demeans women in "Liberty and Pornography."

No. 90-7675

In The

Supreme Court of the United States

October Term, 1991

———————◆———————

R.A.V.,

Petitioner,

v.

CITY OF ST. PAUL, MINNESOTA,

Respondent.

———————◆———————

On Writ Of Certiorari
To The Minnesota Supreme Court

———————◆———————

BRIEF *AMICUS CURIAE* OF THE
NATIONAL BLACK WOMEN'S HEALTH PROJECT
IN SUPPORT OF RESPONDENT

———————◆———————

CATHARINE A. MACKINNON*
625 S. State Street
Ann Arbor, Michigan 48109-1215
(313) 747-4046

BURKE MARSHALL
127 Wall Street
New Haven, Connecticut 06520
(203) 432-4953

Counsel for Amicus Curiae

*Counsel of Record

197

———————◆———————

SUMMARY OF ARGUMENT

The Minnesota Supreme Court upheld St. Paul Minn. Leg. Code section 292.02 (1990) ("§ 292.02") by authoritatively construing it as limited to "fighting words" under *Chaplinsky v. New Hampshire*, 315 U.S. 568 (1942), thus applying only to expressive conduct which falls outside First Amendment protection. *Matter of Welfare of R.A.V.*, 464 N.W. 2d 507 (Minn. 1991). While accepting this analysis, the National Black Women's Health Project respectfully submits that the ordinance promotes the government's "compelling interest in eradicating discrimination," *Roberts v. U.S. Jaycees*, 468 U.S. 609, 623 (1983) (sex discrimination), *Korematsu v. United States*, 323 U.S. 214, 216 (1944) (racial discrimination constitutionally suspect), *Richmond v. J.A. Croson*, 488 U.S. 469, 494 (1989) (same) in a way which outweighs First Amendment interests.

Crossburning, of which defendant R.A.V. is accused, should be recognized as a terrorist hate practice of intimidation and harassment which, contrary to the purposes of the Fourteenth Amendment, works to institutionalize the civil inequality of protected groups. As applied to petitioner and others who engage in related practices, the statute in question does not violate the First Amendment because social inequality, including through expressive conduct, is a harm for which states are entitled leeway in regulation. *New York v. Ferber*, 458 U.S. 747 (1982) (harm to mental and physical health of children used in child pornography justifies its regulation); *Pittsburgh Press Co. v. Pittsburgh Comm'n. on Human Relations*, 413 U.S. 376 (1973) (interest in eradicating sex discrimination outweighs First Amendment interest in sex-segregated advertising); *U.S. v. O'Brien*, 391 U.S. 367, 376-377 (1968) (communicative conduct may be regulated under specific conditions). The goal of eradicating inequality is advanced narrowly, leaving ample room for less coercive and harassing means of expressing the same message.

Applied, as here, to discriminatory expressive action, § 292.02 significantly advances equality and damages freedom of expression virtually not at all. The compelling interest in eradicating discrimination justifies any impact that application of the statute, as narrowed by the Minnesota Supreme Court and justified herein, may have on the expressive freedoms of perpetrators of symbolic acts of bigotry. Because the legitimate reach of § 292.02 dwarfs any arguably impermissible applications, *Broadrick v. Oklahoma*, 413 U.S. 601 (1973), the ordinance is not unconstitutionally overbroad.

———————◆———————

ARGUMENT

I. THE CHALLENGED ORDiNANCE PROMOIES THE COMPELLING GOVERNMENTAL INTEREST IN EQUALITY, OUTWEIGHING FIRST AMEND-MENT CONCERNS.

A. The Ordinance Prohibits Discriminatory Practices Which Violate And Undermine The Equality Rights Of Target Groups.

On its face, § 292.02 prohibits, with qualifications, the placing of "a symbol, object, appellation, characterization or graffiti, including but not limited to, a burning cross or Nazi swastika" on public or private property. The qualifications include a *scienter* requirement ("knows or has reasonable grounds to know"), injurious or dangercus consequences ("arouses anger, alarm, or resentment in others"), and a traditional prohibited basis on "race, color, creed, religion, or gender." This case applies the statute to an incident in which white youths allegedly burned a cross on the lawn of the one African American family in a St. Paul neighborhood. *Matter of Welfare of R.A.V.*, 464 N.W. 2d 507 (Minn. 1991).

The flaming cross is a well-recognized symbcl of racial and religious hatred and instrument of persecution and intimidation, historically directed principaily against Blacks and Jews. By the 1920's, the Ku Klux Klan -- a white supremacist racial hate organization which is secret, violent, authoritarian, xenophobic, and rabidly prejudiced – made it the emblem of its presence and the precursor of arson, firebombing, torture, and lynching. See generally Wade, THE FIERY CROSS (1987); Goldberg, HOODED EMPIRE (1981); Alexander, THE KU KLUX

KLAN IN THE SOUTHWEST (1965); Katz, THE INVISI-
BLE EMPIRE (1986). One federal district court found that

> .... to attain its end, the klan exploits the forces
> of hate, prejudice, and ignorance. We find that
> the klan relies on systematic economic coercion,
> varieties of intimidation, and physical violence
> in attempting to frustrate the national policy
> expressed in civil rights legislation.
> . . . [K]lansmen pledge their first allegiance to
> their Konstitution and give their first loyalty to
> a cross in flames. *U.S. v. Original Knights of the
> Ku Klux Klan*, 250 F. Supp. 330, 334, 335 (E.D. La.
> 1965).

Crossburning was also directed against Jews by the Nazis
in Germany in the 1930s. Wade, 185. Crossburning, coupled with violence, motivated by invidious animus, has
continued to the present day, escalating in recent years.
McMullen v. Carson, 754 F.2d 936, 938 (11th Cir. 1985);
Marshall v. Bramer, 110 F.R.D. 232, 235-237 (W.D. Ky. 1985)
(collecting cases); Padgett, Racially-Motivated Violence
and Intimidation: Inadequate State Enforcement and Federal Civil Rights Remedies, 75 J. Crim. L. 103 (1984).

Courts have recognized that crossburning threatens violence, *Stevens v. Tillman*, 855 F.2d 394 (7th Cir. 1988), and is a
"particularly invidious act when directed against a black
American," *U.S. v. Salyer*, 893 F.2d 113, 117 (6th Cir. 1989),
one which produces "fear, anxiety, and apprehension for
safety" among Black men, *Ford v. Hollowell*, 385 F. Supp. 1392,
1397 (N.D. Miss. 1974). The Eleventh Circuit, in a case
involving a conviction for crossburning, recognized that
crossburning sought to intimidate a Black family. *U.S. v.
Worthy*, 915 F.2d 1514, 1515 (11th Cir. 1990). The Eighth
Circuit recently concluded that a "cross burning was an

especially intrusive act which invaded the substantial privacy interests of its victims in an essentially intolerable manner." *U.S. v. Lee*, 935 F.2d 952, 956 (8th Cir. 1991). The Sixth Circuit observed similarly that "a black American would be particularly susceptible to the threat of cross burning because of the historical connotations of violence associated with the act." *Salyer*, 893 F.2d 116. That crossburning is a threatening act on the basis of race is uncontested.

Indeed, there is no doubt in anyone's mind what crossburning connotes, conveys, portends, or does. In *U.S. v. Lee*, Lonetta Miller, a seventy-one year old Black woman testified on cross-examination as follows:

> Q: Could you tell the ladies and gentlemen of the jury what a cross burning means, whether it is in the south or anywhere else?

> A: Well it is a form of intimidation; the ku klux klan uses it for threats; promises of violence, and that sort of thing. From what I understand a lot of the cross burnings in the south during the civil rights movement preceded hangings and that sort of thing. 935 F.2d, 956 n.5.

The Eighth Circuit observed there that defendants' crossburning "was tantamount to intimidation by threat of physical violence. It was not mere advocacy, but rather an overt act of intimidation which, because of its historical context, is often considered a precursor to or a promise of violence against black people." 935 F.2d, 956.

All of the cases discussed above involved complaints of crossburning in a context of inequality claims. Crosses have been found burned to intimidate Blacks out of voter registration in a jury selection case, *Ford v. Hollowell,*

385 F. Supp. 1392 (N.D. Miss. 197.); to induce targets to refrain from exercising federally assured rights such as travel, association, and speech under 42 U.S.C. § 1985(3), *Stevens v. Tillman*, 855 F.2d 394 (7th Cir. 1988); and to threaten and intimidate citizens from the free exercise or enjoyment of a civil right under 42 U.S.C. § 241, *U.S. v. Salyer*, 893 F.2d 113 (6th Cir. 1989), *U.S. v. Worthy*, 915 F.2d 1514 (11th Cir. 1990).

Two recent Court of Appeals decisions are particularly apposite to the instant case. In one, the defendant was charged with conspiracy to interfere with housing rights by force or threat of force for burning a cross within sight of an African American family's home. *U.S. v. Lee*, 935 F.2d 952 (8th Cir. 1991) (upholding civil rights claim under 42 U.S.C. § 3631(a) over First Amendment defense). In another, the defendant pled guilty, *inter alia*, to interference with housing rights, stating in the plea agreement that defendants "decided to burn the cross in the victims' yard 'because of the family's race and their presence in the neighborhood . . .' " *U.S. v. Long*, 935 F.2d 1207, 1209 (11th Cir. 1991) (allowing race to be taken into account as a fact in sentencing enhancement).[1]

Existing equality law has long recognized similar practices as violations of civil rights. Title 42 U.S.C. § 1971(b) provides that "no person . . . shall intimidate, threaten, coerce, or attempt to intimidate, threaten, or coerce any other person for the purpose of interfering

---

[1] Some of these cases, such as *Worthy*, also invoke 18 U.S.C. § 844(h)(1), use of fire in the commission of a federal felony. *See e.g.*, *U.S. v. Gresser*, 935 F.2d 96 (6th Cir. 1991).

with the right of such other person to vote or to vote as he may choose . . . " Where sharecropper-tenants in possession of real estate under contract are threatened, intimidated or coerced by landlords for the purpose of interfering with their rights of franchise, *U.S. v. Bruce*, 353 F.2d 474 (5th Cir. 1965); *U.S. v. Beaty*, 288 F.2d 653 (6th Cir. 1961), burning a cross to attempt to intimidate a person out of their voting rights should clearly be covered as well. Similarly, 42 U.S.C. § 2000b provides for an action for threatened loss of equal access to public facilities, under which burning a cross would obviously be included. Crossburning to exclude from housing rights, as in the case at bar, is covered under 42 U.S.C. Section 3631(a), which prevents intimidation of "any person because of his race, color, religion, sex . . . " from exercising rights to fair housing. *See also* 42 U.S.C. § 3617 (1991).

In upholding Title II of the Civil Rights Act of 1964's equal accommodations provision, this Court emphasized that its "fundamental object . . . was to vindicate the deprivation of personal dignity that surely accompanies denials of equal access . . . " *Heart of Atlanta Motel, Inc. v. U.S.*, 379 U.S. 241, 250 (1964). Cowering in terror at night with your family on the floor of your own home in the light of a terrorist cross burning on your lawn is surely a deprivation of personal dignity equal to not being permitted to stay overnight in a motel on the road.

Other civil rights rubrics have long permitted civil actions for conduct covered under § 292.02. Behavior such as hanging a noose over a desk, *Vance v. Southern Bell*, 863 F.2d 1503 (11th Cir. 1989) or in a supply room, *Taylor v. Jones*, 653 F.2d 1196 (8th Cir. 1981), or writing "KKK" on a tool shed in a workplace, *Vaughn v. Pool*

Offshore Co., 683 F.2d 922 (5th Cir. 1982) are legally action-able as discriminatory harassment on the basis of race. Placing pornography in the workplace, arguably a type of conduct based on gender under § 292.02, has been recognized as discriminatory sexual harassment under Title VII. *Robinson v. Jacksonville Shipyards*, 760 F. Supp. 1486 (M.D. Fla. 1991) (posting sex pictures is sexual harassment over First Amendment defense); *but cf. Rabidue v. Osceola Refining Co.*, 805 F.2d 611 (6th Cir. 1986) (posting sex pictures is not sexual harassment because pornography is pervasive; no First Amendment defense raised).

Purely verbal harassment is unproblematically actionable as racial or sexual discrimination or both under state and federal human rights laws. *Rogers v. EEOC*, 454 F.2d 234 (5th Cir. 1971), *cert. denied*, 406 U.S. 957 (1972) (racial epithets); *Friend v. Leidinger*, 446 F. Supp. 361 (E.D. Va. 1977), *aff'd.*, 588 F.2d 61 (4th Cir. 1978) (racial harassment); *Weiss v. U.S.*, 595 F. Supp. 1052 (E.D. Va. 1984) (anti-Semitic epithets). Examples of sexual harassment include *Meritor Savings Bank v. Vinson*, 477 U.S. 57, 65 (1986); *Henson v. City of Dundee*, 682 F.2d 897 (11th Cir. 1982); *Bohen v. East Chicago*, 799 F.2d 1180, 1189 (7th Cir. 1986) (Posner, J., concurring) (sexual abuse and vilification); *Hicks v. Gates Rubber*, 928 F.2d 966 (10th Cir. 1991) (racial and sexual harassment); *Continental Can v. State*, 297 N.W.2d 241, 245-246 (Minn. 1980) (defendant "wished slavery days would return so that he could sexually train [plaintiff] and she would be his bitch," in action for sexual harassment under state human rights law).

Discrimination, it should be noted, is typically effectuated through words like "you're fired;" "it was essential that the understudy to my administrative assistant be a man," *Davis v. Passman*, 422 U.S. 228, 230 (1971); and posted signs stating "whites only." *See, e.g., Palmer v. Thompson*, 403 U.S. 217 (1971); *Jones v. Alfred H. Mayer Co.*, 392 U.S. 409 (1968); *Blow v. North Carolina*, 379 U.S. 684 (1965); *Watson v. Memphis*, 373 U.S. 526 (1963); *see also Pierson v. Ray*, 386 U.S. 547 (1967). Other common examples include "did you get any over the weekend?" *Morgan v. Hertz Corp.*, 542 F. Supp. 123, 128 (W.D. Tenn. 1981), "sleep with me and I'll give you an A," *Alexander v. Yale Univ.*, 459 F. Supp. 1, 3-4 (D. Conn. 1977), *aff'd.*, 631 F.2d 178 (2d Cir. 1980), and "walk more femininely, talk more femininely, dress more femininely, wear makeup, have [your] hair styled, and wear jewelry," *Price Waterhouse v. Hopkins*, 490 U.S. 228, 235 (1989). Nearly every time a refusal to hire or promote or accommodate is based on a prohibited group ground, some verbal act either constitutes the discrimination or proves it.

To the knowledge of *amicus*, the First Amendment has been raised as a defense in none of these cases, other than to be rejected in *Robinson* (pornography) and *Lee* (crossburning). Section 292.02 merely covers by express language a small subset of facts that civil rights statutes and rubrics have, without First Amendment controversy, been permitted to cover under far broader prohibitions for decades.

The civil rights approach favors the prohibition of all invidious treatment that has as its consequence "implying inferiority in civil society" for individuals on the basis of their membership in identifiable social groups. *Strauder v.*

West Virginia, 100 U.S. (10 Otto) 303, 308 (1880). In a context of social inequality, the practices prohibited by § 292.02 form integral links in systematic social discrimination. They work to keep target groups in socially isolated, stigmatized, and disadvantaged positions through the promotion of fear, intolerance, segregation, exclusion, disparagement, vilification, degradation, violence, and genocide. The harms range from immediate psychic wounding and attack, Matsuda, Public Response to Racist Speech: Considering the Victim's Story, 87 Mich. L. Rev. 2320, 2365-66 (1989), to well-documented consequent physical aggression. *Increasing Violence Against Minorities: Hearing Before the Subcomm. on Crime of the House Comm. on the Judiciary*, 96th Cong., 2d Sess. 124-25 (1980). As terrorist acts of social subordination, they effectuate inequality through coercion, intimidation and harassment.

In this approach, the placing of Nazi swastikas promotes the inequality of Jews on the basis of religion (and creates a false racial identification that has had genocide as its consequence). Crossburnings promote white supremacy – in this case, the inequality of African-Americans to whites – on the basis of race and color. Such symbolic acts of social inequality are thus discriminatory practices, an expressive form inequality takes. In the instant case, the threat, although group-based, was directed against a specific family. Their injuries were not merely subjective, nor can their fears be said to be unfounded. *See e.g. Marshall v. Bramer*, 110 F.R.D. 232 (W.D. Ky. 1985) (Black couple whose home was destroyed by arson after cross burning brings § 1985(3) action against Klan as an organization). The statute's "alarm" translates into moving out to avoid getting killed, its "anger" and "resentment" could well, in a healthy person, become striking back in self-defense or in defense of one's human dignity. "There is no persuasive reason to wipe the statute from the books, unless we want to encourage victims of such verbal assaults to seek their own private redress." *Gooding v. Wilson,* 405 U.S. 518, 530 (1972) (Burger, J., dissenting).

At minimum, acts such as crossburnings further the social construction of a group as inferior, unequal, and rightly disadvantaged. On a material level, many African Americans were driven out of the South and forced to relocate in places like Minnesota as a result of such acts. Systematic liquidation due to membership in a group, as occurred to Jews and others during the Holocaust, is the ultimate inequality of which acts such as crossburning are an integral part. In the case at bar, the crossburning is an act of exclusion of Black residents from a neighborhood where they have an equality right to live. It is a euphemism to say that this is what such acts communicate when the fact is that this *is* what they *do*.

B. **The Practices Of Inequality Prohibited By § 292.02 Are Not Protected By The First Amendment.**

Crossburning is expressive action which promotes racial inequality through its racist message and impact, engendering terror and effectuating segregation. It inflicts its harm through its meaning, as all threats do. Intimidation by threats of physical violence is not protected by the First Amendment. *See, e.g., Watts v. United*

States, 394 U.S. 705, 707 (1969); *U.S. v. Orozco-Santilian,* 903 F.2d 1262, 1265 (9th Cir. 1990). But physical violence does not mark the constitutional line beyond which legislation is impermissible. *U.S. v. Lee,* 935 F.2d 952, 956 (8th Cir. 1991). Where the harm the expression does to the emotional, physical, and mental health of vulnerable groups – groups the state has an interest in protecting – outweighs its expressive value, even pure speech, on balance, can be restricted. *New York v. Ferber,* 458 U.S. 747 (1982). Where the state interest is in eradicating discrimination, and the speech interest is not of the highest order, even written words can be regulated. *Pittsburgh Press v. Pittsburgh Comm'n. on Human Relations,* 413 U.S. 376 (1973). With expressive conduct, a compelling governmental interest, narrowly pursued, can outweigh a First Amendment interest. *U.S. v. O'Brien,* 391 U.S. 367 (1968). Assuming *arguendo* that crossburning, a public show of force, falls within the scope of the First Amendment, under these combined tests, crossburning may readily be prohibited as under § 292.02.

The traditional approach to a statute such as § 292.02 is to construe it as kind of a prohibition on group defamation, as petitioner and his *amici* ACLU *et al.* have done. This fails to recognize the overriding importance of equality interests where the treatment of suspect classes based on race or gender are involved. When abused through speech, the victim's harm – hence the state's interest in regulation – has traditionally been conceived as protection of sensibilities from offense or guarding of emotional tranquility. *Cohen v. California,* 403 U.S. 15 (1971); *Street v. New York,* 394 U.S. 576, 592 (1969). The harm of the type of conduct covered by § 292.02 has traditionally sounded more in defamation – injury to group reputation – than discrimination – injury to group status and treatment. While defamation recognizes damage, its damage is more ideational and less material than the damage of discrimination, which recognizes the harm of second-class citizenship and inferior social standing with attendant material deprivation of access to resources, voice, and power. Certainly, being treated as a second-class citizen furthers the second-class reputation of the group of which one is a member, even as a demeaned reputation permits and encourages social denigration and exclusion. But equality is an interest of Constitutional dimension; repute, however weighty, is not. The failure to recognize the equality interest at stake in "group libel" statutes, see e.g. Collin v. Smith, 578 F.2d 1197, 1199 (7th Cir. 1978) (ordinance prohibiting parade permit for assemblies which, inter alia, incite violence, hatred, abuse or hostility "by reason of reference to religious, racial, ethnic, national or regional affiliation") cert. denied, 439 U.S. 916 (1978), has trivialized the harm and obscured the state interest, disabling the constitutional defense of such laws against First Amendment attack.

In the civil rights context, it should be noted that segregated lunch counters or toilets or water fountains were not defended because of what they said – that is, as symbolic speech or as expressions of political opinion – although they were arguably both expressive and political. Racial segregation in education was not regarded as protected speech to the extent it required verbal forms, such as laws and directives, to create and sustain it, nor was it legally regarded as actionable defamation against

African Americans, although a substantial part of its harm was the message of inferiority it conveyed, as well as its impact on the self-concept of Black children. *Brown v. Board of Education*, 347 U.S. 483, 494 (1954); *see also* Lawrence, If He Hollers Let Him Go: Regulating Racist Speech on Campus, 1990 Duke Law Journal 901 (*Brown* may be read as regulating the content of racist speech). Yet the harm of segregation and other racist practices is at least as much what it says as what it does, just as with crossburning, what it says is indistinguishable from what it does.

Where equality interests in regulating speech have been explicitly articulated, overwhelmingly they have prevailed. In *Pittsburgh Press*, because sex-segregated job advertisements "indicat[ed]" sex discrimination in employment, this Court concluded that such speech "signaled that the advertisers were likely to show an illegal sex preference in their hiring decisions." *Pittsburgh Press v. Pittsburgh Comm'n. on Human Relations*, 413 U.S. 376, 389 (1973). A burning cross "signals" just as powerfully that African Americans are not welcome in the neighborhood. *See also Roberts v. U.S. Jaycees*, 468 U.S. 609 (1984); *Hishon v. King & Spalding*, 467 U.S. 69 (1983).

Where the harm of symbolic conduct is real rather than symbolic, the value of the expression should be weighed against the harm done. *New York v. Ferber*, 458 U.S. 757, 763-64 (1982) (harm of child pornography outweighs its expressive value). The value of crossburnings "is exceedingly modest, if not *de minimus.*" 459 U.S. 762. Indeed, its only value lies in the harm it does.[2]

In the civil rights context, courts have increasingly rejected First Amendment protections for racist harassment and intimidation, including through symbolic means. In the *Vietnamese Fishermen's* case, the court enjoined defendants from engaging in acts of violence, intimidation, or harassment under 42 U.S.C. §§ 1981, 1983 and 1985 for symbolic acts including hanging an effigy of a Vietnamese fisherman, walking around with guns, and "burning crosses on property within the geographic area where members of plaintiffs' class live and/or work without the consent of the owner of said property." *Vietnamese Fishermen's Ass'n. v. Knights of the Ku Klux Klan,* 543 F. Supp. 198, 220 (S. D. Tex. 1982). Similarly, in the *Lac du Flambeau Indians* case, the court, finding a claim under 42 U.S.C. § 1985(3) based on a "campaign driven by racial hostility toward Indians" as evidenced by verbal racial insults, found an injunction against such activities outside First Amendment scope. *Lac du Flambeau Indians v. Stop Treaty Abuse-Wis.,* 759 F. Supp. 1339, 1349, 1353 (W.D. Wis. 1991).

In a related recognition, the Supreme Court of Georgia recently upheld an anti-mask law against a free

---

2 Outside the recognized civil rights context, but invoking similar concerns, Justice Souter, concurring in *Barnes v. Glen Theatres, Inc.,* expressed a similar rationale for upholding a restriction on nude dancing based on its "secondary effects," there, increased prostitution and sexual assault. 111 S.Ct. 2456, 2470. In the instant case, racial exclusion and intimidation is the primary, indeed only, effect of the expression, making its avoidance even weightier.

speech challenge, recognizing that the Klan's practice of wearing masks worked to "intimidate, threaten, or create an environment for impending violence," hence was not protected speech, in a factual context in which the mask-wearing "helped to create a climate of fear that prevented Georgia citizens from exercising their civil rights." *State v. Miller*, 398 S.E.2d 547, 550 (1990). Crossburnings are at least as harassing, intimidating, and obstructive of protected rights.

Conduct that communicates may invoke the First Amendment but is not necessarily protected speech. This Court permits expressive conduct to be regulated more readily than other expression. It looks to see if such regulation "furthers an important or substantial governmental interest; if the governmental interest is unrelated to the suppression of free expression; and if the incidental restriction on alleged First Amendment freedom is no greater than is essential to the furtherance of that interest." *U.S. v. O'Brien*, 391 U.S. 367, 376-377 (1968). *See also Barnes v. Glen Theatre, Inc.*, 111 S.Ct. 2456 (1991) (nude dancing case, reaffirming and adumbrating *O'Brien*). Harm to a state interest does not become protected as speech because it makes a statement in inflicting an injury. As clarified in *Texas v. Johnson*, "a law directed at the communicative nature of the conduct must . . . be justified by the substantial showing of need that the First Amendment requires . . . It is, in short, not simply the verbal or nonverbal nature of the expression, but the governmental interest at stake, that helps to determine whether a restriction on that expression is valid." *Texas v. Johnson*, 491 U.S. 397, 406-407 (1989) (flag-burning case).

The recent cases on flag-burning found the statutes regulating it impermissible because they lacked a sufficient governmental interest other than that of suppressing a particular form of criticism of the government. The expression of an idea through conduct may not be regulated "simply because society finds the idea itself offensive or disagreeable." *Johnson*, 491 U.S., 414. The Court in *dicta* emphasized the inadequacy of offensiveness as a harm: "[w]e are aware that desecration of the flag is deeply offensive to many. But the same might be said, for example, of virulent ethnic and religious epithets . . . " *U.S. v. Eichman*, 110 S. Ct. 2402, 2410 (1990). Protected groups are not in a position of power comparable to that of the government, and, in reality, nothing is done to the country when its symbol is burned. By contrast, crossburning, if unpunished, is tantamount to racial supremacy and exclusion, like a "white only" sign only nonverbal. Like most acts, crossburning expresses an idea, but unlike other expressions of ideas, it is threatening and coercive conduct on the basis of race. As noted by the Seventh Circuit in *Collin v. Smith*, "It bears noting that we are not viewing here a law which prohibits action designed to impede the equal exercise of guaranteed rights . . . or even a conspiracy to harass or intimidate others and subject them thus to racial or religious hatred . . . If we were, we would have a very different case." 578 F.2d, at 1204, n.13. Creating a First Amendment exception for an injured flag is not the same as recognizing the state interest in protecting from discrimination terrorized and constructively evicted Black citizens awaiting what may well be a firebombing or a lynch mob.

This Court has made clear that, "concepts virtually sacred to our Nation as a whole – such as the principle that discrimination on the basis of race is odious and destructive" must, as a matter of principle, remain disputed in the marketplace of ideas. *Johnson*, 491 U.S., 417. The marketplace of ideas cannot be assumed to be an equal place in a society in which some groups are systematically unequal to others. But this reality need not be confronted here, since the idea of racial equality can remain disputed in St. Paul. The city, through § 292.02, does not enforce its views in a dialogue on racial equality, nor has St. Paul here adopted the instant regulation of crossburning "because of disagreement with the message it conveys." *Community for Creative Non-Violence v. Watt*, 468 U.S. 288, 295 (1984). Rather, this expressive conduct is prohibited because it inflicts inequality through the delivery of its message. As this Court observed in *Jaycees*, upholding an equality claim over a First Amendment association challenge, "acts of invidious discrimination in the distribution of publicly available goods, services, and other advantages cause unique evils that government has a compelling interest to prevent – wholly apart from the point of view such conduct may transmit . . . Accordingly . . . such practices are entitled to no constitutional protection." *Roberts v. U.S. Jaycees*, 468 U.S. 609, 628 (1984). That the content of the message is politically racist does not, *ipso facto*, make it protected speech. "[I]nvidious private discrimination may be characterized as a form of exercising freedom . . . protected by the First Amendment, but it has never been accorded affirmative constitutional protection." *Norwood v. Harrison*, 413 U.S. 455, 470 (1973). This case is not the time to start.

For St. Paul to side with equality as a basis for public policy is not the same as officially imposing a conclusion on a dialogue. A crossburning is not a dialogue, it is a discriminatory act. The state need not remain neutral when racial inequality is practiced, including through expressive conduct. A law against crossburning means only that second-class citizenship may not be imposed in this way. When equality is a constitutional mandate, the idea that some people are inferior to others on the basis of group membership has been authoritatively rejected as the basis for public policy. Practices based on this idea are not insulated from regulation on the ground that the ideas they express cannot be rejected by law, nor are legislative attempts to address such practices invalid because they take a position in favor of human equality.

Burning crosses, placing Nazi swastikas, and posting pornography in workplaces serve none of the purposes for which speech is protected, any more than verbal racial and sexual harassment or "white only" signs do. Free speech is valued because it encourages political dissent, debate, and participation in self-government, Emerson, THE SYSTEM OF FREEDOM OF EXPRESSION 6-7 (1970), Meiklejohn, FREE SPEECH AND ITS RELATION TO SELF-GOVERNMENT 27 (1948); promotes diversity, tolerance, and self-restraint, Bollinger, THE TOLERANT SOCIETY 9-11 (1986); manages social change and social conflict, Emerson, at 7; advances knowledge and promotes the discovery of truth, Mill, ON LIBERTY 16-52 (A. Castell ed. 1947); and promotes individual self-fulfillment, Baker, Scope of the First Amendment Freedom of Speech, 25 U.C.L.A. L. Rev. 964, 995-996 (1978). The acts prohibited by § 292.02, by contrast, quash dissent by silencing the voices of disadvantaged groups through terrorism, often insuring that the victims are so intimidated that the most aggressive and coercive verbal attacks upon them never become "fighting words" because they cannot or do not fight back.[3] Such acts also inhibit truth-seeking because they intimidate disadvantaged groups from asserting their truth and their point of view. They undermine social diversity through exclusion and discourage community participation by demeaning the human worth and self-esteem of their targets. If bigots are fulfilled through such acts, it is at the expense of a welcoming and tolerant environment for others.

The hatemongering prohibited by § 292.02 silences the speech of the less powerful as it marginalizes and segregates them. The official imprimatur of approval that would be secured for such conduct by protecting it as expression would do incalculable harm to the "hearts and minds," *Brown v. Board of Education*, 347 U.S. 483, 494 (1954), of its victims, inhibiting progress toward civil equality, and delegitimating the First Amendment.

In prohibiting such practices, the St. Paul ordinance "responds precisely to the substantive problem which legitimately concerns" government and abridges no more freedom of speech than necessary to accomplish that purpose. *See City Council of Los Angeles v. Taxpayers for Vincent*, 466 U.S. 789, 810 (1984); *Ward v. Rock Against Racism*, 491 U.S. 781 (1989). Moreover, the provision aims

---

[3] This is to suggest that the "fighting words" doctrine implicitly assumes an equality of social vulnerability, safety, and state solicitude that cannot be assumed for groups that have historically been the targets of discrimination.

to stop intimidation from protected rights and to advance equality, not to suppress dissident speech. While the content of the message of a burning cross may represent dissent from the national consensus reflected in legal mandates of equality, it offers no dissent from the overwhelming reality of racial inequality that continues to afflict social life. Bell, AND WE ARE NOT SAVED: THE ELUSIVE QUEST FOR RACIAL JUSTICE (1987). Cross-burning should not be romanticized as a lonely and unheeded critique of a powerful *status quo*. Its racism entrenches, embodies, and advances society's most repressive and antiegalitarian norms, indefensible in a society that has equality as a constitutional guarantee.

If St. Paul burned a cross at an official ceremony, it would discriminate on the basis of race in violation of the Fourteenth Amendment. The fact the conduct was expressive would be no defense. This would be as virulent and shocking an act "designed to maintain White Supremacy" as has ever been seen. *Loving v. Virginia*, 388 U.S. 1, 11 (1967) (invalidating antimiscegenation laws). What would be discriminatory for government to do can be recognized as discriminatory in society through legislation. By prohibiting such conduct when it occurs between its citizens, the city acts against socially institutionalized inequality and, indirectly, against the negative group animus that drives it.

Section 292.02 is as much an equality provision as if it were part of the human rights code. Like the provision upheld over First Amendment concerns in *Jaycees*, the ordinance reflects Minnesota's historically "strong commitment to eliminating discrimination and assuring its citizens equal access to publicly available goods and services." *Roberts v. U.S. Jaycees*, 468 U.S. 609, 624 (1984). Had equality been recognized as the constitutional interest at stake in group defamation, it would have supported Justice Frankfurter's opinion upholding Illinois' statute in *Beauharnais*, not overruled to this day, that "a man's job and his educational opportunities and the dignity accorded him may depend as much on the reputation of the racial and religious group to which he willy-nilly belongs, as on his own merits." *Beauharnais v. Illinois*, 343 U.S. 250, 263 (1952). It would also support the reservations based on *Beauharnais* expressed by some members of this Court in the *Skokie* case. *Smith v. Collin*, 439 U.S. 916 (1978) (Blackmun, J., with whom White, J., joins, dissenting from denial of *cert*. to resolve possible conflict with *Beauharnais*). See also *R. v. Keegstra*, [1991] 2 W.W.R. 1 (Supreme Court of Canada upholding hate propaganda statute on equality rationale under *Canadian Charter of Rights and Freedoms*). As the Eighth Circuit concluded in an action for a crossburning, "[t]o protect the inhabitants of this nation from such an attack on civil rights does not violate the spirit of the first amendment." *U.S. v. Lee*, 935 F.2d 952, 956 (8th Cir. 1991).

R.A.V., Petitioner,

v.

CITY OF ST. PAUL, MINNESOTA.

No. 90–7675.

Argued Dec. 4, 1991.

Decided June 22, 1992.

Syllabus *

After allegedly burning a cross on a black family's lawn, petitioner R.A.V. was charged under, *inter alia*, the St. Paul, Minnesota, Bias–Motivated Crime Ordinance, which prohibits the display of a symbol which one knows or has reason to know "arouses anger, alarm or resentment in others on the basis of race, color, creed, religion or gender." The trial court dismissed this charge on the ground that the ordinance was substantially overbroad and impermissibly content-based, but the State Supreme Court reversed. It rejected the overbreadth claim because the phrase "arouses anger, alarm or resentment in others" had been construed in earlier state cases to limit the ordinance's reach to "fighting words" within the meaning of this Court's decision in *Chaplinsky v. New Hampshire*, 315 U.S. 568, 572, 62 S.Ct. 766, 769, 86 L.Ed. 1031 a category of expression unprotected by the First Amendment. The court also concluded that the ordinance was not impermissibly content-based because it was narrowly tailored to serve a compelling governmental interest in protecting the community against bias-motivated threats to public safety and order.

Held: The ordinance is facially invalid under the First Amendment. Pp. 2542–2550.

(a) This Court is bound by the state court's construction of the ordinance as reaching only expressions constituting "fighting words." However, R.A.V.'s request that the scope of the *Chaplinsky* formulation be modified, thereby invalidating the ordinance as substantially overbroad, need not be reached, since the ordinance unconstitutionally prohibits speech on the basis of the subjects the speech addresses. P. 2542.

(b) A few limited categories of speech, such as obscenity, defamation, and fighting words, may be regulated *because of their constitutionally proscribable content.* However, these categories are not entirely invisible to the Constitution, and government may not regulate them based on hostility, or favoritism, towards a nonproscribable message they contain. Thus the regulation of "fighting words" may not be based on nonproscribable content. It may, however, be underinclusive, addressing some offensive instances and leaving other, equally offensive, ones alone, so long as the selective prescription is not based on content, or there is no realistic possibility that regulation of ideas is afoot. Pp. 2542–2547.

(c) The ordinance, even as narrowly construed by the State Supreme Court, is facially unconstitutional because it imposes special prohibitions on those speakers who express views on the disfavored subjects of "race, color, creed, religion or gender." At the same time, it permits displays containing abusive invective if they are not addressed to those topics. Moreover, in its practical operation the ordinance goes beyond mere content, to actual viewpoint, discrimination. Displays containing "fighting words" that do not invoke the disfavored subjects would seemingly be useable *ad libitum* by those arguing in favor of racial, color, etc. tolerance and equality, but not by their opponents. St. Paul's desire to communicate to minority groups that it does not condone the "group hatred" of bias-motivated speech does not justify selectively silencing speech on the basis of its content. Pp. 2547–2549.

(d) The content-based discrimination reflected in the ordinance does not rest upon the very reasons why the particular class of speech at issue is proscribable, it is not aimed only at the "secondary effects"

---

* The syllabus constitutes no part of the opinion of the Court but has been prepared by the Reporter of Decisions for the convenience of the reader. See *United States v. Detroit Lumber Co.*, 200 U.S. 321, 337, 26 S.Ct. 282, 287, 50 L.Ed. 499.

of speech within the meaning of *Renton v. Playtime Theatres, Inc.*, 475 U.S. 41, 106 S.Ct. 925, 89 L.Ed.2d 29, and it is not for any other reason the sort that does not threaten censorship of ideas. In addition, the ordinance's content discrimination is not justified on the ground that the ordinance is narrowly tailored to serve a compelling state interest in ensuring the basic human rights of groups historically discriminated against, since an ordinance not limited to the favored topics would have precisely the same beneficial effect. Pp. 2549–2550.

464 N.W.2d 507 (Minn.1991), reversed and remanded.

SCALIA, J., delivered the opinion of the Court, in which REHNQUIST, C.J., and KENNEDY, SOUTER, and THOMAS, JJ., joined. WHITE, J., filed an opinion concurring in the judgment, in which BLACKMUN and O'CONNOR, JJ., joined, and in which STEVENS, J., joined except as to Part I–A. BLACKMUN, J., filed an opinion concurring in the judgment. STEVENS, J., filed an opinion concurring in the judgment, in Part I of which WHITE and BLACKMUN, JJ., joined.

Justice SCALIA delivered the opinion of the Court.

In the predawn hours of June 21, 1990, petitioner and several other teenagers allegedly assembled a crudely-made cross by taping together broken chair legs. They then allegedly burned the cross inside the fenced yard of a black family that lived across the street from the house where petitioner was staying. Although this conduct could have been punished under any of a number of laws,[1] one of the two provisions under which respondent city of St. Paul chose to charge petitioner (then a juvenile) was the St. Paul Bias–Motivated Crime Ordinance, St. Paul, Minn.Legis.Code § 292.02 (1990), which provides:

> "Whoever places on public or private property a symbol, object, appellation, characterization or graffiti, including, but not limited to, a burning cross or Nazi swastika, which one knows or has reasonable grounds to know arouses anger, alarm or resentment in others on the basis of race, color, creed, religion or gender commits disorderly conduct and shall be guilty of a misdemeanor."

Petitioner moved to dismiss this count on the ground that the St. Paul ordinance was substantially overbroad and impermissibly content-based and therefore facially invalid under the First Amendment.[2] The trial court granted this motion, but the Minnesota Supreme Court reversed. That court rejected petitioner's overbreadth claim because, as construed in prior Minnesota cases, see, *e.g.*, *In re Welfare of S.L.J.*, 263 N.W.2d 412 (Minn.1978), the modifying phrase "arouses anger, alarm or resentment in others" limited the reach of the ordinance to conduct that amounts to "fighting words," *i.e.*, "conduct that itself inflicts injury or tends to incite immediate violence ...," *In re Welfare of R.A.V.*, 464 N.W.2d 507, 510 (Minn.1991) (citing *Chaplinsky v. New Hampshire*, 315 U.S. 568, 572, 62 S.Ct. 766, 769, 86 L.Ed. 1031 (1942)), and therefore the ordinance reached only expression "that the first amendment does not protect." 464 N.W.2d, at 511. The court also concluded that the ordinance was not impermissibly content-based because, in its view, "the ordinance is a narrowly tailored means toward accomplishing the compelling governmental interest in protecting the community against bias-motivated

---

1. The conduct might have violated Minnesota statutes carrying significant penalties. See, *e.g.*, Minn.Stat. § 609.713(1) (1987) (providing for up to five years in prison for terroristic threats); § 609.563 (arson) (providing for up to five years and a $10,000 fine, depending on the value of the property intended to be damaged); § 609.-595 (Supp.1992) (criminal damage to property) (providing for up to one year and a $3,000 fine,

depending upon the extent of the damage to the property).

2. Petitioner has also been charged, in Count I of the delinquency petition, with a violation of Minn.Stat. § 609.2231(4) (Supp.1990) (racially motivated assaults). Petitioner did not challenge this count.

threats to public safety and order." *Ibid.*
We granted certiorari, 501 U.S. ——, 111
S.Ct. 2795, 115 L.Ed.2d 969 (1991).

I

[1] In construing the St. Paul ordinance, we are bound by the construction
given to it by the Minnesota court. *Posadas de Puerto Rico Associates v. Tourism
Co. of Puerto Rico,* 478 U.S. 328, 339, 106
S.Ct. 2968, 2975–2976, 92 L.Ed.2d 266
(1986); *New York v. Ferber,* 458 U.S. 747,
769, n. 24, 102 S.Ct. 3348, 3361, n. 24, 73
L.Ed.2d 1113 (1982); *Terminiello v. Chicago,* 337 U.S. 1, 4, 69 S.Ct. 894, 895–896, 93
L.Ed. 1131 (1949). Accordingly, we accept
the Minnesota Supreme Court's authoritative statement that the ordinance reaches only those expressions that constitute
"fighting words" within the meaning of
Chaplinsky. 464 N.W.2d, at 510–511. Petitioner and his *amici* urge us to modify
the scope of the *Chaplinsky* formulation,
thereby invalidating the ordinance as "substantially overbroad," *Broadrick v. Oklahoma,* 413 U.S. 601, 610, 93 S.Ct. 2908,
2914–2915, 37 L.Ed.2d 830 (1973). We find
it unnecessary to consider this issue. Assuming, *arguendo,* that all of the expression reached by the ordinance is proscriba-

ble under the "fighting words" doctrine,
we nonetheless conclude that the ordinance
is facially unconstitutional in that it prohibits otherwise permitted speech solely on the
basis of the subjects the speech addresses.[3]

[2, 3] The First Amendment generally
prevents government from proscribing
speech, see, *e.g., Cantwell v. Connecticut,*
310 U.S. 296, 309–311, 60 S.Ct. 900, 905–
906, 84 L.Ed. 1213 (1940), or even expressive conduct, see, *e.g., Texas v. Johnson,*
491 U.S. 397, 406, 109 S.Ct. 2533, 2540, 105
L.Ed.2d 342 (1989), because of disapproval
of the ideas expressed. Content-based regulations are presumptively invalid. *Simon
& Schuster, Inc. v. Members of N.Y. State
Crime Victims Bd.,* 502 U.S. ——, ——
——, 112 S.Ct. 501, ——–——, 116
L.Ed.2d 476 (1991) *id.,* at ——–——, 112
S.Ct., at ——–—— (KENNEDY, J., concurring in judgment); *Consolidated Edison Co. of N.Y. v. Public Serv. Comm'n of
N.Y.,* 447 U.S. 530, 536, 100 S.Ct. 2326,
2332–2333, 65 L.Ed.2d 319 (1980); *Police
Dept. of Chicago v. Mosley,* 408 U.S. 92,
95, 92 S.Ct. 2286, 2289–2290, 33 L.Ed.2d
212 (1972). From 1791 to the present, however, our society, like other free but civi-

---

3. Contrary to Justice WHITE's suggestion, *post,*
at 2550–2551, petitioner's claim is "fairly included" within the questions presented in the petition for certiorari, see this Court's Rule 14.1(a).
It was clear from the petition and from petitioner's other filings in this Court (and in the courts
below) that his assertion that the St. Paul ordinance "violat[es] overbreadth ... principles of
the First Amendment," Pet. for Cert. i, was *not*
just a technical "overbreadth" claim—*i.e.,* a
claim that the ordinance violated the rights of
too many third parties—but included the contention that the ordinance was "overbroad" in
the sense of restricting more speech than the
Constitution permits, even in its application to
him, because it is content-based. An important
component of petitioner's argument is, and has
been all along, that narrowly construing the
ordinance to cover only "fighting words" cannot
cure this fundamental defect. *Id.,* at 12, 14, 15–
16. In his briefs in this Court, petitioner argued
that a narrowing construction was ineffective
because (1) its boundaries were vague, Brief for
Petitioner 26, and because (2) denominating
particular expression a "fighting word" because
of the impact of its ideological content upon the

audience is inconsistent with the First Amendment, Reply Brief for Petitioner 5; *id.,* at 13
("[The ordinance] is overbroad, *viewpoint discriminatory* and vague as 'narrowly construed'") (emphasis added). At oral argument,
counsel for Petitioner reiterated this second
point: "It is ... one of my positions, that in
[punishing only some fighting words and not
others], even though it is a subcategory, technically, of unprotected conduct, [the ordinance]
still is picking out an opinion, a disfavored
message, and making that clear through the
State." Tr. of Oral Arg. 8. In resting our judgment upon this contention, we have not departed from our criteria of what is "fairly included"
within the petition. See *Arkansas Electric Cooperative Corp. v. Arkansas Pub. Serv. Comm'n,*
461 U.S. 375, 382, n. 6, 103 S.Ct. 1905, 1911–
1912, n. 6, 76 L.Ed.2d 1 (1983); *Brown v. Socialist Workers '74 Campaign Comm.,* 459 U.S. 87,
94, n. 9, 103 S.Ct. 416, 421, n. 9, 74 L.Ed.2d 250
(1982); *Eddings v. Oklahoma,* 455 U.S. 104, 113,
n. 9, 102 S.Ct. 869, 876, n. 9, 71 L.Ed.2d 1 (1982);
see generally R. Stern, E. Gressman, & S. Shapi-
ro, Supreme Court Practice 361 (6th ed. 1986).

lized societies, has permitted restrictions upon the content of speech in a few limited areas, which are "of such slight social value as a step to truth that any benefit that may be derived from them is clearly outweighed by the social interest in order and morality." *Chaplinsky, supra,* 315 U.S., at 572, 62 S.Ct. at 762. We have recognized that "the freedom of speech" referred to by the First Amendment does not include a freedom to disregard these traditional limitations. See, *e.g., Roth v. United States,* 354 U.S. 476, 77 S.Ct. 1304, 1 L.Ed.2d 1498 (1957) (obscenity); *Beauharnais v. Illinois,* 343 U.S. 250, 72 S.Ct. 725, 96 L.Ed. 919 (1952) (defamation); *Chaplinsky v. New Hampshire, supra,* ("fighting words"); see generally *Simon & Schuster, supra,* 502 U.S., at ——, 112 S.Ct., at —— (KENNEDY, J., concurring in judgment). Our decisions since the 1960's have narrowed the scope of the traditional categorical exceptions for defamation, see *New York Times Co. v. Sullivan,* 376 U.S. 254, 84 S.Ct. 710, 11 L.Ed.2d 686 (1964); *Gertz v. Robert Welch, Inc.,* 418 U.S. 323, 94 S.Ct. 2997, 41 L.Ed.2d 789 (1974); see generally *Milkovich v. Lorain Journal Co.,* 497 U.S. 1, 13–17, 110 S.Ct. 2695, ——, 111 L.Ed.2d 1 (1990), and for obscenity, see *Miller v. California,* 413 U.S. 15, 93 S.Ct. 2607, 37 L.Ed.2d 419 (1973), but a limited categorical approach has remained an important part of our First Amendment jurisprudence.

[4] We have sometimes said that these categories of expression are "not within the area of constitutionally protected speech," *Roth, supra,* 354 U.S., at 483, 77 S.Ct., at 1308; *Beauharnais, supra,* 343 U.S., at 266, 72 S.Ct., at 735; *Chaplinsky, supra,* 315 U.S., at 571–572, 62 S.Ct., at 768–769; or that the "protection of the First Amendment does not extend" to them, *Bose Corp. v. Consumers Union of United States, Inc.,* 466 U.S. 485, 504, 104 S.Ct. 1949, 1961, 80 L.Ed.2d 502 (1984); *Sable Communications of Cal., Inc. v.*

FCC, 492 U.S. 115, 124, 109 S.Ct. 2829, 2835, 106 L.Ed.2d 93 (1989). Such statements must be taken in context, however, and are no more literally true than is the occasionally repeated shorthand characterizing obscenity "as not being speech at all," Sunstein, Pornography and the First Amendment, 1986 Duke L.J. 589, 615, n. 146. What they mean is that these areas of speech can, consistently with the First Amendment, be regulated *because of their constitutionally proscribable content* (obscenity, defamation, etc.)—not that they are categories of speech entirely invisible to the Constitution, so that they may be made the vehicles for content discrimination unrelated to their distinctively proscribable content. Thus, the government may proscribe libel; but it may not make the further content discrimination of proscribing *only* libel critical of the government. We recently acknowledged this distinction in *Ferber,* 458 U.S., at 763, 102 S.Ct., at 3357–3358, where, in upholding New York's child pornography law, we expressly recognized that there was no "question here of censoring a particular literary theme...." See also *id.,* at 775, 102 S.Ct., at 3364 (O'CONNOR, J., concurring) ("As drafted, New York's statute does not attempt to suppress the communication of particular ideas").

Our cases surely do not establish the proposition that the First Amendment imposes no obstacle whatsoever to regulation of particular instances of such proscribable expression, so that the government "may regulate [them] freely," *post,* at 2552 (WHITE, J., concurring in judgment). That would mean that a city council could enact an ordinance prohibiting only those legally obscene works that contain criticism of the city government or, indeed, that do not include endorsement of the city government. Such a simplistic, all-or-nothing-at-all approach to First Amendment protection is at odds with common sense and with our jurisprudence as well.[4] It is not true

4. Justice WHITE concedes that a city council   cannot prohibit only those legally obscene

that "fighting words" have at most a *"de minimis"* expressive content, *ibid.*, or that their content is *in all respects* "worthless and undeserving of constitutional protection," *post,* at 2553; sometimes they are quite expressive indeed. We have not said that they constitute *"no* part of the expression of ideas," but only that they constitute "no *essential* part of any exposition of ideas." *Chaplinsky,* 315 U.S., at 572, 62 S.Ct., at 769 (emphasis added).

The proposition that a particular instance of speech can be proscribable on the basis of one feature (*e.g.,* obscenity) but not on the basis of another (*e.g.,* opposition to the city government) is commonplace, and has found application in many contexts. We have long held, for example, that nonverbal expressive activity can be banned because of the action it entails, but not because of the ideas it expresses—so that burning a flag in violation of an ordinance against outdoor fires could be punishable, whereas burning a flag in violation of an ordinance against dishonoring the flag is not. See *Johnson,* 491 U.S., at 406–407, 109 S.Ct., at 2540–2541. See also *Barnes v. Glen Theatre, Inc.,* 501 U.S. ——, —— – ——, 111 S.Ct. 2456, 2460–2461, 115 L.Ed.2d 504

works that contain criticism of the city government, *post,* at 2555, but asserts that to be the consequence, not of the First Amendment, but of the Equal Protection Clause. Such content-based discrimination would not, he asserts, "be rationally related to a legitimate government interest," *ibid.* But of course the only *reason* that government interest is not a "legitimate" one is that it violates the First Amendment. This Court itself has occasionally fused the First Amendment into the Equal Protection Clause in this fashion, but at least with the acknowledgment (which Justice WHITE cannot afford to make) that the First Amendment underlies its analysis. See *Police Dept. of Chicago v. Mosley,* 408 U.S. 92, 95, 92 S.Ct. 2286, 2289–2290, 33 L.Ed.2d 212 (1972) (ordinance prohibiting only nonlabor picketing violated the Equal Protection Clause because there was no "appropriate governmental interest" supporting the distinction inasmuch as "the First Amendment means that government has no power to restrict expression because of its message, its ideas, its subject matter, or its content"); *Carey v. Brown,* 447 U.S. 455, 100 S.Ct. 2286, 65 L.Ed.2d 263 (1980). See generally *Simon & Schuster, Inc. v.*

(1991) (plurality); *id.,* at —— – ——, 111 S.Ct., at 2465–2466 (SCALIA, J., concurring in judgment); *id.,* at —— – ——, 111 S.Ct., at 2468–2469 (SOUTER, J., concurring in judgment); *United States v. O'Brien,* 391 U.S. 367, 376–377, 88 S.Ct. 1673, 1678–1679, 20 L.Ed.2d 672 (1968). Similarly, we have upheld reasonable "time, place, or manner" restrictions, but only if they are "justified without reference to the content of the regulated speech." *Ward v. Rock Against Racism,* 491 U.S. 781, 791, 109 S.Ct. 2746, 2753–2754, 105 L.Ed.2d 661 (1989) (internal quotation marks omitted); see also *Clark v. Community for Creative Non-Violence,* 468 U.S. 288, 298, 104 S.Ct. 3065, 3071, 82 L.Ed.2d 221 (1984) (noting that the *O'Brien* test differs little from the standard applied to time, place, or manner restrictions). And just as the power to proscribe particular speech on the basis of a noncontent element (*e.g.,* noise) does not entail the power to proscribe the same speech on the basis of a content element; so also, the power to proscribe it on the basis of *one* content element (*e.g.,* obscenity) does not entail the power to proscribe it on the basis of *other* content elements.

Members of N.Y. State Crime Victims Bd., 502 U.S. ——, —— – ——, 112 S.Ct. 501, 514, 116 L.Ed.2d 476 (1991) (KENNEDY, J., concurring in judgment).

Justice STEVENS seeks to avoid the point by dismissing the notion of obscene anti-government speech as "fantastical," *post,* at 2562, apparently believing that any reference to politics prevents a finding of obscenity. Unfortunately for the purveyors of obscenity, that is obviously false. A shockingly hard core pornographic movie that contains a model sporting a political tattoo can be found, *"taken as a whole* [to] lac[k] serious literary, artistic, political, or scientific value." *Miller v. California,* 413 U.S. 15, 24, 93 S.Ct. 2607, 2614–2615, 37 L.Ed.2d 419 (1973) (emphasis added). Anyway, it is easy enough to come up with other illustrations of a content-based restriction upon "unprotected speech" that is obviously invalid: the anti-government libel illustration mentioned earlier, for one. See *supra,* at 2543. And of course the concept of racist fighting words is, unfortunately, anything but a "highly speculative hypothetica[l]," *post,* at 2562.

[5, 6] In other words, the exclusion of "fighting words" from the scope of the First Amendment simply means that, for purposes of that Amendment, the unprotected features of the words are, despite their verbal character, essentially a "nonspeech" element of communication. Fighting words are thus analogous to a noisy sound truck: Each is, as Justice Frankfurter recognized, a "mode of speech," *Niemotko v. Maryland*, 340 U.S. 268, 282, 71 S.Ct. 325, 333, 95 L.Ed. 267 (1951) (Frankfurter, J., concurring in result); both can be used to convey an idea; but neither has, in and of itself, a claim upon the First Amendment. As with the sound truck, however, so also with fighting words: The government may not regulate use based on hostility—or favoritism—towards the underlying message expressed. Compare *Frisby v. Schultz*, 487 U.S. 474, 108 S.Ct. 2495, 101 L.Ed.2d 420 (1988) (upholding, against facial challenge, a content-neutral ban on targeted residential picketing) with *Carey v. Brown*, 447 U.S. 455, 100 S.Ct. 2286, 65 L.Ed.2d 263 (1980) (invalidating a ban on residential picketing that exempted labor picketing).[5]

The concurrences describe us as setting forth a new First Amendment principle that prohibition of constitutionally proscribable speech cannot be "underinclusiv[e]," *post*, at 2553 (WHITE, J., concurring in judgment)—a First Amendment "absolutism" whereby "within a particular 'proscribable' category of expression, ... a government must either proscribe *all* speech or no speech at all," *post*, at 2562 (STEVENS, J., concurring in judgment). That easy target is of the concurrences' own invention. In our view, the First Amendment imposes not an "underinclusiveness" limitation but a "content discrimination" limitation upon a State's prohibition of proscribable speech. There is no problem whatever, for example, with a State's prohibiting obscenity (and other forms of proscribable expression) only in certain media or markets, for although that prohibition would be "underinclusive," it would not discriminate on the basis of content. See, *e.g., Sable Communications*, 492 U.S., at 124–126, 109 S.Ct., at 2835–2836 (upholding 47 U.S.C. § 223(b)(1) (1988), which prohibits obscene *telephone* communications).

Even the prohibition against content discrimination that we assert the First Amendment requires is not absolute. It applies differently in the context of proscribable speech than in the area of fully protected speech. The rationale of the general prohibition, after all, is that content discrimination "rais[es] the specter that the Government may effectively drive certain ideas or viewpoints from the marketplace," *Simon & Schuster*, 502 U.S., at ——, 112 S.Ct., at 508; *Leathers v. Medlock*, 499 U.S. ——, ——, 111 S.Ct. 1438, 1444, 113 L.Ed.2d 494 (1991); *FCC v. League of Women Voters of California*, 468 U.S. 364, 383–384, 104 S.Ct. 3106, 3119–3120, 82 L.Ed.2d 278 (1984); *Consolidated Edison Co.*, 447 U.S., at 536, 100 S.Ct., at 2333; *Police Dept. of Chicago v. Mosley*, 408 U.S., at 95–98, 92 S.Ct., at 2289–2292. But content discrimination among various instances of a class of proscribable speech often does not pose this threat.

When the basis for the content discrimination consists entirely of the very reason the entire class of speech at issue is proscribable, no significant danger of idea or viewpoint discrimination exists. Such a reason, having been adjudged neutral enough to support exclusion of the entire class of speech from First Amendment protection, is also neutral enough to form the

---

5. Although Justice WHITE asserts that our analysis disregards "established principles of First Amendment law," *post*, at 2560, he cites not a single case (and we are aware of none) that even involved, much less considered and resolved, the issue of content discrimination through regulation of "unprotected" speech— though we plainly *recognized* that as an issue in *Ferber*. It is of course contrary to all traditions of our jurisprudence to consider the law on this point conclusively resolved by broad language in cases where the issue was not presented or even envisioned.

basis of distinction within the class. To illustrate: A State might choose to prohibit only that obscenity which is the most patently offensive *in its prurience—i.e.,* that which involves the most lascivious displays of sexual activity. But it may not prohibit, for example, only that obscenity which includes offensive *political* messages. See *Kucharek v. Hanaway,* 902 F.2d 513, 517 (CA7 1990), cert. denied, 498 U.S. ——, 111 S.Ct. 713, 112 L.Ed.2d 702 (1991). And the Federal Government can criminalize only those threats of violence that are directed against the President, see 18 U.S.C. § 871—since the reasons why threats of violence are outside the First Amendment (protecting individuals from the fear of violence, from the disruption that fear engenders, and from the possibility that the threatened violence will occur) have special force when applied to the person of the President. See *Watts v. United States,* 394 U.S. 705, 707, 89 S.Ct. 1399, 1401, 22 L.Ed.2d 664 (1969) (upholding the facial validity of § 871 because of the "overwhelmin[g] interest in protecting the safety of [the] Chief Executive and in allowing him to perform his duties without interference from threats of physical violence"). But the Federal Government may not criminalize only those threats against the President that mention his policy on aid to inner cities. And to take a final example (one mentioned by Justice STEVENS, *post,* at 2563–2564), a State may choose to regulate price advertising in one industry but not in others, because the risk of fraud (one of the characteristics of commercial speech that justifies depriving it of full First Amendment protection, see *Virginia Pharmacy Bd. v. Virginia Citizens Consumer Council, Inc.,* 425 U.S. 748, 771–772, 96 S.Ct. 1817, 1830–1831, 48 L.Ed.2d 346 (1976)) is in its view greater there. Cf. *Morales v. Trans World Airlines, Inc.,* 504 U.S. ——, 112 S.Ct. 2031, 119 L.Ed.2d 157 (1992) (state regulation of airline advertising); *Ohralik v. Ohio State Bar Assn.,* 436 U.S. 447, 98 S.Ct. 1912, 56 L.Ed.2d 444 (1978) (state regulation of lawyer advertising). But a State may not prohibit only that commercial advertising that depicts men in a demeaning fashion, see, *e.g.,* L.A. Times, Aug. 8, 1989, section 4, p. 6, col. 1.

Another valid basis for according differential treatment to even a content-defined subclass of proscribable speech is that the subclass happens to be associated with particular "secondary effects" of the speech, so that the regulation is *"justified* without reference to the content of the . . . speech," *Renton v. Playtime Theatres, Inc.,* 475 U.S. 41, 48, 106 S.Ct. 925, 929, 89 L.Ed.2d 29 (1986) (quoting, with emphasis, *Virginia Pharmacy Bd., supra,* 425 U.S., at 771, 96 S.Ct., at 1830); see also *Young v. American Mini Theatres, Inc.,* 427 U.S. 50, 71, n. 34, 96 S.Ct. 2440, 2453, n. 34, 49 L.Ed.2d 310 (1976) (plurality); *id.,* at 80–82, 96 S.Ct., at 2457–2458 (Powell, J., concurring); *Barnes,* 501 U.S., at —— – ——, 111 S.Ct., at 2469–2471 (SOUTER, J., concurring in judgment). A State could, for example, permit all obscene live performances except those involving minors. Moreover, since words can in some circumstances violate laws directed not against speech but against conduct (a law against treason, for example, is violated by telling the enemy the nation's defense secrets), a particular content-based subcategory of a proscribable class of speech can be swept up incidentally within the reach of a statute directed at conduct rather than speech. See *id.,* at ——, 111 S.Ct., at 2460 (plurality); *id.,* at —— – ——, 111 S.Ct., at 2465–2466 (SCALIA, J., concurring in judgment); *id.,* at —— – ——, 111 S.Ct., at 2468–2469 (SOUTER, J., concurring in judgment); *FTC v. Superior Court Trial Lawyers Assn.,* 493 U.S. 411, 425–432, 110 S.Ct. 768, 776–780, 107 L.Ed.2d 851 (1990); *O'Brien,* 391 U.S., at 376–377, 88 S.Ct., at 1678–1679. Thus, for example, sexually derogatory "fighting words," among other words, may produce a violation of Title VII's general prohibition against sexual discrimination in employment practices, 42 U.S.C. § 2000e–2; 29 CFR § 1604.11 (1991). See also 18 U.S.C. § 242; 42 U.S.C. §§ 1981, 1982. Where the government does not target conduct on the basis of its expressive content, acts are not shielded from regulation merely because they express a discriminatory idea or philosophy.

These bases for distinction refute the proposition that the selectivity of the restriction is "even arguably 'conditioned upon the sovereign's agreement with what a speaker may intend to say.'" *Metromedia, Inc. v. San Diego,* 453 U.S. 490, 555, 101 S.Ct. 2882, 2917, 69 L.Ed.2d 800 (1981) (STEVENS, J., dissenting in part) (citation omitted). There may be other such bases as well. Indeed, to validate such selectivity (where totally proscribable speech is at issue) it may not even be necessary to identify any particular "neutral" basis, so long as the nature of the content discrimination is such that there is no realistic possibility that official suppression of ideas is afoot. (We cannot think of any First Amendment interest that would stand in the way of a State's prohibiting only those obscene motion pictures with blue-eyed actresses.) Save for that limitation, the regulation of "fighting words," like the regulation of noisy speech, may address some offensive instances and leave other, equally offensive, instances alone. See *Posadas de Puerto Rico,* 478 U.S., at 342–343, 106 S.Ct., at 2977–2978.[6]

II

[7, 8] Applying these principles to the St. Paul ordinance, we conclude that, even as narrowly construed by the Minnesota

Supreme Court, the ordinance is facially unconstitutional. Although the phrase in the ordinance, "arouses anger, alarm or resentment in others," has been limited by the Minnesota Supreme Court's construction to reach only those symbols or displays that amount to "fighting words," the remaining, unmodified terms make clear that the ordinance applies only to "fighting words" that insult, or provoke violence, "on the basis of race, color, creed, religion or gender." Displays containing abusive invective, no matter how vicious or severe, are permissible unless they are addressed to one of the specified disfavored topics. Those who wish to use "fighting words" in connection with other ideas—to express hostility, for example, on the basis of political affiliation, union membership, or homosexuality—are not covered. The First Amendment does not permit St. Paul to impose special prohibitions on those speakers who express views on disfavored subjects. See *Simon & Schuster,* 502 U.S., at —— – ——, 112 S.Ct., at —— – ——; *Arkansas Writers' Project, Inc. v. Ragland,* 481 U.S. 221, 229–230, 107 S.Ct. 1722, 1727–1728, 95 L.Ed.2d 209 (1987).

In its practical operation, moreover, the ordinance goes even beyond mere content discrimination, to actual viewpoint discrimination. Displays containing some words—odious racial epithets, for example—would be prohibited to proponents of all views. But "fighting words" that do not themselves invoke race, color, creed, religion, or

6. Justice STEVENS cites a string of opinions as supporting his assertion that "selective regulation of speech based on content" is not presumptively invalid. *Post,* at 2563–2564. Analysis reveals, however, that they do not support it. To begin with, three of them did not command a majority of the Court, *Young v. American Mini Theatres, Inc.,* 427 U.S. 50, 63–73, 96 S.Ct. 2440, 2448–2454, 49 L.Ed.2d 310 (1976) (plurality); *FCC v. Pacifica Foundation,* 438 U.S. 726, 744–748, 98 S.Ct. 3026, 3037–3040, 57 L.Ed.2d 1073 (1978) (plurality); *Lehman v. City of Shaker Heights,* 418 U.S. 298, 94 S.Ct. 2714, 41 L.Ed.2d 770 (1974) (plurality), and two others did not even discuss the First Amendment, *Morales v. Trans World Airlines, Inc.,* 504 U.S. ——, 112 S.Ct. 2031, 119 L.Ed.2d 157 (1992); *Jacob Siegel*

Co. v. FTC, 327 U.S. 608, 66 S.Ct. 758, 90 L.Ed. 888 (1946). In any event, all that their contents establish is what we readily concede: that presumptive invalidity does not mean invariable invalidity, leaving room for such exceptions as reasonable and viewpoint-neutral content-based discrimination in nonpublic forums, see *Lehman, supra,* 418 U.S., at 301–304, 94 S.Ct., at 2716–2718; see also *Cornelius v. NAACP Legal Defense & Educational Fund, Inc.,* 473 U.S. 788, 806, 105 S.Ct. 3439, 3451, 87 L.Ed.2d 567 (1985), or with respect to certain speech by government employees, see *Broadrick v. Oklahoma,* 413 U.S. 601, 93 S.Ct. 2908, 37 L.Ed.2d 830 (1973); see also *CSC v. Letter Carriers,* 413 U.S. 548, 564–567, 93 S.Ct. 2880, 2889–2891, 37 L.Ed.2d 796 (1973).

gender—aspersions upon a person's mother, for example—would seemingly be usable *ad libitum* in the placards of those arguing *in favor* of racial, color, etc. tolerance and equality, but could not be used by that speaker's opponents. One could hold up a sign saying, for example, that all "anti-Catholic bigots" are misbegotten; but not that all "papists" are, for that would insult and provoke violence "on the basis of religion." St. Paul has no such authority to license one side of a debate to fight freestyle, while requiring the other to follow Marquis of Queensbury Rules.

What we have here, it must be emphasized, is not a prohibition of fighting words that are directed at certain persons or groups (which would be *facially* valid if it met the requirements of the Equal Protection Clause); but rather, a prohibition of fighting words that contain (as the Minnesota Supreme Court repeatedly emphasized) messages of "bias-motivated" hatred and in particular, as applied to this case, messages "based on virulent notions of racial supremacy." 464 N.W.2d, at 508, 511. One must wholeheartedly agree with the Minnesota Supreme Court that "[i]t is the responsibility, even the obligation, of diverse communities to confront such notions in whatever form they appear," *ibid.*, but the manner of that confrontation cannot consist of selective limitations upon speech. St. Paul's brief asserts that a general "fighting words" law would not meet the city's needs because only a content-specific measure can communicate to minority groups that the "group hatred" aspect of such speech "is not condoned by the majority." Brief for Respondent 25. The point of the First Amendment is that majority preferences must be expressed in some fashion other than silencing speech on the basis of its content.

Despite the fact that the Minnesota Supreme Court and St. Paul acknowledge that the ordinance is directed at expression of group hatred, Justice STEVENS suggests that this "fundamentally misreads" the ordinance. *Post*, at 2570. It is directed, he

claims, not to speech of a particular content, but to particular "injur[ies]" that are "qualitatively different" from other injuries. *Post*, at 2565. This is word-play. What makes the anger, fear, sense of dishonor, etc. produced by violation of this ordinance distinct from the anger, fear, sense of dishonor, etc. produced by other fighting words is nothing other than the fact that it is caused by a distinctive idea, conveyed by a distinctive message. The First Amendment cannot be evaded that easily. It is obvious that the symbols which will arouse "anger, alarm or resentment in others on the basis of race, color, creed, religion or gender" are those symbols that communicate a message of hostility based on one of these characteristics. St. Paul concedes in its brief that the ordinance applies only to "racial, religious, or gender-specific symbols" such as "a burning cross, Nazi swastika or other instrumentality of like import." Brief for Respondent 8. Indeed, St. Paul argued in the Juvenile Court that "[t]he burning of a cross does express a message and it is, in fact, the content of that message which the St. Paul Ordinance attempts to legislate." Memorandum from the Ramsey County Attorney to the Honorable Charles A. Flinn, Jr., dated July 13, 1990, in *In re Welfare of R.A.V.*, No. 89–D–1231 (Ramsey Cty. Juvenile Ct.), p. 1, reprinted in App. to Brief for Petitioner C–1.

The content-based discrimination reflected in the St. Paul ordinance comes within neither any of the specific exceptions to the First Amendment prohibition we discussed earlier, nor within a more general exception for content discrimination that does not threaten censorship of ideas. It assuredly does not fall within the exception for content discrimination based on the very reasons why the particular class of speech at issue (here, fighting words) is proscribable. As explained earlier, see *supra*, at 2545, the reason why fighting words are categorically excluded from the protection of the First Amendment is not that their content communicates any particular idea, but that their content embodies a particularly intolerable (and socially unnecessary) *mode* of expressing *whatever* idea the speaker wishes to convey. St. Paul has not singled out an especially offensive mode of expression—it has not, for example, selected for prohibition only those fighting words that communicate ideas in a threatening (as opposed to a merely obnoxious) manner. Rather, it has proscribed fighting words of whatever manner that communicate messages of racial, gender, or religious intolerance. Selectivity of this sort creates the possibility that the city is seeking to handicap the expression of particular ideas. That possibility would alone be enough to render the ordinance presumptively invalid, but St. Paul's comments and concessions in this case elevate the possibility to a certainty.

St. Paul argues that the ordinance comes within another of the specific exceptions we mentioned, the one that allows content discrimination aimed only at the "secondary effects" of the speech, see *Renton v. Playtime Theatres, Inc.*, 475 U.S. 41, 106 S.Ct. 925, 89 L.Ed.2d 29 (1986). According to St. Paul, the ordinance is intended, "not to impact on [*sic*] the right of free expression of the accused," but rather to "protect against the victimization of a person or persons who are particularly vulnerable because of their membership in a group that historically has been discriminated against." Brief for Respondent 28. Even assuming that an ordinance that completely proscribes, rather than merely regulates, a specified category of speech can ever be considered to be directed only to the secondary effects of such speech, it is clear that the St. Paul ordinance is not directed to secondary effects within the meaning of

Renton. As we said in *Boos v. Barry*, 485 U.S. 312, 108 S.Ct. 1157, 99 L.Ed.2d 333 (1988), "[l]isteners' reactions to speech are not the type of 'secondary effects' we referred to in *Renton*." *Id.*, at 321, 108 S.Ct., at 1163–1164. "The emotive impact of speech on its audience is not a 'secondary effect.'" *Ibid.* See also *id.*, at 334, 108 S.Ct., at 1170–1171. (opinion of Brennan, J.).[7]

It hardly needs discussion that the ordinance does not fall within some more general exception permitting *all* selectivity that for any reason is beyond the suspicion of official suppression of ideas. The statements of St. Paul in this very case afford ample basis for, if not full confirmation of, that suspicion.

[9] Finally, St. Paul and its *amici* defend the conclusion of the Minnesota Supreme Court that, even if the ordinance regulates expression based on hostility towards its protected ideological content, this discrimination is nonetheless justified because it is narrowly tailored to serve compelling state interests. Specifically, they assert that the ordinance helps to ensure the basic human rights of members of groups that have historically been subjected to discrimination, including the right of such group members to live in peace where they wish. We do not doubt that these interests are compelling, and that the ordinance can be said to promote them. But the "danger of censorship" presented by a facially content-based statute, *Leathers v. Medlock*, 499 U.S. ——, ——, 111 S.Ct. 1438, 1444, 113 L.Ed.2d 494 (1991), requires that that weapon be employed only where it is "*necessary* to serve the asserted [compelling] interest," *Burson v. Freeman*, 504

---

7. St. Paul has not argued in this case that the ordinance merely regulates that subclass of fighting words which is most likely to provoke a violent response. But even if one assumes (as appears unlikely) that the categories selected may be so described, that would not justify selective regulation under a "secondary effects" theory. The only reason why such expressive conduct would be especially correlated with violence is that it conveys a particularly odious

message; because the "chain of causation" thus *necessarily* "run[s] through the persuasive effect of the expressive component" of the conduct, *Barnes v. Glen Theatre*, 501 U.S. ——, ——, 111 S.Ct. 2456, 2470–2471, 115 L.Ed.2d 504 (1991) (SOUTER, J., concurring in judgment), it is clear that the St. Paul ordinance regulates on the basis of the "primary" effect of the speech—*i.e.*, its persuasive (or repellant) force.

U.S. ——, ——, 112 S.Ct. 1846, 1852, 119 L.Ed.2d 5 (1992) (plurality) (emphasis added); *Perry Education Assn. v. Perry Local Educators' Assn.*, 460 U.S. 37, 45, 103 S.Ct. 948, 954–955, 74 L.Ed.2d 794 (1983). The existence of adequate content-neutral alternatives thus "undercut[s] significantly" any defense of such a statute, *Boos v. Barry, supra*, 485 U.S., at 329, 108 S.Ct., at 1168, casting considerable doubt on the government's protestations that "the asserted justification is in fact an accurate description of the purpose and effect of the law," *Burson, supra*, 504 U.S., at ——, 112 S.Ct., at 1859 (KENNEDY, J., concurring). See *Boos, supra*, 485 U.S., at 324–329, 108 S.Ct., at 1165–1168; cf. *Minneapolis Star & Tribune Co. v. Minnesota Comm'r of Revenue*, 460 U.S. 575, 586–587, 103 S.Ct. 1365, 1372–1373, 75 L.Ed.2d 295 (1983). The dispositive question in this case, therefore, is whether content discrimination is reasonably necessary to achieve St. Paul's compelling interests; it plainly is not. An ordinance not limited to the favored topics, for example, would have precisely the same beneficial effect. In fact the only interest distinctively served by the content limitation is that of displaying the city council's special hostility towards the particular biases thus singled out.[8] That is precisely what the First Amendment forbids. The politicians of St. Paul are entitled to express that hostility—but not through the means of imposing unique limitations upon

speakers who (however benightedly) disagree.

•   •   •

Let there be no mistake about our belief that burning a cross in someone's front yard is reprehensible. But St. Paul has sufficient means at its disposal to prevent such behavior without adding the First Amendment to the fire.

The judgment of the Minnesota Supreme Court is reversed, and the case is remanded for proceedings not inconsistent with this opinion.

It is so ordered.

Justice WHITE, with whom Justice BLACKMUN and Justice O'CONNOR join, and with whom Justice STEVENS joins except as to Part I(A), concurring in the judgment.

I agree with the majority that the judgment of the Minnesota Supreme Court should be reversed. However, our agreement ends there.

This case could easily be decided within the contours of established First Amendment law by holding, as petitioner argues, that the St. Paul ordinance is fatally overbroad because it criminalizes not only unprotected expression but expression protected by the First Amendment. See Part II, *infra.* Instead, "find[ing] it unnecessary" to consider the questions upon which we granted review,[1] *ante*, at 2542, the

---

8. A plurality of the Court reached a different conclusion with regard to the Tennessee anti-electioneering statute considered earlier this Term in *Burson v. Freeman*, 504 U.S. ——, 112 S.Ct. 1846, 119 L.Ed.2d 5 (1992). In light of the "logical connection" between electioneering and the State's compelling interest in preventing voter intimidation and election fraud—an inherent connection borne out by a "long history" and a "wide-spread and time-tested consensus," *id.*, at —— – ——, 112 S.Ct., at 1855–1858—the plurality concluded that it was faced with one of those "rare case[s]" in which the use of a facially content-based restriction was justified by interests unrelated to the suppression of ideas, *id.*, at ——, 112 S.Ct., at 1857–1858; see also *id.*, at ——, 112 S.Ct., at 1859 (KENNEDY, J., concurring). Justice WHITE and Justice STEVENS are therefore quite mistaken when they seek to

convert the *Burson* plurality's passing comment that "[t]he First Amendment does not require States to regulate for problems that do not exist," *id.*, at ——, 112 S.Ct., at 1856, into endorsement of the revolutionary proposition that the suppression of particular ideas can be justified when only those ideas have been a source of trouble in the past. *Post*, at 2555 (WHITE, J.); *post*, at 2570 (STEVENS, J.).

1. The Court granted certiorari to review the following questions:

"1. May a local government enact a content-based, 'hate-crime' ordinance prohibiting the display of symbols, including a Nazi swastika or a burning cross, on public or private property, which one knows or has reason to know arouses anger, alarm, or resentment in others on the

Court holds the ordinance facially unconstitutional on a ground that was never presented to the Minnesota Supreme Court, a ground that has not been briefed by the parties before this Court, a ground that requires serious departures from the teaching of prior cases and is inconsistent with the plurality opinion in *Burson v. Freeman*, 504 U.S. ——, 112 S.Ct. 1846, 119 L.Ed.2d 5 (1992), which was joined by two of the five Justices in the majority in the present case.

This Court ordinarily is not so eager to abandon its precedents. Twice within the past month, the Court has declined to overturn longstanding but controversial decisions on questions of constitutional law. See *Allied Signal, Inc. v. Director, Division of Taxation*, 504 U.S. ——, 112 S.Ct. 2251, —— L.Ed.2d —— (1992); *Quill Corp. v. North Dakota*, 504 U.S. ——, 112 S.Ct. 1904, 119 L.Ed.2d 91 (1992). In each case, we had the benefit of full briefing on the critical issue, so that the parties and amici had the opportunity to apprise us of the impact of a change in the law. And in each case, the Court declined to abandon its precedents, invoking the principle of *stare decisis*. *Allied Signal, Inc., supra,* —— U.S., at —— – ——, 112 S.Ct., at 2261;

Quill Corp., supra, —— U.S., at ——, 112 S.Ct., at 1915–1916.

But in the present case, the majority casts aside long-established First Amendment doctrine without the benefit of briefing and adopts an untried theory. This is hardly a judicious way of proceeding, and the Court's reasoning in reaching its result is transparently wrong.

I

A

This Court's decisions have plainly stated that expression falling within certain limited categories so lacks the values the First Amendment was designed to protect that the Constitution affords no protection to that expression. *Chaplinsky v. New Hampshire*, 315 U.S. 568, 62 S.Ct. 766, 86 L.Ed. 1031 (1942), made the point in the clearest possible terms:

"There are certain well-defined and narrowly limited classes of speech, the prevention and punishment of which have never been thought to raise any Constitutional problem.... It has been well observed that such utterances are no essential part of any exposition of ideas, and are of such slight social value as a step to truth that any benefit that may be

---

basis of race, color, creed, religion, or gender without violating overbreadth and vagueness principles of the First Amendment to the United States Constitution?

"2. Can the constitutionality of such a vague and substantially overbroad content-based restraint of expression be saved by a limiting construction, like that used to save the vague and overbroad content-neutral laws, restricting its application to 'fighting words' or 'imminent lawless action?'" Pet. for Cert. i.

It has long been the rule of this Court that "[o]nly the questions set forth in the petition, or fairly included therein, will be considered by the Court." This Court's Rule 14.1(a). This Rule has served to focus the issues presented for review. But the majority reads the Rule so expansively that any First Amendment theory would appear to be "fairly included" within the questions quoted above.

Contrary to the impression the majority attempts to create through its selective quotation of petitioner's briefs, see *ante,* at 2542, n. 3, petitioner did not present to this Court or the

Minnesota Supreme Court anything approximating the novel theory the majority adopts today. Most certainly petitioner did not "reiterat[e]" such a claim at argument; he responded to a question from the bench. Tr. of Oral Arg. 8. Previously, this Court has shown the restraint to refrain from deciding cases on the basis of its own theories when they have not been pressed or passed upon by a state court of last resort. See, *e.g., Illinois v. Gates*, 462 U.S. 213, 217–224, 103 S.Ct. 2317, 2321–2325, 76 L.Ed.2d 527 (1983).

Given this threshold issue, it is my view that the Court lacks jurisdiction to decide the case on the majority rationale. Cf. *Arkansas Elec. Cooperative Corp. v. Arkansas Public Serv. Comm'n*, 461 U.S. 375, 382, n. 6, 103 S.Ct. 1905, 1911, n. 6, 76 L.Ed.2d 1 (1983). Certainly the preliminary jurisdictional and prudential concerns are sufficiently weighty that we would never have granted certiorari, had petitioner sought review of a question based on the majority's decisional theory.

derived from them is clearly outweighed by the social interest in order and morality." *Id.,* at 571–572, 62 S.Ct., at 769. See also *Bose Corp. v. Consumers Union of United States, Inc.,* 466 U.S. 485, 504, 104 S.Ct. 1949, 1961, 80 L.Ed.2d 502 (1984) (citing *Chaplinsky*).

Thus, as the majority concedes, see *ante,* at 2543, this Court has long held certain discrete categories of expression to be proscribable on the basis of their content. For instance, the Court has held that the individual who falsely shouts "fire" in a crowded theatre may not claim the protection of the First Amendment. *Schenck v. United States,* 249 U.S. 47, 52, 39 S.Ct. 247, 249, 63 L.Ed. 470 (1919). The Court has concluded that neither child pornography, nor obscenity, is protected by the First Amendment. *New York v. Ferber,* 458 U.S. 747, 764, 102 S.Ct. 3348, 3358, 73 L.Ed.2d 1113 (1982); *Miller v. California,* 413 U.S. 15, 20, 93 S.Ct. 2607, 2612, 37 L.Ed.2d 419 (1973); *Roth v. United States,* 354 U.S. 476, 484–485, 77 S.Ct. 1304, 1308–1309, 1 L.Ed.2d 1498 (1957). And the Court has observed that, "[l]eaving aside the special considerations when public officials [and public figures] are the target, a libelous publication is not protected by the Constitution." *Ferber, supra,* 458 U.S., at 763, 102 S.Ct., at 3358 (citations omitted).

All of these categories are content based. But the Court has held that First Amendment does not apply to them because their expressive content is worthless or of *de minimis* value to society. *Chaplinsky, supra,* 315 U.S., at 571–572, 62 S.Ct., at 768–769. We have not departed from this principle, emphasizing repeatedly that, "within the confines of [these] given classification[s], the evil to be restricted so overwhelmingly outweighs the expressive interests, if any, at stake, that no process of case-by-case adjudication is required."

2. "In each of these areas, the limits of the unprotected category, as well as the unprotected character of particular communications, have been determined by the judicial evaluation of special facts that have been deemed to have

Ferber, supra, 458 U.S., at 763–764, 102 S.Ct., at 3358–3359; *Bigelow v. Virginia,* 421 U.S. 809, 819, 95 S.Ct. 2222, 2231, 44 L.Ed.2d 600 (1975). This categorical approach has provided a principled and narrowly focused means for distinguishing between expression that the government may regulate freely and that which it may regulate on the basis of content only upon a showing of compelling need.[2]

Today, however, the Court announces that earlier Courts did not mean their repeated statements that certain categories of expression are "not within the area of constitutionally protected speech." *Roth, supra,* 354 U.S., at 483, 77 S.Ct., at 1308. See *ante,* at 2543, citing *Beauharnais v. Illinois,* 343 U.S. 250, 266, 72 S.Ct. 725, 735, 96 L.Ed. 919 (1952); *Chaplinsky, supra,* 315 U.S., at 571–572, 62 S.Ct., at 768–769; *Bose Corp., supra,* 466 U.S., at 504, 104 S.Ct., at 1961; *Sable Communications of Cal., Inc. v. FCC,* 492 U.S. 115, 124, 109 S.Ct. 2829, 2835, 106 L.Ed.2d 93 (1989). The present Court submits that such clear statements "must be taken in context" and are not "literally true." *Ante,* at 2543.

To the contrary, those statements meant precisely what they said: The categorical approach is a firmly entrenched part of our First Amendment jurisprudence. Indeed, the Court in *Roth* reviewed the guarantees of freedom of expression in effect at the time of the ratification of the Constitution and concluded, "[i]n light of this history, it is apparent that the unconditional phrasing of the First Amendment was not intended to protect every utterance." 354 U.S., at 482–483, 77 S.Ct., at 1308.

In its decision today, the Court points to "[n]othing ... in this Court's precedents warrant[ing] disregard of this longstanding tradition." *Burson,* 504 U.S., at ——, 112 S.Ct., at 1860 (SCALIA, J., concurring in judgment); *Allied Signal, Inc., supra,* ——

constitutional significance." *Bose Corp. v. Consumers Union of United States, Inc.,* 466 U.S. 485, 504–505, 104 S.Ct. 1949, 1961–1962, 80 L.Ed.2d 502 (1948).

U.S., at ——, 112 S.Ct., at 2261. Nevertheless, the majority holds that the First Amendment protects those narrow categories of expression long held to be undeserving of First Amendment protection—at least to the extent that lawmakers may not regulate some fighting words more strictly than others because of their content. The Court announces that such content-based distinctions violate the First Amendment because "the government may not regulate use based on hostility—or favoritism—towards the underlying message expressed." *Ante*, at 2545. Should the government want to criminalize certain fighting words, the Court now requires it to criminalize all fighting words.

To borrow a phrase, "Such a simplistic, all-or-nothing-at-all approach to First Amendment protection is at odds with common sense and with our jurisprudence as well." *Ante*, at 2543. It is inconsistent to hold that the government may proscribe an entire category of speech because the content of that speech is evil, *Ferber, supra,* 458 U.S., at 763–764, 102 S.Ct., at 3358–3359; but that the government may not treat a subset of that category differently without violating the First Amendment; the content of the subset is by definition worthless and undeserving of constitutional protection.

The majority's observation that fighting words are "quite expressive indeed," *ante,* at 2544, is no answer. Fighting words are not a means of exchanging views, rallying supporters, or registering a protest; they are directed against individuals to provoke violence or to inflict injury. *Chaplinsky,* 315 U.S., at 572, 62 S.Ct., at 769. Therefore, a ban on all fighting words or on a subset of the fighting words category

would restrict only the social evil of hate speech, without creating the danger of driving viewpoints from the marketplace. See *ante,* at 2545.

Therefore, the Court's insistence on inventing its brand of First Amendment underinclusiveness puzzles me.[3] The overbreadth doctrine has the redeeming virtue of attempting to avoid the chilling of protected expression, *Broadrick v. Oklahoma,* 413 U.S. 601, 612, 93 S.Ct. 2908, 2915, 37 L.Ed.2d 830 (1973); *Osborne v. Ohio,* 495 U.S. 103, 112, n. 8, 110 S.Ct. 1691, 1697, n. 8, 109 L.Ed.2d 98 (1990); *Brockett v. Spokane Arcades, Inc.,* 472 U.S. 491, 503, 105 S.Ct. 2794, 2801, 86 L.Ed.2d 394 (1985); *Ferber, supra,* 458 U.S., at 772, 102 S.Ct., at 3362, but the Court's new "underbreadth" creation serves no desirable function. Instead, it permits, indeed invites, the continuation of expressive conduct that in this case is evil and worthless in First Amendment terms, see *Ferber, supra,* at 763–764, 102 S.Ct., at 3358–3359; *Chaplinsky, supra,* 315 U.S., at 571–572, 62 S.Ct., at 768–769, until the city of St. Paul cures the underbreadth by adding to its ordinance a catch-all phrase such as "and all other fighting words that may constitutionally be subject to this ordinance."

Any contribution of this holding to First Amendment jurisprudence is surely a negative one, since it necessarily signals that expressions of violence, such as the message of intimidation and racial hatred conveyed by burning a cross on someone's lawn, are of sufficient value to outweigh the social interest in order and morality that has traditionally placed such fighting words outside the First Amendment.[4] Indeed, by characterizing fighting words as a form of "debate," *ante,* at 2548, the majori-

---

3. The assortment of exceptions the Court attaches to its rule belies the majority's claim, see *ante,* at 2545, that its new theory is truly concerned with content discrimination. See Part I(C), *infra* (discussing the exceptions).

4. This does not suggest, of course, that cross burning is always unprotected. Burning a cross at a political rally would almost certainly be

protected expression. Cf. *Brandenburg v. Ohio,* 395 U.S. 444, 445, 89 S.Ct. 1827, 1828, 23 L.Ed.2d 430 (1969). But in such a context, the cross burning could not be characterized as a "direct personal insult or an invitation to exchange fisticuffs," *Texas v. Johnson,* 491 U.S. 397, 409, 109 S.Ct. 2533, 2542, 105 L.Ed.2d 342 (1989), to which the fighting words doctrine, see Part II, *infra,* applies.

ty legitimates hate speech as a form of public discussion.

Furthermore, the Court obscures the line between speech that could be regulated freely on the basis of content (*i.e.*, the narrow categories of expression falling outside the First Amendment) and that which could be regulated on the basis of content only upon a showing of a compelling state interest (*i.e.*, all remaining expression). By placing fighting words, which the Court has long held to be valueless, on at least equal constitutional footing with political discourse and other forms of speech that we have deemed to have the greatest social value, the majority devalues the latter category. See *Burson v. Freeman, supra,* —— at ——, 112 S.Ct., at 1849–1850; *Eu v. San Francisco County Democratic Central Comm.*, 489 U.S. 214, 222–223, 109 S.Ct. 1013, 1019–1020, 103 L.Ed.2d 271 (1989).

B

In a second break with precedent, the Court refuses to sustain the ordinance even though it would survive under the strict scrutiny applicable to other protected expression. Assuming, *arguendo*, that the St. Paul ordinance is a content-based regulation of protected expression, it nevertheless would pass First Amendment review under settled law upon a showing that the regulation " 'is necessary to serve a compelling state interest and is narrowly drawn to achieve that end.' " *Simon &*

Schuster, Inc. v. New York Crime Victims Board, 502 U.S. ——, ——, 112 S.Ct. 501, 509, 116 L.Ed.2d 476 (1991) (quoting *Arkansas Writers' Project, Inc., v. Ragland*, 481 U.S. 221, 231, 107 S.Ct. 1722, 1728, 95 L.Ed.2d 209 (1987)). St. Paul has urged that its ordinance, in the words of the majority, "helps to ensure the basic human rights of members of groups that have historically been subjected to discrimination...." *Ante*, at ——. The Court expressly concedes that this interest is compelling and is promoted by the ordinance. *Ibid.* Nevertheless, the Court treats strict scrutiny analysis as irrelevant to the constitutionality of the legislation:

> "The dispositive question ... is whether content discrimination is reasonably necessary in order to achieve St. Paul's compelling interests; it plainly is not. An ordinance not limited to the favored topics would have precisely the same beneficial effect." *Ibid.*

Under the majority's view, a narrowly drawn, content-based ordinance could never pass constitutional muster if the object of that legislation could be accomplished by banning a wider category of speech. This appears to be a general renunciation of strict scrutiny review, a fundamental tool of First Amendment analysis.[5]

This abandonment of the doctrine is inexplicable in light of our decision in *Burson v. Freeman, supra,* which was handed down just a month ago.[6] In *Burson*, seven

---

5. The majority relies on *Boos v. Barry*, 485 U.S. 312, 108 S.Ct. 1157, 99 L.Ed.2d 333 (1988), in arguing that the availability of content-neutral alternatives " 'undercut[s] significantly' " a claim that content-based legislation is " '*necessary* to serve the asserted [compelling] interest.' " *Ante*, at 2549–2550 (quoting *Boos, supra*, at 329, 108 S.Ct., at 1168, and *Burson v. Freeman*, 504 U.S. ——, ——, 112 S.Ct. 1846, 1852, 119 L.Ed.2d 5 (plurality)). *Boos* does not support the majority's analysis. In *Boos*, Congress already had decided that the challenged legislation was not necessary, and the Court pointedly deferred to this choice. 485 U.S., at 329, 108 S.Ct., at 1168. St. Paul lawmakers have made no such legislative choice.

Moreover, in *Boos*, the Court held that the challenged statute was not narrowly tailored

because a less restrictive alternative was available. *Ibid.* But the Court's analysis today turns *Boos* inside-out by substituting the majority's policy judgment that a *more* restrictive alternative could adequately serve the compelling need identified by St. Paul lawmakers. The result would be: (a) a statute that was not tailored to fit the need identified by the government; and (b) a greater restriction on fighting words, even though the Court clearly believes that fighting words have protected expressive content. *Ante*, at 2544.

6. Earlier this Term, seven of the eight participating members of the Court agreed that strict scrutiny analysis applied in *Simon & Schuster*, 502 U.S. ——, 112 S.Ct. 501, 116 L.Ed.2d 476 (1991), in which we struck down New York's

of the eight participating members of the Court agreed that the strict scrutiny standard applied in a case involving a First Amendment challenge to a content-based statute. See *id.*, at ——, 112 S.Ct., at 1851; *id.*, at ——, 112 S.Ct., at 1848 (STEVENS, J., dissenting).[7] The statute at issue prohibited the solicitation of votes and the display or distribution of campaign materials within 100 feet of the entrance to a polling place. The plurality concluded that the legislation survived strict scrutiny because the State had asserted a compelling interest in regulating electioneering near polling places and because the statute at issue was narrowly tailored to accomplish that goal. *Id.*, at ——, 112 S.Ct., at 1856–1857.

Significantly, the statute in *Burson* did not proscribe all speech near polling places; it restricted only political speech. *Id.*, at ——, 112 S.Ct., at 1850. The *Burson* plurality, which included THE CHIEF JUSTICE and Justice KENNEDY, concluded that the distinction between types of speech required application of strict scrutiny, but it squarely rejected the proposition that the legislation failed First Amendment review because it could have been drafted in broader, content-neutral terms:

"States adopt laws to address the problems that confront them. *The First Amendment does not require States to regulate for problems that do not exist.*" *Id.*, at ——, 112 S.Ct., at 1856 (emphasis added).

This reasoning is in direct conflict with the majority's analysis in the present case,

which leaves two options to lawmakers attempting to regulate expressions of violence: (1) enact a sweeping prohibition on an entire class of speech (thereby requiring "regulat[ion] for problems that do not exist"); or (2) not legislate at all.

Had the analysis adopted by the majority in the present case been applied in *Burson*, the challenged election law would have failed constitutional review, for its content-based distinction between political and nonpolitical speech could not have been characterized as "reasonably necessary," *ante*, at 2550, to achieve the State's interest in regulating polling place premises.[8]

As with its rejection of the Court's categorical analysis, the majority offers no reasoned basis for discarding our firmly established strict scrutiny analysis at this time. The majority appears to believe that its doctrinal revisionism is necessary to prevent our elected lawmakers from prohibiting libel against members of one political party but not another and from enacting similarly preposterous laws. *Ante*, at 2543. The majority is misguided.

Although the First Amendment does not apply to categories of unprotected speech, such as fighting words, the Equal Protection Clause requires that the regulation of unprotected speech be rationally related to a legitimate government interest. A defamation statute that drew distinctions on the basis of political affiliation or "an ordinance prohibiting only those legally obscene works that contain criticism of the

---

"Son of Sam" law, which required "that an accused or convicted criminal's income from works describing his crime be deposited in an escrow account." *Id.*, at ——, 112 S.Ct., at 504.

7. The *Burson* dissenters did not complain that the plurality erred in applying strict scrutiny; they objected that the plurality was not sufficiently rigorous in its review. 504 U.S., at ——, 112 S.Ct., at 1865 (STEVENS, J., dissenting).

8. Justice SCALIA concurred in the judgment in *Burson*, reasoning that the statute, "though content-based, is constitutional [as] a reasonable, viewpoint-neutral regulation of a nonpublic forum." *Id.*, at ——, 112 S.Ct., at 1848. However,

nothing in his reasoning in the present case suggests that a content-based ban on fighting words would be constitutional were that ban limited to nonpublic fora. Taken together, the two opinions suggest that, in some settings, political speech, to which "the First Amendment 'has its fullest and most urgent application,'" is entitled to less constitutional protection than fighting words. *Eu v. San Francisco County Democratic Central Comm.*, 489 U.S. 214, 223, 109 S.Ct. 1013, 1020, 103 L.Ed.2d 271 (1989) (quoting *Monitor Patriot Co. v. Roy*, 401 U.S. 265, 272, 91 S.Ct. 621, 625, 28 L.Ed.2d 35 (1971)).

city government," *ante*, at 2543, would unquestionably fail rational basis review.[9]

Turning to the St. Paul ordinance and assuming *arguendo*, as the majority does, that the ordinance is not constitutionally overbroad (but see Part II, *infra*), there is no question that it would pass equal protection review. The ordinance proscribes a subset of "fighting words," those that injure "on the basis of race, color, creed, religion or gender." This selective regulation reflects the City's judgment that harms based on race, color, creed, religion, or gender are more pressing public concerns than the harms caused by other fighting words. In light of our Nation's long and painful experience with discrimination, this determination is plainly reasonable. Indeed, as the majority concedes, the interest is compelling. *Ante*, at 2549.

C

The Court has patched up its argument with an apparently nonexhaustive list of ad hoc exceptions, in what can be viewed either as an attempt to confine the effects of its decision to the facts of this case, see *post*, at 2560–2561 (BLACKMUN, J., concurring in judgment), or as an effort to anticipate some of the questions that will arise from its radical revision of First Amendment law.

For instance, if the majority were to give general application to the rule on which it decides this case, today's decision would call into question the constitutionality of the statute making it illegal to threaten the life of the President. 18 U.S.C. § 871. See *Watts v. United States*, 394 U.S. 705, 89 S.Ct. 1399, 22 L.Ed.2d 664 (1969) (*per cu-*

riam). Surely, this statute, by singling out certain threats, incorporates a content-based distinction; it indicates that the Government especially disfavors threats against the President as opposed to threats against all others.[10] See *ante*, at 2547. But because the Government could prohibit all threats and not just those directed against the President, under the Court's theory, the compelling reasons justifying the enactment of special legislation to safeguard the President would be irrelevant, and the statute would fail First Amendment review.

To save the statute, the majority has engrafted the following exception onto its newly announced First Amendment rule: Content-based distinctions may be drawn within an unprotected category of speech if the basis for the distinctions is "the very reason the entire class of speech at issue is proscribable." *Ante*, at 2545. Thus, the argument goes, the statute making it illegal to threaten the life of the President is constitutional, "since the reasons why threats of violence are outside the First Amendment (protecting individuals from the fear of violence, from the disruption that fear engenders, and from the possibility that the threatened violence will occur) have special force when applied to the person of the President." *Ante*, at 2546.

The exception swallows the majority's rule. Certainly, it should apply to the St. Paul ordinance, since "the reasons why [fighting words] are outside the First Amendment ... have special force when applied to [groups that have historically been subjected to discrimination]."

To avoid the result of its own analysis, the Court suggests that fighting words are

---

9. The majority is mistaken in stating that a ban on obscene works critical of government would fail equal protection review only because the ban would violate the First Amendment. *Ante*, at 2541, n. 2. While decisions such as *Police Dept. of Chicago v. Mosley*, 408 U.S. 92, 92 S.Ct. 2286, 33 L.Ed.2d 212 (1972), recognize that First Amendment principles may be relevant to an equal protection claim challenging distinctions that impact on protected expression, *id.*, at 95–99, 92 S.Ct., at 2289–2292, there is no basis for

linking First and Fourteenth Amendment analysis in a case involving unprotected expression. Certainly, one need not resort to First Amendment principles to conclude that the sort of improbable legislation the majority hypothesizes is based on senseless distinctions.

10. Indeed, such a law is content based in and of itself because it distinguishes between threatening and nonthreatening speech.

simply a mode of communication, rather than a content-based category, and that the St. Paul ordinance has not singled out a particularly objectionable mode of communication. *Ante*, at 2545, 2548. Again, the majority confuses the issue. A prohibition on fighting words is not a time, place, or manner restriction; it is a ban on a class of speech that conveys an overriding message of personal injury and imminent violence, *Chaplinsky, supra*, 315 U.S., at 572, 62 S.Ct., at 769, a message that is at its ugliest when directed against groups that have long been the targets of discrimination. Accordingly, the ordinance falls within the first exception to the majority's theory.

As its second exception, the Court posits that certain content-based regulations will survive under the new regime if the regulated subclass "happens to be associated with particular 'secondary effects' of the speech ...," *ante*, at 2546, which the majority treats as encompassing instances in which "words can ... violate laws directed not against speech but against conduct ..." *Ante*, at 2546.[11] Again, there is a simple explanation for the Court's eagerness to craft an exception to its new First Amendment rule: Under the general rule the Court applies in this case, Title VII hostile work environment claims would suddenly be unconstitutional.

Title VII makes it unlawful to discriminate "because of [an] individual's race, color, religion, sex, or national origin," 42 U.S.C. § 2000e–2(a)(1), and the regulations covering hostile workplace claims forbid "sexual harassment," which includes "[u]nwelcome sexual advances, requests for sexual favors, and other verbal or physical conduct of a sexual nature" which creates "an intimidating, hostile, or offensive working environment." 29 CFR § 1604.11(a) (1991). The regulation does not prohibit workplace harassment generally; it focuses on what the majority would characterize

as the "disfavored topi[c]" of sexual harassment. *Ante*, at 2547. In this way, Title VII is similar to the St. Paul ordinance that the majority condemns because it "impose[s] special prohibitions on those speakers who express views on disfavored subjects." *Ibid.* Under the broad principle the Court uses to decide the present case, hostile work environment claims based on sexual harassment should fail First Amendment review; because a general ban on harassment in the workplace would cover the problem of sexual harassment, any attempt to proscribe the subcategory of sexually harassing expression would violate the First Amendment.

Hence, the majority's second exception, which the Court indicates would insulate a Title VII hostile work environment claim from an underinclusiveness challenge because "sexually derogatory 'fighting words' ... may produce a violation of Title VII's general prohibition against sexual discrimination in employment practices." *Ante*, at 2546. But application of this exception to a hostile work environment claim does not hold up under close examination.

First, the hostile work environment regulation is not keyed to the presence or absence of an economic *quid pro quo, Meritor Savings Bank v. Vinson*, 477 U.S. 57, 65, 106 S.Ct. 2399, 2404, 91 L.Ed.2d 49 (1986), but to the impact of the speech on the victimized worker. Consequently, the regulation would no more fall within a secondary effects exception than does the St. Paul ordinance. *Ante*, at 2549. Second, the majority's focus on the statute's general prohibition on discrimination glosses over the language of the specific regulation governing hostile working environment, which reaches beyond any "incidental" effect on speech. *United States v. O'Brien*, 391 U.S. 367, 376, 88 S.Ct. 1673, 1678, 20 L.Ed.2d 672 (1968). If the relationship be-

---

11. The consequences of the majority's conflation of the rarely-used secondary effects standard and the *O'Brien* test for conduct incorporating "speech" and "nonspeech" elements, see generally *United States v. O'Brien*, 391 U.S. 367,

376–377, 88 S.Ct. 1673, 1678–1679, 20 L.Ed.2d 672 (1968), present another question that I fear will haunt us and the lower courts in the aftermath of the majority's opinion.

tween the broader statute and specific regulation is sufficient to bring the Title VII regulation within *O'Brien*, then all St. Paul need do to bring its ordinance within this exception is to add some prefatory language concerning discrimination generally.

As the third exception to the Court's theory for deciding this case, the majority concocts a catchall exclusion to protect against unforeseen problems, a concern that is heightened here given the lack of briefing on the majority's decisional theory. This final exception would apply in cases in which "there is no realistic possibility that official suppression of ideas is afoot." *Ante*, at 2547. As I have demonstrated, this case does not concern the official suppression of ideas. See *supra*, at 2553. The majority discards this notion out-of-hand. *Ante*, at 2549.

As I see it, the Court's theory does not work and will do nothing more than confuse the law. Its selection of this case to rewrite First Amendment law is particularly inexplicable, because the whole problem could have been avoided by deciding this case under settled First Amendment principles.

II

Although I disagree with the Court's analysis, I do agree with its conclusion: The St. Paul ordinance is unconstitutional. However, I would decide the case on overbreadth grounds.

We have emphasized time and again that overbreadth doctrine is an exception to the established principle that "a person to whom a statute may constitutionally be applied will not be heard to challenge that statute on the ground that it may conceivably be applied unconstitutionally to others, in other situations not before the Court." *Broadrick v. Oklahoma*, 413 U.S., at 610, 93 S.Ct., at 2915; *Brockett v. Spokane Arcades, Inc.*, 472 U.S., at 503–504, 105 S.Ct., at 2801–2802. A defendant being prosecuted for speech or expressive conduct may challenge the law on its face if it

reaches protected expression, even when that person's activities are not protected by the First Amendment. This is because "the possible harm to society in permitting some unprotected speech to go unpunished is outweighed by the possibility that protected speech of others may be muted." *Broadrick, supra*, 413 U.S., at 612, 93 S.Ct., at 2916; *Osborne v. Ohio*, 495 U.S., at 112, n. 8, 110 S.Ct., at 169, n. 8; *New York v. Ferber, supra*, 458 U.S., at 768–769, 102 S.Ct. at 3360–3361; *Schaumburg v. Citizens for a Better Environment*, 444 U.S. 620, 634, 100 S.Ct. 826, 834, 63 L.Ed.2d 73 (1980); *Gooding v. Wilson*, 405 U.S. 518, 521, 92 S.Ct. 1103, 1105, 31 L.Ed.2d 408 (1972).

However, we have consistently held that, because overbreadth analysis is "strong medicine," it may be invoked to strike an entire statute only when the overbreadth of the statute is not only "real, but substantial as well, judged in relation to the statute's plainly legitimate sweep," *Broadrick*, 413 U.S., at 615, 93 S.Ct., at 2917, and when the statute is not susceptible to limitation or partial invalidation. *Id.*, at 613, 93 S.Ct., at 2916; *Board of Airport Comm'rs of Los Angeles v. Jews for Jesus, Inc.*, 482 U.S. 569, 574, 107 S.Ct. 2568, 2571, 96 L.Ed.2d 500 (1987). "When a federal court is dealing with a federal statute challenged as overbroad, it should ... construe the statute to avoid constitutional problems, if the statute is subject to a limiting construction." *Ferber*, 458 U.S., at 769, n. 24, 102 S.Ct., at 3361, n. 24. Of course, "[a] state court is also free to deal with a state statute in the same way." *Ibid.* See, *e.g.*, *Osborne*, 495 U.S. at 113–114, 110 S.Ct., at 1698–1699.

Petitioner contends that the St. Paul ordinance is not susceptible to a narrowing construction and that the ordinance therefore should be considered as written, and not as construed by the Minnesota Supreme Court. Petitioner is wrong. Where a state court has interpreted a provision of state law, we cannot ignore that interpretation, even if it is not one that we would have reached if we were construing the statute in the first instance. *Ibid.; Kolender v. Lawson*, 461 U.S. 352, 355, 103 S.Ct. 1855, 1856, 75 L.Ed.2d 903 (1983); *Hoffman Estates v. Flipside, Hoffman Estates, Inc.*, 455 U.S. 489, 494, n. 5, 102 S.Ct. 1186, 1191, n. 5, 71 L.Ed.2d 362 (1982).[12]

Of course, the mere presence of a state court interpretation does not insulate a statute from overbreadth review. We have stricken legislation when the construction supplied by the state court failed to cure the overbreadth problem. See, *e.g., Lewis v. City of New Orleans*, 415 U.S. 130, 132–133, 94 S.Ct. 970, 972, 39 L.Ed.2d 214 (1974); *Gooding, supra*, 405 U.S., at 524–525, 92 S.Ct., at 1107–1108. But in such cases, we have looked to the statute as construed in determining whether it contravened the First Amendment. Here, the Minnesota Supreme Court has provided an authoritative construction of the St. Paul antibias ordinance. Consideration of petitioner's overbreadth claim must be based on that interpretation.

I agree with petitioner that the ordinance is invalid on its face. Although the ordinance as construed reaches categories of speech that are constitutionally unprotected, it also criminalizes a substantial amount of expression that—however repugnant—is shielded by the First Amendment.

In attempting to narrow the scope of the St. Paul antibias ordinance, the Minnesota Supreme Court relied upon two of the categories of speech and expressive conduct that fall outside the First Amendment's protective sphere: words that incite "imminent lawless action," *Brandenburg v. Ohio*, 395 U.S. 444, 449, 89 S.Ct. 1827,

1830, 23 L.Ed.2d 430 (1969), and "fighting" words, *Chaplinsky v. New Hampshire*, 315 U.S., at 571–572, 62 S.Ct., at 768–769. The Minnesota Supreme Court erred in its application of the *Chaplinsky* fighting words test and consequently interpreted the St. Paul ordinance in a fashion that rendered the ordinance facially overbroad.

In construing the St. Paul ordinance, the Minnesota Supreme Court drew upon the definition of fighting words that appears in *Chaplinsky*—words "which by their very utterance inflict injury or tend to incite an immediate breach of the peace." *Id.*, at 572, 62 S.Ct., at 769. However, the Minnesota court was far from clear in identifying the "injur[ies]" inflicted by the expression that St. Paul sought to regulate. Indeed, the Minnesota court emphasized (tracking the language of the ordinance) that "the ordinance censors only those displays that one knows or should know will create anger, alarm or resentment based on racial, ethnic, gender or religious bias." *In re Welfare of R.A.V.*, 464 N.W.2d 507, 510 (1991). I therefore understand the court to have ruled that St. Paul may constitutionally prohibit expression that "by its very utterance" causes "anger, alarm or resentment."

Our fighting words cases have made clear, however, that such generalized reactions are not sufficient to strip expression of its constitutional protection. The mere fact that expressive activity causes hurt feelings, offense, or resentment does not render the expression unprotected. See *United States v. Eichman*, 496 U.S. 310, 319, 110 S.Ct. 2404, 2410, 110 L.Ed.2d 287 (1990); *Texas v. Johnson*, 491 U.S. 397,

---

12. Petitioner can derive no support from our statement in *Virginia v. American Bookseller's Assn.*, 484 U.S. 383, 397, 108 S.Ct. 636, 645, 98 L.Ed.2d 782 (1988), that "the statute must be 'readily susceptible' to the limitation; we will not rewrite a state law to conform it to constitutional requirements." In *American Bookseller's*, no state court had construed the language in dispute. In that instance, we certified a question to the state court so that it would have an opportunity to provide a narrowing interpreta-

tion. *Ibid.* In *Erznoznik v. City of Jacksonville*, 422 U.S. 205, 216, 95 S.Ct. 2268, 2276, 45 L.Ed.2d 125 (1975), the other case upon which petitioner principally relies, we observed not only that the ordinance at issue was not "by its plain terms ... easily susceptible of a narrowing construction," but that the state courts had made no effort to restrict the scope of the statute when it was challenged on overbreadth grounds.

409, 414, 109 S.Ct. 2533, 2541, 2544, 105 L.Ed.2d 342 (1989); *Hustler Magazine, Inc. v. Falwell*, 485 U.S. 46, 55–56, 108 S.Ct. 876, 881–882, 99 L.Ed.2d 41 (1988); *FCC v. Pacifica Foundation*, 438 U.S. 726, 745, 98 S.Ct. 3026, 3038, 57 L.Ed.2d 1073 (1978); *Hess v. Indiana*, 414 U.S. 105, 107–108, 94 S.Ct. 326, 328–329, 38 L.Ed.2d 303 (1973); *Cohen v. California*, 403 U.S. 15, 20, 91 S.Ct. 1780, 1785–1786, 29 L.Ed.2d 284 (1971); *Street v. New York*, 394 U.S. 576, 592, 89 S.Ct. 1354, 1365–1366, 22 L.Ed.2d 572 (1969); *Terminiello v. Chicago*, 337 U.S. 1, 69 S.Ct. 894, 93 L.Ed. 1131 (1949).

In the First Amendment context, "[c]riminal statutes must be scrutinized with particular care; those that make unlawful a substantial amount of constitutionally protected conduct may be held facially invalid even if they also have legitimate application." *Houston v. Hill*, 482 U.S. 451, 459, 107 S.Ct. 2502, 2508, 96 L.Ed.2d 398 (1987) (citation omitted). The St. Paul antibias ordinance is such a law. Although the ordinance reaches conduct that is unprotected, it also makes criminal expressive conduct that causes only hurt feelings, offense, or resentment, and is protected by the First Amendment. Cf. *Lewis, supra*, 415 U.S., at 132, 94 S.Ct., at 972.[13] The ordinance is therefore fatally overbroad and invalid on its face.

III

Today, the Court has disregarded two established principles of First Amendment law without providing a coherent replacement theory. Its decision is an arid, doctrinaire interpretation, driven by the frequently irresistible impulse of judges to tinker with the First Amendment. The decision is mischievous at best and will surely confuse the lower courts. I join the judgment, but not the folly of the opinion.

Justice BLACKMUN, concurring in the judgment.

I regret what the Court has done in this case. The majority opinion signals one of two possibilities: it will serve as precedent for future cases, or it will not. Either result is disheartening.

In the first instance, by deciding that a State cannot regulate speech that causes great harm unless it also regulates speech that does not (setting law and logic on their heads), the Court seems to abandon the categorical approach, and inevitably to relax the level of scrutiny applicable to content-based laws. As Justice WHITE points out, this weakens the traditional protections of speech. If all expressive activity must be accorded the same protection, that protection will be scant. The simple reality is that the Court will never provide child pornography or cigarette advertising the level of protection customarily granted political speech. If we are forbidden from categorizing, as the Court has done here, we shall reduce protection across the board. It is sad that in its effort to reach a satisfying result in this case, the Court is willing to weaken First Amendment protections.

In the second instance is the possibility that this case will not significantly alter First Amendment jurisprudence, but, instead, will be regarded as an aberration—a case where the Court manipulated doctrine to strike down an ordinance whose premise it opposed, namely, that racial threats and

---

13. Although the First Amendment protects offensive speech, *Johnson v. Texas*, 491 U.S., at 414, 109 S.Ct., at 2544, it does not require us to be subjected to such expression at all times, in all settings. We have held that such expression may be proscribed when it intrudes upon a "captive audience." *Frisby v. Schultz*, 487 U.S. 474, 484–485, 108 S.Ct. 2495, 2502–2503, 101 L.Ed.2d 420 (1988); *FCC v. Pacifica Foundation*, 438 U.S. 726, 748–749, 98 S.Ct. 3026, 3040–3041, 57 L.Ed.2d 1073 (1978). And expression may be limited when it merges into conduct. *United States v. O'Brien*, 391 U.S. 367, 88 S.Ct. 1673, 20 L.Ed.2d 672 (1968); cf. *Meritor Savings Bank v. Vinson*, 477 U.S. 57, 65, 106 S.Ct. 2399, 2404, 91 L.Ed.2d 49 (1986). However, because of the manner in which the Minnesota Supreme Court construed the St. Paul ordinance, those issues are not before us in this case.

verbal assaults are of greater harm than other fighting words. I fear that the Court has been distracted from its proper mission by the temptation to decide the issue over "politically correct speech" and "cultural diversity," neither of which is presented here. If this is the meaning of today's opinion, it is perhaps even more regrettable.

I see no First Amendment values that are compromised by a law that prohibits hoodlums from driving minorities out of their homes by burning crosses on their lawns, but I see great harm in preventing the people of Saint Paul from specifically punishing the race-based fighting words that so prejudice their community.

I concur in the judgment, however, because I agree with Justice WHITE that this particular ordinance reaches beyond fighting words to speech protected by the First Amendment.

Justice STEVENS, with whom Justice WHITE and Justice BLACKMUN join as to Part I, concurring in the judgment.

Conduct that creates special risks or causes special harms may be prohibited by special rules. Lighting a fire near an ammunition dump or a gasoline storage tank is especially dangerous; such behavior may be punished more severely than burning trash in a vacant lot. Threatening someone because of her race or religious beliefs may cause particularly severe trauma or touch off a riot, and threatening a high public official may cause substantial social disruption; such threats may be punished more severely than threats against someone based on, say, his support of a particular athletic team. There are legitimate, reasonable, and neutral justifications for such special rules.

This case involves the constitutionality of one such ordinance. Because the regulated conduct has some communicative content— a message of racial, religious or gender hostility—the ordinance raises two quite different First Amendment questions. Is the ordinance "overbroad" because it prohibits too much speech? If not, is it "underbroad" because it does not prohibit enough speech?

In answering these questions, my colleagues today wrestle with two broad principles: first, that certain "categories of expression [including 'fighting words'] are 'not within the area of constitutionally protected speech,'" *ante*, at 2553 (WHITE, J., concurring in judgment); and second, that "[c]ontent-based regulations [of expression] are presumptively invalid." *Ante*, at 2542 (Opinion of the Court). Although in past opinions the Court has repeated both of these maxims, it has—quite rightly— adhered to neither with the absolutism suggested by my colleagues. Thus, while I agree that the St. Paul ordinance is unconstitutionally overbroad for the reasons stated in Part II of Justice WHITE's opinion, I write separately to suggest how the allure of absolute principles has skewed the analysis of both the majority and concurring opinions.

I

Fifty years ago, the Court articulated a categorical approach to First Amendment jurisprudence.

"There are certain well-defined and narrowly limited classes of speech, the prevention and punishment of which have never been thought to raise any Constitutional problem.... It has been well observed that such utterances are no essential part of any exposition of ideas, and are of such slight social value as a step to truth that any benefit that may be derived from them is clearly outweighed by the social interest in order and morality." *Chaplinsky v. New Hampshire*, 315 U.S. 568, 571–572, 62 S.Ct. 766, 769, 86 L.Ed. 1031 (1942).

We have, as Justice WHITE observes, often described such categories of expression as "not within the area of constitutionally protected speech." *Roth v. United States*, 354 U.S. 476, 483, 77 S.Ct. 1304, 1308, 1 L.Ed.2d 1498 (1957).

The Court today revises this categorical approach. It is not, the Court rules, that certain "categories" of expression are "unprotected," but rather that certain "elements" of expression are wholly "proscribable." To the Court, an expressive act, like a chemical compound, consists of more than one element. Although the act may be regulated because it contains a proscribable element, it may not be regulated on the basis of another (nonproscribable) element it also contains. Thus, obscene antigovernment speech may be regulated because it is obscene, but not because it is antigovernment. *Ante*, at 2543. It is this revision of the categorical approach that allows the Court to assume that the St. Paul ordinance proscribes *only* fighting words, while at the same time concluding that the ordinance is invalid because it imposes a content-based regulation on expressive activity.

As an initial matter, the Court's revision of the categorical approach seems to me something of an adventure in a doctrinal wonderland, for the concept of "obscene anti-government" speech is fantastical. The category of the obscene is very narrow; to be obscene, expression must be found by the trier of fact to "appea[l] to the prurient interest, ... depic[t] or describ[e], in a patently offensive way, sexual conduct, [and] taken as a whole, *lac[k] serious literary, artistic, political or scientific value.*" *Miller v. California,* 413 U.S. 15, 24, 93 S.Ct. 2607, 2614–2615, 37 L.Ed.2d 419 (1973) (emphasis added). "Obscene antigovernment" speech, then, is a contradiction in terms: If expression is antigovernment, it does not "lac[k] serious ... political ... value" and cannot be obscene.

The Court attempts to bolster its argument by likening its novel analysis to that applied to restrictions on the time, place, or manner of expression or on expressive conduct. It is true that loud speech in favor of the Republican Party can be regulated because it is loud, but not because it is pro-Republican; and it is true that the public burning of the American flag can be regulated because it involves public burning and not because it involves the flag. But these analogies are inapposite. In each of these examples, the two elements (*e.g.,* loudness and pro-Republican orientation) can coexist; in the case of "obscene antigovernment" speech, however, the presence of one element ("obscenity") by definition means the absence of the other. To my mind, it is unwise and unsound to craft a new doctrine based on such highly speculative hypotheticals.

I am, however, even more troubled by the second step of the Court's analysis—namely, its conclusion that the St. Paul ordinance is an unconstitutional content-based regulation of speech. Drawing on broadly worded *dicta,* the Court establishes a near-absolute ban on content-based regulations of expression and holds that the First Amendment prohibits the regulation of fighting words by subject matter. Thus, while the Court rejects the "all-or-nothing-at-all" nature of the categorical approach, *ante,* at 2543, it promptly embraces an absolutism of its own: within a particular "proscribable" category of expression, the Court holds, a government must either proscribe *all* speech or no speech at all.[1] This aspect of the Court's ruling fundamentally misunderstands the role and constitutional status of content-based regulations

1. The Court disputes this characterization because it has crafted two exceptions, one for "certain media or markets" and the other for content discrimination based upon "the very reason that the entire class of speech at issue is proscribable." *Ante,* at 2545. These exceptions are, at best, ill-defined. The Court does not tell us whether, with respect to the former, fighting words such as cross-burning could be proscribed only in certain neighborhoods where the threat of violence is particularly severe, or whether, with respect to the second category, fighting words that create a particular risk of harm (such as a race riot) would be proscribable. The hypothetical and illusory category of these two exceptions persuades me that either my description of the Court's analysis is accurate or that the Court does not in fact mean much of what it says in its opinion.

on speech, conflicts with the very nature of First Amendment jurisprudence, and disrupts well-settled principles of First Amendment law.

Although the Court has, on occasion, declared that content-based regulations of speech are "never permitted," *Police Dept. of Chicago v. Mosley*, 408 U.S. 92, 99, 92 S.Ct. 2286, 2292, 33 L.Ed.2d 212 (1972), such claims are overstated. Indeed, in *Mosley* itself, the Court indicated that Chicago's selective proscription of nonlabor picketing was not *per se* unconstitutional, but rather could be upheld if the City demonstrated that nonlabor picketing was "clearly more disruptive than [labor] picketing." *Id.*, at 100, 92 S.Ct., at 2292. Contrary to the broad *dicta* in *Mosley* and elsewhere, our decisions demonstrate that content-based distinctions, far from being presumptively invalid, are an inevitable and indispensable aspect of a coherent understanding of the First Amendment.

This is true at every level of First Amendment law. In broadest terms, our entire First Amendment jurisprudence creates a regime based on the content of speech. The scope of the First Amendment is determined by the content of expressive activity: Although the First Amendment broadly protects "speech," it does not protect the right to "fix prices, breach contracts, make false warranties, place bets with bookies, threaten, [or] extort." Schauer, Categories and the First Amendment: A Play in Three Acts, 34 Vand. L.Rev. 265, 270 (1981). Whether an agreement among competitors is a violation of the Sherman Act or protected activity under the *Noerr–Pennington* doctrine [2] hinges upon the content of the agreement. Similarly, "the line between permissible advocacy and impermissible incitation to crime or violence depends, not merely on the setting in which the speech occurs, but also on exactly what the speaker had to say." *Young v. American Mini Theatres,*

Inc., 427 U.S. 50, 66, 96 S.Ct. 2440, 2450, 49 L.Ed.2d 310 (1976) (plurality opinion); see also *Musser v. Utah*, 333 U.S. 95, 100–103, 68 S.Ct. 397, 399–401, 92 L.Ed. 562 (1948) (Rutledge, J., dissenting).

Likewise, whether speech falls within one of the categories of "unprotected" or "proscribable" expression is determined, in part, by its content. Whether a magazine is obscene, a gesture a fighting word, or a photograph child pornography is determined, in part, by its content. Even within categories of protected expression, the First Amendment status of speech is fixed by its content. *New York Times Co. v. Sullivan*, 376 U.S. 254, 84 S.Ct. 710, 11 L.Ed.2d 686 (1964), and *Dun & Bradstreet, Inc. v. Greenmoss Builders, Inc.*, 472 U.S. 749, 105 S.Ct. 2939, 86 L.Ed.2d 593 (1985), establish that the level of protection given to speech depends upon its subject matter: speech about public officials or matters of public concern receives greater protection than speech about other topics. It can, therefore, scarcely be said that the regulation of expressive activity cannot be predicated on its content: much of our First Amendment jurisprudence is premised on the assumption that content makes a difference.

Consistent with this general premise, we have frequently upheld content-based regulations of speech. For example, in *Young v. American Mini Theatres*, the Court upheld zoning ordinances that regulated movie theaters based on the content of the films shown. In *FCC v. Pacifica Foundation*, 438 U.S. 726, 98 S.Ct. 3026, 57 L.Ed.2d 1073 (1978) (plurality opinion), we upheld a restriction on the broadcast of *specific* indecent words. In *Lehman v. City of Shaker Heights*, 418 U.S. 298, 94 S.Ct. 2714, 41 L.Ed.2d 770 (1974) (plurality opinion), we upheld a city law that permitted commercial advertising, but prohibited political advertising, on city buses. In *Broadrick v. Oklahoma*, 413 U.S. 601, 93

2. See *Mine Workers v. Pennington*, 381 U.S. 657, 85 S.Ct. 1585, 14 L.Ed.2d 626 (1965); *Eastern Railroad Presidents Conference v. Noerr Motor*

Freight, Inc., 365 U.S. 127, 81 S.Ct. 523, 5 L.Ed.2d 464 (1961).

S.Ct. 2908, 37 L.Ed.2d 830 (1973), we upheld a state law that restricted the speech of state employees, but only as concerned partisan political matters. We have long recognized the power of the Federal Trade Commission to regulate misleading advertising and labeling, see, *e.g., Jacob Siegel Co. v. FTC,* 327 U.S. 608, 66 S.Ct. 758, 90 L.Ed. 888 (1946), and the National Labor Relations Board's power to regulate an employer's election-related speech on the basis of its content. See, *e.g., NLRB v. Gissel Packing Co.,* 395 U.S. 575, 616–618, 89 S.Ct. 1918, 1942–1943, 23 L.Ed.2d 547 (1969). It is also beyond question that the Government may choose to limit advertisements for cigarettes, see 15 U.S.C. §§ 1331–1340,[3] but not for cigars; choose to regulate airline advertising, see *Morales v. Trans World Airlines,* 504 U.S. ——, 112 S.Ct. 2031, 119 L.Ed.2d 157 (1992), but not bus advertising; or choose to monitor solicitation by lawyers, see *Ohralik v. Ohio State Bar Assn.,* 436 U.S. 447, 98 S.Ct. 1912, 56 L.Ed.2d 444 (1978), but not by doctors.

All of these cases involved the selective regulation of speech based on content—precisely the sort of regulation the Court invalidates today. Such selective regulations are unavoidably content based, but they are not, in my opinion, "presumptively invalid." As these many decisions and examples demonstrate, the prohibition on content-based regulations is not nearly as total as the *Mosley* dictum suggests.

Disregarding this vast body of case law, the Court today goes beyond even the overstatement in *Mosley* and applies the prohibition on content-based regulation to speech that the Court had until today considered wholly "unprotected" by the First Amendment—namely, fighting words. This new absolutism in the prohibition of content-based regulations severely contorts the fabric of settled First Amendment law.

Our First Amendment decisions have created a rough hierarchy in the constitutional protection of speech. Core political speech occupies the highest, most protected position; commercial speech and nonobscene, sexually explicit speech are regarded as a sort of second-class expression; obscenity and fighting words receive the least protection of all. Assuming that the Court is correct that this last class of speech is not wholly "unprotected," it certainly does not follow that fighting words and obscenity receive the *same* sort of protection afforded core political speech. Yet in ruling that proscribable speech cannot be regulated based on subject matter, the Court does just that.[4] Perversely, this gives fighting words *greater* protection than is afforded commercial speech. If Congress can prohibit false advertising directed at airline passengers without also prohibiting false advertising directed at bus passengers and if a city can prohibit political advertisements in its buses while allowing other advertisements, it is ironic to hold that a city cannot regulate fighting words based on "race, color, creed, religion or gender" while leaving unregulated fighting words based on "union membership or homosexuality." *Ante,* at 2547. The Court today turns First Amendment law on its head: Communication that was once entirely unprotected (and that still can be wholly proscribed) is now entitled to greater protection than commercial speech—and possibly greater protection than core political

---

3. See also *Packer Corp v. Utah,* 285 U.S. 105, 52 S.Ct. 273, 76 L.Ed. 643 (1932) (Brandeis, J.) (upholding a statute that prohibited the advertisement of cigarettes on billboards and streetcar placards).

4. The Court states that the prohibition on content-based regulations "applies differently in the context of proscribable speech" than in the context of other speech, *ante,* at 2545, but its analy-

sis belies that claim. The Court strikes down the St. Paul ordinance because it regulates fighting words based on subject matter, despite the fact that, as demonstrated above, we have long upheld regulations of commercial speech based on subject matter. The Court's self-description is inapt: By prohibiting the regulation of fighting words based on its subject matter, the Court provides the same protection to fighting words as is currently provided to core political speech.

speech. See *Burson v. Freeman*, 504 U.S. ——, ——, 112 S.Ct. 1846, ——, 119 L.Ed.2d 5 (1992).

Perhaps because the Court recognizes these perversities, it quickly offers some ad hoc limitations on its newly extended prohibition on content-based regulations. First, the Court states that a content-based regulation is valid "[w]hen the content discrimination is based upon the very reason the entire class of speech ... is proscribable." In a pivotal passage, the Court writes

"the Federal Government can criminalize only those physical threats that are directed against the President, see 18 U.S.C. § 871—since the reasons why threats of violence are outside the First Amendment (protecting individuals from the fear of violence, from the disruption that fear engenders, and from the possibility that the threatened violence will occur) have special force when applied to the ... President." *Ante*, at 2546.

As I understand this opaque passage, Congress may choose from the set of unprotected speech (all threats) to proscribe only a subset (threats against the President) because those threats are particularly likely to cause "fear of violence," "disruption," and actual "violence."

Precisely this same reasoning, however, compels the conclusion that St. Paul's ordinance is constitutional. Just as Congress may determine that threats against the President entail more severe consequences than other threats, so St. Paul's City Council may determine that threats based on the target's race, religion, or gender cause more severe harm to both the target and to society than other threats. This latter judgment—that harms caused by racial, religious, and gender-based invective are qualitatively different from that caused by other fighting words—seems to me eminently reasonable and realistic.

Next, the Court recognizes that a State may regulate advertising in one industry but not another because "the risk of fraud (one of the characteristics that justifies depriving [commercial speech] of full First Amendment protection ...)" in the regulated industry is "greater" than in other industries. *Ante*, at 2546. Again, the same reasoning demonstrates the constitutionality of St. Paul's ordinance. "[O]ne of the characteristics that justifies" the constitutional status of fighting words is that such words "by their very utterance inflict injury or tend to incite an immediate breach of the peace." *Chaplinsky*, 315 U.S., at 572, 62 S.Ct., at 762. Certainly a legislature that may determine that the risk of fraud is greater in the legal trade than in the medical trade may determine that the risk of injury or breach of peace created by race-based threats is greater than that created by other threats.

Similarly, it is impossible to reconcile the Court's analysis of the St. Paul ordinance with its recognition that "a prohibition of fighting words that are directed at certain persons or groups ... would be facially valid." *Ante*, at 2548 (emphasis deleted). A selective proscription of unprotected expression designed to protect "certain persons or groups" (for example, a law proscribing threats directed at the elderly) would be constitutional if it were based on a legitimate determination that the harm created by the regulated expression differs from that created by the unregulated expression (that is, if the elderly are more severely injured by threats than are the nonelderly). Such selective protection is no different from a law prohibiting minors (and only minors) from obtaining obscene publications. See *Ginsberg v. New York*, 390 U.S. 629, 88 S.Ct. 1274, 20 L.Ed.2d 195 (1968). St. Paul has determined—reasonably in my judgment—that fighting-word injuries "based on race, color, creed, religion or gender" are qualitatively different and more severe than fighting-word injuries based on other characteristics. Whether the selective proscription of proscribable speech is defined by the protected target ("certain persons or groups") or the basis of the harm (injuries "based on race, color, creed, religion or gender") makes no constitutional difference: what matters is whether the legislature's selection is based on a legitimate, neutral, and reasonable distinction.

In sum, the central premise of the Court's ruling—that "[c]ontent-based regulations are presumptively invalid"—has simplistic appeal, but lacks support in our First Amendment jurisprudence. To make matters worse, the Court today extends this overstated claim to reach categories of hitherto unprotected speech and, in doing so, wreaks havoc in an area of settled law. Finally, although the Court recognizes exceptions to its new principle, those exceptions undermine its very conclusion that the St. Paul ordinance is unconstitutional. Stated directly, the majority's position cannot withstand scrutiny.

II

Although I agree with much of Justice WHITE's analysis, I do not join Part I-A of his opinion because I have reservations about the "categorical approach" to the First Amendment. These concerns, which I have noted on other occasions, see, *e.g.*, *New York v. Ferber*, 458 U.S. 747, 778, 102 S.Ct. 3348, 3365–3366, 73 L.Ed.2d 1113 (1982) (STEVENS, J., concurring in judgment), lead me to find Justice WHITE's response to the Court's analysis unsatisfying.

Admittedly, the categorical approach to the First Amendment has some appeal: either expression is protected or it is not— the categories create safe harbors for governments and speakers alike. But this approach sacrifices subtlety for clarity and is, I am convinced, ultimately unsound. As an initial matter, the concept of "categories" fits poorly with the complex reality of expression. Few dividing lines in First Amendment law are straight and unwavering, and efforts at categorization inevitably give rise only to fuzzy boundaries. Our

definitions of "obscenity," see, *e.g.*, *Marks v. United States*, 430 U.S. 188, 198, 97 S.Ct. 990, 996, 51 L.Ed.2d 260 (1977) (STEVENS, J., concurring in part and dissenting in part), and "public forum," see, *e.g.*, *United States Postal Service v. Council of Greenburgh Civic Assns.*, 453 U.S. 114, 126–131, 101 S.Ct. 2676, 2683–2686, 69 L.Ed.2d 517 (1981); *id.*, at 136–140, 101 S.Ct., at 2688–2691 (Brennan, J., concurring in judgment); *id.*, at 147–151, 101 S.Ct., at 2694–2696 (Marshall, J., dissenting); 152–154, 101 S.Ct. at 2696–2698 (STEVENS, J., dissenting) (all debating the definition of "public forum"), illustrate this all too well. The quest for doctrinal certainty through the definition of categories and subcategories is, in my opinion, destined to fail.

Moreover, the categorical approach does not take seriously the importance of *context*. The meaning of any expression and the legitimacy of its regulation can only be determined in context.[5] Whether, for example, a picture or a sentence is obscene cannot be judged in the abstract, but rather only in the context of its setting, its use, and its audience. Similarly, although legislatures may freely regulate most nonobscene child pornography, such pornography that is part of "a serious work of art, a documentary on behavioral problems, or a medical or psychiatric teaching device," may be entitled to constitutional protection; the "question whether a specific act of communication is protected by the First Amendment always requires some consideration of both its content and its context." *Ferber*, 458 U.S. at 778, 102 S.Ct., at 3366 (STEVENS, J., concurring in judgment); see also *Smith v. United States*, 431 U.S. 291, 311–321, 97 S.Ct. 1756, 1769–1774, 52 L.Ed.2d 324 (1977) (STEVENS, J., dissenting). The categorical approach sweeps too broadly when it declares that all such ex-

---

5. "A word," as Justice Holmes has noted, "is not a crystal, transparent and unchanged, it is the skin of a living thought and may vary greatly in color and content according to the circumstances and the time in which it is used." *Towne v. Eisner*, 245 U.S. 418, 425, 38 S.Ct. 158, 159, 62 L.Ed. 372 (1918); see also *Jacobellis v. Ohio*, 378 U.S. 184, 201, 84 S.Ct. 1676, 1685, 12 L.Ed.2d 793 (1964) (Warren, C.J., dissenting).

pression is beyond the protection of the First Amendment.

Perhaps sensing the limits of such an all-or-nothing approach, the Court has applied its analysis less categorically than its doctrinal statements suggest. The Court has recognized intermediate categories of speech (for example, for indecent nonobscene speech and commercial speech) and geographic categories of speech (public fora, limited public fora, nonpublic fora) entitled to varying levels of protection. The Court has also stringently delimited the categories of unprotected speech. While we once declared that "[l]ibelous utterances [are] not ... within the area of constitutionally protected speech," *Beauharnais v. Illinois*, 343 U.S. 250, 266, 72 S.Ct. 725, 735, 96 L.Ed. 919 (1952), our rulings in *New York Times Co. v. Sullivan*, 376 U.S. 254, 84 S.Ct. 710, 11 L.Ed.2d 686 (1964); *Gertz v. Robert Welch, Inc.*, 418 U.S. 323, 94 S.Ct. 2997, 41 L.Ed.2d 789 (1974), and *Dun & Bradstreet, Inc. v. Greenmoss Builders, Inc.*, 472 U.S. 749, 105 S.Ct. 2939, 86 L.Ed.2d 593 (1985), have substantially qualified this broad claim. Similarly, we have consistently construed the "fighting words" exception set forth in *Chaplinsky* narrowly. See, *e.g.*, *Houston v. Hill*, 482 U.S. 451, 107 S.Ct. 2502, 96 L.Ed.2d 398 (1987); *Lewis v. City of New Orleans*, 415 U.S. 130, 94 S.Ct. 970, 39 L.Ed.2d 214 (1974); *Cohen v. California*, 403 U.S. 15, 91 S.Ct. 1780, 29 L.Ed.2d 284 (1971). In the case of commercial speech, our ruling that "the Constitution imposes no ... restraint on government [regulation] as respects purely commercial advertising," *Valentine v. Chrestensen*, 316 U.S. 52, 54, 62 S.Ct. 920, 921, 86 L.Ed. 1262 (1942), was expressly repudiated in *Virginia Bd. of Pharmacy v. Virginia Citizens Consumer Council, Inc.*, 425 U.S. 748, 96 S.Ct. 1817, 48 L.Ed.2d 346 (1976). In short, the history of the categorical approach is largely the history of narrowing the categories of unprotected speech.

This evolution, I believe, indicates that the categorical approach is unworkable and the quest for absolute categories of "protected" and "unprotected" speech ultimately futile. My analysis of the faults and limits of this approach persuades me that the categorical approach presented in Part I-A of Justice WHITE's opinion is not an adequate response to the novel "underbreadth" analysis the Court sets forth today.

III

As the foregoing suggests, I disagree with both the Court's and part of Justice WHITE's analysis of the constitutionality St. Paul ordinance. Unlike the Court, I do not believe that all content-based regulations are equally infirm and presumptively invalid; unlike Justice WHITE, I do not believe that fighting words are wholly unprotected by the First Amendment. To the contrary, I believe our decisions establish a more complex and subtle analysis, one that considers the content and context of the regulated speech, and the nature and scope of the restriction on speech. Applying this analysis and assuming *arguendo* (as the Court does) that the St. Paul ordinance is *not* overbroad, I conclude that such a selective, subject-matter regulation on proscribable speech is constitutional.

Not all content-based regulations are alike; our decisions clearly recognize that some content-based restrictions raise more constitutional questions than others. Although the Court's analysis of content-based regulations cannot be reduced to a simple formula, we have considered a number of factors in determining the validity of such regulations.

First, as suggested above, the scope of protection provided expressive activity depends in part upon its content and character. We have long recognized that when government regulates political speech or "the expression of editorial opinion on matters of public importance," *FCC v. League of Women Voters of California*, 468 U.S. 364, 375–376, 104 S.Ct. 3106, 3114–3115, 82 L.Ed.2d 278 (1984), "First Amendment protectio[n] is 'at its zenith.'" *Meyer v.*

Grant, 486 U.S. 414, 425, 108 S.Ct. 1886, 1894, 100 L.Ed.2d 425 (1988). In comparison, we have recognized that "commercial speech receives a limited form of First Amendment protection," *Posadas de Puerto Rico Associates v. Tourism Co. of Puerto Rico*, 478 U.S. 328, 340, 106 S.Ct. 2968, 2976, 92 L.Ed.2d 266 (1986), and that "society's interest in protecting [sexually explicit films] is of a wholly different, and lesser magnitude than [its] interest in untrammeled political debate." *Young v. American Mini Theatres*, 427 U.S., at 70, 96 S.Ct., at 2452; see also *FCC v. Pacifica Foundation*, 438 U.S. 726, 98 S.Ct. 3026, 57 L.Ed.2d 1073 (1978). The character of expressive activity also weighs in our consideration of its constitutional status. As we have frequently noted, "[t]he government generally has a freer hand in restricting expressive conduct than it has in restricting the written or spoken word." *Texas v. Johnson*, 491 U.S. 397, 406, 109 S.Ct. 2533, 2540, 105 L.Ed.2d 342 (1989); see also *United States v. O'Brien*, 391 U.S. 367, 88 S.Ct. 1673, 20 L.Ed.2d 672 (1968).

The protection afforded expression turns as well on the context of the regulated speech. We have noted, for example, that "[a]ny assessment of the precise scope of employer expression, of course, must be made in the context of its labor relations setting ... [and] must take into account the economic dependence of the employees on their employers." *NLRB v. Gissel Packing Co.*, 395 U.S., at 617, 89 S.Ct., at 1942. Similarly, the distinctive character of a university environment, see *Widmar v. Vincent*, 454 U.S. 263, 277–280, 102 S.Ct. 269, 278–280, 70 L.Ed.2d 440 (1981) (STEVENS, J., concurring in judgment), or a secondary school environment, see *Hazelwood School Dist. v. Kuhlmeier*, 484 U.S. 260, 108 S.Ct. 592, 98 L.Ed.2d 562 (1988), influences our First Amendment analysis. The same is true of the presence of a "'captive audience[, one] there as a matter

of necessity, not of choice.'" *Lehman v. City of Shaker Heights*, 418 U.S., at 302, 94 S.Ct., at 2717 (citation omitted).[6] Perhaps the most familiar embodiment of the relevance of context is our "fora" jurisprudence, differentiating the levels of protection afforded speech in different locations.

The nature of a contested restriction of speech also informs our evaluation of its constitutionality. Thus, for example, "[a]ny system of prior restraints of expression comes to this Court bearing a heavy presumption against its constitutional validity." *Bantam Books, Inc. v. Sullivan*, 372 U.S. 58, 70, 83 S.Ct. 631, 639, 9 L.Ed.2d 584 (1963). More particularly to the matter of content-based regulations, we have implicitly distinguished between restrictions on expression based on *subject matter* and restrictions based on *viewpoint*, indicating that the latter are particularly pernicious. "If there is a bedrock principle underlying the First Amendment, it is that the Government may not prohibit the expression of an idea simply because society finds the idea itself offensive or disagreeable." *Texas v. Johnson*, 491 U.S., at 414, 109 S.Ct., at 2544. "Viewpoint discrimination is censorship in its purest form," *Perry Education Assn. v. Perry Local Educators' Assn.*, 460 U.S. 37, 62, 103 S.Ct. 948, 964, 74 L.Ed.2d 794 (1983) (Brennan, J., dissenting), and requires particular scrutiny, in part because such regulation often indicates a legislative effort to skew public debate on an issue. See, *e.g.*, *Schacht v. United States*, 398 U.S. 58, 63, 90 S.Ct. 1555, 1559, 26 L.Ed.2d 44 (1970). "Especially where ... the legislature's suppression of speech suggests an attempt to give one side of a debatable public question an advantage in expressing its views to the people, the First Amendment is plainly offended." *First National Bank of Boston v. Bellotti*, 435 U.S. 765, 785–786, 98 S.Ct. 1407, 1420–1421, 55 L.Ed.2d 707 (1978).

---

6. Cf. *In re Chase*, 468 F.2d 128, 139–140 (CA7 1972) (Stevens, J., dissenting) (arguing that defendant who, for reasons of religious belief, refused to rise and stand as the trial judge entered the courtroom was not subject to contempt proceedings because he was not present in the courtroom "as a matter of choice").

Thus, although a regulation that on its face regulates speech by subject matter may in some instances effectively suppress particular viewpoints, see, *e.g.*, *Consolidated Edison Co. of N.Y. v. Public Service Comm'n of N.Y.*, 447 U.S. 530, 546–547, 100 S.Ct. 2326, 2338, 65 L.Ed.2d 319 (1980) (STEVENS, J., concurring in judgment), in general, viewpoint-based restrictions on expression require greater scrutiny than subject-matter based restrictions.[7]

Finally, in considering the validity of content-based regulations we have also looked more broadly at the scope of the restrictions. For example, in *Young v. American Mini Theatres*, 427 U.S., at 71, 96 S.Ct., at 2452–2453, we found significant the fact that "what [was] ultimately at stake [was] nothing more than a limitation on the place where adult films may be exhibited." Similarly, in *FCC v. Pacifica Foundation*, the Court emphasized two dimensions of the limited scope of the FCC ruling. First, the ruling concerned only broadcast material which presents particular problems because it "confronts the citizen ... in the privacy of the home"; second, the ruling was not a complete ban on the use of selected offensive words, but rather merely a limitation on the times such speech could be broadcast. 438 U.S., at 748–750, 98 S.Ct., at 3039–3041.

All of these factors play some role in our evaluation of content-based regulations on expression. Such a multi-faceted analysis cannot be conflated into two dimensions. Whatever the allure of absolute doctrines, it is just too simple to declare expression "protected" or "unprotected" or to proclaim a regulation "content-based" or "content-neutral."

In applying this analysis to the St. Paul ordinance, I assume *arguendo*—as the Court does—that the ordinance regulates *only* fighting words and therefore is *not* overbroad. Looking to the content and character of the regulated activity, two things are clear. First, by hypothesis the ordinance bars only low-value speech, namely, fighting words. By definition such expression constitutes "no essential part of any exposition of ideas, and [is] of such slight social value as a step to truth that any benefit that may be derived from [it] is clearly outweighed by the social interest in order and morality." *Chaplinsky*, 315 U.S., at 572, 62 S.Ct., at 769. Second, the ordinance regulates "expressive conduct [rather] than ... the written or spoken word." *Texas v. Johnson*, 491 U.S., at 406, 109 S.Ct., at 2540.

Looking to the context of the regulated activity, it is again significant that the statute (by hypothesis) regulates *only* fighting words. Whether words are fighting words is determined in part by their context. Fighting words are not words that merely cause offense; fighting words must be directed at individuals so as to "by their very utterance inflict injury." By hypothesis, then, the St. Paul ordinance restricts speech in confrontational and potentially violent situations. The case at hand is illustrative. The cross-burning in this case—directed as it was to a single African–American family trapped in their home—was nothing more than a crude form of physical intimidation. That this cross-burning sends a message of racial hostility does not automatically endow it with complete constitutional protection.[8]

7. Although the Court has sometimes suggested that subject-matter based and viewpoint-based regulations are equally problematic, see, *e.g.*, *Consolidated Edison Co. of N.Y. v. Public Service Comm'n of N.Y.*, 447 U.S., at 537, 100 S.Ct., at 2338, our decisions belie such claims.

8. The Court makes much of St. Paul's description of the ordinance as regulating "a message." *Ante*, at 2548. As always, however, St. Paul's argument must be read in context:

"Finally, we ask the Court to reflect on the 'content' of the 'expressive conduct' represented by a 'burning cross.' It is no less than the first step in an act of racial violence. It was and unfortunately still is the equivalent of [the] waving of a knife before the thrust, the pointing of a gun before it is fired, the lighting of the match before the arson, the hanging of the noose before the lynching. It is not a political statement, or even a cowardly statement of hatred. It is the first step in an act of assault. It can be

Significantly, the St. Paul ordinance regulates speech not on the basis of its subject matter or the viewpoint expressed, but rather on the basis of the *harm* the speech causes. In this regard, the Court fundamentally misreads the St. Paul ordinance. The Court describes the St. Paul ordinance as regulating expression "addressed to one of [several] specified disfavored *topics,*" *ante,* at 2547 (emphasis supplied), as policing "disfavored *subjects,*" *ibid.* (emphasis supplied), and as "prohibit[ing] ... speech solely on the basis of the *subjects* the speech addresses." *Ante,* at 2542 (emphasis supplied). Contrary to the Court's suggestion, the ordinance regulates only a subcategory of expression that causes *injuries based on* "race, color, creed, religion or gender," not a subcategory that involves *discussions* that concern those characteristics.[9] The ordinance, as construed by the Court, criminalizes expression that "one knows ... [by its very utterance inflicts injury on] others on the basis of race, color, creed, religion or gender." In this regard, the ordinance resembles the child pornography law at issue in *Ferber,* which in effect singled out child pornography because those publications caused far greater harms than pornography involving adults.

Moreover, even if the St. Paul ordinance did regulate fighting words based on its subject matter, such a regulation would, in my opinion, be constitutional. As noted above, subject-matter based regulations on commercial speech are widespread and largely unproblematic. As we have long recognized, subject-matter regulations generally do not raise the same concerns of government censorship and the distortion of public discourse presented by viewpoint regulations. Thus, in upholding subject-matter regulations we have carefully noted that viewpoint-based discrimination was not implicated. See *Young v. American Mini Theatres,* 427 U.S., at 67, 96 S.Ct., at 2450–2451 (emphasizing "the need for absolute neutrality by the government," and observing that the contested statute was not animated by "hostility for the point of view" of the theatres); *FCC v. Pacifica Foundation,* 438 U.S., at 745–746, 98 S.Ct., at 3038–3039 (stressing that "government must remain neutral in the marketplace of ideas"); see also *FCC v. League of Women's Voters of California,* 468 U.S., at 412–417, 104 S.Ct., at 3134–3137 (STEVENS, J., dissenting); *Metromedia, Inc. v. City of San Diego,* 453 U.S. 490, 554–555, 101 S.Ct. 2882, 2916–2917, 69 L.Ed.2d 800 (1981) (STEVENS, J., dissenting in part). Indeed, some subject-matter restrictions are a functional necessity in contemporary governance: "The First Amendment does not require States to regulate for problems that do not exist." *Burson v. Freeman,* 504 U.S. ——, ——, 112 S.Ct. 1846, 1856, 119 L.Ed.2d 5 (1992).

Contrary to the suggestion of the majority, the St. Paul ordinance does *not* regulate expression based on viewpoint. The Court contends that the ordinance requires proponents of racial intolerance to "follow the

---

no more protected than holding a gun to a victim['s] head. It is perhaps the ultimate expression of 'fighting words.'" App. to Brief for Petitioner C–6.

9. The Court contends that this distinction is "wordplay," reasoning that "[w]hat makes [the harms caused by race-based threats] distinct from [the harms] produced by other fighting words is ... the fact that [the former are] caused by a *distinctive idea.*" *Ante,* at 2548 (emphasis added). In this way, the Court concludes that regulating speech based on the injury it causes is no different from regulating speech based on its subject matter. This analysis fundamentally miscomprehends the role of

"race, color, creed, religion [and] gender" in contemporary American society. One need look no further than the recent social unrest in the Nation's cities to see that race-based threats may cause more harm to society and to individuals than other threats. Just as the statute prohibiting threats against the President is justifiable because of the place of the President in our social and political order, so a statute prohibiting race-based threats is justifiable because of the place of race in our social and political order. Although it is regrettable that race occupies such a place and is so incendiary an issue, until the Nation matures beyond that condition, laws such as St. Paul's ordinance will remain reasonable and justifiable.

Marquis of Queensbury Rules" while allowing advocates of racial tolerance to "fight freestyle." The law does no such thing.

The Court writes:

"One could hold up a sign saying, for example, that all 'anti-Catholic bigots' are misbegotten; but not that all 'papists' are, for that would insult and provoke violence 'on the basis of religion.'" *Ante*, at 2548.

This may be true, but it hardly proves the Court's point. The Court's reasoning is asymmetrical. The response to a sign saying that "all [religious] bigots are misbegotten" is a sign saying that "all advocates of religious tolerance are misbegotten." Assuming such signs could be fighting words (which seems to me extremely unlikely), neither sign would be banned by the ordinance for the attacks were not "based on ... religion" but rather on one's beliefs about tolerance. Conversely (and again assuming such signs are fighting words), just as the ordinance would prohibit a Muslim from hoisting a sign claiming that all Catholics were misbegotten, so the ordinance would bar a Catholic from hoisting a similar sign attacking Muslims.

The St. Paul ordinance is evenhanded. In a battle between advocates of tolerance and advocates of intolerance, the ordinance does not prevent either side from hurling fighting words at the other on the basis of their conflicting ideas, but it does bar *both* sides from hurling such words on the basis of the target's "race, color, creed, religion or gender." To extend the Court's pugilistic metaphor, the St. Paul ordinance simply bans punches "below the belt"—*by either party*. It does not, therefore, favor one side of any debate.[10]

Finally, it is noteworthy that the St. Paul ordinance is, as construed by the Court today, quite narrow. The St. Paul ordinance does not ban all "hate speech," nor does it ban, say, all cross-burnings or all swastika displays. Rather it only bans a subcategory of the already narrow category of fighting words. Such a limited ordinance leaves open and protected a vast range of expression on the subjects of racial, religious, and gender equality. As construed by the Court today, the ordinance certainly does not " 'raise the specter that the Government may effectively drive certain ideas or viewpoints from the marketplace.' " *Ante*, at 2545. Petitioner is free to burn a cross to announce a rally or to express his views about racial supremacy, he may do so on private property or public land, at day or at night, so long as the burning is not so threatening and so directed at an individual as to "by its very [execution] inflict injury." Such a limited proscription scarcely offends the First Amendment.

In sum, the St. Paul ordinance (as construed by the Court) regulates expressive activity that is wholly proscribable and does so not on the basis of viewpoint, but rather in recognition of the different harms caused by such activity. Taken together, these several considerations persuade me that the St. Paul ordinance is not an unconstitutional content-based regulation of speech. Thus, were the ordinance not overbroad, I would vote to uphold it.

---

10. Cf. *FCC v. League of Women Voters of California*, 468 U.S. 364, 418, 104 S.Ct. 3106, 3137, 82 L.Ed.2d 278 (1984) (STEVENS, J., dissenting) ("In this case ... the regulation applies ... to a defined class of ... licensees [who] represent heterogenous points of view. There is simply no sensible basis for considering this regulation a viewpoint restriction—or ... to condemn it as 'content-based'—because it applies equally to station owners of all shades of opinion").

COMMENT

THE CASE OF THE MISSING AMENDMENTS:
R.A.V. v. CITY OF ST. PAUL

*Akhil Reed Amar**

All nine Justices analyzed cross burning and other forms of racial hate speech by focusing almost exclusively on the First Amendment. They all seemed to have forgotten that it is a *Constitution* they are expounding, and that the Constitution contains not just the First Amendment, but the Thirteenth and Fourteenth Amendments as well.

B. Missing the Thirteenth Amendment

For Justices White and Stevens, the key Reconstruction Amendment to have emphasized was not the Fourteenth, but the Thirteenth. The Thirteenth Amendment's abolition of slavery and involuntary servitude speaks directly to private, as well as governmental, misconduct; indeed, it authorizes governmental regulation in order to abolish all of the vestiges, "badges[,] and incidents" of the slavery system.[168] The White Four could well have argued that the burning cross erected by R.A.V. was such a badge.

Although the Thirteenth Amendment's second section explicitly empowers only Congress to enforce its anti-slavery vision,[169] states are not powerless to act. Without Section 2, Congress might have lacked the specific enumerated power to eliminate the vestiges of slavery, but states generally need no such specific enumeration before they can act. Rather, state lawmakers typically may support the Constitution's mandates using their general police power under their state constitution, and in keeping with a specific invitation in Article VI's Supremacy Clause and Supremacy Oath.[170]

Might not the kind of harassment alleged in R.A.V. be deemed an obvious legacy of slavery — the Klan rising again to terrorize free blacks? Consider the following evocative sentence from Justice Stevens's opinion: "The cross-burning in this case — directed as it was to a single African-American family trapped in their home — was nothing more than a crude form of physical intimidation."[171] If cast as a First Amendment argument, this imagery suggests why the speech at issue should not have been protected — it threatened violence and involved an unwilling private audience, unable to avoid an unwanted message, thereby violating the autonomy principle. Furthermore, it was not directed in any way at a larger political audience as part of

---

[168] The Civil Rights Cases, 109 U.S. 3, 35–36 (1883) (Harlan, J., dissenting).

[169] "Congress shall have power to enforce this article by appropriate legislation." U.S. CONST. amend. XIII, § 2.

[170] State power is subject, of course, both to legitimate congressional pre-emption and the affirmative restrictions imposed on states by provisions like Article I, § 10, and § 1 of the Fourteenth Amendment.

[171] R.A.V., 112 S. Ct. at 2569 (Stevens, J., concurring in the judgment).

a legitimate exercise of political persuasion[172] and thereby fails the Meiklejohn-popular sovereignty test.[173] The incident was, in short, a classic example of the fighting words category of unprotected expression.

But the First Amendment packaging fails to explain why race-based fighting words directed at African-Americans should be treated differently from *other* fighting words. Consider how Stevens's evocative sentence takes on a new color if placed in a Thirteenth Amendment frame. The threat of white racist violence against blacks calls to mind an especially vivid set of historical images — slavery — and the otherwise stale First Amendment metaphor of a *"captive* audience" suddenly springs to life, poetic and ominous. Now we have a focused *constitutional* response to questions about why race might be different, and why a burning cross — or the word "nigger" — might be different.[174] *These,* Justice Stevens might have argued, are badges — symbols — of servitude, and the Constitution allows legislatures to treat them differently from other kinds of speech.[175]

Two important qualifications are in order. First, Section 1 of the Thirteenth Amendment is not logically tied to race; it protects persons of all races against slavery and involuntary servitude.[176] However, the Supreme Court has long recognized — both before the Thirteenth Amendment in the infamous *Dred Scott* case[177] and thereafter[178] — the important connections between slavery and race in America. And from the Civil Rights Act of 1866 to the present, Congress has treated *race-based* oppression as a unique badge and incident of slavery that may be specially targeted and punished. The Act of 1866 — the

---

[172] This assumes, of course, that Justice Stevens was correct in his factual assertion that the cross-burning was directed *only* at the trapped family.

[173] *See* MEIKLEJOHN, *supra* note 46.

[174] "'The term "nigger" . . . hark[s] back to slavery days.'" Richard Delgado, *Words That Wound: A Tort Action for Racial Insults, Epithets and Name-Calling,* 17 HARV. C.R.-C.L. L. REV. 133, 158 (1982) (quoting Bradshaw v. Swagerty, 563 P.2d 511, 514 (Kan. Ct. App. 1977)); *id.* at 174 (arguing that "[w]ords such as 'nigger' . . . are badges of degradation").

[175] If taken at face value, the suggestive phrase "badge of servitude" seems naturally to encompass words like "nigger" and symbols like burning crosses. More historical research, however, is needed to trace the usage of this key phrase among abolitionists, freedmen, and Reconstruction Republicans. Perhaps the phrase had some narrow and precise meaning wholly irrelevant to private racist oppression conducted via words and symbols.

[176] I have emphasized this theme elsewhere. *See* Akhil Reed Amar & Daniel Widawsky, *Child Abuse as Slavery: A Thirteenth Amendment Response to DeShaney,* 105 HARV. L. REV. 1359, 1359–60, 1365–66, 1368 & n.30 (*But cf. id.* at 1368 n.30 (noting explicitly the special relevance of race in analyzing the "'badges and incidents' of slavery" that may be legislatively proscribed beyond the self-executing core of § 1 of the Thirteenth Amendment (quoting The Civil Rights Cases, 109 U.S. 3, 35–36 (1883) (Harlan, J., dissenting))).

[177] Dred Scott v. Sandford, 60 U.S. (19 How.) 393 (1857).

[178] *See, e.g.,* Jones v. Alfred H. Mayer Co., 392 U.S. 409, 437–44 (1968) (holding that private race-based discrimination may be prohibited as a "'badge[] and incident[]' of slavery" (quoting *The Civil Rights Cases,* 109 U.S. at 35–36 (Harlan, J., dissenting))).

precursor of section 1982 — is especially significant here, as it was purposely drafted pursuant to the Thirteenth Amendment, and yet it prohibited *race-based* misconduct even in formerly free states (such as Minnesota).[179]

Second, the argument sketched out thus far in no way authorizes states to betray the basic principles of the Fourteenth Amendment — including its protection of free speech — simply by purporting to enforce the Thirteenth.[180] Laws that regulate only fighting words, properly defined, may present no realistic threat to the hard core of free speech. But perhaps the Thirteenth Amendment might allow word regulation beyond the fighting words category. For example, the Court has upheld legislation under the Thirteenth Amendment that bars, among other things, the use of words such as "For Whites Only" on a residential "For Sale" sign.[181] As noted earlier, Justice Scalia seemed to allow for such restrictions if the words are "swept up incidentally within the reach of a statute directed at conduct rather than speech," such as the private racial discrimination in housing prohibited by section 1982, which Justice Scalia cited on this point.[182]

---

[179] *See* Act of Apr. 9, 1866, ch. 31, § 1, 14 Stat. 27, 27 (1866). The relevant texts of the Act of 1866 and of § 1982 are as follows: The Act of 1866 states that "citizens of every race and color . . . shall have the same right, in every State and Territory in the United States . . . to inherit, purchase, lease, sell, hold, and convey real and personal property . . . as is enjoyed by white citizens." *Id.* Section 1982 states that "[a]ll citizens of the United States shall have the same right, in every State and Territory, as is enjoyed by white citizens thereof to inherit, purchase, lease, sell, hold, and convey real and personal property." 42 U.S.C. § 1982 (1988).

[180] The argument does suggest, however, that doctrinal rules implementing the Fourteenth Amendment's basic principles must be sensitively crafted in light of Thirteenth Amendment principles. Neither Amendment "trumps" the other; rather they must be synthesized into a coherent doctrinal whole.

[181] *See Jones*, 392 U.S. at 437–44. As *Jones* reminds us, the key constitutional provision is § 2 of the Thirteenth Amendment, which focuses on legislative implementation of an anti-slavery ethos. For a more recent reminder, see United States v. Lee, 935 F.2d 952 (8th Cir.), *vacated in part, reh'g en banc granted in part*, 1991 U.S. App. LEXIS 19740 (Aug. 14, 1991), in which the court upheld as constitutional under the First Amendment an act passed as "an exercise of the power of Congress to enforce the Thirteenth Amendment by and through legislation." *Id.* at 955.

The anti-hate-speech academic literature has instead tended to stress the Equal Protection Clause of the Fourteenth Amendment. *But cf.* Richard Delgado, *Campus Antiracism Rules: Constitutional Narratives in Collision*, 85 Nw. U. L. Rev. 343, 346, 381 n.321, 384 (1991) (discussing both the Thirteenth and Fourteenth Amendments). Although obviously relevant when public universities are concerned — and much of the hate speech debate has been fought out on that ground — the Equal Protection Clause creates monumental state action hurdles that a Thirteenth Amendment approach avoids. The Thirteenth Amendment has an additional advantage for those who favor an asymmetric approach to hate speech. Whereas the abstract language of equality can easily be assimilated into doctrine stressing formal symmetry, the Thirteenth Amendment differs in subtle ways. Its evocative words conjure up vivid images of asymmetric social, political, and economic power — images of masters and slaves, images more congenial to openly asymmetric attempts to right past imbalances. *See infra* pp. 159–60.

[182] *See R.A.V.*, 112 S. Ct. at 2546. Indeed, the facts of *R.A.V.* seem close to the core of

But if mere refusal to deal with another on the basis of race can constitute a badge of servitude, surely the intentional racial harassment of blacks can constitute a badge of servitude as well. Under this theory, the intentional trapping of a captive audience of blacks, in order to subject them to face-to-face degradation and dehumanization on the basis of their race, might be proscribed as "incidental" to a general statute designed to eliminate all "badges and incidents" of the legacy of slavery. Intentional trapping — temporary involuntary servitude, a sliver of slavery — is arguably more like conduct than like speech, akin to (and arguably much worse than) refusal to deal on the basis of race.[183]

Of course, any incidental regulation of words imposed by these anti-slavery laws would be quite narrow. Consistent with the hard core of the First and Fourteenth Amendments, white supremacists, for example, would still be free to publicly urge the legislature to repeal such hate-speech laws and to use ugly, offensive, racist language in the course of their urging. Indeed, had the St. Paul ordinance explicitly stated that the city would *not* punish racist speakers engaged in offensive but peaceful public discourse, and moreover would fully protect such racist speakers from any possible violence by private hecklers, the Scalia Five would have had less reason to suspect

---

§ 1982's concerns: the cross burning occurred less than three months after the targeted black family had moved into a predominantly white neighborhood. *See* Terry, *supra* note 18, at A16.

[183] The premise of the analysis here — that mere refusal to deal on the basis of race can legitimately be treated as a "badge" of servitude, *see supra* note 178 — can be questioned. *See, e.g.*, EARL M. MALTZ, CIVIL RIGHTS, THE CONSTITUTION, AND CONGRESS 1863–1869, at 70–78 (1990). The Court, however, is unlikely to reverse Jones v. Alfred Mayer Co., 392 U.S. 409 (1968), which embraces this premise. In any event, the kind of intentional racial harassment at issue in *R.A.V.* seems much closer to the core of the slave system. That this relic of slavery occurs through words and symbols is not the end of the inquiry: extortion also occurs through words. The word "nigger" hurled face-to-face at a captive target is usually not meant to persuade — it is often meant to dominate and degrade. Arguably it is a flaunting of power — "I can do this and get away with it" — as were many verbal epithets uttered by masters to degrade antebellum slaves. Black victims of such epithets may lack symmetric power — for there may be no analogous badges of servitude against whites, no words weighted with the history and stigma associated with slave degradation. And by hypothesis, there is no place for the target to escape or avert her eyes — where was the black family in *R.A.V.* to go? "Intentional trapping," as I am using the term, occurs precisely when the degradation is unwanted and unavoidable.

On captivity, see Frisby v. Schultz, 487 U.S. 474 (1988), which states that "[t]here simply is no right to force speech into the home of an unwilling listener." *Id.* at 485. On harassment, see Boos v. Barry, 485 U.S. 312 (1988), which comments favorably on a law that "only prohibits activity undertaken to 'intimidate, coerce, threaten, or harass.'" *Id.* at 326. On unwanted insults, see Kent Greenawalt, *Insults and Epithets: Are They Protected Speech?*, 42 RUTGERS L. REV. 287 (1990), which notes that "[r]emarks whose dominant object is to hurt and humiliate, not to assert facts or values, have very limited expressive value. . . . [P]enalties are proper when . . . someone has initiated contact with a person just to harass him or her . . . ." *Id.* at 298.

that "official suppression of ideas [was] afoot."[184] In effect, St. Paul would have made clear that it was trying to ban only certain conduct rather than offensive words and ideas.

Had the Justices focused on the Reconstruction Amendments, they would have been forced to think more clearly about whether gender-based and religion-based hate speech warranted similar treatment to race-based hate speech and whether, within each category, symmetry or asymmetry should obtain. On the first issue, they would have had to consider that American slavery was originally rooted in religious discrimination — only non-Christians were enslaved — and that like blacks, women have suffered deeply entrenched and systematic status-based subordination based on physical traits fixed at birth. On the other hand, they could have noted that by the time of the Thirteenth Amendment's adoption, American slavery had lost its connection to discrimination against non-Christians[185] and that, thus far, the Court and Congress have both linked slavery only to race, not to gender or religion. Section 1982, for example, prohibits only race-based residential discrimination.

On the symmetry issue, the Justices would have had to deal squarely with a question they slid past all too quickly: could the ordinance be applied *against* racial minorities? If so, why were the anti-Scalia Justices so unconcerned, and why did Justice White's and Justice Blackmun's opinions use language focused only on racial hate speech directed at — rather than spoken by — racial minorities? If, on the other hand, Justices White, Blackmun, and O'Connor were willing to uphold an ordinance they read as asymmetric, that too required explanation. Perhaps they might have emphasized that this form of "affirmative action" for racial minorities did not threaten any "innocent whites" and possibly would not involve courts in the tricky task of administering rules based on the percentages of racial blood in a person's veins.[186] In other affirmative action contexts, the government must decide who counts as sufficiently "black," for example, to qualify for race-based benefits. Under the St. Paul ordinance, however, perhaps prosecution might well lie even if the trapped family was not black, as long as R.A.V. *thought* they were, or even if a light-skinned mulatto sought to denigrate a darker Jamaican as "black scum." In any event, the Thirteenth Amendment approach raises an interesting possibility not easily visible through a conventional First

---

[184] *R.A.V.*, 112 S. Ct. at 2547. Various statements of St. Paul officials apparently worried the Court. *See id.* at 2548–49.

[185] The connection lapsed in part because, early on in American slavery, the master class proved unwilling to emancipate slaves who converted to Christianity. *See* KENNETH M. STAMPP, THE PECULIAR INSTITUTION 16–17, 19, 156 (1956).

[186] *See* Massaro, *supra* note 150, at 242 (discussing the problems raised by making criminal or civil liability "hinge on the race of the speaker and the victim").

Amendment lens: openly asymmetric regulation of racial hate speech may be less, rather than more, constitutionally troubling.

There is, of course, no guarantee that the Scalia Five would have embraced the Thirteenth Amendment approach had it been vigorously pressed in *R.A.V.* But the Court, one hopes, would at least have been obliged to speak with much greater clarity than it did about the differences it saw between the St. Paul ordinance and section 1982. In the process, it might have clarified exactly how far legislation under the Thirteenth Amendment can go without running afoul of freedom of speech under the First and Fourteenth Amendments.

In any event, my purpose here has not been to resolve definitively the issues raised by *R.A.V.*, but to show how more careful attention to Reconstruction might have enabled all the Justices in *R.A.V.* to write sharper and more persuasive opinions.[187]

---

[187] How might St. Paul have drafted a sharper and more defensible ordinance? Here are a few tentative suggestions:

1.   State explicitly that the ordinance is designed to implement the Thirteenth Amendment by eliminating various badges and incidents of slavery and caste-based subordination.

2.   Limit the ordinance to intentional harassment of a captive and unwilling audience that either: (A) threatens unlawful violence directed at the captive, or (B) tries to affix a badge of slavery on the captive. A "captive" audience in this context connotes one who cannot easily avert her eyes or ears to avoid the harassing message targeted at her.

3.   Define "badge of slavery": (A) narrowly to include only racial subordination, or (B) more broadly to include gender subordination as well.

(A) is easier to fit into standard Thirteenth Amendment doctrine; but (B) may broaden the political coalition necessary to secure the ordinance's passage. If (A), the ordinance may define "badge of slavery" to include words, pictures, symbols, and the like, targeted at captive members of historic racial outgroups, such as African-Americans, designed to degrade and dehumanize them, or suggest their untouchability, on the basis of their group membership. If (B), the ordinance would need to be broader, encompassing badges designed to degrade, dehumanize, and subjugate based on the captive's membership from birth in an historically subordinated racial or gender group that harasser seeks to convert into an untouchable and degraded caste. The ordinance should specify that a history of legally imposed disabilities shall be highly probative of the existence of an "historic racial outgroup" under (A) or "an historically subordinated racial or gender group" under (B).

4.   Make explicit that if a harasser is mistaken about the captive's actual racial or gender identity, this mistake of fact shall constitute no defense. This helps solve the problem noted above at p. 159.

5.   Make clear that speech that does not involve an unwilling captive audience, especially if part of political discourse, is absolutely protected against both public censors and private hecklers threatening violence towards speakers, and that government will intervene to protect offensive speech against private intimidation.

Liberalism and Campus Hate Speech: A Philosophical Examination*

Andrew Altman

INTRODUCTION

In recent years a vigorous public debate has developed over freedom of speech within the academic community. The immediate stimulus for the debate has been the enactment by a number of colleges and universities of rules against hate speech. While some have defended these rules as essential for protecting the equal dignity of all members of the academic community, others have condemned them as intolerable efforts to impose ideological conformity on the academy.

Liberals can be found on both sides of this debate. Many see campus hate-speech regulation as a form of illegitimate control by the community over individual liberty of expression. They argue that hate-speech rules violate the important liberal principle that any regulation of speech be viewpoint-neutral. But other liberals see hate-speech regulation as a justifiable part of the effort to help rid society of discrimination and subordination based on such characteristics as race, religion, ethnicity, gender, and sexual preference.

In this article, I develop a liberal argument in favor of certain narrowly drawn rules prohibiting hate speech. The argument steers a middle course between those who reject all forms of campus hate-speech regulation and those who favor relatively sweeping forms of regulation. Like those who reject all regulation, I argue that rules against hate speech are not viewpoint-neutral. Like those who favor sweeping regulation, I accept the claim that hate speech can cause serious psychological harm to those at whom it is directed. However, I do not believe that such harm can justify regulation, sweeping or otherwise. Instead, I argue that some forms of hate speech inflict on their victims a certain kind of wrong, and it is on the basis of this wrong that regulation can be justified. The kind of wrong in question

* For valuable comments and criticisms on earlier drafts of this article, I am grateful to Steven Lee, Kent Greenawalt, Peter Caws, David DeGrazia, the members of the Human Sciences Seminar at George Washington University, and an anonymous reviewer for this journal and its associate editors.

Ethics 103 (January 1993): 302–317

is one that is inflicted in virtue of the performance of a certain kind of speech-act characteristic of some forms of hate speech, and I argue that rules targeting this speech-act wrong will be relatively narrow in scope.[1]

HATE SPEECH, HARASSMENT, AND NEUTRALITY

Hate-speech regulations typically provide for disciplinary action against students for making racist, sexist, or homophobic utterances or for engaging in behavior that expresses the same kinds of discriminatory attitudes.[2] The stimulus for the regulations has been an apparent upsurge in racist, sexist, and homophobic incidents on college campuses over the past decade. The regulations that have actually been proposed or enacted vary widely in the scope of what they prohibit.

The rules at Stanford University are narrow in scope. They require that speech meet three conditions before it falls into the proscribed zone: the speaker must intend to insult or stigmatize another on the basis of certain characteristics such as race, gender, or sexual orientation; the speech must be addressed directly to those whom it is intended to stigmatize; and the speech must employ epithets or terms that similarly convey "visceral hate or contempt" for the people at whom it is directed.[3]

On the other hand, the rules of the University of Connecticut, in their original form, were relatively sweeping in scope. According to these rules, "Every member of the University is obligated to

1. In a discussion of the strictly legal issues surrounding the regulation of campus hate speech, the distinction between private and public universities would be an important one. The philosophical considerations on which this article focuses, however, apply both to public and private institutions.

2. In this article I will focus on the restriction of racist (understood broadly to include anti-Semitic), sexist, and homophobic expression. In addition to such expression, regulations typically prohibit discriminatory utterances based on ethnicity, religion, and physical appearance. The argument I develop in favor of regulation applies noncontroversially to ethnicity and religion, as well as to race, gender, and sexual preference. But in a later section I argue against the prohibition of discriminatory remarks based on appearance. I understand 'speech' as whatever has nonnatural meaning according to Grice's account, i.e., any utterances or actions having the following nested intentions behind them: the intention to produce a certain effect in the audience, to have the audience recognize that intention, and to have that recognition be the reason for the production of the effect. See Paul Grice, "Meaning," in his *Studies in the Way of Words* (Cambridge, Mass.: Harvard University Press, 1989), pp. 220–21. On this Gricean account, not only verbal utterances but also the display of symbols or flags, gestures, drawings, and more will count as speech. Although some commentators have produced counterexamples to this account of speaker's meaning, I do not believe that they pose insurmountable problems. See Robert Fogelin, "Review of Grice, *Studies in the Way of Words*," *Journal of Philosophy* 88 (1991): 217.

3. The full text of the Stanford regulations is in Thomas Grey, "Civil Rights v. Civil Liberties: The Case of Discriminatory Verbal Harassment," *Social Philosophy and Policy* 8 (1991): 106–7.

refrain from actions that intimidate, humiliate or demean persons or groups or that undermine their security or self-esteem." Explicitly mentioned as examples of proscribed speech were "making inconsiderate jokes . . . stereotyping the experiences, background, and skills of individuals, . . . imitating stereotypes in speech or mannerisms [and] attributing objections to any of the above actions to 'hypersensitivity' of the targeted individual or group."[4]

Even the narrower forms of hate-speech regulation, such as we find at Stanford, must be distinguished from a simple prohibition of verbal harassment. As commonly understood, harassment involves a pattern of conduct that is intended to annoy a person so much as to disrupt substantially her activities.[5] No one questions the authority of universities to enact regulations that prohibit such conduct, whether the conduct be verbal or not. There are three principal differences between hate-speech rules and rules against harassment. First, hate-speech rules do not require a pattern of conduct: a single incident is sufficient to incur liability. Second, hate-speech rules describe the offending conduct in ways that refer to the moral and political viewpoint it expresses. The conduct is not simply annoying or disturbing; it is racist, sexist, or homophobic.

The third difference is tied closely to the second and is the most important one: rules against hate speech are not viewpoint-neutral. Such rules rest on the view that racism, sexism, and homophobia are morally wrong. The liberal principle of viewpoint-neutrality holds that those in authority should not be permitted to limit speech on the ground that it expresses a viewpoint that is wrong, evil, or otherwise deficient. Yet, hate-speech rules rest on precisely such a basis. Rules against harassment, on the other hand, are not viewpoint-based. Anyone in our society could accept the prohibition of harassment because it would not violate their normative political or moral beliefs to do so.[6] The same cannot be said for hate-speech rules because they embody

---

4. The University of Connecticut's original regulations are found in the pamphlet "Protect Campus Pluralism," published under the auspices of the Department of Student Affairs, the Dean of Students Office, and the Division of Student Affairs and Services. The regulations have since been rescinded in response to a legal challenge and replaced by ones similar to those in effect at Stanford. See *University of Connecticut Student Handbook* (Storrs: University of Connecticut, 1990–91), p. 62.

5. Kingsley Browne points out that the legal understanding of harassment as conceived under current interpretations of Title VII of the Civil Rights Act of 1964 departs from the ordinary understanding in important ways. See Kingsley Browne, "Title VII as Censorship: Hostile Environment Harassment and the First Amendment," *Ohio State Law Journal* 52 (1991): 486.

6. Laws against the defamation of individuals are essentially viewpoint-neutral for the same reason: anyone in society can accept them, regardless of their moral or political viewpoint.

a view of race, gender, and homosexuality contrary to the normative viewpoints held by some people.[7]

If I am correct in claiming that hate-speech regulations are not viewpoint-neutral, this will raise a strong prima facie case against them from a liberal perspective. Contrary to my claim, however, Thomas Grey, author of Stanford's hate-speech policy, argues that his regulations are viewpoint-neutral. He claims that the policy "preserves practical neutrality—that is, it does not differentially deprive any significant element in American political life of its rhetorical capital. . . . The Right has no special stake in the free face-to-face use of epithets that perform no other function except to portray whole classes of Americans as subhuman and unworthy of full citizenship."[8]

I cannot agree with Grey's contentions on this score. The implicit identification of groups such as the neo-Nazis and the KKK as insignificant presupposes a value judgment that is not viewpoint-neutral, namely, that the views of such groups have no significant merit. If Grey claims that he is simply making the factual judgment that the influence of these groups on the political process is nil, it is not clear why that is relevant (even assuming its truth—which is debatable). Certainly, such groups aim to become significant influences on the process, and their use of language that would violate Stanford's rules is a significant part of their rhetoric. In fact, I will argue later that the use of such language is tied in an especially close way to their substantive moral and political views.

Grey might be suggesting that our public political discourse does not tolerate the sorts of slurs and epithets his rules proscribe: public debate proceeds with an unwritten prohibition on that kind of language. Such a suggestion is certainly correct, as can be seen by the fact that racists who enter the public arena must rely on "code words" to get their message across. But from the racists' point of view, this is just further evidence of how our public political discourse has been captured by "liberals" and is biased against their view.

Viewpoint-neutrality is not simply a matter of the effects of speech regulation on the liberty of various groups to express their views in the language they prefer. It is also concerned with the kinds of justification that must be offered for speech regulation. The fact is that any plausible justification of hate-speech regulation hinges on the premise that racism, sexism, and homophobia are wrong. Without that premise there would be no basis for arguing that the viewpoint-neutral proscription of verbal harassment is insufficient to protect the rights of minorities and women. The liberal who favors hate-speech

7. Compare Kent Greenawalt. "Insults and Epithets." *Rutgers Law Review* 24 (1990): 306–7.

8. Grey, pp. 103–4.

regulations, no matter how narrowly drawn, must therefore be prepared to carve out an exception to the principle of viewpoint-neutrality.

THE HARMS OF HATE SPEECH

Many of the proponents of campus hate-speech regulation defend their position by arguing that hate speech causes serious harm to those who are the targets of such speech. Among the most basic of these harms are psychological ones. Even when it involves no direct threat of violence, hate speech can cause abiding feelings of fear, anxiety, and insecurity in those at whom it is targeted. As Mari Matsuda has argued, this is in part because many forms of such speech tacitly draw on a history of violence against certain groups.[9] The symbols and language of hate speech call up historical memories of violent persecution and may encourage fears of current violence. Moreover, hate speech can cause a variety of other harms, from feelings of isolation, to a loss of self-confidence, to physical problems associated with serious psychological disturbance.[10]

The question is whether or not the potential for inflicting these harms is sufficient ground for some sort of hate-speech regulation. As powerful as these appeals to the harms of hate speech are, there is a fundamental sticking point in accepting them as justification for regulation, from a liberal point of view. The basic problem is that the proposed justification sweeps too broadly for a liberal to countenance it. Forms of racist, sexist, or homophobic speech that the liberal is committed to protecting may cause precisely the kinds of harm that the proposed justification invokes.

The liberal will not accept the regulation of racist, sexist, or homophobic speech couched in a scientific, religious, philosophical, or political mode of discourse. The regulation of such speech would not merely carve out a minor exception to the principle of viewpoint-neutrality but would, rather, eviscerate it in a way unacceptable to any liberal. Yet, those forms of hate speech can surely cause in minorities the harms that are invoked to justify regulation: insecurity, anxiety, isolation, loss of self-confidence, and so on. Thus, the liberal must invoke something beyond these kinds of harm in order to justify any hate-speech regulation.

Liberals who favor regulation typically add to their argument the contention that the value to society of the hate speech they would proscribe is virtually nil, while scientific, religious, philosophical, and

---

9. Mari Matsuda, "Legal Storytelling: Public Response to Racist Speech: Considering the Victim's Story," *Michigan Law Review* 87 (1989): 2329–34, 2352.

10. See Richard Delgado, "Words That Wound: A Tort Action for Racial Insults, Epithets and Name-Calling," *Harvard Civil Rights–Civil Liberties Law Review* 17 (1982): 137, 146.

political forms of hate speech have at least some significant value. Thus, Mary Ellen Gale says that the forms she would prohibit "neither advance knowledge, seek truth, expose government abuses, initiate dialogue, encourage participation, further tolerance of divergent views, nor enhance the victim's individual dignity or self respect."[11] As an example of such worthless hate speech Gale cites an incident of white students writing a message on the mirror in the dorm room of blacks: "African monkeys, why don't you go back to the jungle."[12] But she would protect a great deal of racist or sexist speech, such as a meeting of neo-Nazi students at which swastikas are publicly displayed and speeches made that condemn the presence of Jews and blacks on campus.[13]

Although Gale ends up defending relatively narrow regulations, I believe liberals should be very hesitant to accept her argument for distinguishing regulable from nonregulable hate speech. One problem is that she omits from her list of the values that valuable speech serves one which liberals have long considered important, especially for speech that upsets and disturbs others. Such speech, it is argued, enables the speaker to "blow off steam" in a relatively nondestructive and nonviolent way. Calling particular blacks "African monkeys" might serve as a psychological substitute for harming them in a much more serious way, for example, by lynchings or beatings.

Gale could respond that slurring blacks might just as well serve as an encouragement and prelude to the more serious harms. But the same can be said of forms of hate speech that Gale would protect from regulation, for example, the speech at the neo-Nazi student meeting. Moreover, liberals should argue that it is the job of legal rules against assault, battery, conspiracy, rape, and so on to protect people from violence. It is, at best, highly speculative that hate speech on campus contributes to violence against minorities or women. And while the claim about blowing off steam is also a highly speculative one, the liberal tradition clearly puts a substantial burden of proof on those who would silence speech.

There is a more basic problem with any effort to draw the line between regulable and nonregulable hate speech by appealing to the value of speech. Such appeals invariably involve substantial departures from the principle of viewpoint-neutrality. There is no way to make differential judgments about the value of different types of hate speech without taking one or another moral and political viewpoint. Gale's criteria clearly illustrate this as they are heavily

---

11. Mary Ellen Gale, "Reimagining the First Amendment: Racist Speech and Equal Liberty," *St. John's Law Review* 65 (1991): 179–80.

12. Ibid., p. 176.

13. Ibid.

tilted against the values of racists and sexists, and yet she does not adequately address the question of how a liberal position can accommodate such substantial departures from viewpoint-neutrality.

Gale contends that existing legal rules and regulations against sexual and racial harassment in the workplace should serve as the model in terms of which campus hate-speech regulations can be justified.[14] Those rules are based on an interpretation of Title VII of the Civil Rights Act of 1964, outlawing discrimination in the terms and conditions of employment, and they prohibit a hostile or offensive work environment. But there are three problems with appealing to these harassment rules. First, almost all legal cases involving claims of a hostile work environment have required more than simply hostile verbal conduct for a finding of a violation.[15] Second, it is doubtful that the context of a student at a university is sufficiently similar to that of a worker in the workplace to assume that the exact same rules should apply for both settings. Freedom of expression is far more vital to the role of the university than it is to that of the typical workplace, and so it is reasonable to think that university rules should be less restrictive of expression. Third, even if the university context is sufficiently similar to that of the typical workplace, Gale's invocation of the existing rules covering workplace harassment begs the crucial question of whether the current interpretation of Title VII itself involves an unjustifiably sweeping departure from viewpoint-neutrality.[16]

I do not assume that the principle of viewpoint-neutrality is an absolute or ultimate one within the liberal framework. Liberals do defend some types of speech regulation that seem to rely on viewpoint-based claims. For example, they would not reject copyright laws, even if it could be shown—as seems plausible—that those laws are biased against the views of people who regard private property as theft.[17] Moreover, the viewpoint-neutrality principle itself rests on deeper liberal concerns which it is thought to serve. Ideally, a liberal argument for the regulation of hate speech would show that regulations can be developed that accommodate these deeper concerns and that simultaneously serve important liberal values. I believe that there is such a liberal argument. In order to show this, however, it is necessary to examine a kind of wrong committed by hate speakers that is quite different from the harmful psychological effects of their speech.

14. Ibid., pp. 174–75.
15. See Browne, p. 483.
16. Ibid., pp. 491–501, 547.
17. I think liberals could argue that the deviation of copyright laws from viewpoint-neutrality is both minor and reasonable, given the extreme rarity of the antiproperty view in our society and given the great social value that such laws are seen as serving.

SUBORDINATION AND SPEECH ACTS

Some proponents of regulation claim that there is an especially close connection between hate speech and the subordination of minorities. Thus, Charles Lawrence contends, "all racist speech constructs the social reality that constrains the liberty of non-whites because of their race."[18] Along the same lines, Mari Matsuda claims, "racist speech is particularly harmful because it is a mechanism of subordination."[19]

The position of Lawrence and Matsuda can be clarified and elaborated using J. L. Austin's distinction between perlocutionary effects and illocutionary force.[20] The perlocutionary effects of an utterance consist of its causal effects on the hearer: infuriating her, persuading her, frightening her, and so on. The illocutionary force of an utterance consists of the kind of speech act one is performing in making the utterance: advising, warning, stating, claiming, arguing, and so on. Lawrence and Matsuda are not simply suggesting that the direct perlocutionary effects of racist speech constitute harm. Nor are they simply suggesting that hate speech can persuade listeners to accept beliefs that then motivate them to commit acts of harm against racial minorities. That again is a matter of the perlocutionary effects of hate speech. Rather, I believe that they are suggesting that hate speech can inflict a wrong in virtue of its illocutionary acts, the very speech acts performed in the utterances of such speech.[21]

What exactly does this speech-act wrong amount to? My suggestion is that it is the wrong of treating a person as having inferior moral standing. In other words, hate speech involves the performance of a

18. Charles Lawrence. "If He Hollers Let Him Go: Regulating Racist Speech on Campus." *Duke Law Journal* (1990). p. 444.

19. Matsuda. p. 2357.

20. J. L. Austin. *How to Do Things with Words* (New York: Oxford University Press. 1962). pp. 98 ff. The concept of an illocutionary act has been refined and elaborated by John Searle in a series of works starting with "Austin on Locutionary and Illocutionary Acts." *Philosophical Review* 77 (1968): 420–21. Also see his *Speech Acts* (New York: Cambridge University Press. 1969), p. 31. and *Expression and Meaning* (New York: Cambridge University Press. 1979); and John Searle and D. Vanderveken. *Foundations of Illocutionary Logic* (New York: Cambridge University Press. 1985).

21. Both Lawrence and Matsuda describe racist speech as a unique form of speech in its internal relation to subordination. See Lawrence. p. 440, n. 42; and Matsuda. p. 2356. I do not think that their view is correct. Homophobic and sexist speech, e.g., can also be subordinating. In fact, Lawrence and Matsuda are applying to racist speech essentially the same idea that several feminist writers have applied to pornography. These feminists argue that pornography does not simply depict the subordination of women; it actually subordinates them. See Melinda Vadas. "A First Look at the Pornography/Civil Rights Ordinance: Could Pornography Be the Subordination of Women?" *Journal of Philosophy* 84 (1987): 487–511.

certain kind of illocutionary act, namely, the act of treating someone as a moral subordinate.[22]

Treating persons as moral subordinates means treating them in a way that takes their interests to be intrinsically less important, and their lives inherently less valuable, than the interests and lives of those who belong to some reference group. There are many ways of treating people as moral subordinates that are natural as opposed to conventional: the status of these acts as acts of subordination depend solely on universal principles of morality and not on the conventions of a given society. Slavery and genocide, for example, treat people as having inferior moral standing simply in virtue of the affront of such practices to universal moral principles.

Other ways of treating people as moral subordinates have both natural and conventional elements. The practice of racial segregation is an example. It is subordinating because the conditions imposed on blacks by such treatment violate moral principles but also because the act of separation is a convention for putting the minority group in its (supposedly) proper, subordinate place.

I believe that the language of racist, sexist, and homophobic slurs and epithets provides wholly conventional ways of treating people as moral subordinates. Terms such as 'kike', 'faggot', 'spic', and 'nigger' are verbal instruments of subordination. They are used not only to express hatred or contempt for people but also to "put them in their place," that is, to treat them as having inferior moral standing.

It is commonly recognized that through language we can "put people down," to use the vernacular expression. There are many different modes of putting people down: putting them down as less intelligent or less clever or less articulate or less skillful. Putting people down in these ways is not identical to treating them as moral subordinates, and the ordinary put-down does not involve regarding someone as having inferior moral standing.[23] The put-downs that are accomplished

22. Lawrence and Matsuda argue that all racist speech is subordinating. I reject their argument below and claim that the speech act of treating someone as a moral subordinate is not characteristic of all forms of racist speech. They also describe the wrong of speech-act subordination as a "harm." But the wrong does not in itself interfere with a person's formulation and pursuit of her plans and purposes. On that basis, I have been persuaded by my colleague Peter Caws that it is better to avoid the term 'harm' when describing speech-act subordination. Why such speech acts are, from a liberal perspective, wrongs is explained below.

23. The distinction which I am drawing between putting someone down as a moral subordinate and putting him down in other ways is an instance of a more general moral distinction. That general distinction is described in different ways: as one between respect and esteem, or between two forms of respect, or between worth and merit. See, e.g., Gregory Vlastos, "Human Worth, Merit, and Equality," in *Moral Concepts* ed. Joel Feinberg (New York: Oxford University Press, 1969); Larry Thomas, "Morality and Our Self-Concept," *Journal of Value Inquiry* 12 (1978): 258–68; and David Sachs, "How

with the slurs and epithets of hate speech are different from the ordinary verbal put-down in that respect, even though both sorts of put-down are done through language.

I have contended that the primary verbal instruments for treating people as moral subordinates are the slurs and epithets of hate speech. In order to see this more clearly, consider the difference between derisively calling someone a "faggot" and saying to that person, with equal derision, "You are contemptible for being homosexual." Both utterances can treat the homosexual as a moral subordinate, but the former accomplishes it much more powerfully than the latter. This is, I believe, because the conventional rules of language make the epithet 'faggot' a term whose principal purpose is precisely to treat homosexuals as having inferior moral standing.

I do not believe that a clean and neat line can be drawn around those forms of hate speech that treat their targets as moral subordinates. Slurs and epithets are certainly used that way often, but not always, as is evidenced by the fact that sometimes victimized groups seize on the slurs that historically have subordinated them and seek to "transvalue" the terms. For example, homosexuals have done this with the term 'queer', seeking to turn it into a term of pride rather than one of subordination.

Hate speech in modes such as the scientific or philosophical typically would not involve illocutionary acts of moral subordination. This is because speech in those modes usually involves essentially different kinds of speech acts: describing, asserting, stating, arguing, and so forth. To assert or argue that blacks are genetically inferior to whites is not to perform a speech act that itself consists of treating blacks as inferior.[21] Yet, language is often ambiguous and used for multiple purposes, and I would not rule out a priori that in certain contexts even scientific or philosophical hate speech is used in part to subordinate.

The absence of a neat and clean line around those forms of hate speech that subordinate through speech acts does not entail that it is futile to attempt to formulate regulations that target such hate speech. Rules and regulations rarely have an exact fit with what they aim to prevent: over- and underinclusiveness are pervasive in any system of rules that seeks to regulate conduct. The problem is to develop rules

---

to Distinguish Self-Respect from Self-Esteem." *Philosophy and Public Affairs* 10 (1981): 346–60. I do not believe that liberal claims about the equal moral status of persons can make sense without presupposing some such distinction.

24. Thus I agree with Marcy Strauss's claim that there is a viable distinction between speech that discriminates and speech that advocates discrimination, but I reject the way she draws the distinction. She attempts to do it by appealing to differences in what amounts to perlocutionary effects, failing to realize that the essential difference lies in the illocutionary act. See Marcy Strauss, "Sexist Speech in the Workplace," *Harvard Civil Rights–Civil Liberties Law Review* 25 (1990): 39–40.

that have a reasonably good fit. Later I argue that there are hate-speech regulations that target subordinating hate speech reasonably well. But first I must argue that such speech commits a wrong that may be legitimately targeted by regulation.

SPEECH-ACT WRONG

I have argued that some forms of hate speech treat their targets as moral subordinates on account of race, gender, or sexual preference. Such treatment runs counter to the central liberal idea of persons as free and equal. To that extent, it constitutes a wrong, a speech-act wrong inflicted on those whom it addresses. However, it does not follow that it is a wrong that may be legitimately targeted by regulation. A liberal republic is not a republic of virtue in which the authorities prohibit every conceivable wrong. The liberal republic protects a substantial zone of liberty around the individual in which she is free from authoritative intrusion even to do some things that are wrong.

Yet, the wrongs of subordination based on such characteristics as race, gender, and sexual preference are not just any old wrongs. Historically, they are among the principal wrongs that have prevented—and continue to prevent—Western liberal democracies from living up to their ideals and principles. As such, these wrongs are especially appropriate targets of regulation in our liberal republic. Liberals recognize the special importance of combating such wrongs in their strong support for laws prohibiting discrimination in employment, housing, and public accommodations. And even if the regulation of speech-act subordination on campus is not regarded as mandatory for universities, it does seem that the choice of an institution to regulate that type of subordination on campus is at least justifiable within a liberal framework.

In opposition, it may be argued that subordination is a serious wrong that should be targeted but that the line should be drawn when it comes to subordination through speech. There, viewpoint-neutrality must govern. But I believe that the principle of viewpoint-neutrality must be understood as resting on deeper liberal concerns. Other things being equal, a departure from viewpoint-neutrality will be justified if it can accommodate these deeper concerns while at the same time serving the liberal principle of the equality of persons.

The concerns fall into three basic categories. First is the Millian idea that speech can promote individual development and contribute to the public political dialogue, even when it is wrong, misguided, or otherwise deficient.[25] Second is the Madisonian reason that the authorities cannot be trusted with formulating and enforcing rules that silence certain views: they will be too tempted to abuse such rules in

---

25. See Robert Post, "Racist Speech, Democracy, and the First Amendment," *William and Mary Law Review* 32 (1991): 290–91.

order to promote their own advantage or their own sectarian viewpoint.[26] Third is the idea that any departures from viewpoint-neutrality might serve as precedents that could be seized upon by would-be censors with antiliberal agendas to further their broad efforts to silence speech and expression.[27]

These concerns that underlie viewpoint-neutrality must be accommodated for hate-speech regulation to be justifiable from a liberal perspective. But that cannot be done in the abstract. It needs to be done in the context of a particular set of regulations. In the next section, I argue that there are regulations that target reasonably well those forms of hate speech that subordinate, and in the following section I argue that such regulations accommodate the concerns that underlie the liberal endorsement of the viewpoint-neutrality principle.

TARGETING SPEECH-ACT WRONG

If I am right in thinking that the slurs and epithets of hate speech are the principal instruments of the speech-act wrong of treating someone as a moral subordinate and that such a wrong is a legitimate target of regulation, then it will not be difficult to formulate rules that have a reasonably good fit with the wrong they legitimately seek to regulate. In general, what are needed are rules that prohibit speech that (*a*) employs slurs and epithets conventionally used to subordinate persons on account of their race, gender, religion, ethnicity, or sexual preference, (*b*) is addressed to particular persons, and (*c*) is expressed with the intention of degrading such persons on account of their race, gender, religion, ethnicity, or sexual preference. With some modification, this is essentially what one finds in the regulations drafted by Grey for Stanford.[28]

Restricting the prohibition to slurs and epithets addressed to specific persons will capture many speech-act wrongs of subordination. But it will not capture them all. Slurs and epithets are not necessary for such speech acts, as I conceded earlier. In addition, it may be possible to treat someone as a moral subordinate through a speech act, even though the utterance is not addressing that person. However, prohibiting more than slurs and epithets would run a high risk of serious over-inclusiveness, capturing much speech that performs legitimate speech acts such as stating and arguing. And prohibiting all use of slurs and epithets, whatever the context, would mandate a degree of intrusiveness

26. See Frederick Schauer, "The Second-Best First Amendment," *William and Mary Law Review* 31 (1989): 1–2.

27. Peter Linzer, "White Liberal Looks at Racist Speech," *St. John's Law Review* 65 (1991): 219.

28. Stanford describes the intent that is needed for a hate speaker to be liable as the intent to insult or stigmatize. My reservations about formulating the requisite intent in terms of 'insult' are given below.

into the private lives of students that would be difficult for liberals to license.

The regulations should identify examples of the kinds of terms that count as epithets or slurs conventionally used to perform speech acts of subordination. This is required in order to give people sufficient fair warning. But because the terms of natural languages are not precise, univocal, and unchanging, it is not possible to give an exhaustive list, nor is it mandatory to try. Individuals who innocently use an epithet that conventionally subordinates can plead lack of the requisite intent.

The intent requirement is needed to accommodate cases in which an epithet or slur is not used with any intent to treat the addressee as a moral subordinate. These cases cover a wide range, including the efforts of some minorities to capture and transvalue terms historically used to subordinate them. There are several different ways in which the required intent could be described: the intent to stigmatize or to demean or to insult or to degrade and so on. I think that 'degrade' does the best job of capturing the idea of treating someone as a moral subordinate in language the average person will find familiar and understandable. 'Insult' does the poorest job and should be avoided. Insulting someone typically does not involve treating the person as a moral subordinate. Rather, it involves putting someone down in other ways: as less skillful, less intelligent, less clever, and the like.

The regulations at some universities extend beyond what I have defended and prohibit speech that demeans on the basis of physical appearance. I do not believe that such regulations can be justified within the liberal framework I have developed here. Speech can certainly be used to demean people based on physical appearance. 'Slob', 'dog', 'beast', 'pig': these are some examples of terms that are used in such verbal put-downs.[29] But I do not believe that they are used to treat people as moral subordinates, and thus the terms do not inflict the kind of speech-act wrong that justifies the regulation of racist, sexist, or homophobic slurs and epithets.

It should not be surprising that terms which demean on the basis of appearance do not morally subordinate, since the belief that full human moral standing depends on good looks is one that few people, if any, hold.[30] The terms that put people down for their appearance are thus fundamentally different from racist, sexist, or homophobic

29. Most such terms are conventionally understood as applying to women and not to men, a clear reflection of our culture's way of perceiving men and women.

30. Some people believe that being overweight is the result of a failure of self-control and thus a kind of moral failing. But that is quite different from thinking that the rights and interests of overweight people are morally less important than those of people who are not overweight. See n. 23 above.

slurs and epithets. The latter terms do reflect beliefs that are held by many about the lower moral standing of certain groups.

ACCOMMODATING LIBERAL CONCERNS

I have argued that regulations should target those forms of hate speech that inflict the speech-act wrong of subordination on their victims. This wrong is distinct from the psychological harm that hate speech causes. In targeting speech-act subordination, the aim of regulation is not to prohibit speech that has undesirable psychological effects on individuals but, rather, to prohibit speech that treats people as moral subordinates. To target speech that has undesirable psychological effects is invariably to target certain ideas, since it is through the communication of ideas that the psychological harm occurs. In contrast, targeting speech-act subordination does not target ideas. Any idea would be free from regulation as long as it was expressed through a speech act other than one which subordinates: stating, arguing, claiming, defending, and so on would all be free of regulation.[31]

Because of these differences, regulations that target speech-act subordination can accommodate the liberal concerns underlying viewpoint-neutrality, while regulations that sweep more broadly cannot. Consider the important Millian idea that individual development requires that people be left free to say things that are wrong and to learn from their mistakes. Under the sort of regulation I endorse, people would be perfectly free to make racist, sexist, and homophobic assertions and arguments and to learn of the deficiencies of their views from the counterassertions and counterarguments of others. And the equally important Millian point that public dialogue gains even through the expression of false ideas is accommodated in a similar way. Whatever contribution a racist viewpoint can bring to public discussion can be made under regulations that only target speech-act subordination.

The liberal fear of trusting the authorities is somewhat more worrisome. Some liberals have argued that the authorities cannot be trusted with impartial enforcement of hate-speech regulations. Nadine Strossen, for example, claims that the hate-speech regulations at the University of Michigan have been applied in a biased manner, punishing the racist and homophobic speech of blacks but not of whites.[32] Still,

31. A similar argument was made by some supporters of a legal ban on desecrating the American flag through such acts as burning it: to the extent that the ban would prohibit some people from expressing their political viewpoints, it was only a minor departure from viewpoint-neutrality, since those people had an array of other ways to express their views. But the critical difference between the flag-burning case and the hate-speech case is that flag burning is not an act that treats anyone as a moral subordinate.

32. Nadine Strossen, "Regulating Racist Speech on Campus: A Modest Proposal?" *Duke Law Journal* (1990), pp. 557–58. Eric Barendt argues that the British criminal law against racist speech "has often been used to convict militant black spokesmen" (Eric Barendt, *Freedom of Speech* [Oxford: Clarendon, 1985], p. 163).

it is not at all clear that the biased application of rules is any more of a problem with rules that are not viewpoint-neutral than with those that are. A neutral rule against harassment can also be enforced in a racially discriminatory manner. There is no reason to think a priori that narrowly drawn hate-speech rules would be any more liable to such abuse. Of course, if it did turn out that there was a pervasive problem with the biased enforcement of hate-speech rules, any sensible liberal would advocate rescinding them. But absent a good reason for thinking that this is likely to happen—not just that it could conceivably happen—the potential for abusive enforcement is no basis for rejecting the kind of regulation I have defended.

Still remaining is the problem of precedent: even narrowly drawn regulations targeting only speech-act subordination could be cited as precedent for more sweeping, antiliberal restrictions by those at other universities or in the community at large who are not committed to liberal values.[33] In response to this concern, it should be argued that narrowly drawn rules will not serve well as precedents for would-be censors with antiliberal agendas. Those who wish to silence socialists, for example, on the ground that socialism is as discredited as racism will find scant precedential support from regulations that allow the expression of racist opinions as long as they are not couched in slurs and epithets directed at specific individuals.

There may be some precedent-setting risk in such narrow regulations. Those who wish to censor the arts, for example, might draw an analogy between the epithets that narrow hate-speech regulations proscribe and the "trash" they would proscribe: both forms of expression are indecent, ugly, and repulsive to the average American, or so the argument might go.

Yet, would-be art censors already have precedents at their disposal providing much closer analogies in antiobscenity laws. Hate-speech regulations are not likely to give would-be censors of the arts any additional ammunition. To this, a liberal opponent of any hate-speech regulation might reply that there is no reason to take the risk. But the response will be that there is a good reason, namely, to prevent the wrong of speech-act subordination that is inflicted by certain forms of hate speech.

---

33. This concern should be distinguished from the idea that any hate-speech regulation is a step down the slippery slope to the totalitarian control of ideas. That idea is difficult to take seriously. Even for nations that have gone much farther in regulating hate speech than anything envisioned by liberal proponents of regulation in the United States, countries such as England, France, and Germany, the idea that they are on the road to totalitarianism is preposterous. A summary of the laws against racist speech in Britain, France, and Germany can be found in Barendt, pp. 161–66.

CONCLUSION

There is a defensible liberal middle ground between those who oppose all campus hate-speech regulation and those who favor the sweeping regulation of such speech. But the best defense of this middle ground requires the recognition that speech acts of subordination are at the heart of the hate-speech issue. Some forms of hate speech do wrong to people by treating them as moral subordinates. This is the wrong that can and should be the target of campus hate-speech regulations.

Political Studies (1993), XLI, 453–470

Harm Principle, Offence Principle, and the Skokie Affair*

RAPHAEL COHEN-ALMAGOR

The Hebrew University of Jerusalem

The primary aims are to formulate principles conducive to safeguarding fundamental civil rights and to employ the theory to analyse the Skokie affair. The focus is on the ethical question of the constraints on speech. I advance two arguments relating to the 'Harm Principle' and the 'Offence Principle'. Under the 'Harm Principle', restrictions on liberty may be prescribed when there are sheer threats of immediate violence against some individuals or groups. Under the 'Offence Principle', expressions which intend to inflict psychological offence are morally on a par with physical harm and thus there are grounds for abridging them. Moving from theory to practice, in the light of the formulated principles, the ruling of the Illinois Supreme Court which permitted the Nazis to hold a demonstration in Skokie is argued to be flawed.

The aim of this essay is to confront the ethical question of the constraints of speech. Can we say that sometimes, the harm or the offence brought about by a certain speech constitutes such an injury that it cannot be tolerated? More specifically, under what conditions can preventing offence provide adequate reason for limiting freedom of expression?

The discussion will be divided into theoretical and practical parts. First I shall try to formulate the restrictions on freedom of expression in the clearest and most precise fashion possible. Too vague a definition might lead to administrative abuse on the part of the government in its attempt to silence 'inconvenient' views. An imprecise definition might have a snowball effect, paving the way for a syndrome whereby freedom of speech might become the exception rather than the rule. Moreover, the restrictions cannot be occasional. We have to seek a criterion that could serve both as an evaluative guideline and be suitable for a range of cases, covering different types of speech (racist, ethnic, religious etc.). In doing so, I shall avail myself of the Millian theory on liberty, discussing in brief the well versed Harm Principle and then proceed by formulating the Offence Principle.

* I wish to thank Ronald Dworkin, Geoffrey Marshall, Eric Barendt, Chris McCrudden, Jan Sieckmann, and Sir Zelman Cowen for their enlightening comments on previous drafts of this essay. I have also benefited from discussions with Joel Feinberg, G. A. Cohen and Michael Freeden on various aspects of this essay and from the comments of the two anonymous referees of *Political Studies*. In addition I express deep gratitude to the Ben-Gurion Foundation and Bernard Susser for their support.

Second. I shall attend to a legal case which arouses much controversy, the Skokie case, evaluating the court decision in the light of the two principles. My suggestion will be that there are grounds for abridging expression not only when the speech is intended to bring about physical harm but also when it is designed to inflict psychological offence, which is morally on a par with physical harm, provided that the circumstances are such that the target group cannot avoid being exposed to it. The term 'morally on a par with physical harm' comes to mean that just as we view the infliction of physical pain as a wrongful deed, seeing it as the right and the duty of the state to prohibit such an infliction, so we should put boundaries to expressions designed to cause psychological offence to some target group. It will be argued that in either case, when physical harm *or* psychological offence is inflicted upon others, four considerations are pertinent:

The content of the speech.[1]
The manner in which the speech is expressed.
The intentions and the motives of the speaker.
The circumstances in which the speech takes place.

I will further assert that when no consideration is paid to these aspects, then freedom of speech might be abused in a way which contradicts fundamental background rights to human dignity and equality of concern and respect, which underlie a free democratic society.[2] The view enunciated in this study is similar, in various respects, to that of German law. Article 5 of the Basic Law limits the right to freedom of expression by the right to inviolability of personal honour.[3] The German Penal Code (section 130) also makes it an offence to attack the dignity of other people (*inter alia*, by inciting to racial hatred) and thus prevents the possibility of exploiting democratic principles.[4]

Before contemplating the Millian theory, one preliminary methodological note has to be made concerning the Offence Principle. The common liberal interpretation of Mill is that any speech which falls under the category of 'advocacy' is immune to restrictions. Only forms of instigation which bring about instant harm are punishable and these cases constitute the exception to the free speech principle. My view is different. I shall argue that Mill introduced an exception to advocacy, holding that there is a category of cases of advocacy that has to be restricted. This category of cases is concerned with offensive conduct which is done in public. I will show that *there are* certain offensive expressions which may be considered as advocacy which nevertheless should be prohibited. However, it seems that my view and the common liberal view differ only in terminology, not in essence. That is, there are certain utterances which do not induce anyone to take a harmful action but which should still be excluded from the protection of the free speech principle because of their imminent offensive

---

[1] When people speak of the content of the speech, they may refer to its *truthfulness* or to its *consequences* or to both. Here I refer not to the truthfulness of the speech but to the consequences that it is intended to bring about.

[2] R. M. Dworkin, *Taking Rights Seriously* (London, Duckworth, 1977), pp. 266–78; 'Liberalism', in *A Matter of Principle* (Oxford, Clarendon Press, 1985), pp. 181–204.

[3] The view is that the right to freedom of expression has to be balanced against the right to personal honour. Cf. the German Federal Constitutional Court's decision from 7 December 1976 BVerfGE, Vol. 43, 130 (at 137, 139).

[4] Article 1 of the *Grundgesetz* provides: 'The dignity of man shall be inviolable. To respect and protect it shall be the duty of all state authority'. Cf. Eric Barendt, *Freedom of Speech* (Oxford, Clarendon Press, 1985), p. 165.

effects on those who are exposed to it. Some liberals would probably not agree with my vocabulary and would not consider what I call advocacy to be advocacy. They would rather designate it instigative speech but I think that they would agree with my conclusions.

The Millian Theory and Freedom of Expression

Mill proffered two main qualifications in *On Liberty* for the immunity which freedom of expression should, as a general rule, enjoy and in an earlier article concerning freedom of the press he formulated two other qualifications.[5] He did not introduce them in a systematic manner but in an *ad hoc* way, allowing for interference in what he conceived to be special cases. The first qualification proposed in *On Liberty* is concerned with the case of instigative speech. The second qualification considers the case of indecent conduct that is performed in public. Let us first examine the case of instigation.

As a consequentialist, Mill acknowledged that speech loses its immunity when it constitutes an instigation to some harmful action. In his corn-dealer example, Mill asserted that opinions lose their absolute immunity when the circumstances in which they are expressed are such as to constitute by their expression a positive instigation to some mischievous act. Thus, the opinion that corn-dealers are starvers of the poor may be prevented from being delivered orally to 'an excited mob assembled before the house of a corn-dealer, or when handed about among the same mob in the form of a placard'.[6] Nevertheless, that same opinion ought to go unmolested when simply circulated through the press. Accordingly, we may deduce that Mill considered as instigation a speech which intends to lead to some mischievous action, in circumstances which are conducive to the taking of that action. It seems that in instances such as that of the corn-dealer, Mill would regard certain speech as instigation irrespective of whether overt harmful action follows. Though he did not explicitly say so, Mill implied that the intention to lead people to take a harmful action constitutes an instigation.[7] However, advocacy which does not induce someone to take an action, which is voiced as a matter of ethical conviction, is protected under Mill's theory. This is one of his major contributions to the free speech literature. Mill was the first to distinguish between speech (or discussion) as a matter of ethical conviction and instigation.

The essential distinction between 'instigation' and 'advocacy' or 'teaching' is that those to whom the instigation is addressed must be urged to *do* something now or in the immediate future, rather than merely to believe in something. In other words, instigation is speech which is closely linked to action. Mill in the corn-dealer example implicitly opined that when an audience has no time for

---

[5] The two qualifications that were presented in the article are quite problematic because it is difficult to reconcile them with his arguments in *On Liberty*. One qualification is concerned with telling 'the truth', when that 'truth, without being of any advantage to the public, is calculated to give annoyance to private individuals.' The other qualification is concerned with the publication of false statements of facts. Cf. 'Law and libel and liberty of the press', in Geraint L. Williams, (ed.), *John S. Mill on Politics and Society* (Glasgow, Fontana, 1976), pp. 143–69.

[6] J. S. Mill, *On Liberty* (London, Dent, Everyman's Edition, 1948), p. 114.

[7] Mill acknowledged the importance of intentions in other places. Thus, for instance, speaking of employing military commanders by ministers, Mill said that as long as a minister trusts his military commander he does not send him instructions how to fight. He holds him responsible only for intentions and results. Cf. 'Appendix', in *Dissertations and Discussions*, Vol. I, (New York, Haskell House, 1973), pp. 471–2.

© Political Studies Association, 1993

careful and rational reflection before it pursues the course of action urged on it, then this speech falls outside the protection of the free speech principle, since the people are too excited to be responsible for their acts.[8] Mill did not restrict the advocating of certain opinions *per se*. Rather, it is the combination of the content of the opinion, its manner, the intentions of the speaker and the circumstances that necessitates the restriction. In the corn-dealer example the harmful results of a breach of the peace, disorder and harm to others were imminent and likely. Therefore, they outweigh the importance of free expression.

In parenthesis, two clarifications have to be made. One relates to the factor of 'intention', the other to 'manner'. As to 'intention', one may question the relevance of intention to Mill's argument about instigation. One may argue that the relevant consideration is whether circumstances are such that a speech will cause a riot; that would seem sufficient reason for intervention, even when the speaker does not intend to cause a riot. I am not convinced. The very usage of the word 'instigation' implies that the intention exists to provoke a riot. I agree that there might be unintended riots but it seems to me odd to use the term 'instigation' in that context.

The second point relates to 'manner'. This factor characterizes the way expressions are made, be it in oral or symbolic speech. We can think of situations in which the manner is not so important, yet the three other factors are sufficient to constitute an instigation. Consider a leader of a fundamentalist religious sect who urges his followers to some mischievous act in a very cool and quiet tone. In this case it seems that Mill would have had no qualms to classify such a speech under the heading of 'instigation'. I discuss this issue later.

The implications of the instigation reasoning are that it will be incorrect to say that all opinions bring the same results. It seems, then, that Justice Holmes's assertion '[E]very idea is an incitement' is too hasty.[9] Rather, we may concede that words which express an opinion in one context can become incendiary when addressed to an inflammable audience. The peculiarity of cases of instigation is that the likelihood of an immediate danger is high and there is little or no opportunity to conduct discussion in the open, and to bring conflicting considerations into play which may reduce the effects of the speech. Holmes J. agreed that in certain circumstances, when speech is closely related to action and might induce harmful consequences, it should be curtailed. In a similar way to the Millian corn-dealer example, Holmes J. asserted in a renowned opinion that we cannot allow falsely shouting '*Fire!*' in a crowded theatre.[10] Here too a restriction on speech is justified on the grounds that the content of the speech (its effects, not its intrinsic value), the manner of the speech, and the intentions of the agent are aimed to bring about harm. The audience is under conditions which diminish its ability to deliberate in a rational manner, so such a shout might lead it to act in a manner harmful to themselves as well as to others.[11] Hence, to the extent that speech entails an immediate effect, the arguments which assign special status to

[8] Similar reasoning, as far as shortage of time is concerned, guided Mill in supporting interference in the other's freedom in the case of the unsafe bridge.

[9] *Gitlow v. New York* 268 U.S. 652, 673 (1925).

[10] *Schenck v. U.S.* 249 U.S. 47 (1919).

[11] Note that in this instance it does not matter whether the intention of the actor was only to do this specific act and not to bring about harmful consequences. The actor may say that he only wanted to break the silence or to attract public attention and that he did not think of creating panic. Still he will be held accountable for his action. The same reasoning guides us in prosecuting those who press emergency buttons in trains just because they could not resist the temptation.

© Political Studies Association, 1993

freedom of speech are less compelling. Boundaries have to be introduced in accordance with the context of the speech, otherwise the results could be too risky. 'Smoking is all right, but not in a powder magazine'.[12]

Incorporating the four conditions of content, manner, intention and circumstances into the Millian and the Holmesian examples, the following argument may be deduced:

> *Argument number one*: Any speech which *instigates* (in the sense of meeting the four criteria of content, manner, intention and circumstances) to cause physical harm to certain individuals or groups ought to be curtailed. Notice that this argument is a much more decisive version of the Millian Harm Principle.[13]

Let us now move on to examine Mill's second exception which qualifies, in my opinion, the immunity Mill generally granted to advocacy. This exception considers the case of indecent conduct performed in public. Although Mill spoke of 'conduct' and did not explicitly mention speech, it is plausible to argue that he included utterances, as well as acts, under this qualification. Mill implied that there are certain cases which fall within the scope of social regulation and people not only have the right but the duty to put a stop to those individuals' activities. In a brief paragraph he discussed a category of actions which being directly injurious only to the agents themselves, ought not to be legally interdicted, but which, 'if done publicly, are a violation of good manners, and coming thus within the category of offenses against others, may rightly be prohibited'.[14] This argument is in accordance with Mill's position on the importance of autonomy. There are intimate matters which do not concern anyone but the individual, so long as they are done in private. When they are done publicly, then they might cause offence to others, and the State may legitimately control them.[15] Mill said, offenses against decency were of this kind.

Hence, in certain situations, one is culpable not because of the act done, though this act might be morally wrong, but because of its *circumstances* and its *consequences*. Mill assumed that one can evaluate the rightness and wrongness of an action by considering its consequences, believing that the morality of an action depends on the consequences which it is likely to produce.[16] Since one is to judge before acting, then one must weight the probable results of one's doing, given the specific conditions of the situation.

From these arguments we may infer that it is usually not the act itself which is crucial for taking a stand on this subject but the forum in which it is done. A certain conduct in itself does not necessarily provide sufficient grounds for interference. But if that same conduct is being done in public then it might be counted as morally wrong. It constitutes an offence, and hence it is legitimate to

[12] Z. Chafee, *Free Speech in the U.S.* (Cambridge, Mass., Harvard University Press, 1946), p. 397.

[13] The Millian Harm Principle holds that something is *eligible* for restriction only if it causes harm to others. Whether it ought to be restricted remains to be calculated. Whereas this argument provides conditions in which a harm *ought* to be restricted.

[14] Mill, *On Liberty*, p. 153.

[15] John Skorupski, *John Stuart Mill* (London, Routledge, 1989) pp. 347-59, speaks of the concept of moral freedom which is conceived by Mill as rational autonomy. The autonomy which one values as an independent part of one's own good is the freedom to lead one's own life but this is not just 'freedom to do as one likes' either. Autonomy is sovereignty over one's own life, not sovereignty over anyone else's.

[16] Mill, 'Bentham', in *Dissertations and Discussions*. Vol. I, p. 386.

† Political Studies Association, 1993.

curtail it. Enforcement of sanctions may be justified when conduct causes offence to others.[17]

To sum up: the two exceptions brought forward by Mill touch upon the time factor which distinguishes speech from action. Thus, action – if it endangers the public or part of it – might have immediate consequences; whereas speech, if it has any endangering effect, would have it in most cases sometime in the near or more remote future, thus allowing us much wider room for manoeuvre.[18] Even if a specific view might cause harm or risk of harm to others but the danger is not immediate, then free speech has to be allowed. However, in some circumstances the time factor might lose its distinctiveness, with the result that the effects of the expression in question are *immediate*. Indeed, both in the case of instigation as well as in cases of moral offence (say when one vulgarly praises in public the sexual qualities of one's next door neighbour, knowing the anguish that the neighbour might suffer as a result), the effects of the expression are instantaneous and thus might bring about hurtful consequences *now*, rather than at some remote point in the future. That is, when we discuss the issue of obscene speech or defamation,[19] the line between conduct and speech, according to the criterion of time, becomes blurred and consequently these utterances are not protected under the principle of freedom of speech.

The preliminary argument (*number one*) included the term 'physical'. I have formulated the argument, using this term, in order to avoid at that stage the question of whether the formula ought to include other sorts of harm. I have now argued that in both the cases of instigation and cases of indecent conduct done in public, the effects of the communication are immediate. Yet, such conduct does not necessarily fall under the first argument, for offenses against decency may not be physical. There seem to be other notions of injury that Mill articulated when he introduced this qualification. The expression in question may fall under the rubric of 'advocacy', in the sense that it does not induce anyone to take an harmful action. Nevertheless, the expression may still be excluded from the protection of the free speech principle because of its offensive effects on those who are exposed to it. This is the only exception that is implied in Mill's theory with regard to advocacy. It is the combination of the content of the advocacy, its manner, the intentions of the speaker, and the fact that it is done publicly which gives grounds for restriction. Certain types of advocacy constitute a violation of good manners, thus coming within the category of offenses and, may rightly be prohibited. In order to understand what notions of injury may be included under

---

[17] In *Utilitarianism* (p. 45) Mill explained: 'We do not call anything wrong, unless we mean to imply that a person ought to be punished in some way or other for doing it; if not by law, by the opinion of his fellow-creatures; if not by opinion, by the reproaches of his own conscience. This seems the real turning point of the distinction between morality and simple expediency. It is a part of the notion of Duty in every one of its forms, that a person may rightfully be compelled to fulfil it . . .'.

[18] One of the arguments that is commonly made, following Mill, is that action – if it endangers the public or part of it – might have its consequences immediately; whereas speech, if it has any endangering effect, would have it in most cases sometime in the future, thus allowing us a much wider range of manoeuvres. The assumption is that an opinion does not necessarily entail action, and that, in most cases, opinions do not automatically translate into action, therefore there is enough time to stop ideas before they materialize into harmful action. Even if a specific view might cause harm or risk of harm to others, the danger is not immediate, so free speech has to be allowed.

[19] There are situations in which the offence that is done by the defamatory remarks is immediate and irreparable, so there is no time for a reply. An example would be the publication of false accusations against a rival candidate on the eve of elections.

© Political Studies Association, 1993

this qualification, which may be put under the heading of the Offence Principle, it is necessary to explain the distinction between 'harm' and 'offence'.

Feinberg: The Offence Principle

Feinberg explains that like the word 'harm', the word 'offence' has both a general and a specifically normative sense, the former including in its reference any or all of a miscellany of disliked mental states (disgust, shame, hurt, anxiety, etc), while the latter refers to those states only when caused by the wrongful (right-violating) conduct of others. He postulates that offence takes place when three criteria are present: one is offended when one suffers a disliked state; attributes that state to the wrongful conduct of another and resents the other for his role in causing one to be in that state.[20] Feinberg maintains that the seriousness of the offensiveness would be determined by three standards: (1) 'the extent of offensive standard', meaning the intensity and durability of the repugnance produced and the extent to which repugnance could be anticipated to be the general reaction of strangers to the conduct displayed; (2) 'the reasonable avoidability standard', which refers to the ease with which unwilling witnesses can avoid the offensive displays; and (3) 'the *Volenti* standard', which considers whether or not the witnesses have willingly taken the risk of being offended either through curiosity or the anticipation of pleasure.[21] Standards (2) and (3) are of relevance when we examine the circumstances in which an offensive speech is expressed.

Feinberg categorically asserts that offence is a less serious thing than harm and thus ignores the possibility that psychological offenses might amount to physical harm, with the same serious implications. The next section specifically reflects on this subject through consideration of Feinberg's standards. Here, if we return to Mill's second qualification, we may say that morally wrong actions which concern others cause one to suffer a disliked state, which one attributes to the doer's conduct. Consequently one resents the doer for his acts. Nevertheless, offenses against decency are problematic, since what is offensive to one may not be regarded as offensive at all by another. If we want to make the Offence Principle an intelligible principle, the offence has to be explicit, and it has to be more than emotional distress, inconvenience, embarrassment, or annoyance. We cannot outlaw *anything* that causes some sort of offence to others. If the Offence Principle is broadened to include annoyance, then it would become too weak to serve as a guideline in political theory, for almost every action can be said to cause some nuisance to others. Cultural norms and prejudices, for instance, might irritate some people. Liberal views may cause some discomfort to conservatives; and conservative opinions might distress liberals. Some, for instance, might be offended when hearing a woman shouting commands, or just by the sight of black and white people holding hands. This is not to say that these sorts of behaviour should be curbed because of some people who are 'over-sensitive' to gender or inter-racial relations. Similarly, if someone is easily offended by pornographic material, one can easily avoid the pain by not buying magazines marked by the warning: 'The content may be offensive to some'. Under Feinberg's 'reasonable avoidability' and '*Volenti*' standards the offence cannot be considered to be serious. Injuries, to be restricted under the Offence Principle, must involve serious

[20] Joel Feinberg. *Offense to Others* (New York, Oxford University Press, 1985), pp. 1–2.
[21] Feinberg. *Offense to Others*, p. 26.

Political Studies Association, 1993.

offence to be infringed. By 'serious offence' is meant that consideration has to be given to the 'reasonable avoidability', the '*Volenti*' as well as the 'extent of offensive' standards. The repugnance produced has to be severe so as to cause an irremediable offence which might affect the ability of the listeners to function in their lives.

Under Feinberg's 'reasonable avoidability standard' and Mill's argument regarding public immoral actions, the offence has to be committed in such circumstances that those offended cannot possibly avoid it in order to supply grounds for restriction. Hence, for example, if a person at Hyde Park Corner advocates getting rid of Parliament, throwing out all Indians, expressing his desire to become the new Stalin of tomorrow or claiming that yesterday he was Napoleon, the offence at that point cannot be considered as more than annoying, or to cause more than an inconvenience to the listeners, for they can simply leave the place and free themselves of the speaker's presence, as well as of his speech. We are not able to say that the audience interest in 'having a good environment' is more important than the speaker's interest in conveying his thoughts.[22] Also, the argument that this communication does not carry substantive content cannot serve as sufficient reason for abridging it, for then we might supply grounds for curtailing many other speeches that just repeat familiar stands. In addition, 'the extent of offence standard', determined by the content and manner of the speech, and 'the *Volenti* standard', do not provide reasons for restriction.

The situation is different, however, when the avoidance of offensive conduct in itself constitutes a weighty pain. Then we may say that the matter is open to dispute. If those who are offended by a speech feel an obligation to stay because they think that they would suffer more were they to avoid the speech by going away, then there are grounds for putting restrictions on speech, provided that the extent of the offence is considerable. In any event, it is the combination of the content and manner of the speech, the evil intention of the speaker *and* unavoidable circumstances, that warrants the introduction of sanctions.

In the next section I shall discuss the Nazi's decision to march in Skokie as an illustration of this argument. In this case the conflict over freedom of expression involves the issue of freedom of assembly. I shall assess the preliminary court decisions to ban the march, as well as the Illinois Supreme Court ruling which allowed the demonstration, and explore whether the Offence Principle supplies us with grounds for supporting one over the other. A prior clarification is needed. In applying the Offence Principle to Skokie I do not claim that racist speech should be considered a distinct case, as some philosophers and commentators urge, thus excluding it from the protection usually accorded to expression.[23] It may be suggested that, as a matter of principle, racist speech is incompatible with liberal democracy and hence should be outlawed. My reluctance to accept this line of reasoning derives from two basic considerations. First, I do not see why verbal attacks on race, colour or religion should be regarded as a unique type of speech

[22] Cf. T. M. Scanlon, 'Freedom of expression and categories of expression', *University of Pittsburgh Law Review* 40 (1979), 527.

[23] Cf. David Kretzmer, 'Freedom of speech and racism'. *Cardozo Law Review* 8 (1987), 445–513. See also Jean-Paul Sartre, who wrote that anti-Semitism does not fall within the category of ideas protected by the right of free expression (*Réflexions sur la Question Juive*, Gallimard, 2nd ed, 1954). In addition, several international law treaties justify restricting racist speech on the grounds of the possible connection between racist expressions and discrimination. Cf. *Universal Declaration on Human Rights*, Art. 7; *Convention on the Elimination of all Forms of Racial Discrimination*, Art. 4; *International Covenant on Civil and Political Rights*, Art 20(2).

Political Studies Association, 1993

which does not deserve protection. I find it difficult to see why racist expressions should be thought different from verbal attacks on one's most fundamental ethical and moral convictions – as, for instance, in the abortion or the euthanasia cases. I do not see why dignity or equal respect and concern is more at stake in the former than in the latter. Second, there is lack of agreement on the meaning of the term 'racism'. Different countries and forums put under the heading of 'racism' different types of speech. Thus by excluding racist expressions, we might open the way to curtailing expressions which we may want to defend.

My intention is to formulate general criteria to be applied consistently not only in cases of racial hatred but also to other categories of offensive speech. Any speech, be it on religious, ethnic, cultural, national, social or moral grounds, should be submitted to the confines of the two principles that are suggested.[24] Speech which instigates the causing of immediate harm to the target group, and speech which is designed to offend the sensibilities of the target group, – in circumstances which are bound to expose the target group to a serious offence which is morally on a par with physical pain – should be restricted.

Applying the Offence Principle: the Skokie Controversy

What came to be known as 'the Skokie case' began in April 1977, when Frank Collin, the leader of the National Socialist Party of America (NSPA) announced that a march would be held in Skokie, one of the outskirts of Chicago, inhabited mostly by Jews; some hundreds of them being survivors of Nazi concentration camps.[25] The Skokie citizens obtained an injunction in court that banned the march. Referring to the *Brandenburg* case, they contended that the display of the Nazi uniform and the swastika were the symbolic equivalents of a public call to kill all Jews, and consequently that it constituted a 'direct incitement to immediate mass murder'.[26] After a long legal struggle which lasted until January 1978, the Illinois Supreme Court, in a 7 to 1 decision, ruled in favour of Collin.[27] The main argument was the 'content neutrality rule' according to which political speech shall not be abridged because of its content, even if that content is verbally abusive. Speech can be restricted only when it interferes in a physical way with other legitimate activities; when it is thrust upon a 'captive' audience, or when it directly incites immediate harmful conduct. Otherwise, no matter what the content of the speech, the intention of the speaker and the impact of the speech on non-captive listeners, the speech is protected under the First Amendment to the Constitution.[28]

The Court dismissed the main arguments of the citizens of Skokie, enunciating that the display of the swastika was symbolic political speech, which was

[24] Accordingly, pornography may be dealt with under the Offence Principle. This issue, however, requires a separate analysis.
[25] Skokie has the highest number of Holocaust survivors of any city in the United States, outside the city of New York.
[26] In *Brandenburg v. Ohio* 395 U.S. 444 (1969) the court ruled that the expression of a particular idea may not be suppressed unless it is both directed to and likely to incite or produce imminent unlawful conduct. See also *Hess v. Indiana* 414 U.S. 105 (1973).
[27] Clark J. dissented without submitting any explanation.
[28] *Skokie v. NSPA*, 373 N.E. 2d, 21 (1978). Chief Justice Vinson wrote in *Dennis v. U.S.* 341 U.S. 494 (1951) that the basis of the First amendment is the hypothesis that speech can rebut speech, propaganda will answer propaganda, free debate of ideas will result in the widest governmental policies. Powell J. argued in *Gertz v. Robert Welch* 418 U.S. 323 (1974) that under this amendment there is no such thing as a false idea.

© Political Studies Association, 1993

intended to convey the ideas of the NSPA, even if these ideas were offensive. Similarly it was argued that the plaintiffs' wearing uniforms need not meet standards of acceptability. The judges further concluded that anticipation of a hostile audience could not justify prior restraint when the audience was not 'captive'. Freedom of speech cannot be abridged because the listeners are intolerant of its content.[29]

The 'Avoidability Standard'

Two basic things concerning this case are plain and generally agreed upon. First, Skokie was not a case of a captive audience because there was advance notification of the Nazis' intentions. Second, the argument that the Nazi march or speech was designed to convince some members of the audience to embrace all or part of the Nazi ideology, was not an issue. It was obvious that Collin's aim was not to convince his audience but rather to offend the Jewish population in Skokie. Nevertheless, the Illinois Supreme Court ruled that it was not a case of 'fighting words',[30] because the display of the swastika did not fall within the confines of that doctrine[31] and because it was no longer the prevailing view that it was up to the court to assess the *value* of utterances. The Court ruled that the wearing of Nazi uniforms and the display of the swastika constituted political speech that was protected under the Free Speech clause.[32]

In his examination of the Skokie decisions, Feinberg lays emphasis on the contention that given the relative ease with which the malicious and spiteful Nazi insults could be avoided, there was not an exceptionally weighty case for legal interference. Since the Nazis announced the demonstration well in advance, it could easily be avoided by all those who wished to do so, in most cases with minimal inconvenience.[33] Feinberg reiterates the reasoning of the Illinois

---

[*] Under constitutional precedents, the threat of violence could not serve as an argument to prevent assemblies, rallies, and the like. Cf. *Terminiello v. Chicago* 337 U.S. 1 (1949); *Feiner v. New York* 340 U.S. 315 (1951); *Edwards v. South Carolina* 372 U.S. 229 (1963); *Street v. New York* 394 U.S. 576 (1969); *Tinker v. Des Moines* 393 U.S. 503 (1969); and *Bachellar v. Maryland* 397 U.S. 564 (1970). In England the most notable case is *Beatty v. Gillbanks* 9 QBD 308 (1882). The reasoning of the British courts on this issue is similar to that of the American courts, holding that the hostile audience problem should not serve as grounds for suppression of demonstrations.

[*] *Chaplinsky v. New Hampshire* 315 U.S. 568 (1942). See also *Cohen v. California* 403 U.S. 15 (1971). In Britain the 'fighting words' doctrine came into expression in Lord Parker's phraseology, that a speaker must insult his audience in the sense of 'hitting them with words' for an offence to be committed (*Jordan v. Burgoyne* 2 QB 744, 1963).

[*] The 'fighting words' doctrine is not applicable to Skokie for it gives grounds to punish a person who, in a face-to-face encounter, states something so provocative and insulting as to cause an immediate violent response. This was not the case in Skokie.

[*] One may suggest, following *Chaplinsky*, that there may be a place for a 'fighting symbols' doctrine. I tend to disagree. The crux of the matter in the 'fighting words' doctrine is that certain utterances are seen as having no essential part of any exposition of ideas, or rather utterances which do not communicate any ideas. Therefore they are ruled out of the Free Speech clause of the Constitution. On the other hand, the very using of a symbol intends to convey a certain idea, otherwise it would not be considered a symbol. It may be intended to insult or intimidate but one cannot employ the reasoning of *Chaplinsky* here: 'fighting words' seem to contain no idea; symbols, by their very characterization as such, *do* contain a certain idea.

[*] Feinberg, *Offense to Others*, pp. 87–88. I find Feinberg's arguments confusing, for he also writes that the feelings of a Jewish survivor of a Nazi death camp as a small band of American Nazis strut down the main street of his town 'cannot be wholly escaped merely by withdrawing one's attention, by locking one's door, pulling the window blinds, and putting plugs in one's ears'. Feinberg maintains that the offended state of mind is at least to some degree independent of what is directly perceived (at p. 52).

Supreme Court in favour of the NSPA, in accordance with his 'reasonable avoidability standard'. He maintains that 'the scales would tip the other way' if their behaviour were to become more frequent, for the constant need to avoid public places at certain times can become a major nuisance quickly.[34] Since the issue concerned only one demonstration, the solution is easy enough: those likely to be offended simply have to be elsewhere when it is held. These assertions are in accordance with the Feinberg's emphasis on the intensity and the durability of the repugnance produced.[35]

The crux of the matter lies in the 'avoidability standard': the Jews can ignore the offence. The Jews did not *have* to attend the rally. However, not attending the march was no solution at all for these Jews, because it took them back to the days when they had to hide from the Nazis. The survivors of the Holocaust learned the lesson not to keep silent, not to wait until another 'wave of hatred' was over. The lesson of 1933 was enlightening enough. Hiding and running away was their solution in Europe, when they could not do anything else. That solution, they thought, was over and done with when they came, after the war, to live in the United States. For them as Jews, when the Nazi phenomenon is at issue, there is no other way but to resist it, especially when the Nazis decide to come to their own neighbourhood with the intention of awakening fear. Therefore, the suggestion that the Nazis would march in their own front yard without them being present was intolerable. It is not a matter of a 'nuisance' to avoid 'public places' as Feinberg suggests; it is neither a mere nuisance, nor a public place.

If the Nazis were to march elsewhere in Chicago (say in the city centre), their right to be heard is granted protection under the free speech principle.[36] Then one can say that this march is equally offensive to the Jews of Chicago, New York or Tel-Aviv.[37] But this is not the case when Nazis come to a populated Jewish neighbourhood, when the clear and deliberate intention is to offend and excite the inhabitants, especially knowing that many of them are survivors of the Holocaust. Intentions and motives do matter because they may lead to a wrong interpretation being given to the real motives of the agent. Indeed, the same conduct may be interpreted in different ways, according to the motives of the doer[38] but here there is no fear of such possible confusion. It is not a case of

<hr>

[34] For a similar line of argument see Lee C. Bollinger, *The Tolerant Society* (Oxford, Clarendon Press, 1986), p. 60. Bollinger further argues that we should grant a wide latitude to freedom of expression although the speech in question might be harmful because of the societal benefits derived from the lessons learned through toleration (p. 198). The contesting argument holds that to tolerate speech abusing racial groups is to lend respectability to racist attitudes, which in their turn may foster an eventual breakdown of public order. Cf. Barendt, *Freedom of Speech*, p. 161.

[35] Quite surprisingly, and without much explanation, Feinberg does not justify the decision which allowed the march. He states that one can have sympathy for the A.C.L.U. decision to back the Nazis but that he disagrees with this stand (*Offense to Others*, p. 93). In a private discussion he admitted that he did not make his position explicit enough and expressed regret for not fully clarifying his reasoning.

[36] Those who hold the 'fighting words' doctrine (or the 'hitting with words' doctrine) as valid may argue that certain types of speech *as such* should be restricted, no matter where they are pronounced. I do not endorse this view.

[37] Cf. Feinberg, *Offense to Others*, p. 87.

[38] The same conduct can be interpreted in totally different ways, according to the motives of the agent. Witness a farmer who takes his old donkey to be killed. If he wishes that the donkey not be subjected to further pain, we would regard this as a humanitarian act. But if the same farmer takes his old donkey to be killed in front of the gates of the White House, in protest at the high interest that the farmers of the South are required to pay, which brings many of them to bankruptcy, stating that a similar end awaits the Democrat donkey (referring to the Democrat president), then this is surely a political act and many humanitarians are likely to protest.

© Political Studies Association, 1993.

interpretation at all, for the Nazis voiced their reasons for coming to Skokie. It has to be emphasized that the intentions and motives were manifested by Collin himself, who said that he had decided to march in Skokie in order to offend the Jews. Under such circumstances, refraining from attending the march was not a solution for the Jews, as Feinberg suggests, for it would not evade the injury. It might even increase it.

Clearly Collin did not mean to persuade the Jews that his ideas were justified.[39] He chose Skokie not only because there was a big community whom he could offend but also because he wanted to gain public attention. As Dworkin has suggested,[40] it was the grotesqueness of the venue that gained attention. This is, of course, true. The choosing of a venue is cardinal to the success of the demonstration. Protests are made where they convey their message best. For example, we do not seriously consider a demonstration against sending troops to Saudi Arabia in a zoo. We would expect such a demonstration to take place outside the draft offices, or opposite *10 Downing Street*. By the same logic, we would expect a Nazi to propagate his ideas in a Jewish neighbourhood. The question is, however, whether or not our understanding of Collin's motives in choosing Skokie to attract public attention and media coverage should convince us to allow the march. My conclusive answer is 'No'. I repeat once again: when the offence is serious, the intentions of the offender are clear, and the target group is not in a position to avoid the offence, then democracy should draw the line and constrain freedom of expression.

Furthermore, these arguments do not intend to suggest that only demonstrations that are meant to persuade should be allowed, whereas those that mean to offend should be prohibited. The intentions of the demonstrators are only *one* of the considerations that we should bear in mind when deciding on boundaries of freedom of expression. No less important are the seriousness of the offence and the circumstances in which the protest is being made: that is, whether or not the target group can avoid the demonstration without being hurt by the very act of going away. In this context, historical experience is of relevance.

Thus, the Skokie Jews were put in such a position that in either case they would have been offended: if attending the demonstration, they would have to see the swastika and the Nazi uniform and if not, they would have allowed Nazism to 'pass' in their own vicinity. However, an acceptance of that conclusion only denies the main argument of the Illinois Supreme Court, later to be adopted by Feinberg. It does not in itself constitute sufficient grounds to imply that the Nazi right to freedom of expression had to be curtailed in that instance. What we have tried to establish is that the offence was severe according to 'the *Volenti* standard' and 'the reasonable avoidability standard'. We still have to clarify the scope of 'the extent of the offence standard' and explain how serious the offence has to be so as to make it liable to restriction. The fact that Skokie was not a case of instigation might have been a sufficient reason to protect the expression and allow the march, *unless* we can say that the expression in itself constitutes pain that can be considered morally on a par with physical harm. In other words, while it is true that Skokie cannot fall within the confines of our argument from the Harm Principle, nevertheless, if strong argument would be provided that the very utterance of the Nazi speech constitutes *psychological* damage that can be

---

[39] It would not make any difference if the Nazis were primarily concerned to persuade the Skokie Jews of their views rather than deliberately to cause offence.

[40] In a private communication made to me on an earlier version of this paper.

© Political Studies Association, 1993

equated with physical pain, then we may provide a strong case against tolerance under the Offence Principle and in accordance with 'the extent of offence standard'. Then we may say, contrary to Feinberg's presupposition, that an offence might be as serious as harm.[41]

Psychological Offence, Morally on a Par with Physical Harm

The issue of psychological damage is problematic for two reasons. First there is the general claim that the law is an inappropriate instrument for dealing with expression which produces mental distress or whose targets are the beliefs and values of an audience.[42] Second, speaking of psychological damage necessarily involves drawing a distinction between annoyance or some emotional distress, and a significant offence to the mental framework of people.

As for the first claim, Haiman postulates that individuals in a free society 'are not objects which can be *triggered* into action by symbolic stimuli but human beings who *decide* how they will respond to the communication they see and hear'.[43] He conceives people as rational human beings, who carefully weigh arguments and decide according to them. He does not acknowledge that people also have feelings, drives and emotions, which are sometimes so powerful as to dominate their view regarding a certain object, or a phenomenon, or other people. He is not willing to concede that a personal trauma, for example, might prevent an autonomous person, who is usually able to reason and make choices, from developing a rational line of thought about the causes of his trauma. As far as Haiman is concerned, the anguish experienced by those exposed to scenes that remind people of their trauma is a price that must be paid for freedom of speech. He admits that it is difficult not to seem callous in holding this position, but he 'must take that risk and so argue'.[44] Otherwise, those who display Nazi symbols would have to be prohibited from appearing not only in front of the Skokie Village Hall but in any other public place where it might be expected that they would be seen by survivors of the Holocaust. Furthermore, a television documentary examining and vividly portraying neo-Nazi activity might have to be censored because of its impact on Holocaust survivors.[45]

Both arguments, however, are not sufficient to explain why the law should not deal with expressions which produce mental distress, for the 'avoidability standard' takes the sting out of them. The Offence Principle, as postulated, does not supply grounds to restrict either of Haiman's examples. One can switch one's television off or intentionally avoid an encounter with an offensive phenomenon in the city centre. Either of these acts may be deemed necessary to keep one's peace of mind. However, deliberately avoiding an offensive phenomenon occurring in one's own neighbourhood may be seen by some as surrender. This Haiman, like the Illinois Supreme Court and others, fails to understand.

With regard to the second issue, the distinction between annoyance or some emotional distress and a severe offence to one's psyche, is not clear-cut and it is bound to awaken controversy. For the task obviously requires professional

---

[41] Cf. Feinberg, *Offense to Others*, p. 2.
[42] Franklin S. Haiman, *Speech and Law in a Free Society* (Chicago, University of Chicago Press, 1981), p. 425.
[43] Haiman, *Speech and Law in a Free Society*, pp. 425–6 (Haiman's emphasis).
[44] Haiman, *Speech and Law in a Free Society*, p. 97.
[45] Haiman, *Speech and Law in a Free Society*, p. 154.

judgments, which further complicates this issue. These reasons, among others, have influenced the literature to the effect that it lacks sufficient consideration regarding the potential psychological injury that certain speech-acts might cause. These difficulties should not make us overlook the issue. Rather, because we are aware of the complexities that are involved, we must make the qualifications as conclusive as possible and the requirements equally stringent, in order not to open avenues to further suppression of freedom of expression. As previously stated, we must insist that restrictions on freedom of expression be as clear as possible, for otherwise they might become counter-productive. Instead of protecting our liberties, they will assist in their denial. Hence, there should be no doubt that when we speak of a psychological offence, we refer to an offence which is well beyond inconvenience, irritation or some other marginal form of emotional distress. Only considerable pain, one which is not speculative and which is preferably backed by material evidence, may provide us with a reason to restrict freedom of expression under the Offence Principle, assuming that the circumstances make the offence inescapable. With regard to Skokie our task, therefore, is to establish that the offence was such as to constitute an injury which outweighed the special status reserved for freedom of expression.

There was testimony by psychologists on the possible injuries many Jews would suffer as a result of the march. They argued that this speech-act might be regarded as the equivalent of a *physical assault*.[46] This entails that the speech-act was properly subject to regulation (if we recall Scanlon's theory of free speech) as was any physical attack.[47] Thus, in opposition to the *Brandenburg* and *Skokie* decisions, the argument being advanced here is that the content of speech *is* of significance. In emphasizing the importance of content, the focus is put not on the truth of the speech but rather on its *effects*. When the content and the purpose of expression are overlooked, freedom of speech may be exploited in a way that rebuts fundamental principles which underlie a democratic society. Indeed, the U.S. Supreme Court recognized in a series of cases several classes of speech as having 'low' value and thus deserving only limited constitutional protection.[48] The Court held that otherwise speech can be exercised wilfully to inflict injury upon the target persons and groups, thus transforming freedom of speech into a means of curtailing the freedoms of others. Therefore, we should bear in mind the content of speeches. When they are designed to inflict psychological damage upon their target group, then there is a basis to consider their constraint. Here it is worth mentioning the Illinois Appellate Court ruling, later to be overruled by the Illinois Supreme Court, which justified the restriction of the Nazi march because of the likelihood of such injury. The court said that:

[46] Bollinger, *The Tolerant Society*, pp. 197–200. See also *New York Times*, 7.2.1978, (Dr. William Niederland's letter); D. A. Downs, *Nazis in Skokie* (Notre Dame, Indiana, University of Notre Dame Press, 1985), chs. 1, 8; and the statement of Sol Goldstein, a concentration camp survivor whose mother was killed by the Nazis, in Neier, *Defending My Enemy* (New York, Dutton, 1979), p. 46.

[47] Scanlon ('A theory of freedom of expression', in R. Dworkin (ed.), *The Philosophy and Law*, Oxford, Oxford University Press, 1977) contemplates that an assault is committed when one person intentionally places another in apprehension of imminent bodily harm. He maintains that instances of assault necessarily involve expressions since an element of successful communication must be present (p. 158).

[48] There were several occasions in which the United States Supreme Court considered whether certain types of speech are of only 'low' First Amendment value. Among them are the 'fighting words' doctrine (*Chaplinsky v. New Hampshire* 315 U.S. 568, 1942); incitement (*Dennis v. U.S.* 341 U.S. 494, 1951); obscenity (*Miller v. California* 413 U.S. 15, 1973); and false statements of fact (*Gertz v. Robert Welch* 418 U.S. 323, 1974). Cf. Geoffrey R. Stone, 'Content regulation and the First Amendment', *William and Mary Law Review* 25 (1983), 189–252.

⊢ Political Studies Association, 1993

'the tens of thousands of Skokie's Jewish residents must feel gross revulsion
for the swastika and would immediately respond to the personally abusive
epithets slung their way in the form of the defendants' chosen symbol, the
swastika . . . '.[49]

It maintained that the swastika was a personal affront to every member of the
Jewish faith, especially to the survivors. These beliefs were powerful enough to
rule in favour of Skokie's residents and against Collin. However, this ruling
supplies a weaker standard than the one that was just declared to restrict free
speech. 'Gross revulsion' and 'personally abusive epithets' set a more general
standard for constraining freedom of speech. People may feel gross revulsion
when watching a commercial featuring a woman in a bathing suit. We cannot
extend the scope of the Offence Principle so as to include any potential reaction of
disgust on the part of some people. Therefore, we ought to insist on the more
stringent requirement, the one which holds that a restriction on freedom of
speech under the Offence Principle is permissible only if we can show that the
speech in question causes psychological offence, which may be equated with
physical pain.

Now, we face the problem of making this distinction between an offence which
causes 'emotional distress' or 'personal affront', and an offence which causes
'psychological injury' amounting to physical pain, an intelligible distinction.
Offensive acts in general cause unpleasant distressful psychological states to some
degree. To be offended is, by definition, to suffer distress or anguish.[50] So the
Offence Principle allows infringement of freedom of speech only in specific cases,
when the damage is deemed to be irreversible. Skokie is a relevant case because
racist utterances have a damaging psychological impact on the target group
which is difficult to overcome or to reverse. Consequently 'the extent of offence
standard' is satisfied to a degree that Feinberg himself does not acknowledge
when formulating his standards. In some instances the seriousness of the offence
is such that it can be viewed as morally on a par with physical harm.

A further clarification is called for in order to make the argument under the
Offence Principle more precise. The Principle does not provide grounds to restrict
racial hatred *as such*. It insists that we should take into consideration the
circumstances in which the speech is made. In this respect my view is somewhat
different from criminal codes of some European countries, such as Britain or
Sweden.[51] With regard to the British stance, sections 5 and 18 of the Public Order
Act 1986 are of specific relevance.[52] Section 5 prohibits threatening, abusive or

[49] *Village of Skokie v. NSPA.* 366 N.E. 2d 347 (1977), at 357.

[50] Donald Vandeveer, 'Coercive restraint of offensive actions'. *Philosophy & Public Affairs,* 8 (1979), 177.

[51] Chapter 16, section 8 of the Swedish Criminal Code (amended in 1982) reads: 'Anyone who publicly or otherwise in a declaration or other statement which is disseminated to the public threatens or expresses contempt for an ethnic group or some similar group of persons, with allusion to race, colour, national or ethnic origin or religious creed, shall be sentenced for agitation against ethnic groups by imprisonment of up to two years or, if the crime is petty, to a fine'. On the laws of other countries concerning racist speech see Bollinger, *The Tolerant Society,* 1986, pp. 253-6.

[52] In addition, under the Race Relations Act of 1976 a speaker can theoretically be prosecuted if he is using in public threatening, abusive or insulting words. Section 70 of this Act inserted a new section (5A) into the Public Order Act 1936. The section made it an offence for any person to publish or distribute written matter or to use in any public place or at any public meeting words which were threatening, abusive or insulting in a case where hatred was likely to be stirred up against any racial group. This law altered the previous law in that it was no longer necessary, as it had been under section 6 of the Race Relations Act (1965), to prove that the accused intended to stir up racial hatred.

⌐ Political Studies Association, 1993

insulting speech likely to cause harassment, alarm or distress.[53] There need be no intention to insult: it is sufficient that an ordinary person might feel so insulted.[54] In turn, section 18 of the 1986 Act reads:

> '(1) A person who uses threatening, abusive or insulting words or behaviour, or displays any written material which is threatening, abusive or insulting, is guilty of an offence if (a) he intends thereby to stir up racial hatred, or (b) having regard to all the circumstances racial hatred is likely to be stirred up thereby'.[55]

If we are to follow the British reasoning, then grounds might be provided to prohibit a Hyde Park speaker from conveying racist opinions, although we have argued that he should not be denied expression because the listeners are free to leave the place thereby avoiding the offence. Relying on the Millian formulation of the Offence Principle which speaks of a combination of consequences *and* circumstances, and also on Feinberg's standards which determine the seriousness of the offensiveness, it is emphasized that the fact that some types of speech (such as racial and discriminatory advocacy) create great psychological distress is *not* in itself a sufficiently compelling reason to override free speech. The Home Affairs Committee of the House of Commons in its fifth report (1979–1980) recommended against banning marches where there was a likelihood of racial incitement. Barendt, concurring, writes:

> "... however distasteful the views of these [racist] organizations may be, they are entitled to the same freedom of speech as those with more orthodox opinions, and the suppression of such views may be the first slide down the 'slippery slope' towards total government control of political discourse".[56]

There is no disagreement that prescribing boundaries to freedom of expression has to be a painstaking effort, to avoid sliding down the slippery slope. I must, nevertheless, express reservations about the traditional British position which solely emphasizes the fear of provoking a breach of the peace. This reasoning comes close to *argument number one*. Indeed, looking at the way the British authorities have dealt with facist and racist demonstrations over the years, one can assume that this reasoning would have been invoked in order to ban a Skokie-like demonstration.[57] Thus it seems that the British approach is at variance to that adopted in the United States.

It did not, however, confer any powers to ban demonstrations or meetings by racialist organizations. It should also be said that prosecutions for incitement to racial hatred require the consent of the Attorney-General.

[53] A number of speakers in Parliament justified the legislation prohibiting racist expressions on the grounds of the fear, alarm and distress caused to members of minority groups. Cf. W. J. Wolffe, 'Values in conflict: incitement to racial hatred and the Public Order Act 1986', *Public Law* (1987), p. 94.

[54] Cf. *Parkin v. Norman* (1982) 3 W.L.R. 523.

[55] Cf. part III, 'Racial Hatred'. According to the Attorney General fifteen prosecutions for incitement to racial hatred have been brought between March 1986 and November 1990 under part III of the 1986 Act, or under section 5A of the 1936 Act, (180 *Parliamentary Debates*, 1990–1, p. 88W).

[56] Fifth Report of the Home Affairs Committee of the House of Commons 1979–80, HC 756, para 51. Cf. Barendt, *Freedom of Speech*, p. 198.

[57] In 1948 the Home Secretary invoked the Public Order Act to ban all political marches in London for three months after the Fascists marched through Jewish areas of London. The same reaction reoccurred in the 1970s after the National Front decided to march through immigrant areas.

In Britain, unlike the United States, there is no guaranteed right to demonstrate. The view is that public processions and *peaceful* demonstrations are lawful.[58] Accordingly, a procession may only be banned on the ground that it is likely to cause 'serious public disorder'.[59] Here lies my disagreement with the British stance. The apprehension of serious public disorder should not be the sole ground for the prohibition of processions and assemblies.[60] The British authorities considered the Offence Principle in the Green Paper of 1980 and the White Paper of 1985 and rejected it on both occasions.[61]

One additional comment has to be made before formulating our argument under the Offence Principle. Among the justifications voiced for the *Skokie* decision was the contention that if the Nazis were denied free expression, this would jeopardize the entire structure of free speech rights. To permit Skokie to ban this speech because of its offensiveness would mean that Southern whites could ban civil rights marches, especially those that are held by blacks.[62] Let us assume that it is plausible to argue that the degree of irritation resulting in this case amounted to psychological offence. Then Southern whites could claim that these demonstrators acted in a manner which they found to be seriously offensive: that they maliciously, recklessly or negligently disregarded their interest in not being harmed by seriously offensive actions, such as marching in 'their' territory; that the corollary of these marches was severe injury of those whites who were offended.

The Offence Principle, however, is intended as protection against the abuse of freedom by those who deny respect for others. It is not to assist those whose motivation is to cause harm to others, whose aim is either to intimidate or to discriminate and to deny rights to others.[63] There is a set of values that underlie a liberal society and we judge in accordance with it. The fact that some individuals are offended by a speech which advocates equal rights is not sufficient reason for

---

[58] Note that international treaties speak of 'the right to freedom of *peaceful* assembly' (emphasis mine). Cf. Article 11 of the *European Convention of Human Rights*; Article 20 of the *Universal Declaration of Human Rights*; and Article 21 of the *UN International Covenant on Civil and Political Rights*.

[59] Home Office, *Review of Public Order Law*, Cmmd. 9510 (White Paper). May 1985, pp. 23–4.

[60] It may be of interest to note that part II of the Public Order Act 1986 speaks of imposing conditions on public processions, holding that if a senior police officer reasonably believes that the procession in question 'may result in serious public disorder, serious damage to property or *serious disruption to the life of the community* . . . he may give directions imposing on the persons organising or taking part in the procession such conditions as appear to him necessary to prevent such disorder, damage, disruption or intimidation' (sect. 12, emphasis mine). The courts, it seems, interpret the above as being in line with the 'breach of the peace' reasoning.

[61] Cf. Home Office, *Review of Public Order Act 1936* (The Green Paper), April 1980, esp. pp. 11–2, and Home Office, *Review of Public Order Law* (The White Paper), May 1985, esp. p. 23. In both papers it was reiterated that considerations of public order were the sole test for banning of processions. For my part, I do not see why in delicate or (if we resort to familiar phraseology) 'hard' cases – such as Skokie – it has to be left for the police to decide whether or not to allow the demonstration in question. Moreover, this reasoning does not fully consider the extent of harm that is inflicted upon the target group which cannot avoid being exposed to the offensive utterances.

[62] Bollinger, *The Tolerant Society*, p. 34. In the same vein, Aryeh Neier (*Defending My Enemy*, p. 142) rightly contends that speakers characteristically carry their messages to places where their views are anathema. He, however, fails to distinguish incidents of protest from demonstrations aiming to offend a specific target group, who cannot avoid being exposed to it.

[63] By discrimination is meant 'any distinction, exclusion, restriction or preference based on race, colour, descent, or national or ethnic origin which has the purpose or effect of nullifying or impairing the recognition, enjoyment or exercise, on an equal footing, of human rights and fundamental freedoms in the political, economic, social, cultural or any other field of public life'. Cf. *International Convention on the Elimination of All Forms of Racial Discrimination*, Article 1 (1).

⊹ Political Studies Association 1993

its restriction. The Principle affects freedom of expression when the speech in question contradicts fundamental background rights to human dignity and to equality of concern and respect.[54] Otherwise, every speech which some might find psychologically offensive may be curtailed. Members of the civil rights movement who come to demonstrate in the Southern United States do not deny the rights of any group of people. In contrast to the Nazis in Skokie, they are not deliberately setting out to upset Southern whites. The intentions of the civil rights marchers are not to offend but rather to protect the rights of those who are discriminated against by those who now claim that they are being offended. The right to freedom of speech is here exercised out of respect for others, aiming to preach values that are in accordance with the moral codes of a liberal society, not values which deny these accepted moral codes. Those who are offended by the values adopted by the entire society implicitly argue when wishing to prevent the demonstration that their problem is not with the march as such. Rather, their problem is a matter of principle which concerns their own place within a liberal society.

Hence, we may suggest four major elements to be taken into account when we come to restrict expression on the grounds of psychological offence: the content of the expression; the tenor and the manner of the expression; the intentions and the motive of the speaker; and the objective circumstances in which the advocacy is to take place. Accordingly we can now lay down our second qualification of free speech. This restriction is made under the Offence Principle. The argument is:

> *Argument number two*: Under the Offence Principle, when the content and/or manner of a certain speech is are designed to cause psychological offence to a target group, and the objective circumstances are such that make the target group inescapably exposed to that offence, then the speech in question should be restricted. Notice that this argument differs from my reconstruction of the Millian Harm Principle in two crucial respects: it covers damage that is not physical, and it restricts certain types of speeches that fall within the category of 'advocacy', as distinguished from 'instigation'.

To sum up, we ought not to tolerate every speech, whatever it might be, for then we elevate the value of freedom of expression, and indeed, of tolerance, over other values which are of no less importance, such as human dignity and equality of concern and respect. Tolerance which conceives the right to freedom of expression as *carte blanche* allowing any speech, in any circumstances, might be counter productive, assisting the flourishing of anti-tolerant opinions and movements.[65] Therefore, we have to be aware of the dangers of words, and restrict certain forms of expression which lead to harmful, discriminatory actions; for words, to a great extent, are prescriptions for actions.

---

[54] R. M. Dworkin, *Taking Rights Seriously*, 1977, pp. 266–78; 'Liberalism', in *A Matter of Principle*, 1985, pp. 181–204.

[65] A similar line of reasoning guided the framers of the European Convention on Human Rights when they enacted Articles 9, 10 and 17. Notice in particular the language of Article 17: 'Nothing in this Convention may be interpreted as implying for any State, group or person any right to engage in any activity or perform any act aimed at the destruction of any of the rights and freedoms set forth herein or at their limitation to a greater extent than is provided for in the Convention'. A case in point concerning the right to freedom of expression in general and freedom of expression in the context of elections in particular is *Glimmerveen and Hagenbeek v the Netherlands* (1980) 18 *Decisions and Reports*, E. Comm. H. R., pp. 187–208.

© Political Studies Association, 1993

In 1990 the French National Assembly passed new laws to toughen the existing measures against racism. At the time people were in an uproar over the desecration of Jewish graves, and the newspapers were full of concern about France's extremist right wing and the revival of anti-Semitism in Europe and the Soviet Union. So the new legislation surprised no one. But there was something disturbing in it, passed over incidentally, as though hardly worth mentioning, in newspaper accounts like this one: "The measures also outlaw 'revisionism'—a historical tendency rife among extreme right-wing activists which consists of questioning the truth of the Jewish Holocaust in World War II."

Taken by itself, the French action was a curious and vaguely troubling incident, but little more. But the French action could not be taken by itself. It was part of a pattern.

In Australia the New South Wales parliament amended the Anti-Discrimination Act in 1989 to ban public racial vilification. Since most people are against racial vilification, most could sympathize with the legislature's intentions. But it was hard to be enthusiastic about the mechanism. Reports Tony Katsigiannis in the Australian magazine *Policy*: "The law invests in the Anti-Discrimination Board the power to determine whether a report is 'fair,' and whether a discussion is 'reasonable,' 'in good faith,' and 'in the public interest.' The Board will pronounce upon the acceptability of artistic expression, research papers, academic controversy, and scientific questions. An unfair (i.e., inaccurate) report of a public act may expose the reporter and the publisher to damages of up to $40,000."

In Denmark the national civil-rights law forbids "threatening, humiliating, or degrading" someone in public on the basis of race, religion, ethnic background, or sexual orientation. When a woman wrote letters to a newspaper calling the national domestic-partnership law "ungodly" and homosexuality "the ugliest kind of adultery," she and the editor who published her letters were targeted for prosecution.

In Canada a reputable research psychologist named Jean Philippe Rushton presented a paper in 1989 in which he looked at three very broad racial groups and hypothesized that, on average, blacks' reproductive strategy tends to emphasize high birth rates, Asians' tends toward intensive parental nurturing, and whites' tends to fall in between. The man was vilified in the press, he was denounced on national television (to his face) as a neo-Nazi, and his graduate students were advised to find a new mentor. That was not all. The Ontario provincial police promptly launched a six-month investigation of Rushton under Canada's hate-speech prohibition. They questioned his colleagues, demanded tapes of his debates and media appearances,

and so on. "The provincial police officially assessed the question of whether Rushton might be subject to two years in prison for such actions as 'using questionable source data.' " In the end, the attorney general decided not to prosecute and settled for denouncing Rushton's ideas as "loony."

So it goes in France, Australia, Denmark, Canada—and the United States. The U.S. Constitution, however, makes government regulation of upsetting talk difficult, so in America the movement against hurtful speech has been primarily moral rather than legal, and nongovernmental institutions, especially colleges and universities, have taken the lead. All around the country, universities have set up anti-harassment rules prohibiting, and establishing punishments for, "speech or other expression" (this is from Stanford's policy, adopted in 1990 and more or less representative) that "is intended to insult or stigmatize an individual or a small number of individuals on the basis of their sex, race, color, handicap, religion, sexual orientation or national and ethnic origin."

One case generated a lawsuit in the federal courts, which eventually struck down the rule in question. At the University of Michigan, a student said in a classroom discussion that he considered homosexuality a disease treatable with therapy. Now, as of this writing the evidence is abundant that the student's hypothesis is wrong, and any gay man or woman in America can attest to the harm that this particular hypothesis has inflicted over the years. But people at Michigan went further than to refute the student or ignore him. They summoned him to a formal disciplinary hearing for violating the school's policy prohibiting speech that "victimizes" people on the basis of "sexual orientation."

Such cases have drawn their share of outrage from civil libertarians. To understand these incidents as raising only civil-liberties issues, however, is to miss the bigger point. A very dangerous principle is now being established as a social right: Thou shalt not hurt others with words. This principle is a menace—and not just to civil liberties. At bottom it threatens liberal inquiry—that is, science itself.

THE HUMANITARIAN THREAT TO FREE INQUIRY

By Jonathan Rauch

On May 10, 1989, the Nashville *Tennessean* reported that George Darden, a city councilman, had filed a resolution asking the city to build a landing pad for unidentified flying objects. "What it was," he said, "people were reporting all these strange creatures coming to town, and they have nowhere to land." He said that he had never seen the creatures himself but that he was "very serious." He wanted to know, "When people see them, do you want to just cast them off as a lunatic?"

295

George Darden was no clown. He was raising nothing less than what philosophers refer to as the problem of knowledge: What is the right standard for distinguishing the few true beliefs from the many false ones? And who should set that standard? Everybody laughed at Darden—but he deserves an answer. To the central question of how to sort true beliefs from the "lunatic" ones, here are five answers, five decision-making principles—not the only ones by any means, but the most important contenders right now:

☛ The Fundamentalist Principle: Those who know the truth should decide who is right.

☛ The Simple Egalitarian Principle: All sincere persons' beliefs have equal claims to respect.

☛ The Radical Egalitarian Principle: Like the simple egalitarian principle, but the beliefs of persons in historically oppressed classes or groups get special consideration.

☛ The Humanitarian Principle: Any of the above, but with the condition that the first priority be to cause no hurt.

☛ The Liberal Principle: Checking of each by each through public criticism is the only legitimate way to decide who is right.

The last principle is the only one that is acceptable, but it is now losing ground to the others. Impelled by the notions that science is oppression and criticism is violence, the central regulation of debate and inquiry is returning to respectability—this time in a humanitarian disguise. The old principle of the Inquisition is being revived: People who hold wrong and hurtful opinions should be punished for the good of society. To see why, you have to look at fundamentals.

W e have standard labels for the liberal political and economic systems—democracy and capitalism. Oddly, however, we have no name for the liberal intellectual system, whose activities range from physics to history to journalism. I use the term "liberal science." The very need to invent a label for our public idea-sorting system speaks volumes about the system's success. Establishing the two basic rules on which liberal science is based required a social revolution; yet so effective have those rules been, and so beneficent, that most of us take them for granted. Put them into effect, and you have laid the groundwork for a knowledge-producing and dispute-resolving system that beats all competitors hands down. They are the basis of liberal inquiry and of science.

First, the skeptical rule: *No one gets the final say.* No idea, however wise and insightful its proponent, can ever have any claim to be exempt from criticism by anyone, no matter how

stupid and grubby-minded the critic. A statement is established as knowledge only if it can be debunked, in principle, and only insofar as it withstands attempts to debunk it.

This is, more or less, what the great 20th-century philosopher of science Karl R. Popper and his followers have called the principle of falsifiability. Science is distinctive not because it proves true statements but because it seeks systematically to disprove false ones. In practice, of course, it is sometimes hard, if not impossible, to say whether a given statement is falsifiable or not. But what counts is the way the rule directs us to try to *act.* If you do not try to check ideas by trying to debunk them, then you are not practicing science.

Second, the empirical rule: *No one has personal authority.* No one gets special say simply on the basis of who he happens to be. A statement is established as knowledge only if the method used to check it gives the same result regardless of the identity of the checker and regardless of the source of the statement. *Who* you are doesn't count; the rules apply to everybody, regardless of identity.

THE CENTRAL REGULATION OF DEBATE AND INQUIRY IS RETURNING TO RESPECTABILITY, THIS TIME IN A HUMANITARIAN DISGUISE.

"T he liberation of the human mind," H. L. Mencken once wrote, "has been best furthered by gay fellows who heaved dead cats into sanctuaries and then went roistering down the highways of the world, proving to all men that doubt, after all, was safe—that the god in the sanctuary was a fraud. One horse-laugh is worth ten thousand syllogisms."

Mencken stood in a great American tradition: a tradition of doubt and inquiry and rowdy reformulation of truth. "All of my work hangs together, once the main ideas under it are discerned," he said. "These ideas are chiefly of a skeptical character. I believe that nothing is unconditionally true, and hence I am opposed to every statement of positive truth and every man who states it." No final say—that was Mencken, down to the soles of his feet.

Americans have enough Menckenian instinct in their guts to be frightened by overt intellectual authoritarianism, even if they don't always precisely understand the nature of the threat. The war whoops of Khomeini and his raging supporters have awakened many snoozing Westerners to the fact that tens or hundreds of millions of people really do detest liberalism. At home, religious fundamentalism is a minority interest, not very powerful—weak enough, in fact, to be treated with arrogance and contempt by the intellectual establishment when it is worthy instead of respectful enmity.

Where religious true believers are concerned, we are pretty vigilant. The greater threat is embracing authoritarianism in the name of fairness and compassion. Having been at last rousted out of politics and economics by the disaster of communism, the authoritarian Rasputin has now come calling on liberal science, and he already has his foot in the door.

To begin with, I should be clear about what I mean by intellectual egalitarianism. In one sense, liberal science is as egalitarian as any system could be. Where the game of science is properly played, no one is granted personal authority simply because of who he happens to be—period. The rules apply to everybody. It is quite true that for most of history (and not just in the West) women, blacks, and others were denied equal access to the intellectual and scientific establishment, as they were denied equal access to so much else. But that represents not the failure of liberalism but the failure to embrace it. To renounce liberal science because the society in which it was embedded tended to shut out women is as silly as it would have been to renounce democracy in 1910 because women were not allowed to vote.

Science, when it works the way it is supposed to, is an equal-opportunity knowledge maker. But that is very different—radically, fundamentally different—from being an equal-*results* knowledge maker. Some people who understand the difference clamor for equal results—for instance, people on the political left who demand an equal place in the canon of knowledge for minority groups' points of view. Many more people, however, simply misunderstand. They don't realize that there is a wide gulf between equal access to a knowledge-making system and equal results. Their misunderstanding has the potential for grave consequences.

One of the most troubling examples of such misunderstanding is *Edwards v. Aguillard*, whose attack on intellectual liberalism was subscribed to by two justices of the U.S. Supreme Court. The state of Louisiana had passed a statute (the Balanced Treatment for Creation-Science and Evolution-Science in Public School Instruction Act) requiring that wherever in public schools the theory of evolution was taught, "scientific creationism" was to be taught along with it. The act did not require that either one be taught; only that if one was, so must be the other. The bill's sponsors felt that students were being indoctrinated with one (disputed) view of how humanity came to be. They thus demanded that the evidence on both sides be presented if the subject were to be broached. One state senator stressed that to teach religion in disguise was not his intent: "My intent is to see to it that our textbooks are not censored."

In 1987 the Supreme Court struck down the law as unconstitutional. But Justice Antonin Scalia, one of the brightest judges on the American bench, strongly dissented; he was joined by the chief justice, William Rehnquist. Scalia's dissent aimed straight at what liberal intellectual standards are all about. And it is a mark of the egalitarian fallacy's seductiveness that the conservative Scalia and the still more conservative Rehnquist tumbled right into bed with the left-wing people who say that to insist on science is to oppress minority traditions.

The question of constitutionality was central to the Court, but not to the egalitarian attack. What was central there was the background view of knowledge that informed Scalia's dissent: that the Louisiana legislature was seeking to ensure academic freedom, and that academic freedom could be advanced by requiring that evidence for all beliefs, or at least more than one, be presented. It is important to see that you could apply that argument to secular beliefs just as easily as to religious ones. If states began passing laws requiring equal time for astrology—and it's a wonder they haven't—Scalia's egalitarian view of knowledge would say they were doing the fair thing. Scalia said that the evidence for evolution was not conclusive, and that the law's supporters had presented testimony that creationism had scientific support. Therefore throwing out a state's attempt to give both sides a hearing, he said, was "illiberal." "In this case," he said, "it seems to me the Court's position is the repressive one."

That, of course, is just what the complaints from the left assert: The Western view of objective knowledge and the scientific order built upon it are both "repressive." The egalitarian line of thinking holds that since any standard for truth is biased and political, no one's standard should get special privileges, but rather all should be equal.

For instance, "The monocultural perspective of traditional American education *restricts the scope of knowledge*" (my italics). That is from the report by New York State's 1989 task force on minorities and education. The report continues, "It acts as a constraint on the critical thinking of African American, Asian American, Native American, and Puerto Rican/Latino youth because of its hidden assumptions of 'white supremacy' and 'white nationalism.'"

Only the particulars are left-wing. The charge itself—that "the monocultural perspective of traditional American education restricts the scope of knowledge"—could just as easily have come from the creationist right. The bill of particulars might just as easily have read, "It acts as a constraint on the critical thinking of American youth because of its hidden assumptions of 'Darwinist supremacy' and 'secular

TO REQUIRE "EQUAL TIME" FOR CREATIONISM IN THE NAME OF ACADEMIC FREEDOM IS TO MISCONSTRUE HOW LIBERAL INQUIRY WORKS.

humanism.' " Either way, the argument is the same: The establishment's view of what the "facts" are and how to find them has excluded someone, and the way to ensure intellectual freedom (broaden "the scope of knowledge") is to rewrite the texts so as to let that someone in. That the left-wing and right-wing intellectual egalitarians have so far failed to make common cause is a function merely of expediency, not principle.

On its face Scalia's argument is plausible, especially since it appeals to one of Americans' most laudable principles, namely the principle of political equality. There is no doubt that the argument is impelled by decency. But in fact it is very dangerous. It cuts out, with a surgeon's precision, the heart of a peculiar and subtle distinction on which all of Western intellectual life—I do not exaggerate—depends. That distinction is as follows: To believe incorrectly is never a crime, *but simply to believe is never to have knowledge.*

In liberal science, there is positively no right to have one's opinions, however heartfelt, taken seriously as knowledge. Just the contrary: Liberal science is nothing other than a selection process whose mission is to test beliefs and reject the ones that fail. A liberal intellectual regime says that if you want to believe the moon is made of green cheese, fine. But if you want your belief recognized as knowledge, there are things you must *do.* You must run your belief through the science game for checking. And if your belief is a loser, it will not be included in the science texts. It probably won't even be taken seriously by most respectable intellectuals. In a liberal society, knowledge is the rolling critical consensus of a decentralized community of checkers. That is so not by the power of law but by the deeper power of a common liberal morality.

And who decides what the critical consensus actually is? The critical society does, arguing about itself. That is why scholars spend so much time and energy "surveying the literature" (i.e., assessing the consensus so far). Then they argue about their assessments. The process is long and arduous, but there you are. Academic freedom would be trampled instead of advanced by, say, requiring that state-financed universities put creationists on their biology faculties or give Afrocentrists rebuttal space in their journals. When a state legislature or a curriculum committee or any other political body decrees that anything in particular is, or has equal claim to be, our knowl-· edge, it wrests control over truth from the liberal community of checkers and places it in the hands of central political authorities. And *that* is illiberal.

IF YOU WANT TO BELIEVE THE MOON IS MADE OF GREEN CHEESE, FINE. BUT TO HAVE YOUR BELIEF ACCEPTED AS KNOWLEDGE, THERE ARE CERTAIN THINGS YOU MUST DO.

Intellectual liberalism is not intellectual majoritarianism or egalitarianism. You do not have a claim to knowledge either because 51 percent of the public agrees with you or because your "group" was historically left out; you have a claim to knowledge only to the extent that your opinion still stands up after prolonged exposure to withering public testing. Now, it is true that when we talk about knowledge being a scientific consensus we are talking about a majority of scientists. But we are not talking about a mere majority. For a theory to go into a textbook as knowledge, it does not need the unanimity of checkers' assent, but it does need far more than a bare majority's. It should be generally recognized as having stood up better than any competitor to most of the tests that various critical debunkers have tried.

Today it is possible that a majority of climatologists believe that global warming is a fact (one can't say for sure, since scientists don't vote on these things), but global warming is far from well enough established to be presented as fact in textbooks. The point extends beyond natural science. The critical consensus of historians is that many minority groups did not make much of a contribution to the writing of the Constitution. Attempts to find a role for them and install them in the textbooks may make some people feel better. But it would betray the community of critical checkers. It would also lead to factional warfare as other political groups took up the cry and demanded *their* share.

For various minorities, the answer is to do just what many black and feminist historians are doing, namely to propose new hypotheses about the role of, say, blacks and women in American history. But only after those hypotheses have stood up to extensive checking, only after each has convinced each, is it time to rewrite the texts.

Further, only after an idea has survived checking is it deserving of respect. Not long ago, I heard an activist say at a public meeting that her opinion deserved at least respect. The audience gave her a big round of applause. But she and they had it backwards. Respect was the most, not the least, that she could have demanded for her opinion. Except insofar as an opinion earns its stripes in the science game, it is entitled to no respect whatever. This point matters, because respectability is the coin in which liberal science rewards ideas that are duly put up for checking and pass the test. That is why it is so important that creationists and alien-watchers and radical Afrocentrists and white supremacists be granted every entitlement to speak but no entitlement to have their opinions respected.

Liberal science cannot exert discipline if it cannot drive unsupported or bogus beliefs from the agenda by marginalizing them. When you pass laws requiring equal time for

298

somebody's excluded belief, you effectively make marginalization illegal. You say, "In our society, a belief is respectable—and will be taught and treated respectfully—if the politically powerful say it is."

Once you have said that, you face a very stark choice. You can open the textbooks only to those "oppressed" beliefs whose proponents have political pull. Or you can take the principled egalitarian position, and open the books and the schools to *all* sincere beliefs. If you do the former, then you have replaced science with power politics. If you do the latter, then you have no principled choice but to teach, for example, "Holocaust revisionism" as an "alternative theory" held by an "excluded minority"—which means, in practice, not teaching 20th-century history at all. Either way, you have taken in hand silly and even execrable opinions and ushered them from the fringes of debate to the very center. At a single stroke, you have disabled liberal society's mechanism for marginalizing foolish ideas, and you have sent those ideas straight to the top of the social agenda with a safe-conduct pass.

As knowledge-making regimes go, nothing is as successful or as respectful of diversity or as humane as liberal science. The trouble is that liberal science often does not look very humane. It uses sticks as well as carrots. The carrots are the respectability, frequent use, and public credit that it bestows on the opinions that it validates; the sticks are the disrespect and the silent treatment that it inflicts on the opinions that fail. Those sticks are nonviolent, true. But it is unconscionable not to acknowledge that denying respectability is a very serious matter indeed. It causes pain and outrage—outrage to which Scalia's humane impulses reached out in *Edwards v. Aguillard*. Here is where the door opens to the most formidable attack on liberal science—the humanitarian attack.

"Well," goes the argument, "we must, it appears, have intellectual standards. But what should our standards be? Obviously it is desirable to have standards that minimize pain. And a lot of beliefs cause pain. Racist beliefs cause pain. Anti-Semitic and sexist and homophobic beliefs cause pain. So do anti-American and anti-religious beliefs. If we're going to have a social system for weeding out beliefs, it should start by weeding out beliefs that cause pain. Intellectuals should be like doctors. They should first do no harm."

The empathetic spirit from which that line of thinking springs is admirable. But the principle to which it leads is nothing but dreadful. The right principle, and the only one consonant with liberal science, is: Cause no pain solely in order

BY ITS OWN LIGHTS THE INQUISITION WAS A HUMANITARIAN ACTION, SINCE HERETICS THREATENED PEACE, STABILITY, AND OTHER PEOPLE'S SOULS.

to hurt. The wrong principle, but the one that has increasingly taken the place of the right one, is: Allow no pain to be caused.

The social system does not and never can exist that allows no harm to come to anybody. Conflict of impulse and desire is an inescapable fact of human existence, and where there is conflict there will always be losers and wounds. Utopian systems premised on a world of loving harmony—communism, for instance—fail because in the attempt to obliterate conflict they obliterate freedom. The chore of a social regime is not to obliterate conflict but to manage it, so as to put it to good use while causing a minimum of hurt and abuse.

Liberal systems, although far from perfect, have at least two great advantages: They can channel conflict rather than obliterate it, and they give a certain degree of protection from centrally administered abuse. The liberal intellectual system is no exception. It causes pain to people whose views are criticized, still more to those whose views fail to check out and so are rejected. But there are two important consolations. First, no one gets to run the system to his own advantage or stay in charge for long. Whatever you can do to me, I can do to you. Those who are criticized may give as good as they get. Second, the books are never closed, and the game is never over. Sometimes rejected ideas (continental drift, for one) make sensational comebacks.

Humanitarians, though, remain unsatisfied. Their hope, which is no less appealing for being futile, is that somehow the harm can be prevented in the first place. Their worry is that the harm may emanate in two directions, one social and the other individual.

Social harm accrues to society as a whole from the spread of bad ideas; held to be especially vulnerable are minorities or groups seen as lacking power. "AIDS comes from homosexuals," "Jews fabricated the Holocaust," "blacks are less intelligent than whites"—those ideas and others like them can do real mischief.

Though the special concern for minorities as groups is a new twist, this argument is an old and highly principled one. It was used, in all good conscience, by the Inquisition. The heretic, in those days, endangered the peace and stability of the whole society by challenging the rightful authority of the church. The Inquisition was a policing action. But by its own lights it was a humanitarian action, too. The heretic endangered the faith of believers and so threatened to drag others with him to an eternity of suffering in perdition; not least of all, he threw away his own soul. To allow such a person to destroy souls seemed at least as indecent as allowing racist hate speech seems today.

Humane motives, however, could not save the Inquisition from the same problem that faces humanitarians today: Although allowing mistakes is risky, suppressing them is much riskier, because then a "mistake" becomes whatever it is that the authorities don't like to hear. Suppressing offensiveness, too, comes at a high cost, since offensiveness is not the same thing as wrongness—often just the contrary. Sometimes patently "offensive" verbiage turns out to be telling the unpopular truth. "All the durable truths that have come into the world within historic times," said Mencken, "have been opposed as bitterly as if they were so many waves of smallpox."

The other, and much newer, strand of intellectual humanitarianism is intuitively more appealing and emotionally harder to resist. It says that wrongheaded opinions and harsh words are hurtful to *individuals*. And here liberal science has been put squarely on the defensive, for the first time in more than 100 years; for here you have, not the cold-blooded public censor raising bureaucratic objections on behalf of "society," but an identifiable person saying "*I* am hurt" and speaking for his own dignity. In today's world the second kind of claim, like all human-rights claims, seems compelling. Facing it means owning up to the truth about knowledge and about the system that best produces it.

So let us be frank, once and for all: Creating knowledge is painful, for the same reason that it can also be exhilarating. Knowledge does not come free to any of us; we have to suffer for it. We have to stand naked before the court of critical checkers and watch our most cherished beliefs come under fire. Sometimes we have to watch while our notion of evident truth gets tossed in the gutter. Sometimes we feel we are treated rudely, even viciously. As others prod and test and criticize our ideas, we feel angry, hurt, embarrassed.

We would all like to think that knowledge could be separated from hurt. We would all like to think that painful but useful and thus "legitimate" criticism is objectively distinguishable from criticism that is merely ugly and hurtful. But the fact is that even the most "scientific" criticism can be horribly hurtful, devastatingly so. The physicist Ludwig Boltzmann was so depressed by the harshness of F. W. Ostwald's and Ernst Mach's attacks on his ideas that he committed suicide.

In the pursuit of knowledge many people—probably most of us at one time or another—will be hurt, and this is a reality that no amount of wishing or regulating can ever change. It is

IT'S CLEAR WHAT COMES AFTER "OFFENSIVE WORDS ARE BULLETS": YOU HURT ME WITH WORDS, I REPLY WITH BULLETS.

not good to offend people, but it is necessary. A no-offense society is a no-knowledge society.

And what should we require be done to assuage the feelings of people who have been offended, to recompense them for their hurt and punish their tormentors? This and only this: *absolutely nothing.* Nothing at all.

The standard answer to people who say they are offended should be: "Is there any casualty other than your feelings? Are you or others being threatened with violence or vandalism? No? Then it's a shame your feelings are hurt, but that's too bad. You'll live." If one is going to enjoy the benefits of living in a liberal society without being shamelessly hypocritical, one must try to be thick-skinned.

The alternative is to reward people for being upset. And as soon as people learn they can get something if they raise Cain about being offended, they go into the business of professional offendedness. If that sounds callous, remember that the establishment of a right not to be offended would lead not to a more civil culture but to a lot of shouting matches over who was being offensive to whom, and who could claim to be more offended. All we will do that way is to shut ourselves up.

In one sense the rise of intellectual humanitarianism represents an advance of honesty: It drops the pretense that liberal science is a painless and purely mechanistic process, like doing crossword puzzles. But the conclusion that the humanitarians draw—that the hurting must be stopped—is all wrong. Impelling them toward their wrong conclusion is a dreadful error: the notion that hurtful words are a form of violence.

Offensive speech hurts, say the humanitarians. It constitutes "words that wound" (writes one law professor); it does "real harm to real people" who deserve protection and redress (writes another law professor). When a law student at Georgetown University published an article charging that the academic credentials of white and black students accepted at Georgetown were "dramatically unequal," a number of students demanded that the writer be punished. And note carefully the terms of the condemnation: "I think the article is assaultive. People were injured. I think that kind of speech is outrageous." The notion of "assaultive speech" is no rarity today. A University of Michigan law professor said: "To me, racial epithets are not speech. They are bullets."

This, finally, is where the humanitarian line leads: to the erasure of the distinction, in principle and ultimately also in practice, between discussion and bloodshed. You do not have to be a genius to see what comes after "offensive words are bullets": If you hurt me with words, I reply with bullets, and the exchange is even. Words are bullets; fair is fair.

In February 1989 fundamentalist Moslems rose up against the British writer Salman Rushdie, who had written a novel they regarded as deeply, shockingly offensive to Islam's holy truths and to the Moslem community. As they understood it, the novel implied that Mohammed had made up the Koran, an outrageous (to them) slander against their holy book's divine origin. The novel fantasized about a whorehouse where each whore takes on the name, even the personality, of one of Mohammed's wives. It suggested that Mohammed might have bent his divine inspirations to suit his political needs or even his convenience. It referred to him as "Mahound." This is what they saw.

The Ayatollah Ruhollah Khomeini proclaimed it the duty of all good Moslems to kill Salman Rushdie: "It is incumbent on every Moslem to employ everything he has got, his life and his wealth, to send him to hell." Rushdie went underground. "I feel as if I have been plunged, like Alice, into the world beyond the looking glass," he wrote a year later, "where nonsense is the only available sense. And I wonder if I'll ever be able to climb back through."

The attack itself was not so very singular; fundamentalists have made a hobby of harassing the unorthodox for centuries. The surprise was that the reply from the liberal democracies was muttered and utterly incoherent. A long week of silence passed before President George Bush got around to saying, unimpressively, that the death threat was "deeply offensive."

In the end the Rushdie affair showed us graphically two things, one that we already knew and one that we did not know at all. What we already knew was that fundamentalism—and not just religious fundamentalism but any fundamentalist system for settling differences of opinion—is the enemy of free thought. More frightening was what we had not known: Western intellectuals did not have a clear answer to the challenge that Khomeini set before them.

This challenge was twofold (at least). First, it was a restatement of the creationists' challenge, the angry outsiders' cry from the heart: "Who gave you, the arrogant West, the right to make the rules? You are imperialists with your view of truth, with your insistence on the intellectual ways of secularism and of science. How dare you flout and mock our view of truth?"

The point was noted at the time. What was not so widely noted was the second dimension of Khomeini's challenge: the humanitarian dimension. This is not to say that Khomeini was a humanitarian, only that the argument that his supporters commonly made was humanitarian in principle: "You have *hurt* us with these evil words, these impious words, disrespectfully and needlessly written in utter disregard of Moslem sensibili-

ties. You have caused pain and offense to many people. And this you have no right to do."

Liberals will never be able to answer these complaints honestly or consistently until we grit our teeth and admit the truth. Yes, Rushdie's words caused many people anger and pain. *And that is all right.* But no such honest admission was forthcoming. People often did not seem even to know what it was—free speech? science? religious liberty? nonviolence? respect for other cultures?—that they were defending. A lot of people seemed to have the impression that the Western intellectual system is a kind of anything-goes pluralism in which all ways of believing are created equal and the only rule is: "Be nice."

"Well," quite a few people said apologetically at the time of the Rushdie incident, "for Khomeini to have ordered Rushdie's death was of course bad, and he shouldn't have done that, but Rushdie certainly did write a book that was offensive to Islamic truths, and he shouldn't have done that, either." The chief rabbi of Great Britain said that the book should not have been published: "Both Mr. Rushdie and the Ayatollah have abused freedom of speech."

The Rushdie affair was a defining moment. It showed how readily Westerners could be backed away from a fundamental principle of intellectual liberalism, namely that there is nothing whatever wrong with offending—hurting people's feelings—in pursuit of truth.

The credo of liberal science imposes upon each of us two moral obligations: to allow everybody to err and criticize, even obnoxiously, and to submit everybody's beliefs—including our own—to public checking before claiming that they deserve to be accepted as knowledge. Today, activists and moralists are assailing both halves of the creed. They are assailing the right to err and criticize, when the error seems outrageous or the criticism seems hurtful; they are assailing the requirement for public checking, when the result is to reject someone's belief. They have a right to pursue their attack (nonviolently), but they, and we, should understand that they are enemies of science itself, and even, ultimately, of freedom of thought. And those of us who hold sacred the right to err and the duty to check need to understand that our defense of liberal science must preach not only toleration but discipline: the hard self-discipline that requires us to live with offense. ⌐

Jonathan Rauch is a contributing editor of National Journal. *This article is excerpted from* Kindly Inquisitors: The New Attacks on Free Thought, *a Cato Institute book to be published this month by the University of Chicago Press. By arrangement with the University of Chicago Press. Copyright © 1993 by the Cato Institute.*

WHEN YOU PASS LAWS REQUIRING EQUAL TIME FOR SOMEONE'S EXCLUDED BELIEF, YOU ELIMINATE THE INTELLECTUAL DISCIPLINE IMPOSED BY MARGINALIZATION.

THE NEW REPUBLIC

SEPTEMBER 20 AND 27, 1993

LET THEM TALK: WHY CIVIL LIBERTIES POSE NO THREAT TO CIVIL RIGHTS

HENRY LOUIS GATES JR. *

I.

"As a thumbnail summary of the last two or three decades of speech issues in the Supreme Court," the great First Amendment scholar Harry Kalven Jr. wrote in 1965 in *The Negro and the First Amendment*, "we may come to see the Negro as winning back for us the freedoms the Communists seemed to have lost for us." Surveying the legal scene in the heyday of the civil rights era, Kalven was confident that civil rights and civil liberties were marching in unison; that their mutual expansion represented, for a nation in a time of tumult, an intertwined destiny. He might have been surprised had he lived to witness the shifting nature of their relations. Today the partnership named in the title of his classic book seems hopelessly in disrepair. Civil liberties are regarded by many as a chief obstacle to civil rights. To be sure, blacks are still on the front lines of First Amendment jurisprudence—but this time we soldier on the other side. The byword among many black activists and black intellectuals is no longer the political imperative to protect free speech; it is the moral imperative to suppress "hate speech."

Like such phrases as "pro-choice" and "pro-life," the phrase "hate speech" is ideology in spansule form. It is the term-of-art of a movement, most active on college campuses and in liberal municipalities, that has caused many civil rights activists to rethink their allegiance to the First Amendment, the very amendment that licensed the protests, the rallies, the organization and the agitation that galvanized the nation in a recent, bygone era. Addressing the concerns of a very different time, the hate speech movement has enlisted the energies of some of our most engaged and interesting legal scholars. The result has been the proliferation of campus speech codes as well as municipal statutes enhancing penalties for bias crimes.

No less important, however, is the opportunity that this movement has provided, for those outside it, to clarify and to

---

* HENRY LOUIS GATES JR. is W.E.B. Du Bois Professor of the Humanities at Harvard University and co-editor of *Transition*. Reviewing Mari J. Matsuda, Charles R. Lawrence III, Richard Delgado and Kimberlè Williams Crenshaw, *Words That Wound: Critical Race Theory, Assaultive Speech and the First Amendment*.

rethink the meaning of their commitment to the freedom of expression. It is an opportunity, I must say, that we have miserably bungled. Content with soundbites and one-liners, our deliberations on the subject have had all the heft of a talk-show monologue. Free speech? You get what you pay for.

The irony that lurks behind this debate, of course, is that the First Amendment may be the central article of faith in the civil religion of America, if America has a civic religion. "It's a free country," we say, and shrug; and what we usually mean is that you can say what you please. "Sticks and stones can break my bones," we are taught to chant as children, "but words can never hurt me." As Catharine MacKinnon writes with some asperity in *Only Words*, her new book, Americans

> are taught this view by about the fourth grade, and continue to absorb it through osmosis from everything around them for the rest of their lives . . . to the point that those who embrace it think it is their own personal faith, their own original view, and trot it out like something learned from their own personal lives every time a problem is denominated one of "speech," whether it really fits or not.

The strongest argument for regulating hate speech is the unreflective stupidity of most of the arguments for the other side. I do not refer to the debate as it has proceeded in the law reviews, where you find a quality of caution, clarity and tentativeness that has made few inroads into the larger public discourse; the law professors who offer the best analysis of public discourse exert very little influence on it. And this leaves us with a familiar stale-

mate. On the one side are those who speak of "hate speech," a phrase that alludes to an argument instead of making it; and to insist on probing further is to admit that you "just don't get it." On the other side are those who invoke the First Amendment like a mantra and seem immediately to fall into a trance, so oblivious are they to further discussion and evidence. A small number of anecdotes, about racism on campus or about P.C. inquisitions on campus, are endlessly recycled, and a University of Pennsylvania undergraduate named Eden Jacobowitz, of "water buffalo" fame, becomes a Dreyfus *de nos jours*.

There is also a practical reason to worry about the impoverishment of the national discourse on free speech. If we keep losing the arguments, then we may slowly lose the liberties that they were meant to defend. We may come to think that the bad arguments are the only arguments, and when someone finally disabuses us of them, we may switch sides without ever considering the better arguments for staying put. That is why, for all the pleasures of demonology, the burgeoning literature urging the regulation of racist speech has a serious claim on our attention.

Now Westview Press has conveniently collected the three most widely cited and influential papers making the case for the regulation of racist speech. (The collection also includes a provocative essay by Kimberlè Williams Crenshaw about the conflicting allegiances posed by race and gender.) Gathered together for the first time, these essays—which originally appeared in law reviews over the past several years, and were circulated more widely through the samizdat of the photocopier—complement each other surprisingly well. Their proximity to each other casts light on their strengths and their weaknesses.

The authors of these proposals are "minority" law professors who teach at mainstream institutions—Mari J. Matsuda and Charles R. Lawrence III at Georgetown and Richard Delgado at the University of Colorado. They write vigorous and accessible prose. They are, one can fairly say, the legal eagles of the crusade against racist hate speech. But they are also, as the subtitle of their collection suggests, the principal architects of critical race theory, which is one of the most widely discussed trends in the contemporary legal academy; and their jointly written introduction to the volume serves as the clearest manifesto that the movement has yet received.

Critical race theory, we learn, owes its "social origins" to a student boycott of a Harvard Law School course in 1981. The course was called "Race, Racism and American Law," and the university failed to accede to student demands that it be taught by a person of color. Organizing an informal alternative course, students invited lawyers and law professors of color to lecture weekly on the topic. Crenshaw was one of the student organizers of the alternative course, Matsuda was one of its participants and Delgado and Lawrence were among its guest lecturers. And thus was formed the nucleus of "a small but growing group of scholars committed to finding new ways to think about and act in pursuit of racial justice."

The intellectual ancestry of the movement is more complicated, but its two main progenitors are the brand of feminist theory associated with MacKinnon and the radical skepticism toward traditional blackletter pieties associated with critical legal studies. Almost invariably, the literature arguing for hate speech regulation cites MacKinnon as an authority and a model, and takes on one or more of the traditional legal distinctions (such as the distinction between "private" and "public") whose dismantling is a staple of critical legal studies. So it is no surprise that conservative pundits denounce these theorists of hate speech as faddish foes of freedom. In fact, one could more accurately describe their approach as neotraditional. And those conservatives who dream of turning the cultural clock back to the '50s should realize that the First Amendment law of those years is precisely what these supposedly faddish scholars wish to revive.

For the conventional lay defense of free speech absolutism, and its concomitant attack on those who would curtail free speech, suffers from a bad case of historical amnesia. Just as Samuel Johnson thought he could refute Bishop Berkeley just by kicking a stone, the armchair absolutists often think that they can win the debate just by adducing the authority of the First Amendment itself. The invocation is generally folded together with a vague sort of historical argument. The First Amendment, we are told, has stood us in good stead through more than two centuries; and our greatness as a society may depend on it. The framers of the Constitution knew what they were doing, and (this is directed to those inclined to bog down in interpretative quibbles) in the end the First Amendment means what it says.

The only flaw of this uplifting and well-rehearsed argument is that it is false. Indeed, the notion that the First Amendment has been a historical mainstay of American liberty is an exemplary instance of invented tradition. To begin with, the First Amendment was not conceived as a protection of the free speech of citizens until 1931. Before then, the Court took the amendment at its word: "*Congress* shall make no law . . . ." Congress could not; but states and municipalities could do what they liked. And so it is no surprise that once the Supreme Court recognized freedom of expression as a right held by citizens, the interpretation of its scope still remained quite narrow. This changed after World War II, when the Warren Court gradually ushered in a more generous vision of civil liberties. So the expansive ethic that we call the First Amendment, the eternal verity that people either celebrate or bemoan, is really only a few decades old.

But the hate speech movement is not content with rehearsing the weaknesses in the absolutist position. It has also aligned itself with earlier traditions of jurisprudence—here the movement's atavism is most obvious—by showing that the sort of speech it wishes to restrict falls into two expressive categories that the Supreme Court has previously held (and, the advocates of restrictions argue, correctly held) to be undeserving of First Amendment protection. The categories are those of "fighting words" and group defamation, as exemplified by cases decided in 1942 and 1952.

The doctrine of "fighting words" was promulgated by the Supreme Court in *Chaplinsky v. New Hampshire* (1942), in which the Court held that the Constitution did not protect "insulting or 'fighting' words—those that by their very utterance inflict injury or tend to incite an immediate breach of the peace." "Such utterances are no essential part of any exposition of ideas," Justice Murphy wrote for the majority, "and are of such slight social value as a step to truth that any benefit that may be derived from them is clearly outweighed by the social interest in order and morality." Those who would regulate hate speech argue that racist abuse is a variety of, or "functionally equivalent to," the sort of

language that the *Chaplinsky* decision declared to be unprotected; indeed, the carefully drafted speech code adopted by Stanford University in 1990 explicitly extends only to "fighting words" or symbols, thus wearing its claim to constitutionality on its face. If *Chaplinsky* can shoulder the legal and ethical burdens placed upon it, the regulationists have a powerful weapon on their side.

Can it? Probably not. To begin with, it is an open question whether *Chaplinsky* remains, as they say, "good law." For the Supreme Court, in the fifty years since *Chaplinsky*, has never once affirmed a conviction for uttering either "fighting words" or words that "by their very utterance inflict injury." Indeed, in part because of this functional desuetude, in part because of the supposed male bias of the "breach of the peace" prong (men being more likely than women to throw a punch), the editors of the *Harvard Law Review* recently issued a call for the doctrine's explicit interment. So much for the doctrine's judicial value.

The young scholars at the *Harvard Law Review* also note, with others, that statutes prohibiting "fighting words" have had discriminatory effects. An apparently not atypical conviction, upheld by the Louisiana state court, was occasioned by the following exchange between a white police officer and the black mother of a young suspect. He: "Get your black ass in the goddamned car." She: "You goddamn motherfucking police—I am going to [the superintendent of police] about this." No prize for guessing who was convicted for "fighting words." As the legal scholar Kenneth Karst reports, "Statutes proscribing abusive words are applied to members of racial and political minorities more frequently than can be wholly explained by any special proclivity of those people to speak abusively." So much for the doctrine's political value.

Even if we finally reject the appeal to *Chaplinsky,* the hate speech movement can still link itself to constitutional precedent through the alternative model of group defamation. Indeed, the defamation model is more central, more weighty, in these arguments. And note that these are alternatives, not just different ways of describing the same thing. The "fighting words" or "assaultive speech" paradigm compares racist expression to physical assault: at its simplest, it characterizes an act of aggression between two individuals, victim and victimizer. The defamation paradigm, by contrast, compares racist speech to libel, which is an assault on dignity or reputation. The harm is essentially social; to be defamed is to be defamed in the eyes of other people.

Here the guiding precedent is Justice Frankfurter's majority opinion in the case of *Beauharnais v. Illinois* (1952), in which the Court upheld a conviction under an Illinois group libel ordinance. The ordinance was clumsily written, but it essentially prohibited public expression that "portrays depravity, criminality, unchastity or lack of virtue in a class of citizens of any race, color, creed or religion," thereby exposing them to "contempt, derision or obloquy." In Frankfurter's opinion: "If an utterance directed at an individual may be the object of criminal sanctions we cannot deny to a state power to punish the same utterance directed at a defined group," at least as long as the restriction related to the peace and well-being of the state.

Beauharnais v. Illinois has since fallen into judicial disrepute, having been reversed in its particulars by subsequent cases like the celebrated *Sullivan v. New York*

Times. Indeed, more widely cited than Justice Frankfurter's opinion is Justice Black's dissent: "If there be minority groups who hail this holding as their victory, they might consider the possible relevancy of this ancient remark: 'Another such victory and I am undone.'" And yet Frankfurter's claim for the congruence of individual libel and group libel is not implausible, and many critical race theorists argue for its resurrection. Thus MacKinnon urges "the rather obvious reality that groups are made up of individuals." That is why "libel of groups multiplies rather than avoids the very same damage through reputation which the law of individual libel recognizes when done one at a time, as well as inflicting some of its own."

What is wrong with the basic claim, endorsed by judges and scholars across the ideological spectrum, that group libel is just individual libel multiplied? Begin with the assumption that individual libel involves the publication of information about someone that is both damaging and false. Charles Lawrence III inadvertently directs us to the source of the problem. The racial epithet, he writes, "is invoked as an assault, not as a statement of fact that may be proven true or false." But that suggests that the evaluative judgments characteristic of racial invective do not lend themselves to factual verification—and this is where the comparison with individual libel breaks down. The same problem emerges when MacKinnon identifies pornography as an instance of group defamation whose message is (roughly) that it would be nice if women were available for sexual exploitation. A proposition of that form may be right or wrong, but it cannot be true or false. You cannot libel someone by saying, "I despise you"; but that is precisely the message common to most racial epithets. "Nigger," used in the vocative, is not usefully treated as group libel for the same reason that it is not usefully treated as individual libel.

II.

Critical race theory is strongest not when it seeks to establish a bridgehead with constitutional precedent, but when it frontally contests what has recently emerged as a central aspect of Supreme Court First Amendment doctrine: the principle of content and viewpoint neutrality. That principle is meant to serve as a guide to how speech can permissibly be regulated, ensuring basic fairness by preventing the law from favoring one partisan interest over another. So, for example, a law forbidding the discussion of race would violate the principle of content-neutrality, which is held to be a bad thing; a law forbidding the advocacy of black supremacy would violate the principle of viewpoint-neutrality, which is held to be a worse thing. When the Minnesota Supreme Court affirmed the content-sensitive hate speech ordinance at issue in *RAV v. St. Paul*, it cited Mari J. Matsuda's work in reaching its conclusions. When Justice Scalia reversed and invalidated the ordinance on the grounds of viewpoint discrimination, he was implicitly writing against Matsuda's argument. These are not mere conflicts of academic vision; these are arguments with judicial consequences.

Matsuda's rejection of what she calls the "neutrality trap" is, to my mind, the most powerful element of her argument. Rather than trying to fashion neutral laws to further our social objectives, why not put our cards on the table and acknowledge what we know? As an example of where the neutrality trap leads, Matsuda cites the anti-mask statutes that many states passed "in a barely disguised effort to limit Ku Klux Klan activities":

> These statutes purportedly cover the wearing of masks in general, with no specific mention of the intent to control the Klan. Neutral reasons such as the need to prevent pickpockets from moving unidentified through crowds or the need to unmask burglars or bank robbers are proffered for such statutes. The result of forgetting—or pretending to forget—the real reason for anti-mask legislation is farcical. Masks are used in protest against terrorist regimes for reasons both of symbolism and personal safety. Iranian students wearing masks and opposing human rights violations by the Shah of Iran, for example, were prosecuted under a California anti-mask statute.

I call here for an end of such unknowing. We know why state legislatures—those quirkily populist institutions—have passed anti-mask statutes. It is more honest, and less cynically manipulative of legal doctrine to legislate openly against the worst forms of racist speech, allowing ourselves to know what we know.

What makes Matsuda's position particularly attractive is that she offers a pragmatic, pro-civil liberties argument for content-specificity:

> The alternative to recognizing racist speech as qualitatively different because of its content is to continue to stretch existing First Amendment exceptions, such as the "fighting words" doctrine and the "content/conduct" distinction. This stretching ultimately

weakens the First Amendment fabric, creating neutral holes that remove protection for many forms of speech. Setting aside the worst forms of racist speech for special treatment is a non-neutral, value-laden approach that will better preserve free speech.

At the very least, this approach would promise a quick solution to the abuse of "fighting words" ordinances. Consider Matsuda's own approach to legal sanctions for racist speech. By way of distinguishing "the worst, paradigm example of racist hate messages from other forms of racist and non-racist speech," she offers three identifying characteristics:

(1) The message is of racial inferiority.
(2) The message is directed against a historically oppressed group.
(3) The message is persecutory, hateful and degrading.

The third element, she says, is "related to the 'fighting words' idea"; and the first "is the primary identifier of racist speech"; but it is the second element that "attempts to further define racism by recognizing the connection of racism to power and subordination."

The second element is the one that most radically departs from the current requirement that law be neutral as to content and viewpoint. But it would seem to forestall some of the abuses to which earlier speech ordinances have been put, simply by requiring the victim of the penalized speech to be a member of a "historically oppressed group." Surely there is something refreshingly straightforward about the call for "an end to unknowing."

Is Matsuda on to something? Not quite. Ironically enough, what trips up the con-

tent-specific approach is that it can never be content-specific enough. Take a second look at Matsuda's three identifying characteristics of paradigm hate speech. First, recall, that the message is of racial inferiority. Now, Matsuda is clear that she wants her definition to encompass, inter alia, anti-Semitic and anti-Asian prejudice; but anti-Semitism (as the philosopher Laurence Thomas, who is black and Jewish, observes) traditionally imputes to its object not inferiority, but iniquity. Moreover, anti-Asian prejudice often more closely resembles anti-Semitic prejudice than it does anti-black prejudice. Surely anti-Asian prejudice that depicts Asians as menacingly superior, and therefore as a threat to "us," is just as likely to arouse the sort of violence that notoriously claimed the life of Vincent Chin ten years ago in Detroit.

More obviously, the test of membership in a "historically oppressed" group is either too narrow (just blacks) or too broad (just about everybody). Are poor Appalachians, a group I knew well from growing up in a West Virginia mill town, "historically oppressed" or "dominant group members"? Once we adopt the "historically oppressed" proviso, I suspect, it is a matter of time before a group of black women in Chicago are arraigned for calling a policeman a "dumb Polak." Evidence that Poles are a historically oppressed group in Chicago will be in plentiful supply; the policeman's grandmother will offer poignant firsthand testimony to that.

III.

The critique of neutrality would affect not simply how we draft our ordinances, but also how we conduct our litigation. One quickly moves from asking whether our statutes can or should be neutral to asking whether the adjudication of these statutes can or should be neutral. Indeed, many legal pragmatists, mainstream scholars and critical race theorists converge in their affirmation of the balancing approach toward the First Amendment and their corresponding skepticism toward what could be called the "Skokie school" of jurisprudence. When the American Civil Liberties Union defended the right of neo-Nazis to march in Skokie, a predominantly Jewish suburb of Chicago where a number of Holocaust survivors lived, they wished to protect and to fortify the constitutional right at issue. Indeed, they may have reasoned, if a civil liberty can be tested and upheld in so odious an exercise of it, then the precedent will strengthen it for all the less obnoxious cases where it may be disputed in the future. Hard cases harden laws.

The strategy of the Skokie school relies on a number of presuppositions that critical legal theorists and others regard as doubtful. Most importantly, it is premised on the neutral operation of principle in judicial decisionmaking. But what if judges really decided matters in an unprincipled and political way, and invoked principles only by way of window dressing? In cases close-run enough to require the Supreme Court to decide them, precedent and principle are elastic enough, or complex enough, that justices can often decide either way without brazenly contradicting themselves. And even if the justices want to make principled decisions, it may turn out that the facts of the case—in the real-world cases that come before them—are too various and complicated ever to be overdetermined by the rule of precedent, *stare decisis*. In either event, it could turn out that defending neo-Nazis was just defending neo-Nazis.

Moreover, it may be that the sort of formal liberties vouchsafed by this process are not the sort of liberties that we need most. Perhaps we have been overly impressed by the frisson of defending bad people for good causes, when the good consequences are at best conjectural and the bad ones real and immediate. Perhaps, these critics conclude, it is time to give up the pursuit of abstract principles and instead defend victims against victimizers, achieving your results in the here-and-now, not in the sweet hereafter.

There is something to this position, but it is, like the position it is meant to rebuff, overstated. Nadine Strossen of the ACLU can show, for example, that the organization's winning First Amendment defense of the racist Father Terminiello in 1949 bore Fourteenth Amendment fruit when the ACLU was able to use the landmark *Terminiello* decision to defend the free speech rights of civil rights protesters in the '60s and '70s. Granted, this may not constitute proof, which is an elusive thing in historical argument, but such cases do provide good prima facie reason to think that the Skokie school has pragmatic justification, not just blind faith, on its side.

Another problem with the abandonment of principled adjudication is what it leaves in its wake: the case-by-case balancing of interests. My point is not that "normal" First Amendment jurisprudence can completely eschew balancing, but there is a difference between employing it in background or *in extremis* and employing it as the first and only approach. An unfettered regime of balancing admits too much to judicial inspection. What we miss when we dwell on the rarefied workings of high court decisionmaking is the way in which laws exert their effects lower down the legal food chain. It's been pointed out that when police arrest somebody for loitering or disorderly conduct, the experience of arrest—being hauled off to the station and fingerprinted before being released—often is the punishment. And "fighting words" ordinances have lent themselves to similar abuse. Anthony D'Amato, a law professor at Northwestern, makes a crucial and often overlooked point when he argues: "In some areas of law we do not want judges to decide cases at all—not justly or any other way. In these areas, the mere possibility of judicial decisionmaking exerts a chilling effect that can undermine what we want the law to achieve."

But what if that chilling effect is precisely what the law is designed for? After all, one person's chill is another person's civility. It is clear, in any event, that all manner of punitive speech regulations are meant to have effects far beyond the classic triad of deterrence, reform and retribution.

IV.

The main appeal of speech codes usually turns out to be expressive or symbolic rather than consequential. That is, their advocates do not depend on the claim that a speech-code statute will spare certain groups some foreseeable amount of psychic trauma. They say, rather, that such a statute expresses a university's opposition to hate speech and bigotry; and more positively, that it symbolizes a commitment to tolerance, to the creation of an educational environment in which mutual colloquy and comity are preserved.

In this spirit Matsuda writes that "a legal response to racist speech is a *statement* that victims of racism are valued members of our polity," and that "in a society that *expresses* its moral judgments through the law," the "absence of laws against racist speech is telling." In this same spirit Delgado suggests that a tort action for racist speech would have the effect of "*communicating* to the perpetrator and to society that such abuse will not be tolerated either by its victims or by the courts" (italics mine). And also in this spirit Thomas Grey, the Stanford law professor who helped draft the campus speech regulations there, counsels that "authorities make the most effective statement when they are honestly concerned to do something *beyond* making a statement," thus "putting their money where their mouth is." The punitive function of speech codes is thus enlisted to expressive means, as a means of bolstering the credibility of the anti-racist statement.

Still, once we have admitted that the regulation of racist speech is partly or wholly a symbolic act, we must register the force of the other symbolic considerations that may come into play. Thus, even if you think that the notion of free speech contains logical inconsistencies, you need to register the symbolic force of its further abridgement. And it is this level of scrutiny that may tip the balance in the other direction. The controversy over flag-burning is a good illustration of the two-edged nature of symbolic arguments. Safeguarding the flag may symbolize something nice for some of us, but safeguarding our freedom to burn the flag symbolizes something nicer for others of us.

Note, too, that the expressivist position suffers from an uncomfortable contradiction. A university administration that merely condemns hate speech, without mobilizing punitive sanctions, is held to have done little, to have offered "mere words." And yet this skepticism about the power of "mere words" comports oddly with the attempt to regulate "mere words" that, since they are spoken by those not in a position of authority, would seem to have even less symbolic force. Why is it "mere words" when a university only condemns racist speech, but not "mere words" that the student utters in the first place? Whose words are "only words"? Why are racist words deeds, but anti-racist words just lip service?

And is the verbal situation really as asymmetrical as it first appears? Surely the rebuke "racist" also has the power to wound. One of the cases that arose under the University of Michigan speech code involved a group discussion at the beginning of a dentistry class, in which the teacher, a black woman, sought to "identify concerns of students." A student reported that he had heard, from his roommate, who was a minority, that minority students had a hard time in the class and were not treated fairly. In response, the outraged teacher lodged a complaint against the student for having accused her (as she perceived it) of racism. For this black woman, at least, even an indirect accusation of racism apparently had the brunt of racial stigmatization.

One other paradox fissures the hate speech movement. Because these scholars wish to show that substantial restrictions on racist speech are consistent with the Constitution, they must make the case that racist speech is sui generis among offensive or injurious utterances; otherwise the domain of unprotected speech would mushroom beyond the point of constitutional and political plausibility. "Words That Wound," the title of Delgado's pioneering essay, designates a category that includes racist speech but is scarcely exhausted by it. Nor could we maintain that racist insults, which tend to be generic, are necessarily more wounding than an insult tailor-made to hurt someone: being jeered at for your acne or your obesity may be far more hurtful than being jeered at for your race or your religion.

Alert to this consideration, scholars like Matsuda, Lawrence and Delgado argue that racist speech is peculiarly deserving of curtailment precisely because it participates in (and is at least partly constitutive of) the larger structures of racism that are "hegemonic" in our society. "Black folks know that no racial incident is 'isolated' in the United States," writes Lawrence:

That is what makes the incidents so horrible, so scary. It is the knowledge that they are not the isolated unpopular speech of a dissident few that makes them so frightening. These incidents are manifestations of a ubiquitous and deeply ingrained cultural belief system, an American way of life.

To this consideration Matsuda annexes the further argument that what distinguishes racist speech from other forms of unpopular speech is "the universal acceptance of the wrongness of the doctrine of racial supremacy." Unlike Marxist speech, say, racist speech is "universally condemned."

At first blush, this is a surprising claim. After all, if racist speech really were universally rejected, ordinances against it would be an exercise in antiquarianism. And yet there is something in what Matsuda says: a shared assumption about the weight of the anti-racist consensus, a conviction that at least overt racists are an unpopular minority, that authority is likely to side with *us* against *them*. This hopeful conviction about the magnitude of racist expression in America provides the hidden and rather unexpected foundation for the hate speech movement. Why would you entrust authority with enlarged powers of regulating the speech of unpopular minorities, unless you were confident that the unpopular minorities would be racists, not blacks? Lawrence may know that racial incidents are never "isolated," but he must also believe them to be less than wholly systemic. You don't go to the teacher to complain about the school bully unless you know that the teacher is on your side.

The tacit confidence of critical race theory in the anti-racist consensus also enables its criticism of neutral principles. This becomes clear when one considers the best arguments in favor of such principles. Thus David Coles, a law professor at Georgetown University, suggests that

> in a democratic society the only speech government is likely to succeed in regulating will be that of the politically marginalized. If an idea is sufficiently popular, a representative government will lack the political wherewithal to suppress it, irrespective of the First Amendment. But if an idea is unpopular, the only thing that may protect it from the majority is a strong constitutional norm of content-neutrality.

Reverse his assumptions about whose speech is marginalized and you stand the argument on its head. If blatantly racist speech is unpopular and stigmatized, a strong constitutional norm of content-neutrality may be its best hope for protection. For these critics, however, that is a damning argument *against* content-neutrality.

This, then, is the political ambiguity that haunts the new academic activism. "Our colleagues of color, struggling to carry the multiple burdens of token representative, role model and change agent in increasingly hostile environments, needed to know that the institutions in which they worked stood behind them," declare our critical race theorists in their joint manifesto. *Needed to know that the institutions in which they worked stood behind them*: I have difficulty imagining this sentiment expressed by activists in the '60s, who defined themselves in a proudly adversarial relation to authority and its institutions. Here is the crucial difference this time around. The contemporary aim is not to resist power, but to enlist power.

V.

"Critical race theory challenges ahistoricism and insists on a contextual/historical analysis of the law." So states the manifesto, and it is not necessarily a bad principle. What it suggests to me, however, is that we get down to cases, and consider, as these theorists do not, the actual results of various regimes of hate speech regulation.

Surveying United Nations conventions urging the criminalization of racist speech, Matsuda bemoans the fact that the United States, out of First Amendment scruple, has declined fully to endorse such resolutions. By contrast, she commends to our attention nations such as Canada and the United Kingdom. Canada's appeal to the hate speech movement is obvious; after all, the new Canadian Bill of Rights has not been allowed (as Matsuda observes) to interfere with its national statutes governing hate propaganda. And Canada's Supreme Court has recently promulgated MacKinnon's statutory definition of pornography as the law of the land. What you don't hear from the hate speech theorists is that the first casualty of the MacKinnonite anti-obscenity ruling was a gay and lesbian bookshop in Toronto, which was raided by the police because of a lesbian magazine it carried. (Homosexual literature is a frequent target of Canada's restrictions on free expression.) Nor are they likely to mention that in June copies of *Black Looks: Race and Representation* by the well-known black feminist scholar Bell Hooks, a book widely assigned in women's studies courses, was confiscated by Canadian authorities as possible "hate literature." Is the Canadian system really a beacon of hope?

Even more perplexing, especially in the context of an insistence on challenging ahistoricism and attending to context, is the nomination of Britain as an exemplar of a more enlightened free speech jurisprudence. Does anyone believe that racism has subsided in Britain since the adoption of the 1965 Race Relations Act forbidding racial defamation? Or that the legal climate in that country is more conducive to searching political debate? Ask any British newspaperman about that. When Harry Evans, then editor of the London *Times,* famously proclaimed that the British press was, by comparison to ours, only "half-free," he was not exaggerating much. The result of Britain's judicial climate is to make the country a net importer of libel suits launched by tycoons who are displeased with their biographers. Everyone knows that a British libel suit is like a Reno divorce. It is rather a mordant irony that American progressives should propose Britain, and its underdeveloped protection of expression, as a model to emulate at a time when many progressives in Britain are agitating for a bill of rights and broad First Amendment-style protections.

And what of speech codes on American campuses? The record may surprise some advocates of regulations. "When the ACLU enters the debate by challenging the University of Michigan's efforts to provide a safe harbor for its Black, Latino and Asian students," Lawrence writes, "we should not be surprised that nonwhite students feel abandoned." In light of the actual record of enforcement, however, the situation might be viewed differently. During the year in which Michigan's speech code was enforced, more than twenty blacks were charged—by whites—with racist speech. As Strossen notes, not a single instance of white racist speech was punished, a fact that makes Lawrence's talk of a "safe harbor" seem more wishful than informed.

At Michigan, a full disciplinary hearing was conducted only in the case of a black social work student who was charged with saying, in a class discussion of research projects, that he believed homosexuality was an illness, and that he was developing a social work approach to move homosexuals toward heterosexuality. ("These charges will haunt me for the rest of my life," the student claimed in a court affidavit.) By my lights, this is a good example of how speech codes kill critique. I think that the student's views about homosexuality (which may or may not have been well-intentioned) are both widespread and unlikely to survive intellectual scrutiny. Regrettably, we have not yet achieved a public consensus in this country on the moral legitimacy (or, more precisely, the moral indifference) of homosexuality. Yet it may well be that a class on social work is not an inappropriate forum for a rational discussion of why the "disease" model of sexual difference has lost credibility among social scientists. (In a class on social work, this isn't P.C. brainwashing, this is education.) The trouble is, you cannot begin to conduct this conversation when you outlaw the expression of the view that you would criticize.

Critical race theorists are fond of the

ideal of conversation. "This chapter attempts to begin a conversation about the First Amendment," Matsuda writes toward the end of her contribution. "Most important, we must continue this discussion," Lawrence writes toward the end of his. It is too easy to lose sight of the fact that the conversation to which they are devoted is aimed at limiting conversation. If there are costs to speech, then there are costs also to curtailing speech, often unpredictable ones.

Speech codes, to be sure, may be more narrowly and responsibly tailored, and the Stanford rules—carefully drafted by scholars, like Thomas Grey, with civil libertarian sympathies—have rightly been taken as a model of such careful delimitation. For rather than following the arguments against racist speech to their natural conclusion, the Stanford rules prohibit only insulting expression that conveys "direct and visceral hatred or contempt" for people on the basis of their sex, race, color, handicap, religion, sexual orientation or national and ethnic origin, and that is "addressed directly to the individual or individuals whom it insults or stigmatizes."

Chances are, the Stanford rule won't do much harm. Chances are, too, it won't do much good. As long as the eminently reasonable Grey is drafting and enforcing the restrictions, I won't lose much sleep over it. Yet we must be clear how inadequate the code is as a response to the powerful arguments that were marshaled to support it. Contrast the following two statements addressed to a black freshman at Stanford:

(A) LeVon, if you find yourself struggling in your classes here, you should realize it isn't your fault. It's simply that you're the beneficiary of a disruptive policy of affirmative action that places underqualified, underprepared and often undertalented black students in demanding educational environments like this one. The policy's egalitarian aims may be well-intentioned, but given the fact that aptitude tests place African Americans almost a full standard deviation below the mean, even controlling for socioeconomic disparities, they are also profoundly misguided. The truth is, you probably don't belong here, and your college experience will be a long downhill slide.

(B) Out of my face, jungle bunny.

Surely there is no doubt which is likely to be more "wounding" and alienating to its intended audience. Under the Stanford speech regulations, however, the first is protected speech, and the second may well not be: a result that makes a mockery of the words-that-wound rationale.

If you really want to penalize such wounding words, it makes no sense to single out gutter epithets—which, on many college campuses, are more likely to stigmatize the speaker than their intended victim—and leave the far more painful disquisition alone. In American society today, the real power commanded by racism is likely to vary inversely with the vulgarity with which it is expressed. Black professionals soon learn that it is the socially disfranchised—the lower class, the homeless—who are most likely to hail them as "niggers." The circles of power have long since switched to a vocabulary of indirection. Unfortunately, those who pit the First Amendment against the Fourteenth Amendment invite us to worry more about speech codes than coded speech.

I suspect that many of those liberals who supported Stanford's restrictions on abusive language did so because they thought it was the civil thing to do. Few imagined that, say, the graduation rates or GPAs of Stanford's blacks (or Asians, gays, and so on) are likely to rise significantly as a result. Few imagined, that is, that the restrictions would lead to substantive rights or minority empowerment. They just believed that gutter epithets violate the sort of civility that ought to prevail on campus. In spirit, then, the new regulations were little different from the rules about curfews, drinking or the after-hours presence of women in male dormitories that once governed America's campuses and preoccupied their disciplinary committees.

Not that rules about civility are without value. Lawrence charges that civil libertarians who disagree with him about speech regulations may be "unconscious racists." I don't doubt this is so; I don't doubt that some of those who support speech codes are unconscious racists. What I doubt is whether the imputation of racism is the most effective way to advance the debate between civil rights and civil liberties.

VI.

"What is ultimately at stake in this debate is our vision for this society," write the authors of *Words That Wound,* and they are right. In parsing the reasoning of the movement against hate speech, it is essential that we not miss the civic forest for the legal trees. Far beyond the wrangling over particular statutes and codes lies an encompassing vision of state and civil society. And its wellsprings are to be found not in legal scholarship or critical theory, but in the more powerful cultural currents identified with the "recovery movement."

At the vital center of the hate speech movement is the seductive vision of the therapeutic state. This vision is presaged in the manifesto itself:

Too often victims of hate speech find themselves without the words to articulate what they see, feel and know. In the absence of theory and analysis that give them a diagnosis and a name for the injury they have suffered, they internalize the injury done them and are rendered silent in the fact of continuing injury. Critical race theory names the injury and identifies its origins.

This sounds, of course, like a popular primer on how psychotherapy is supposed to work; with a few changes, the passage might be addressed to survivors of toxic parenting. Indeed, "alexathymia"—the inability to name and articulate one's feelings—is a faddish diagnosis in psychiatry these days. Nor is critical race theory's affinity with the booming recovery industry a matter of chance. These days the recovery movement is perhaps the principal source of resistance to the older and much-beleaguered American tradition of individualism.

"When the ideology is deconstructed and injury is named, subordinated victims find their voices," the manifesto asserts. "They discover they are not alone in their subordination. They are empowered." Here the recovery/survivor-group paradigm leads to a puzzling contradiction. We are told that victims of racist speech are cured—that is, empowered—when they learn they are "not alone" in their subordination, but subordinated as a group. But elsewhere we are told that what makes racist speech peculiarly wounding is that it conveys precisely the message that you are a member

315

of a subordinated group. How can the suggestion of group subordination be the poison *and* the antidote?

The therapeutic claims made for critical race theory cut against the hate speech offensive in more important ways. For if we took these claims at face value, critical race theory would not buttress speech regulations, it would obviate the need for them. The problem about which Lawrence worries, that racist speech "silenc[es] members of those groups who are its targets," would naturally be addressed not through bureaucratic regulations, but through the sort of deconstruction and critique that will enable victims, according to critical race theory, to "find their voices." And here lies another painful irony. All this sounds very much like Justice Brandeis's hoary and much-scorned prescription for redressing harmful speech: "more speech."

Scholars such as Delgado and Matsuda understandably emphasize the adverse psychological effects of racial abuse. "Because they constantly hear racist messages, minority children, not surprisingly, come to question their competence, intelligence and worth," Delgado writes. And he further notes that the psychic injuries incurred by racist speech have additional costs down the road: "The person who is timid, withdrawn, bitter, hypertense or psychotic will almost certainly fare poorly in employment settings." (As a member of the Harvard faculty, I would venture that there are exceptions to this rule.) But the proposed therapeutic regime is no mere talking cure. Indeed, in the Republic of Self-Esteem, we are invited to conceive of the lawsuit as therapy. "When victimized by racist language," Delgado explains, "victims must be able to threaten and institute legal action, thereby relieving the sense of helplessness that leads to psychological harm."

A similar therapeutic function could be played by criminal proceedings, in Matsuda's view. When the government does nothing about racist speech, she argues, it actually causes a second injury. "The second injury is the pain of knowing that the government provides no remedy and offers no recognition of the dehumanizing experience that victims of hate propaganda are subjected to." In fact, "The government's denial of personhood through its denial of legal recourse may even be more painful than the initial act of hatred." Of course, what this grievance presupposes is that the state is there, *in loco parentis*, to confer personhood in the first place. Finally Matsuda must repair not to an instrumental conception of the state, but to a conception of it as the "official embodiment of the society we live in," which is rather remote and abstracted from the realities of our heterogeneous populace, with its conflicting norms and jostling values.

Psychotherapy cannot do the hard work of politics. Yet a similar therapeutic vision animates the more broad-gauged campus regulations such as those adopted in the late 1980s at the University of Connecticut. These rules sought to proscribe such behavior as, inter alia:

> Treating people differently solely because they are in some way different from the majority. . . .

> Imitating stereotypes in speech or mannerisms. . . .

> Attributing objections to any of the above actions to "hypersensitivity" of the targeted individual or group.

That last provision was especially cunning. It meant that even if you believed that a complainant was overreacting to an innocuous remark, the attempt to defend yourself in this way would serve only as proof of your guilt.

The rationale of the university's rules was made explicit in its general prohibition on actions that undermined the "security or self-esteem" of persons or groups. (Would awarding low grades count?) Not surprisingly, the university's expressed objective was to provide "a positive environment in which everyone feels comfortable working or living." It was unclear whether any provisions were to be made for those who did not feel "comfortable" working or living under such restrictive regulations. In any event, they were later dropped under threat of legal action.

It may be that widespread skepticism about the distinction between the public and the private made it inevitable that the recovery movement would translate into a politics; and that this politics would center on a vocabulary of trauma and abuse, in which the verbal forms and the physical forms are seen as equivalent. Perhaps it was inevitable that the citizen at the center of the political theory of the Enlightenment would be replaced by the infant at the center of modern depth psychology and its popular therapeutic variants. The inner child may hurt and grieve, as we have been advised. But may the inner child also vote?

VII.

What cannot be sidestepped, finally, is the larger question, the political question, of how we came to decide that our energies were best directed not at strengthening our position in the field of public discourse, but at trying to move its boundary posts. I detect two motivations.

In the academy, there has been increased attention to the formative power of language in the construction of our social reality, to language as "performative," as itself counting as action and constituting a "speech act." These are phrases and ideas that are owed to ordinary language philosophy, of the kind that the Oxford philosopher J.L. Austin developed in the middle of the century, but now MacKinnon adds them to her argumentative arsenal in her latest book. The notion of the speech act certainly acquires new force when the act in question is rape.

MacKinnon's emphasis on the realness, the act-like nature, of expression receives an interesting twist in the attempt by some hate speech theorists to "textualize" the Fourteenth Amendment. If expression is act, then act must be expression. If the First Amendment is about speech, then so, too, is the Fourteenth Amendment. Following this reasoning, Lawrence has proposed in an influential reinterpretation of legal history that *Brown v. Board,* and, by analogy, all subsequent civil rights decisions and legislation, are in fact prohibitions on expressive behavior. In Lawrence's reading, they forbid not racism, but the expression of racism. In line with this argument, he tells us that "discriminatory conduct is not racist unless it also conveys the message of white supremacy," thus contributing to the social construction of racism.

This is a bold and unsettling claim, which commits Lawrence to the view that in the case of discriminatory conduct, the only crime is to get caught. By this logic, racial redlining by bankers is not racist unless people find out about it. And the crusading district attorney who uncovers hidden evidence of those bankers' discrimination is not to be hailed as a friend of justice, after all: by bringing it to light, he was only activating the racist potential of those misdeeds. Should anti-discrimination policy be founded, then, on the principle of "don't ask, don't tell"?

Lawrence's analysis of segregation reaches the same surprising conclusion: "The nonspeech elements are byproducts of the main message rather than the message being simply a by-product of unlawful conduct." By this logic, poverty is not really about material deprivation; it is really about the message of class inequality. We might conclude, then, that the problem of economic inequality would most naturally be redressed by promulgating a self-affirmative lower-class identity along the lines of Poverty Is Beautiful. Words may not be cheap, but they are much less costly than AFDC and job training programs.

Something, let us agree, has gone very wrong. The pendulum has swung from the absurd position that words don't matter to the equally absurd position that only words matter. Critical race theory, it appears, has fallen under the sway of a species of academic nominalism. Yes, speech is a species of action. Yes, there are some acts that only speech can perform. But there are some acts that speech alone cannot accomplish. You cannot heal the sick by pronouncing them well. You cannot lift up the poor by declaring them rich.

In their manifesto, the authors of *Words That Wound* identify their fight as "a fight for a constitutional community where freedom does not implicate a right to degrade and humiliate another human being." These are heady words. Like much sweepingly utopian rhetoric, however, they invite a regime so heavily policed as to be incompatible with democracy. Once we are forbidden verbally to degrade and to humiliate, will we retain the moral autonomy to

elevate and to affirm?

In the end, the preference for the substantive liberties supposedly vouchsafed by the Fourteenth Amendment over the formal ones enshrined in the First Amendment rehearses the classic disjunction that Isaiah Berlin analyzed a generation ago in "Two Conceptions of Liberty," but without having learned from him. Berlin's words have aged little. "Negative" liberty, the simple freedom from external coercion, seemed to him

> a truer and more humane ideal than the goals of those who seek in the great, disciplined, authoritarian structures the ideal of "positive" self-mastery by classes, or peoples or the whole of mankind. It is truer, because it recognizes the fact that human goals are many, not all of them commensurable, and in perpetual rivalry with one another.

To suggest, as the critical race theorists do, that equality must precede liberty is simply to jettison the latter without securing the former. The First Amendment may not secure us substantive liberties, but neither will its abrogation.

It is not hard to explain the disenchantment among minority critics with such liberal mainstays as the "marketplace of ideas" and the ideal of public discourse. I take their disenchantment to be a part of a larger crisis of faith. The civil rights era witnessed the development of a national consensus—hammered out noisily, and against significant resistance—that racism, at least overt racism, was wrong. Amazingly enough, things like reason, argument and moral suasion did play a significant role in changing attitudes toward "race relations." But what have they done for us lately?

For all his good sense, Harry Kalven Jr. was spectacularly wrong when he wrote: "One is tempted to say that it will be a sign that the Negro problem has basically been solved when the Negro begins to worry about group libel protection." Quite the contrary. The disillusionment with liberal ideology that is now rampant among many minority scholars and activists stems from the lack of progress in the struggle for racial equality over the past fifteen years. Liberalism's principle of formal equality seems to have led us so far, but no further. As Patricia J. Williams observes, it "put the vampire back in its coffin but it was no silver stake."

The problem may be that the continuing economic and material inequality between black America and white America, and the continuing immiseration of large segments of black America, cannot be erased simply through better racial attitudes. Poverty, white and black, can take on a life of its own, to the point that removing the conditions that caused it can do little to alleviate it. The '80s may have been the "Cosby Decade," but you wouldn't know it from the South Bronx. It has become clear, in other words, that the political economy of race and poverty can no longer be reduced to a mirror of what whites think of blacks.

In some ways the intellectuals have not caught up to this changing reality. Generals are not the only ones who are prone to fight the last war. Rather than responding to the grim new situation with new and subtler modes of socioeconomic analysis, we have finessed the gap between rhetoric and reality by forging new and subtler definitions of the word "racism." Hence a new model of institutional racism is one that can operate in the ab-

sence of actual racists. By redefining our terms, we can always say of the economic gap between black and white America: the problem is still racism . . . and, by stipulation, it would be true. But the grip of this vocabulary has tended to foreclose the more sophisticated models of political economy that we so desperately need. I cannot otherwise explain why some of our brightest legal minds believe that substantive liberties can be vouchsafed and substantive inequities redressed by punishing rude remarks; or why their analysis of racism owes more to the totalizing theory of Catharine MacKinnon than to the work of scholar-investigators like Douglas Massey or William Julius Wilson or Gary Orfield—people who, whatever their differences, are attempting to discover how things work in the real world, never confusing the empirical with the merely anecdotal.

Critical race theory has served, then, as a labor-saving device. For if racism can be fully textualized, if its real existence is in its articulation, then racial inequity can be prized free from the moss and soil of political economy. "Gender is sexual," MacKinnon wrote in *Toward a Feminist Theory of the State.* "Pornography constitutes the meaning of that sexuality." By extension, racist speech must prove to be the real content of racial subordination: banish it, and you banish subordination. The perverse result is a see-no-evil, hear-no-evil approach toward racial inequality. Unfortunately, even if hate did disappear, aggregative patterns of segregation and segmentation in housing and employment would not disappear. And conversely, in the absence of this material and economic gap, not many people would care about racist speech.

Beliefs that go untested and unchallenged cannot prosper. The critical race theorists must be credited with helping to reinvigorate the debate about freedom of expression; the intelligence, the innovation and the thoughtfulness of their best work deserve a reasoned response, and not, as so often happens, demonization and dismissal. And yet, for all the passion and all the scholarship that the critical race theorists have expended upon the problem of hate speech, I cannot believe that it will capture their attention for very much longer. "It is strange how rapidly things change," wrote Kalven in 1965. "Just a little more than a decade ago we were all concerned with devising legal controls for the libeling of groups. . . . Ironically, once the victory was won, the momentum for such legal measures seemed to dissipate, and the problem has all but disappeared from view." It is strange how rapidly things change—and change back. But the results, I suspect, will be similar this time around. The advocates of speech restrictions will grow disenchanted not with their failures, but with their victo-

ries, and the movement will come to seem yet another curious byway in the long history of our racial desperation.

And yet the movement will not have been without its political costs. I cannot put it better than Charles Lawrence himself, who writes: "I fear that by framing the debate as we have—as one in which the liberty of free speech is in conflict with the elimination of racism—we have advanced the cause of racial oppression and placed the bigot on the moral high ground, fanning the rising flames of racism." He does not intend it as such, but I read this passage as a harsh rebuke to the movement itself. As the critical race theory manifesto acknowledges, "This debate has deeply divided the liberal civil rights/civil liberties community." And so it has. It has created hostility between old allies and fractured longtime coalitions. Was it worth it? Justice Black's words may return, like the sound of an unheeded tocsin, to haunt us: "Another such victory and I am undone."

WISCONSIN, Petitioner,

v.

Todd MITCHELL.

No. 92–515.

Argued April 21, 1993.

Decided June 11, 1993.

Syllabus *

Pursuant to a Wisconsin statute, respondent Mitchell's sentence for aggravated battery was enhanced because he intentionally selected his victim on account of the victim's race. The State Court of Appeals rejected his challenge to the law's constitutionality, but the State Supreme Court reversed. Relying on *R.A.V. v. St. Paul,* 505 U.S. ——, 112 S.Ct. 2538, 120 L.Ed.2d 305 it held that the statute violates the First Amendment by punishing what the legislature has deemed to be offensive thought and rejected the State's contention that the law punishes only the conduct of intentional victim selection. It also found that the statute was unconstitutionally overbroad because the evidentiary use of a defendant's prior speech would have a chilling effect on those who fear they may be prosecuted for offenses subject to penalty enhancement. Finally, it distinguished antidiscrimination laws, which have long been held constitutional, on the ground that they prohibit objective acts of discrimination, whereas the state statute punishes the subjective mental process.

Held: Mitchell's First Amendment rights were not violated by the application of the penalty-enhancement provision in sentencing him. Pp. 2198–2202.

(a) While Mitchell correctly notes that this Court is bound by a state court's interpretation of a state statute, the State Supreme Court did not construe the instant statute in the sense of defining the meaning of a particular word or phrase. Rather, it characterized the statute's practical effect for First Amendment purposes. Thus, after resolving any ambiguities in the statute's meaning, this Court may form its own judgment about the law's operative effect. The State's argument that the statute punishes only conduct does not dispose of Mitchell's claim, since the fact remains that the same criminal conduct is more heavily punished if the victim is selected

The syllabus constitutes no part of the opinion of the Court but has been prepared by the Reporter of Decisions for the convenience of the reader. See *United States v. Detroit Lumber Co.,* 200 U.S. 321, 337, 26 S.Ct. 282, 287, 50 L.Ed. 499.

because of his protected status than if no such motive obtains. Pp. 2198–99.

(b) In determining what sentence to impose, sentencing judges have traditionally considered a wide variety of factors in addition to evidence bearing on guilt, including a defendant's motive for committing the offense. While it is equally true that a sentencing judge may not take into consideration a defendant's abstract beliefs, however obnoxious to most people, the Constitution does not erect a *per se* barrier to the admission of evidence concerning one's beliefs and associations at sentencing simply because they are protected by the First Amendment. *Dawson v. Delaware*, 503 U.S. ——, 112 S.Ct. 1093, 117 L.Ed.2d 309; *Barclay v. Florida*, 463 U.S. 939, 103 S.Ct. 3418, 77 L.Ed.2d 1134 (plurality opinion). That *Dawson* and *Barclay* did not involve the application of a penalty-enhancement provision does not make them inapposite. *Barclay* involved the consideration of racial animus in determining whether to sentence a defendant to death, the most severe "enhancement" of all; and the state legislature has the primary responsibility for fixing criminal penalties. Motive plays the same role under the state statute as it does under federal and state antidiscrimination laws, which have been upheld against constitutional challenge. Nothing in *R.A.V. v. St. Paul, supra*, compels a different result here. The ordinance at issue there was explicitly directed at speech, while the one here is aimed at conduct unprotected by the First Amendment. Moreover, the State's desire to redress what it sees as the greater individual and societal harm inflicted by bias-inspired conduct provides an adequate explanation for the provision over and above mere disagreement with offenders' beliefs or biases. Pp. 2199–2201.

(c) Because the statute has no "chilling effect" on free speech, it is not unconstitutionally overbroad. The prospect of a citizen suppressing his bigoted beliefs for fear that evidence of those beliefs will be introduced against him at trial if he commits a serious offense against person or property is too speculative a hypothesis to support this claim. Moreover, the First Amendment permits the admission of previous declarations or statements to establish the elements of a crime or to prove motive or intent, subject to evidentiary rules dealing with relevancy, reliability, and the like. *Haupt v. United States*, 330 U.S. 631, 67 S.Ct. 874, 91 L.Ed. 1145. Pp. 2201–02.

169 Wis.2d 153, 485 N.W.2d 807 (1992), reversed and remanded.

REHNQUIST, C.J., delivered the opinion for a unanimous Court.

———

James E. Doyle, Madison, WI, for petitioner.

Michael R. Dreeben, Washington, DC, for the U.S. as amicus curiae, by special leave of the Court.

Lynn S. Adelman, Milwaukee, WI, for respondent.

Chief Justice REHNQUIST delivered the opinion of the Court.

Respondent Todd Mitchell's sentence for aggravated battery was enhanced because he intentionally selected his victim on account of the victim's race. The question presented in this case is whether this penalty enhancement is prohibited by the First and Fourteenth Amendments. We hold that it is not.

On the evening of October 7, 1989, a group of young black men and boys, including Mitchell, gathered at an apartment complex in Kenosha, Wisconsin. Several members of the group discussed a scene from the motion picture "Mississippi Burning," in which a white man beat a young black boy who was praying. The group moved outside and Mitchell asked them: " 'Do you all feel hyped up to move on some white people?' " Brief for Petitioner 4. Shortly thereafter, a young white boy approached the group on the opposite side of the street where they were standing. As the boy walked by, Mitchell said: " 'You all want to fuck somebody up? There goes a white boy; go get him.'" *Id.*, at 4–5. Mitchell counted to three and pointed in the boy's direction. The group ran towards the boy, beat him severely, and stole his tennis shoes. The boy was rendered unconscious and remained in a coma for four days.

After a jury trial in the Circuit Court for Kenosha County, Mitchell was convicted of aggravated battery. Wis.Stat. §§ 939.05 and 940.19(1m) (1989–1990). That offense ordinarily carries a maximum sentence of two years' imprisonment. §§ 940.19(1m) and 939.50(3)(e). But because the jury found that Mitchell had intentionally selected his victim because of the boy's race, the maximum sentence for Mitchell's offense was increased to seven years under § 939.-645. That provision enhances the maximum penalty for an offense whenever the defendant "[i]ntentionally selects the person against whom the crime ... is committed ... because of the race, religion, color, disability, sexual orientation, national origin or ancestry of that person...." § 939.645(1)(b).[1] The Circuit Court sen-

tenced Mitchell to four years' imprisonment for the aggravated battery.

Mitchell unsuccessfully sought postconviction relief in the Circuit Court. Then he appealed his conviction and sentence, challenging the constitutionality of Wisconsin's penalty-enhancement provision on First Amendment grounds.[2] The Wisconsin Court of Appeals rejected Mitchell's challenge, 163 Wis.2d 652, 473 N.W.2d 1 (1991), but the Wisconsin Supreme Court reversed. The Supreme Court held that the statute "violates the First Amendment directly by punishing what the legislature has deemed to be offensive thought." 169 Wis.2d 153, 163, 485 N.W.2d 807, 811 (1992). It rejected the State's contention "that the statute punishes only the 'conduct' of intentional selection of a victim." *Id.*, at 164, 485 N.W.2d, at 812. According to the court, "[t]he statute punishes the 'because of' aspect of the defendant's selection, the *reason* the defendant selected the victim, the *motive* behind the selection." *Ibid.* (emphasis in original). And under *R.A.V. v. St. Paul*, 505 U.S. ——, 112 S.Ct. 2538, 120 L.Ed.2d 305 (1992), "the Wisconsin legisla-

---

1. At the time of Mitchell's trial, the Wisconsin penalty-enhancement statute provided:

"(1) If a person does all of the following, the penalties for the underlying crime are increased as provided in sub. (2):

"(a) Commits a crime under chs. 939 to 948.

"(b) Intentionally selects the person against whom the crime under par. (a) is committed or selects the property which is damaged or otherwise affected by the crime under par. (a) because of the race, religion, color, disability, sexual orientation, national origin or ancestry of that person or the owner or occupant of that property.

"(2)(a) If the crime committed under sub. (1) is ordinarily a misdemeanor other than a Class A misdemeanor, the revised maximum fine is $10,000 and the revised maximum period of imprisonment is one year in the county jail.

"(b) If the crime committed under sub. (1) is ordinarily a Class A misdemeanor, the penalty increase under this section changes the status of the crime to a felony and the revised maximum fine is $10,000 and the revised maximum period of imprisonment is 2 years.

"(c) If the crime committed under sub. (1) is a felony, the maximum fine prescribed by law for the crime may be increased by not more than $5,000 and the maximum period of impris-

onment prescribed by law for the crime may be increased by not more than 5 years.

"(3) This section provides for the enhancement of the penalties applicable for the underlying crime. The court shall direct that the trier of fact find a special verdict as to all of the issues specified in sub. (1).

"(4) This section does not apply to any crime if proof of race, religion, color, disability, sexual orientation, national origin or ancestry is required for a conviction for that crime." Wis. Stat. § 939.645 (1989–1990). The statute was amended in 1992, but the amendments are not at issue in this case.

2. Mitchell also challenged the statute on Fourteenth Amendment equal protection and vagueness grounds. The Wisconsin Court of Appeals held that Mitchell waived his equal protection claim and rejected his vagueness challenge outright. 163 Wis.2d 652, 473 N.W.2d 1 (1991). The Wisconsin Supreme Court declined to address both claims. 169 Wis.2d 153, 158, n. 2, 485 N.W.2d 807, 809, n. 2 (1992). Mitchell renews his Fourteenth Amendment claims in this Court. But since they were not developed below and plainly fall outside of the question on which we granted certiorari, we do not reach them either.

ture cannot criminalize bigoted thought with which it disagrees." 169 Wis.2d, at 171, 485 N.W.2d, at 815.

The Supreme Court also held that the penalty-enhancement statute was unconstitutionally overbroad. It reasoned that, in order to prove that a defendant intentionally selected his victim because of the victim's protected status, the State would often have to introduce evidence of the defendant's prior speech, such as racial epithets he may have uttered before the commission of the offense. This evidentiary use of protected speech, the court thought, would have a "chilling effect" on those who feared the possibility of prosecution for offenses subject to penalty enhancement. See *id.*, at 174, 485 N.W.2d, at 816. Finally, the court distinguished antidiscrimination laws, which have long been held constitutional, on the ground that the Wisconsin statute punishes the "subjective mental process" of selecting a victim because of his protected status, whereas antidiscrimination laws prohibit "objective acts of discrimination." *Id.*, at 176, 485 N.W.2d, at 817.[3]

We granted certiorari because of the importance of the question presented and the existence of a conflict of authority among

state high courts on the constitutionality of statutes similar to Wisconsin's penalty-enhancement provision.[4] 506 U.S. ——, 113 S.Ct. 810, 121 L.Ed.2d 683 (1992). We reverse.

[1, 2] Mitchell argues that we are bound by the Wisconsin Supreme Court's conclusion that the statute punishes bigoted thought and not conduct. There is no doubt that we are bound by a state court's construction of a state statute. *R.A.V., supra,* at —— - ——, 112 S.Ct., at 2541–2542; *New York v. Ferber,* 458 U.S. 747, 769, n. 24, 102 S.Ct. 3348, 3361, n. 24, 73 L.Ed.2d 1113 (1982); *Terminiello v. Chicago.* 337 U.S. 1, 4, 69 S.Ct. 894, 895, 93 L.Ed. 1131 (1949). In *Terminiello,* for example, the Illinois courts had defined the term " 'breach of the peace,' " in a city ordinance prohibiting disorderly conduct, to include " 'stirs the public to anger ... or creates a disturbance.' " *Id.*, at 4, 69 S.Ct., at 895. We held this construction to be binding on us. But here the Wisconsin Supreme Court did not, strictly speaking, construe the Wisconsin statute in the sense of defining the meaning of a particular statutory word or phrase. Rather, it merely characterized the "practical effect" of the statute for First Amendment purposes. See 169

---

3. Two justices dissented. They concluded that the statute punished discriminatory acts, and not beliefs, and therefore would have upheld it. See 169 Wis.2d at 181, 485 N.W.2d, at 819 (Abrahamson, J.); *id.,* at 187–195, 485 N.W.2d at 821–825 (Bablitch, J.).

4. Several States have enacted penalty-enhancement provisions similar to the Wisconsin statute at issue in this case. See, *e.g.,* Cal.Penal Code Ann. § 422.7 (West 1988 and Supp.1993); Fla. Stat. § 775.085 (1991); Mont.Code Ann. § 45–5–222 (1992); Vt.Stat.Ann., Tit. 13, § 1455 (Supp. 1992). Proposed federal legislation to the same effect passed the House of Representatives in 1992, H.R. 4797, 102d Cong., 2d Sess. (1992), but failed to pass the Senate, S. 2522, 102d Cong., 2d Sess. (1992). The state high courts are divided over the constitutionality of penalty-enhancement statutes and analogous statutes covering bias-motivated offenses. Compare, *e.g., State v. Plowman,* 314 Or. 157, 838 P.2d 558 (1992) (upholding Oregon statute), with *State v. Wyant,* 64 Ohio St.3d 566, 597 N.E.2d 450 (1992) (striking

down Ohio statute); 169 Wis.2d 153, 485 N.W.2d 807 (1992) (striking down Wisconsin statute). According to *amici,* bias-motivated violence is on the rise throughout the United States. See, *e.g.,* Brief for the National Asian Pacific American Legal Consortium et al. as *Amici Curiae* 5–11; Brief for the Anti–Defamation League et al. as *Amici Curiae* 4–7; Brief for Atlanta et al. as *Amici Curiae* 3–12. In 1990, Congress enacted the Hate Crimes Statistics Act, Pub.L. 101–275. § 1(b)(1), 104 Stat. 140, codified at 28 U.S.C. § 534 (note) (1988 ed., Supp. III), directing the Attorney General to compile data "about crimes that manifest evidence of prejudice based on race, religion, sexual orientation, or ethnicity." Pursuant to the Act, the Federal Bureau of Investigation reported in January 1993, that 4,558 bias-motivated offenses were committed in 1991, including 1,614 incidents of intimidation, 1,301 incidents of vandalism, 796 simple assaults, 773 aggravated assaults, and 12 murders. See Brief for the Crown Heights Coalition et al. as *Amici Curiae* 1A–7A.

Wis.2d, at 166–167, 485 N.W.2d, at 813 ("Merely because the statute refers in a literal sense to the intentional 'conduct' of selecting, does not mean the court must turn a blind eye to the intent and practical effect of the law—punishment of motive or thought"). This assessment does not bind us. Once any ambiguities as to the meaning of the statute are resolved, we may form our own judgment as to its operative effect.

[3, 4] The State argues that the statute does not punish bigoted thought, as the Supreme Court of Wisconsin said, but instead punishes only conduct. While this argument is literally correct, it does not dispose of Mitchell's First Amendment challenge. To be sure, our cases reject the "view that an apparently limitless variety of conduct can be labeled 'speech' whenever the person engaging in the conduct intends thereby to express an idea." *United States v. O'Brien*, 391 U.S. 367, 376, 88 S.Ct. 1673, 1678, 20 L.Ed.2d 672 (1968); accord, *R.A.V.*, 505 U.S., at ——, 112 S.Ct., at 2544; *Spence v. Washington*, 418 U.S. 405, 409, 94 S.Ct. 2727, 2729, 41 L.Ed.2d 842 (1974) (*per curiam*); *Cox v. Louisiana*, 379 U.S. 536, 555, 85 S.Ct. 453, 464, 13 L.Ed.2d 471 (1965). Thus, a physical assault is not by any stretch of the imagination expressive conduct protected by the First Amendment. See *Roberts v. United States Jaycees*, 468 U.S. 609, 628, 104 S.Ct. 3244, 3255, 82 L.Ed.2d 462 (1984) ("[V]iolence or other types of potentially expressive activities that produce special harms distinct from their communicative impact . . . are entitled to no constitutional protection"); *NAACP v. Claiborne Hardware Co.*, 458 U.S. 886, 916, 102 S.Ct. 3409, 3427, 73 L.Ed.2d 1215 (1982) ("The First Amendment does not protect violence").

[5] But the fact remains that under the Wisconsin statute the same criminal conduct may be more heavily punished if the victim is selected because of his race or other protected status than if no such motive obtained. Thus, although the statute punishes criminal conduct, it enhances the maximum penalty for conduct motivated by a discriminatory point of view more severely than the same conduct engaged in for some other reason or for no reason at all. Because the only reason for the enhancement is the defendant's discriminatory motive for selecting his victim, Mitchell argues (and the Wisconsin Supreme Court held) that the statute violates the First Amendment by punishing offenders' bigoted beliefs.

[6, 7] Traditionally, sentencing judges have considered a wide variety of factors in addition to evidence bearing on guilt in determining what sentence to impose on a convicted defendant. See *Payne v. Tennessee*, 501 U.S. ——, ——, 111 S.Ct. 2597, 2605, 115 L.Ed.2d 720 (1991); *United States v. Tucker*, 404 U.S. 443, 446, 92 S.Ct. 589, 591, 30 L.Ed.2d 592 (1972); *Williams v. New York*, 337 U.S. 241, 246, 69 S.Ct. 1079, 1082, 93 L.Ed. 1337 (1949). The defendant's motive for committing the offense is one important factor. See 1 W. LeFave & A. Scott, Substantive Criminal Law § 3.6(b), p. 324 (1986) ("Motives are most relevant when the trial judge sets the defendant's sentence, and it is not uncommon for a defendant to receive a minimum sentence because he was acting with good motives, or a rather high sentence because of his bad motives"); cf. *Tison v. Arizona*, 481 U.S. 137, 156, 107 S.Ct. 1676, 1687, 95 L.Ed.2d 127 (1987) ("Deeply ingrained in our legal tradition is the idea that the more purposeful is the criminal conduct, the more serious is the offense, and, therefore, the more severely it ought to be punished"). Thus, in many States the commission of a murder, or other capital offense, for pecuniary gain is a separate aggravating circumstance under the capital-sentencing statute. See, *e.g.*, Ariz.Rev. Stat.Ann. § 13–703(F)(5) (1989); Fla.Stat. § 921.141(5)(f) (Supp.1992); Miss.Code Ann. § 99–19–101(5)(f) (Supp.1992); N.C.Gen. Stat. § 15A–2000(e)(6) (1992); Wyo.Stat. § 6–2–102(h)(vi) (Supp.1992).

[8, 9] But it is equally true that a defendant's abstract beliefs, however obnoxious to most people, may not be taken into consideration by a sentencing judge. *Dawson v. Delaware*, 503 U.S. ——, 112 S.Ct. 1093, 117 L.Ed.2d 309 (1992). In *Dawson*, the State introduced evidence at a capital-sentencing hearing that the defendant was a member of a white supremacist prison gang. Because "the evidence proved nothing more than [the defendant's] abstract beliefs," we held that its admission violated the defendant's First Amendment rights. *Id.*, at ——, 112 S.Ct., at 1098. In so holding, however, we emphasized that "the Constitution does not erect a *per se* barrier to the admission of evidence concerning one's beliefs and associations at sentencing simply because those beliefs and associations are protected by the First Amendment." *Id.*, at ——, 112 S.Ct., at 1094. Thus, in *Barclay v. Florida*, 463 U.S. 939, 103 S.Ct. 3418, 77 L.Ed.2d 1134 (1983) (plurality opinion), we allowed the sentencing judge to take into account the defendant's racial animus towards his victim. The evidence in that case showed that the defendant's membership in the Black Liberation Army and desire to provoke a "race war" were related to the murder of a white man for which he was convicted. See *id.*, at 942–944, 103 S.Ct., at 3421–3422. Because "the elements of racial hatred in [the] murder" were relevant to several aggravating factors, we held that the trial judge permissibly took this evidence into account in sentencing the defendant to death. *Id.*, at 949, and n. 7, 103 S.Ct., at 3424, and n. 7.

[10] Mitchell suggests that *Dawson* and *Barclay* are inapposite because they did not involve application of a penalty-enhancement provision. But in *Barclay* we held that it was permissible for the sentencing court to consider the defendant's racial animus in determining whether he should be sentenced to death, surely the most severe "enhancement" of all. And the fact that the Wisconsin Legislature has decided, as a general matter, that bias-motivated offenses warrant greater maximum penalties across the board does not alter the result here. For the primary responsibility for fixing criminal penalties lies with the legislature. *Rummel v. Estelle*, 445 U.S. 263, 274, 100 S.Ct. 1133, 1139, 63 L.Ed.2d 382 (1980); *Gore v. United States*, 357 U.S. 386, 393, 78 S.Ct. 1280, 1284, 2 L.Ed.2d 1405 (1958).

Mitchell argues that the Wisconsin penalty-enhancement statute is invalid because it punishes the defendant's discriminatory motive, or reason, for acting. But motive plays the same role under the Wisconsin statute as it does under federal and state antidiscrimination laws, which we have previously upheld against constitutional challenge. See *Roberts v. Jaycees*, 468 U.S., at 628, 104 S.Ct., at 3255; *Hishon v. King & Spalding*, 467 U.S. 69, 78, 104 S.Ct. 2229, 2235, 81 L.Ed.2d 59 (1984); *Runyon v. McCrary*, 427 U.S. 160, 176, 96 S.Ct. 2586, 2597, 49 L.Ed.2d 415 (1976). Title VII, for example, makes it unlawful for an employer to discriminate against an employee "*because of* such individual's race, color, religion, sex, or national origin." 42 U.S.C. § 2000e–2(a)(1) (emphasis added). In *Hishon*, we rejected the argument that Title VII infringed employers' First Amendment rights. And more recently, in *R.A.V. v. St. Paul*, 505 U.S., at ——, 112 S.Ct., at 2546, we cited Title VII (as well as 18 U.S.C. § 242 and 42 U.S.C. §§ 1981 and 1982) as an example of a permissible content-neutral regulation of conduct.

Nothing in our decision last Term in *R.A.V.* compels a different result here. That case involved a First Amendment challenge to a municipal ordinance prohibiting the use of " 'fighting words' that insult, or provoke violence, 'on the basis of race, color, creed, religion or gender.' " 505 U.S., at ——, 112 S.Ct., at 2547 (quoting St. Paul Bias–Motivated Crime Ordinance, St. Paul, Minn., Legis.Code § 292.02 (1990)). Because the ordinance only proscribed a class of "fighting words" deemed particularly offensive by the city—*i.e.*, those "that contain ... messages of 'bias-motivated' hatred," 505 U.S., at ——, 112 S.Ct., at

2547 we held that it violated the rule against content-based discrimination. See *id.*, at ——, 112 S.Ct., at 2547–2548. But whereas the ordinance struck down in *R.A.V.* was explicitly directed at expression (*i.e.*, "speech" or "messages," *id.*, at ——, 112 S.Ct., at 2547, the statute in this case is aimed at conduct unprotected by the First Amendment.

Moreover, the Wisconsin statute singles out for enhancement bias-inspired conduct because this conduct is thought to inflict greater individual and societal harm. For example, according to the State and its *amici*, bias-motivated crimes are more likely to provoke retaliatory crimes, inflict distinct emotional harms on their victims, and incite community unrest. See, *e.g.*, Brief for Petitioner 24–27; Brief for United States as *Amicus Curiae* 13–15; Brief for Lawyers' Committee for Civil Rights Under Law as *Amicus Curiae* 18–22; Brief for the American Civil Liberties Union as *Amicus Curiae* 17–19; Brief for the Anti-Defamation League et al. as *Amici Curiae* 9–10; Brief for Congressman Charles E. Schumer et al. as *Amici Curiae* 8–9. The State's desire to redress these perceived harms provides an adequate explanation for its penalty-enhancement provision over and above mere disagreement with offenders' beliefs or biases. As Blackstone said long ago, "it is but reasonable that among crimes of different natures those should be most severely punished, which are the most destructive of the public safety and happiness." 4 W. Blackstone, Commentaries *16.

[11] Finally, there remains to be considered Mitchell's argument that the Wisconsin statute is unconstitutionally overbroad because of its "chilling effect" on free speech. Mitchell argues (and the Wisconsin Supreme Court agreed) that the statute is "overbroad" because evidence of the defendant's prior speech or associations may be used to prove that the defendant intentionally selected his victim on account of the victim's protected status. Consequently, the argument goes, the statute impermissibly chills free expression with respect to such matters by those concerned about the possibility of enhanced sentences if they should in the future commit a criminal offense covered by the statute. We find no merit in this contention.

The sort of chill envisioned here is far more attenuated and unlikely than that contemplated in traditional "overbreadth" cases. We must conjure up a vision of a Wisconsin citizen suppressing his unpopular bigoted opinions for fear that if he later commits an offense covered by the statute, these opinions will be offered at trial to establish that he selected his victim on account of the victim's protected status, thus qualifying him for penalty-enhancement. To stay within the realm of rationality, we must surely put to one side minor misdemeanor offenses covered by the statute, such as negligent operation of a motor vehicle (Wis.Stat. § 941.01 (1989–1990)); for it is difficult, if not impossible, to conceive of a situation where such offenses would be racially motivated. We are left, then, with the prospect of a citizen suppressing his bigoted beliefs for fear that evidence of such beliefs will be introduced against him at trial if he commits a more serious offense against person or property. This is simply too speculative a hypothesis to support Mitchell's overbreadth claim.

[12] The First Amendment, moreover, does not prohibit the evidentiary use of speech to establish the elements of a crime or to prove motive or intent. Evidence of a defendant's previous declarations or statements is commonly admitted in criminal trials subject to evidentiary rules dealing with relevancy, reliability, and the like. Nearly half a century ago, in *Haupt v. United States*, 330 U.S. 631, 67 S.Ct. 874, 91 L.Ed. 1145 (1947), we rejected a contention similar to that advanced by Mitchell here. Haupt was tried for the offense of treason, which, as defined by the Constitution (Art. III, § 3), may depend very much on proof of motive. To prove that the acts in question were committed out of "adher-

ence to the enemy" rather than "parental solicitude," *id.*, at 641, 67 S.Ct., at 878, the Government introduced evidence of conversations that had taken place long prior to the indictment, some of which consisted of statements showing Haupt's sympathy with Germany and Hitler and hostility towards the United States. We rejected Haupt's argument that this evidence was improperly admitted. While "[s]uch testimony is to be scrutinized with care to be certain the statements are not expressions of mere lawful and permissible difference of opinion with our own government or quite proper appreciation of the land of birth," we held that "these statements ... clearly were admissible on the question of intent and adherence to the enemy." *Id.*, at 642, 67 S.Ct., at 879. See also *Price Waterhouse v. Hopkins,* 490 U.S. 228, 251–252, 109 S.Ct. 1775, 1791–1792, 104 L.Ed.2d 268 (1989) (plurality opinion) (allowing evidentiary use of defendant's speech in evaluating Title VII discrimination claim); *Street v. New York,* 394 U.S. 576, 594, 89 S.Ct. 1354, 1366–1367, 22 L.Ed.2d 572 (1969).

For the foregoing reasons, we hold that Mitchell's First Amendment rights were not violated by the application of the Wisconsin penalty-enhancement provision in sentencing him. The judgment of the Supreme Court of Wisconsin is therefore reversed, and the case is remanded for further proceedings not inconsistent with this opinion.

It is so ordered.

The University of Chicago Law Review

VOLUME 60   NUMBERS 3 & 4
SUMMER/FALL 1993

© 1993 by The University of Chicago

Words, Conduct, Caste

Cass R. Sunstein†

B. Hate Speech

Are restrictions on hate speech impermissibly selective? In
R.A.V. v City of St. Paul,[94] the Court invalidated a law directed
against a certain kind of hate speech, principally on the ground
that it discriminated on the basis of subject matter. As interpreted
by the Minnesota Supreme Court, the relevant law banned any
fighting words that produced anger or resentment on the basis of
race, religion, or gender.[95] The *R.A.V.* Court emphasized that the
law at issue was not a broad or general proscription of fighting
words.[96] Instead, the law reflected a decision to single out a certain
category of "fighting words," defined in terms of audience reactions *to speech about certain topics*.[97] Is this constitutionally ille-

---

[94] 112 S Ct 2538 (1992).
[95] Id at 2541.
[96] Id at 2547-48.
[97] Id.

gitimate? The point bears on almost all efforts to regulate hate speech.[98]

Subject matter restrictions are not all the same. We can imagine subject matter restrictions that are questionable ("no one may discuss homosexuality on the subway") and subject matter restrictions that seem legitimate ("no high-level CIA employee may speak publicly about classified matters relating to the clandestine affairs of the American government."[99]) As a class, subject matter restrictions appear to occupy a point somewhere between viewpoint-based restrictions and content-neutral ones. Sometimes courts uphold such restrictions as a form of permissible content regulation. For example, the Court has permitted prohibitions of political advertising on buses[100] and of partisan political speech at army bases.[101] These cases show that there is no per se ban on subject matter restrictions. When the Court upholds subject matter restrictions, it is either because the line drawn by government gives no real reason for fear about lurking viewpoint discrimination, or (what is close to the same thing) because government is able to invoke neutral, harm-based justifications for treating certain subjects differently from others. In raising this issue, hate speech restrictions pose many of the same problems discussed above in connection with pornography.

If the subject matter restriction in the cross-burning case is acceptable, it must be because the specified catalogue of regulated speech is sufficiently neutral and does not alert the judge to possible concerns about viewpoint discrimination, or because (again a closely overlapping point) it is plausible to argue that the harms, in the specific covered cases, are sufficiently severe and distinctive to justify special treatment. This was the issue that in the end divided the Supreme Court.

In his separate opinion in *R.A.V.*, Justice Stevens argued that the harms were indeed sufficiently distinctive. He wrote: "Just as Congress may determine that threats against the President entail more severe consequences than other threats, so St. Paul's City

---

[98] In the following discussion, I draw on Cass R. Sunstein, *On Analogical Reasoning*, 106 Harv L Rev 741, 759-66 (1993), though I have made a number of new points here. See also Sunstein, *Democracy and the Problem of Free Expression* ch 7 (cited in note 22), which discusses *R.A.V.* and the issue of viewpoint discrimination in more detail.

[99] This example comes from *Snepp v United States*, 444 US 507, 510-13 (1980) (per curiam) (upholding the imposition of a constructive trust on a book produced by a former CIA agent in contravention of a nondisclosure agreement with the government).

[100] *Lehman v Shaker Heights*, 418 US 298, 304 (1974).

[101] *Greer v Spock*, 424 US 828, 838 (1976).

Council may determine that threats based on the target's race, religion, or gender cause more severe harm to both the target and society than other threats."[102] In his view, "[t]hreatening someone because of her race or religious beliefs may cause particularly severe trauma or touch off a riot . . . such threats may be punished more severely than threats against someone based on, for example, his support of a particular athletic team."[103] Thus there were "legitimate, reasonable, and neutral justifications" for the special rule.[104] Justice Stevens' argument is highly reminiscent of the claim that antipornography legislation should be seen as an acceptable response to harm rather than an imposition of a point of view.

In its response, the Court said that this argument "is word-play."[105] The reason that a race-based threat is different "is nothing other than the fact that it is caused by a distinctive idea, conveyed by a distinctive method. The First Amendment cannot be evaded that easily."[106] But at first glance, it seems that a legislature could reasonably decide that the harms produced by this narrow category of hate speech are sufficiently severe as to deserve separate treatment. Surely it seems plausible to say that cross-burning, swastikas, and the like are an especially distinctive kind of "fighting word"—distinctive because of the objective and subjective harm they inflict on their victims and on society in general. An incident of cross-burning can have large and corrosive social consequences. A reasonable and sufficiently neutral government could decide that the same is not true for a hateful attack on someone's parents, union affiliation, or political convictions.

A harm-based argument of this kind suggests that in singling out a certain kind of regulable speech for special controls, the legislature is responding not to ideological message, but to real-world consequences. Unlike in most cases of viewpoint discrimination, it appears that we have no special reason for suspecting government's motives. According to Justice Stevens, a state is acting neutrally if it singles out cross-burning for special punishment, because this

---

[102] *R.A.V.*, 112 S Ct at 2565 (Stevens concurring in the judgment). The relevant statute is 18 USC § 871 (1988). See also 18 USC § 879 (1988) (regulating threats against former presidents). Justice Stevens was responding to the majority's argument that laws increasing the penalty for threats against the President are permissible because the reasons for these laws relate to the justification for punishing threats in the first place. See text accompanying note 92.

[103] 112 S Ct at 2561 (Stevens concurring in the judgment).

[104] Id.

[105] Id at 2548 (majority opinion).

[106] Id.

kind of "fighting word" has especially severe social consequences. According to the Court, on the other hand, a state cannot legitimately decide that cross-burning is worse than (for example) a vicious attack on your political convictions or your parents. A decision to this effect violates neutrality. But the Court's conception of neutrality seems wrong. There is nothing partisan or illegitimate in recognizing that this unusual class of fighting words causes distinctive harms.

My claim here is very narrow; I do not argue for broad bans on hate speech. Most such bans would indeed violate the First Amendment because they would forbid a good deal of speech that is intended and received as a contribution to public deliberation. But here we are dealing with hate speech limited to the exceedingly narrow category of admittedly unprotected fighting words. The argument on behalf of this kind of restriction might benefit from Justice Stevens's analogy to the especially severe legal penalties directed toward threats against the President.[107] Everyone seems to agree that this restriction is permissible, because threats against the President cause distinctive harms and can therefore be punished more severely. But if the government can single out one category of threats for special sanction because of the distinctive harm that those particular threats cause, why cannot the same be said for the fighting words at issue here?

Justice Scalia's response is probably the best that can be offered: "[T]he reasons why threats of violence are outside the First Amendment (protecting individuals from fear of violence, from the disruption that fear engenders, and from the possibility that threatened violence will occur) have special force when applied to the President."[108] But exactly the same could be said of the hate speech ordinance under discussion: the justification for the fighting words exemption has special force because of the context of racial injustice. Here, as in cases involving threats against the President, we are dealing with a subcategory of unprotected speech challenged as involving impermissible selectivity, and the justification for the selectivity involves the particular harms of the unprotected speech at issue. That justification seems sufficiently neutral.

Consider another analogy. Supplemental criminal penalties for racially-motivated "hate crimes" seem to be a well-established part of current law, appearing in the statutes of the vast majority of

---

[107] Id at 2565-66 (Stevens concurring in the judgment). See note 102.
[108] Id at 2546 (majority opinion).

states.[109] Do those penalties violate the First Amendment? In *Wisconsin v Mitchell*,[110] a unanimous Supreme Court said that they do not, and I believe the Court was right. But consider the fact that the government imposes the additional penalty because it thinks that hate crimes create distinctive subjective and objective harm. The distinctive harm is produced in part because of the symbolic or expressive nature of hate crimes. This justification is the same as that in the cross-burning case. This does not mean that it is impossible to draw distinctions between enhanced penalty statutes and "hate speech" laws. But it does mean that if the justification for the hate crimes measures is sufficiently neutral, the same should be said for narrow restrictions on hate speech.

Perhaps we can respond to this claim with the suggestion that hate crimes are not speech—not because of discredited versions of the "speech/conduct" distinction, but because hate crimes are not intended and received as contributions to deliberation about anything and do not communicate ideas of any kind.[111] This was one of the Supreme Court's major arguments in the *Mitchell* case. According to the Court, cross-burning is speech, whereas hate crimes are unprotected conduct.[112] Perhaps laws that regulate conduct are permissible even if some of the relevant conduct is communicative. Moreover, it may well be true that most hate crimes do not have a communicative intention or effect. But some certainly do. The lynching of black people, for example, is thoroughly communicative. When a hate crime has a communicative purpose, are enhanced penalties invalid if the reason for enhancement is what I have described? I do not believe that there is anything illegitimate about the state's belief that the subjective and objective harm justify enhancement.

In *Mitchell*, the Supreme Court relied heavily on this belief.[113] For this reason, the line between *R.A.V.* and *Mitchell* seems quite thin. As I have emphasized, all the justices in *R.A.V.* agreed that

---

[109] See, for example, 46 Fla Stat Ann § 775.085 (West 1992); 720 ILCS 5/12-7.1 (West 1993); 76 Utah Code 1953 ch 3 § 203.3 (Michie 1992 Supp). As of June 23, 1992, forty-six states had enacted some form of hate crime statute. David G. Savage, *Hate Crime Law is Struck Down*, LA Times A1 (June 23, 1992). A penalty-enhancement bill for federal criminal cases is currently pending in Congress. Hate Crimes Sentencing Enhancement Act of 1993, HR 1152, 103d Cong, 1st Sess (March 1, 1993). See also Hate Crimes Sentencing Enhancement Act of 1992, Hearing on HR 4797 before the Subcommittee on Crime and Criminal Justice of the House Committee on the Judiciary, 102d Cong, 2d Sess (1992).

[110] 113 S Ct 2194 (1993).

[111] See Section IV.A.

[112] 113 S Ct at 2199.

[113] Id at 2200-01.

the expressive acts at issue were unprotected by the First Amendment, because the state court had said that the statute was limited to unprotected "fighting words." *R.A.V.* therefore involved constitutionally unprotected acts, just as *Mitchell* did. And everyone in *Mitchell* agreed that the First Amendment issue did not disappear simply because conduct was involved. The Court said that "a physical assault is not by any stretch of the imagination expressive conduct protected by the First Amendment"[114]; but it rightly added that a genuine First Amendment issue is raised when a state "enhances the maximum penalty for conduct motivated by a discriminatory point of view."[115]

Understood in these terms, *R.A.V.* and *Mitchell* are very close, and the Court did not adequately explain the difference between them. Perhaps the major distinction between the two cases is that the Minnesota law in *R.A.V.* covered speech as well as expressive conduct, and cross-burning is characteristically expressive —whereas the enhancement statute was directed only at conduct, and many hate crimes are not intended or received as a communication on anything at all. For this reason, the enhancement penalty can perhaps be seen as a content-neutral restriction on conduct that is not ordinarily expressive, while the Minnesota law was a content-based restriction on speech, including expressive conduct. This is a reasonable distinction. But it is not clear that the distinction really rescues the *R.A.V.* outcome. The question remains whether the state had a legitimate justification for doing what it did. The *Mitchell* Court emphasized that the state treated "bias-inspired" conduct more severely because that conduct inflicts "greater individual and societal harm."[116] This was Justice Stevens's argument in *R.A.V.*, and it seems to have equal weight in both cases.

One final analogy seems to suggest that *R.A.V.* is wrong on the neutrality issue. The civil rights laws say that you may not fire someone because of his race, even though you may fire him for many other reasons.[117] On one view, the civil rights laws are therefore unconstitutional, because they penalize someone for his politi-

---

[114] Id at 2199.
[115] Id.
[116] Id at 2201.
[117] See Civil Rights Act of 1964, § 703(a)(1), as amended, codified at 42 USC § 2000e-2(a)(1) (1988); *McDonnell Douglas Corp. v Green*, 411 US 792, 800-03 (1973) (discussing burdens of proof in employment discrimination cases and noting that although an employee does not have a right to a job, she has the right to a workplace free from unfair discrimination).

cal convictions. In this respect, they are similar to a prohibition on flag-burning. They single out conduct (or mere words) for special penalty simply because of the message communicated by that conduct.

To be sure, most discriminatory discharges are not intended to communicate a general political message, but some discharges do have such an intention. It would be most adventurous, to say the least, to claim that the First Amendment prohibits application of the civil rights laws to politically-motivated discrimination. But if *R.A.V.* is right on the issue of neutrality, it is not simple to explain why the civil rights laws survive constitutional attack. Perhaps it could be said that most discriminatory discharges are not communicative in nature, and that the claim that such discharges are distinctly harmful has a sufficiently neutral justification. Perhaps it could be said that the civil rights laws sweep up communicative discharges as an incidental part of an effort to prevent a class of activities defined in terms of conduct rather than expression. But if the justification behind the civil rights laws is in fact sufficiently neutral, the same seems to be true of the statute in the *R.A.V.* case.

The arguments from these analogies are not decisive. Plausible distinctions can be drawn. But some of the distinctions seem thin. I conclude that as the *Mitchell* Court held, the First Amendment is not violated by laws enhancing the punishment of hate crime. I also conclude that no serious First Amendment problem is raised by the civil rights laws, even though those laws sometimes punish speech. And a restriction on cross-burning and other symbolic hate speech is a permissible subject-matter classification, so long as the restriction is narrowed in the way described.

In *R.A.V.* the Supreme Court offered a tempting and clever response:

> In its practical operation, moreover, the ordinance goes even beyond mere content discrimination to actual viewpoint discrimination. Displays containing some words—odious racial epithets, for example—would be prohibited to proponents of all views. But 'fighting words' that do not themselves invoke race, color, creed, religion, or gender—aspersions based upon a person's mother, for example—would be seemingly usable ad libitum in the placards of those arguing in favor of racial, color, etc. tolerance and equality, but could not be used by that speaker's opponents. . . . St. Paul has no such authority

to license one side of a debate to fight freestyle, while requiring the other to follow Marquis of Queensbury Rules.[118]

The short answer to this argument is that the ordinance at issue does not embody viewpoint discrimination as that term is ordinarily understood. Viewpoint discrimination occurs if the government takes one side in a debate, as in, for example, a law saying that libel of the President will be punished more severely than libel of anyone else. Viewpoint discrimination is not established by the fact that in some hypotheticals, one side has greater means of expression than another, at least—and this is the critical point—if the restriction on means has legitimate, neutral justifications.

We can make this point by reference to the fact that it is a federal crime to threaten the life of the President. Recall that the Supreme Court said in *R.A.V.* that such statutes are permissible even though they make distinctions within the category of unprotected threats. Imagine the following conversation: John: "I will kill the President." Jill: "I will kill anyone who threatens to kill the President." John has committed a federal crime; Jill has not. In this sense, the presidential threat case involves the same kind of de facto viewpoint discrimination as the *R.A.V.* case. If it is not unconstitutional for that reason[119]—and the Court indicated that it is not—the Court should not have found the statute in *R.A.V.* viewpoint discriminatory.

The point has general implications. It suggests that the state can attack hate speech dealing with certain matters, as Stanford has done, without running afoul of the prohibition on impermissible selectivity. It also suggests that some narrowly drawn viewpoint discriminatory restrictions—protecting against hate speech directed at blacks or women—might well be permissible.[120] Thus, for example, a locality might decide that cross-burning and hate speech directed against blacks pose special risks not posed by hate speech directed against whites. For the reasons I have outlined, I do not believe that there is anything illegitimate about a public judgment that hate speech against blacks creates distinctive subjective and objective harm.

---

[118] 112 S Ct at 2547-48.

[119] See the discussion of pornography in Section III.A.

[120] See Amar, 106 Harv L Rev at 151-61 (cited in note 21).

Freedom of Speech and International Norms: A Response to Hate Speech

ELIZABETH F. DEFEIS*

Nearly all other countries have adopted a position that facilitates free speech, yet recognizes the interdependence of the rights, duties and responsibilities of individuals. The international conventions adopted after World War II are direct re-

* Professor of Law, Seton Hall University School of Law. The author wishes to thank Professor Ignatius M. Rautenbach, Rand Afrikaans University, South Africa; Professor Rosario Domingue, University of Birmingham, England, and Dr. Jean-Bernard Marie for their initial collaboration at the International Institute of Human Rights, Strasbourg, France (Summer Session 1991), and Professors Eugene Gressman, Malvina Halberstam, Joseph Lynch, and Catherine McCauliff for their helpful critiques of the drafts of this article. The author also wishes to thank Seton Hall University School of Law students Paul R. Clementi, Class of 1993, and Garo Bakmazian, Class of 1994, for their excellent research assistance, and Linda Murph for her assistance.

sponses to the horror of genocide perpetrated against Jews and other minorities before and during World War II. The international community approved these documents to ensure that such atrocities could not occur again. Equality and non-discrimination are central themes of these international documents and no international human rights norm is more clearly established by the United Nations Charter than the one against discrimination.[58] The preamble of the Universal Declaration also recognizes the equal and inalienable rights of all and provides that all are "entitled to equal protection against any discrimination in violation of this Declaration and against any incitement to such discrimination."[59] Similarly, the International Convention on the Protection of Civil and Political Rights provides for equality before the law and requires that "the law shall prohibit any discrimination and guarantee to all persons equal and effective protection against discrimination."[60] Together with the Covenant on Economic and Social Rights, these documents are commonly referred to as the International Bill of Human Rights. The principles of equality and non-discrimination are now recognized as constituting customary international law.[61]

---

[58] *See* RICHARD B. LILLICH, INTERNATIONAL HUMAN RIGHTS 229 (2d ed. 1991) [hereinafter INTERNATIONAL HUMAN RIGHTS]; LOUIS HENKIN, THE INTERNATIONAL BILL OF RIGHTS 20 (1981) [hereinafter INTERNATIONAL BILL OF RIGHTS].

[59] Universal Declaration, *supra* note 6, art 7.

[60] Rights Covenant, *supra* note 1, at 52.

[61] *See* B. G. Ramcharan, *Equality and Non Discrimination, in* INTERNATIONAL BILL OF RIGHTS, *supra* note 58, at 249.

II. INTERNATIONAL INSTRUMENTS AND NORMS

Human rights featured prominently in the planning and drafting of the United Nations Charter.[93] The preamble of the Char-

---

[93] Although sporadic humanitarian interventions occurred during the nineteenth
century, these limited efforts focused on self-determination of people, the prohibition of
slavery, religious freedom, and the regulation of prohibitions against war. *See* Matthew
Lippman, *Human Rights Revisited,* 10 CAL. W. INT'L L.J. 450 (1980). In addition, the
League of Nations, through its mandate system, recognized an international concern for
some human rights. An accepted principle of international law was that a country's
treatment of its own citizens was not a matter of international concern. *See* RIGHTS OF

ter reaffirms "faith in the fundamental human rights, . . . in the dignity and worth of the human person," and in the "equal rights of men and women."[94] Among the purposes of the United Nations is international cooperation "in promoting and encouraging respect for human rights and fundamental freedom for all without distinction as to race, sex, language, or religion."[95] Two weaknesses of the Charter are its failure to define human rights in specific terms and its failure to establish a mechanism to enforce these rights. The drafters expected that subsequent documents would delineate those rights and provide for protection through binding international conventions.[96]

Freedom of opinion and expression were among the basic human rights to be protected and were the subject of several General Assembly resolutions. At its first session, the United Nations General Assembly, in calling for an International Conference on Freedom of Information, declared:

> Freedom of information is a fundamental right and is the touchstone of all freedoms to which the United Nations is consecrated; freedom of information requires as an indispensable element the willingness and capacity to employ its privileges without abuse. It requires as a basic discipline the moral obligation to seek facts without prejudice

Man, *supra* note 63; Hersh Lauterpacht, International Law and Human Rights 166-220 (1950).

[94] U. N. Charter pmbl.

[95] U.N. Charter arts. 1(3), 5. Some countries sought to include in the charter a bill of rights. However, the efforts failed mainly because the United States, the Soviet Union, France and the United Kingdom did not favor a strong statement on human rights. Thomas Buergenthal, *The Human Rights Revolution*, 23 St. Mary's L.J. 3, 7 (1991).

[96] Although early drafts of the United Nations Charter proposed by the U.S. Department of State included a bill of rights to which all nations were required to subscribe, disagreement arose over the inclusion of social and economic rights and methods of implementation. Efforts to include a bill of rights therefore were abandoned. *See* Lippman, *supra* note 93, at 459. At the San Francisco Conference, various proposals were put forth for the inclusion of the bill of rights in the Charter. *See* John Huston, *Human Rights, Enforcement Issue of the United Nations Conference on International Organizations*, 53 Iowa L. Rev. 272 (1967).

At the San Francisco Conference, President Harry Truman echoed the sentiment of the conference in the expectation that a bill of rights was forthcoming. He stated:

> Under this document [the Charter] we have good reason to expect an international bill of rights acceptable to all nations involved. That bill of rights will be as much a part of international life as our own Bill of Rights is part of our Constitution. The Charter is dedicated to the achievement and observance of human rights and fundamental freedoms. Unless we can attain those objectives for all men and women everywhere without regard to race, language or religion, we can not have permanent peace and security in the world.

1 U.N.C.I.O. Docs. 717 (1945).

and to spread knowledge without malicious intent.[97]

In turn, at its first meeting, the Human Rights Commission of the United Nations commenced the task of drafting a bill of rights.[98] Initially, discussion centered on whether a declaration of the General Assembly with no legally binding effect would be sufficient and feasible, or whether a legally binding convention was necessary. The Commission decided to proceed by drafting simultaneously a Declaration and a Covenant.[99]

A. *The Universal Declaration of Human Rights*

The Universal Declaration of Human Rights, unanimously adopted by the General Assembly in 1948, sets forth specific inalienable rights and freedoms which cannot be abridged by any nation. Although technically non-binding as a source of international law, the Universal Declaration was intended to serve as a common standard of achievement to which all states should aspire.[100]

Provision for freedom of expression is contained in Article 19 of the Universal Declaration which states:

Everyone has the right to freedom of opinion and expres-

---

[97] *Calling of an International Conference on Freedom of Information*, G.A. Res. 59(I), U.N. Doc. A/64/Add.1 (1947), *reprinted in* 1 UNITED NATIONS RESOLUTIONS, SER. I 82 (Dusan J. Djonovich ed. 1973). The primary concern of the United Nations during the post World War II era was not so much the freedom of expression, but the freedom of dissemination of information. The goal of such freedom was to provide a forum for internal opposition to oppressive regimes and to allow foreign governments greater access to evaluate human rights abuses.

[98] The first meeting, chaired by Eleanor Roosevelt, took place on January 27, 1947. The committee produced a final draft which was submitted to the General Assembly on September 21, 1947. Lippman, *supra* note 93, at 456-59.

[99] Vratislav Pechota, *The Development of the Covenant on Civil and Political Rights*, in INTERNATIONAL BILL OF RIGHTS, *supra* note 58, at 32.

[100] *See* RIGHTS OF MAN, *supra* note 63, at 1. The vote on the Declaration was forty-eight in favor, zero votes against, eight abstentions and two were absent. The dissenting votes were from five Eastern European Community bloc countries, Saudi Arabia, and South Africa. The rights contained in the Declaration have been compared in significance to the Magna Carta. *See* U.N. GAOR 3d Sess., pt. 1, at 262 (1948). The text of the pronouncement has been incorporated in national legislation. *See* UNITED NATIONS OFFICE OF PUBLIC INFORMATION, THE UNITED NATIONS AND HUMAN RIGHTS, U.N. Doc. OPI/621, at 166 (1978).

Although when adopted the Declaration was understood to be non-binding, some noted scholars have taken the position that the provisions are binding as customary international law or as part of the Charter obligations of member states. For example, Professor Louis Sohn states that the Universal Declaration of Human Rights has "become a part of the common law of the world community; and, together with the Charter of the United Nations, it has achieved the character of the world law superior to all other international instruments and to domestic laws." Louis B. Sohn, *The Universal Declaration of Human Rights*, 8 J. INT'L COMMISSION JURISTS 17, 26 (1967).

sion; this right includes freedom to hold opinions without interference and to seek, receive and impart information and ideas through any media and regardless of frontiers.[101]

Although the Declaration does not contain a specific restriction clause with respect to hate speech, its general limitation clause, Article 29(3), states: "These rights and freedoms may in no case be exercised contrary to the purposes and principles of the United Nations."[102] A significant goal of the United Nations is to promote and encourage respect for human rights and fundamental freedoms "without distinction as to race, sex, language, or religion."[103] This Article can reasonably be interpreted as limiting protection for speech that promotes racial, sexual, linguistic, or religious discrimination.

Furthermore, Article 30 of the Declaration reads: "Nothing in this Declaration may be interpreted as implying for any State, group or person any right to engage in any activity or to perform any act aimed at the destruction of any of the rights and freedoms set forth herein."[104] Because rights can be abused sometimes to destroy or deny the rights of others, this provision authorizes states, under certain circumstances, to derogate, limit, or restrict the rights it proclaims.[105]

The Universal Declaration stresses the rights of equality and non-discrimination throughout. It recognizes in the Preamble the inherent dignity and "the equal and inalienable rights of all members of the human family" as the "foundation of freedom, justice and peace in the world."[106] Furthermore, Article I provides that all human beings are born free and equal in dignity and rights.[107] Article II provides for non-discrimination in the exercise of such rights and freedoms.[108] Today the view that

---

[101] Universal Declaration, *supra* note 6, art. 19.

[102] *Id.* art. 29(3).

[103] U.N. CHARTER art. 1(3).

[104] Universal Declaration, *supra* note 6, art. 30.

[105] The original draft of Article 30 referred only to the actions taken by individuals. The drafters' concern was to protect the state from any individual who might misapply the rights guaranteed in the Declaration as a means of promoting the establishment of a totalitarian regime. However, the inclusion of groups and states substantially broadens the scope of Article 30. Professor Thomas Buergenthal notes that this modification now prevents any government from inhibiting an existing right. *See* Thomas Buergenthal, *State Obligations and Permissible Derogations, in* INTERNATIONAL BILL OF RIGHTS, *supra* note 58, at 86.

[106] Universal Declaration, *supra* note 6, pmbl.

[107] *Id.* art. 1.

[108] *Id.* art. 2.

equality and non-discrimination are part of international law and must be respected together with other civil rights enjoys wide support.[109]

No express limitation pertaining to hate speech exists in the Universal Declaration. Nevertheless, in view of the historic setting of the drafting of the Universal Declaration, the Commission's review of relevant state practice, the emphasis on equality and non-discrimination and the recognition of the interdependence of rights, the Universal Declaration implicitly does not protect hate speech.

B. *The Covenant on Civil and Political Rights*

After approving the Universal Declaration, the UN General Assembly and Secretariat sought to implement the rights embodied in the Universal Declaration through binding agreements. The Commission on Human Rights, chaired by Eleanor Roosevelt, was charged with the task of drafting these documents.[110] The difficulty of obtaining a universal agreement on either the content or the form of the convention was immediately apparent. For example, while the British favored exacting language throughout the covenant, the United States advocated general principles that more closely resembled a declaration.[111] In addition, the United States delegation was wary that the covenant might contain language that would be inconsistent with United States constitutional law as it related to freedom of

---

109 *See* B.G. Ramcharan, *supra* note 61, at 247. Mr. Ramcharan provides a compressive analysis of the development of the concept of equality as an international human right. Quoted in the essay is an address by the Head of the Federal Political Department of Switzerland at the opening of the World Conference to Combat Racism and Racial Discrimination on August 14, 1978 which states:

> Of all human rights, the right to equality is one of the most important. It is linked to the concepts of liberty and justice, and is manifested through the observance of two fundamental and complementary principles of international law. The first of these principles, that "all human beings are born free and equal in dignity and rights," appears in the 1948 Universal Declaration of Human Rights; the second, the principle of nondiscrimination, has been solemnly reaffirmed in Article I of the Charter of the United Nations. It is upon those two principles that all the instruments on human rights adopted since 1945 are based. . . . The prohibition of discrimination has become a norm of positive law.

110 Although the Commission on Human Rights initially was instructed to draft a covenant that would include not only civil and political rights, but also economic and social rights, the General Assembly subsequently instructed the Commission to draft two covenants, GA. Res. 41E (V), Dec. 4, 1950 and GA Res. 543 (VI), Feb. 5, 1952. *See* Lippman, *supra* note 93, at 471 n.90.

111 *See infra* text accompanying note 112.

expression.[112]

The general principle that everyone shall have the right to freedom of expression was not in itself a controversial issue, yet differences of opinion arose regarding the scope and substance of freedom of expression.[113] The debate centered on whether the document should provide specifically that the right to freedom of expression is coupled with duties and responsibilities. Those supporting this proposal argued that freedom of expression is a "precious heritage" and, in view of the powerful influence of the media on thought and international affairs, the duties and responsibilities in the exercise of freedom of expression should be emphasized.[114] Other states countered that because each right carries a corresponding duty, and that in no other article was the corresponding duty set out, no such exception should be imposed.[115] Ultimately, the Commission adopted the clause with the word "special" before "duties and responsibilities."[116]

The Commission also debated whether the guarantee of freedom of expression in the Covenant on Civil and Political Rights (Rights Covenant) should protect the individual against governmental actions only or against other individuals' actions as well. Efforts to restrict the guarantee to government interference through specific reference failed.[117] The Rights Covenant's guarantee therefore protects individuals against actions by government and by other individuals as well.

Perhaps the most significant debate centered on the question of permissible restrictions or limitations on speech rights. Several states introduced amendments which would further restrict the exercise of the rights and in particular the right to dissemi-

---

[112] See JOHN P. HUMPHREY, HUMAN RIGHTS AND THE UNITED NATIONS: A GREAT ADVENTURE 38-40 (1984). Fighting involving various nations, the United States in particular, ensued as the drafters of the Covenant included provisions which conflicted with the First Amendment to the Constitution. See also Pechota, *supra* note 99, at 44.

[113] See MARC J. BOSSUYT, GUIDE TO THE "TRAVAUX PRÉPARATOIRES" OF THE INTERNATIONAL COVENANT ON CIVIL AND POLITICAL RIGHTS 376 (1987).

[114] The nations which called for specific limitations on expression " . . . laid stress on the continued existence of such evils as national, racial, and religious hatred or prejudices. . . [arguing that] States should therefore be able to prohibit such activities." *Id.* at 393. Consequently, more than 30 specific limitations were proposed by various nations. Among the limitations suggested by one such proposal were "[e]xpressions which are obscene" and "[e]xpressions about other persons, natural or legal, which defame their reputations or are otherwise injurious to them without benefiting the public. . . ." *Id.* at 387.

[115] Further, opponents of the proposal argued that the purpose of the Covenant was to set forth and protect rights rather than impose duties and responsibilities. *Id.* at 386.

[116] *Id.* at 387.

[117] *Id.* at 379.

nate information. These restrictions included those necessary
for the prevention of war propaganda, incitement to enmity
among nations and the "dissemination of slanderous rumors."[118]
The controversy centered on balancing the need for governmental interference or censorship against the need to maintain freedom of information.

The Commission decided to preserve Article 19 but to introduce a new provision dealing with specific limitations.[119] As finally drafted, freedom of expression in Article 19 of the Rights
Covenant reads as follows:

> 1. Everyone shall have the right to hold opinions without
> interference.
> 2. Everyone shall have the right to freedom of expres-
> sion; this right shall include freedom to seek, receive and
> impart information and ideas of all kinds, regardless of
> frontiers, either orally, in writing or in print, in the form of
> art, or through any other media of his choice.
> 3. The exercise of the rights provided for in paragraph 2
> of this article carries with it special duties and responsibili-
> ties. It may therefore be subject to certain restrictions, but
> these shall only be such as are provided by law and are
> necessary:
> > (a) For respect of the rights or reputations of others;
> > (b) For the protection of national security or of pub-
> > lic order (public ordre), or of public health or
> > morals.[120]

Article 19 contains the essential and universally relevant elements of the right to freedom of expression. All subsequent regional treaties contain these major elements.[121]

Some states had argued that additional specific restrictions
should be included in Article 19. They argued that the restric-

---

[118] BOSSUYT, *supra* note 113, at 392.

[119] Pechota, *supra* note 99, at 59.

[120] BOSSUYT, *supra* note 113, at 380-81, 386. This was a more general limitation than
that proposed by Great Britain. The British proposal reads:

The exercise of these freedoms carries with it duties and responsibility and may
therefore be subject to certain penalties, liabilities, and restrictions provided by
law, which are necessary in the interests of national security, for prevention of
disorder or crime, for the protection of public safety, health or morals, for the
protection of the reputations or rights of other persons, for preventing the disclosure of information received in confidence, or for maintaining the authority
and impartiality of the judiciary.

Id. at 386.

[121] *See* DANILO TURK, U.N COMM'N ON HUMAN RIGHTS, PRELIMINARY REPORT ON THE
REALIZATION OF ECONOMIC, SOCIAL AND CULTURAL RIGHTS, U.N. Doc. E/CN.4/Sub.2/
1989/19 (1989).

tions were necessary because of the continued existence of such evils as national, racial and religious hatred and prejudices, and the danger these presented to friendly relations among nations.[122]

The United States expressed strong doubts concerning the wisdom of a prohibition of content-based speech because such a prohibition would prejudice the right of freedom of expression and opinion.[123] However, the position that states must take affirmative steps to prohibit such expression prevailed, and the debate then centered on the parameters of the speech which each state would be required to prohibit.[124]

As a result, Article 20 specifically limits speech by requiring a state to prohibit hate speech. It provides: "Any propaganda for war shall be prohibited by law. Any advocacy of national, racial, or religious hatred that constitutes incitement to discrimination, hostility or violence shall be prohibited by law."[125]

Upon ratification or accession to the Rights Covenant several states entered reservations or declarations to these articles. Several European countries indicated that Article 19 would be applied in the context of the provisions and restrictions of the Convention for the Protection of Human Rights and Fundamental Freedoms.[126] Interpretations or reservations to Article 20 centered on the prohibition against war propaganda and on the necessity for additional legislation in view of existing domestic legislation on the subject.[127]

---

[122] BOSSUYT, *supra* note 113, at 393. The United States proposed the following amendment to Article 19 to exclude protection for expression that promotes national or religious hatred:

"The above mentioned rights shall not be subject to any restrictions except those which . . . are necessary . . . to prevent incitement to violence by fostering, national, racial or religious hatred, and are consistent with other rights recognized in this covenant." *Id.* at 395. This formulation would have been consistent with U.S. Supreme Court opinions. *See* Brandenburg v. Ohio, 395 U.S. 444 (1969).

[123] BOSSUYT, *supra* note 113, at 406. The United States was opposed to the inclusion of this article.

[124] The words "shall be prohibited by the law of the state" were chosen in preference to the words "constitutes a crime and shall be punished under the law of the State." *Id.* at 405-06.

[125] *Id.* at 403.

[126] For example, see the declarations and reservations of Austria, Belgium and France, *in* UNITED NATIONS SECRETARIAT, MULTILATERAL TREATIES DEPOSITED WITH THE SECRETARY GENERAL at 131, 133, U.N. Doc. ST/LEG/SER.E/9, U.N. Sales No. E.91.V.8 (1990) [hereinafter U.N. TREATIES].

[127] For example, France stated: "The Government of the Republic declares that the term 'war,' appearing in Article 20, paragraph 1, is to be understood to mean war in contravention of international law and considers, in any case, that French legislation in

Several states have expressed concerns regarding the limitations on the right to freedom of expression contained in Articles 19 and 20. In general, however, nations agree that limitations in the Rights Covenant, particularly limitations on the right to freedom of speech and expression, must be construed narrowly, with a presumption in favor of freedom of expression.[128]

This requirement of strict construction of the limitation clause on freedom of expression as well as limitation clauses on other rights guaranteed in the convention is reinforced by Article 5(1) of the Rights Covenant which states:

> Nothing in the present Covenant may be interpreted as implying for any State, group or person any right to engage in any activity or perform any act aimed at the destruction of any of the rights and freedoms recognized herein or at their limitation to a greater extent than is provided for in the present Covenant.[129]

Article 5(1) implicitly authorizes states to limit or restrict rights of individuals who engage in activities aimed at destroying rights

this matter is adequate." *Id.* at 133. *See also* the reservations of Finland, *id.* at 133, and the Netherlands, *id.* at 142.

[128] *See The Siracusa Principles on the Limitation and Derogation Provisions in the International Covenant on Civil and Political Rights,* 7 HUM. RTS. Q. 3, 4-5 (1985). The Siracusa Principles state the general rules and principles justifying speech limitations. Principle 3 requires all limitation provisions to be interpreted "strictly in favor of the rights at issue." Principle 2 states that no limitation clause shall be interpreted "so as to jeopardize the essence of the rights concerned." Furthermore, Principle 10 requires that all limitation clauses be "necessary" infringement of a specified right. Principle 10 defines necessary to mean that all limitations must be grounded within a justification found within the Covenant, acted upon "in response to a pressing public or social need," and motivated by a legitimate aim.

The Principles also outline a framework for interpreting the limitation provisions within the context of other international human rights accords and the Rights Covenant itself. According to Principle 1, no limitations may be imposed on a fundamental right unless the Covenant specifically provides for the limitation. The Principles list preservation of the public order, public health, and "rights and reputations of others" as possible justifications for limiting speech. *See* Principles 19-23, 37. Principle 27 states that public morals also may justify a limitation on freedom of speech. Principle 28 requires that for this limitation to be justified, the limitation must be "essential to the maintenance of the respect for fundamental values of the community."

Moreover, Principle 14 states that no limitation within the Rights Covenant may "restrict the exercise of any human right protected to a greater extent by any other international obligation binding upon the state."

[129] Rights Covenant, *supra* note 1, art. 5(1). *See also* Alexandre Charles Kiss, *Permissible Limitations on Rights,* in INTERNATIONAL BILL OF RIGHTS, *supra* note 58, at 290.

The wording of Article 5(1) closely tracks the language of Article 30 of the Universal Declaration. Recognizing its broad scope, the United States delegation challenged Article 5(1) as "vague, unnecessary, and open for abuse." BOSSUYT, *supra* note 113, at 106. Specifically, the United States expressed its concern with regard to the Article's potential impact on the freedom of speech provision of the Rights Covenant.

guaranteed in the Convention, and the Human Rights Committee has upheld these restrictions in several cases.

In *M.A. v. Italy*,[130] the Human Rights Committee ruled inadmissible a complaint that a conviction for reorganizing the dissolved Fascist Party in violation of Italian law violated speech and association rights under the Rights Covenant. The Committee stated that the acts punished were of a kind which are removed from the protection of the Rights Covenant by Article 5 and which were, in any event, justifiably prohibited by Italian law.[131] The limitations invoked by the Committee were those on freedom to manifest one's religion or beliefs (Article 18(3)), freedom of expression (Article 19(3)), freedom of association (Article 22(2)) and freedom to take part in the conduct of public affairs (Article 25).[132]

Similarly, in *F.R.T. and the W.G. Party v. Canada*,[133] the Committee rejected the contention that Canada violated the petitioners' freedom of expression under Article 19(2) of the Rights Covenant. The Commission stated:

> [N]ot only is the author's 'right' to communicate racist ideas not protected by the Covenant, it is in fact incompatible with its provisions . . . [T]he opinions which [the applicant] seeks to disseminate through the telephone system clearly constitute the advocacy of racial or religious hatred which Canada has an obligation under Article 20(2) of the Covenant to prohibit.[134]

The Human Rights Committee held, in effect, that the freedom of expression granted by Article 19 is compatible with prohibitions required by Article 20, and that the exercise of freedom of expression carries special duties and responsibilities.[135]

Although the United States participated in the drafting of the Rights Covenant, in 1954 it declared its intention not to ratify the Convention. However, in 1978, President Jimmy Carter transmitted the Rights Covenant together with three other treaties to the Senate for its advice and consent, subject to certain reserva-

---

[130] Report of the Human Rights Committee, GAOR 39th Sess., Supp. No. 40, at 190, U.N. Doc. A/39/40 (1984) [hereinafter "Committee Report 1984"]. *See also* Richard Delgado, *supra* note 21, at 570.

[131] Committee Report 1984, *supra* note 130, at 196.

[132] *See* P. R. Ghandi, *The Human Rights Committee and the Rights of Individual Communication*, 1986 BRIT. Y.B. INT'L L. 201, 239.

[133] *Id.* at 240.

[134] *Id.*, citing Report of the Human Rights Committee, U.N. GAOR 38th Sess., Supp. No. 40, at 234, 236, U.N. Doc. A/38/40 (1983).

[135] *Id.*

tions, understandings, and declarations.[136] President Carter acknowledged that "[t]he great majority of the substantive provisions of these four treaties are entirely consistent with the letter and the spirit of the United States Constitution and Laws."[137] However, the Department of State and the Department of Justice recommended a specific reservation to Article 20 as follows:

> The Constitution of the United States and Article 19 of the International Covenant on Civil and Political Rights contain provisions for the protection of individual rights, including the right of free speech, and nothing in this Covenant shall be deemed to require or to authorize legislation or other action by the United States which would restrict the right of free speech protected by the Constitution, laws, and practice of the United States.[138]

On April 2, 1992, the United States Senate ratified the treaty with the reservation to Article 20 as proposed, as well as several other amendments relating to the self-executing nature of the treaty and the so-called federal-state reservation.[139]

---

[136] Also transmitted were the Convention on the Elimination of All Forms of Racial Discrimination, the Covenant on Economic Social and Cultural Rights and the American Convention on Human Rights. *See* Jimmy Carter, Message from the President of the United States Transmitting Four Treaties Pertaining to Human Rights, S. Exec. Docs. C, D, E AND F, No. 95-2, 95th Cong., 2d. Sess. (1978), *reprinted in* U.S. RATIFICATION OF HUMAN RIGHTS TREATIES: WITH OR WITHOUT RESERVATIONS 83 (Richard B. Lillich ed., 1981) [hereinafter Message from the President]. In his Letter of Transmittal, President Carter stated: "The two human rights Covenants are based upon the Universal Declaration of Human Rights, in whose conception, formulation and adoption, the United States played a central role." *Id.* at 85.

[137] *Id.* at 86.

[138] Letter from Warren Christopher to the President (Dec. 17, 1977), *in* Message from the President, *supra* note 136, at 95. Professor Louis Henkin had advocated that the United States ratify the Covenant stating, "[T]here are no constitutional objections based on federalism or the separation of powers or on some notion that the subject is not of international concern." *See* Louis Henkin, *The Covenant on Civil and Political Rights, in* U.S. RATIFICATION OF HUMAN RIGHTS TREATIES: WITH OR WITHOUT RESERVATIONS, *supra* note 136, at 21 (1981). However, Henkin indicated that Article 20 would require a reservation regarding the advocacy of racial hatred if it were to conform to present interpretation of First Amendment rights. *Id.* at 22.

The United States has been consistent in its position with respect to provisions in the various international treaties and declarations that might impact speech rights. For example, in 1979, the General Assembly issued the Declaration on the Preparation of Societies for Life in Peace, the so-called Right to Peace Declaration. The Declaration was adopted by 138 states, with only the United States and Israel abstaining. The United States' abstention was due primarily to the concern that the Declaration's prohibition of propaganda for wars of aggression implied a threat to the freedom of speech. G.A. Res. 33/73, U.N. Press Release, G.A/5942 at 109 (1979), *discussed in* Louis B. Sohn, *The New International Law: Protection of the Rights of Individuals Rather Than States*, 32 AM. U. L. REV. 1, 58 (1982).

[139] 138 CONG. REC. S4783-84 (daily ed. Apr. 2, 1992).

C. *The International Covenant on the Elimination of All Forms of
    Racial Discrimination*

Following adoption of the Universal Declaration, the Commission on Human Rights commenced drafting binding legal
covenants to implement the guarantees of the Declaration. However, developing concurrently with the drafting of the comprehensive human rights agreements were agreements pertaining to
specific categories of persons and regional human rights
instruments.[140]

In 1963 the UN General Assembly adopted the United Nations Declaration on the Elimination of all Forms of Racial Discrimination (Discrimination Declaration),[141] which provided that
all incitements to violence on account of color or ethnic origin
shall be punishable by law.[142] Like the Universal Declaration, the
Discrimination Declaration was not binding on member states

[140] *See, e.g.*, Convention Relating to the Status of Refugees, July 28, 1951, 189
U.N.T.S. 150; Convention on the Political Rights of Women, Mar. 31, 1953, 27 U.S.T.
1909, 193 U.N.T.S. 135; Convention Relating to the Status of Stateless Persons, Sept.
28, 1954, No. 5158, 118, 360 U.N.T.S. 122.

[141] Prior to the U.N. Declaration in 1963, the General Assembly had in 1960
adopted a resolution condemning all manifestations of racial, religious and national hatred. Nevertheless, it decided to adopt two separate declarations and conventions; one
pertaining to racial discrimination and one to religious discrimination. The decision to
separate the instruments was made to meet the objections of the Arab and Communist
delegates. To date, little progress has been made with respect to a Convention on Religious Intolerance. During the debate on the Racial Convention at the twentieth session
of the Commission on Human Rights, the United States offered an amendment to condemn anti-Semitism. This amendment was defeated.

[142] U.N. Declaration on the Elimination of All Forms of Racial Discrimination, G.A.
Res. 1904 (XVIII), U.N. GAOR, 18th Sess., Supp. No. 15, at 35-37, U.N. Doc. A/5515
(1963). Article 9 of this Declaration reads:
    1. All propaganda and organizations based on ideas or theories of the superi-
    ority of one race or group of persons of one color or ethnic origin with a view
    to justifying or promoting racial discrimination in any form shall be severely
    condemned.
    2. All incitement to or acts of violence, whether by individuals or organiza-
    tions, against any race or group of persons of another color or ethnic origin
    shall be considered an offence against society and punishable under law.
    3. In order to put into effect the purposes and principles of the present Decla-
    ration, all States shall take immediate and positive measures, including legisla-
    tive and other measures, to prosecute and/or outlaw organizations which
    promote or incite to racial discrimination, or incite to use violence for purposes
    of discrimination based on race, color or ethnic origin.
The General Assembly adopted the Declaration on November 20, 1963, and the
Convention on December 21, 1965. Commenting on the swiftness of the U.N. action in
this area, the President of the General Assembly, Amintore Fanfani stated: "States Members of the United Nations attach special importance to the fight against racial discrimination, thus stressing one of the most urgent and crucial problems that have arisen in
the matter of protecting human rights." NATAN LERNER, THE U.N. CONVENTION ON THE
ELIMINATION OF ALL FORMS OF RACIAL DISCRIMINATION 21 (1970).

but soon was followed by the Convention on the Elimination of all Forms of Racial Discrimination (Discrimination Convention),[143] which was intended to be binding on member states.

The Discrimination Convention and the Discrimination Declaration were drafted simultaneously, and the Convention was adopted by the General Assembly only two years after the Declaration. During this period a plethora of newly independent African states joined the United Nations. These nations desired to have human rights issues serve an expanded role in the post-colonial world. The civil rights movement in the United States also was underway at this time. Many provisions in the Discrimination Convention stemmed from the events unfolding in the United States and indeed are similar to the provisions contained in the United States Civil Rights Act of 1964.[144]

Racial discrimination is defined in Article I of the Discrimination Convention as:

> any distinction, exclusion, restriction or preference based on race, color, descent, or national or ethnic origin which has the purpose or effect of nullifying or impairing the recognition, enjoyment or exercise, on an equal footing, of human rights and fundamental freedoms in the political, economic, social, cultural or any other field of public life.[145]

Article 4 pertains to racist propaganda and speech. It attempts to balance restrictions on speech and assembly with rights of free speech and association. Article 4 reads:

> States Parties condemn all propaganda and all organizations which are based on ideas or theories of superiority of one race or group of persons of one color or ethnic origin, or which attempt to justify or promote racial hatred and discrimination in any form, and undertake to adopt immediate and positive measures designed to eradicate all incitement to, or acts of, such discrimination and, to this end, with due regard to the principles embodied in the Universal Declaration of Human Rights and the rights expressly set forth in Article 5 of this Convention, *inter alia*:
> (a) Shall declare an offence punishable by law all dissemi-

---

[143] Discrimination Convention, *supra* note 9.

[144] Clyde Ferguson, *International Convention on the Elimination of All Forms of Racial Discrimination, in* U.S. RATIFICATION OF HUMAN RIGHTS TREATIES: WITH OR WITHOUT RESERVATIONS, *supra* note 136, at 41, 43. The Convention and the Civil Rights Act of 1964 are related in that the Convention reflects significantly the work of two United States citizen members of the Committee.

[145] Discrimination Convention, *supra* note 9, art. 1.

nation of ideas based on racial superiority or hatred, incitement to racial discrimination, as well as all acts of violence or incitement to such acts against any race or group of persons of another color or ethnic origin, and also the provision of any assistance to racist activities, including the financing thereof;

(b) Shall declare illegal and prohibit organizations, and also organized and all other propaganda activities, which promote and incite racial discrimination, and shall recognize participation in such organizations or activities as an offence punishable by law;

(c) Shall not permit public authorities or public institutions, national or local, to promote or incite racial discrimination.[146]

As one of the delegates in the General Assembly stated, Article 4 "was the outcome of a difficult compromise after hours, and even days, of discussion, drafting and redrafting."[147] Objections to the Convention in the General Assembly centered on the fact that the Discrimination Convention went further than the Discrimination Declaration on the Elimination of all Forms of Racial Discrimination and condemned not only propaganda and organizations which promote racial discrimination, but also racial hatred.[148] Furthermore, the Discrimination Convention requires that states undertake to punish not only incitement to racial discrimination, but also the dissemination of ideas based on racial superiority or hatred. The United States stated its understanding that Article 4 of the Discrimination Convention imposed "no obligation on any party to take any measures which are not fully consistent with its constitutional guarantees of freedom, including freedom of speech and association."[149] Colombia referred to Article 4 as a "throwback to the past" because "punishing ideas . . . is to aid and abet tyranny, and leads to abuse of power."[150]

In order to balance the right of free speech with the restric-

---

[146] *Id.* art. 4.

[147] Delegate of Ghana, Mr. Lamptey, at 7, *in* LERNER, *supra* note 142, at 58.

[148] LERNER, *supra* note 142, at 59.

[149] Statement in the General Assembly by the representative of the United States of America, *in* LERNER, *supra* note 142, at 60. Despite participation in drafting the Convention, the United States is not a party. Although most commentators have suggested that ratification of the Convention without reservation would jeopardize First Amendment rights, other commentators argue that the Convention could be adopted without infringing U.S. Constitutional values. *See* Thomas Jones, *Article 4 of the International Convention on the Elimination of All Forms of Racial Discrimination and the First Amendment,* 23 HOW. L.J. 429, 433 (1980).

[150] LERNER, *supra* note 142, at 59.

tions on speech mandated in the Discrimination Convention and to allay expressed concerns, Article 4 provides that legislation to implement the Convention be enacted "with due regard to the principles embodied in the Universal Declaration of Human Rights."[151] In the Sub-Commission discussion on Article 4, Morris Abram, the United States delegate, submitted a text that declared "all incitement to racial hatred and discrimination resulting in or likely to cause acts of violence, whether by individuals or organizations, as an offense against society and punishable under law."[152] Nevertheless, upon ratification or accession of the Convention, several states made declarations or reservations with respect to Article 4.[153]

The Discrimination Convention also provides: "Each State Party shall prohibit and bring to an end by all appropriate means, including legislation as required by circumstances, racial discrim-

---

[151] *See supra* text accompanying note 9.

[152] LERNER, *supra* note 142, at 56.

[153] UNITED NATIONS, HUMAN RIGHTS: STATUS OF INTERNATIONAL INSTRUMENTS 1987, ST/HR/5, at 100 [hereinafter INTERNATIONAL INSTRUMENTS]. For example, Austria declared:

> Article 4 of the International Convention on the Elimination of All Forms of Racial Discrimination provides that the measures specifically described in subparagraphs (a), (b) and (c) shall be undertaken with due regard to the principles embodied in the Universal Declaration of Human Rights and the rights expressly set forth in article 5 of the Convention. The Republic of Austria therefore considers that through such measures the right to freedom of opinion and expression and the right to freedom of peaceful assembly and association may not be jeopardized. These rights are laid down in articles 19 and 20 of the Universal Declaration of Human Rights; they were reaffirmed by the General Assembly of the United Nations when it adopted articles 19 and 21 of the International Covenant on Civil and Political Rights and are referred to in article 5 (d) (viii) and ix) of the present Convention.

Id.

Belgium, France and Italy made similar declarations. *Id.* at 101, 105-06, 108. The United Kingdom attached its interpretation of Article 4 as follows:

> [T]he United Kingdom wishes to state its understanding of certain articles in the Convention. It interprets article 4 as requiring a party to the Convention to adopt further legislative measures in the fields covered by subparagraphs (a), (b) and (c) of that article only in so far as it may consider with due regard to the principles embodied in the Universal Declaration of Human Rights and the rights expressly set forth in article 5 of the Convention (in particular the right to freedom of opinion and expression and the right to freedom of peaceful assembly and association) that some legislative addition to or variation of existing law and practice in those fields is necessary for the attainment of the end specified in the earlier part of article 4.

Id. at 116.

Malta, Papua, New Guinea and Tonga also made declarations. *Id.* at 110, 112, 114. The Bahamas, Barbados and Jamaica made reservations that acceptance of the Convention implied acceptance of obligations going beyond domestic constitutional limits. *Id.* at 100, 101, 109.

ination by any persons, group or organization."[154] The Committee on the Elimination of Racial Discrimination focused on the interpretation of state compliance with Article 4 and the effect of the declarations, reservations and interpretations of the state parties. Although some states argued that alternatives to criminal punishment are consistent with Article 4, the Committee rejected this position.[155] The Committee also rejected arguments that no legislation was required because racial bias did not exist in the country in question.[156]

Article 20(2) of the Rights Covenant merely requires that the advocacy of hatred which constitutes incitement to hostility, discrimination, or violence be prohibited but not necessarily made a crime; Article 4 of the Discrimination Convention goes much further. It obligates states to punish "all dissemination of ideas based on racial superiority or hatred . . . with due regard to the principles embodied in the Universal Declaration of Human Rights." This divergence between the two instruments may not be of great practical importance as the great majority of states have ratified both.[157]

Together with the Rights Covenant, President Carter transmitted this treaty to the Senate for its advice and consent and stated: "The racial discrimination convention deals with a problem which in the past has been identified with the United States; ratification of this treaty will attest to our enormous progress in this field . . . ."[158] However, the United States proposed the following reservation with respect to the speech provisions:

> The Constitution of the United States and Article 5 of this Convention contain provisions for the protection of individual rights, including the right to free speech, and nothing in this Convention shall be deemed to require or to authorize legislation or other action by the United States which would restrict the right of speech protected by the

---

154 Discrimination Convention, *supra* note 9, art. 2(1)(d).

155 Drew Mahalic & Joan Gambee Mahalic, *The Limitation Provisions of the International Convention on the Elimination on All Forms of Discrimination*, 9 Hum. Rts. Q. 74, 85-93 (1987). Several states have also taken the position that because racial discrimination does not exist in the nation, criminal legislation is not required. The Committee has not been receptive to this argument. *Id.* at 86.

156 *Id.* at 86-87.

157 *See* Karl Joseph Partsch, *Freedom of Conscience and Expression and Political Freedoms,* in International Bill of Rights, *supra* note 58, at 229.

158 Message from the President, *supra* note 136, at 85.

Constitution, laws, and practice of the United States.[159]
To date the Senate has not acted on this treaty.[160]

D. *Convention on the Prevention and Punishment of the Crime of Genocide*

The first human rights convention adopted by the General Assembly was the Convention on the Prevention and Punishment of the Crime of Genocide (Genocide Convention).[161] The Nuremberg Charter,[162] which prompted the Genocide Convention, was adopted by the General Assembly at the end of World War II. The Charter created an *ad hoc* international court at Nuremberg, Germany[163] and established the criminal responsibility of states and individuals for participating in crimes against peace, war crimes, and crimes against humanity. Pre-war offenses were not within the jurisdiction of the Charter. Therefore, only inhumane crimes against civilians committed in connection with war

[159] Letter from Warren Christopher to the President (Dec. 17, 1977), *in* Message from the President, *supra* note 136, at 91.

[160] *The International Convention on the Suppression and Punishment of the Crime of Apartheid*, G.A. Res. 3068 (XXVIII), 28 U.N. GAOR Supp. (No. 30) at 75, U.N. Doc. A/9030 (1973), *reprinted in* 13 I.L.M. 56 (1974), is also relevant. This Convention was adopted by the General Assembly in 1973 and entered into force in 1976. Apartheid, already referred to in Article 3(a) of the Convention of the Elimination of all Forms of Racial Discrimination, is the only form of racial discrimination which has been addressed specifically in a separate Convention.

Article 2 of the Convention defines apartheid to include "similar policies and practices of racial segregation and discrimination as practiced in southern Africa." Article 3, *inter alia*, provides that international criminal responsibility shall apply in the case of "incitement" to commit the crime of Apartheid. Moreover, Article 4(a) reads: "The States Parties to the present Convention undertake:

(a) to adopt any legislative or other measures necessary to suppress as well as to prevent any encouragement of the crime of apartheid and similar segregationist policies or their manifestations and to punish persons guilty of that crime . . . ."

To date 86 states have ratified or acceded to the Convention. U.N. TREATIES, *supra* note 126, at 162.

[161] Genocide Convention, *supra* note 8.

[162] Charter of the International Military Tribunal, Aug. 8, 1945, 59 Stat. 1546, 82 U.N.T.S. 279, *reprinted in* 3 BEVANS 1238 [hereinafter Nuremberg Charter]. This tribunal was created August 8, 1945 by the United States, France, USSR, and Britain to try Nazi officers for war crimes.

[163] Nuremburg Charter, *supra* note 162. *See generally* The Statute of the Nuremberg Tribunal, 13 DEP'T ST. BULL. 222, 224 (1945). Acts that violate the Nuremberg Charter include:

murder, extermination, enslavement, deportation and other inhumane acts committed against any civilian population, before or during any war; or persecutions on political, racial or religious grounds in execution of or in connection with any crime within the jurisdiction of the tribunal, whether or not in violation of the domestic law of the country where perpetrated.

Nuremberg Charter, at 1242.

were punishable.[164]

The public outrage concerning the crimes against humanity committed by the Nazis spurred international action to prevent such atrocities from reoccurring. In 1946 the United Nations unanimously adopted Resolution 96(I) proclaiming genocide a crime under international law[165] and urged the adoption of a legally binding Convention on the subject.[166] On December 9, 1948, one day prior to the adoption of the Universal Declaration, the UN General Assembly unanimously adopted the Genocide Convention.[167]

The Genocide Convention defines genocide as any "acts committed with intent to destroy, in whole or in part, a national, ethnical [sic], racial or religious groups [sic]"[168] regardless of whether such acts are undertaken in peacetime or in wartime. Parties to the Genocide Convention affirm that genocide is a crime and that all persons who commit or conspire to commit genocide within their public or private capacity are criminally liable.[169] Furthermore, Article III of the Genocide Convention provides that "[d]irect and public incitement to commit genocide" shall be punishable.[170]

More than 100 states have ratified or acceded to the Genocide Convention, which entered into force in 1951.[171] Several states entered reservations with respect to Article IX, which confers jurisdiction on the International Court of Justice in all disputes relating to the Genocide Convention and other provisions relating to jurisdiction. No states, except the United States, objected to or limited the substantive provisions of the Genocide Convention.[172]

---

[164] Raphael Lemkin, *Genocide as a Crime Under International Law*, 41 Am. J. Int'l L. 145 (1947); Barry M. Schiller, *Life in a Symbolic Universe: Comments on the Genocide Convention and International Law*, 9 Sw. U. L. Rev. 47, 49 (1977).

[165] U.N. Res. 96(I), U.N. Doc A/64/Add.1, at 188 (1946).

[166] G.A. Res. 217 (III)A, U.N. GAOR, 3d Sess., pt. 1, at 71, U.N. Doc. A/810 (1948), *reprinted in* 45 Am. J. Int'l L. 7-10 (Supp. 1951). The word "genocide" was created by Raphael I. Lemkin, who lost fifty relatives in the Holocaust, and who by himself lobbied to force the international community to denounce the commission of such atrocities as those perpetrated against Jews in Nazi Germany. *See* Marian N. Leich, *Contemporary Practice of the United States Relating to International Law*, 80 Am. J. Int'l L. 612, 618 (1986).

[167] Genocide Convention, *supra* note 8. *See also Genocide: A Commentary to the Convention*, 58 Yale L.J. 1142 (1949).

[168] Genocide Convention, *supra* note 8, art. II.

[169] *Id.* art. I.

[170] *Id.* art. III.

[171] U.N. Treaties, *supra* note 126, at 95.

[172] *Id.* at 96-103.

Even though the United States was an original signatory to the Genocide Convention, it did not ratify it until 1986.[173] This thirty-eight year delay was attributable in part to the caution and opposition within the legal community[174] and in part to the general arguments made in connection with human rights treaties that ratification might infringe on constitutional guarantees and threaten the United States' sovereignty.[175]

Among the organizations that opposed ratification was the American Bar Association (ABA), which objected that ratification would constitute an abuse of treaty power and federal encroachment on state rights.[176] The ABA reaffirmed its position in 1970 when President Nixon called upon the Senate for its advice and consent in ratifying the Genocide Convention.[177] However, in 1976, the ABA reversed its opposition and supported ratification.[178] The final vote to reverse the ABA position was qualified upon understandings that were identical to the understandings adopted by the Senate for its own consent to the ratification of the Genocide Convention in 1973.[179] Opposition centering on the argument that the phrase "incitement to commit genocide" included in Article III of the Convention was a threat to the First Amendment protection of freedom of speech[180] continued until the 1980's. Those urging ratification countered that Article III must be read within the context of other treaty provisions and

---

[173] *Genocide Convention Implementation Act of 1987*, Pub. L. No. 100-606, 102 Stat. 3045, (codified at 18 U.S.C. § 1091 (1988)), *reprinted in* 28 I.L.M. 754 (1989) [hereinafter Proxmire Act].

[174] *See* Frank W. Grinnell, *The Action of the American Bar Association in Regard to the "Genocide" Treaty Pending Before the Senate of the United States and the Reasons For It*, 34 MASS. L. Q. 28 (1949); Jennifer A. Post, *The United States and the Genocide Treaty: Returning Genocide to Sovereign Concerns*, 13 SUFFOLK TRANSNAT'L L.J. 686 (1990).

[175] Grinnell, *supra* note 174. The ABA argued that article VI of the Convention was a threat to the supremacy of the Constitution because upon ratification the Convention would become the supreme law of the land. *Id.* at 30-31. *See also* U.S. CONST. art. VI, cl. 2. (Treaties shall be supreme law of the land). The ABA stated that the ratification would remove from states the jurisdiction over crimes which may be forbidden under the Genocide Convention, and that it would alter state and federal government. Grinnell, *supra* note 174, at 31.

[176] Grinnell, *supra* note 174, at 31-32. *But see* Bruno V. Bitker, *Genocide Revisited*, 56 A.B.A. J. 71, 73 (1970). Article V of the Genocide Convention requires legislation for criminal prosecution. It also states that parties agree to give effect to the treaty by enacting domestic legislation. *See* Genocide Convention, *supra* note 8, art. V.

[177] Schiller, *supra* note 164, at 58.

[178] *Id.* at 56.

[179] *Id.*

[180] Schiller, *supra* note 164, at 58. The opponent's argument was that "incitement to commit genocide," included in Article II of the Genocide Convention, is unconstitutionally vague. *Id. See also* Arthur J. Goldberg and Richard N. Gardner, *Time to Act on the Genocide Convention*, 58 A.B.A.J. 141-45 (1972).

existing First Amendment protection, and thus the speech right would not be affected.[181] Furthermore, the proponents argued that ratification would not limit or impair the sovereignty of the United States because the United States would always defer to constitutional mandates.[182] The February, 1986, Senate approval of the ratification of the Genocide Convention ultimately was subject to two reservations, five understandings, and one declaration.[183] On November 4, 1988 President Reagan signed the Genocide Convention Implementation Act.[184]

One of the reservations provides that "nothing in the Convention requires or authorizes legislation or other actions by The United States of America prohibited by the Constitution of the United States as interpreted by the United States."[185] The Senate Committee on Foreign Affairs stated:

Conflict is most likely to occur between the [F]irst [A]mendment's proscription on legislation abridging free speech and Article III's requirement that 'direct and public incitement to commit genocide' be punished. The contours of the latter remain to be defined. In response to a request for an advisory opinion, or as a result of a proceeding under Article IX, the ICJ could interpret Article III in a way inconsistent with the First Amendment.[186]

---

[181] Goldberg and Gardner, *supra* note 180, at 144. As one commentator noted:
The principal question about the meaning of Article III [of the Genocide Convention] concerned the relationship of the words "direct and public incitement to genocide" to the freedom of speech guarantees of the [F]irst [A]mendment. This question was raised with then Assistant Attorney General William H. Rehnquist in the 1970's as follows:
Senator Church. In other words, you are satisfied that such constitutional protection, as presently exists in the field of free speech, would not be adversely affected in any way by the terms of this convention?
Mr. Rehnquist. I am satisfied, first, that they would not be and, second, that they could not be.
Marian N. Leich, *Contemporary Practice of the United States Relating to International Law*, 79 AM. J. INT'L L. 116, 121 (1985).

[182] The Supreme Court "has regularly and uniformly recognized the supremacy of the constitution over a treaty." Reid v. Covert, 354 U.S. 1, 17 (1956). Thus some legal scholars argue that the claim that the Genocide Convention will supersede or set aside the Constitution of the United States is false.

[183] The United States Senate, by a vote of 83 to 11, with 6 Senators absent and not voting, gave its advice and consent to U.S. ratification of the Genocide Convention. Leich, *supra* note 166, at 612. The text of the ratification was identical with that recommended by the Senate Committee on Foreign Relations in its report on the Genocide Convention issued July 18, 1985. *See* S. EXEC. REP. No. 2, 99th Cong., 2d. Sess. (1985).

[184] Proxmire Act, *supra* note 173.

[185] *Id.* at 774.

[186] *Id.* at 771.

The Senate Committee further justified its reservation by stating that:

> The Genocide Convention is unique among the treaties the committee has reviewed in that it touches upon such fundamental matters as the relationship between criminal law and the right of free speech. No other type of treaty, be it one of friendship and commerce, taxation or the like, raises these kinds of issues. Accordingly, unlike any other treaty that has come before the Senate, the Committee finds that a constitutional reservation is appropriate.[187]

The Committee further limited the scope of the Genocide Convention in the United States through its understanding of the term "mental harm" of Article II(b) of the Genocide Convention to mean "permanent impairment of mental faculties through drugs, torture, or similar techniques."[188] Thus hate speech directed toward national, ethnic, racial, or religious groups does not fall within the proscribed activity of the Genocide Convention as understood by the United States.

---

[187] *Id.*
[188] *Id.* at 774.

REGINA V. KEEGSTRA*

EDITED BY LORRAINE E. WEINRIB

[p.16] DICKSON C.J.C. (WILSON, L'HEUREUX-DUBÉ, and GONTHIER JJ. concurring):—This appeal. . .raises a delicate and highly controversial issue as to the constitutional validity of s. 319(2) of the *Criminal Code*, R.S.C., 1985, c. C-46, a legislative provision which prohibits the wilful promotion of hatred, other than in private conversation, towards any section of the [p.17] public distinguished by colour, race, religion or ethnic origin. In particular, the Court must decide whether this section infringes the guarantee of freedom of expression found in s. 2(b) of the *Canadian Charter of Rights and Freedoms* in a manner that cannot be justified under s. 1 of the Charter. A secondary issue arises as to whether the presumption of innocence protected in the Charter's s. 11(d) is unjustifiably breached by reason of s. 319(3)(a) of the Code, which affords a defence of "truth" to the wilful promotion of hatred, but only where the accused proves the truth of the communicated statements on the balance of probabilities.

I. FACTS

Mr. James Keegstra was a high school teacher in Eckville, Alberta from the early 1970s until his dismissal in 1982. In 1984 Mr. Keegstra was charged under s. 319(2) (then 281.2(2)) of the *Criminal Code* with unlawfully promoting hatred against an identifiable group by communicating anti-semitic statements to his students . . .

. . . Mr. Keegstra's teachings attributed various evil qualities to Jews. He thus described Jews to his pupils as "treacherous", "subversive", "sadistic", "money-loving", "power hungry" and "child killers". He taught his classes that Jewish people seek to destroy Christianity and are responsible for depressions, anarchy, chaos, wars and revolution. . . . Mr. Keegstra expected his students to reproduce his teachings in class and on exams. If they failed to do so, their marks suffered.

Prior to his trial, Mr. Keegstra applied to the Court of Queen's Bench in Alberta for an order quashing the charge on a number of grounds, the primary one being that s. 319(2) of the *Criminal Code* unjustifiably infringed his freedom of expression as guaranteed by s. 2(b) of the Charter. Among the other grounds of appeal was the allegation that the defence of truth found in s. 319(3)(a) of the Code violates the Charter's presumption of innocence. The application was dismissed by Quigley J., and Mr. Keegstra was thereafter tried and convicted. He then appealed his conviction to the Alberta Court of Appeal, raising the same Charter issues. The Court of Appeal unanimously accepted his argument, and it is from this judgment that the Crown appeals . . .

* [1990] 3 S.C.R. 697, 61 C.C.C. (3d) 1, [1991] 2 W.W.R. 1 (Canada). Available in LEXIS, Canada library, Ccrim file. Page numbers in brackets refer to W.W.R.

[p.18]

III. RELEVANT STATUTORY AND CONSTITUTIONAL PROVISIONS

The relevant legislative and Charter provisions are set out below:

Criminal Code 319 . . .

(2) Every one who, by communicating statements, other than in private conversation, wilfully promotes hatred against any identifiable group is guilty of

(a) an indictable offence and is liable to imprisonment for a term not exceeding two years; or

(b) an offence punishable on summary conviction.

[p.19] (3) No person shall be convicted of an offence under subsection (2)

(a) if he establishes that the statements communicated were true;

(b) if, in good faith, he expressed or attempted to establish by argument an opinion upon a religious subject;

(c) if the statements were relevant to any subject of public interest, the discussion of which was for the public benefit, and if on reasonable grounds he believed them to be true; or

(d) if, in good faith, he intended to point out, for the purpose of removal, matters producing or tending to produce feelings of hatred towards an identifiable group in Canada . . .

(7) In this section,

"communicating" includes communicating by telephone, broadcasting or other audible or visible means;

"identifiable group" has the same meaning as in section 318;

"public place" includes any place to which the public have access as of right or by invitation, express or implied;

"statements" includes words spoken or written or recorded electronically or electro-magnetically or otherwise, and gestures, signs or other visible representations.

318 . . .

(4) In this section, "identifiable group" means any section of the public distinguished by colour, race, religion or ethnic origin. . .

[p.20] *Canadian Charter of Rights and Freedoms*

1. The *Canadian Charter of Rights and Freedoms* guarantees the rights and freedoms set out in it subject only to such reasonable limits prescribed by law as can be demonstrably justified in a free and democratic society.

2. Everyone has the following fundamental freedoms: . . .

(b) freedom of thought, belief, opinion and expression, including freedom of the press and other media of communication . . .

11. Any person charged with an offence has the right . . .

(d) to be presumed innocent until proven guilty according to law in a fair and public hearing by an independent and impartial tribunal . . .

15. (1) Every individual is equal before and under the law and has the right to the equal protection and equal benefit of the law without discrimination and, in particular, without discrimination based on race, national and ethnic origin, colour, religion, sex, age or mental or physical disability . . .

27. This Charter shall be interpreted in a manner consistent with the preservation and enhancement of the multicultural heritage of Canadians . . .

[p.23]

V. The History of Hate Propaganda Crimes in Canada

[Dickson C.J.C. discusses the concern in Canada following the Second World War to protect human rights and to guard against discrimination. This concern led to the creation of the Special Committee on Hate Propaganda in Canada (the "Cohen Committee") in 1953. In its 1966 Report, the Committee recommended the adoption of a number of new criminal offences, including advocacy of genocide, public incitement of hatred likely to lead to a breach of the peace and the provision in issue here, public wilful promotion of hatred. These recommendations resulted in a number of amendments to the *Criminal Code*, including s. 319(2).]

[p.26]

VI. Section 2(b) of the Charter — Freedom of Expression

Having briefly set out the history of attempts to prohibit hate propaganda, I can now address the constitutional questions arising for decision in this appeal. The first of these concerns whether the Charter guarantee of freedom of expression is infringed by s. 319(2) of the Criminal Code. Before looking to the specific facts of this appeal, however, I would like to comment upon the nature of the s. 2(b) guarantee. Obviously, one's conception of the freedom of expression provides a crucial backdrop to any s. 2(b) inquiry; the values promoted by the freedom help not only to define the ambit of s. 2(b), but also come to the forefront when discussing how competing interests might co-exist with the freedom under s. 1 of the Charter . . .

[p.27] . . . [T]he reach of s.2(b) is potentially very wide, expression being deserving of protection if "it serves indi-

vidual and societal values in a free and democratic society". . . [p.28] Moreover, the Court has attempted to articulate more precisely some of the convictions fueling the freedom of expression, these being summarized in *Irwin Toy*, [1989] 1 S.C.R. 927 at p. 976, 58 D.L.R. (4th) 577, 25 C.P.R. (3d) 417, as follows: (1) seeking and attaining truth is an inherently good activity; (2) participation in social and political decision-making is to be fostered and encouraged; and (3) diversity in forms of individual self-fulfilment and human flourishing ought to be cultivated in a tolerant and welcoming environment for the sake of both those who convey a meaning and those to whom meaning is conveyed . . .

[p.29] The first step in the *Irwin Toy* analysis involves asking whether the activity of the litigant who alleges an infringement of the freedom of expression falls within the protected s. 2(b) sphere . . . .[T]he term "expression" as used in s. 2(b) of the Charter embraces all content of expression irrespective of the particular meaning or message sought to be conveyed (*Reference re ss. 193 and 195.1(1)(c) of the Criminal Code*, [1990] 1 S.C.R. 1123 at p. 1181 per Lamer J., 56 C.C.C. (3d) 65, 4 W.W.R 481).

The second step in the analysis outlined in *Irwin Toy* is to determine whether the purpose of the impugned government action is to restrict freedom of expression. The guarantee of freedom of expression will necessarily be infringed by government action having such a purpose. If, however, it is the effect of the action, rather than the purpose, that restricts an activity, s. 2(b) is not brought into play unless it can be demonstrated by the party alleging an infringement that the activity supports rather than undermines the prin-

363

ciples and values upon which freedom of expression is based.

. . . Communications which wilfully promote hatred against an identifiable group without doubt convey a meaning, and are intended to do so by those who make them. Because *Irwin Toy* stresses that the type of meaning conveyed is irrelevant to the question of whether s. 2(b) is infringed, that the expression covered by s. 319(2) is invidious and obnoxious is beside the point. [p.30] It is enough that those who publicly and wilfully promote hatred convey or attempt to convey a meaning, and it must therefore be concluded that the first step of the *Irwin Toy* test is satisfied.

Moving to the second stage of the s. 2(b) inquiry, one notes that the prohibition in s. 319(2) aims directly at words — in this appeal, Mr. Keegstra's teachings — that have as their content and objective the promotion of racial or religious hatred. The purpose of s. 319(2) can consequently be formulated as follows: to restrict the content of expression by singling out particular meanings that are not to be conveyed. Section 319(2) therefore overtly seeks to prevent the communication of expression, and hence meets the second requirement of the *Irwin Toy* test . . .

[p.32]. . . It has been argued in support of excluding hate propaganda from the coverage of s. 2(b) that the use of ss. 15 and 27 of the Charter—dealing respectively with equality and multiculturalism—and Canada's acceptance of international agreements requiring the prohibition of racist statements make s. 319(2) incompatible with even a large and liberal definition of the freedom. . . . The general tenor of this argument is that these interpretive aids inextricably infuse each constitutional guarantee with values supporting equal societal participation and the

security and dignity of all persons. Consequently, it is said that s. 2(b) must be curtailed so as not to extend to communications which seriously undermine the equality, security and dignity of others.

. . . It is, in my opinion, inappropriate to attenuate the s. 2(b) freedom on the grounds that a *particular* context requires such; the large and liberal interpretation given the freedom of expression in *Irwin Toy* indicates that the preferable course is to weigh the various contextual values and factors in s. 1.

[p.33] I thus conclude on the issue of s. 2(b) by finding that s. 319(2) of the Criminal Code constitutes an infringement of the Charter guarantee of freedom of expression, and turn to examine whether such an infringement is justifiable under s. 1 as a reasonable limit in a free and democratic society.

VII. SECTION 1 ANALYSIS OF S. 319(2)

A. General Approach to Section 1

Though the language of s. 1 appears earlier in these reasons, it is appropriate to repeat its words:

1. The *Canadian Charter of Rights and Freedoms* guarantees the rights and freedoms set out in it subject only to such reasonable limits prescribed by law as can be demonstrably justified in a free and democratic society.

In *R. v. Oakes*, [1986] 1 S.C.R. 103, 24 C.C.C. (3d) 321, 26 D.L.R. (4th) 200, this Court offered a course of analysis to be employed in determining whether a limit on a right or freedom can be demonstrably justified in a free and democratic society. Under the approach in *Oakes*, it must first be established that impugned state action

364

has an objective of pressing and substantial concern in a free and democratic society. Only such an objective is of sufficient stature to warrant overriding a constitutionally protected right or freedom (p. 138). The second feature of the *Oakes* test involves assessing the proportionality between the objective and the impugned measure. The inquiry as to proportionality attempts to guide the balancing of individual and group interests protected in s. 1, and in *Oakes* was broken down into the following three segments (at p. 139):

First, the measures adopted must be carefully designed to achieve the objective in question. They must not be arbitrary, unfair or based on irrational considerations. In short, they must be rationally connected to the objective. Secondly, the means, even if rationally connected to the objective in this first sense, should impair "as little as possible" the right or freedom in question . . . Thirdly, there must be a proportionality between the effects of the measures which are responsible for limiting the Charter right or freedom, and the objective which has been identified as of "sufficient importance" . . .

[p.34] In the words of s. 1 are brought together the fundamental values and aspirations of Canadian society. As this Court has said before, the premier article of the Charter has a dual function, operating both to activate Charter rights and freedoms and to permit such reasonable limits as a free and democratic society may have occasion to place upon them (*Oakes*, at pp. 133-34). What seems to me to be of significance in this dual function is the commonality that links the guarantee of rights and freedoms to their limitation. This commonality lies in the phrase "free and democratic society". As was stated by the majority in *Slaight Communications Inc. v. Davidson*, [1989] 1 S.C.R. 1038 at 1056, 26 C.C.E.L. 85, 59 D.L.R. (4th) 416:

The underlying values of a free and democratic society both guarantee the rights in the *Charter* and, in appropriate circumstances, justify limitations upon those rights.

Obviously, a practical application of s. 1 requires more than an incantation of the words "free and democratic society". These words require some definition, an elucidation as to the values that they invoke. . . . [I]n *Oakes* I commented upon some of the ideals that inform our understanding of a free and democratic society, saying (at p. 136):

The Court must be guided by the values and principles essential to a free and democratic society which I believe embody, to name but a few, respect for the inherent dignity of the human person, commitment to social justice and equality, accommodation of a wide variety of beliefs, respect for cultural and group identity, and faith in social and political institutions which enhance the participation of individuals and groups in society. The underlying values and principles of a free and democratic society are the genesis of the rights and freedoms guaranteed by the Charter and the ultimate standard against which a limit on a right or freedom must be shown, despite its effect, to be reasonable and demonstrably justified.

Undoubtedly these values and principles are numerous, covering the guarantees enumerated in the Charter and more. Equally, they may well deserve different emphases, and certainly will assume varying degrees of importance depending upon the circumstances of a particular case.

[p.35]. . . . Clearly, the proper judicial perspective under s. 1 must be derived from an awareness of the synergetic relation between two elements: the values underlying the Charter and the circumstances of the particular case.

From the discussion so far, I hope it is clear that a rigid or formalistic approach to the application of s. 1 must be avoided. The ability to use s. 1 as a gauge which is sensitive to the values and circumstances particular to an appeal has been identified as vital in past cases . . .

[p.36]

B. The Use of American Constitutional Jurisprudence

[Dickson C.J.C. then considers American First Amendment jurisprudence, in which freedom of expression may be curtailed only when there exists a "clear and present danger" of violence or insurrection. He concludes that it is doubtful whether this doctrine can be applied in the context of a challenge to hate propaganda legislation in Canada.]

[p.40] [T]here is much to be learned from First Amendment jurisprudence with regard to freedom of expression and hate propaganda. It would be rash, however, to see First Amendment doctrine as demanding the striking down of s. 319(2). Not only are the precedents somewhat mixed, but the relaxation of the prohibition against content-based regulation of expression in certain areas indicates that American courts are not loath to permit the suppression of ideas in some circumstances. Most importantly, the nature of the s. 1 test as applied in the context of a challenge to s. 319(2) may well demand a perspective particular to Canadian constitutional jurisprudence when weighing competing interests. If values fundamental to the Canadian conception of a free and democratic society suggest an approach that denies hate propaganda the highest degree of constitutional protection, it is this approach which must be employed.

C. Objective of s. 319(2)

. . . According to *Oakes*, the first [p.41] aspect of the s. 1 analysis is to examine the objective of the impugned legislation. Only if the objective relates to concerns which are pressing and substantial in a free and democratic society can the legislative limit on a right or freedom hope to be permissible under the Charter. In examining the objective of s. 319(2), I will begin by discussing the harm caused by hate propaganda as identified by the Cohen Committee and subsequent study groups, and then review in turn the impact upon this objective of international human rights instruments and ss. 15 and 27 of the Charter.

(i) Harm caused by expression promoting the hatred of identifiable groups

Looking to the legislation challenged in this appeal, one must ask whether the amount of hate propaganda in Canada causes sufficient harm to justify legislative intervention of some type. The Cohen Committee, speaking in 1965, found that the incidence of hate propaganda in Canada was not insignificant . . .

In 1984, the House of Commons Special Committee on Participation of Visible Minorities in Canadian Society. . . found that the prevalence and scope of such material had risen since the Cohen Committee made its report, stating (at p. 69):

[p.42] There has been a recent upsurge in hate propaganda. It has been found in virtually every part of Canada. Not only is it anti-semitic and antiblack, as in the 1960s, but it is also now anti-Roman Catholic, anti-East Indian, anti-aboriginal people and anti-French. Some of this material is imported from the United States but much of it is produced in Canada. Most worrisome of all is that in recent years Canada has become a major source of supply of hate propaganda that finds its way to Europe, and especially to West Germany.

[T]he presence of hate propaganda in Canada is sufficiently substantial to warrant concern. Disquiet caused by the existence of such material is not simply the product of its offensiveness, however, but stems from the very real harm which it causes. Essentially, there are two sorts of injury caused by hate propaganda. First, there is harm done to members of the target group. It is indisputable that the emotional damage caused by words may be of grave psychological and social consequence . . .

. . . This impact may cause target group members to take drastic measures in reaction, perhaps avoiding activities which bring them into contact with non-group members or adopting attitudes and postures directed towards blending in with the majority. Such consequences bear heavily in a nation that prides itself on tolerance and the fostering of human dignity through, among other things, respect for the many racial, religious and cultural groups in our society.

A second harmful effect of hate propaganda which is of pressing and substantial concern is its influence upon society at large. . . .[p.43] It is . . . not inconceivable that the active dissemination of hate propaganda can attract individuals to its cause, and in the process create serious discord between various cultural groups in society. Moreover, the alteration of views held by the recipients of hate propaganda may occur subtly, and is not always attendant upon conscious acceptance of the communicated ideas. Even if the message of hate propaganda is outwardly rejected, there is evidence that its premise of racial or religious inferiority may persist in a recipient's mind as an idea that holds some truth . . .

The threat to the self-dignity of target group members is thus matched by the possibility that prejudiced messages will gain some credence, with the attendant result of discrimination, and perhaps even violence, against minority groups in Canadian society . . .[p.44] As noted previously, in articulating concern about hate propaganda and its contribution to racial and religious tension in Canada, the Cohen Committee recommended that Parliament use the Criminal Code in order to prohibit wilful, hate-promoting expression and underline Canada's commitment to end prejudice and intolerance.

The close connection between the recommendations of the Cohen Committee and the hate propaganda amendments to the Criminal Code made in 1970 indicates that in enacting s. 319(2) Parliament's purpose was to prevent the harm identified by the Committee as being caused by hate-promoting expression. More recent reports have echoed the findings and concerns of the Cohen Committee, lending further support to the substantial nature of the legislative objective . . .

*(ii) International human rights
instruments*

[p.45] Generally speaking, the international human rights obligations taken on by Canada reflect the values and principles of a free and democratic society, and thus those values and principles that underlie the Charter itself. . . . Moreover, international human rights law and Canada's commitments in that area are of particular significance in assessing the importance of Parliament's objective under s. 1 . . .

No aspect of international human rights has been given attention greater than that focused upon discrimination. . . . This high concern regarding discrimination has led to the presence in two international human rights documents of articles forbidding the dissemination of hate propaganda.

[Dickson C.J.C. then discusses two United Nations documents to which Canada is a signatory: the International Convention on the Elimination of All Forms of Racial Discrimination (CERD), Can. T.S. 1970, No. 28 and the International Covenant on Civil and Political Rights (ICCPR), 999 U.N.T.S. 171 (1966). Both documents call for the elimination of racial discrimination and the prohibition by law of expression based upon racial hatred or constituting incitement to racial discrimination.]

[p.48] CERD and ICCPR demonstrate that the prohibition of hate-promoting expression is considered to be not only compatible with a signatory nation's guarantee of human rights, but is as well an obligatory aspect of this guarantee. . . . Canada, along with other members of the international community, has indicated a commitment to prohibiting hate propaganda, and in my opinion this Court must have regard to that commitment in investigating the nature of the government objective

behind s. 319(2) of the Criminal Code. That the international community has collectively acted to condemn hate propaganda, and to oblige State Parties to CERD and ICCPR to prohibit such expression, thus emphasizes the importance of the objective behind s. 319(2) and the principles of equality and the inherent dignity of all persons that infuse both international human rights and the Charter.

(iii) Other provisions of the Charter

Significant indicia of the strength of the objective behind s. 319(2) are gleaned not only from the international arena, but are also expressly [p.49] evident in various provisions of the Charter itself . . . Most importantly for the purposes of this appeal, ss. 15 and 27 represent a strong commitment to the values of equality and multiculturalism, and hence underline the great importance of Parliament's objective in prohibiting hate propaganda.

[p.50]. . . In light of the Charter commitment to equality, and the reflection of this commitment in the framework of s. 1, the objective of the impugned legislation is enhanced insofar as it seeks to ensure the equality of all individuals in Canadian society. The message of the expressive activity covered by s. 319(2) is that members of identifiable groups are not to be given equal standing in society, and are not human beings equally deserving of concern, respect and consideration. The harms caused by this message run directly counter to the values central to a free and democratic society, and in restricting the promotion of hatred Parliament is therefore seeking to bolster the notion of mutual respect necessary in a nation which venerates the equality of all persons.

Section 15 is not the only Charter

provision which emphasizes values both important to a free and democratic society and pertinent to the disposition of this appeal under s. 1 . . . I am of the belief that s. 27 and the commitment to a multicultural vision of our nation bears notice in [p.51] emphasizing the acute importance of the objective of eradicating hate propaganda from society . . . Indeed, the sense that an individual can be affected by treatment of a group to which he or she belongs is clearly evident in a number of other Charter provisions not yet mentioned, including ss. 16 to 23 (language rights), s. 25 (aboriginal rights), s. 28 (gender equality) and s. 29 (denominational schools).

When the prohibition of expressive activity that promotes hatred of groups identifiable on the basis of colour, race, religion, or ethnic origin is considered in light of s. 27, the legitimacy and substantial nature of the government objective is therefore considerably strengthened.

(iv) Conclusion Respecting Objective of s. 319(2)
In my opinion, it would be impossible to deny that Parliament's objective in enacting s. 319(2) is of the utmost importance. Parliament has recognized the substantial harm that can flow from hate propaganda, and in trying to prevent the pain suffered by target group members and to reduce racial, ethnic and religious tension in Canada has decided to suppress the wilful promotion of hatred against identifiable groups. The nature of Parliament's objective is supported not only by the work of numerous study groups, but also by our collective historical knowledge of the potentially catastrophic effects of the promotion of hatred . . . Additionally, the international commitment to eradicate hate propaganda and the stress placed upon equality and multiculturalism in the Charter strongly buttress the importance of this objective. I consequently find that the first part of the test [p.52] under s. 1 of the Charter is easily satisfied and that a powerfully convincing legislative objective exists such as to justify some limit on freedom of expression.

D. Proportionality

The second branch of the *Oakes* test—proportionality—poses the most challenging questions with respect to the validity of s. 319(2) as a reasonable limit on freedom of expression in a free and democratic society . . .

i) Relation of the expression at stake to free expression values
[T]he interpretation of s. 2(b) under *Irwin Toy*, supra, gives protection to a very wide range of expression. Content is irrelevant to this interpretation, the result of a high value being placed upon freedom of expression [p.53] in the abstract. . . . In my opinion, however, the s. 1 analysis of a limit upon s. 2(b) cannot ignore the nature of the expressive activity which the state seeks to restrict. While we must guard carefully against judging expression according to its popularity, it is equally destructive of free expression values, as well as the other values which underlie a free and democratic society, to treat all expression as equally crucial to those principles at the core of s. 2(b).

[p.54] From the outset, I wish to make clear that in my opinion the expression prohibited by s. 319(2) is not closely linked to the rationale underlying s. 2(b) . . .

At the core of freedom of expression lies the need to ensure that truth and the common good are attained, whether in scientific and artistic endeavours or in the process of determining the best course to take in our political affairs . . . [p.55] [E]xpression can be used to the detriment of our search for truth; the state should not be the sole arbiter of truth, but neither should we overplay the view that rationality will overcome all falsehoods in the unregulated marketplace of ideas. There is very little chance that statements intended to promote hatred against an identifiable group are true, or that their vision of society will lead to a better world. To portray such statements as crucial to truth and the betterment of the political and social milieu is therefore misguided.

Another component central to the rationale underlying s. 2(b) concerns the vital role of free expression as a means of ensuring individuals the ability to gain self-fulfilment by developing and articulating thoughts and ideas as they see fit. It is true that s. 319(2) inhibits this process among those individuals whose expression it limits, and hence arguably works against freedom of expression values. On the other hand, such self autonomy stems in large part from one's ability to articulate and nurture an identity derived from membership in a cultural or religious group. The message put forth by individuals who fall within the ambit of s. 319(2) represents a most extreme opposition to the idea that members of identifiable groups should enjoy this aspect of the s. 2(b) benefit. The extent to which the unhindered promotion of this message furthers free expression values must therefore be tempered insofar as it advocates with inordinate vitriol an intolerance and prejudice which views as execrable the process of individual self-development and human flourishing among all members of society.

Moving on to a third strain of thought said to justify the protection of free ex-

pression, one's attention is brought specifically to the political realm. The connection between freedom of expression and the political process is perhaps the linchpin of the s. 2(b) guarantee, and the nature of this connection is largely derived from the Canadian commitment to democracy. Freedom of expression is a crucial aspect of the democratic commitment, not merely because it permits the best policies to be chosen from among a wide array of proffered options, but additionally because it helps to ensure that participation in the political process is open to all persons . . .

[p.56] The suppression of hate propaganda undeniably muzzles the participation of a few individuals in the democratic process, and hence detracts somewhat from free expression values, but the degree of this limitation is not substantial. I am aware that the use of strong language in political and social debate—indeed, perhaps even language intended to promote hatred—is an unavoidable part of the democratic process. Moreover, I recognize that hate propaganda is expression of a type which would generally be categorized as "political", thus putatively placing it at the very heart of the principle extolling freedom of expression as vital to the democratic process. Nonetheless, expression can work to undermine our commitment to democracy where employed to propagate ideas anathemic to democratic values. Hate propaganda works in just such a way, arguing as it does for a society in which the democratic process is subverted and individuals are denied respect and dignity simply because of racial or religious characteristics. This brand of expressive activity is thus wholly inimical to the democratic aspirations of the free expression guarantee.

Indeed, one may quite plausibly contend that it is through rejecting hate propaganda that the state can best encourage the protection of values central to freedom of expression, while simultaneously demonstrating dislike for the vision forwarded by hate-mongers . . . [O]ne must be careful not to accept blindly that the suppression of expression must always and unremittingly detract from values central to freedom of expression . . .

I am very reluctant to attach anything but the highest importance to expression relevant to political matters. But[p.57] I am unable to see the protection of such expression as integral to the democratic ideal so central to the s. 2(b) rationale. . . In my view, hate propaganda should not be accorded the greatest of weight in the s. 1 analysis.

[p.58] Having made some preliminary comments as to the nature of the expression at stake in this appeal, it is now possible to ask whether s. 319(2) is an acceptably proportional response to Parliament's valid objective. As stated above, the proportionality aspect of the Oakes test requires the Court to decide whether the impugned state action: i) is rationally connected to the objective; ii) minimally impairs the Charter right or freedom at issue; and iii) does not produce effects of such severity so as to make the impairment unjustifiable. . . .

ii) Rational connection

. . . Those who would uphold the provision argue that the criminal prohibition of hate propaganda obviously bears a rational connection to the legitimate Parliamentary objective of protecting target group members and fostering harmonious social relations in a community dedicated to equality and multiculturalism. I agree, for in my opinion it would be difficult to deny that the suppression of hate propaganda reduces the harm such expression does to individuals who belong to identifiable groups and to relations between various cultural and religious groups in Canadian society.

Doubts have been raised, however, as to whether the actual effect of s. 319(2) is to undermine any rational connection between it and Parliament's objective. As stated in the reasons of McLachlin J., there are three primary ways in which the effect of the impugned legislation might be seen as an irrational means of carrying out the Parliamentary purpose. [p.59] First, it is argued that the provision may actually promote the cause of hatemongers by earning them extensive media attention. In this vein, it is also suggested that persons accused of intentionally promoting hatred often see themselves as martyrs, and may actually generate sympathy from the community in the role of underdogs engaged in battle against the immense powers of the state. Second, the public may view the suppression of expression by the government with suspicion, making it possible that such expression—even if it be hate propaganda—is perceived as containing an element of truth. Finally, it is often noted, citing the writings of Aryeh Neier, *Defending My Enemy: American Nazis, the Skokie Case, and the Risks of Freedom* (1979), that Germany of the 1920s and 1930s possessed and used hate propaganda laws similar to those existing in Canada, and yet these laws did nothing to stop the triumph of a racist philosophy under the Nazis.

. . . I recognize that the effect of s. 319(2) is impossible to define with exact precision—the same can be said for many laws, criminal or otherwise. In my view, however, the position that there is no strong and evident connection between the

371

criminalization of hate propaganda and its suppression is unconvincing. I come to this conclusion for a number of reasons, and will elucidate these by answering in turn the three arguments just mentioned.

It is undeniable that media attention has been extensive on those occasions when s. 319(2) has been used. Yet from my perspective, s. 319(2) serves to illustrate to the public the severe reprobation with which society holds messages of hate directed towards racial and religious groups. The existence of a particular criminal law, and the process of holding a trial when that law is used, is thus itself a form of expression, and the message sent out is that hate propaganda is harmful to target group members and threatening to a harmonious society . . . [p.60] The many, many Canadians who belong to identifiable groups surely gain a great deal of comfort from the knowledge that the hatemonger is criminally prosecuted and his or her ideas rejected. Equally, the community as a whole is reminded of the importance of diversity and multiculturalism in Canada, the value of equality and the worth and dignity of each human person being particularly emphasized.

In this context, it can also be said that government suppression of hate propaganda will not make the expression attractive and hence increase acceptance of its content. Similarly, it is very doubtful that Canadians will have sympathy for either propagators of hatred or their ideas. Governmental disapproval of hate propaganda does not invariably result in dignifying the suppressed ideology. Pornography is not dignified by its suppression, nor are defamatory statements against individuals seen as meritorious because the common law lends its support to their prohibition. Again, I stress my belief that hate propa-

ganda legislation and trials are a means by which the values beneficial to a free and democratic society can be publicized. In this context, no dignity will be unwittingly foisted upon the convicted hatemonger or his or her philosophy, and that a hatemonger might see him or herself as a martyr is of no matter to the content of the state's message.

As for the use of hate propaganda laws in pre-World War Two Germany, I am skeptical as to the relevance of the observation that legislation similar to s. 319(2) proved ineffective in curbing the racism of the Nazis. No one is contending that hate propaganda laws can in themselves prevent the tragedy of a Holocaust; conditions particular to Germany made the rise of Nazi ideology possible despite the existence and use of these laws. . . . Rather, hate propaganda laws are one part of a free and democratic society's bid to prevent the spread of racism, and their rational connection to this objective must be seen in such a context. Certainly West Germany has not reacted to the failure of prewar laws by seeking their removal, a new set of criminal offences having been implemented as recently as 1985: see Eric Stein, "History Against Free Speech: The New German Law Against 'Auschwitz'—and other—'Lies'", 85 Mich. L. Rev. 277 (1987). Nor, as has been discussed, has the international community regarded the promulgation of laws suppressing hate propaganda as futile or counter-productive. Indeed, this court's attention has been drawn to the fact that a great many countries possess legislation similar to that found in Canada: see, e.g.: England and Wales, *Public Order Act, 1986*, (U.K.), c. 64, ss. 17 to 23; New Zealand, *Race Relations Act, 1971* (N.Z.), s. 25; Sweden, *Penal Code*, c. 16, s. 8, as amended; Netherlands, *Penal Code*, ss. 137c, 137d and 137e; India, *Penal Code*, ss. 153-A and 153-B. . . .

[p.61] In sum, having found that the purpose of the challenged legislation is valid, I also find that the means chosen to further this purpose are rational in both theory and operation, and therefore conclude that the first branch of the proportionality test has been met . . .

iii) Minimal impairment of the s. 2(b) freedom

The criminal nature of the impugned provision, involving the associated risks of prejudice through prosecution, conviction and the imposition of up to two years imprisonment, indicates that the means embodied in hate propaganda legislation should be carefully tailored so as to minimize impairment of the freedom of expression. It therefore must be shown that s. 319(2) is a measured and appropriate response to the phenomenon of hate propaganda, and that it does not overly circumscribe the s. 2(b) guarantee.

The main argument of those who would strike down s. 319(2) is that it creates a real possibility of punishing expression that is not hate propaganda. It is thus submitted that the legislation is overbroad, its terms so wide as to include expression which does not relate to Parliament's objective, and also unduly vague, in that a lack of clarity and precision in its words prevents individuals from discerning its meaning with any accuracy. In either instance, it is said that the effect of s. 319(2) is to limit the expression of merely unpopular or unconventional communications. . . . [p.62] Accordingly, those attacking the validity of s. 319(2) contend that vigorous debate on important political and social issues, so highly valued in a society that prizes a diversity of ideas, is unacceptably suppressed by the provision.

. . . In order to . . . determine whether s. 319(2) minimally impairs the freedom of expression, the nature and impact of specific features of the provision must be examined in some detail. These features relate to both the terms of the offence and the available defences enumerated in s. 319(3). . . . As well, in examining this aspect of the proportionality test I will comment upon the relevance of alternative modes of combatting the harm caused by hate propaganda.

a. Terms of s. 319(2)

In assessing the constitutionality of s. 319(2), especially as concerns arguments of overbreadth and vagueness, an immediate observation is that . . . [t]he provision . . . does not prohibit views expressed with an intention to promote hatred if made privately, indicating Parliament's concern not to intrude upon the privacy of the individual . . .

[p.63] A second important element of s. 319(2) is its requirement that the promotion of hatred be "wilful". The nature of this mental element was explored by Martin J.A. in *R. v. Buzzanga and Durocher* (1979), 49 C.C.C. (2d) 369, 101 D.L.R. (3d) 488, 25 O.R. (2d) 705 (Ont. C.A.). . . .

[p.64] . . . Martin J.A. conclud[ed] that this mental element is satisfied only where an accused subjectively desires the promotion of hatred or foresees such a consequence as certain or substantially certain to result from an act done in order to achieve some other purpose (pp. 384-85) . . .

The interpretation of "wilfully" in *Buzzanga* has great bearing upon the extent to which s. 319(2) limits the freedom of expression. This mental element, requiring more than merely negligence or recklessness as to result, significantly restricts the reach of the provision, and thereby reduces the scope of the targeted expression. . . . It is clear that the word "wilfully" imports a difficult burden for the Crown to meet and, in so doing, serves to minimize the impairment of freedom of expression.

It has been argued, however, that even a demanding mens rea component fails to give s. 319(2) a constitutionally acceptable breadth. The problem is said to lie in the failure of the offence to require proof of actual hatred resulting from a communication, the assumption being that only such proof can demonstrate a harm serious enough to justify limiting the freedom of expression under s. 1. . . .

[p.65] While mindful of the dangers . . . I do not find them sufficiently grave to compel striking down s. 319(2). First, to predicate the limitation of free expression upon proof of actual hatred gives insufficient attention to the severe psychological trauma suffered by members of those identifiable groups targeted by hate propaganda. Second, it is clearly difficult to prove a causative link between a specific statement and hatred of an identifiable group. In fact, to require direct proof of hatred in listeners would severely debilitate the effectiveness of s. 319(2) in achieving Parliament's aim. It is well-accepted that Parliament can use the criminal law to prevent the risk of serious harms, a leading example being the drinking and driving provisions in the *Criminal Code*. The conclusions of the Cohen Committee and subsequent study groups show that the risk of hatred caused by hate propaganda is very real, and in view of the grievous harm to be avoided in the context of this appeal, I conclude that proof of actual hatred is not required in order to justify a limit under s. 1.

The meaning of "hatred" remains to be elucidated. Just as "wilfully" must be interpreted in the setting of s. 319(2), so must the word "hatred" be defined according to the context in which it is found. . . . Noting the purpose of s. 319(2), in my opinion the term "hatred" connotes emotion of an intense and extreme nature that is clearly associated with vilification and detestation. . . .[p.66] Hatred in this sense is a most extreme emotion that belies reason; an emotion that, if exercised against members of an identifiable group, implies that those individuals are to be despised, scorned, denied respect and made subject to ill-treatment on the basis of group affiliation.

Those who argue that s. 319(2) should be struck down submit that it is impossible to define with care and precision a term like "hatred". Yet, as I have stated, the sense in which "hatred" is used in s. 319(2) does not denote a wide range of diverse emotions, but is circumscribed so as to cover only the most intense form of dislike . . .

b. The defences to s. 319(2)

The factors mentioned above suggest that s. 319(2) does not unduly [p.67] restrict the s. 2(b) guarantee. The terms of the offence, as I have defined them, rather indicate that s. 319(2) possesses definitional limits which act as safeguards to ensure that it will capture only expressive activity which is openly hostile to Parliament's objective, and will thus attack only the harm at which the prohibition is targeted. The specific defences provided are further glosses on the purview of the offence. . . .

[T]he three defences which include elements of good faith or honest belief — namely, ss. 319(3) (b), (c) and (d) — would seem to operate to negate directly the mens rea in the offence, for only rarely will one who intends to promote hatred be acting in good faith or upon honest belief. These defences are hence intended to aid in making the scope of the wilful promotion of hatred more explicit; individuals engaging in the type of expression described are thus given a strong signal that their activity will not be swept into the ambit of the offence. The result is that what danger exists that s. 319(2) is overbroad or unduly vague, or will be perceived as such, is significantly reduced. . . .

The overlap between s. 319(2) and the defences is less pronounced in the case of the defence of truth, s. 319(3)(a) being more likely than the other defences to excuse the wilful promotion of hatred. This increased [p.68] likelihood reveals the defence in paragraph (a) to be an especially poignant indicator of Parliament's cautionary approach and care in protecting freedom of expression. Of course, if statements of truth are made without the intention to promote hatred towards identifiable groups, the offence as defined in s. 319(2) has not been committed. On the other hand, if a situation arises where an individual uses statements of truth in order to promote hatred against identifiable groups, the accused is acquitted despite the existence of the harm which Parliament seeks to prevent. Excusing the accused who intentionally promotes hatred through the communication of truthful statements is thus a circumspect measure associated with the importance attributed to truth—and hence to free expression—in our society.

It has been forcefully argued before us that the defence of truth is insufficient protection against an overly broad hate propaganda law. In this vein, it is rightly pointed out that many (if not most) of the communications coming within s. 319(2) are not susceptible to a true/false categorization, existing instead as ideas or opinions in the mind of the communicator. The accused could therefore sincerely believe in the worth of his or her viewpoint and yet be unable to utilize the s. 319(3)(a) defence. Moreover, it is said that, even where a statement is capable of categorization as true or false, the individual honestly mistaken as to the validity of his or her position (even if innocently so) is left unprotected, a result which dangerously restricts freedom of expression, causing a "chill" on communications as those who fear that their statements may be false exercise self-censorship. Finally, one might wonder if the courts are not on dangerous ground in attempting to distinguish between truthfulness and falsehood. The potential for bias in making such a determination, be it intentional or subconscious, is a danger frequently noted in freedom of expression theory (this potential is equally evident in s. 319(3)(c), insofar as ideas are assessed in light of "reasonableness" and the "public benefit").

[p.69] Because the presence of truth, though legally a defence to a charge under s. 319(2), does not change the fact that the accused has intended to promote the hatred of an identifiable group, I cannot find excessive impairment of the freedom of expression merely because s. 319(3)(a) does not cover negligent or innocent error. Whether or not a statement is susceptible to classification as true or false, my inclination is therefore to accept that such error should not excuse an accused who has wilfully used a statement in order to promote hatred against an identifiable group. That the legislative line is drawn so as to convict the accused who is negligent or even innocent regarding the accuracy of his or her statements is perfectly acceptable, for the mistake is not as to the use to which the information is put, namely, the promotion of hatred against an identifiable group. As for the argument that the courts and legislature should not involve themselves in the evaluation of "truth", "reasonable grounds for finding truth" or "public interest", the same response applies. Where the likelihood of truth or benefit from an idea diminishes to the point of vanishing, and the statement in question has harmful consequences inimical to the most central values of a free and democratic society, it is not excessively problematic to make a judgment that involves limiting expression.

. . . I should comment on a final argument marshalled in support of striking down s. 319(2) because of overbreadth or vagueness. It is said that the presence of the [p.70] legislation has led authorities to interfere with a diverse range of political, educational and artistic expression, demonstrating only too well the way in which overbreadth and vagueness can result in undue intrusion and the threat of persecution. In this regard, a number of incidents are cited where authorities appear to have been overzealous in their interpretation of the law, including the arrest of individuals distributing pamphlets admonishing Americans to leave the country and the temporary holdup at the border of a film entitled *Nelson Mandela* and Salman Rushdie's novel *Satanic Verses* (1988) (. . . note that the latter two examples involve not s. 319(2), but similar wording found in *Customs Tariff*, S.C. 1987, c. 49, s. 114, and Schedule VII, Code 9956(b)).

That s. 319(2) may in the past have led authorities to restrict expression offering valuable contributions to the arts, education or politics in Canada is surely worrying. I hope, however, that my comments as to the scope of the provision make it obvious that only the most intentionally extreme forms of expression will find a place within s. 319(2). In this light, one can safely say that the incidents mentioned above illustrate not overexpansive breadth and vagueness in the law, but rather actions by the state which cannot be lawfully taken pursuant to s. 319(2). The possibility of illegal police harassment clearly has minimal bearing on the proportionality of hate propaganda legislation to legitimate Parliamentary objectives, and hence the argument based on such harassment can be rejected.

c. Alternative modes of furthering Parliament's objective

. . . [I]t is said that non-criminal responses can more effectively combat the harm caused by hate propaganda. Most generally, it is said that discriminatory ideas can best be met with information and education programmes extolling the merits of tolerance and cooperation between racial and religious groups. As for the prohibition of hate propaganda, human rights statutes are pointed to as being a less severe and more effective response than the criminal law. Such statutes not only subject the disseminator of hate propaganda to reduced stigma and punishment, but also take a less confrontational approach to the suppression of such expression. [p.71] This conciliatory tack is said to be preferable to penal sanction because an incentive is offered the disseminator to cooperate with human rights tribunals and thus to amend his or her conduct.

. . . It is important, in my opinion, not

to hold any illusions about the ability of this one provision to rid our society of hate propaganda and its associated harms. Indeed, to become overly complacent, forgetting that there are a great many ways in which to address the problem of racial and religious intolerance, could be dangerous. Obviously, a variety of measures need be employed in the quest to achieve such lofty and important goals.

In assessing the proportionality of a legislative enactment to a valid governmental objective, however, s. 1 should not operate in every instance so as to force the government to rely upon only the mode of intervention least intrusive of a Charter right or freedom. It may be that a number of courses of action are available in the furtherance of a pressing and substantial objective, each imposing a varying degree of restriction upon a right or freedom. In such circumstances, the government may legitimately employ a more restrictive measure, either alone or as part of a larger programme of action, if that measure is not redundant, furthering the objective in ways that alternative responses could not, and is in all other respects proportionate to a valid s. 1 aim.

Though the fostering of tolerant attitudes among Canadians will be best achieved through a combination of diverse measures, the harm done through hate propaganda may require that especially stringent responses be taken to suppress and prohibit a modicum of expressive activity. At the moment, for example, the state has the option of responding to hate propaganda by acting under either the *Criminal Code* or human rights provisions. In my view, having both avenues of redress at the state's disposal is justified in a free and democratic society. . . .

[p.72] d. Conclusion as to minimal impairment

. . . I find that the terms of s. 319(2) create a narrowly confined offence which suffers from neither overbreadth nor vagueness . . .

iv) Effects of the limitation

The third branch of the proportionality test entails a weighing of the importance of the state objective against the effect of limits imposed upon a Charter right or guarantee. Even if the purpose of the limiting measure is substantial and the first two components of the proportionality [p.73] test are satisfied, the deleterious effects of a limit may be too great to permit the infringement of the right or guarantee in issue.

. . . It will by now be quite clear that I do not view the infringement of s. 2(b) by s. 319(2) as a restriction of the most serious kind. The expressive activity at which this provision aims is of a special category, a category only tenuously connected with the values underlying the guarantee of freedom of speech. Moreover, the narrowly drawn terms of s. 319(2) and its defences prevent the prohibition of expression lying outside of this narrow category. Consequently, the suppression of hate propaganda affected by s. 319(2) represents an impairment of the individual's freedom of expression which is not of a most serious nature.

It is also apposite to stress yet again the enormous importance of the objective fuelling s. 319(2), an objective of such magnitude as to support even the severe response of criminal prohibition. Few concerns can be as central to the concept of a free and democratic society as the dissipation of racism, and the especially strong value which Canadian society attaches to this goal must never be forgotten in assessing the effects of an impugned legislative measure. When the purpose of s. 319(2) is thus recognized, I have little trouble in finding that its effects, involving as they do the restriction of expression largely removed from the heart of free expression values, are not of such a deleterious nature as to outweigh any advantage gleaned from the limitation of s. 2(b).

E. Analysis of Section 319(2) Under Section 1 of the Charter: Conclusion

I find that the infringement of the respondent's freedom of expression as guaranteed by s. 2(b) should be upheld as a reasonable limit prescribed by law in a free and democratic society. Furthering an immensely important objective and directed at expression distant from the core of free expression values, s. 319(2) satisfies each of the components of the proportionality inquiry. . . .

VIII. SECTION 319(3)(A) AND THE PRESUMPTION OF INNOCENCE

As already noted, s. 319(3)(a) of the *Criminal Code* provides that no person shall be convicted of wilfully promoting hatred "if he establishes [p.74] that the statements communicated were true". This provision is challenged as breaching the presumption of innocence guaranteed in s. 11(d) of the Charter . . .

[Dickson C.J.C. then applies the test of *R. v. Whyte* [1988], 2 S.C.R. 3, 42 C.C.C. (3d) 97, 5 W.W.R. 26: an infringement of s. 11(d) will occur whenever the accused is liable to be convicted despite the existence of a reasonable doubt as to guilt in the mind of the trier of fact. He finds that s. 319(3)(a) creates a reverse onus provision which leaves room for such a doubt and that the legislation therefore violates s. 11(d). He concludes that the

legislation may nonetheless be upheld as a reasonable limit under s. 1:]

[p.78] . . . The reverse onus found in the truth defence represents the only way in which the defence can be [p.79] offered while still enabling Parliament to prohibit effectively hate-promoting expression through criminal legislation; to require that the state prove beyond a reasonable doubt the falsity of a statement would excuse much of the harmful expressive activity caught by s. 319(2) despite minimal proof as to its worth. In my opinion, justification for this reverse onus must therefore reside in the fact that it only applies where the Crown has proven beyond a reasonable doubt an intent to promote harm-causing hatred, and in the recognition that excessive deference to the possibility that a statement is true will undermine Parliament's objective.

[p.79]

IX. CONCLUSION

Insofar as its purpose is to prohibit the expression of certain meanings, s. 319(2) of the *Criminal Code* infringes the guarantee of freedom of expression found in s. 2(b) of the Charter. Given the importance of Parliament's purpose in preventing the dissemination of hate propaganda and the tenuous connection such expression has with s. 2(b) values, however, I have found the narrowly drawn parameters of s. 319(2) to be justifiable under s. 1. Similarly, although the reverse onus provision contained in s. 319(3)(a) conflicts with the s. 11(d) presumption of innocence, it can be seen as a justifiable means of excusing truthful statements without undermining the objective of preventing harm caused by the intentional promotion of hatred.

Appeal Allowed

[p.80] McLachin J. (dissenting) (Sopinka J. concurring): [McLachlin J. agrees that s. 319 (2) violates s. 2(b) of the Charter. However, she concludes that the legislation may not be upheld as a reasonable limit under s. 1. While the objective of s. 319(2) is pressing and substantial, McLachlin J. finds that it does not pass the proportionality test.

[Under rational connection, McLachlin J. finds a tenuous link between the criminalization of hate propaganda and its suppression. Prosecution of hate-mongers might actually promote their cause by providing publicity and invoking sympathy from the public. Moreover, the history of pre-Hitler Germany shows that the existence of hate propaganda laws may be ineffective in promoting multiculturalism and equality.

[In terms of minimal impairment, McLachlin J. finds that s. 319(2) is overbroad and capable of catching a wide variety of expression. This may also produce a "chilling effect" in stifling expression and debate among individuals who fear the possibility of criminal prosecution. Furthermore, equally effective means of prohibition were open to the government besides criminal prosecution, such as human rights legislation.

[Under the third branch of the *Oakes* proportionality test, McLachlin J. finds that the extent of the infringement of s. 2(b) is severe due to its potential to catch legitimate expression. She argues that this infringement touches on values at the core of s. 2(b), such as vigorous and open debate, the promotion of a marketplace of ideas and human flourishing. Such a violation of s. 2(b) could only be justified by a countervailing state interest of the most compelling nature, but the claims of the gains to be achieved by s. 319(2) are tenuous: the legislation does not necessarily promote social harmony, individual dignity or multiculturalism and equality. Indeed, it might operate to further the cause of hate-mongers.

[McLachlin J. therefore concludes that the objectives of the legislation are valid and important but that the means chosen to achieve them are not proportionate to these ends. S. 319(2) thus violates s. 2(b) of the Charter and is not saved under s. 1.

[McLachlin J. also finds that s. 319(3)(a) violates the presumption of innocence under s. 11(d) of the Charter and is not saved under s. 1, due to a similar lack of proportionality regarding the means chosen to achieve the valid objectives of the legislation.

[La Forest J. also dissents, agreeing with McLachlin J. that s. 319(2) is unconstitutional but concluding that it is therefore unnecessary to consider issues respecting the presumption of innocence.]

Subsequent Developments

[The case was subsequently remitted to the Alberta Court of Appeal. On March 15, 1991, the Court of Appeal quashed Mr. Keegstra's conviction and ordered a new trial, on the grounds that Mr. Keegstra's counsel had been denied the right to challenge jurors for cause at trial. On July 10, 1992, Mr. Keegstra was convicted in the Alberta Court of Queen's Bench of wilfully promoting hatred and fined $3,000. He once again appealed. On September 8, 1994, the Alberta Court of Appeal quashed the conviction, this time on the grounds that the trial judge had erred in failing to respond to the jury's requests for transcripts of testimony and help in understanding the *Criminal Code*. On September 22, the Alberta government announced its intention to appeal this decision to the

Supreme Court of Canada. This appeal has not yet been heard (as of May 30, 1995).

[The Liberal government of Jean Chrétien has meanwhile sought to introduce amendments to the *Criminal Code* that would expand sentencing powers in cases of hate crime. The government's proposed Bill C-41 provides for increased punishment in "crimes based on race, nationality, colour, religion, sex, age, mental or physical disability or sexual orientation of the victim". The amendments would only come into play once the accused was convicted of a separate criminal offence.

The Bill has faced opposition in the House of Commons from both Reform Party MPs and a small number of dissidents within the Liberal Party itself. These MPs primarily oppose the "sexual orientation" provision of the Bill and what they see as a government endorsement of homosexual lifestyles and the provision of "special rights" to gays and lesbians. As of May 30, 1995, the Bill was scheduled for its third and final reading. Prime Minister Chrétien expected it to be passed by the House of Commons before Parliament's June recess.]

Hate Promotion in a Free and Democratic Society:
R. v. Keegstra

Lorraine Eisenstat Weinrib *

> Where s. 1 operates to accentuate a uniquely Canadian vision of a free and dem-
> ocratic society...we must not hesitate to depart from the path taken in the United
> States.[1]

> [T]he provisions of the *Charter*, though drawing on a political and social philos-
> ophy shared with other democratic societies, are uniquely Canadian.[2]

Introduction

R. v. Keegstra[3] deals with an issue fundamental to a free and democratic
society: is hate propaganda constitutionally protected?

Mr. Keegstra was a secondary school teacher who used his classroom to
inculcate anti-semitism. He taught that Jews were personally odious ("sadistic,"
"manipulative," "deceptive," "money-loving," "child killers," "inherently
evil")[4] and politically dangerous ("treacherous," "subversive," "power hungry,"
"revolutionists," "communists").[5] He faulted them for attempting to destroy
Christianity through a variety of world calamities, including "depressions,
anarchy, chaos, wars and revolution."[6] Students could obtain good marks by
regurgitating this mesh of anti-semitic myth and diatribe, poor marks for doing
otherwise.[7]

Mr. Keegstra was prosecuted for promoting hatred contrary to s. 319(2)
of the *Criminal Code*.[8] As is evident from the debate which preceded its adop-

---

* Of the Faculty of Law, University of Toronto.

© McGill Law Journal 1991
  Revue de droit de McGill

[1] *R. v. Keegstra*, [1990] 3 S.C.R. 697, [1991] 2 W.W.R. 1 at 40 (S.C.C.), Dickson C.J. [hereinafter
Keegstra cited to W.W.R.].

[2] *Ibid.* at 112, McLachlin J. (dissenting).

[3] *Ibid.*

[4] *Ibid.* at 17, Dickson C.J., and at 81, McLachlin J.

[5] *Ibid.*

[6] *Ibid.* at 17.

[7] *Ibid.* at 81. The factum submitted to the Supreme Court on his behalf gives a chilling sense of
Mr. Keegstra's Christian crusade against "evil."

[8] S. 319 of the *Criminal Code*, R.S.C. 1985, c. C-46 [hereinafter s. 319], provides as follows:
  (2) Everyone who, by communicating statements, other than ... in private conversation, wilfully promotes hatred against any identifiable group is guilty of

tion and the numerous studies that have deliberated upon its retention, this section is complex and controversial. Its many twists and turns reflect the tension between Canada's national commitment to freedom of expression and our awareness of the corrosive effects of racial, religious and ethnic hatred.

In a 4-3 decision, the Supreme Court of Canada upheld the constitutionality of s. 319(2). The majority and the dissent agreed that the section infringed s. 2(b) of the *Charter*,[9] but disagreed as to whether the provision could be saved by s. 1. The two judgments canvass many issues of both substance and method. What kinds of expression should be protected by the *Charter*? On what basis can the state abridge expression? How should a court of law determine the scope of a constitutionally protected right? And behind these specific questions lies a puzzle about the place of the *Charter* in the corpus of rights-protecting documents. Is the *Charter* modelled on the text and jurisprudence of the American *Bill of Rights*,[10] or on the international commitment to human rights that arose in response to the experience of the Second World War?

(a) an indictable offence and is liable to imprisonment for a term not exceeding two years; or

(b) an offence punishable on summary conviction.

(3) No person shall be convicted of an offence under subsection (2)

(a) if he establishes that the statements communicated were true;

(b) if, in good faith, he expressed or attempted to establish by argument an opinion upon a religious subject;

(c) if the statements were relevant to a subject of public interest, the discussion of which was for the public benefit, and if on reasonable grounds he believed them to be true; or

(d) if, in good faith, he intended to point out, for the purpose of removal, matters producing or tending to produce feelings of hatred towards an identifiable group in Canada.

(6) No proceeding for an offence under subsection (2) shall be instituted without the consent of the Attorney General.

(7) In this section,

"communicating" includes communicating by telephone, broadcasting or other audible or visible means;

"identifiable group" [incorporated from s. 318] means any section of the public distinguished by colour, race, religion or ethnic origin ...

"public place" includes any place to which the public have access as of right or by invitation, express or implied; "statements" includes words spoken or written or recorded electronically or electro-magnetically or otherwise, and gestures, signs or other visible representations.

[9]*Canadian Charter of Rights and Freedoms*, Part I of the *Constitution Act, 1982*, being Schedule B of the *Canada Act 1982* (U.K.), 1982, c. 11 [hereinafter *Charter*].

[10]U.S. Const., amend I.

While both the majority and the dissent in *Keegstra* find the guarantee of freedom of expression in s. 2(b)[11] of the *Charter* to be infringed by s. 319(2), the mode of analysis in the two opinions differs dramatically. Resting its discussion on doctrinal precedent, the majority comes to the conclusion that s. 2(b) brooks no content-based restrictions; the dissent reads the right to freedom of expression as a prerequisite to an open, democratic and progressive polity. The respective s. 1 analyses reflect even more profound disagreement. The majority understands s. 1 analysis as normative, forwarding the *Charter*'s promise of a free and democratic society imbued with the public values of equal respect for all individuals. The dissent, in contrast, takes an empirical approach, insisting upon proof of the effectiveness of s. 319(2) to eradicate the evil it was enacted to address without chilling expressive activity beyond its actual reach.

I.   The Majority Judgment

The majority judgment, written by Chief Justice Dickson (Wilson, L'Heureux-Dubé and Gonthier JJ. concurring), follows the two-stage analysis now standard to *Charter* cases. The first stage focuses on the scope of the right and the fact of its infringement; the second seeks to ascertain whether the infringement constitutes a justified limitation under s. 1. The two stages of the majority opinion in *Keegstra* differ remarkably in tone and technique. The first part of Dickson C.J.C.'s reasons for judgment relies mechanically and superficially on recent precedent. Only the second part exhibits the now familiar and welcome characteristics of the Chief Justice's other leading *Charter* judgments: detailed, well-researched and sensitive presentations of the history and policy underlying both the *Charter* and the impugned legal rules; a deep concern for those whose lives are marked by disadvantage or discrimination; and an awareness that the *Charter* is a testament to Canada's commitment to the values underlying the family of post-war rights-protecting instruments.

A.   *The Scope of Freedom of Expression*

The first issue addressed by the Chief Justice is whether the public, wilful promotion of hatred, proscribed by s. 319(2) of the *Criminal Code*, is expression protected under the guarantee set out in s. 2(b) of the *Charter*. The majority answers this question in the affirmative, relying on the Court's determination in a previous case that the guarantee of freedom of expression in the *Charter* embraces "all content ... irrespective of the particular meaning or message

---

[11]S. 2(b) of the *Charter*:

    Everyone has the following fundamental freedoms:

        (b) freedom of thought, belief, opinion and expression, including freedom of the press and other media of communication ...

sought to be conveyed."[12] The only relevant exception to the otherwise comprehensive constitutional protection of communicated meaning is for expression communicated directly through physical harm.[13] Hate promotion does not fall under this exception. It is criminalized for the repugnancy of its *meaning*, not because any direct physical harm is consequent on its utterance. With meaning, therefore, comes constitutional protection.

The Chief Justice's view that the guarantee of freedom of expression protects all communicated meaning that lacks violent form is a function of his comprehensive approach to the rationales for the protection of freedom of expression. Citing previous case law,[14] Dickson C.J. sets out these values as: (1) the protection of the "inherently good activity" of "seeking and attaining truth"; (2) the fostering and encouragement of "participation in social and political decision-making;" and (3) the cultivation of "diversity in forms of individual self-fulfilment and human flourishing" in a society that is "tolerant and welcoming," so as to benefit speaker and listener alike.[15]

Despite the broad range of the values he advances as underlying the guarantee of freedom of expression, Dickson C.J.'s conception of the right is surprisingly dessicated. These stated values play only a perfunctory role in his elucidation of that right in the general sense, and no role in the specific context of the wilful promotion of hatred. In his discussion of the scope of the guarantee, the Chief Justice considers neither the plausibility of the three rationales he has enumerated, nor their inter-relationship, nor the degree to which the propagation of hatred instantiates them, nor the extent to which the specific text of s. 319(2) and (3) conforms to them. Only when he reaches the second stage of *Charter* analysis, and comes to consider the justification for the impugned provision, does he acknowledge that the three rationales are in tension with one another, that their formulation derives from a jurisprudence that is marginal to our own,[16]

---

[12]*Supra*, note 1 at 29, referring to *Reference re ss 193 and 195.1(1)(c) of the Criminal Code of Canada (Man.)*, [1990] 1 S.C.R. 1123 at 1181, 4 W.W.R. 481.

[13]*Irwin Toy v. A.G. Quebec*, [1989] 1 S.C.R. 927, 58 D.L.R. (4th) 577 at 607 & 614 [hereinafter *Irwin Toy* cited to D.L.R.] formulated this exception. In *Keegstra, ibid.* at 31-32, Dickson C.J. differentiates the idea of physical harm from mere threats, which are content specific and thus protected by s. 2(b): "threats of violence can only be ... classified by reference to the content of their meaning. As such, they do not fall within the exception ..." The violent form exception would exclude, *e.g.*, acts of murder or rape that carry a communicative message. See, *infra*, note 89, for McLachlin J.'s view that threats are not protected expression.

[14]*Irwin Toy, ibid.* at 612.

[15]*Supra*, note 1 at 28.

[16]The majority, in its s. 1 discussion, takes the view that the *Charter* is sufficiently different from the American mode of rights protection to warrant different results in similar cases. See *Reference Re S. 94(2) of the Motor Vehicle Act*, [1985] 1 W.W.R. 481, 24 D.L.R. (4th) 536 [hereinafter *B.C. Motor Vehicle*], where Lamer J. (as he then was) stated:

> We would, in my view, do our own Constitution a disservice to simply allow the American debate to define the issue for us, all the while ignoring the truly fundamental structural differences between the two constitutions.

that the argument based on democratic process cuts both ways,[17] and that the truth-seeking rationale is no longer credible.[18] Only then, also, does he demonstrate how the careful drafting of s. 319(2) and (3) of the *Criminal Code* respects the values for which freedom of expression is protected. Like Penelope forestalling her suitors, the Chief Justice weaves and then unravels before our eyes the right to propagate hatred.

Dickson C.J.'s broad-brush approach to the delineation of the right to freedom of expression precludes careful examination of the relationship between s. 2(b) and other *Charter* provisions. Thus, although the Chief Justice concludes that the guarantee in s. 2(b) protects the wilful promotion of hatred against identifiable groups "distinguished by colour, race, religion or ethnic origin" (s. 319(2)), he does not relate that designation of identifiable groups to the *Charter* proscription against state discrimination in s. 15, on grounds that include colour, race, religion and ethnic origin.[19] Moreover, he denies s. 27 of the *Charter* any role in delineating the scope of s. 2(b), even though this section mandates an interpretation of *Charter* rights that is favourable to our multicultural heritage — and hence the colour, race, religion and ethnic origin — of Canadians.[20]

Similarly, the Chief Justice refuses to consider in the first stage of his analysis the international agreements on rights-protection to which Canada is a

---

[17]Democracy can be used to support an argument both for and against regulation of expression. Some would argue that democracy can flourish only if expression is unchecked. Others would argue that democracy can function properly only when the state regulates to eliminate excesses and manipulation. See O.M. Fiss, "Free Speech and Social Structure" (1986) 71 Iowa L. Rev. 1405 and "Why the State?" (1986) 100 Harvard L. Rev. 781.

[18]The Chief Justice does note in *Keegstra, supra,* note 1 at 28, perhaps critically, that *Irwin Toy,* "perhaps goes further towards stressing as primary the 'democratic commitment'". He appears to prefer the formulation that s. 2(b) protects more than political expression in service of democracy, because "it serves individual and societal values in a free and democratic society." For a discussion of the conceptual difficulties posed by these rationales for protecting expression, see L.E. Weinrib, "Does Money Talk? Commercial Expression in the Canadian Constitutional Context" in D. Schneiderman, ed., *Freedom of Expression and the Charter* (Toronto: Carswell, 1991) [hereinafter "Does Money Talk?"].

[19]S. 15 of the *Charter* provides:

(1) Every individual is equal before and under the law and has the right to the equal protection and equal benefit of the law without discrimination and, in particular, without discrimination based on race, national or ethnic origin, colour, religion, sex, age or mental or physical disability.

(2) Subsection (1) does not preclude any law, program or activity that has as its objective the amelioration of conditions of disadvantaged individuals or groups including those that are disadvantaged because of race, national or ethnic origin, colour, religion, sex, age or mental or physical disability.

[20]S. 27 of the *Charter* provides:

This *Charter* shall be interpreted in a manner consistent with the preservation and enhancement of the multicultural heritage of Canadians.

signatory. To do so in the course of articulating the *Charter* right, he contends, would diminish the large and liberal interpretation made possible by s. 1 balancing. He therefore relegates consideration of these instruments to the second stage of his analysis, that of "weighing of contextual values"[21] to set limits on protected rights.

According to the majority judgment, then, the first stage of *Charter* adjudication excludes textual, contextual and comparative analysis. The Court is to read the values underlying the right or freedom as expansively as possible, leaving aside any consideration of the currency or mutual consistency of these values, the broader significance of the *Charter* text and its interpretive provisions, as well as the interpretive resources provided by similar systems of rights protection elsewhere in the world. This, says the Chief Justice, is the "large and liberal interpretation"[22] of *Charter* rights.

While this approach may be "large and liberal," it is certainly not the "purposive" approach as originally articulated in *R. v. Big M Drug Mart*.[23] Far from directing the Court to raise values at the initial stage of *Charter* analysis that turn out to be irrelevant at the justification stage, or to ignore the rest of the *Charter* text or other rights-protecting documents simply because s. 1 offers the Court a second bite, the purposive approach allowed for reference to:

> the character and the larger objects of the *Charter* itself, to the language chosen to articulate the specific right or freedom, to the historical origins of the concepts enshrined, and where applicable, to the meaning and purpose of the other specific rights and freedoms, with which it is associated within the text of the *Charter*. The interpretation should be ... a generous rather than a legalistic one, aimed at fulfilling the purpose of the guarantee and securing for individuals the full benefit of the *Charter*'s protection. [In order not to overshoot the purpose of the right or freedom, the *Charter* must] be placed in its proper linguistic, philosophic and historical contexts.[24]

Compared to the formulation in *Big M*, the Chief Justice in *Keegstra* takes an extremely narrow view of the values that are relevant to the characterization of the scope of freedom of expression.

On the basis of the purposive approach dictated in *Big M*, a court might still have reached the Chief Justice's conclusion that wilful promotion of hatred is protected by s. 2(b) of the *Charter*, but in so doing, it would have taken into

---

[21]*Supra*, note 1 at 32.

[22]*Ibid.*

[23][1985] 1 S.C.R. 295, 18 D.L.R. (4th) 321 [hereinafter *Big M* or *Big M Drug Mart* cited to S.C.R.]. P.W. Hogg, "Interpreting the Charter of Rights: Generosity and Justification" (1990) 28 Osgoode Hall L.J. 817 also makes the distinction between a broad or generous approach to interpreting the scope of a right and an approach tied to its underlying purposes. D. Beatty, "A Conservative Court: The Politicization of Law" (1991) 41 U.T.L.J. 147 traces the development of the case law on rights and limits.

[24]*Big M, ibid.* at 344.

account the following factors. First, the *Big M* formulation encourages consideration of the language chosen to articulate the s. 2(b) guarantee. The *Charter*, like the international instruments, employs the word "expression," rather than the word "speech," which appears in the First Amendment to the United States' *Bill of Rights*. The *Charter*'s departure from the American terminology, twinned with the provision in s. 1 of an express limitation clause under which the state bears the burden of persuasion, gives s. 2(b) a particular significance. "Expression" connotes emotive behaviour rather than rational discourse. It focuses on the interests of the speaker, leaving the interests of the audience or of other affected parties to be considered under the expressly provided limitation clause, which directs justification to the demands of a free and democratic society.

Second, *Big M* directs the Court to examine critically the historical origins of the concepts enshrined in the *Charter*. Historically, politically and socially, international rights-protecting documents are more relevant to the Canadian experience than is the American one. Much of the American commitment to unrestrained freedom of speech was developed in the course of and in the *ex post* legitimation of a revolution, which had been fomented by public speeches, letter writing and pamphleteering. This background explains the republican ideal of a sovereign, homogeneous people creating and sustaining self-government, which continues to inform speech rights in the United States.[25] Moreover, the precise ideas underlying the rationales for freedom of expression, as developed in this century, remain matters of contention. For example, does the free trade in ideas stand for a truth-seeking enterprise, libertarian ideals, autonomy, self-fulfilment or individual dignity?[26]

The American background should not provide an unexamined paradigm for the development of freedom of expression in Canadian constitutional law. On the contrary, it should highlight the contrast with Canadian loyalty to the Crown and faith in the state as promoter of the conditions of collective life in a system of parliamentary democracy. Instead of accepting the American approach to free speech, Canadian courts should have recourse to the ideas that underlie freedom of expression in a more relevant context. The international

---

[25]See, *e.g.*, L.H. Cohen, "Creating a Usable Future: The Revolutionary Historians" in J.P. Greene, ed., *The American Revolution: Its Character and Limits* (New York: New York University Press, 1987); B. Bailyn, *The Ideological Limits of the American Revolution* (Cambridge: Harvard University Press, 1967); G.S. Wood, *The Creation of the American Republic* (New York: Norton, 1969); and D.A. Richards, *Foundations of American Constitutionalism* (New York: Oxford University Press, 1989) at 172-201.

[26]See M.H. Redich & G. Lippman, "Freedom of Expression and the Civic Republican Revival in Constitutional Theory: The Ominous Implications" (1991) 79 Calif. L. Rev. 267, D. Cole, "Agon at Agora: Creative Misreadings of the First Amendment Tradition" (1986) 95 Yale L.J. 857, and P. Lahav, "Holmes and Brandeis: Libertarian and Republican Justifications for Free Speech" (1988) 4 J. of L. & Politics 451.

instruments, the other available paradigm, reflect a more current and more relevant agenda with respect to expression rights. In particular, the international model is more relevant to Canada than the American one because it is contextualized in the post-war project of maintaining democratic stability in nation states with mixed racial, religious and ethnic populations.

Third, the *Big M* methodology renders relevant other provisions of the *Charter* text.[27] In particular, the values embodied in s. 15 (the equality section) and s. 27 (the multiculturalism section) bear on the constitutional status of the wilful promotion of hatred. S. 15 proscribes state discrimination, with a proviso for affirmative action programmes, directed at (or affecting) individuals with characteristics similar to those listed in s. 319(2). Accordingly, one might argue, a speaker must be given wide latitude with respect to public comment on the activities, claims and interests of persons identified by those constitutionally significant characteristics, because the *Charter* considers these characteristics to be of great public importance. Furthermore, the possible application of the directive in s. 27 to ss 1, 2(b) & 15 gives additional weight to the recognition of a prima facie right to expression which touches on these categories of persons.

The majority in *Keegstra* invokes precedent to relegate these considerations to the second stage of their analysis. The choice of precedent, however, reflects interpretive preference. The majority relies heavily on *Irwin Toy* for the rule that all expression attracts protection regardless of content, based upon its uncritical adoption of the three rationales noted earlier.[28] An alternative was available, however. Dickson C.J. might have emulated the reasoning in the *Ford* case,[29] where the Court had focussed in the first stage of *Charter* analysis not on expression in the general sense, but instead upon the particular claim asserted. With this focus, the Court in *Ford* considered whether s. 2(b) protected the right to speak in the language of one's choice in the context of a modern democracy grappling with the problem of the varied linguistic usages of its inhabitants. In *Ford*, unlike *Keegstra*, the Court analyzed other sections of the *Charter*, as well as international human rights jurisprudence, to reach its conclusion that choice of language found protection under s. 2(b) because of the unde-

---

[27]See *Dubois* v. *R.*, [1985] 2 S.C.R. 350 at 365, [1986] 1 W.W.R. 193, Lamer J. (as he then was), for the view that the *Charter* must be construed so that each component gives meaning to the whole and *vice versa*: "[t]he courts must interpret each section of the *Charter* in relation to the others."

[28]For comment on *Irwin Toy* and its progeny, *e.g.*, *Royal College of Dental Surgeons* v. *Rocket*, [1990] 2 S.C.R. 232, 71 D.L.R. (4th) 68 [hereinafter *Rocket* cited to S.C.R.], see "Does Money Talk?," *supra*, note 18 and R. Moon, "Lifestyle Advertising and Classical Freedom of Expression Doctrine" (1991) 36 McGill L.J. 76.

[29]*Ford* v. *A.G. Quebec*, [1988] 2 S.C.R. 712, 54 D.L.R. (4th) 577 [hereinafter *Ford* cited to D.L.R.].

niable links between individual identity, group affiliation and the expressive content of language.[30]

The majority in *Keegstra* abandoned the methodology of *Big M* without explanatory comment. Instead of elucidating broadly those factors relevant to discerning the purpose of a right in the context of the *Charter* text, its history and value structure, the Court adopted an expansive analysis of the particular right, isolated from the rest of the *Charter* text.

The Court's "large and liberal" approach bears certain methodological costs. First, it sets s. 2(b) off from the other rights already elaborated by the Court using the purposive approach. The Court has interpreted most other sections of the *Charter*, not by parading unexamined values, as did the majority in *Keegstra*, but by discerning the values for the sake of which we have set the right above the political fray.[31] By exempting s. 2(b) from this methodology, the majority in *Keegstra* suggests that freedom of expression has higher standing than other *Charter* rights. This may in turn suggest that the main goal of the *Charter* is to support the democratic political function, rather than to affirm individual human flourishing in a free *and* democratic society.[32] While orienting the *Charter* agenda towards the political process may appear to be rights-forwarding, it may in reality be a post-*Charter* expression of anti-entrenchment

---

[30]*Ibid.* at 604-09, where the Court quotes from *Reference re Language Rights under Manitoba Act, 1870*, [1985] 1 S.C.R. 721, 19 D.L.R. (4th) 1 at 19, for reference to the same values of individual dignity and equality that Dickson C.J. later invokes in his s. 1 analysis in *Keegstra*:

> The importance of language rights is grounded in the essential role that language plays in human existence, development and dignity. It is through language that we are able to form concepts; to structure and order the world around us. Language bridges the gap between isolation and community, allowing humans to delineate the rights and duties they hold in respect of one another, and thus to live in society.

The reasons for judgment in *Ford* refer to other sections of the Canadian *Charter*, to the preamble of the *Quebec Charter of the French Language*, R.S.Q. 1977, c. C-11, ss 1 & 58, and to the views of the European Commission of Human Rights and the European Court of Human Rights. While the conclusion in *Ford* was that choice of language is protected because of its inextricable relationship with content and meaning, the benchmark values in the case were individual dignity and equality.

[31]See, *e.g.*: for s. 2(a), *Big M Drug Mart*; for s. 7, *B.C. Motor Vehicle* and *R. v. Morgentaler*, [1988] 1 S.C.R. 30, 44 D.L.R. (4th) 385 [hereinafter *Morgentaler* cited to D.L.R.]; for the legal rights, *R. v. Strachan*, [1988] 2 S.C.R. 980, 25 D.L.R. (4th) 567, *R. v. Vaillancourt*, [1987] 2 S.C.R. 636, 47 D.L.R. (4th) 399, and *R. v. Oakes*, [1986] 1 S.C.R. 103, 26 D.L.R. (4th) 200 [hereinafter *Oakes* cited to S.C.R.]; and for s. 15, *Andrews* v. *Law Society of B.C.*, [1989] 1 S.C.R. 143, 56 D.L.R. (4th) 1. P.W. Hogg, *supra*, note 23, suggests that the Court's more recent abandonment of the purposive approach will be reversed. *Keegstra* and *McKinney* v. *Univ. of Guelph*, [1990] 3 S.C.R. 229, 76 D.L.R. (4th) 545 [hereinafter *McKinney* cited to D.L.R.], to the extent that they demonstrate the future direction of the Court, reconstituted after a number of retirements, suggest otherwise.

[32]For the view that the *Charter* protects democratic values, see P. Monahan, *Politics and the Constitution* (Toronto: Carswell, 1987), who follows the line of thinking developed in the American context by J.H. Ely, *Democracy and Distrust* (Cambridge: Harvard University Press, 1980).

sentiment, because it introduces into *Charter* adjudication a methodology that favours claims to expression, particularly in the political arena, and little else.

Second, the approach of the majority in *Keegstra* undermines the normativity of *Charter* rights. When the reasons for protecting rights are not fully articulated or critically examined by the Court, the currency of rights-protection is debased. What is essential in the first stage of *Charter* argument is that the Court explain why certain activities, here speech acts, are *prima facie* beyond the range of our representative and politically accountable institutions. The purposive approach of *Big M* should focus our attention on Mr. Keegstra's right to spew racist venom without being hindered by the state, not on the claims of his listeners (to listen) and his targets (to stop him). It should make us realize, whatever our views about s. 319(2) of the *Criminal Code*, the sense in which Mr. Keegstra's interests are *our* interests. This, the real reason for content-neutral protection of expression under s. 2(b), is the message that the Chief Justice's "large and liberal" approach fails to deliver.[33]

Finally, when the right is not brought home to us by the Court as a right that we must each hold in order to enjoy and maintain a free and democratic society, then s. 1 justification in the second stage of *Charter* analysis becomes blurred.[34] Unless the holder of the right comes into clear focus in the first stage, the broader and more varied viewpoints appropriate to the second stage do not come alive. How can we tell what might justify limiting the right if we lack a well-considered appreciation of its grounds? The Chief Justice's approach in *Keegstra* in effect reduces the difference between the two stages to a shift in onus, from the rights-claimant to the proponent of the impugned legislation. The change in the burden of persuasion is without significance, however, if the same arguments arise at both stages and cancel each other out.

B. Limitation under Section 1

When the Chief Justice turns from articulating the scope of s. 2(b) to s. 1 justification, he revisits the themes of truth-seeking, democratic process and human fulfilment, which he earlier found to underlie the guarantee of freedom of expression. Now, he regards these values with a critical eye. In a startling retreat from the jurisprudence that constrained his s.2(b) analysis, and in stark contrast to the s. 1 analysis offered by the dissent, the Chief Justice uses the second stage of *Charter* adjudication to forge a new resolution of the tension

---

[33]D.A.J. Richards, *Toleration and the Constitution* (New York: Oxford University Press, 1989) at 192 presents a ringing affirmation of the missing appeal: "the state's restriction of ... speech by group libel laws is inconsistent with the place respect for conscience holds in our constitutional traditions"; "communicative integrity, grounded in the fuller expression of its background right of critical conscience, is not one that can be abridged on grounds of offence, which would sanitize authentic exercises of the moral powers of free people" (at 195).

[34]See T. Macklem, "Putting Heart into Expression" (1991) 1 M.C.L.R. 341 at 347ff.

between vibrant, even heated, public debate, and restrictions on freedom of expression.

1.   Methodology

The Chief Justice introduces the second part of his judgment with a methodological preface. He warns at the outset that it would be "dangerously misleading to conceive of s. 1 as rigid and technical," "rigid or formalistic," or "mechanical."[35] While the target of these dreaded adjectives is not fully explicit, he seems to be criticizing the view that the justificatory undertaking in s. 1 pertains solely to the values "expressly set out in the *Charter*."[36] Dickson C.J. prefers a "flexible," "contextual," "sensitive" approach,[37] summarized in the following quotation from an earlier judgment of Justice La Forest in *U.S.A.* v. *Cotroni*:

> While the rights guaranteed by the *Charter* must be given priority in the equation, the underlying values must be sensitively weighed in a particular context against other values of a free and democratic society sought to be promoted by the legislature.[38]

Although the metaphors are mixed, if not garbled, the message here is clear: *Charter* values are not the exclusive pre-occupation of s. 1 analysis. Under the case law embodied in and evolved from this quotation, s. 1 justification is free-form balancing — a decidedly subjective exercise, serviced by a superficial utilitarian cost-benefit analysis, informed by a less-than-rigorous attitude to facts and data, and deferential in the extreme to majoritarian policy formation.[39] A free and democratic society, for Justice La Forest, is defined in the mind of the legislature.[40]

One can contrast the La Forest quote with the Court's approach in *Oakes*.[41] The *Oakes* test focused s. 1 justification on *Charter* values, so that a free and

---

[35]*Supra*, note 1 at 33.

[36]*Ibid.* at 33-35. See, *ibid.* at 58 for attribution of these negative characteristics to American analysis based on levels of scrutiny.

[37]*Ibid.* at 35.

[38][1989] 1 S.C.R. 1469 at 1489-90, 48 C.C.C. (3d) 193 [hereinafter *Cotroni* cited to S.C.R.], quoted by Dickson C.J. in *Keegstra, ibid.* at 35. In the *Keegstra* case itself, La Forest J. concurs with the dissenting reasons of McLachlin J. This quote from *Cotroni* is adopted by La Forest J. in his majority judgment in *McKinney, supra,* note 31 at 647-48, as epitomizing the balancing function under s. 1.

[39]For an application of this methodology, see *McKinney*. Judgment was rendered in that case on December 6, 1990, one week before *Keegstra*.

[40]*McKinney, ibid.* at 676. This approach to s. 1 would have accorded well with versions of its text that pre-dated its final draft, *e.g.*, "reasonable limits as are generally accepted in a free and democratic society" or "reasonable limits as are generally acceptable in a free society living under a parliamentary democracy." See A.F. Bayefsky, *Canada's Constitution Act, 1982 and Amendments: A Documentary History* (Toronto: McGraw-Hill Ryerson, 1989) at 669 & 678.

[41]*Supra*, note 31. The first section of the *Charter* states:

The *Canadian Charter of Rights and Freedoms* guarantees the rights and freedoms set

democratic society is one which honours the values that underlie *Charter* rights and freedoms, in both stages of *Charter* adjudication. Despite his invocation of the La Forest quotation, the Chief Justice in fact follows the *Oakes* approach. He rehearses the most significant interpretive component of the *Oakes* case, namely, the dual function of s. 1 as the source of both the guarantee and its limitation. In *Oakes*, Dickson C.J. had inferred from this dual function that the concept of a "free and democratic society" was both the "genesis of the rights and freedoms guaranteed by the *Charter*,"[42] and "the ultimate standard against which a limit on a right or freedom must be shown, despite its effect, to be reasonable and demonstrably justified."[43] On this reading the values underlying *Charter* rights are decisive in justifying their limitation.

The use of the *Oakes* test, in turn, allows the majority in *Keegstra* to rely heavily on international human rights instruments. Both the *Charter* and these international instruments build upon the idea that rights protection and limitation are joined in the common venture of affirming individual dignity and equality.[44] So understood, the relationship between the *Charter* and the international instruments means that one need not go beyond the *Charter*'s own values in *Keegstra*. And Dickson C.J. does not.

The majority judgment manifests no trace of the deferential, utilitarian and empirically suspect arguments, championed by Justice La Forest and referred to with favour by the Chief Justice at the beginning of his judgment. Indeed, Dickson C.J. applies the method he just decried as "mechanistic," "formalistic" and "technical." In so doing, he demonstrates it to be as "sensitive," "contextual"

---

out in it subject only to such reasonable limits prescribed by law as can be demonstrably justified in a free and democratic society.

[42]*Oakes, ibid.* at 136. See L.E. Weinrib, "The Supreme Court of Canada and Section One of the Charter" (1988) 10 Sup. Ct. L. Rev. 469 for an elaboration of this view of s. 1.

[43]Oakes, *ibid.* at 136, quoted in *Keegstra, supra,* note 1 at 34. Accordingly, each and every strand of the *Oakes* test was tied to the values of a free and democratic society. See "The Supreme Court of Canada and Section One of the Charter," *ibid.* for the full development of this approach to the *Charter* as a matter of theory as well as doctrinal development. In that article, I attribute this approach to Wilson J., and argue that she has been its most consistent adherent.

[44]Particularly helpful sources on this point are: J. M. Ross,'Limitations on Human Rights in International Law: Their Relevance to the Canadian Charter of Rights and Freedoms" (1986) 6 Human Rights Q. 180; A.C. Kiss, "Permissible Limitations on Rights" in L. Henkin, ed., *The International Bill of Rights: The Covenant on Civil and Political Rights* (New York: Columbia University Press, 1981) 290; and the Siracusa Principles on the Limitation and Derogation Provisions in the International Covenant on Civil and Political Rights, E/CN.4/1985/4 Annex (reprinted in (1985) 7 Human Rts Q.). This embrace of international rights-protection as the model for justification of limitation upon freedom of expression marks a rejection of the American jurisprudence on free speech. To soften the sharp departure from previous Supreme Court decisions, which imported without criticism the American rationales for freedom of speech, the focus is narrowed. Dickson C.J. indicates that he doubts the unmitigated commitment to content neutrality in that body of law, and therefore does not read that jurisprudence as inexorably mandating the invalidation of hate promotion laws: *Keegstra, ibid.* at 38-39.

and "flexible" an analytic approach as one might desire. Justice La Forest's preferred methodology is to be found in the dissent.

2.   The *Oakes* test applied

a.   *Pressing and substantial objective*

The first part of the *Oakes* test requires that the objective of the impugned legislation be pressing and substantial. In a detailed and sensitive discussion, Dickson C.J. finds adequate foundation for the enactment of s. 319(2) in a series of parliamentary reports, dating from the 1965 *Report of the Special Committee on Hate Propaganda in Canada*,[45] to the Working Paper entitled *Hate Propaganda*, issued by the Law Reform Commission of Canada in 1986.[46]

The Chief Justice begins his survey of the literature by observing that racial tension, even at low levels, constitutes a breeding ground for sentiments inimical to civilized society. Originally evidenced in anti-semitic and anti-black prejudice, hatred of individuals identified by particular characteristics has expanded with the diversification of Canada's population. The harm inflicted by the preaching of racial and religious contempt begins with an affront to the target individuals' "sense of human dignity and belonging to the community at large."[47] An individual's feeling of acceptance into Canadian society correlates with that society's concern for the group with which the individual identifies.[48] The majority judgment underscores the pivotal role of "connection" and "belonging." Dickson C.J. takes the concern encompassed in the "chilling effect" doctrine, favoured by the dissent, for speakers who may be silenced beyond the actual application of a restrictive law, and re-directs it to the targets of wilfully promoted hatred, whose entry into the larger community may be thwarted.

---

[45]*Report to the Minister of Justice of the Special Committee on Hate Propaganda in Canada* (Chair: M. Cohen) (Ottawa: Queen's Printer, 1966) [hereinafter *Cohen Report*].

[46]Law Reform Commission of Canada, *Hate Propaganda* (Working Paper No. 50) (Ottawa: The Commission, 1986) at 36, quoted in *Keegstra*, *supra*, note 1 at 41-44. The work of these expert bodies provides the Chief Justice with the basis for his skepticism, in this part of his analysis, of the "marketplace of ideas" and the democratic function rationales for freedom of expression, which he relied upon in the earlier part of his opinion.

[47]*Keegstra*, *ibid.* at 42.

[48]*Ibid.*, at 42-43 and also at 35 & 55. At 42, Dickson C.J. refers to I. Berlin, "Two Concepts of Liberty" in *Four Essays on Liberty* (London: Oxford University Press, 1969) 118 at 155, and at 51 he cites J. Magnet "Multiculturalism and Collective Rights: Approaches to Section 27" in G.-A. Beaudoin & E. Ratushny, eds, *The Canadian Charter of Rights and Freedoms* (Toronto: Carswell, 1989) 739, as well as Cory J.A.'s judgment, in the Ontario Court of Appeal, in *R. v. Andrews* (1988), 43 C.C.C. (3d) 193 at 213, 28 O.A.C. 161. For a Rawlsian elaboration of the issues, see the Factum filed by the Intervenor, Interamicus in *Keegstra*.

Dickson C.J. is keenly aware that the community at large, and thus majoritarian politics, can fall prey to the poison of hatred because human beings are
not solely or simply rational, truth-seeking creatures. He candidly notes that
emotion can displace reason, at least in the short run and particularly at the non-
conscious level. He makes reference to two examples: modern advertising and
Hitler's propaganda machine.[49] He therefore questions the reliability of both the
democratic process and the marketplace of ideas to protect society from the
harm inflicted by the wilful promotion of hatred — although he had earlier
accepted these as rationales for the constitutional protection of expression.

Such rejection also informs international rights protecting instruments
adopted after the Second World War. For this reason, these documents offer a
model. One is reminded of the Chief Justice's earlier pronouncement on the relevance of international conventions:

> Since the close of the Second World War, the protection of the fundamental rights
> and freedoms of groups and individuals has become a matter of international con-
> cern. A body of treaties (or conventions) and customary norms now constitutes an
> international law of human rights under which the nations of the world have
> undertaken to adhere to the standards and principles necessary for ensuring free-
> dom, dignity and social justice for their citizens. The *Charter* conforms to the
> spirit of this contemporary international human rights movement, and it incorpo-
> rates many of the policies and prescriptions of the various international documents
> pertaining to human rights. The various sources of international human rights law
> ... must, in my opinion be relevant and persuasive sources for interpretation of the
> *Charter*'s provisions.[50]

The international approach is to protect freedom of expression, while also committing signatory states, including Canada, to legislate against hate propaganda.
This approach does not manifest a lesser allegience to democracy. Rather, it
rests upon the understanding that a nation must have healthy public relationships between the individual, the identified group, and the community at large,

---

[49]*Keegstra, ibid.* at 43. This reference to advertising stands in stark contrast to the Supreme
Court's consideration of advertising in the context of *Charter* cases. See "Does Money Talk,"
supra, note 18; Moon, *supra,* note 28; *Irwin Toy;* and *Rocket.* In addition, Dickson C.J. does not
comment on the degree to which mass media and advertising concerns now shape politics.

[50]*Re Public Service Employee Relations Act (Alta.),* [1987] 1 S.C.R. 313, 38 D.L.R. (4th) 161
at 184, Dickson C.J., dissenting. I am indebted to Mordechai Wasserman for bringing this quote
to my attention, and for general discussions on the line of argument developed in this paper. In *Slaight Communications* v. *Davidson,* [1989] 1 S.C.R. 1038 at 1056-57, 93 N.R. 183, Chief Justice
Dickson stated:

> Given the dual function of s. 1 identified in *Oakes,* Canada's international human rights
> obligations should inform not only the interpretation of the content of the rights guar-
> anteed by the *Charter* but also the interpretation of what can constitute pressing and
> substantial s. 1 objectives which may justify restrictions upon those rights.

For a detailed account of the reliance in *Charter* cases upon the international law of rights and limitations, see W.A. Schabas, *International Human Rights Law and the Canadian Charter: A Manual
for the Practitioner* (Toronto: Carswell, 1991) at 65-126.

to ensure that all members of society may take part in the democratic process. The commitment is to the dignity and equality of individuals, regardless of group identification, through the eradication of hate propaganda, so that all are members of a free and democratic society.[51]

The Chief Justice understands the *Charter* to reflect this commitment to inherent dignity and equality in a democratic society. Acordingly, he treats the values of equality and multiculturalism promoted in ss 15 and 27 as informing the justification exercise under s. 1.[52] He also adduces other sections of the *Charter*, to highlight the connection of the individual to cultural groups by providing, for example, language and denominational education rights, aboriginal rights, and guarantees of gender equality.[53] These sections, of course, do not apply independently to the issue at hand. Rather, they provide a value structure for the judicial evaluation of arguments proffered to justify limits on *Charter* rights and freedoms. Their role follows from the understanding that the sole justificatory criterion of limitation is the idea of a free and democratic society, which is itself the genesis of the rights.[54]

b.	*Proportionality*

Having recognized the objective of s. 319(2) as "of the utmost impor-

---

[51]*Keegstra, supra,* note 1 at 45ff, referring to the *International Convention on the Elimination of All Forms of Racial Discrimination* ("CERD"), Can T.S. 1970, No. 28, Art. 4 and the *International Covenant on Civil and Political Rights,* 999 U.N.T.S. 171 (1966), arts. 19 & 20. In addition, the Chief Justice refers to *Taylor and Western Guard Party* v. *Canada,* Communication No. R. 24-104, Report of the Human Rights Committee, 38 U.N. GAOR, Supp. No. 40 (A/38/40) 231 (1983), para. 8(b). The latter decision of the United Nations Human Rights Committee rejects the argument that s. 13(1) of the *Canadian Human Rights Act,* S.C. 1976-66, c. 33 — prohibiting the communication of hate messages by telephone — violates art. 20. To mark the general approach of international human rights documents, the Chief Justice also refers to the *European Convention for the Protection of Human Rights and Fundamental Freedoms,* 213 U.N.T.S. 221 (1950), art. 10 and its interpretation. The argument with respect to CERD, to the extent that it is an argument about Canada's international legal obligations, is diminished by the fact, unmentioned in the judgment by either the Chief Justice or McLachlin J., that Canada has not acted on para. (b) of art. 4 of the CERD, even though it made no reservation or interpretive declaration at the time of ratification: see *Hate Propaganda, supra,* note 44 at 18-19, nn 65-67. This paragraph requires adhering states to declare illegal organizations and organized activities, including membership therein, that promote and incite racial discrimination. The Chief Justice refers to this study in *Keegstra, supra,* at 44.

[52]*Keegstra, ibid.* at 49-51. Reference is made to *Singh* v. *Minister of Employment and Immigration,* [1985] 1 S.C.R. 177 at 218, 17 D.L.R. (4th) 422, Wilson J., where she states: "it is important to remember that the courts are conducting this inquiry [under s. 1] in light of a commitment to uphold the rights and freedoms set out in other sections of the *Charter*." This idea, picked up in *Oakes* is part of the orientation of s. 1 towards exclusively right-based values, discussed *supra,* note 23 and accompanying text.

[53]*Keegstra, ibid.* at 50. The *Charter* sections referred to are ss 16-23, 25, 28 & 29.

[54]See, *supra,* notes 40-43 and accompanying text.

tance,"[55] the first part of s. 1 justification is satisfied and the Chief Justice turns to consider the provision's proportionality to its objective.

First, he finds a rational connection between the stated objective of s. 319(2) and its terms. He rejects the contention that criminal prosecution undermines the stated objective by providing the hate-monger a free public forum and lending legitimacy to the message. He also rejects the proferred historical example of Weimar Germany, which prosecuted hate-mongers and nevertheless descended into totalitarianism and genocide based on the type of category found in s. 319(2) as identifying groups.[56] The Chief Justice adopts a normative stance, in contrast to the dissent's more empirical approach. The criminal law, he stresses, embodies society's highest form of disapprobation, and when it condemns expression that undercuts diversity and multiculturalism, it sheds no glimmer of respectability or veracity. Furthermore, the historical example of Weimar Germany does not attest to the futility of such laws, but to the multi-faceted nature of the factors that work for and against societal tolerance. More instructive on this point is the fact that post-war Germany, as well as a number of other countries, maintain comparable laws today.[57]

The Chief Justice turns next to the contention that s. 319(2) is vague and overbroad, and exceeds the minimal impairment test laid down in *Oakes*. After detailed review of the impugned provision, Dickson C.J. rejects these arguments. In particular, he notes the following constricting features in the section: the offence does not attach to statements made "in private conversation"; prosecution is made more difficult by the Crown's need to prove subjective *mens rea*; the accused must either "subjectively desire" to promote hatred or "foresee such a consequence as certain or substantially certain to follow" from his actions; there must be active support or instigation of hatred, rather than mere encouragement or advancement; the need for an "identifiable group" precludes prosecution for fostering hatred against individuals; and "hatred" denotes only a most extreme emotion that ousts reason, rather than a wide range of diverse emotions.[58]

The defences afforded under s. 319(3) further narrow the range of activity proscribed.[59] Specifically, an accused may avoid conviction by establishing that the statements were true, or good faith opinions on a religious subject, or commentary on a subject of public interest reasonably believed to be true, or good

---

[55]*Supra*, note 1 at 51.

[56]*Ibid.* at 60.

[57]*Ibid.* at 60-61. While comparison to legislative arrangements in other free and democratic societies is not cogent as legal argument, such references should at least alert the reader to the fact that the American aversion to content-based regulation of hate speech is not standard in Western democracies, and has not been adopted in a number of countries that have post-war constitutions.

[58]*Ibid.* at 62ff.

[59]*Ibid.* at 67ff. For the text of s. 319(3), see *supra*, note 8.

faith comments for the purpose of countering hatred towards identifiable groups.[60] The Chief Justice takes the view that the defence afforded for true statements is not mandated by the *Charter*, but is to be understood as a Parliamentary concession to truthful freedom of expression even though it may have harmful results. This conclusion meshes well with Dickson C.J.'s skepticism as to the rationality of human behaviour, but appears to call into question the legitimacy of the truth-seeking rationale said to underlie s. 2(b). The first and second stages of the argument lack integration with respect to this important consideration.

Once again, empirical considerations bow to *Charter* values in Dickson C.J.'s analysis. The fact that the state has unsuccessfully tried to use s. 319(2) in unwarranted circumstances is illustrative of unlawful action, not of legislative meaning for the purposes of *Charter* analysis. Moreover, the availability of non-criminal measures, even if more effective, does not undermine the use of the criminal sanction. The minimal impairment test under s. 1 does not require the state to choose one of a number of alternatives where multiple approaches are indicated, as long as the more restrictive measure is not redundant.[61]

The Chief Justice concludes his analysis under s. 1 by finding that the limitation upon s. 2(b) freedoms effected by s. 319(2) does not outweigh its legislative objective. This conclusion follows from the finding that the expressive activity proscribed is remote from the values that underlie the guarantee in s. 2(b), while the objective of the proscription reflects these values. The limitation, in other words, is more faithful to *Charter* values than is the crystallized right expressed in the document itself.

The majority's s. 1 analysis as a whole is lucid, cogent and principled. It belies the apprehension initially expressed by the Chief Justice that, were *Charter* values alone to drive s. 1 analysis, the exercise would become "mechanical" or "formalistic." These opprobrious adjectives are out of place. The *Charter* shares the values of other post-war rights-protecting instruments, which promote stable democratic political functioning by rejecting the excesses that can deprive certain members of the community of their self-dignity and the will to take part in public life. The Court's s. 1 analysis is of high calibre. It would have been a worthy counterpart for a purposive interpretation of s. 2(b), which was inexplicably lacking in the earlier part of the majority judgment.

---

[60]Space precludes discussion of the consideration of s. 11(d) of the *Charter*, the presumption of innocence.

[61]*Supra*, note 1 at 70-72. Also, the division of powers under ss 91 & 92 of the *Constitution Act, 1867* (U.K.), 30 & 31 Vict., c. 3 would limit Parliament's power to legislate to areas within its jurisdiction. Reliance on the possibility of provincial schemes would be an unrealistic, as well as novel, approach under the "minimal impairment" test.

III. The Significance of *Keegstra*

The *Keegstra* judgment lays bare the two very different value structures underpinning the right to freedom of expression in a free and democratic society.

The Chief Justice reads s. 2(b) as forwarding the *Charter*'s general concern for individual dignity and equality. In his examination of the *Criminal Code* provision against hate propaganda, Dickson C.J.'s sympathy lies with those who are or might be the targets of hate propaganda. He is apprehensive that wilful, public hatemongering, in both the short and long term, poisons the atmosphere of public life, so that members of target groups will be reluctant or unable to emerge from negative parochial identification into the larger social and political arena. He requires neither empirical proof of this effect, nor statistical evidence of its likelihood. He is not daunted by the possibility that this criminal offence might stifle heated public debate. He is secure in this approach because his conception of free and democratic society, as an aspiration to a public world of equality and individual dignity, builds upon the knowledge that human beings are not invariably rational and that, even if they were, rationality takes time. It is therefore permissible for the state to attach its highest form of disapprobation to wilful promotion of hatred in the knowledge that there is ample national and international recognition that this kind of communicative activity is inimical to the stability in multicultural statehood of the post-war world.

McLachlin J.'s allegiance to the values underlying s. 2(b) may appear to lie with potential speakers, whose expression stands to be curtailed or chilled by provisions like s. 319(2). Yet she speaks very little about the rights of speakers, or even about the rights of Mr. Keegstra himself. Her primary concern is to preserve a social order that can absorb the fortuities of unregulated expression, for the benefit of the vitality and progress that such expression facilitates. State interference in expression is forbidden, unless one can establish that there is violence at hand, or an empirical link between the offensive communication and harm to members of the target group. Her metaphor is the marketplace of ideas, in which rational beings trade their wares and true value emerges. She ignores the fact that the trade in virulent anti-semitism and debased racism can precipitate market failure at exorbitant tangible and intangible cost.

The *Keegstra* decision is the swan song of Chief Justice Dickson, who wrote, and Justice Wilson, who concurred. It may mark the final invocation of an understanding of the common values forwarded in *Charter* rights guarantees and their limitation, the original vision of purposive rights and justified limitation under the *Charter*.[132] In that vision, the text of the *Charter* encapsulates the rights and freedoms that are intrinsic to liberal democracy, and permits the justification of limits that give priority to individual dignity and equality. The legacy of the *Keegstra* judgment is not that expression rights are feeble. On the contrary, restrictions on promoting hatred against identifiable groups both publicly and wilfully manifest a commitment to vibrant democracy in a diverse and far flung land.[133]

---

[132]This is likely given that the majority's generous overtures to La Forest and McLachlin JJ. were ineffective to secure a less sharply divided bench. See *supra*, note 1 at 35 & 53-54. Cory J., before his appointment to the Supreme Court, delivered a judgment much like the majority in *Keegstra*: see *supra*, note 47. Stevenson J. was a member of the Alberta Court of Appeal panel that invalidated s. 319(2).

[133]For a similar approach in the American context, see H. Arkes, *The Philosopher in the City: The Moral Dimensions of Urban Life* (Princeton: Princeton University Press, 1981), c. 2 & 3.

Chapter 18

INCITEMENT TO NATIONAL AND RACIAL HATRED: THE LEGAL SITUATION IN GERMANY

Rainer Hofmann

INTRODUCTION

Europe is presently experiencing a strong, and in many aspects frightening, revival of openly nationalistic and xenophobic tendencies. This statement applies in particular to many of the former socialist countries of Eastern Europe where, subsequent to the collapse of socialist rule, conflicts between different nations have arisen again, resulting in outbreaks of violence against members of minority groups or even, in the case of what used to be Yugoslavia, outright war. Fortunately, such developments of massive and widespread violence have not occurred as yet in Western Europe.[1]

There is, however, quite a considerable increase in support for political parties which call, with clearly racist undertones, for restrictions on further immigration of aliens in general and asylum-seekers in particular, and which oppose measures to improve the situation of existing alien populations.[2] Acts of violence against aliens and asylum-seekers are reported with increasing frequency in Austria, France, Germany and the United Kingdom. Reports of racist violence have even come from societies once considered almost immune to violent xenophobia, such as Sweden. These developments clearly pose a serious threat to the peaceful internal order of the societies concerned, and constitute gross and flagrant violations of basic human rights and the fundamental principles of tolerance and pluralism upon which Western democracies are founded.

Such developments raise with utmost urgency questions as to the legal and political relationship between freedom of speech, an essential element of any democratic constitutional order, and the need to protect the people who are targets of violent acts instigated by incitement to national or racial hatred. This question relates, moreover, to the fundamental problem as to whether and to what extent provisions of criminal law penalizing racist speech should be enacted in order to prevent the outbreak of violence against persons defined by their nationality or ethnicity, and whether and to what extent such provisions, once enacted, prove to be effective as regards the achievement of this aim.

A completely satisfactory answer to these questions, in particular the latter one, presupposes the existence of pertinent in-depth studies, preferably performed by experts in legal sociology. Since I am a constitutional lawyer and not a sociologist, this report is confined to a descriptive analysis of the relevant provisions of the German Criminal Code, their implications under German constitutional law and the relevant court practice. I do not assess Germany's compliance with its

---

1 Since violence in Northern Ireland and the Spanish Basque Country seems to be characterized by acts of politically motivated terrorism, these situations should, at least in the present context, be considered as fundamentally different.

2 Examples include the 1991 general elections in Belgium and Sweden, and the recent regional elections in France and the German *Länder* of Baden-Württemberg and Schleswig-Holstein.

obligations under various international human rights treaties;[3] rather, my examination is confined to Germany's internal legal order. I will not venture into any evaluation as to whether the recent outbreaks of violence against asylum-seekers throughout Germany could have been completely, or even partially, prevented if there had been "tougher" anti-racist legal provisions. Nor will I discuss whether the wide media coverage of such acts of violence and the negative reaction of the general public have had an unwelcome counter-effect, as some commentators have suggested, of encouraging even more violent acts against aliens and asylum-seekers.

FREEDOM OF EXPRESSION AND INCITEMENT TO NATIONAL AND RACIAL HATRED IN GERMANY

There can be no doubt that freedom of opinion and speech constitutes an essential element of any democratic society. On the other hand, it is equally obvious that rights and freedoms can be, and in fact are, abused to the detriment of other persons and their basic human rights. This explains why most constitutions and all international human rights instruments provide for the possibility of lawfully restricting freedom of speech.[4]

The German experience as regards the abuse of rights and freedoms has been particularly traumatic; abuse of the right to free expression contributed considerably to the demise of the Weimar Republic, and human rights were totally suppressed by the National Socialist regime. These experiences had a deep impact upon the drafting of the *Grundgesetz*, the Constitution of the Federal Republic of Germany, and subsequent legislation. In particular, a fundamental aspect of the German constitutional order is the concept of *wehrhafte Demokratie* (militant democracy) which not only allows for but even demands limitations on the exercise of human rights by those persons who abuse such rights in order to destroy the democratic order of the country. The notion of *wehrhafte Demokratie* can only be understood if one takes into consideration Germany's recent history.[5]

"Nothing in the present Covenant may be interpreted as implying for any ... group or person any right to engage in any activity or perform any act aimed at the destruction of any of the rights and freedoms recognized herein ... ."

---

3 For an excellent discussion of Germany's compliance with Art. 4 of the International Convention on the Elimination of All Forms of Racial Discrimination, *see* Rüdiger Wolfrum, "Das Verbot der Rassendiskriminierung im Spannungsfeld zwischen dem Schutz individueller Freiheitsrechte und der Verpflichtung des einzelnen im Allgemeininteresse," (The Prohibition of Racial Discrimination in the Area of Tension between the Protection of Individual Rights and the Obligation of the Individual towards the Common Interest), in E Denninger et al., eds., *Kritik und Vertrauen: Festschrift für Peter Schneider* (1990). Prof. Wolfrum concludes that, by and large, Germany has implemented its obligations under the CERD Convention, but more as a result of the practice of the courts than the activities of the legislature. *Id.* at 525. Some lacunae remain, such as the failure to prohibit the exclusion of ethnic and national groups from public establishments. *Id.*

4 *See, e.g.,* Art. 19(3) and Art. 20 of the ICCPR; Art. 10(2) of the ECHR; Art. 13 of the ACHR; and Art. 9(2) of the ACHPR, the texts of which are reproduced in Annexe A.

5 For this reason, this concept of a "militant democracy" is generally considered to permit greater restrictions on individual rights in the interest of protecting the rights of others than is permitted by Article 5(1) of the ICCPR which reads, in relevant part: "Nothing in the present Covenant may be interpreted as implying for any ... group or person any right to engage in any activity or perform any act aimed at the destruction of any of the rights and freedoms recognized herein ... ."

Article 5 of the *Grundgesetz*, the provision which protects freedom of opinion and expression, expressly permits limitation of the right "by the provisions of the general laws".[6] The "general laws" include the Criminal Code.

Article 9(2), Article 21(2) and Article 18 of the *Grundgesetz* go much further. Article 9(2) outlaws associations whose activities aim to undermine the criminal law, the constitutional order or international understanding.[7] However, contrary to what might be deduced from its actual wording, this provision is generally construed not to outlaw *per se* associations which conduct such activities but rather to authorize administrative decisions outlawing these associations. The relevant provisions stipulating the legal conditions for such decisions and regulating procedural questions, including means of recourse to administrative tribunals, are to be found in the *Vereinsgesetz* (Act on Associations) of 5 August 1964.[8] According to Section 3 of this law, the decision to outlaw such an association is to be taken by the *Bundesminister des Innern* (Federal Minister of the Interior) and to be published in the *Bundesanzeiger*. Financial assets and other properties of such associations may be seized and confiscated. Since 1964, there have been only 12 such decisions, eight concerning extreme right-wing groups and four concerning extreme left-wing groups. It should be added that, according to prevailing opinion, the competent minister of the interior acts within a margin of appreciation when deciding whether to outlaw an association.

Under Article 21(2) of the *Grundgesetz* political parties may be declared unconstitutional by the Federal Constitutional Court if their objectives include the obstruction or abolition of the democratic order.[9] The power to institute such proceedings before the Federal Constitutional Court is vested with the *Bundestag* (Federal Parliament), the *Bundesrat* (Federal Council), which represents the Governments of the *Länder*, and the Federal Government.[10] The Federal Constitutional Court may also order that all assets and properties of such political parties be seized and confiscated.[11] The organs competent to institute such proceedings operate within a margin of appreciation in deciding whether to take such a step. In the 1950s,

---

6 Art. 5 reads:
"(1) Everyone shall have the right to freely express and disseminate his opinion by speech, writing and pictures and to freely inform himself from generally accessible sources. Freedom of the press and freedom of reporting by means of broadcasts and films are guaranteed. There shall be no censorship.
(2) These rights are limited by the provisions of the general laws, the provisions of law for the protection of youth, and by the right to inviolability of personal honour.
(3) Art and science, research and teaching, shall be free. Freedom of teaching shall not absolve from loyalty to the Constitution."
Translation published by the Press and Information Office of the Federal Government (Bonn: 1987).

7 Art. 9(2) reads: "Associations, the purposes or activities of which conflict with criminal laws or which are directed against the constitutional order or the concept of international understanding, are prohibited."

8 *Bundesgesetzblatt* I, 593 (1964), as subsequently amended.

9 Art. 21(2) reads: "Parties which, by reason of their aims or the behaviour of their adherents, seek to impair or abolish the free democratic basic order or to endanger the existence of the Federal Republic of Germany, shall be unconstitutional. The Federal Constitutional Court shall decide on the question of unconstitutionality."

10 *See* Section 13 No. 2 of the *Bundesverfassungsgerichtsgesetz* (Act on the Federal Constitutional Court), in the wording of 12 Dec. 1985, in connection with Section 43, *Bundesgesetzblatt* I, 327 (1989).

11 *Id.* Further regulations in this context are to be found in Sections 32 and 33 of the *Parteiengesetz* (Act on Political Parties) in the wording of 3 Mar. 1989.

it was generally considered that such political parties should be outlawed. Thus, in 1952 the Sozialistische Reichspartei[12] (generally perceived as a successor to the National Socialist Party) and in 1956 the Kommunistische Partei Deutschlands[13] were declared unconstitutional. In contrast, the opinion prevailing since the mid-1960s, when the Nationaldemokratische Partei Deutschlands and the Deutsche Kommunistische Partei were founded, is that extremist parties should be countered politically rather than banned by a decision of the Federal Constitutional Court.

Article 18 of the *Grundgesetz* declares that individuals who abuse the exercise of their basic human rights, including freedom of expression, "in order to combat the free democratic order", forfeit those rights.[14] Again, such a decision is to be taken exclusively by the Federal Constitutional Court in a proceeding which may be instituted by the Federal Parliament, the Federal Government or a *Land* Government. This provision has, however, been of minor practical relevance. Only two proceedings have been instituted under this article, the first one in 1960 against the former president of the Sozialistische Reichspartei, Otto-Ernst Remer, and the second one in 1974 against Dr Gerhard Frey, a known right-wing publisher. Both cases were dismissed by the Federal Constitutional Court because neither individual was found to be a threat to the democratic order.[15] Given the historical background to the drafting of the *Grundgesetz*, it is evident that these articles were intended to give a solid anti-fascist foundation to the new Federal Republic. Subsequent practice, notably influenced by the "Cold War", reveals, however, a broader anti-totalitarian aim directed against both left-wing and right-wing extremism.

Among Germany's numerous legal provisions limiting human rights in general and freedom of speech in particular, the Criminal Code contains several provisions which effectively restrict racist speech. The provisions, their constitutional implications and relevant court practice are discussed in the following sections.

The Pertinent Provisions of the German Criminal Code

The pertinent provisions of the *Strafgesetzbuch* (German Criminal Code) are Articles 130 and 131, both of which constitute serious crimes against "public peace", and Article 185 which makes punishable "insult" or offences against personal honour.

Article 130. Article 130 replaced a provision of the Criminal Code of the German Empire which penalized breaches of the public peace by incitement to class

---

12 Judgement of 23 Oct. 1952, *Bundesverfassungsgerichtsentscheidungen* (BVerfGE) (Decisions of the Federal Constitutional Court) Vol. 2, 1 *et seq.*

13 Judgement of 17 Aug. 1956, BVerfGE Vol. 5, 85 *et seq.*

14 Art. 18 reads: "Whoever abuses freedom of expression or opinion, in particular, freedom of the press (Art. 5(1)), freedom of teaching (Art. 5(3)), freedom of assembly (Art.8), freedom of association (Art. 9), privacy of posts and telecommunication (Art.10), property (Art.14), or the right to asylum (Art. 16(2)) in order to combat the free democratic basic order, shall forfeit these basic rights. Such forfeiture and the extent thereof shall be pronounced by the Federal Constitutional Court.

15 *See* Judgement of 25 July 1960, BVerfGE Vol. 11, 282 *et seq.* (Remer case); and Judgement of 2 July 1974, BVerfGE Vol. 38, 23 *et seq.* (Frey case). Presently, Dr Frey is president of the Deutsche Volksunion, an extremist right-wing political party which, in the regional elections of 5 April 1992 in Schleswig-Holstein, obtained more than 6 per cent of the votes.

hatred.[16] The new version was adopted in 1960 as a legislative reaction to a wave of desecration of synagogues and cemeteries in 1959 and 1960. These events brought about a radical change in the legislative atmosphere and swept away all arguments that such specific legislation was neither necessary nor desirable.[17] The motivation behind the new version of Article 130 was the appreciation that, although the courts in most cases were able to impose punishment under the prevailing law, that law did not "strike at the core of the evil ... that is, the attack on humanity, human dignity, and general public peace."[18] Thus, rather than being concerned exclusively with the protection of private or group honour, safeguarded by the provisions concerning *Beleidigung* (criminal libel) in Article 185, the new version of Article 130 aims to promote the public interest in safeguarding public peace.[19]

The key notion of Article 130 is the concept of *Menschenwürde* (human dignity), enshrined in Article 1(1) of the *Grundgesetz* as a fundamental principle of the German Constitutional order.[20] Prohibited are attacks on human dignity which are likely to breach the public peace, committed in the form of acts of particular gravity against parts of the population.[21] The proscribed acts consist of:

(1) incitement to hatred, which is described as "stirring up enmity in an invasive manner, beyond mere rejection or contempt";

(2) provocation to violent or arbitrary acts, described as "acts of violence or lawlessness against personal freedom"; and

(3) insult, ridicule and defamation, which must amount to more than "mere expression of disrespect" or "disparaging assertions, the truth or untruth of which cannot be proven".[22]

The concept of an attack on human dignity presupposes an attack "on the core area of the victim's personality, a denial of the victim's right to life as an equal in the community" or a person's treatment as an inferior which has the effect of excluding him or her from the protection of the constitution".[23] It should be stressed,

---

16 Art. 130 reads: "Whosoever attacks the human dignity of others in a manner liable to disturb the public peace by:
1. inciting hatred against a certain part of the population,
2. inciting to violent or arbitrary acts against such part of the population, or
3. insulting, maliciously ridiculing or defaming such part,
shall be punished by a term of imprisonment of not less than three months and not exceeding five years." (Author's translation.)

17 *See, in particular*, Von Bubnoff, "Commentary on Article 130 StGB", in *Strafgesetzbuch, Leipziger Kommentar* (10th ed. 1988), Vol. IV; Schafheutle, *Das Sechste Strafrechtsänderungsgesetz. Juristenzeitung* 15 (1960), 470 *et seq.*; Wolfrum, supra note 3, at 521-23.For an excellent presentation in English, *see* E Stein, "History Against Free Speech: The New German Law Against the Auschwitz - and Other - Lies," 85 *Mich. L. Rev.* 277, 282 (1986).

18 Schafheutle, *supra* note 17, at 471.

19 This is a well-established interpretation in German jurisprudence and doctrine. *See, e.g.*, Von Bubnoff, *supra* note 17, at No. 1; and Lackner, "Commentary on Article 130 StGB", in *Strafgesetzbuch* (18th ed. 1989), 648 *et seq.* , with further references.

20 Art. 1(1) provides: "The dignity of man shall be inviolable."

21 It should be mentioned that this notion not only includes German citizens belonging to an ethnic, linguistic, racial, religious or social minority, but also aliens residing in Germany such as, *e.g.*, migrant workers; *see* Von Bubnoff, *supra* note 17, at No. 3 *et seq.* and Lackner, *supra* note 19, at No. 2, both with further references.

22 Stein, *supra* note 17, at 284.

23 *See*, Von Bubnoff, *supra* note 17, at No. 4; and Lackner, *supra* note 19, at 3; both with further references.

moreover, that Article 130 applies not only to attacks on human dignity which in fact breach or threaten the public peace but also to attacks which might result in a sense of threat among persons belonging to the particular group under attack, on the one hand, or in an increase in an existing predisposition to commit such attacks among those persons likely to be incited to acts of verbal or physical violence, on the other hand.[24]

Article 131. Article 131 was introduced into the Criminal Code in 1973 as part of the Fourth Law to Reform the Penal Code.[25] It penalizes the dissemination, display and production of depictions "of violence against people in a cruel or otherwise inhuman manner" with the intent to glorify or seek to minimize the cruelty or to incite racial hatred. Reports on contemporary events or history are expressly exempted from punishment by Article 131(3). Violations are punishable by up to one year's imprisonment or a fine. The objective of Article 131 is the maintenance of social harmony to which incitement to racial hatred is considered to pose a serious threat.

Article 131 was introduced because the government was of the view that Article 130 did not adequately implement Article 4 of the International Convention on the Elimination of All Forms of Racial Discrimination (which entered into force for the Federal Republic of Germany on 15 June 1969), notwithstanding the fact that many scholars considered that racially motivated acts were punishable under other provisions of the Criminal Code.

Prosecutions under Article 131 are comparatively rare. This might be explained by the fact that large parts of the German legal community[26] in the field of criminal law consider this provision, due to its rather vague wording, problematic with respect to the fundamental principle of *Bestimmtheitsgrundsatz* (legal certainty) enshrined in Article 103(2) of the *Grundgesetz*.[27] On the other hand it should be emphasized that German legal doctrine unanimously holds that publications of an anti-Semitic character are prime examples of "writings" in the sense of Article 131,[28] notwithstanding that there is some discussion as to whether the sale of "classical anti-Semitic works" such as books by Chamberlain or Gobineau, would be prohibited by this provision.[29]

---

24 *See* Von Bubnoff, *supra* note 17, at No. 5, with further references.

25 Art. 131 of StGB reads: "(1) Whosoever 1. disseminates, 2. publicly exhibits, posts, demonstrates, or otherwise makes accessible, 3. offers or makes available or accessible to a person below the age of eighteen, or 4. produces, procures, supplies, keeps in stock, offers, advertises, recommends, undertakes to import into, or export out of, the territory in which this law applies, in order to use them, or pieces derived from them, in the manner indicated in numbers 1 to 3 above, or to enable others to do so, writings, sound or picture recordings, illustrations or representations which show acts of violence against people in a cruel or otherwise inhuman manner and this in order to glorify or to seek to minimize the cruelty of such acts of violence or to incite racial hatred, shall be punished by a term of imprisonment of up to one year or by a fine. (2) Whosoever disseminates, by radio broadcasts, such representations as indicated in sub-paragraph 1 will be penalized in like manner. (3) Sub-paragraphs (1) and (2) do not apply when the act is in the service of reporting on current events or history. (4)Sub-paragraph (1)3 is not to be applied if done by the legal guardian of the person involved. "(Author's translation.)

26 *See. e.g.,* Von Bubnoff, *supra* note 17, at No 1.

27 This principle requires that penal laws are to be worded in such a clear and unambiguous way as to exclude, to the extent possible, any doubt as to whether a certain behaviour falls under a given penal provision.

28 *See* Von Bubnoff, *supra* note 17, at No. 19.

Article 185. Article 185 has been part of the Criminal Code since 1875. It makes punishable an offence against personal honour.[30] According to Article 192, proof of the truth of a statement is no defence under Article 185 "when the insult arises from the manner in which the assertion was made or disseminated or from the circumstances in which it was made".

Until 1945, the *Reichsgericht* (German Supreme Court) consistently refused to apply Article 185 to insults against Jews as a group. This approach changed in 1949. In the leading decision on this matter,[31] the Federal Supreme Court confirmed that the Jewish citizens of the Federal Republic of Germany have become "at least since the special legislation of the National Socialist State ... a sharply demarcated group" who consequently may be insulted as a group.[32] So far, there have been no decisions of the Federal Supreme Court extending the applicability of Article 185 to other racially or ethnically determined groups.[33]

Subsequent to a sharp increase in extremist right-wing activities including, in particular, the publication of pseudo-scientific writings attempting to prove that there had been no concentration camps and that the number of Jews and other people murdered in those camps had been grossly exaggerated (the so-called "Auschwitz-lie"), legislative attempts to deal with these writings were initiated in the early 1980s. The main legal problem to be solved arose from the wording of Article 194 of the *Strafgesetzbuch* which required a private petition to initiate prosecution under Article 185. After a lengthy and rather animated debate in the media and in Parliament,[34] the 21st Law Modifying the Criminal Law finally came into effect on 1 August 1985.[35]

The new law eliminates the need for a private petition for prosecutions in cases where the insult was made in a document which was publicly disseminated or accessible, or in an assembly, or in broadcasting, if the insulted individual is a member of a group which was persecuted under the National Socialist or another violent and arbitrary dominance, and if that group is at the time of the act a part of the population of the Federal Republic of Germany.[36] The new wording of Article

---

29 *Id.* at No. 26.

30 Art. 185 reads: "Insult shall be punished by a term of imprisonment of up to one year or by a fine, and, if the insult is committed by a physical act, by a term of imprisonment of up to two years or by a fine."

31 Judgement of 18 Sept. 1975, *Bundesgerichtshof in Zivilsachen* (BGHZ) (the Official Collection of Decisions of the Federal Supreme Court in Private Law Matters) Vol. 75, 160 *et seq.* It should be stressed that in the case in question the proceedings were founded under a provision of the German Civil Code, seeking compensation for the tort of defamation. This decision confirmed and clarified the previous jurisprudence of the Federal Supreme Court's Criminal Law Panels, in particular the decisions of 28 Feb. 1958, *Entscheidungen des Bundesgerichtshofs in Strafsachen* (BGHSt) (the Official Collection of Decisions of the Federal Supreme Court in Criminal Matters) Vol. 11, 207 *et seq.*, and the decision of 21 Apr. 1961, BGHSt Vol. 16, 49 *et seq.*

32 *See* Stein, *supra* note 17, at 301-03.

33 *See* Lackner, *supra* note 19, Commentary on Article 185 StGB, *Vorbemerkung* No.2, with further references. *Compare* the application of Arts. 130 and 131 to various ethnic, national and social groups, including Gypsies, black students, and migrant workers. *See infra*, notes 51-52.

34 *See* Stein, *supra* note 17, at 305 *et seq.*

35 21 *Strafrechtsänderungsgesetz* in *Bundesgesetzblatt* I, 965 (1985).

36 Art. 194 now reads:
"(1) Prosecution for insult shall be instituted only upon petition. When the act is committed by disseminating or by making publicly accessible a writing (Article 11, paragraph 3), or in an assembly or by means of a broadcasting, a petition is not required, if the insulted person was persecuted as a

194 has met with considerable criticism from German criminal lawyers for being too vague. Lawyers have also criticized the requirement that the person insulted must be an individual who was personally a victim of such persecution.[37]

Implementation of the Provisions of the *Strafgesetzbuch.* Articles 130 and 131 have been of limited importance for the actual work of the German courts. In 1982 only 12 per cent of prosecutions against right-wing extremists took place under these provisions. Forty-four per cent of prosecutions were brought under Articles 86 and 86a of the Criminal Code for the dissemination of propaganda and the use of emblems of anti-constitutional organizations; 32.5 per cent of charges were brought for violations of articles of the Criminal Code connected with violence. The remaining 11.5 per cent of prosecutions were divided between convictions for criminal defamation under Article 185 and for condemnation of the President of the Federal Republic, the State, its symbols and constitutional organs under Article 90.

It is perhaps worthy of note that there has been no imbalance in prosecution of left and right-wing activities. For instance, in 1987, 1,855 prosecutions related to left-wing extremism and 1,447 cases to right-wing extremism.

The Prohibition of Racist Speech as a Problem of Constitutional Law

To penalize certain cases of public speech and publications due to their racial connotations obviously raises problems under constitutional law with regard to the guarantee of freedom of expression. As mentioned above, the particular German experience of abuse of such rights as the rights to freedom of expression and association resulted in the introduction into the *Grundgesetz* of a provision allowing rights to be limited "by the general laws". For foreign lawyers, in particular those familiar with the jurisprudence of the United States Supreme Court concerning freedom of speech, it might be surprising that there has in fact been very little scholarly discussion as to the compatibility of Articles 130, 131 and 185 of the *Strafgesetzbuch* with Article 5(1) and 5(2) of the *Grundgesetz.* Generally speaking, German constitutional and criminal lawyers share the opinion that acts by private persons likely to incite racial hatred are not protected by the right to freedom of speech.

---

member of a group under the National Socialist or another violent and arbitrary dominance, if the group is a part of the population and if the insult is connected with such persecution. However, there shall be no prosecution *ex officio* if the injured person opposes it. The opposition may not be withdrawn. If the injured person dies, the right of petition and of opposition passes to the next of kin as specified in Article 77, paragraph 2.

(2) If the memory of a deceased person is disparaged, the next of kin as specified in Article 77, paragraph 2 shall have the right to lodge a petition. If the act is committed by disseminating or by making publicly accessible a writing (Article 11, paragraph 3), or in an assembly or by means of a broadcasting, a petition is not required, if the insulted person was persecuted as a member of a group under National Socialist or another violent and arbitrary dominance and the disparagement is connected with it. However, there shall be no prosecution *ex officio* if the person entitled to lodge a petition opposes it. The opposition may not be withdrawn."

37 *See* Lackner, *supra* note 19, Commentary on Article 194 StGB No. 2, with further references. For a thorough discussion of the new law *see* Stein, *supra* note 17, at 314 *et seq.,* and Kohler, "Zur Frage der Strafbarkeit des Leugnens von Völkermordtaten",*Neue Juristische Wochenschrift*, Vol. 38, 2389 (1985), *et seq.*; Ostendorf, "Im Streit: Die Strafrechtliche Verfolgung der 'Auschwitzlüge'", *Neue Juristische Wochenschrift*, Vol. 38, 1062 (1985), *et seq.* and Vogelgesang, "Die Neuregelung zur sogenannten 'Auschwitzlüge' -Beitrag zur Bewältigung der Vergangenheit oder 'Widerliche Aufrechnung'?", *Neue Juristische Wochenschrift* Vol. 38, 2388 (1985), *et seq.*

Obviously, this general statement does not mean that there are no legal problems as to whether a specific conviction under Articles 130, 131 or 185 will be constitutional, bearing in mind that, according to the established jurisprudence of the Federal Constitutional Court, in situations where human rights conflict, these rights have to be balanced in such a way as to permit only those limitations which are necessary to protect the core of the conflicting rights. Moreover, this jurisprudence can only be understood in the light of Article 19(2) of the *Grundgesetz* which expressly prohibits violations of the *Wesensgehalt* (basic core) of a given human right.[38]

Under German constitutional law, the power to declare a law in breach of the *Grundgesetz* and therefore null and void, is vested exclusively with the Federal Constitutional Court. So far, this Court has not been called upon to decide whether Articles 130, 131 or 185 are unconstitutional as such. Nor is such a development to be expected. From a more practical point of view, however, cases may arise in which the Court is called on to decide whether the application of these provisions in a specific case amounts to a violation of the speaker's or author's constitutionally protected right to freedom of expression. The Court would have jurisdiction because, under German constitutional law, any person who alleges that his or her human rights have been violated by public authority is entitled to file a *Verfassungsbeschwerde* (constitutional complaint) with the Federal Constitutional Court.[39]

It is perhaps surprising that there has been only one reported case in which the Federal Constitutional Court was in fact faced with such a challenge. In the case, the applicant had been found guilty of an attack on human dignity in conjunction with incitement to race hatred by carrying, at a public event, a sign which read:

I, a donkey, still believe that Jews were "gassed" in German concentration camps. I, a donkey, believe the "gassing" lies and want to pay, pay, pay to Israel. I, a donkey, still believe the propaganda lies of the "victors".[40]

In a preliminary proceeding, the screening committee of the Federal Constitutional Court rejected the application on the ground that it had no prospect of success, since the interpretation and application of Articles 130 and 131 by the competent courts did not disclose any violation of basic rights.[41] The Court also rejected the allegation that the lower courts had violated the applicant's human rights by disregarding his offers of "evidence". The Court held:

The applicant, who does not deal even with the numerous generally accessible sources about the mass destruction of the Jews, not to speak of trying to reach an independent opinion through a thorough consider-

---

38 Art. 19(2) reads: "In no case may the essential content of a basic right be encroached upon."

39 *See* Art. 93(1) No. 4a of the *Grundgesetz* which reads: "The Federal Constitutional Court shall decide: ... on complaints of constitutionality, which may be entered by any person who claims that one of his basic rights or one of his rights under paragraph (4) of Article 20, under Article 33, 38, 101, 103, or 104 has been violated by public authority." As to this topic *see, e.g.,* Oellers-Frahm, "Review of Constitutionality of Legal Norms and Acts of Public Authorities in the Federal Republic of Germany," in Bernhardt & Beyerhin, eds., *Reports on German Public Law and Public International Law* (1986), 49 *et seq.*

40 For a discussion, *see* Stein, *supra* note 17, at 287.

41 Decision of 27 Apr. 1982, reported in 35 *Neue Juristische Wochenschrift* 1803 (1982).

ation, is not impaired either in his right to a hearing nor to an effective protection of law when the courts judge this mass destruction to be commonly known and consider irrelevant the mere offering of the names of individual witnesses.[42]

If the courts competent to decide criminal matters consider the question of constitutionality at all, they usually declare that defendants accused under Articles 130 and 131 are not in a position to invoke the guarantee of freedom of speech in Article 5(1) of the *Grundgesetz*.[43] Although this could be challenged as incorrect from a strictly constitutional law point of view on the ground that such defendants have claims under the limitation clause of Article 5(2) the criminal courts have consistently assumed the constitutionality of Articles 130 and 131.

Another problem to be mentioned in this context concerns the relationship between Articles 130 and 131 and Article 5(3) of the *Grundgesetz* which provides that "Art and science, research and teaching, shall be free."[44] Prevailing legal opinion, shared by the courts,[45] regards incitement to racial hatred as, by definition, beyond the scope of what might be considered to be art, science, research or teaching within the meaning of Article 5(3). This approach is based upon the argument that, since the fundamental aim of the *Grundgesetz* is the protection of human dignity, art, science, research and teaching may not violate human dignity. It goes without saying that this approach could raise considerable problems if applied strictly.[46]

The Pertinent Practice of the Courts

Courts dealing with charges brought under Articles 130 and 131 will usually have to decide upon the following issues: What is an attack on human dignity? When is an act likely to breach public peace? What constitutes incitement to race hatred? Which groups of persons are to be considered a race for purposes of Article 131, or a "part of the population" for purposes of Article 130?

In what might be considered the leading case in this context, the *Bundesgerichtshof* (Federal Supreme Court) in 1981 developed its definition of an "attack on human dignity".[47] In that case, the defendant was charged with distributing a pamphlet which denied the occurrence of the Holocaust in particularly vile language, and suggested that the Jews had tortured and blackmailed others to give false testimony. The trial court convicted the pamphleteer of a violation of Article 131 but not of the more serious charge under Article 130. The Federal Supreme Court upheld the conviction under Article 131 and ruled that Article 130 had also been

---

42 This translation is taken from Stein, *supra* note 17, at 287.

43 For references *see, e.g.,* Stein, *supra* note 17, at 288.

44 *See supra* note 5, for full text of Article 5(3).

45 For references *see* Von Bubnoff, *supra* note 17, at No. 26.

46 For instance, Shakespeare's treatment of Shylock could remove the Merchant of Venice from the category of "art". Another problem which has not yet been dealt with by German courts concerns the legal standing of anti-Semitic publications of doubtful scholarly foundation, such as the works of Chamberlain or Gobineau, or the large number of older publications which present "scientific" evidence of the inferiority of people of colour.

47 Judgement of 14 Jan. 1981, BGHSt, reported in *Neue Zeitschrift für Strafrecht* (1981), at 258; for a discussion in English, *see* Stein, *supra* note 17, at 291-92.

violated. The Court confirmed that an "attack on human dignity" exists only if it is directed against the *unverzichtbar kern* (unrenounceable core) of the personality of another person, against him as a human being, and only if it denies his value as a human being.[48] Such an attack had been committed in this case because the pamphlet "was apt to provoke an emotional, hostile stance toward the Jews." The argument that Jews in Germany should not reasonably feel threatened by such a pamphlet was not considered relevant.

The Court furthermore ruled that Jews form a race for purposes of Article 131, although based upon reasoning which reflects a greater interest in genetic characteristics than is found in the jurisprudence of many other European countries. The Court declared that the concept of race hatred

> proceeds from merely an approximate anthropological classification of humanity into human races, that is, according to common hereditary, predominantly physical characteristics, as a starting point for a theory pursuant to which biological diversity of the "races" is supposed to be the cause of their relative superiority or inferiority and corresponding different value. The emotionally heightened hostility of the provocation against the Jews is one of the phenomena of the incitement to race hatred which the lawmaker wanted to include in article 131.[49]

The notion "parts of the population" found in Article 130 has been interpreted by German courts so as to include German citizens belonging to an ethnic, linguistic, racial, religious or social minority,[50] and also to aliens residing in Germany.[51]

As to the question of the conditions under which an act is to be considered likely to breach public peace, the Federal Supreme Court held in its decision of 21 April 1961[52] that the act in question does not in fact need to breach public peace or to constitute an imminent and concrete threat to public peace. It is sufficient if there are objective grounds for believing that the publication will shatter confidence in legal security, even if this is felt only by that part of the population against which the publication is directed.[53]

Although trial court opinions are generally not published, trial courts have been inclined to acquit defendants of charges of anti-Semitism under Articles 130 and 131 while state appellate courts and the Federal Supreme Court have tended to

---

48 This definition is firmly established in German jurisprudence. *See* Von Bubnoff, *supra* note 17, at No.4; and Lackner, *supra* note 19, at No. 3.; both with further references.

49 Translation taken from Stein, *supra* note 17, at 292. This definition is well-accepted in German doctrine. *See*, Von Bubnoff, *supra* note 17, at No. 18 and Lackner, *supra* note 19, at No. 3, both with further references.

50 Jews are considered to form a "part of the population" for purposes of Art. 130, *see* BGHSt (*Entscheidungen des Bundesgerichtshofs in Strafsachen*, the Official Collection of Decisions of the Federal Supreme Court in Criminal Matters) Vol. 21, at 371 and Vol. 31, at 226), as are Gypsies, *see* Oberlandesgericht Karlsruhe, reported in 39 *Neue Juristische Wochenschrift* 1276 (1986).

51 For instance, black students are protected by Art. 130, *see* Oberlandesgericht Hamburg, reported in 28 *Neue Juristische Wochenschrift* 1088 (1975), as are migrant workers, *see* Oberlandesgericht Celle, reported in 23 *Neue Juristische Wochenschrift* 2257 (1970)). In contrast to the protection afforded to these groups against incitement to hatred, there are lacunae in the law which have permitted the barring of such groups as blacks and Turks from restaurants and other public establishments. *See* Wolfrum, *supra* note 3, at 525.

52 BGHSt Vol. 16, 49 *et seq.*; for a discussion in English, *see* Stein, *supra* note 17, at 293.

53 This principle is well accepted in German doctrine. *See* Von Bubnoff, *supra* note 17, at No. 5; and Lackner, *supra* note 19, at No. 4; both with further references.

reverse the acquittals. One commentator has speculated about this pattern of judicial interaction:

> For one thing, trial judges are generally of a younger generation, without oppressive memories and - understandably - without a sense of personal guilt. Lacking extensive experience, they may feel less confident in handing down convictions for a distinctly political crime. Perhaps they also are more in tune with local attitudes than the higher-level judiciary, and are less responsive to the national policy that has reflected both the recent historical experience and a sensitivity to international considerations.[54]

CONCLUSION

In the author's opinion, Articles 130 and 131 of the *Strafgesetzbuch*, which make punishable racist speech and incitement to racial hatred, constitute an acceptable attempt to strike a fair balance between the state's obligation, resulting from Article 1(1) of the *Grundgesetz*, to protect human dignity, and its obligation, resulting from Article 5 of the *Grundgesetz*, to protect freedom of speech. Obviously, this statement does not mean that the practice of German courts in interpreting and applying these provisions of the Criminal Code in specific cases does not call for critique. However, it is submitted that the jurisprudence of the Federal Supreme Court appears largely satisfactory.

In this author's opinion, it would be to overestimate the role of the courts if the recent, and increasing, cases of violence against non-Germans, and in particular asylum-seekers, in Germany were to be taken as proof of the failure of the judiciary or of the laws. Obviously, it remains to be seen what the reaction of the courts will be and whether police and prosecuting authorities will act as promptly and efficiently as necessary.[55] Thus, notwithstanding the undoubted importance of criminal law in the fight against racial hatred, it seems as if profound changes in the political climate with regard to aliens in general and asylum-seekers in particular are of even greater significance. Substantial parts of the German political establishment and public opinion, although unequivocally condemning acts of violence, openly promote the idea that "something has to be done against the abuse of the right to asylum" and that "Germany is not a country of immigration". As long as such public statements continue, and are not met with equally forceful statements about the need to respect the human dignity of all those within Germany's borders, it is hardly surprising that certain parts of the population, although still very small, are attracted by groups which aggressively proclaim nationalistic and neo-Nazi ideologies.

---

54 Stein, *supra* note 17, at 299.

55 According to a report in *Süddeutsche Zeitung* of 5 Dec. 1991 at 7, in the first trial against participants of the riots directed against Romanian asylum-seekers in the city of Hoyerswerda (Saxony) on 21 Sept. 1991, the *Kreisgericht Bautzen* sentenced a person to a term of 15 months' imprisonment (not suspended) for a breach of Art. 125a of the StGB (*Schwerer Landfriedensbruch*, an especially aggravated breach of the peace) in conjunction with a breach of Art. 130 of the StGB.

ESSAY

CONFRONTING RACISM BY LAW IN ISRAEL— PROMISES AND PITFALLS

Amos Shapira *

By any accepted international yardstick, Israel is essentially a stable democracy,[1] one of about thirty true liberal democracies of the contemporary world. This is no small feat, considering the existential dilemmas of physical survival and nation-building that have confronted the State of Israel from day one of its sovereign independence. However, there exist several major foci of actual and potential peril to Israel's democracy, which are both exacerbated by and result in latent racist attitudes within Israeli society. These attitudes have been aggravated by Rabbi Meir Kahane[2] and his followers.

First and foremost is the persisting Arab-Israeli conflict and its devastating impact on the relations between Jews and Arabs. Such relations have been marred by mutual anxiety, hostility, and fear. The Jewish majority in Israel displays attitudes of suspicion and dis-

---

* Kalman Lubowski Professor of Law and Biomedical Ethics, Tel Aviv University; Former Dean of the Faculty of Law, Tel Aviv University; M. Jur., 1962, Hebrew University, Jerusalem; M.C.L., 1963, Columbia University; J.S.D., 1968, Yale University.

[1] Israel is a parliamentary democracy in which the 120-member Parliament—called the Knesset—is supreme. W. Frankel, Israel Observed: An Anatomy of the State 13 (1980). The courts, the executive, and the President are all subordinate to the Knesset. The President has no power to veto legislation and the courts cannot declare any law passed by the Knesset unconstitutional. Id. at 15. Although the Knesset prescribes the law, policy is made by the Prime Minister and his Cabinet. Id.

Elections for the Knesset are held at least once every four years. Id. at 19. Voters vote for a party list and not for an individual candidate. Id. at 20. Vacancies are filled by the persons highest on the party list. Id. at 21.

[2] Kahane was born in Brooklyn, New York in August 1932. After college he attended Mirrer Yeshiva where he was ordained as a rabbi. In 1968, he and Bertram Zwiebon founded the Jewish Defense League ("JDL") for the purpose of protecting Jews from antisemitic acts by whatever means necessary. See Kaufman, The Complex Past of Meir Kahane, N.Y. Times, Jan. 24, 1971, at A1, col. 5. Kahane resigned as head of the organization in 1985.

Since 1971, Kahane has spent most of his time in Israel and has become a fanatic political figure with a substantial following. He casts aside liberal democratic values in favor of a society run by Jewish law. It is his belief that the Arab population in Israel, through its high birthrate, will eventually outnumber the Jews and will have a majority vote sufficient to control Israel eventually. In Kahane's view, this potential situation is intolerable, as the State of Israel was created for and should be governed by Jews. Consequently, he advocates the expulsion of all Arabs from the State of Israel. Friedman, Kahane Appeal to Oust Arabs Gains in Israel, N.Y. Times, Aug. 5, 1985, at A1, col. 5.

trust towards the Arab minority, a group which views itself—and is certainly regarded by Israeli Jews—as part of a regional Arab majority that is essentially hostile to Israel.[3] While many Israelis react with apathy or bewilderment to this complex conflict, the nationalistic thrust of the Kahane movement carries the existing sentiments of anxiety and distrust to an extreme by openly advocating expulsion of the Arabs from Israel.

Second, the long-lasting debate over religion and state confronts Israeli society with yet another existential dilemma. Sharply differing views regarding the normative implications of Israel's Jewish character have turned the ominous prospect of a Kulturkampf[4] into a constant threat to Israeli communal life. Moreover, tensions between the religious and secular communities are mounting, occasionally throwing the entire political system into turmoil.[5] Religious fanaticism, frequently coupled with nationalist extremism, has been on the rise in recent years. Some fanatic groups assert divine injunctions as justification for conduct that is in flagrant violation of the law. These groups pose a threat to the liberal-democratic values cherished by most enlightened Israelis, by supporting Kahane's goal to make Israel a theocracy.

Problems relating to national survival and identity in Israel are exacerbated by ethnic tensions that are triggered by the lingering socio-economic and cultural-psychological gap between the Ashkenazi and Sephardic[6] communities. Despite the impressive progress made in a consistent effort to close this gap, frustration and alienation still constitute a disturbing feature of Israeli society.

---

[3] The situation has been complicated further by the territorial and demographic realities evolving since the 1967 Six Day War, when Israel found itself in control of a vast population of Palestinian Arabs living under military administration in the West Bank and the Gaza strip.

[4] A Kulturkampf is a conflict between religious and civil authorities. The term was popularized during the struggle to subject the Roman Catholic Church to state controls of the German Empire under Bismarck. See The New Columbia Encyclopedia 1506 (4th ed. 1975).

[5] Since the inception of the State of Israel, no party has ever won an overall majority. Instead, coalition governments are formed. See W. Frankel, supra note 1, at 24. As the withdrawal of one party from the coalition may be sufficient to undermine the majority position of the government, each party within the coalition has significant influence. Consequently, the Prime Minister and his dominant party have the task of balancing the interests of all political factions in the coalition.

[6] Ashkenazi is a term for Jews of European descent—most notably from Germany, France, and Poland. 3 Encyclopedia Judaica 719 (1972). Sephardi generally means all non-Ashkenazi Jews but specifically refers to Jews who descend from the Spanish and Portugese Jews who immigrated to North Africa and Turkey in the 1500's. 14 Encyclopedia Judaica, supra, at 1164. While the cultural development of these two groups is different, their belief in the basic tenets of Judaism is the same. In Israel, Jews of European origin have traditionally been socio-economically more advantaged than the Sephardic Jews.

Kahane's extreme anti-Arab rhetoric clearly appeals to the less afflu-
ent, underachieving segments of Israeli society, which are generally
associated with the Sephardic community. Here, as elsewhere, socio-
economically weak populations tend to find in racist ideology an out-
let through which they can vent feelings of inferiority and
discrimination.[7]

Finally, one must realize that Israel's sovereign statehood is still
young and its democratic fabric vulnerable. The bulk of Jewish immi-
grants to the country—not only those from the Arab states of the
Middle East and North Africa but also those coming from many
Eastern and Central European countries—arrived with little or no experience with democratic political traditions. Thus, the concept of
democracy is perceived by many, including government officials, in
simplistic terms of majority rule. Commitment to the ideas of inalienable civil rights and individual freedoms, coupled with a measure of
healthy skepticism as to governmental credibility, still requires careful
nurturing. The conspicuous absence of a written constitution, complete with an entrenched Bill of Rights, is significant and telling in
this connection.

The young Israeli liberal democracy is thus faced with a myriad
of difficulties: the physical struggle for national survival, the dilemma
concerning the appropriate place of religious values, practices, and
institutions in the life of the nation, the socio-ethnic tensions generated in the process of ingathering exiles from all four corners of the
earth, and the constitutional deficiencies of the political system. The
abominable phenomenon of racist incitement and discrimination is an
extreme manifestation of such difficulties. Patently, any serious en-
deavor to erase the symptoms of racism in Israeli society requires a
thorough treatment of the problem. This would include a sustained
educational effort at all levels of the education system, a rigorous public opinion campaign mobilizing the mass-communication media, an
active involvement of the intelligentsia, academia, and free profes-
sions, a genuine commitment to the values of liberal democracy on
the part of the political establishment, and the introduction of certain
constitutional reforms. In the final analysis, to effectively combat racial bigotry and hatred, one must have faith in the ultimate triumph
of human rationality and goodwill. The law has a relevant role to
play in bringing about such a victory. Indeed, the State of Israel has

---

[7] The message of Kahanism expresses a racial supremacy of Jews over the Arabs, and it is
no wonder that this message is being accepted by the less privileged segments of the population
who have no other supremacy with which to pride themselves, save for the automatic
supremacy promised them as their birthright.

adopted legal measures restricting the right to run in Knesset elections[8] and the rights of Knesset members,[9] and has made incitement to racism a crime.[10]

I. Pros and Cons of Legislation

Lawyers are conditioned, by schooling and training, to believe in the omnipotence of legal prescription as a problem-solving device. Immersed in the thought patterns of their vocation, they sometimes lose sight of the true desirability or feasibility of legal ordering in a given area. Therefore, before reviewing certain specific legal measures recently taken with a view to containing racist phenomena in Israel, the main arguments both for and against such legislation should be examined.

The case against antiracist legislation starts with a fundamental query: Should we, in a genuine democracy, condition freedom of political expression and action on one's faithful commitment to the underlying precepts of democracy? This inquiry leads to consideration of the weight that should be accorded freedom of political expression[11] and association in a liberal democracy. To be meaningful, the freedom of expression regime ought to accommodate points of view considered unpopular and even damaging. The answer to dangerous speech should be more speech. Sound governmental discretion and good faith can never be completely trusted when government purports to restrict, for whatever reason, freedom of political expression. One must always be mindful of the perils of the slippery-slope syndrome: today Kahane is silenced, but who will it be tomorrow? A precedent once established is likely to have a snowballing effect, particularly in a legal system which habitually bows to precedents. And where does one stop to limit undesirable socio-political expression? Do we intend to punish every racist utterance, including colloquial jokes about Scottish stinginess or Jewish greed? Even if one manages to escape the slippery-slope menace, does not the attempt to counter racism with prohibitory legislation amount to treating an irritating symptom rather than trying to cure the disease itself?

Further, lawyers are forever concerned with definitional predica-

---

[8] See infra text accompanying notes 23-32.

[9] See infra text accompanying notes 13-22.

[10] See infra text accompanying notes 33-39.

[11] The principle of freedom of expression is supported by widely recognized rationales. Such freedom provides a pluralistic marketplace of ideas facilitating truthfinding and rational judgment, an open arena where public opinion can be freely molded and the will of the people crystallized and voiced.

ments, especially in the province of legislation. Indeed, concepts such as "incitement to racial hatred" or "racial discrimination" are hardly amenable to easy statutory formulation. A law penalizing racist incitement or discrimination must not be defined too broadly lest it unduly encroach on the domain of legitimate socio-political conduct. However, while one should certainly shy away from punishing people solely for their opinions and ideas, too narrow a definition could leave instances of racist behavior which one feels ought to be censured unchecked, especially since racist incitement and discrimination are practiced with ever-growing subtlety and sophistication. In light of these and other legislative complexities, it is frequently argued that existing laws, such as the penal prohibition of sedition and the libel law importing both civil and criminal liability for individual and group libel, should suffice to cope with the problem.

The possibility of selective use, overuse, misuse, or even outright abuse of laws against racism must also be considered. The definitional dilemmas noted above, coupled with the inherent dynamics and shortcomings of law enforcement, exacerbate the risk that such laws will be applied—whether intentionally or unwittingly—in situations not initially contemplated as falling within the purview of the antiracist legislation. Can the prosecuting authorities and the courts be trusted with the delicate task of responsibly enforcing these laws strictly for their designated purposes, without any selective manipulation or spillover? To the anticipated difficulties in draftsmanship and application, the skeptics are bound to add serious doubts regarding the expected effectiveness of laws against racism. The actual effectiveness of such laws can be measured, for instance, by comparing the socio-political situation with respect to incitement to racial hatred prevailing prior to the enactment of the legislation and subsequent to it.[12]

The case against antiracist legislation rests on weighty considerations that point to serious deficiencies of law prescription and enforcement in this sphere. Yet the arguments in support of legislation are even more compelling. Democracy rests on a fundamental social contract and on accepted political ground rules. No one wishing to play an active role in the democratic arena has the right to undermine the foundations of this rudimentary pact and break the rules of the game.

---

[12] Among the relevant inquiries to be made in this connection are the following: Who was indicted? For what types of behavior? Who was acquitted? Who was convicted and what penalties were meted out? Who was not indicted in the first place? Has the criminal process really achieved its asserted goals of deterrence and prevention or, conversely, has it been proven to be ineffectual or even counterproductive—by, for instance, providing racists with a highly visible platform from which to trumpet their hate propaganda while becoming martyrs in the eyes of their followers?

Freedom of expression ought not be guaranteed to those striving to silence everyone else. While it is legitimate in a democracy to espouse all points of view, no matter how extreme and revolting they may be, the shield of legitimacy should not be made available to a group whose stated goal is to deny freedom of expression to anyone disagreeing with it. In addition, the actual purpose of a law forbidding incitement to racism is not to cleanse the minds and hearts of confirmed racists, but rather to prevent them from disseminating their racial beliefs. It is well beyond the power of the law to uproot deeply-seated sentiments of racial hostility and hatred. Yet, it can strive to halt or limit the malignant spreading of such sentiments.

One can argue further that it is the legitimate business of the law to provide victims of racism the necessary safeguards from real and substantial injury to their feelings, privacy, and human dignity. Thus, preventive or remedial legal measures may appropriately be invoked with a view to minimizing the damage inflicted upon the political, social, economic, professional, and cultural rights of the population at which racial discrimination is aimed. It is also proper for the law to try to thwart the danger to public peace which may result from a violent confrontation between the victims of racism and their victimizers. Put in general terms, a "defensive democracy" (let alone a fighting one) should not hesitate to take adequate steps calculated to frustrate any and all attempts to shake the foundations of the democratic order.

Even the most ardent advocates of legislation against racial incitement and discrimination cannot deny the difficulties of fashioning and implementing such legislation. But the absence of an impeccable definition for the terms "racism" and "incitement" is hardly a compelling reason to abandon the law completely when considering an overall societal initiative to contain the racist peril. Similarly, misapplication of the law is a dangerous possibility lurking whenever the legislature invests the executive branch of government with discretionary powers. The appropriate, though never perfect, remedy may lie in statutorily defining the powers thus granted as tightly as possible and in promoting a reliable process of public control, including vigorous judicial review. Despite the skepticism voiced concerning the effectiveness of law enforcement in this area, it must be acknowledged that ineffectiveness of law enforcement is scarcely a rare phenomenon and should not stand in the way of an attempt to curtail racism by law.

As to the desired scope of the legal prohibition against racist incitement and discrimination, one may choose between a narrow or a

broad legislative design. A narrow design would involve the prevention of breach of the public peace likely to be triggered by incitement
to racism and the victims' reaction thereto. A legal measure geared
solely to that limited end must consider the degree of causal connection between the racist act and breach of the peace that would be
sufficient to justify curtailment of certain liberties, e.g., freedom of
expression, demonstration, and association of racist groups. By a
broader legislative design, all manifestations of racial hatred and discrimination—i.e., impinging upon the feelings, privacy, human dignity, and other legitimate interests of the victims of racism and
generally shaking the foundations of the democratic order—can be
viewed as a per se justification of restrictive legal control. In this
scheme, racist behavior could become a proper target of prohibitory
legislation even in the absence of a sufficiently close causal relationship between such behavior and the danger of violent breach of the
public peace.

Proponents of antiracism legislation should fully acknowledge
the exacting cost of a heavy-handed interference with the fundamental
freedoms of expression and association. In view of this unavoidable
cost, one must seek to receive in return a truly balanced law, that will
actually prevent or minimize racist phenomena without generating
excessively risky side effects which might damage the healthy tissue of
society. Such a law can also be expected to serve a useful declaratory
and educational purpose, by explicitly setting a binding norm for society, stating an obligatory modus operandi for all branches of government, and solemnly reaffirming the fundamental values of democracy.

II. LEGISLATIVE ATTACK ON RACISM

The State of Israel has recently adopted legislation in an effort to
confront racism. While the legislative measures are in fact prompted
by the fanatacism of Kahane and his followers, they serve to establish
a mechanism to curtail racist attitudes within Israeli society regardless of their source.

The first legal step taken against Kahane was to deny him a special privilege granted by law to Knesset members: complete freedom
of movement throughout Israel.[13] Shortly after starting his term as a
member of the Knesset, Kahane waged a campaign of provocative

---

13 The pertinent provision of Israeli law states: "A direction prohibiting or restricting access to any place within the State other than private property shall not apply to a member of
the Knesset unless the prohibition or restriction is motivated by considerations of State security or military security." 80 Sefer Ha-Chukkim 228, 229, 5 Laws of the State of Israel 149, 151
(authorized trans. Oct. 25, 1950-Sept. 26, 1951).

visits to Arab communities with the declared aim of "persuading" the local inhabitants to pack and migrate to some Arab country. Time and again the police labored to prevent a riotous confrontation between the zealous Rabbi, surrounded by a handful of devout followers, and angry Arab villagers.[14] Ultimately, the Knesset passed a resolution withholding the special privilege from Kahane,[15] thus subjecting him—like all ordinary citizens—to possible legal restrictions on mobility in the face of an imminent and substantial danger of a breach of the public peace. It is noteworthy that following the passage of this resolution, the Knesset took a similar step against one of its Arab members[16] in circumstances raising grave doubts as to the justifiability of invoking such an extraordinary measure. The latter episode underscores the perils of the slippery-slope syndrome and the snowballing effect of this kind of precedent.

Another legal measure to confront racism is embodied in a Knesset resolution which amends its standing orders so as to explicitly authorize the speaker to disqualify racist bills proposed by Knesset members.[17] Under Israeli law, a Knesset member may submit a private bill to the speaker, and the latter, after approving it, puts the bill on the Knesset's agenda for a preliminary reading.[18] Kahane proposed a bill[19] under which, inter alia, only Jews may be citizens of the state of Israel and a non-Jewish resident would not be permitted to reside in Jerusalem nor be eligible to vote or to run for any public office. According to another bill also introduced by Kahane,[20] separate public beaches would be created for Jews and non-Jews, non-Jews would be prevented from residing in a Jewish neighborhood except

---

[14] The incident in the town of Um El Fahm typifies the confrontations the Knesset sought to prevent. On August 29, 1984, Kahane and his supporters attempted to enter Um El Fahm, Israel's largest Arab town. Feron, *Kahane Barred from Entering an Arab Town*, N.Y. Times, Aug. 30, 1984, at A1, col. 2. They were stopped by police two miles from town and by town residents who had gathered to block the Rabbi at the town entrance. The protestors included both Arabs and Jews, many of whom wore yellow stars with the Hebrew words for "Racism Won't Pass." *Id.* at A11, col. 1. Violence flared shortly after the Rabbi's expected time of arrival. Stones were thrown at car windows, the police released tear gas in crowds of youths, and the chant of "racist" hung in the air. By the day's end, at least 11 policemen and youths had been injured. *Id.* at A1, col. 2.

[15] Knesset Resolution (unpublished 1985).

[16] The Knesset withheld the same privilege of Knesset member Muhamed Miari of the Progressive Party for Peace.

[17] Knesset Standing Order Amend. § 134(c), 3271 Yalkut Ha-Pirsumim 772 (1985) (amending Standing Order § 134 by adding subsection (c)). Standing orders are the rules prescribing the procedure of the Knesset.

[18] S. Sager, *The Parliamentary System of Israel* 172-73 (1985).

[19] M. Kahane, *The Law of Israeli Citizenship* (1985) (unpublished bill).

[20] M. Kahane, *Law for Prevention of Assimilation between Jews and Non-Jews* (1985) (unpublished bill).

with the consent of the majority of the Jewish dwellers, it would be forbidden for Jewish citizens and residents of the State to marry or to have sexual relations with non-Jews, and couples of existing mixed marriages would be forced to breakup forthwith. The speaker of the Knesset declined to put the bills on the Knesset's agenda for a preliminary reading on the ground that they were racist and offensive to democratic values and to the dignity of the Knesset.

Kahane challenged the legality of the speaker's ruling before the Supreme Court[21] which held that under existing law, the speaker did not possess the authority to prevent deliberation of a proposed private member bill on account of the repugnant nature of its normative content. Reacting to the Supreme Court holding, and following ardent political negotiations, the Knesset resolved to amend its standing orders by expressly vesting the speaker with the specific power to deny a preliminary reading to private member bills which are "essentially racist" or which "negate the existence of the State of Israel as the State of the Jewish people."[22]

To date, the most constitutionally significant and problematic step taken as part of the campaign to counter racism by law was the enactment of an explicit statutory limitation on the right to run for elections.[23] Prior to this enactment, there had been no express legislative mandate in Israeli law for denying a party the right to participate in elections on account of the unacceptable nature of its ideological-political platform.[24] Shortly prior to the elections to the present Knesset, the Central Elections Committee[25] resolved to disqualify both the Kahane list as being antidemocratic and the predominantly Arab Progressive Party for Peace list as being subversive and support-

---

[21] Kahane v. Speaker of the Knesset, High Court of Justice [H.C.] 742/84, 39(4) Piskei Din [P.D.] 85 (1985).

[22] Knesset Standing Order Amend. § 134(c), 3271 Yalkut Ha-Pirsumim 772 (1985). Kahane was quick to petition the Supreme Court with a challenge to the legitimacy of this amendment. Kahane v. Speaker of the Knesset, H.C. 306/85, 39(4) P.D. 486 (1985). On Dec. 1, 1986, the Israeli Supreme Court dismissed Kahane's petition, thereby establishing the amendment's legality. See Kahane v. Speaker of the Knesset, H.C. 669/85, 24/86, 131/86 (1986).

[23] Basic Law: The Knesset, (Amend. 9), 1155 Sefer Ha-Chukkim 196 (1985).

[24] However, in a celebrated and controversial split decision in the case of Yerdor v. Chairman of the Cent. Election Comm., Appell. File 1/65, 19(3) P.D. 365 (1965), the Supreme Court decreed that the Central Elections Committee has the authority—although not anchored specifically in any statutory provision—to disqualify a list of candidates espousing the liquidation of Israel as a sovereign Jewish nation-state. The right to be elected, reasoned the majority justices, could be withheld from an anti-State party. Id. at 366.

[25] The Central Elections Committee is a statutory body made up of delegates of the parties represented in the current Knesset and headed by a Supreme Court justice.

ive of the enemies of the Jewish state.[26] The Supreme Court over-turned the disqualification ruling and sanctioned the right of both lists to run in the elections.[27] Kahane was elected to the Knesset as were two members of the Progressive Party for Peace.

Reacting to Kahane's election, an overwhelming majority of the Knesset adopted Basic Law: The Knesset (Amendment No. 9)[28] which provides:

> A list of candidates shall not participate in Knesset elections if any of the following is expressed or implied in its purposes or deeds:
> (1) Denial of the existence of the State of Israel as the state of the Jewish people;
> (2) Denial of the democratic character of the State;
> (3) Incitement to racism.[29]

The statutory language, which authorizes the barring of a list of candidates from participation in Knesset elections, does not include an explicit requirement for the existence of a sufficiently proximate causal connection, such as "clear and present," "probable," or "reasonably possible," between the "purposes or deeds" of the list of candidates and the stipulated possible harmful consequences[30] as a prerequisite to disqualification. The absence of such an express requirement may lead to the conclusion that the drastic authority to prohibit a party from running for elections may be exercised solely upon a convincing showing of the express or implied repulsive antistate, antidemocratic, or racist nature of that party's goals and actions. However, this conclusion is neither necessary nor, arguably, desirable. In light of the Supreme Court decision[31] referred to above, it may be

---

[26] Decision of the Cent. Election Comm. of June 17, 1984, 39(2) P.D. 238 (1984).

[27] Naiman, Avneri v. Chairman of the Knesset Elections Cent. Comm., Elections Appeal 2, 3/84, 39(2) P.D. 225, 233 (1985).

[28] Basic Law: The Knesset, (Amend. 9), 1155 Sefer Ha-Chukkim 196 (1985).

[29] Id. It was the appearance of Kahanism on the political scene in Israel which actually prompted this legislative measure denying antidemocratic and racist parties the right to participate in Knesset elections. The second and third grounds for disqualification specified in the new law clearly testify to this underlying reason for the legislation. But, as a telling manifestation of the dynamics of ideological symmetry and political bargaining, these two grounds were preceded by the legislature with yet another disqualifying ground phrased in terms of the "denial of the existence of the State of Israel as the state of the Jewish people." Id. The phrase characterizing Israel as "the state of the Jewish people" merely expresses the axiomatic assumption, shared by most Israeli Jews, about the Jewish national essence of the state and need not be interpreted as adversely reflecting on the civil and political rights of non-Jewish Israeli citizens.

[30] Possible harmful consequences are "denial of the existence of . . . Israel as the state of the Jewish people," "denial of the democratic character of the State," and "incitement to racism." Id.

[31] Naiman, Avneri v. Chairman of the Knesset Elections Cent. Comm., Elections Appeal 2, 3/84, 39(2) P.D. 225 (1985).

argued that demonstrating the repugnant character of a party's platform and behavior should not suffice to justify its disqualification. In
addition to such repugnant character, it must be established that the
factual circumstances of the situation point to a probability, or at least
a reasonable possibility, that the party, if allowed to participate in the
electoral process, will actually be able to materialize its offensive
credo. This view requires an established and sufficiently close causal
relationship between the manifested threat and its actual realization
as a precondition to the exercise of the far-reaching power to prevent
a party from running in elections.

As a result of this law, the Central Elections Committee now has
the explicit authority to disqualify a list of candidates from participating in Knesset elections of the list's antistate, antidemocratic, or racist
behavior. It would have been more fitting, I submit, to deposit this
exceptional power of disqualification in the hands of a body that is not
essentially political in its make-up and orientation. True, members of
a disqualified list are entitled to bring an appeal before the Supreme
Court,[32] but appellate supervision has its inherent limitations and can
hardly provide a satisfactory substitute for an institutionally reliable
decisionmaking process in the first instance. Considering the drastic
nature of the authority to deny a political party the right to run in
elections, the wisdom of entrusting such authority to a body forever
suspect of being politically motivated may be doubted. An independent judicial or quasi-judicial organ would appear to be far more suitable for the responsible exercise of delicate constitutional discretion
which is required whenever the typically vague disqualification
grounds have to be interpreted and applied in concrete fact situations.

Finally, yet another legal measure to confront racist phenomena
was proposed in April, 1985,[33] when a bill was introduced in the
Knesset which would add to the Israeli criminal code a new specific
offense titled "incitement to racism." Ultimately, on August 5, 1986,

---

[32] The Supreme Court may also hear appeals lodged by the Attorney General, the chairman of the committee, or at least one quarter of its members, against the approval of a list by
the committee.

[33] 1728 Bills 195 (April 17, 1985) codified as amended at Penal Law Amend. No. 20, 1191
Sefer Ha-Chukkim 219 (1986). According to the proposed bill, incitement to racism or disseminating any matter with intent to bring about racism would constitute a criminal offense
punishable by law. The bill has met with much reservation and criticism. Some have contended that it was not broad enough in that it failed to address itself to racial discrimination,
while others have argued that it was overly sweeping and therefore in need of further narrowing. Various religious groups have voiced grave apprehension that the bill, as drafted, might
be interpreted as attaching a stigma of criminality to certain religious teachings. For all these
reasons the Knesset has dragged its feet in a slow, even reluctant, legislative process.

a revised version of the bill was enacted into law[34] by a substantial majority of Knesset members. The new criminal offense defines the term "racism" in the following manner: "persecution, humiliation, degradation, manifestation of enmity, hostility or violence, or causing strife toward a group of people or segments of the population—because color or affiliation with a race or a national-ethnic origin."[35] The definition of "racism" expressly refers not only to "race" but also to "national-ethnic origin" and "color," which is relevant to relations between Jews and Arabs in Israel and to inter-Jewish relationships respectively.[36]

The new criminal offense is defined as follows: "One who publishes any matter with the purpose of inciting to racism is subject to five years imprisonment."[37] The prescribed elements of the offense are markedly narrow in scope. First, the racially inciting nature—as objectively determined by a "reasonable man" standard—of the matter published will not, by itself, suffice to import criminal responsibility. It is the specific intent to incite to racism which may expose the perpetrator to penal liability. Thus, the highest possible level of mens rea was made a sine qua non of conviction. To win its case, the prosecution must prove beyond a reasonable doubt that racial incitement was the accused's clear-cut purpose. Establishing such a frame of mind is no small feat, as racists are not prone to readily admit such an intention when brought to trial. Nonetheless, a specific intent can occasionally be inferred from the circumstances of the case, sometimes in reliance on the juridical presumption that "one intends the natural consequences of one's act." Also, the prosecution might rely on the principle that if a perpetrator knows that it is practically certain that an illicit consequence, i.e., racial incitement, will inevitably occur (following the publication in question), he is deemed to have acted purposely. However, it is still an open question whether Israeli judges will be prepared to avail themselves of this so-called "knowledge rule" regarding the offense of racial incitement or, conversely, will insist on

---

[34] Penal Law Amend. No. 20, 1191 Sefer Ha-Chukkim 219 (1986).

[35] Id. When compared with the counterpart definition of "racism" in the April 1985 bill, 1728 Bills 195 (April 17, 1985), the absence of the term "religion" is conspicuous. Consequently, persecution, etc. on account of religious affiliation alone is not "racism" in terms of the law as enacted.

[36] The term "national-ethnic origin" refers to an affiliation which is relevant to relations between Jews and Arabs, while the term "color" may render the definition of racism applicable to attitudes towards, e.g., dark-skinned Ethiopian Jews, or the so-called "Hebrew Blacks."

[37] Penal Law Amend. No. 20, 1191 Sefer Ha-Chukkim 219, 220 (1986). Additionally, possession of an illicit publication for purposes of distribution with a view to bringing about racism is punishable by one year imprisonment and confiscation of the publication. Id.

a direct, positive showing that the accused actually intended to incite to racism.

The limited purview of the new proscription is further indicated by the fact that it condemns only publications purposely *inciting* racism but not racist conduct (such as racial discrimination) per se. While a cautious, strict delineation of a legal norm—such as the criminal offense of incitement to racism—curbing freedom of expression is commendable from a civil libertarian viewpoint, it is regrettable that racist activity other than incitement, and particularly racial discrimination, has entirely escaped the proscriptive reach of this novel criminal prohibition.[38]

In the wake of a massive lobbying effort mounted by a host of religious Knesset members, the following clause was incorporated into the statutory text: "Publication of a quotation from religious writings and prayer books, or worshipping a religion, shall not be deemed an offense [of racist incitement] as long as it was not done with the purpose of inciting to racism."[39] In terms of elementary legal logic, this clause appears to be superfluous and meaningless, for if the publication at hand "was not done with the purpose of inciting to racism," it can hardly amount to a prima facie offense. By definition, it fails to satisfy the requirement of publishing any matter "with the purpose of inciting to racism," which lies at the core of the offense in question.

---

[38] Nevertheless, acts of racial discrimination perpetrated by public authorities are subject to nullification by the Israeli Supreme Court when exercising, in its capacity as High Court of Justice, judicial review of administative action. It is also noteworthy that about a month prior to the passage by the Knesset of the law in question, the General Council of the World Zionist Organisation adopted an amendment to the Organisations' constitution which disavows discrimination on grounds of origin, nationality, or race. See World Zionist Organisation Const., June, 1986 Amend. This formulation manifestly forbids not only incitement to racism but also racist behavior.

It is also noteworthy to consider the following treatment of standards regarding antiracist legislation. The International Convention on the Elimination of All Forms of Racial Discrimination 1966 (of which Israel has been a party since 1979) provides in Part I, Article 2 that "State Parties condemn racial discrimination . . . . Each state party shall prohibit . . . by all appropriate means, including legislation . . . racial discrimination by any persons, group or organization . . . ." International Convention on the Elimination of All Forms of Racial Discrimination 1966, reprinted in Basic Documents in International Law 181-82 (I. Brownlie ed. 1967). In addition, Article 4 of the Convention specifically censures racial incitement by stipulating that "State Parties . . . undertake to adopt . . . measures designed to eradicate all incitement to, or acts of, [racial] discrimination . . . [and] shall declare an offence punishable by law all dissemination of ideas based on racial superiority or hatred, incitement to racial discrimination, as well as all acts of violence . . . against any race or group . . . [and] shall declare illegal and prohibit organizations, and . . . activities, which promote and incite racial discrimination . . . [and] shall not permit public authorities or . . . institutions . . . to promote or incite racial discrimination."

[39] Penal Law Amend. No. 20, 1191 Sefer Ha-Chukkin 219, 220 (1986).

Finally, use of the law is further restricted by the requirement that an indictment for the offense of incitement to racism can only be brought with the written consent of the Attorney General. Incitement to racism has thus been added to the short list of select offenses, such as Nazi crimes and offenses committed by high-ranking officials enjoying immunity, the indictment for which require this authorization.

AMERICA'S FIRST "HATE SPEECH" REGULATION

Michael W. McConnell *

Americans have the endearing but frustrating tendency to view every development in public life as if it were happening for the first time. Each issue is a new thing under the sun. Now the issue of "hate speech"—speech that is designed to degrade or injure other people on the basis of their race, ethnic origin, sex, sexual orientation or other sensitive characteristic—is the hot new free speech question. The law reviews are filled with learned analyses. Task forces have been appointed. Colleges and universities are debating the question. Legislation has been introduced in Congress.

Yet to my knowledge, none of the scholarly analyses of the issue has attempted to draw on the American historical experience with this problem. "Hate speech" is one of the oldest public issues in America; the first law was enacted almost 350 years ago. The question traditionally has been framed in these terms: to what extent does a liberal society require social conditions of mutual respect and toleration, and to what extent may the force of law be employed to attain or preserve those conditions? Attention to historical experience may help us to appreciate both the roots of hate speech regulation and some of its pitfalls.

The first hate speech regulation in America was Maryland's Toleration Act of 1649.[1] Maryland had been founded a few years earlier by a Roman Catholic nobleman and friend of Charles I, Lord Baltimore. Lord Baltimore intended to make Maryland a haven for his fellow Catholics (who at that time were severely persecuted in the mother country) and to extend protection to other dissenters from the Church of England as well. The Toleration Act, which precedes by forty years the famous act of Parliament by that name, was enacted by the colonial legislature, superseding a similar

* Professor of Law, University of Chicago. Thanks are due to Al Alschuler, Anne-Marie Burley, David Currie, Richard Epstein, Abner Greene, Geoffrey Stone, David Strauss, and Cass Sunstein for helpful comments on an earlier draft, to Ruth Bader Ginsburg for encouragement to commit these ideas to paper, and to the Russell Baker Fund and the Class of '49 Dean's Discretionary Fund for financial support.

1. Maryland Acts of Assembly, I, 244, quoted in Sanford H. Cobb, *The Rise of Religious Liberty in America* 376 (1902, reprinted Cooper Square, 1968) ("*Religious Liberty*").

proclamation by Lord Baltimore. As part of legislation establishing the "free exercise" of religion (the first appearance of those words in the laws of this continent), the Act imposed a fine of ten shillings on any person who called another "by such opprobrious terms as, Heretic, Schismatic, Idolator, Puritan, Independent, Presbyterian, Popish priest, Jesuit, Papist, Lutheran, Calvinist, Anabaptist, Brownist, Antinomian, Barrowist, Roundhead, and Separatist."[2] In the only recorded prosecution under the statute or the predecessor proclamation, a Catholic named William Lewis was fined for "interfering by opprobrious reproaches with two Protestants"[3]—an encouraging sign, since most colonial officials at the time were Catholics.

It may be objected that this statute deals with a subject—religion—far removed from today's concerns of race, sex, sexual orientation, and the like. But we must not commit the anachronism of dismissing religion as a private matter of little weight or consequence. Religion was central to the Maryland colonists' identity, and differences in religion were never far from their minds. Religious discord delivered Lord Baltimore's friend, Charles I, to the scaffold, and England to civil war. Moreover, the immediate problem addressed by the Maryland Toleration Act was not unlike that of today's hate speech regulations on campus. Words were used, then as now, to inflict injury, to humiliate, to ostracize, and to subordinate. Historian Sanford Cobb said of religious disputants in seventeenth century Massachusetts that they "made of their tongues weapons harder to bear than clubs."[4] The Maryland Toleration Act is thus an exceedingly close analogy to the regulation of hate speech on modern American campuses.

Unfortunately, we do not have much information about the implementation or effects of the Toleration Act. Following the downfall of the King, a Protestant faction seized power in the colony in 1652 and repealed the Toleration Act two years later, replacing it with a law explicitly denying protection to persons who "profess the exercise of the Popish Religion."[5] Oliver Cromwell forced the colonists to repeal the 1652 Act, thus reinstating the Toleration Act, but in the spirit of the day one would not expect faithful enforcement. Notwithstanding this lack of enforcement, however, three aspects of the Maryland experience seem significant today.

---

2. Cobb, *Religious Liberty*, at 376 (cited in note 1).
3. Id. at 372.
4. Id. at 215.
5. Maryland Acts of Assembly, I, 340, quoted in Cobb, *Religious Liberty* at 379 (cited in note 1).

First, the framers of the Maryland statute obviously thought that outlawing hate speech ("opprobrious terms") was consistent with—not in opposition to—a regime of free speech and religion. Restrictions of this sort would advance free discourse and inquiry, because they would enable persons of all groups, including the most socially despised, to participate on equal terms. The Toleration Act did not view religious freedom as meaning only an absence of governmental coercion; it sought to regulate the private sphere to ensure social conditions of toleration.

The idea that governmental intervention in the realm of speech might promote the liberal society is utterly foreign to modern conceptions of freedom of speech, which are under challenge today mostly from a segment of the post-modern left. Conservatives and ACLU liberals alike share the conviction that the first amendment is a restraint on the power of government and that the social conditions of tolerance, like the social conditions of patriotism, virtue, or other ideals, must take care of themselves without the help of law. The great free speech controversies of the twentieth century have typically involved speakers—Jehovah's Witnesses, Nazis, or Communists—who were themselves intolerant of others.

The post-modern left challenge to the prevailing conception of freedom of speech, of which hate speech regulation is the most conspicuous element, may seem newfangled and paradoxical. How can the principle of freedom of speech empower the *authorities* to restrict the speech of private persons, however hateful that speech may be? Surely such restrictions must be defended on the basis of some goal (perhaps racial equality) *other than* promoting free discourse and inquiry, and must be subjected to a healthy dose of liberal skepticism.

It is helpful to realize that the post-modern left challenge to free speech doctrine is not a new position. The hate speech regulators stand in the honorable shoes of Lord Baltimore and the Maryland colonists, who believed that private intolerance, through the use of hurtful epithets, is a significant obstacle to achievement of a society in which persons of all faiths (today we would say all races, sexes, sexual orientations, and the like) can live together peaceably and equally. In a world in which Catholics, for example, are both seriously outnumbered and socially subordinated, a jurisdiction that wants to offer Catholics a hospitable place in which to live must be concerned with the danger that private intolerance will make that objective unattainable. By the same token, if the desired end is a community of inquiry in which all viewpoints and perspectives can be shared, is it unreasonable for university administrators to think that an interventionist policy is necessary to ensure that some portions of the student body are not silenced and excluded from the discourse?

Second, the framers of the Toleration Act of 1649 had a difficult drafting problem. They were caught between the dangers of vagueness on the one hand and underinclusiveness on the other. How could they define "hate speech" so that they could outlaw it? The problem was particularly difficult because part of the religious exercise they were protecting was the ability to proclaim the faith, which often entails an explanation ("exhortation" might be a better word) of why other religions are false. How could the colonial authorities tell when legitimate discourse ends and "opprobrious terms" begin?

The Maryland drafters did not do a very good job. If their list is taken to be exclusive, there are a number of opprobrious epithets they left out: Socinian, ranter, pagan, Christ-killer, fanatic, hireling, and many more. If the list is taken only to be illustrative, it doesn't solve the vagueness problem. If a Protestant maliciously mocks the Latin of the mass by calling it "hocus-pocus,"[6] is that covered? If a Unitarian sneers at the credulity of those who believe in a virgin birth, is that covered? Conversely, some of the terms in the Maryland Act seem rather innocent. "Presbyterian," for example, is not an obvious example of an opprobrious epithet. And any of the terms, in a certain context, might be perfectly legitimate. That is the problem with legislation by list. If, however, the Maryland legislators had used another approach instead of listing forbidden epithets, they would have had a different set of problems. They might have based the law on the actual intent of the speaker to ostracize or subordinate members of a different faith, which makes it virtually unenforceable. Only the speaker knows his own intent. Or they might have based it on the effect on the hearer, which makes it vaguer than ever, and makes speech vulnerable to the reactions of the most sensitive among us.

Modern campus administrators face much the same problem. Like the Maryland legislators, they, too, could publish a list of forbidden epithets, the modern equivalents of "heretic," "schismatic," "papist," or "roundhead." We can all imagine the contents of the list. But no university has opted for that approach, perhaps for reasons of good manners. Instead they opt for vagueness. The University of Michigan interim code—the one instituted *after* the first effort was held unconstitutional by a federal court—forbids "verbal

---

6. The expression "hocus-pocus" is a corruption of the Latin hoc est corpus, "this is my body," the eucharistic formula.

slurs, invectives or epithets referring to an individual's race, ethnicity, religion, sex, sexual orientation," etc., made with the "purpose of injuring the person to whom the words or actions are directed," but excluding statements made as a part of a "discussion or exchange of an idea, ideology, or philosophy."[7] Try to figure out when that will apply.

Given the difficulties of drafting intelligible standards, it should come as no surprise that the enforcement of hate speech codes has been clumsy and unpredictable. Under the original Michigan code, for example, a graduate student was haled before a disciplinary board to account for his statement in a social work class that he believed homosexuality to be a disease and that he intended to develop a counseling program to help patients to overcome it.[8] Another student was "counseled" and required to apologize for commenting in class that "he had heard that minorities had a difficult time in the course and that he had heard that they were not treated fairly."[9] At the same time, some of the more egregious incidents of racism on campus would apparently fall outside most hate speech codes because they are directed at a general audience rather than at a particular person whom they seek to injure.

Third, the selectivity reflected in the Maryland statute is not random. Several epithets referring to Catholics are listed, because they were precisely the protected class whom the colonial authorities had in mind. There are no epithets pertaining to Jews. There are no epithets pertaining to atheists. There are no epithets pertaining to pagans, Muslims, or other assorted heathen—even though the vast majority of the inhabitants of Maryland in 1649 adhered to religions the legislators would have considered heathen. By interesting contrast, the 1669 Fundamental Constitutions of the Colony of Carolina, drafted in part by John Locke, which was in other respects less liberal in its protection of religious freedom, explicitly extended its protection to "Jews, heathens, and other dissenters from the purity of Christian religion."[10]

It was no accident that the Maryland legislature outlawed some epithets and not others. Maryland was designed as a haven

---

7. University of Michigan Interim Policy on Discrimination and Discriminatory Conduct By Students in the University Environment. at 5.

8. The incident is recounted in *Doe v. University of Michigan*, 721 F. Supp. 852, 865 (E.D. Mich. 1989).

9. 721 F. Supp. at 866.

10. Fundamental Constitutions of Carolina § 107 (1669), reprinted in Mattie Erma Edwards Parker, ed., *North Carolina Charters and Constitutions. 1578-1698* 132, 149 (Carolina Charter Tercentenary Comm'n. 1963).

for religious dissenters, but religious dissenters of a particular kind. Others were not welcome.

We see that same phenomenon in modern hate speech rules, which forbid hate speech directed against certain groups but not against others. You can, for example, call a fellow student a "racist, fascist homophobe," or a "pimply nerd," or a "damn Yankee," with impunity on any campus in America. Epithets like these serve no less to cut off debate, to humiliate, to ostracize, and to exclude; but they are not covered. Modern hate speech rules are intended to protect groups, but only groups of a certain kind. The opinions of significant subgroups of Americans on issues such as race and sexuality are not welcome on most American campuses. And these voices are not often heard. Who wants to be hissed in class?

There is a distinction, one might respond: the Maryland statute leaves out groups that are disfavored by the hegemonic authorities, while the hate speech regulations protect the oppressed and vulnerable in society. With all respect, this reflects a distorted picture of power relations in modern American academia. Most modern colleges and universities are passionately—one might even say religiously—committed to a particular view of race, gender, and sexual orientation. It is not merely a coincidence that the speech protected by the hate speech regulations is speech that is broadly consistent with the reigning orthodoxy, while the speech that is prohibited is contrary to it. Of course, some universities are exceptions; but the exceptional institutions typically have not enacted speech codes.

The University of Michigan rules could just as easily have prohibited "verbal slurs, invective or epithets directed at an individual," with the same requirements of intention to injure and the same exception for words used in course of the discussion or exchange of ideas—*without confining the forbidden epithets to those based on race, ethnicity, sex, sexual orientation, or the like*. Nothing would be lost by dropping the limitations. But I am aware of no college or university that has adopted a hate speech regulation without the list of protected classes. That they do not do so is an indication that their framers are less concerned with hate speech in general than with protecting their own ideological position—just as the particular range of religious faiths protected by the Maryland legislators was an indication of their ideological position.

College administrators sometimes defend selective protection on the ground that racial, sexual, and other invective of the prohibited sort is more wounding than other types of opprobrious language. But how can we know? As an empirical matter I suspect that various forms of personal insult ("pimply nerd") are, if anything, more humiliating—more humiliating precisely because there will be no group to rally round in protest and indignation. Indeed, the very fact that racist, sexist, and homophobic speech is so widely condemned on campus suggests that its victims are not without social support. But even if college administrators could demonstrate that the prohibited forms of invective are *more* harmful, this would not mean that other insults, which are also hurtful, should be excluded from protection. Why not prohibit all insults that have the purpose and effect of silencing, subordinating, or excluding a fellow member of the university community, without drawing dubious distinctions on the basis of content?

It is one thing for the authorities to promote civility in discourse. It is quite another thing to promote civility only selectively—to apply a double standard depending on whether the incivility accords with or opposes the ideological position of the authorities. In this context, the content distinctions are suspiciously congruent with the ideological position of the university. Hate speech regulation can be seen as an effort to disarm one particularly unappealing segment of the university's opponents without disarming any of its ideological allies.

An examination of the Maryland Toleration Act of 1649 thus suggests that we should not accept too quickly the common position of conservatives and ACLU liberals that hate speech regulation is, in principle, contrary to the requirements of a free society. Our early history shows that lawmakers no less committed to a free society than most of us came to the conclusion that a free, equal, and tolerant society must protect its principles from the forces of intolerance, even when they manifest themselves in speech. But even if we become more sympathetic, in principle, to the concept of hate speech regulation, we should also be aware that there are grave, and perhaps insuperable, difficulties in drafting regulations that are broad enough without being vague. We must be ever conscious of the possibility that, in the guise of regulations for the preservation of toleration, the authorities will use their power over speech to advance their own ideological causes at the expense of dissenters.

TOWARD A FIRST AMENDMENT JURISPRUDENCE OF RESPECT: A COMMENT ON GEORGE FLETCHER'S *CONSTITUTIONAL IDENTITY*

*Robin West**

As is now widely recognized, the emerging debate in the United States legal community over the constitutionality of city ordinances and university disciplinary sanctions designed to deter "hate speech" has generated two sharply polarized understandings of the nature of the First Amendment and the scope of the rights that amendment protects. What Professor Fletcher's Article helps us see is that those understandings, in turn, rest on two very different conceptions of what he labels in his Article as our sense of "constitutional identity."[1] Although largely undefined by Fletcher, we might take his phrase "constitutional identity" to refer to that aspect of our collective and individual self-conception which we owe to our shared constitutional heritage, and which at least on occasion determines outcomes in close constitutional cases in ways that "overarching principles of political morality"[2] do not.

The two understandings of our constitutional identity that seem to bolster these conflicting accounts of the constitutional status of hate speech regulations might be called, however unimaginatively, the "liberal" and the "progressive" paradigm. Part I of this Comment briefly characterizes the two polarized positions on the constitutionality (or unconstitutionality) of hate speech ordinances, emphasizing only the aspects of each account that are central to its implicit conception of our constitutional identity. Part II offers a friendly criticism of the now somewhat standard defense of hate speech regulations proffered by progressives, and suggests what may be a more promising line of analysis, largely because it rests on a truer account of our constitutional identity.

And lastly, this Comment will demonstrate both the strength and limitation of Professor Fletcher's fine Article; namely, that while some explicit or implicit conception of our "constitutional identity"

---

* Professor of Law, Georgetown University Law Center. B.A., 1976, University of Maryland; J.D., 1979, University of Maryland School of Law; J.S.M., 1982, Stanford Law School.
[1] George P. Fletcher, *Constitutional Identity*, 14 Cardozo L. Rev. 737, 741 (1993).
[2] *Id.* at 737.

may be what determines *decisions* about constitutional questions in close cases, the mere articulation of such a conception in no way provides definitive *answers* to those questions. Our "constitutional identity" is surely as contestable and as contested as any particular and vague constitutional phrase or standard, the interpretation of which it may indeed partly determine.

Both the liberal and unquestionably dominant account of free speech, and the correlative liberal argument against the constitutionality of hate speech regulations, are deeply familiar. Both were recently affirmed by the Supreme Court,[3] and both are eloquently spelled out in Professor Fletcher's Article.[4] From a liberal perspective, speech is, for the most part, an *expressive* act engaged in by individuals toward the end of the individual's own self-fulfillment. Expression, as well as the thought and opinion that accompany it, is what gives our lives their individual definition and contour; it is what *individuates* us. Constitutional protection of free speech—including, of course, speech that "offends"—is therefore the means by which the state acknowledges our individual dignity, our moral worth, individual moral responsibility, and autonomy. Like prayer in earlier times, expression of our innermost selves is a vital means of self-fulfillment, and hence is itself a moral act of high order. We each bare our individual, our authentic, our innermost souls when we express ourselves. And, because we value individual souls, we protect and value our speech whatever its context or side effects. Indeed, in his defense of the liberal conception, Professor Fletcher makes explicit the connecting thread between the protection historically provided to religious belief and practice and the modern protection of expression.[5] We protect expression today for essentially the same reason we once protected religion; namely, the constitutive role of expressive religion in earlier times, and expressive speech today, in the development of the individual's personality:

> All those who feel strongly about something, all those who experience what we loosely call a commitment of conscience should be able to express themselves freely. In the end, one has no tools for distinguishing the anti-patriotic conscience of Johnson from the anti-public school conscience of the Amish. The locus of special freedom, the rubric under which individuals are exempt from at least some general and nondiscriminatory laws, shifts from one

---

[3] R.A.V. v. City of St. Paul, Minn., 112 S. Ct. 2538 (1992) (striking down St. Paul's hate speech regulation as content-based and thus violative of the First Amendment).

[4] *See* Fletcher, *supra* note 1, at 740-46.

[5] *Id.* at 744-45.

clause of the First Amendment to another, from freedom of religion to freedom of speech.

. . . .

One is left, then, with a view of the First Amendment that invests freedom of speech with a particularly heavy burden. The First Amendment is *the* clause in our Constitution that bears the full weight of individual autonomy, the full burden of individuals bearing their souls and expressing their innermost nature in the face of organized demands of conformity and self-restraint. Here is the American spirit at work again, the irreverence of the ongoing American revolution. . . . If the *Smith* decision survives, religion will no longer generate a legal sphere for appeals to higher law, for submissions to conscience, and for resorts to values over which the state has no control. The values of dissent, freedom of the inner self, and the free flourishing of individuals must be borne as emanations of free speech.[6]

From the small explosion of scholarly and adversarial writing in defense of the constitutionality of regulations designed to curb hate speech, one can discern, among several other differences from the liberal paradigm, a dramatically different understanding of the nature of speech and of its role in the development of individual personality. Speech, from the progressive perspective, is not essentially *expressive* (whether "free" or not). Rather, speech is essentially *communicative.* It creates a bond, a relationship, or a community that was not there previously between speaker and listener or writer and reader, the creation of which is both the primary purpose and primary consequence of the speech. We may or may not be baring our individual souls when we speak, but what we are almost inevitably doing (willy-nilly or quite consciously) is creating a social soul: a different and transformed community. Therefore, the value of speech and the value of speech acts are importantly dependent upon the quality, and particularly the moral quality, of the relationships and communities they engender. Depending on the context, the content, the motive, and a host of other intangibles, speech might strengthen or enrich communities, but it also might not; speech can perpetuate hierarchies, can further subordinate already relatively disempowered peoples, can censure by shocking or scaring a listener into silence, or can render the responsive speech of the listener less free by injuring his or her dignity and self-esteem. For any of these reasons it may constitute, to use Patricia Williams's telling phrase, "spirit murder,"[7] regardless of whether or not it also, and incidentally, bares the speaker's innermost

---

6 *Id.*
7 PATRICIA J. WILLIAMS, THE ALCHEMY OF RACE AND RIGHTS 73 (1991).

soul. When these spiritually murderous utterances are of little or no positive value, and when they cause the harm which is their primary purpose and most identifying consequence, it is not at all obvious, from this perspective, why we should protect them.[8]

Thus, the progressive who supports these ordinances and regulations is consciously, firmly, and perhaps obsessively focused on the very *consequences* of the speech to which the liberal also deliberately, firmly, and perhaps obsessively, is willfully blind. What the progressive sees as central—the possibly belittling, injurious, endangering, subordinating, spirit murdering consequences of speech—the liberal sees as, at most, incidental "offense." The liberal then views such offense, as may be taken by overly sensitive souls, as not only an insufficient reason for regulating hate speech, but on the contrary a reason to heighten its protection.[9] The progressive views that offense as a serious anti-communitarian injury which sharply undercuts the prima facie reason for protecting speech, and hence a sufficient justification for its regulation.

The progressive conception of speech—motivated by an egalitarian political impulse, but tremendously enriched theoretically by philosophical work on the nature and necessity of interpretation[10]— has in turn given rise to a particular argument for the constitutionality of hate speech regulations. It is that argument which may be incomplete. That defense pits our political commitment to equality against our commitment to liberty, and on the constitutional level pits the Fourteenth Amendment against the First. Speech may liberate the abstract individual, as the liberal insists, but it also may oppress the very concrete and particular members of subordinated groups. Hence, gains in individual liberty—liberty to speak, to print, or to pornograph—have come at the cost of equality, and both are constitutionally protected values. When we liberate the private individual we simultaneously subordinate already oppressed peoples. Our commitment to liberty, then, should be tempered or limited by our commitment to equality.

Constitutionally, the progressive argument continues, the First

---

[8] *See, e.g.*, Richard Delgado, *Words that Wound: A Tort Action for Racial Insults, Epithets, and Name-Calling*, HARV. C.R.-C.L. L. REV. 133 (1982); Charles R. Lawrence III, *If He Hollers Let Him Go: Regulating Racist Speech on Campus*, 1990 DUKE L.J. 431; Mari J. Matsuda, *Public Response to Racist Speech: Considering the Victim's Story*, 87 MICH. L. REV. 2320 (1990).

[9] *See, e.g.*, Ronald Dworkin, *The Coming Battles over Free Speech*, N.Y. REV. BOOKS, June 11, 1992, at 56-58, 61.

[10] *See* STANLEY FISH, IS THERE A TEXT IN THIS CLASS? (1980); STANLEY FISH, DOING WHAT COMES NATURALLY (1989).

Amendment's protection of speech must be read through the prism of the Fourteenth Amendment's more or less explicit promise of equality. We should, therefore, read an additional exception into the First Amendment's protection of speech, an exception motivated by a political quest for equality and sanctioned by the Fourteenth Amendment. Such an exception would allow for regulations, if narrowly and skillfully crafted, of speech that is of little expressive value and which does tremendous subordinating harm. We should read the First Amendment as "balanced by" the Fourteenth, and our commitment to liberty as limited by our commitment to equality.

There are a number of problems with this approach from a liberal perspective, but there are also problems from a progressive perspective. From a progressive perspective, the first problem is simply strategic and goes not to the particular argument, but to the wisdom of advocating hate speech ordinances on equality or any other grounds. Particularly given the Court's recent pronouncement on the subject in *R.A.V. v. City of St. Paul, Minn.*,[11] it seems clear that neither this argument nor any other is likely to succeed, and our failure to sustain these ordinances will have very real consequences. At the very least the failure to sustain these ordinances will further trivialize the harms of speech, and further denigrate its victims both in their own eyes and in the eyes of others. It is belittling, even humiliating, and at least ostracizing to sustain an injury, the infliction of which is constitutionally *protected*, where the Constitution possesses as much power as it does in this culture to create our moral, our social, and our legal identity. To complain of an injury caused by a constitutionally protected act is not just whining over "names that can never hurt me," but is also deeply anti-communitarian in ways in which Fletcher's Article helps to illuminate: Even to voice the complaint is an attack on our collective constitutional identity, as understood and articulated by liberalism.[12] Unsuccessful attempts to sustain such regulations may underscore the marginality and outsider status of victims of speech, simply by emphasizing the high constitutional status of the events which cause the injuries they suffer.

Other problems, however, inhere in the "equality versus liberty" construction of the issues surrounding hate speech regulations favored by progressives, and the conception of our constitutional identity that construction implies. Regardless of what the Court ultimately decides, that progressive construction—that "constitutional identity" and its attendant problems—will persist as a minority or dissident tradition in First Amendment jurisprudence. It is therefore imperative that we do what we can to get it right.

The first problem is rhetorical. In popular consciousness, as well as constitutional history, we never have had a political or moral commitment to equality that comes anywhere near the weight or intensity of our commitment to liberty. To use Fletcher's phrase, liberty is at the heart of our "constitutional identity" in a way which equality has never been. Think of the pledge of allegiance, the Star Spangled Banner, or the grade school ditty "My Country 'Tis of Thee," all of which mention liberty, and none of which mention equality. In any popular standoff between equality and liberty, liberty will triumph in the popular mind as well as in constitutional doctrine. The contemptuous tone of the charge of "political correctness" that accompanies arguments against hate speech regulations and also against diversity and multiculturalism in education,[13] can be attributed, in part, to that simple rhetorical fact. The often apologetic tone of defenders of these ordinances and of victims of such speech is a much sadder reminder.

The second problem is descriptive. The progressive understanding of hate speech as harmful because of its adverse consequences for equality misdescribes, or at least does not fully describe, the problem. For it is not only the *equality* of subordinated persons (or the groups to which they belong) that is damaged by hate speech. It is also *liberty*: the liberty to walk the street, the campus, or the workplace undeterred by fear of harassment; the liberty to speak uncensored by the silencing effects of hate; the freedom to live in a community with others or to live in peace with oneself unshackled by the effects of speech which, perhaps uniquely, injures the listener by reducing her to her materiality by negating her noncorporeal existence and by equating her with her physical being—in short, by murdering her spirit. When we characterize the injury of hate speech as one to equality, rather than to liberty, we saddle ourselves not only with a constitutional argument which may well be unsustainable, but also with a description of the injury that rests on an unnecessarily thin vision of social and political life. Equality is not the only value at stake—it is not the only characteristic of an ideal community to which we ought strive—nor is inequality the only harm or evil we should seek to eradicate. The claim that it is rests on a falsely narrow understanding of the community as constituted *only* by politics, by power, by domination, and by subordination. But there is much more to social life than power, and much more to individual thriving than relative equality.

---

[13] *See, e.g.*, Paul Carrington, *Diversity!*, 1992 UTAH L. REV. (forthcoming Jan. 1993).

Lastly, the standard equality-based defense of hate speech concedes what should be contested: namely, an understanding of our constitutional identity that pits abstract individual rights of liberty and speech against harms sustained by concrete members of particular groups. For if the progressive understanding of speech as essentially communicative, rather than expressive, is right, then liberals are wrong to characterize the problem as a standoff between individual "rights of expression" on the one hand, and the interests of members of subordinated groups protecting against subordinating injuries on the other. If the progressive critique is right, then it is the liberal conception of our shared constitutional identity—a constitutional self-image of a community of individuals freely expressing their innermost souls and possessed of rights to do so, and of group members injured by such expressions and possessed of interests and vulnerabilities—and not its favoring of individuals and rights over groups and interests, that is the flawed premise in the liberal argument against hate speech regulations. We need to challenge that conception, not simply argue for a rebalancing of the rights and interests it posits.

We should at least supplement, if not supplant, the current Fourteenth Amendment/equality defense of hate speech regulations with a reinvigorated, reconstructed interpretation of the First Amendment that would take seriously the progressive understanding not just of the magnitude of the harms caused by hate speech, but also of the nature of speech and of our consequent "constitutional identity." That understanding would construe the "point" of the First Amendment, to use Ronald Dworkin's phrase,[14] as the protection and facilitation of *communication* rather than expression, and the well-functioning community, rather than the soul-baring, expressive individual of conscience, as its inherent ideal. Understood as such, the First Amendment would protect much of what it now protects and be subject to many of the same exceptions as under its liberal interpretation. It would also non-problematically weigh in favor of regulations of speech designed to counter the censorial effects on communication of private concentrations of power, whether those concentrations be racial, economic, or sexual. The First Amendment, understood as protecting communication rather than expression, and communities of speakers and listeners rather than soul-baring individuals, would thus protect the listener and potential speaker who sustains and is transformed by the consequences of speech, whether for better or ill, as well as the hateful utterance and its expressing speaker. Viewed as such, it would protect all participants—speakers, listeners, potential

---

[14] *See* Dworkin, *supra* note 9, at 56.

speakers—against not only ill-founded state efforts to enforce a stifling conformity, but also against malicious private attempts to induce a silence born not of a valued privacy, but of a stultifying and strangling self-hatred.

This is not to argue that such a redirection would drastically improve the chances of sustaining these ordinances in court against a First Amendment attack. It would not obviate the danger and risk to victims of hate speech posed by unsuccessful defenses of the constitutionality of ordinances designed for their protection. It might, however, address some of the other problems that now plague progressive arguments for the constitutionality of hate speech regulations. On a rhetorical level, it would be tremendously helpful to begin to fashion an understanding of the First Amendment as being in alignment, rather than in tension, with both the Fourteenth Amendment and with progressive ends. It could only help progressive political efforts to rest on a non-contradictory "constitutional identity," rather than one characterized by paradox, contradiction, and tension.

More importantly, such a recharacterization of the First Amendment might be truer not only to the nature of the injuries victims of hate speech sustain, but also to the progressive constitutional identity the sufferance of those injuries offends. As Rodney King pleaded in the violent aftermath of the hate crime he suffered, we must learn to "get along"[15] with each other. In our current pluralist, multicultural, multiethnic, severely *crowded* times, the contrasting liberal constitutional identity behind standard First Amendment understandings—that we learn to let each other alone to nurture, express, or bare our own individual souls—is increasingly an unattainable, whether or not desirable goal. Rodney King's plea may not only be expressive of a more appealing political vision—a more desirable constitutional identity—but a more realistic one as well.

---

[15] *Riots in Los Angeles: A Plea for Calm*, N.Y. TIMES, May 2, 1992, at 6.

ACKNOWLEDGMENTS

Strossen, Nadine. "Regulating Racist Speech on Campus: A Modest Proposal?" *Duke Law Journal* (1990): 484–573. Reprinted with the permission of the Duke University School of Law.

Grey, Thomas C. "Civil Rights vs. Civil Liberties: The Case of Discriminatory Verbal Harassment." *Social Philosophy and Policy* 8, No.2 (1991): 81–105. Reprinted with the permission of Cambridge University Press (North American Branch).

Post, Robert C. "Racist Speech, Democracy, and the First Amendment." *William and Mary Law Review* 32 (1991): 267–327. Reprinted with the permission of the College of William and Mary.

Fish, Stanley. "There's No Such Thing as Free Speech and It's a Good Thing Too." *Boston Review* (February 1992): 3–4, 23–26. Reprinted with the permission of Boston Critic, Inc.

Dworkin, Ronald. Excerpt from "The Coming Battles over Free Speech." *New York Review of Books* (June 11, 1992): 55–61. Reprinted with permission from *The New York Review of Books*. Copyright 1992 Nyrev, Inc.

"Brief *Amicus Curiae* of the National Black Women's Health Project in Support of Respondent, *R.A.V. v. City of St. Paul.*" pp. 1, 3–24. Reprinted with the permission of the West Publishing Company.

R.A.V. v. City of St. Paul. 112 S.Ct. 2538 (1992): 2538, 2540–71. Reprinted with the permission of the West Publishing Company.

Amar, Akhil Reed. Excerpt from "The Case of the Missing Amendments: *R.A.V. v. City of St. Paul.*" *Harvard Law Review* 106 (1992): 124–25, 155–160. Copyright 1992 by the Harvard Law Review Association.

Altman, Andrew. "Liberalism and Campus Hate Speech: A Philosophical Examination." *Ethics* 103 (1993): 302–17. Reprinted with the permission of the University of Chicago Press.

Cohen-Almagor, Raphael. "Harm Principle, Offence Principle, and the Skokie Affair." *Political Studies* 41 (1993): 453–70. Reprinted with the permission of Blackwell Publishers.

Rauch, Jonathan. "The Humanitarian Threat to Free Inquiry." *Reason* (April 1993): 21–27. Reprinted with permission. Copyright 1993 by the Reason Foundation, 3415 South Sepulveda Blvd, Suite 400, Los Angeles, CA 90034.

Gates, Henry Louis Jr. "Let Them Talk: Why Civil Liberties Pose No Threat to Civil Rights." *The New Republic* (September 20 & 27, 1993): 37–49. Reprinted by permission of *The New Republic*, copyright (1993), The New Republic, Inc.

Wisconsin v. Mitchell, 113 S.Ct. 2194 (1993): 2194, 2195–2202. Reprinted with the permission of the West Publishing Company.

Sunstein, Cass R. Excerpt from "Words, Conduct, Caste." *University of Chicago Law Review* 60, Nos. 3 & 4 (1993): 795, 822–29. Reprinted with the permission of the University of Chicago Law School.

Defeis, Elizabeth F. Excerpt from "Freedom of Speech and International Norms: A Response to Hate Speech." *Stanford Journal of International Law* 29 (1991): 57, 68–9, 74–94. Reprinted with the permission of the Stanford University School of Law, and the author. Copyright 1991 by the Board of Trustees of the Leland Stanford Junior University.

Weinrib, Lorraine E., ed. *Regina v. Keegstra* [1990] 3 S.C.R. 697, 61 C.C.C. (3d) 1, [1991] 2 W.W.R. 1 Canadian Supreme Court Document (1990). Copyright © 1995 by Lorraine E. Weinrib.

Weinrib, Lorraine Eisenstat. Excerpt from "Hate Promotion in a Free and Democratic Society: *R. v. Keegstra*." *McGill Law Journal* 36, No.4 (1991): 1416–32, 1448–49. Reprinted with the permission of the *McGill Law Journal*.

Hofmann, Rainer. "Incitement to National and Racial Hatred: The Legal Situation in Germany." In S. Coliver, ed., *Striking a Balance* (University of Essex, 1992): 159–70. Reprinted with the permission of the University of Essex, Human Rights Center.

Shapira, Amos. "Confronting Racism by Law in Israel—Promises and Pitfalls." *Cardozo Law Review* 8 (1987): 595–608. Reprinted with the permission of the *Cardozo Law Review*.

McConnell, Michael W. "America's First 'Hate Speech' Regulation." *Constitutional Commentary* 9 (1992): 17–23. Reprinted with the permission of *Constitutional Commentary Inc.*

West, Robin. "Toward a First Amendment Jurisprudence of Respect: A Comment on George Fletcher's *Constitutional Identity*." *Cardozo Law Review* 14 (1993):759–66. Reprinted with the permission of the *Cardozo Law Review*.

≣Contents≣
of the Series

THE CONSTITUTION AND THE FLAG

VOLUME 1
The Flag Salute Cases

VOLUME 2
The Flag Burning Cases

PRAYER IN PUBLIC SCHOOLS
AND THE CONSTITUTION, 1961-1992

VOLUME 1
Government-Sponsored Religious Activities
in Public Schools and the Constitution

VOLUME 2
Moments of Silence in Public Schools and the Constitution

VOLUME 3
Protecting Religious Speech in Public Schools:
The Establishment and Free Exercise Clauses in the Public Arena

GUN CONTROL AND THE CONSTITUTION
Sources and Explorations on the Second Amendment

VOLUME 1
The Courts, Congress, and the Second Amendment

VOLUME 2
Advocates and Scholars: The Modern Debate on Gun Control

VOLUME 3
Special Topics on Gun Control

SCHOOL BUSING
Constitutional and Political Developments

VOLUME 1
The Development of School Busing as a Desegregation Remedy

VOLUME 2
The Public Debate over Busing
and Attempts to Restrict Its Use

ABORTION LAW IN THE UNITED STATES
VOLUME 1
The Current Abortion Era
VOLUME 2
Historical Development of Abortion Law
VOLUME 3
Modern Literature on Abortion

HATE SPEECH AND THE CONSTITUTION
VOLUME 1
The Development of the Hate Speech Debate: From Group Libel to Campus Speech Codes
VOLUME 2
The Contemporary Debate: Reconciling Freedom of Expression and Equality of Citizenship